Praise for
Playing with Purpose

As a coach, I'm always looking for both talent and character. *Playing with Purpose: Basketball* will introduce you to several professionals whose faith is as strong as their court presence. You'll love their stories.
MIKE KRZYZEWSKI
HEAD COACH, DUKE UNIVERSITY BLUE DEVILS

This book brings to life the testimonies of ballplayers who are living life and playing the game with a greater purpose and an eternal perspective. *Playing with Purpose: Baseball* will inspire readers.
CLAYTON KERSHAW
2011 CY YOUNG WINNER AND AUTHOR OF *ARISE*

Faith is the basis for a strong presence in the locker room, and leadership on and off the field. *Playing with Purpose: Baseball* describes how many of today's Christian athletes carry these assets of faith in their careers.
MIKE SCHMIDT
BASEBALL HALL OF FAMER

As a former pitcher familiar with the pressures of Major League Baseball, I'm encouraged to see how my brothers in Christ are handling fame and fortune. They are using their gifts to exalt Christ and build His kingdom. This book is a fascinating glimpse into some great players who love Jesus!
FRANK TANANA
TWENTY-YEAR MAJOR LEAGUER AND THREE-TIME ALL STAR

A must-read for everyone who wants to get to know the good guys in baseball.
JEREMY AFFELDT
SAN FRANCISCO GIANT

D0974662

PLAYING
WITH
PURPOSE

INSIDE THE LIVES AND FAITH
OF 27 GREAT FOOTBALL,
BASKETBALL, AND BASEBALL STARS

MIKE YORKEY

WITH JESSE FLORE AND JOSHUA COOLEY

BARBOUR
PUBLISHING

© 2012 by Mike Yorkey with Jesse Florea and Joshua Cooley

Print ISBN 978-1-61626-854-1

eBook Editions:
Adobe Digital Edition (.epub) 978-1-62029-042-2
Kindle and MobiPocket Edition (.prc) 978-1-62029-043-9

Cover images © Tim Tebow: David Drapkin/AP
                Kevin Durant: Tony Gutierrez/AP
                Mariano Riviera: Bill Kostroun/AP

The author is represented by WordServe Literary Group, Ltd., Greg Johnson, Literary Agent, 10152 S. Knoll Circle, Highlands Ranch, CO 80130.

Published by Barbour Publishing, Inc., P.O. Box 719, Uhrichsville, Ohio 44683
www.barbourbooks.com

Our mission is to publish and distribute inspirational products offering exceptional value and biblical encouragement to the masses.

 Member of the
Evangelical Christian
Publishers Association

Printed in the United States of America.

CONTENTS

PLAYING

WITH

PURPOSE

Inside the Lives and Faith of
NFL Quarterbacks—
Sam Bradford, Colt McCoy, and Tim Tebow

MIKE YORKEY

CONTENTS

INTRODUCTION

Their first two seasons are in the books.

During the National Football League's 2010 and 2011 campaigns, we got to sit back in our Stratoloungers and watch three up-and-coming quarterbacks—Sam Bradford, Colt McCoy, and Tim Tebow—make their mark in America's most popular sport. Armed with DirecTV's NFL Sunday Ticket and holding remotes in our hands, many of us had front row seats for all the action.

They experienced varying degrees of success.

Sam Bradford, Colt McCoy, and Tim Tebow—listed here in alphabetical order—came into the league after performing spectacularly at the universities of Oklahoma, Texas, and Florida, respectively. They've been groomed for greatness since high school, and they burst into our living rooms as college freshmen (though only Tim played as a true freshman) when they were handed the responsibility of guiding high-powered NCAA football programs down the field.

Instead of collapsing under the weight of the high expectations placed on their shoulder pads, though, they became folk heroes to their fans and focal points of television and radio coverage on ESPN, CBS, Fox Sports, and—during their college years—regional football networks. They passed, they scored . . . they praised the Lord.

During their storied collegiate careers, the three QBs led their teams to Bowl Championship Series (BCS) National Championship games, set numerous passing records, bounced back from injuries, and fought for the Heisman Trophy. Now they're trying to find their way in the National Football League, and if the 2010 season was any indication, it looks like Sam, Colt, and Tim will make their mark in one way or another.

They're used to generating tons of heat on hundreds, if not thousands, of Internet "fan blogs." The raves, rumors, rants, and outright falsehoods posted in cyberspace weren't a phenomenon just 10 or 15 years ago, but that's the reality of playing today at the most visible and talked-about position in football.

Sam, picked No. 1 in the 2010 NFL Draft by the St. Louis Rams, has seen the most playing time of the Three QBs. He earned the starting role as soon as he signed his record-breaking six-year, $78 million contract. Sam backed it up by having a great rookie year in 2010, taking a 1–15 team in 2009 almost back to the playoffs. His sophomore season in the NFL didn't quite match up, though. Some football experts thought Sam regressed since he threw only six touchdown passes in ten starts, winning only one game. A high ankle strain caused him to miss six contests.

Colt, who had to wait until the third round before the Cleveland Browns picked him, wasn't expected to play during his rookie year, but injuries to the two quarterbacks ahead of him gave Colt an unexpected chance to take over a team heading south in a hurry. Colt performed admirably, which earned the starting position in 2011—but a porous offensive line and lack of a running game allowed defenses to tee off. Colt, like the Browns team, struggled to a 4–12 season. During the 2012 draft, the Browns selected Oklahoma State's Brandon Weeden in the first round, and now Colt is in another battle for playing time in 2012. We'll have to see how things play out near Lake Erie.

And how to sum up Tim Tebow's NFL career so far? He was basically ignored by the Denver Broncos during his rookie season until he came off the bench and sparked the team late in a forgettable year. He didn't look to play much in 2011 until Coach John Fox, in the midst of a 1–3 start, handed Tim the reins to the team. What a magical season for the Broncos, who, with one jaw-dropping fourth-quarter comeback after another, returned to the NFL playoffs. There, Denver upset the mighty Pittsburgh Steelers in overtime on an amazing touchdown play involving Tim and receiver Demaryius Thomas. Then a shocking development during the off-season: The Broncos signed free agent Peyton Manning and declared the Tim Tebow era was over in the Colorado Rockies. Tim was traded to the New York Jets, where he and quarterback Mark Sanchez will fight for playing time. And, once again, we'll have to see how that plays out.

Because of their past successes, dedication to winning, and unique situations with their current teams, the Three QBs will be in the mix—in one way or another—for years to come.

So who are Sam Bradford, Colt McCoy, and Tim Tebow? What makes this triumvirate of quarterback talent so compelling?

You'll find the answers in Playing with Purpose. The following pages will

- describe where Sam, Colt, and Tim came from and how they grew up;
- tell you about how their parents raised them and what their families are like;
- narrate their start in football, including their junior high and high school years;
- recap their stellar collegiate careers;
- chronicle their tough moments;
- discuss the implications of the 2010NFL draft;
- describe how their first two NFL seasons went;
- show their willingness to use their incredible, one-in-a-million platforms to talk about their personal relationship with the Lord of the Universe—Jesus Christ.

All three of these young football players were raised in Christian homes, so none of them has a "hell-raising testimony" to share—thank goodness. But they would tell you they've had their share of ups and downs in life, just like anyone else.

Keep in mind that these three young men have been leading public lives since their senior years in high school. Today, they are caught up in a media vortex where they can't order a second dessert without having this breathtaking news reported on the ESPN crawl.

In a sense, they've grown up before our eyes, and by any measuring stick, they've done themselves and their families proud by the way they've handled themselves following tremendous victories and bone-crushing defeats in some of football's biggest games played before packed stadiums and national television viewers numbering in the tens of millions.

Yet it's also worth noting how these three young quarterbacks have acted when no one was looking. A small but telling example of character: back when Tim Tebow was playing at the University of Florida, two-thirds of the 96 Gators football players who played or were on scholarship in 2009 had received traffic citations since 2006 in Alachua County, home to the Gainesville campus of the University of Florida. The number of traffic citations issued to those players: 251. The number of traffic citations issued to Tim Tebow during his four-year college football career: zero. "Though authorities reportedly look the other way when he jaywalks on water," quipped Dwight Perry of the *Seattle Times.*

Tim Tebow hasn't walked on water, and neither has Sam Bradford or Colt McCoy, but that hasn't stopped them from talking about the Person who *has*—Jesus Christ. The biggest thing that sets the Three QBs apart from their peers is their boldness in sharing their faith in Christ. They did that through high school and college, and they didn't appear to audibilize—change the play at the line of scrimmage—when they entered the pro ranks. Apparently, they learned the invaluable lesson that if you make a stand early on, you only have to make it once.

As any youth pastor will tell you, telling the world you're a Christian—knowing that you'll be mocked and made fun of—takes more guts than completing a fourth-and-goal pass into the end zone when your team is down by four points with five seconds left. But wearing their faith on the sleeves of their football jerseys—or inscribing Bible verses on their eye black, à la Tim Tebow—is part of what makes these three quarterbacks so special.

"I've interviewed all three players, and I can't differentiate them," said Jill Ewert, editor of *Sharing the Victory* magazine, which is published by the Fellowship of Christian Athletes (FCA). "I can't put Tim on a pedestal any higher than Sam or Colt because all three of these guys just knocked my socks off. What's pleased me has been watching them succeed and how God has allowed them to fail in graceful ways."

Reagan Lambert, FCA director at the University of Texas campus, said he's never seen three young men like Sam, Colt, and Tim come along at the same time. "People have used the term 'perfect storm' for a lot of different things," he said, "and I believe that's what we've witnessed with three strong Christian young men, who all played the quarterback position, leading major college programs to national titles and winning Heisman Trophies. I don't think we'll ever see anything like it again."

WHY A BOOK LIKE *PLAYING WITH PURPOSE*?

Like the convergence of three funnel clouds in Tornado Alley, Sam Bradford, Colt McCoy, and Tim Tebow *are* the perfect storm of quarterbacking talent.

Their on- and off-the-field exploits have inspired millions of words to be written about them, and they've been the subjects of hundreds of magazine articles and TV features. They have surely lost count of the number of times they've been interviewed. While they shared large chunks of their life stories over the years, we will have to wait until they decide to write their autobiographies for a full accounting.

Authorized biographies will come—including *Growing Up Colt* by Colt McCoy and his father, Brad, from Barbour Publishing, and *Through My Eyes* by Tim Tebow. This is why their agents undoubtedly instructed them not to cooperate with any earlier book projects, including this one. But since these three have talked extensively with the media ever since their days as high school pups—and people close to them have been interviewed for *Playing with Purpose*—you can enjoy this fascinating book as well.

GAME DAY

Chances are strong that you know football is the most popular and most-watched sport on television in America today. "Game Day" can only mean one thing: there's a big football game to be played—and in today's hyped-up sports culture, *every* football game seems to qualify as being of great importance, momentous, pivotal, crucial, or even historic. If a buck were thrown into the pot every time a football analyst said, "This is a big game for both teams," we could retire the national debt in no time.

In the buildup for the "big game," the spotlight always falls on the quarterback, the most important player on the field. He is the team leader, the player the other 10 members of the offense expect to "move the chains" and lead them into the end zone.

Every play begins with the quarterback crouched underneath the center or positioned five to seven yards behind the line of scrimmage in the "shotgun" formation. His eyes scan the defensive side of the football, and in just a couple of seconds, he must locate where the defensive players are positioned and deduce what the defense will do to stop him and his teammates. He has the ability to change course at the line of scrimmage if he believes the defense is lined up perfectly to stop the play that the offensive coordinator or head coach has called.

Once he barks out signals to his offense and yells "hut" to start the play, the ball is literally in the quarterback's hands. He can hand off the pigskin to a running back, lateral to a teammate, drop back and pass the ball downfield, or run the ball himself. His ability to make split-second decisions, fend off ferocious pass rushes, hit his receivers with precision passes, and take a late hit separates the skill set of a quarterback from those of other players. Because the permutations are countless, and because of their ability to inspire their teammates, execute plays, read defenses, and throw the ball *exactly* where it needs to be, quarterbacks are the most dissected, most discussed, most well-known, and most controversial players on the team.

As the quarterback goes, so goes the team—and that is why football pundits devote so much time to "breaking down" the strengths and weaknesses of the opposing quarterbacks during a pregame buildup. Quarterbacks shoulder the responsibility of whether the team wins or loses, and that role is not for the faint of heart. Simply said, quarterback is the hardest, riskiest, and greatest position in all of sports.

Quarterbacks live under a microscope. The scrutiny never lets up. Fans drive by their homes at all hours of the day, and when they eat at a restaurant, they are constantly interrupted for autographs and pictures. They know that fans form lifelong opinions based upon chance encounters, so they always have to be on their guard. They understand that fans will never tell 20 people that their QB was courteous and nice, but they will tell 20 people that he blew them off.

This is the Faustian bargain that top-flight quarterbacks must accept—the fishbowl existence and the anonymous criticism. Yet, as Green Bay Packers quarterback Aaron Rodgers says, "Anytime I'm recognized and can't just walk around, I remind myself that I haven't had a [real] job in my life."

Do know that quarterbacks work hard—insanely hard. They put an incredible number of hours into becoming the go-to guy on the gridiron. Even though Colt, who turns 25 at the start of the 2011 season, is the oldest of the Three QBs (Tim turned 24 in August and Sam is 24 in November), all three have been doing this quarterback thing for a long time—more than half their lives. They all started playing organized football in elementary school and set their sights on becoming the starting quarterbacks for their high school teams. (Tim's case is a bit different, as you'll discover; he chose his high school because he didn't attend one. If that sounds confusing, it's because he was homeschooled until he enrolled at the University of Florida.)

From the time their voices started to change during puberty through their first pro football training camp, Sam, Colt, and Tim have been throwing down-and-outs and post patterns to their receivers for hours on end. They've learned hundreds of plays and dozens of formations—and practiced them until they became second nature. They've spent their evenings watching game film until their eyeballs hurt. And if they didn't get it right, their coaches chewed them out.

Practice, practice, practice. What football fans see when the curtain is raised on Friday nights, Saturday afternoons, and Sunday afternoons is far different from what they would see during the countless hours of preparation—the pianist's equivalent of practicing hand position, scales, arpeggios, and complete pieces—that take place on the practice field five or six days a week for five to six months a year.

Yet for all the practicing under their coaches' watchful eyes, all three quarterbacks had Achilles' heels leading up to the 2010 NFL draft—all of which involved their shoulders and throwing arms.

Sam injured his throwing shoulder in the 2009 season opener against Brigham Young, causing him to miss the next three games. When he returned, he reinjured his shoulder against Texas and then submitted to season-ending surgery for the reconstruction of his acromioclavicular (AC) joint.

After giving himself time to heal, Sam began the rehabilitation process to strengthen his shoulder so he could impress NFL scouts in the spring of 2010, prior to the draft. At his pro day on March 29, before representatives from 21 NFL teams, Sam hit just about every note, completing 49 of 50 passes with pinpoint precision, tight spirals, and excellent velocity.

Colt McCoy suffered his shoulder injury on college football's biggest stage—the BCS Championship game between Texas and Alabama, which was played at the Rose Bowl on January 7, 2010. On the Longhorns' fifth play from scrimmage, Colt was scrambling to his right when he was hammered by Alabama's defensive lineman Marcel Dareus, who scrunched Colt's right shoulder into the Rose Bowl's grass turf. Colt didn't return to action, and that severely lessened the 'Horns' chances of winning (Texas eventually caved in to the Crimson Tide, losing 37–21). But at his pro day, Colt put on a passing clinic, completing all 55 passes in a controlled workout.

Tim Tebow didn't have a shoulder injury to overcome, but he spent three months early in 2010 reworking his throwing mechanics. CBS television analyst and former Baltimore Ravens coach Brian Billick roundly criticized Tim during his final college game—the 2010 Sugar Bowl—for carrying the ball too low as he dropped back to pass, which resulted in a loopy throwing motion and long windup delivery.

After working with a series of high-profile experts, including former NFL coaches Sam Wyche and Jon Gruden, to eliminate the swooping windup, Tim changed his throwing motion—as well as the conventional wisdom that he was second- or third-round draft material, a "project" destined for an apprenticeship role in the NFL. Tim shook the football world and became easily the biggest surprise of the 2010 NFL draft when the Denver Broncos made him a first-round pick and 25th overall.

Now, after establishing beachheads during their rookie seasons, one thing seems certain: Sam Bradford, Colt McCoy, and Tim Tebow are bona fide football heroes worthy of our interest. They come along at a time when too many football stars disappoint their fans with news reports of the latest paternity suit or run-in at the local strip club.

Yes, Sam, Colt, and Tim are human—regular guys who grew up in intact families—and they would want us to know that. But it will be interesting to follow where they go from here after their promising starts in the NFL.

While Tim Tebow was living in an off-campus apartment as a student at the University of Florida, he kept a framed poem on his wall that included the words, "Little eyes are watching you." That saying, no doubt, was a reminder to Tim that children looked up to him—a college-age quarterback playing every year for a national championship.

Now that Tim, Sam, and Colt have graduated to the NFL, they have become multimillionaires—and with all the riches and fame associated with playing professional football, the world is their oyster.

But thanks to their core values and their strength of character—which we can credit in large part to the way their Christian parents raised them—the feeling here is that none of the Three QBs will forget that little eyes are still watching them.

1

SAM BRADFORD:
THE DYNAMITE DRAFT PICK

He's got that tall, lanky build and that tight, curly hair that reminds you of Napoleon Dynamite, the listless, underachieving star of the cult classic film by the same name.

But that's where the similarity ends.

Sam Bradford, the University of Oklahoma quarterback, could probably throw a football over the mountains, as Napoleon's Uncle Rico bragged he could do in the movie. But Sam's long, long bomb would hit the receiver in midstride.

Napoleon would call that "flippin' sweet."

Sam had the shortest college career of the Three QBs, playing one year less and losing most of the 2009 season to injury. Despite appearing in the fewest games and receiving less national attention than Colt or Tim, he could be the best quarterback of the three. At least that's what the St. Louis Rams were betting when they voted with their checkbook and tabbed Sam as the No. 1 pick in the 2010 NFL draft.

As they say in draft-speak, Sam brings tons of "upside" to the table: excellent height, superior arm, pinpoint accuracy, and rock-solid pocket awareness. He is the tallest of the Three QBs, standing 6 feet, 4¼ inches—the fourth of an inch must be important because it's usually included whenever Sam's height is listed. Since he started his professional career with the St. Louis Rams, he's added 13 pounds of muscle to his frame. Scouts believe the extra bulk will make him more durable in the NFL and that it may even bolster his rocket arm.

The scouting reports also say that Sam is an "elite decision-maker." He processes information quickly and can work through the "progressions" of the play, meaning he can look for receivers in a certain order and then complete the pass to his second or third target if his primary receiver isn't open. When his golden arm unleashes the ball, the pass whizzes through the air like it's attached to a zip line—a frozen rope, the scouts call it.

But Sam didn't always have a monster arm, and of the Three QBs, he's the latest bloomer of the bunch. In fact, he needed a huge break just to get his shot at playing quarterback for the University of Oklahoma.

THE EARLY YEARS

Samuel Jacob Bradford was born November 8, 1987, making him the youngest of the Three QBs by three months—and the only one without siblings. Since Kent and Martha Bradford were married eight years before Sam arrived, one could conjecture that she had a hard time getting pregnant or couldn't have more children. Whatever the reason, they slathered Sam with love and devotion. He was their pride and joy, and his athletic career would benefit from the extra attention they were able to afford him.

WHERE'S RUDY WHEN YOU NEED HIM?

The mid-1970s were glory years for Oklahoma football. When Kent Bradford was a student, back in those pre-BCS days, the Barry Switzer–coached teams captured four Big Eight titles and one national championship.

Before Kent played his junior and senior years for the Sooners, however, he was on the scout team—the scrubs and underclassmen who weren't good enough, or who weren't ready, to suit up on Saturday afternoons. Think Rudy at Notre Dame.

One afternoon during practice, the scout team coach, Steve Barrett, instructed Kent—an offensive tackle—to block starting defensive lineman Lee Roy Selmon.

That was a tall order. At 6 feet, 3 inches tall and weighing 256 pounds, "The Gentle Giant" would go on to become the No. 1 pick in the 1976 NFL draft and fashion a Hall of Fame career playing for the Tampa Bay Buccaneers. The guy was a load.

The play was run, and Lee Roy blew past Kent like he was a cardboard cutout. When the offense retreated to the huddle, Coach Barrett yelled, "Bradford, can't you block that guy?"

"Coach, if I could block him, I'd be starting. I wouldn't be on this scout team," Kent answered. "Besides, you probably don't have anybody who'd have blocked him, either."

Now there's a football player who knows what's happening on the field.

Sam, who was born in Oklahoma City, Oklahoma, got his size from his father, who played as an offensive lineman at the University of Oklahoma for two seasons in 1977–78, during the Barry Switzer era. But don't get the idea that just because Dad was a proud OU alum, baby Sam was dressed in red jumpers with OU insignias. His mom graduated from the intrastate rival Oklahoma State University (where Kent's father, Bill, happened to play football in the 1940s), so they had what those in Oklahoma circles might call a "mixed marriage."

One time, before baby Sam turned a year old, Mom took him to a portrait studio where the photographer had several props, including a pint-sized outfit in orange and black—Oklahoma State's school colors.

Kent arrived late to the shoot and was aghast to find his son—*his son!*—sporting an Oklahoma State outfit. When he pressed Martha for an explanation, she replied that she thought their baby son looked darling in the black-and-orange ensemble.

These days you won't find Sam digging through the photo albums and reminiscing over that incriminating photo. "I don't really like the picture," he said.

Why is that?

"Because of the attire. Wrong colors. It wasn't even Halloween."

There isn't much evidence that Martha tried to dress her son in OSU school colors after that episode. Since the University of Oklahoma is in Norman, 20 miles south of Oklahoma City—and because Kent bled Sooner red—Martha became neutral in what you could call a "Switzer-land" home. Since Kent had been an OU season ticket holder for what seemed like forever, young Sam grew up cheering for Big Red at Oklahoma Memorial Stadium. Even Mom came around during the "Bedlam" games—the annual showdown between OU and OSU—and rooted for the Sooners.

You could say sports were important in the Bradford household. Martha was an elementary school physical education teacher while Kent, who worked as an insurance agent, was former Sooner lineman with a competitive nature. When Sam was a preschooler, they filled his bedroom with different kinds of balls, bats, and gloves. Nothing like getting him started early.

Sam's aunt, Jan Bradford, remembers coming over to the house and having Sam, then a preschooler, lead her to his room so he could show off his ball collection—one ball at a time.

"Here's a football!"

"Here's a baseball!"

"Here's a golf ball!"

The only thing Sam didn't bring out during this show-and-tell was his ice skates. His love affair with the ice started because Kent and Martha enjoyed ice skating at a nearby rink during the winter months. When Sam was five years old, he asked for his own pair of skates for Christmas. He wanted to play hockey because it looked like a fun sport.

Santa did his part, making sure the ice skates were under the tree. The parents did their part by immediately enrolling Sam in skating lessons. But the kindergartner didn't like it when the coach got tough on him. One day, the tearful youngster came home and announced he wanted to quit skating.

Mom hugged her son but remained firm. The family had paid for 12 lessons, so he had to see this through. If he stuck with it, then he could play hockey.

Sam completed his skating lessons, and when he began his elementary school years, he starting playing hockey—but he also liked the Big Three All-American sports: football, basketball, and baseball.

Sam displayed some of his athletic precociousness on the ball field as a nine-year-old when he played for the Putnam City Optimist Ducks, who won the AAU state baseball championship in 1997. Check this out: the Ducks played more than 65 games that year, and their state championship team of third and fourth graders earned a trip to Sherwood, Arkansas, for the national tournament.

NO SOCCER FOR SAM

By the 1990s, youth soccer—played under the auspices of the American Youth Soccer Organization (AYSO)—was taking up every free field between Portland, Maine, and Portland, Oregon. In many households, "bunch ball" was replacing T-ball as the sport of choice.

Sam Bradford played just about every sport under the sun—or on the ice—growing up, but he never played organized soccer. Sure, he outplayed the kids in his class during elementary school recess, but his parents never signed him up to play soccer, most likely because they were running themselves ragged getting Sam to all his football, basketball, baseball, and hockey games.

"I would say if you put me on a soccer field today, I would be clueless," Sam said.

No, Sam, you'd probably figure out the game pretty quickly.

No sooner had Sam thrown his mitt into his bedroom closet at the end of summer than it was time to slip on the shoulder pads and a helmet for youth football. Sam somehow always seemed to play each fall on teams named the "Sooners"—with their fire-engine-red mesh jerseys. Then, by Thanksgiving time, the chilly climate made it easy for Sam to transition into basketball, which was played indoors in gymnasiums. After basketball season was over, the sports merry-go-round started all over again with spring baseball.

And then there was hockey.

CATCHING THE HOCKEY BUG

In those early years, Sam's father would drop by his son's bedroom to tuck him in. Many evenings, he would ask his son to say 10 things to him—positive statements like "I can do anything I think I can." Kent was planting the seed that young Sam could do anything he set his mind to, but realizing his goals meant he would have to work hard. Nothing would be handed to him—on the field or in the classroom. It was up to him to set a goal and go chase after it.

That's one way to build a champion, but if you were to ask Sam what his favorite sport was back in grade school and middle school, he'd tell you it wasn't football, basketball, or baseball. That's because he had caught the hockey bug.

Sam was a multi-sport kid juggling a year-round schedule of games "in season," but he truly loved hockey and displayed a gift for the game. His idol was National Hockey League star Pavel Bure—the "Russian Rocket" who played for the Vancouver Canucks and led the NHL in goals during the 1993–94 season.

Despite the time commitment required to keep his hand in the other three sports, it wasn't long before Sam won a spot on the Oklahoma City Junior Blazers, a competitive "travel team" that either drove or flew to tournaments as far away as St. Louis, Kansas City, Dallas, and Houston.

We're talking serious junior hockey. Canadian-born Mike McEwen, a talented defenseman who helped the New York Islanders win three Stanley Cups in the early 1980s, coached the team.

As Sam developed his love for ice hockey in his middle school years, he adopted the Canucks as his favorite team. He would wake up early and grab the morning newspaper so he could see if Vancouver won and if his hero Pavel Bure scored a goal—or two or three.

Then one day, Sam asked his parents—in all seriousness—if the family could move to Vancouver, Canada, the home of the Canucks, so he could watch Pavel roam the ice in person. And besides, they played the best junior hockey in Canada, eh?

"I told him, 'We can't move to Canada. Our lives are in Oklahoma,' " his father said in *USA Hockey* magazine. "But he was pretty set on it."

Sam's parents' practical thinking prevailed, and the family stayed put in Oklahoma City.

Playing on a hockey travel team was a good news/bad news situation for Sam and his parents—and quite a commitment. The good news was that Sam played a top-flight schedule against the best teams in the Midwest. The bad news was the constant travel, which meant being away from home a couple of weekends a month and competing in tournaments where games could be scheduled for six or seven o'clock in the morning or after nine at night. (Tournament games had to be played morning, noon, and night because of the scarcity of rink time.) Sam's parents said he never griped about the early face-offs, though there were 5 a.m. wake-up calls when they had to stuff Sam's legs into his hockey pants while he was still asleep.

From every indication, though, the family enjoyed their hockey days with Sam. Kent never complained about being a "hockey dad," and Martha never complained about being a "hockey mom." Consequently, Sam didn't grow up a complainer, either.

"I definitely think their attitudes had a great deal of impact on getting me where I am today," Sam told *The Oklahoman*.

Sam played two years on the OC Junior Blazers, and his leadership qualities and ever-improving stick skills landed him the role of team captain. But as high school loomed, decisions had to be made. The start of high school is the time when most athletes have to "specialize" in their best—or favorite—sport. Was Sam going to become a hockey player and chuck football, basketball, and baseball?

Mike McEwen told Kent his kid could one day play in the National Hockey League. Sam was a natural, the coach said. He had good hands, great vision, and played smart on the ice.

Kent listened to the old NHL hockey player make his case, saying nothing as his patronizing smile grew bigger and bigger. The father wouldn't be persuaded. Kent had other things in mind for his son, and they weren't going to happen on a sheet of ice.

MEET SAM BRADFORD, CELLO PLAYER

When he was in fourth grade, Sam started playing the cello, a lower-sounding member of the string family that is held between the knees and played in the seated position. He kept at it through middle school, when he became part of the orchestra at Cooper Middle School.

As is often the case with grade-school musicians, Sam's cello ended up in a closet when he graduated to Putnam City North High School. Too much homework and too many sports: football in the fall, basketball in winter, and baseball or golf in the spring.

Sam's father told the *New York Times* that he played the cello "okay for his age group"—although his football coaches at Putnam North and the University of Oklahoma gushed about the quarterback who played the cello. Some of the media's "cello-playing quarterback" story line was embellished a tad, especially when the writer sought to do a little myth-building.

But Sam Bradford, quarterback/cello player, has a nice ring to it, doesn't it?

THE TRANSITION YEARS

In the 1960s and 1970s, when Kent and Martha were growing up, youth sports weren't nearly as organized as they later became. Youth league presidents risked the wrath of parents if they scheduled baseball, basketball, football, or hockey games on Sunday mornings. That was the time for church. For worshipping God.

That mindset slowly changed in the 1980s as parents sought better and better competition for their children, and by the time Sam was lacing up his cleats, sneakers, or hockey skates in the mid-1990s, all the barriers came crashing down. The advent of "all-star" leagues and travel teams heralded a new era in youth sports, and the Bradfords plugged right into the program. Sam was always playing a sport—against the best competition in his peer group—and Kent and Martha had their share of Sunday morning games to attend. Since the seasons overlapped, they had to make choices about which games Sam would play in. That was the reality they had carved for themselves.

By the time Sam entered fifth grade, Martha noticed something else: even though their son was gaining valuable athletic experience every weekend, he was missing out on something far more important—learning about God. She knew that instilling spiritual values and good morals in Sam would mean a lot more than him learning the fast break, the two-minute offense, or the power play. Mom believed it was time for the family to start going to church. If a game was scheduled for a Sunday morning, the team would have to play without Sam.

"We were playing sports every weekend, and it's not like I didn't know who God was, but it was just something that we really did not have the time to do," Sam told Jenni Carlson, a sports columnist with *The Oklahoman*. "I think my mom finally brought it up and was like, 'Hey, we're going to start going to church.' We started going to a couple of different churches, and finally, we found one where a couple of my friends attended. I give a lot of credit to my friends; they were the ones who got me involved in youth group, got me involved in Confirmation, got me to really stick with it."

When Sam started attending church regularly, he sat with his parents in "big church"—the main congregation—and probably had his share of those fidgety moments any fifth or sixth grader would have. Then his friends asked him if he wanted to join them in the middle school ministry. That's when church became fun and interesting to the youngster.

Hanging out with friends, listening to an engaging middle school pastor, and hearing the gospel was a great package, and it was in seventh grade that Sam made a decision that would affect the direction of the rest of his life. "I remember going every Sunday morning, just listening and learning more about the Lord," he said in an interview with Shawn Brown on the CBN network. "Probably after a couple of months, I really decided that I wanted to give my life to the Lord. And ever since then, it's something that I really try to make a strong point in my life."

Sam was also getting stronger as an athlete as he entered Putnam City North, a four-year public high school of 2,000 students situated in the Bradfords' upper-class neighborhood in Oklahoma City. Putnam City North High was one of three high schools in their district: Putnam City and Putnam City West were the other two. The three Putnam City high schools, which were among the largest in the state, competed in the highest classification in Oklahoma: 6A.

Academically, Putnam North was among the highest-scoring public schools in Oklahoma. Before Sam came along, Putnam North's most famous alumnus was James Marsden (class of '91), an actor who played the superhero Cyclops in the three X-Men films and also appeared in other Hollywood features like *Superman Returns*, *Hairspray*, and *Enchanted*.

Something had to be cut from Sam's top-heavy sports schedule, and the family decided it would have to be ice hockey. That was because of the time-consuming travel and weird practice times associated with hockey, plus the fact that, well, Sam couldn't play the other sports that he was really, *really* good at—like football and basketball.

MAKING A CHOICE

There was another issue to deal with as Sam entered high school: he was growing like prairie tallgrass. His growth spurt started in eighth grade, and his knees were killing him as he ran up and down the basketball floor in a summer league before his freshman year. Sam was growing so fast that Mom couldn't keep him in clothes, especially jeans.

Sam hit 6 feet, 3 inches during his first year of high school, an inch—and a quarter!—under his present height. He was rail thin, as most high school freshmen are. When Sam tried out for quarterback of the ninth-grade football team, he wowed his coaches and teammates. Varsity coach Bob Wilson, who likes to know if he has any good-looking signal-callers in the pipeline, kept his eye on the spindly kid.

Then it was on to basketball season and another freshman team. In seventh and eighth grades, basketball was probably the sport Sam played most. He spent his summers with an AAU traveling team that moved around like the Harlem Globetrotters: tournaments were played in Indiana, Georgia, Virginia, Missouri, Kansas, Colorado, and even Las Vegas. As Sam displayed his talents as a great shooter and rebounder during the first month of the season, the Putnam North coaches bumped him up to the varsity team—as a freshman.

Since Sam didn't get much playing time with the juniors and seniors on the varsity basketball team, he still played in the freshman games—which were scheduled for different days of the week (Monday and Thursday) than the varsity games (Tuesday and Friday).

NO OFF-SEASON

There was no such thing as "downtime" for Sam during his childhood. So was he worried about burnout?

"I'm glad there was never a break," he told Andrew Gilman of *The Oklahoman*. "If I had to think about those season-ending losses for seven months, that would be terrible. This way, I just go right into another sport."

For Kent and Martha Bradford, sitting in the bleachers for four basketball games a week was a piece of cake. They'd been doing that sort of stuff since Sam was in short pants. Then springtime blossomed, the time of year when young boys' hearts turn toward . . . golf.

Golf? What about baseball? Wasn't Sam a flame-throwing pitcher and a big bat at the plate?

Sure, but Sam found golf a welcome change from team sports. The competition was between him and the golf course, not other players, and he got to play with his friends. So yes, Sam was a golfer, too—and golf was *another* sport he excelled at.

That's one of *five* if you're keeping score at home.

By now, you're probably wondering, *When did Sam have time to play golf?* Who knows? But Sam started playing when he was 10 years old and proved himself quite a natural from tee to green.

One time, on a hot summer day when Sam was still in elementary school, Martha Bradford dropped him and a couple of buddies off at a local par-3 course—a nine-holer. A golf marathon was planned for that day, and Sam and his buddies made more than 12 circuits of the municipal track before darkness fell. Total number of holes played: 110.

Sam remembers sleeping well that night.

Then there was the time he got the first of his *four* holes in one. He was just a kid playing a round with his grandfather at the time. They came up to a par-3, where Sam had clanged the ball off the flagstick the day before.

Sam looked at his grandpa. "I hit the pin yesterday," he said. "I'm going to make it today."

His grandfather gave him an encouraging *Be my guest* wave, then watched the boy fashion a swing. The ball rose in flight, landed on the green, and plunked into the cup. In other words, Sam jarred it for a hole in one.

Although the odds of making a hole in one are astronomical—one in 12,750, according to *Golf Digest* magazine—Sam made it look easy. Golf was just another sport where he outshined the competition. By the time he was in high school, Sam regularly shot in the 70s and would become a scratch golfer—someone who could break par for a round of golf.

THE SOPHOMORE WINS THE JOB

Putnam North football coach Bob Wilson was in his early fifties when Sam Bradford arrived in the summer of 2003 for the start of a new season. This was his eleventh year of coaching the Panther football team and his seventeenth high school season overall, so he knew something about coaching boys—including the canyon-wide gap in maturity between sophomores and seniors. That's why his teams usually had a senior quarterback under center.

In his business, that was a no-brainer: 18-year-olds were more responsible and levelheaded than amped-up 15- or 16-year-olds who were learning a complex game with many moving parts. You win games and keep parents happy when seniors play. That's why when you're an underclassman, you wait to play.

Heading into the 2003 season, it was senior Philip Poulsen's turn to play quarterback. Sure, there was this Bradford kid, but all he had under his belt was one year of freshman football. He wasn't used to playing on Friday nights in front of 6,000 friends, classmates, parents, and fans at Putnam City Stadium.

But during summer practices, before the start of school, the whistle nearly dropped out of Coach Wilson's mouth when Sam ran the offense. Throw after throw . . . on the money. Good decision after good decision. And good size—he couldn't overlook that.

Coach Wilson raised some eyebrows when he tabbed Sophomore Sam as his starting quarterback, but the seasoned coach knew he was putting the better athlete on the field. "Sam came in and showed us he was the guy," Wilson said. "I don't remember a whole lot of doubt about starting him. He was a coach's dream because when you taught Sam something, you only had to say it once. He did whatever we asked him to do. He was very coachable."

As they say in the movies, this was the start of a beautiful relationship. For the next three seasons at Putnam North, the Panthers were Sam's team.

Sam was a quarterback who felt comfortable leading by example, not by being a holler-guy. "We didn't get to see Sam a lot in the summer, but he did come into the weight room at 6:30 in the morning to lift weights with the linemen. I'm telling you, linemen respect that, and linemen will block their backsides off for a guy who they feel is one of them," Wilson said.

A month into Sophomore Sam's first season as a high school varsity quarterback, he was invited to the Oklahoma State Fair for a "Midway Challenge" organized by *The Oklahoman* newspaper. With the greasy smell of Indian tacos and deep-fried Twinkies hanging in the air, Sam and three other standout quarterbacks were asked to throw a mini-football at a seven-inch star from a distance of 15 feet. Could any of these star athletes hit the tiny target and win an oversized stuffed bear at the football-toss game on the midway?

Out of 18 total throws from the four quarterbacks, there were only three hits. Guess who took home a green-and-purple dragon and a giant white teddy bear after making two strikes?

Sam Bradford, of course.

A LOVE FOR FOOTBALL

Just a month into his first season, Sam was impressing coaches and sportswriters, the latter declaring that he could be one of the best players in the state—even though he was only a sophomore. The young quarterback led the Panthers to the playoffs, where they lost in the state 6A semifinals. Sam put up some nice stats, too: 1,714 yards in passing and 11 touchdowns for the season.

MEET SAM BRADFORD, HIGH SCHOOL SOPHOMORE QUARTERBACK

Imagine you're 15 years old when an enterprising reporter at the local newspaper asks you to fill in the blanks on a list of questions. Here's how Sam answered a questionnaire from *The Oklahoman* on September 4, 2003—obviously before iPods destroyed the CD player market:

Position: quarterback
Grade: sophomore
Height, weight: 6-4, 180 pounds
Favorite movie: *2 Fast 2 Furious*
Favorite food: steak
Favorite music: rap
What's in your CD player? 50 Cent
If I were a pro wrestler, my name would be: Aztec Warrior
If I could have dinner with one person, it would be: Michael Jordan

---

Football was now Sam's sport. Sure, he continued playing basketball and golf at Putnam North, but his athletic future was now staked on football.

In the summer of 2004, between Sam's sophomore and junior seasons, he attended a football camp at the University of Oklahoma. The two-way street of college football camps is the kickoff of the recruiting process because it serves a dual purpose:

1. Young players improve their skills and conditioning under the watchful eyes of experienced college coaches.
2. Those same coaches take mental notes on players they'll want to recruit later on.

After squeezing the Sooners football camp into his busy schedule, Sam played well early in the 2004 season. As a team, however, the Panthers started slowly. "We were 3–3 but still had the possibility of getting to the playoffs," Coach Wilson said. "But we had to turn things around. Sam and some of the guys came up with a big sign in the locker room that said 'Believe' written on large butcher block paper. That thing crumpled during the season, but we did manage to win the next six out of the next seven games. Our comeback had a lot to do with Sam Bradford."

For someone 16 going on 17, this junior quarterback was creating quite a stir on the Putnam North campus. On the field, Sam upped his production to 1,980 yards passing and 16 touchdowns, and his quarterbacking carried the Panthers to the state playoffs. Students—and teachers—wore No. 14 jerseys to celebrate the new star in their midst. He led the Panthers to the state semifinals for the second year in a row, but the Panthers lost in the last two minutes to top-ranked Jenks, 29–23.

Sam's breakout performance in 2004 placed him squarely on the college football recruiters' radar screens. Now his name was listed on the most influential recruiting websites—Rivals, Scout, SuperPrep, and PrepStar College Recruiting, all of which rank players by position and identify the "bluechippers" certain to be wooed by the major programs.

Sam wasn't at the top of anyone's pecking order, however. Some hotshot from Florida named Tim Tebow was generating a lot of buzz. Nonetheless, the recruiting derby was on. Texas Tech made the first overture in the spring of 2005 when then–head coach Mike Leach—known in the coaching fraternity for his uncanny ability to spot developing quarterbacks—offered Sam a scholarship. Sam's family also knew Texas A&M and Iowa State were sniffing around.

When Bob Wilson heard about Texas Tech's scholarship offer, the Putnam North coach picked up the phone and called his contacts inside the Oklahoma and Oklahoma State coaching staffs. *I've got a tip for you. You've got a special kid in your backyard. You'd better take a look at him before someone else grabs him.*

Chuck Long, then the offensive coordinator at the University of Oklahoma, didn't let much moss grow under his feet. He dropped by Putnam High in May 2005 to watch Sam throw and to meet his family. Long remembered Sam from the summer football camp, and he liked the young QB's "intangibles"—his sideline demeanor, the way he handled himself in the huddle, and his polite responsiveness to coaching. He had a cannon for an arm, but he was every bit as good in the classroom, maintaining a grade-point average of better than 4.0, which placed him in the top 10 percent of his class.

As Long and the Sooners coaching staff looked over their quarterback depth chart, they knew they had landed Rhett Bomar—the nation's No. 1 high school quarterback in the 2004 recruiting season, according to Rivals.com and Scout.com—for the coming season. Coached by his father at Grand Prairie High School in Grand Prairie, Texas, Bomar was labeled the second coming of NFL great John Elway. The Sooners' brain trust expected big things from the rangy Texan when he arrived for summer training camp.

Long and the coaching staff debated whether to toss a Sooner helmet into Sam's recruiting ring. Their thinking was that since they had Bomar, who they believed was destined for greatness, they could bring in Bradford for added depth. Perhaps the Putnam North kid would develop into a starter by his junior or senior year.

Then Long learned something about Sam that sealed the deal. "You dig a little deeper, and [you find out] he's a scratch golfer, he's a basketball player, and he's a four-sport athlete, and you like those guys, especially at the quarterback position," Long said. "But I think the scratch golf, when we found that out, [was the difference]. I learned from a professional coach that if you have a quarterback who's a scratch golfer, he's a good one because he's a strategist. He can think, he can get out of the rough, and he's thinking, 'What's the next shot?'

"Plus, it's like a four-hour match, like a football game, and there are a lot of ups and downs in that match. You have to stay even keel to get through it and play under pressure. That was really the factor that got me on board anyway, though it was a little tougher sell for the staff. But we just felt he was the guy."

Long knew that if Oklahoma waited to see how Sam performed during his senior year at Putnam City before offering him a scholarship, they would risk losing him to a rival school. The stakes were raised even higher when he heard the University of Michigan was ready to offer Sam a full ride.

This called for a preemptive strike. The Oklahoma coaching staff decided to offer Sam a scholarship at the end of his junior year so they could lock him up *before* his last season of high school football. The commitment, however, would be nonbinding since, according to NCAA rules, Sam could not officially accept an athletic scholarship until his senior season was over.

National Signing Day was always the first Wednesday in February of a high school football player's senior year. Any athlete accepting a scholarship offer before National Signing Day, like Sam did, was making an oral commitment that he could later choose to back out of so he could attend a different school. (The school could also rescind the scholarship offer, but that rarely happens with top recruits.)

HOCKEY AND HIKING THE BALL

Oklahoma offensive coordinator Chuck Long liked hearing that Sam Bradford was a scratch golfer because golfers have to learn to get themselves out of jams and bounce back from bad breaks. Sam Bradford also believed his years of youth hockey weren't for naught, either.

"Hockey is so fast and unpredictable that it teaches you to think quickly and make snap decisions," Sam said. "I think that quality translates really well to playing quarterback."

He didn't mention checking, blocking, and blind side hits—other things hockey and football have in common.

The Oklahoma coaches tendered the scholarship offer, and the Bradford family, as you can imagine, was thrilled that the Sooners—*their* Sooners!—wanted their son to play quarterback in Norman. But they didn't give an automatic yes. This was a big decision, and there was no reason to rush. Kent and Martha wanted to think things through with their son.

The family drove 20 miles south to the Oklahoma campus to meet with Long and head coach Bob Stoops. They had read all the hoopla in the newspapers about the pending arrival of Rhett Bomar, and they knew Oklahoma liked to stockpile extra quarterbacks—just in case things didn't work out with the Big Recruit.

As the two sides hashed over the matter, Stoops and Long promised the Bradford family that Sam would be their only quarterback recruit in the 2006 class.

That was what the family wanted to hear. But there was something else Sam desired to get off his chest, and that was to declare his intentions to compete for playing time as soon as he arrived on campus. He wasn't going to take a backseat to anybody, including an ace like Rhett Bomar.

"If I come here, I'm coming to play," Sam said in a story recounted by Thayer Evans of the *New York Times*. Told by the Oklahoma coaches that the Sooners welcomed competition, Sam said, "Okay, that's all I wanted to know."

Everything was falling into place for the high school quarterback who had grown up in a bedroom that doubled as a shrine to Oklahoma Sooners football—mugs, pennants, banners, blankets, and other collectibles covered the walls, shelves, and dressers. He would be attending the college of his dreams, and his parents could easily watch him perform in the same 85,000-seat stadium where they had already made so many memories watching the Sooners play.

That's why Sam looked Coach Stoops and Coach Long in the eyes and said he was coming to Norman to play quarterback—not to hold a clipboard on the sideline.

SOONER DAYS

When Sam arrived at the Oklahoma campus in the summer of 2006, the Sooner football program was in turmoil.

Coach Stoops had just kicked quarterback Rhett Bomar and offensive guard J. D. Quinn off the team. The two had received money from Big Red Sports and Imports, a local car dealership, for doing work they—wink, wink—never performed. Apparently, the two never showed up to wash cars, even though they were clocked in.

"According to reports, Bomar had an arrangement with an OU-friendly car dealership that paid him thousands of dollars for performing little-to-no work," said *Sports Illustrated*'s Stewart Mandel. "It's the kind of thing so brazen in its stupidity that you wonder how on earth the involved parties thought they could get away with it."

Stoops said Bomar and Quinn "knowingly" broke the rules, and since they did so in an era of zero tolerance for violations of NCAA rules, they were dismissed from the team. You could say they were OUt of the picture.

Suddenly, the high school quarterback who was recruited almost as an afterthought had an opening.

Sam was coming off a solid senior year at Putnam North, but a porous offensive line, a lack of a threat at running back, and a sewn-up scholarship offer from Oklahoma painted a white bull's-eye on his cardinal and gold Panther jersey. Constantly harassed and chased from the pocket, Sam threw for "only" 2,029 yards and 17 touchdowns. When Putnam North failed to make the playoffs, some Sooners fans complained that Stoops had blown it when he promised to make Bradford the only quarterback in the 2006 recruiting class.

Welcome to the big leagues, Sam.

With Bomar gone, the Sooners faithful wondered if Stoops would plug the hole at quarterback with an untested true freshman—and eighteen years old, to boot. But the coach held firm and handed Sam his red shirt in training camp, meaning he wouldn't play during the 2006 season. This decision would preserve four years of eligibility, starting in 2007.

The Sooners didn't miss a beat, even with Paul Thompson, who had played wide receiver the previous season, in the quarterback role. Meanwhile, Sam handled the quarterback duties for the scout team during practice. All he could do during games was watch from the sideline, in street clothes, as the Sooners won the Big 12 title and a trip to the Fiesta Bowl, where they lost to Boise State. The Broncos scored on a two-point conversion play in overtime to win 43–42.

It practically killed Sam not to be playing. Remember, he'd been juggling three or four sports year-round for more than a decade, and he'd never been anything less than a key player on every team he was on. So when the start of the 2007 college football season rolled around, Sam wasn't about to spend another season watching someone else standing in the pocket—even if he *was* a redshirt freshman.

During summer training camp, Sam emerged from a three-way battle with sophomore Joey Halzle and first-year freshman Keith "Kid" Nichol to grab the reins of the Oklahoma team. Sam's sharp performances in several team scrimmages made the difference. In addition, the success of a "yearling" quarterback the previous year at the University of Texas—a redshirt freshman named Colt McCoy—increased the Oklahoma coaching staff's confidence that another redshirt freshman was up to the job.

Kent Bradford was on cloud nine. "I just tried to teach him patience and probably play the role of the parent and offer him all the encouragement I could—'Hang in there, buddy,' that kind of thing," he said after learning his son had won the coveted position.

It didn't take long for Sam to prove to Sooners fans that Coach Stoops had made the right decision. In his debut, a home opener against the University of North Texas—a warm-up game, if you will—Sam completed 21 of 23 passes for 363 yards—all in a little over two quarters of work. The reason for the short day at the office: the Sooners won 79–10.

The following week, in a 51–13 home win over the University of Miami Hurricanes, Sam broke 2003 Heisman Trophy winner Jason White's school record for the most consecutive pass completions. The new number to beat: 23.

In the next two games—both big wins—the Sooners racked up 54 and 62 points to run their record to 4–0 and claw their way into the national title picture as the No. 4–ranked team in the nation.

Coach Stoops nicknamed Sam "The Big Easy" for his relaxed personality and unflappable attitude. Many of his teammates also said he was a calming influence in the huddle, no matter how well the offense was moving the ball. Then again, it helps when you're scoring on nearly every series.

Sportswriters noticed that Sam had thrown 25 touchdowns in the Sooners' first nine games, meaning he had a good chance to break the NCAA freshman record of 29 touchdown passes, set by David Neill of the University of Nevada in 1988 and tied by a University of Texas quarterback named—you guessed it—Colt McCoy the year before.

The Sooners were on a roll, but a 27–24 road loss to Colorado in Boulder—after they had led 24–10 in the third quarter—came on a day when Sam had his first poor outing as the OU quarterback. His stats: 8-for-19 passing, 112 yards, one touchdown, and two interceptions.

With the loss, the Sooner bandwagon got caught in a wheel rut—but then Sam led the team on a five-game winning stampede, which included a Red River Rivalry (also known as the Red River Shootout) victory over the University of Texas.

The Red River Rivalry—which gets its name from the Red River, a natural boundary between Texas and Oklahoma—is an interstate game played every season at a "neutral" site—Dallas' Cotton Bowl, where Texas fans are allotted half the tickets and Sooners supporters take the other half.

Against Texas Tech, however, Oklahoma suffered its second loss of the season—and a major reason for the defeat was Sam's first serious injury. OU running back Allen Patrick lost a fumble, which Texas Tech linebacker Marlon Williams picked up. Sam chased after Williams to make a tackle, but he hit his head on the turf when he fell to the ground.

Sam returned for the next series, but when he came off the field, he couldn't remember any of the plays the team had run. He was done for the day, and so were the Sooners' hopes for a win.

Sam was cleared to play the next week in the Bedlam Game—the name for the annual contest against rival Oklahoma State—and he helped the Sooners deliver a sweet 49–17 rout of the Cowboys. Sweeter yet—at least on a personal level—was Sam's two-yard touchdown strike to tight end Joe Jon Finley during the second quarter, which broke the NCAA freshman record for TD passes in a season.

The victory over OSU put the Sooners into the Big 12 championship against the No. 1-ranked team in the country, Missouri. The Tigers' only loss of the season came earlier in the year to Oklahoma, so revenge, as well as a trip to the BCS Championship Game, was on their minds. Sam coolly denied Missouri a chance to play for the national championship, leading OU to a clear-cut 38–17 victory that sent the Sooners to Glendale, Arizona, for a January 2, 2008, matchup against West Virginia in the Fiesta Bowl.

The Mountaineers manhandled the Sooners, 48–28, however. Three sacks in the first half, plus several errant throws from Sam—including an interception—put Oklahoma in deep holes they couldn't dig their way out of. Still, in Sam's first season of college football, the Sooners finished the year ranked eighth in the nation with an 11–3 record, leaving him and Sooners fans believing all the pieces were in place for a run to the top in 2008.

After all, they had one of the nation's top-rated passers in their midst, and he was only going to get better.

BUILDING A HABITAT

They call it "team building."

A week before the start of training camp for the 2007 OU football season—before Sam had won the starting quarterback job—60 Sooners players stepped on a bus and traveled five miles south to Noble, Oklahoma, where the Christian charity Habitat for Humanity was building a house in a sleepy residential neighborhood. Sam Bradford, who had yet to don a red Sooners jersey in an official NCAA game, was on board in more ways than one.

This wasn't a 20-minute photo op for the six o'clock news. The beefy players put in a half-day's work in the stifling heat—a four-hour stretch of pounding nails, hefting lumber, and cleaning up the yard. The three OU quarterbacks—Sam, Joey Halzle, and Keith Nichol—drew weed duty.

Sam had learned the value of plugging into a ministry during his redshirt year in 2006. He arrived at the Oklahoma campus a bit untethered. It was his first time living away from home, of course, so there was that adjustment. Then the Rhett Bomar controversy blew up, which created an air of uncertainty. Remember, too, that Sam thought maybe he might get a chance to play right away as a true freshmen, but when Coach Stoops told Sam Oklahoma would redshirt him, he was thrown off kilter. Now he'd have to wait a whole year before he would have the opportunity to get in a real game.

Sam told CBN's Shawn Brown that his patience and perseverance were tested during his first semester in Norman. "I really struggled," he said. "I really struggled with the Lord because I came here and wasn't getting to play. I was sitting on the bench. I was having to wake up at 5 a.m. to go to workouts. That was a totally new concept to me. Every sport I'd played in, I always played. I never sat on the bench. So I kind of turned my back on the Lord. I was like, 'Why are You doing this to me? Why are You putting me in this situation?' "

Kent Bowles, the leader of the OU chapter of the Fellowship of Christian Athletes (FCA), checked in on the redshirt recruit. The FCA, which was founded in 1954 and is based in Kansas City, Missouri, is a nonprofit, interdenominational ministry that reaches out to young athletes and uses the powerful medium of athletics to impact the world for Jesus Christ.

Sam knew about the FCA because he was part of weekly "Huddle" meetings at Putnam North, which any student could attend. Huddles are where Christian fellowship and spiritual growth occur, but on the Oklahoma campus, Sam had yet to plug into the FCA or any other Christian fellowship group.

Bowles quietly but firmly challenged Sam about his relationship with Christ, saying he needed to get off the sidelines and into the game. Sam listened and got the message. A short time later, he began attending FCA meetings on campus and rekindled his relationship with Christ. He also struck up friendships with other Christians who could bolster him and pray for him.

SAM'S NEW PREGAME RITUAL

Moving ahead nearly a year later to the start of the 2007 season, the untested quarterback was nervous before the Sooners' first game against North Texas. Understandable, since 85,000 fans, including his parents, would be in the stands at Owen Field.

Even for home games, the Sooner team stayed in a hotel for meals and meetings. After the last meeting was over, he walked back to his hotel room and opened his Bible. He flipped some pages and landed in 1 Samuel 17, which tells the story of David and Goliath. He was mesmerized as he read about how David, a scrawny shepherd boy who had the fate of his people in his hands, took on a nine-foot-tall giant—a bruiser named Goliath.

The Bible says David wasn't afraid to take on a foe much taller, much heavier, and much more experienced. Instead, the rookie warrior used guile and his "throwing" skill when he raised his slingshot and whizzed a smooth stone with zip-line speed into the middle of Goliath's forehead. If the Israelites had ESPN *SportsCenter* replaying game highlights back then, the anchor would have praised David for delivering a courageous throw "between the numbers" . . . "when it mattered most" . . . "on the biggest stage" . . . "between two foes who don't like each other—the Philistines and the Israelites." You can see for yourself by reading the David and Goliath story from 1 Samuel 17.

Reading the against-all-odds story of David encouraged Sam and gave him the confidence he needed to take the field against North Texas. Afterward, he decided to make reading the David and Goliath story his pregame ritual throughout his college career at Oklahoma. (We'll see if he continues reading 1 Samuel 17 on Saturday nights or Sunday mornings when he starts playing for the Rams.)

ESPN's Ivan Maisel thinks he knows why Sam liked the David and Goliath story so much: "Bradford said it's not that he identifies with David, even though there are similarities. Like Bradford, David started as a freshman. And like Bradford, David led the FBS (First Book of Samuel) in passing efficiency—David completed his only attempt, a game-winner against favored Goliath."

Okay, we're just having some fun here, but there's a serious side to the David and Goliath story, which, after all, was a fight-to-the-death battle with huge implications for each side. First of all, David focused on God, not on the giant in his path. He could trust in the Lord because He was with him every step of the way. If he looked at giant problems and impossible situations from God's perspective, he could feel confidence in knowing God would fight for him and with him.

Emboldened *on* the field, Sam's spiritual confidence grew *off* the field. He became a fixture at the Tuesday night OU Huddle meetings, where he was "Sam"—just another guy who acted like he wanted to be treated that way.

A Q&A WITH KENT BOWLES OF THE OKLAHOMA FCA

Is the story true that you checked in on Sam his freshman year and quietly but firmly challenged his relationship with Christ?

Kent: Sam was very approachable and easygoing. I just gently nudged him toward FCA, and he seemed excited to find a comfortable setting to plug into spiritually.

When did Sam start attending OU Huddle meetings?

Kent: Second semester of his redshirt freshman year. He attended regularly throughout his college career at Oklahoma, and he joined the FCA Leadership Team his sophomore year.

Where were the meetings held? Who attended them? Could anyone go?

Kent: The FCA meetings were held weekly in the athletic dining hall. We average about 100 students every meeting. Any student or student athlete could attend. We had mostly athletes attend at Oklahoma.

Is it true that Sam would either bring icebreaker games or do the icebreaker games? What were some of those icebreaker games?

Kent: Sam did what all of the other leaders did regularly. He opened in prayer, led games and icebreakers, introduced speakers, etc. Even though he garnered an enormous amount of attention on the field and in many circles of campus life, he was just another student athlete at FCA. Sam was old school. You could always count on him to lead an old-fashioned game of rock/scissors/paper!

What else did Sam contribute to the Huddles?

Kent: Sam made himself available to speak to the FCA Huddles in the Norman community. He also spoke to local churches as well. Sam made time in his schedule to be interviewed by FCA's *Sharing the Victory* magazine, which led to various media-related opportunities for FCA Huddles and students across the country.

What will Sam have to do to keep spiritually grounded in the NFL?

Kent: Sam makes great daily choices. Sam will continue to make those great decisions because he is grounded in his faith. Sam will not be enamored with fame and fortune. The spotlight is nothing new to him, and because he values faith and family, he will be a solid role model in the NFL.

The Three QBs come from solid, intact families, which unfortunately is not the norm these days. Talk about that.

Kent: I know that all three of these guys come from solid Christian families. That is rare these days. Sam has great parents who have raised him in a loving, Christian home.

The norm these days is to see about 6 of 10 athletes come from broken homes where the parents are divorced or never married. It certainly doesn't mean that kids from broken homes can't succeed and become solid in their faith and great Christian men and women. But the example of "family" is so important, and you can see the edge it gives a guy like Sam because it's just one element of life that is not a worry or a burden to overcome.

After the 2007 season, during the doldrums between the last bowl game and the start of spring practice, Coach Stoops dropped by the office of Kevin Wilson, who took over as OU offensive coordinator before the 2006 season. The topic turned to how the Sooners offense—already plenty potent during Sam's first season of college football—could score even *more* points.

Big 12 contests were becoming more like "track meets" than football games—with unstoppable offenses running and passing the ball up and down the field and racking up amazing scores. Unless your offense could keep up in this football version of the arms race, you could easily come out on the short end of a 49–42 score.

Stoops and Wilson both knew half the teams in the Big 12 were using a no-huddle offense—also known as the hurry-up offense—a type of strategy where the offense quickly gets to the line of scrimmage without huddling before running the next play.

Most teams use this strategy in the last two minutes of a half in order to get the ball downfield fast in a short amount of time. But more and more teams in the Big 12, and around the country, were utilizing a no-huddle offense *all* the time, meaning that as soon as the whistle blew the previous play dead, the offense was lining up in formation to start a new play. The quarterback then approached the center or stayed in the shotgun, but before starting the play count, he looked to his sideline for a signal for the next play. The quarterback then cupped his hands over his mouth and yelled out the play—all in coded numbers and phrases.

The no-huddle tires and disorients defenses, conserves valuable clock time, and, from a fan's point of view, makes the game more exciting. Running the no-huddle takes tons of preparation and a quarterback who can process information on the fly and execute it flawlessly when the play starts.

Sam had led the nation in passing efficiency during his freshman season, so the Sooners had the right leader on the field.

Coach Wilson was on board. "If you want to run a no-huddle, I know how to do it," he told Stoops.

That spring, the OU coaches overhauled the offense, and what emerged was an up-tempo, fast-break offensive scheme that utilized multiple personnel groupings during the course of a game. The idea was to get the defense playing on its heels while Sam drilled receiver after receiver for 10- and 20-yard gains.

Although no one knew it at the time, Sam had just been handed the keys to a high-powered offense that would take Oklahoma to the BCS National Championship Game and propel him to the very top of college football's list of elite quarterbacks. The Sooners opened with 57, 52, and 55 points—against Chattanooga, Cincinnati, and Washington, respectively—and by early October they vaulted themselves to the top of the major college football polls as the No. 1 team in the country.

Even though the Sooners were running up tons of points and were at the top of the college football polls, Sam understood the importance of keeping their early-season success in perspective. "At this point, [it means] absolutely nothing," Sam said. "We've still got a way to go before we think about polls."

As the Sooners' prospects skyrocketed, the first whispers that Sam was worthy of consideration for the Heisman Trophy—the award given annually to the outstanding college football player whose performance best exhibits the pursuit of excellence with integrity—started appearing in the press. Sam, predictably, said he wasn't worried about individual awards, just about helping the team win.

The sixth game of the OU season—the Red River Rivalry—matched the unbeaten, top-ranked Sooners and the No. 5 Longhorns. ESPN's *College Game-Day* analysts took turns saying, "This is a *big* game," and talked up the high-noon duel between a pair of Heisman Trophy candidates: Sam Bradford and Colt McCoy.

The Texas quarterback saw the Red River pairing as special. "How fun is it every week to be up against a team that has another great quarterback?" Colt said. "It's a challenge every week to know that, hey, there's another guy across the field that's leading his team and is playing really well. It makes it fun, it makes it exciting."

Even though Sam's and Colt's passing attempts and completions were nearly identical (Sam completed 28 of 39, while Colt was 28 of 35), Sam threw two interceptions, and the Longhorn defense came up with the big stops in a 45–35 UT victory. The Oklahoma Sooners left Dallas that day sure that their BCS championship hopes had been dashed inside the Cotton Bowl.

Then something unexpected happened: Oklahoma's no-huddle offense went ballistic and Sam's passing blew the doors off the season. Check out these scores from the next six games:

- Oklahoma over Kansas State: 58–35
- Oklahoma over Nebraska: 62–28
- Oklahoma over Texas A&M: 66–28
- Oklahoma over Texas Tech: 65–21
- in the Bedlam Game, Oklahoma over Oklahoma State: 61–41

- in the Big 12 Championship Game, Oklahoma over Missouri: 62–41

That season, the Sooners set a modern-day NCAA football record for scoring with 702 points, including at least 60 in each of their last five games. Hitler's tanks couldn't stop them. Defensive coordinators had trouble sleeping nights before games with Oklahoma. The nights after as well.

By virtue of winning the Big 12 and scoring in the 60s so often, the Sooners leapfrogged Texas and Florida in the national polls and grabbed the No. 1 spot. That development didn't sit well with Longhorns fans, whose Texas team beat Oklahoma back in October, but that's what the BCS computers spit out.

Oklahoma was back in the National Championship Game, this time against the University of Florida Gators at Dolphin Stadium in Miami.

The Gators had a great quarterback, too.

His name was Tim Tebow.

THE HEISMAN POSE

Two days after the Big 12 Championship Game, Sam underwent surgery to repair damaged ligaments in his nonthrowing (left) hand, which he suffered during the Oklahoma State game. Coach Stoops told the media he expected Sam to be ready for the BCS Championship Game on January 8, 2009.

During the month-long wait, Sam learned he was a finalist for the Heisman Trophy, which would be awarded on December 13 at the Nokia Theatre in New York City. Two other quarterbacks were also invited to the televised event on ESPN: Colt McCoy, who had bounced back from a subpar sophomore season to put together a superlative junior year at Texas, and Tim Tebow, the Florida quarterback who the year before had become the youngest winner—and first sophomore ever—to win the Heisman Trophy.

Sam and his parents made their first trip together to the Big Apple to attend the Heisman ceremonies. The glare of the epicenter of the media universe was a bit overwhelming for Mom. "Sometimes," she said, her voice cracking, "you just have to pinch yourself and realize what's happening. It's just going so fast. I don't know if I'm taking it all in."

Inside the Nokia Theatre, the Heisman Trophy committee sat Sam, Tim, and Colt next to each other in the front row. The Three QBs, dressed in their Sunday best—jacket and tie—looked comfortable with the moment as previous Heisman winners were introduced and speeches were made.

Earlier, the three of them had sat in the green room together making small talk about their teams and the upcoming bowl games. They knew they were all Christians, so as the Heisman ceremony approached, they bowed their heads, clasped hands, and prayed that God would be glorified that evening. Since Tim had won the Heisman Trophy the year before, Sam asked him how it felt to be selected and what he might say should he win. "Don't forget to thank who was responsible," Tim replied.

When the announcement finally came, near the end of the hour-long event, Sam looked stunned when he heard his name spoken as the winner. He stood up, hugged Tebow and McCoy, then stepped a couple of rows back to grasp his beaming parents and Coach Stoops.

When Sam took the podium, his left hand in a cast covered with Sooners-red gauze, the first sentence out of his mouth was: "I first need to thank God. He has given me so many blessings, He's blessed me with so many opportunities, and He's put so many wonderful people in my life that I give all the credit to Him. Without Him, I'd be nowhere and we'd all be nowhere."

Just sixteen months after being named the starting quarterback at Oklahoma, Sam was the toast of college football as he clutched the illustrious bronze sculpture. He was the second sophomore—after Tim Tebow—to win the famed Heisman Trophy. In the second-closest three-man race in the 73-year history of the award, Sam received 1,726 total points, edging out Colt (with 1,604 points) and Tim (with 1,575 points) to win the Heisman.

Kent and Martha Bradford, whose memory banks must have flashed through the hundreds of peewee ball games and summer road trips to another weekend tournament, watched their son pose for pictures and sign autographs after the ESPN cameras had cut away.

"It's unbelievable," Martha said. "You can dream, but the Heisman . . . it's just on another planet."

Something else neat happened in New York during the Heisman event: Sam clicked with Colt. "I think we just got to talking," Sam said. "We were really similar in the way we were brought up. We both played a lot of sports growing up. I think we've gone through some of the same things. He started as a redshirt freshman. I started as a redshirt freshman."

Colt told Ivan Maisel of ESPN, "We both went to a small [high] school. We both really weren't recruited heavily out of high school. We both went to our in-state university that we loved and had grown up watching. He played all the sports in high school. So did I. We finally got to [high] school and focused on one thing, and that ended up being football."

FOR ALL THE MARBLES

The Bradford family hung around Manhattan a few more days after the Heisman ceremony while Sam made the media rounds, signed 300 footballs for the Heisman Trust, sat for his official Heisman portrait, rang the bell to begin trading at the New York Stock Exchange, and attended a formal Heisman banquet.

Meanwhile, winning the Heisman complicated Sam's life in some ways. Even though he had played only 27 games in a Sooners jersey, he was eligible for the NFL draft because he had spent the required three seasons in college, including his redshirt year. If Sam and the family decided the prudent thing for him to do would be to take the NFL's millions now (versus risking injury while playing another year of college football), they had to declare their intentions by January 15, 2009.

But first, there was another big game to play: the BCS Championship between the universities of Oklahoma and Florida, the top two teams in the country.

The Big 12 versus the Southeastern Conference.

Bob Stoops versus Urban Meyer.

Sam Bradford versus Tim Tebow.

The day after Sam cradled the Heisman Trophy, Jeremy Fowler of the *Orlando Sentinel* laid down a Gator gauntlet when he wrote, "His smirk said he got robbed. His body language said he's going to make Oklahoma feel that pain on January 8 in the national title game."

Fowler was referring, of course, to Tim Tebow, who won the most *first-place* votes in the complicated Heisman voting procedure but still finished a close third. An analysis showed that Tebow took his biggest hit from voters in the Southwest region, which included those from Oklahoma and Texas— folks who would be expected to be "Florida haters." The Heisman snub, Fowler believed, would fuel the fire in Tebow's belly.

The trash talk began when Sooners cornerback Dominique Franks said before the game that if Tim Tebow played in the Big 12, he'd "probably be about the fourth-best quarterback in our conference."

Reporters rushed to Tim's side to ask him if he believed he would *really* be the fourth-best quarterback in the Big 12, which prompted a laugh and a wise "I don't really need to talk about that." Florida linebacker Brandon Spikes, however, couldn't resist the microphone, calling Big 12 defenses "a joke" and saying that when he watches ESPN *SportsCenter*, "I look at the scores, and it's 56–49, just basketball scores."

Oklahoma came into the BCS Championship Game with a 12–1 record and ranked No. 1, while Florida, also 12–1, was ranked No. 2. "Clash of the Titans" was the way the game was billed, a marquee match-up pitting the un-stoppable Sooners offense against the Gators' stiff defense.

Dolphin Stadium was crammed with 78,468 fans, and they watched as the Sooner offense failed to score on several early opportunities. Sometimes OU just stalled and sometimes penalties and mental mistakes stopped the team. The Gators stuffed the Sooners on a fourth-and-goal from the one-yard line, and then, on the six-yard line, with 10 seconds to go in the first half, Sam forced a throw into coverage. The Florida defense tipped and intercepted the pass at the goal line.

The game remained close, though. Early in the fourth quarter, with Flor-ida leading 17–14, Sam was driving his team toward a possible touchdown, and the lead, when the key play of the game took place. Florida defensive back Ahmad Black wrestled the ball out of the hands of Sooners receiver Juaquin Iglesias, who was on a deep pass route. Suddenly, Tim Tebow and the Gators smelled victory, and they embarked on an 11-play, 76-yard scoring drive that took 6:52 off the clock, essentially sealing the game for Florida.

Tebow, who bounced back from a couple of first-half interceptions, was clearly on a mission. Throughout the game, he lowered his shoulder and plowed his way through the Sooner defense. One time he cracked an OU linebacker with a meaty forearm. He executed a nifty "jump pass" late in the fourth quarter to clinch the victory and claim the Gators' second national championship in three seasons and third overall.

"You don't want to wake up a sleeping giant," said Florida running back Percy Harvin after the game.

Sam knew his performance was subpar. "In the second half, when we needed to make plays, we just couldn't do it," he said.

Six days later, back in Norman, Sam announced he would return for his junior year at Oklahoma. The loss to Florida played a "little bit" into his decision, but what he really didn't want to do was cut short his college experience at Oklahoma. There was some unfinished business, and that was bringing home the Sooners' eighth national championship.

But then the game of life would take an unexpected bounce for Sam Bradford.

RISKY BUSINESS

When Sam opted to return for his junior year, Kent Bradford knew his son was taking a calculated risk. A serious injury—even a career-ending one—was always just one play away.

Kent also knew something about insurance policies. As the president of Bradford-Irwin Insurance, that was his business. Although he specialized in commercial insurance, his knowledge of the industry proved invaluable as he researched the types of "doomsday" policies that were out there for his son. They all came with exclusions written in favor of the insurance companies, as well as coverage triggers and rehab requirements, so you had to know what you were doing. Cost of a $2 million policy in the event of a career-ending injury: a hefty $20,000 a year.

Kent declined to state how much insurance the family took out on Sam, but it's worth noting that the families of Colt McCoy and Tim Tebow were thinking along the same lines. The McCoy family purchased a policy for Colt that ranged from $3 million to $5 million, and Tim's was worth an estimated $2 million.

Maybe Kent sensed they would need the insurance policy in their hip pocket, or maybe he likes to sleep better at night.

The first omen that things were going to go south for Sam Bradford and the Sooners took place in training camp, when All-American tight end Jermaine Gresham suffered a knee injury and was lost before the season even began. Also, the offensive line never got settled, and in the season opener against Brigham Young, the inexperienced line committed 12 penalties, missed several blocking assignments, and failed to keep the BYU defensive lineman and linebackers from racing into the Sooner backfield. When Sam stepped back to pass, he never knew if he would have to run for his life or get the ball off before he wanted to.

On one key play, a blitzing BYU linebacker found a free lane and delivered a devastating hit on Sam, slamming him into the turf and knocking him out of the game with a sprained acromioclavicular (AC) joint in the shoulder of his throwing arm. There was no damage to the collarbone, rotator cuff, or ball and socket, but Sam would be out two to four weeks.

His new BFF, Colt McCoy, sent him a text message wishing him a speedy recovery. Colt wanted Sam to recover quickly since the pair had a rematch coming up in a month: Oklahoma versus Texas in the Red River Rivalry at the Cotton Bowl.

With pressure mounting to get back on the field, Sam returned three weeks later to lead a lopsided win over Baylor. Then it was on to Dallas. This time around, the 20th-ranked Sooners were coming in as clear underdogs to the No. 3 Longhorns.

Sam started the Red River Rivalry game, but he wasn't able to finish it. During Oklahoma's second series, speedy Longhorns cornerback Aaron Williams blitzed untouched from the right side and smothered Sam—right on his bum shoulder. For the second time in a month, the Oklahoma quarterback writhed in pain, even falling to his knees. Sam Bradford's junior season was over.

A few days later, Sam announced he would submit to season-ending surgery to repair damaged ligaments in his throwing shoulder. Dr. James Andrews, a renowned sports orthopedic surgeon in Birmingham, Alabama—where many of the pros go when they want the best treatment available—would be performing the operation.

Before traveling to Alabama, Sam dropped by the Sooners' locker room to say good-bye to his teammates, thank his coaches, and conduct a farewell press conference. One of the first questions asked was whether he had any regrets about deciding to return to the University of Oklahoma for the 2009 season.

"No," he shot back. "Absolutely 100 percent no regrets."

He expanded on that thought: "Considering this is where I grew up and this is where I dreamed of playing, to put this in the past is extremely tough. I've been blessed to be here. The past three and a half years have been the best three and a half years of my life. I wouldn't trade a day of it."

In Birmingham, Kent was allowed to witness part of Dr. Andrews' 35-minute procedure on Sam's shoulder, which was termed successful. Later, to the surprise of no one, the family announced that Sam would forgo his senior year at OU and make himself available for the NFL draft in April.

Still, the questions remained. Would the shoulder injury cost Sam millions of dollars? Was he "damaged goods" as far as the NFL was concerned? No one would know the answers to those questions until four to five months of rehabilitation had passed.

One thing was certain, though: the last thing the Bradfords wanted to do was cash in on that insurance policy.

2

COLT McCOY:
THE EYES OF TEXAS ARE UPON HIM

The last time we saw Colt McCoy in a college football uniform, he was standing on the floor of the Rose Bowl, grasping his jersey and shoulder pads with his left hand while ABC's sideline reporter Lisa Salters cocked a microphone below his chin.

Behind him, joyous University of Alabama players danced jigs of celebration while tens of thousands of Crimson Tide fans in attendance reveled in their school's first national championship since 1992. Alabama had beaten the proud University of Texas Longhorns 37–21 in the BCS National Championship Game, held on January 7, 2010.

A blank look of dejection covered Colt's face. The moment he had worked for his entire college football career had slipped through his fingers like a muddy football.

Coming into the game, Colt was in top shape. He had done the necessary work on the practice field and in the weight room. He had spent the month of December studying film for one game against the Crimson Tide. He was ready to lead his No. 2–ranked team to a BCS national championship.

But all his preparation and hard work were taken away in one play.

Shortly after the opening kickoff, Texas safety Blake Gideon intercepted an ill-advised throw on a fake punt, and the Longhorns were in business on the Alabama 37-yard line. Colt quickly moved the Texas offense to the 11-yard line, and on the fifth play of the drive, he took the snap and darted to his left. This was an option play in which he had the choice of flipping the football to his trailing tailback, Tre' Newton, or running the ball into the end zone himself if he saw daylight.

Alabama's sturdy defensive tackle Marcel Dareus, however, slid off a block and jolted Colt, knocking him onto the back of Texas center Chris Hall. The collision didn't look like anything out of the ordinary, but, as ABC color commentator Kirk Herbstreit said during a replay, Marcel Dareus "is 300 pounds coming downhill in a hurry."

Colt didn't waste any time getting back to his feet, but as he got his bearings, he rotated his right shoulder and started jogging toward the Texas sideline. With his left arm, he motioned for someone to replace him while his right arm hung to his side, limp as a flag in still air.

Trainers huddled with Colt on the sideline before escorting him to the Texas locker room, located in the corner of the end zone. His father, Brad McCoy, a Texas high school football coach who had nurtured Colt's football career from day one, left his seat and headed to the bowels of the Rose Bowl to comfort his oldest son.

Brad watched Colt take off his predominantly white Longhorn jersey and shoulder pads and lie down on a table for X-rays. The film was quickly developed, and team doctors peered at the images against a lighted background. "Negative," they agreed. Nothing in his right shoulder was fractured.

Their diagnosis made sense to Colt. The shoulder didn't hurt—but he couldn't feel his arm. Trainers applied bags of ice to the shoulder to stop any inflammation.

Colt pleaded with the team doctors and trainers to return to the game. *I can play. Let me go in. Just give me a chance. My arm is okay.*

Colt had fibbed, and he admitted as much afterward. His arm wasn't okay. The limb felt dead—like he had slept on it all night and just woke up. But his heart was willing. He desperately wanted to play, and his team needed him. From a TV set hanging in a corner of the locker room, everyone could see that Alabama was starting to run away with the game in the second quarter.

Okay, let's see you throw, one of the trainers said.

Inside the Rose Bowl locker room, Colt lined up just seven yards away from his father. How many passes had father and son lobbed back and forth to each other over the years? It seemed like millions to Colt. He was just a toddler when they started playing catch in the backyard of their home. With the passage of time, they moved to the football field of Jim Ned High School in tiny Tuscola, Texas, where the father was the coach and the son became the star quarterback.

Inside the Rose Bowl locker room, however, Colt threw . . . well, like a girl. Nothing on the ball. Afterward, he said his arm felt like a "wet noodle."

The Texas medical personnel shook their heads. *We can't let you play, son.* They explained that he had suffered a pinched nerve in his shoulder—also known as a "stinger" or "burner"—following the violent collision with Dareus. He most likely wouldn't require surgery, but the normal course of treatment was three weeks of rest and rehabilitation.

Colt McCoy's career as a Longhorn was over.

The quarterback who had started every game for Texas over the past four seasons—the ironman who never got hurt—was knocked out of his final game in what should have been the fitting climax to his college football career.

This wasn't the storybook ending Colt had dreamed about. He was supposed to lead the Longhorns of the University of Texas—*his* team—to a BCS national championship, just like another Texas quarterback, Vince Young, had done four years and three days earlier on the same Rose Bowl turf—when Colt was a redshirt noncombatant for the 2006 BCS Championship Game.

During a lull in that game's action, Young approached the kid holding a clipboard. "You need to watch," the celebrated Texas quarterback said. "This is going to be you."

Colt nervously paced the Texas sidelines as the Longhorns, down 38–33, had one last chance to come from behind and snatch victory from the USC Trojans. The game hung in the balance when the Texas offense faced a fourth-and-five from the 8-yard line with less than 30 seconds to go.

Fail to convert, and game over.

Any Longhorn fan can tell you what happened next. Vince Young took the snap, scanned the field, and went through his progressions, but he couldn't find an open receiver. With the screams of 93,986 fans ringing in his ears, Young took off on a diagonal for the right pylon of the end zone and, in a footrace, beat the Trojan linebackers to the goal line. Bedlam—and an improbable come-from-behind victory and national championship for the University of Texas.

Tonight was Colt's moment on the same stage, in the same stadium, and with the same stakes—finishing the season as the No. 1 team in college football. It was Texas versus Alabama for the American Football Coaches Association (AFCA) trophy and a chance to hoist an eight-pound Waterford crystal football above his head. But after taking the shot to his right shoulder early in the game, Colt could barely toss a football across a room to his father.

His teammates would have to win without him.

One of the team doctors instructed him to take a shower and watch the second half in team sweats. Colt ignored the directive and put his pads back on, just in case feeling and strength returned to his arm. If he couldn't play, he decided, then he would at least be the team leader he had always been, encouraging his teammates to never give up and helping out where he could.

The second quarter ended, and a downcast Texas team trudged to the locker room, where they found Colt waiting for them. His replacement at quarterback, Garrett Gilbert—the true freshman who saw only mop-up duty behind Colt during the regular season—looked like a ghost. His play had been a train wreck. After the Texas coaches had ordered him to get in there and replace Colt, he couldn't find his helmet. He rushed throws and frequently bounced passes to his receivers. He looked uncomfortable and out of his element. During the first half, he completed three passes out of 10 throws—with Alabama players making two of those catches.

The last interception took place with 15 seconds to go in the first half, when Marcel Dareus—him again!—deflected and corralled Gilbert's short shovel pass. The beefy 'Bama player rumbled for the end zone, shoving Gilbert aside like he was a rag doll. No wonder Gilbert looked down and depressed as he entered the locker room. Alabama had a huge 24–6 lead at intermission.

"Stay calm out there," Colt counseled Gilbert. "Keep your head up. Keep plugging away and something good is going to happen."

Colt, still in full pads and uniform, returned to the sidelines after halftime and wore a headset to stay involved with the play-calling. Between offensive series, he tutored Gilbert like the freshman quarterback he was.

Something clicked in the second half. The inexperienced quarterback who had lost his way in the first half mounted an improbable comeback. Two well-thrown touchdown passes cut the 24–6 deficit to 24–21 with 6:15 to go in the fourth quarter. A last-gasp effort, however, failed when Gilbert was pressured and fumbled, leading to another Tide touchdown.

That was the game.

When Alabama ran out the clock and the victorious players in red jerseys began rejoicing over their victory, ABC's Lisa Salters and a cameraman chased after Colt to get his reaction. With the camera's red light turned on and millions of TV sets tuned in, Ms. Salters asked him, "What was it like for you to watch this game—the last game in uniform—from a sideline?"

Instead of making a glib reply or falling back on the typical jock clichés, Colt ruefully shook his head. *Twice* he began, "I . . . I . . ." before stopping to regroup. Then he took another long, long moment—an eternity on live TV—to gather himself. It was clear he was fighting his emotions.

Perhaps he was remembering what happened the night before with Jordan Shipley, his best friend, roommate, and wide receiver on the Texas team. On the eve of the Rose Bowl game, they sat in their hotel room and read Isaiah 26:4: "Trust in the LORD always, for the LORD GOD is the eternal Rock" (New Living Translation).

Just when it looked like he had lost his voice—or his nerve—Colt called his own number. "I . . . I love this game," he began in his slight but distinctive Texas twang. "I have a passion for this game. I've done everything I can to contribute to my team, and we made it this far. It's unfortunate that I didn't get to play. I would have given everything I had to be out there with my team. Congratulations to Alabama. I love the way our team fought. Garrett Gilbert stepped in and played as good as he could play. He did a tremendous job. I always give God the glory. I never question why things happen the way they do. God is in control of my life, and I know that . . . I am standing on the Rock."

In addition to his articulateness with the entire sporting nation looking on, the greatest thing about Colt's response was his expression. His face carried an angelic look of happiness and assurance of who he was, in victory or defeat.

In many ways, he was just as ready for this trying moment as he would have been for a Texas victory.

WATCH FOR YOURSELF

If you've never seen Colt's postgame interview with Lisa Salters, or would like to revisit the experience, all it takes is a few minutes to watch online. You can find numerous versions on YouTube by typing in "Colt McCoy Rose Bowl 2010 interview." But perhaps the best viewing experience comes from ESPN. The link is: http://espn.go.com/blog/sportscenter/tag/_/name/lisa-salters

BORN ON TEXAS SOIL

The name Colt McCoy is pure Texan and sounds like a movie character from a 1940s rootin'-tootin' western featuring Colt, who'd insist on playing the role of the gunslinger in a white hat. To carry the Wild West theme a step further, if Sam Bradford has a cannon of an arm, then Colt has a deadly accurate rifle.

In 2008 Colt completed 77.6 percent of his passes to set a new NCAA record for highest single-season completion percentage. He also won more games (45) than any other starting quarterback in NCAA history, and though he never won the Heisman Trophy like Sam Bradford and Tim Tebow did, he played in—and started—more games (53) than either Sam or Tim.

Daniel Colt McCoy was born on September 5, 1986, making him the eldest of the Three QBs. He's nearly a year older than Tim Tebow and fifteen months older than Sam Bradford, and he was a grade ahead in high school.

Colt's parents named him after the Old Testament prophet, but if you ever meet him, don't call him Daniel—or Dan. He *hates* his given name and has gone by Colt all his life, which is why offensive linemen at Texas constantly called him Daniel.

That's not the only way the Longhorn linemen liked to tease Colt. "They also like to torture him by pretending to punch him in the man region before pulling up inches short," wrote Rick Reilly, the hilarious ESPN.com columnist. "If McCoy flinches, they get to slug him hard twice in the shoulder [author's note: it had better be his *left* shoulder], then 'wipe' off these slugs, which means taking one of their meaty hands and wiping it down McCoy's face, in his eyes, up his nostrils, and into his mouth."

Football players love these kinds of silly games, even in the huddle. "I'll be trying to call a play, and one of those guys is sticking his big ol' fingers up my nose. I get no respect," he said.

Colt has been around these types of football hijinks for as long as he can remember because he's the son of a high school football coach. His father, Brad McCoy, got into coaching after playing football at Abilene Christian University in Abilene, Texas.

Colt's father was merely following in the footsteps of *his* father, Burl, a football star at ACU who later became the school's women's basketball coach. Good thing Colt's grandfather moved into basketball. Why? Because you could say Burl recruited Brad's wife.

The story goes that Colt's mom, Debra, had been attending Harding University in Arkansas. She really wanted to play basketball, so she transferred to ACU to play on Burl McCoy's team. One day, Brad dropped by Moody Coliseum when his eyes caught sight of a beautiful young woman bouncing a basketball. He turned to a friend and said, "I don't even know that girl, but I'm going to marry her."

Debra rebuffed Brad's first overtures to go out, but she relented when *she* asked *him* to be her date at a Sadie Hawkins dance. Brad and Debra were an item after that, and Debra went on to capture all-conference honors on the basketball court.

Brad was a wide receiver at Abilene Christian in the early 1980s, where his roommate was running back Bob Shipley. (Don't forget that name.) They became very close friends and talked about everything, from football to their love interests. Bob was dating Sharon Felts, the daughter of Addie Felts, Abilene Christian's first women's track coach, so it seemed like everything was happening in the ACU family.

Following graduation, Brad married Debra and Bob married Sharon, and the two men set off to become high school football coaches. Brad started at just about the lowest rung on the coaching ladder: assistant coach at Lovington High School in Lovington, New Mexico. It wasn't Texas high school football and *Friday Night Lights*, but it was a start.

TRIVIA TIME

Brad McCoy has already coached one player to the NFL. Brian Urlacher, the Chicago Bears linebacker, played for him at Lovington High in the mid-1990s. They have remained good friends, and Brad worked for several years at Urlacher's summer football camp in Albuquerque. The Chicago Bears star has also visited the McCoy family in Texas.

BORN IN TEXAS . . . SORT OF

Lovington, a small city of 10,000 located 17 miles west of the Texas border, is known as the Queen City of the Plains. The main regional hospital, however, was in Hobbs, 20 miles to the southeast, which was fine with Brad McCoy since Hobbs was even closer to Texas—just five miles from the border. This was significant, as you will see.

But five miles is five miles, and Hobbs will always be part of New Mexico. After Debra went through labor and delivered Colt, the infant boy was gingerly placed in a hospital crib. According to a Texas tall tale, Brad drove five miles to the Texas border, where he scooped several handfuls of Lone Star dirt into a shoe box. Then he returned to the hospital, where he placed the cardboard box of Texas red earth underneath Colt's bassinet. He did this because he wanted to tell his family back home that Colt was born on Texas soil.

This story has been repeated so often that it's taken on a life of its own. When Brad was asked to confirm this fable, he smiled and said, "I plead the Fifth," referring to the amendment to the U.S. Constitution that protects him from making self-incriminating statements. Colt was also asked about the "shoe box of Texas dirt" story, but he sidestepped the question as neatly as he evades a blitzing linebacker. "I can't remember," he said. "I was a little baby. That's what my folks say. Nobody's said it wasn't true, so I guess it's true."

With a father as a football coach, you can figure Colt hung around plenty of grassy fields as a preschooler, shagging balls and playing imaginary games. He was probably adopted as the team mascot at times.

When Colt started elementary school, his father would drop him off and say the same two things every morning:

"I love you."

And:

"Do your best and be a leader."

The fatherly advice became a game. Whenever Colt would reach for the car door, his father would remind him that he loved him. "Do your best—"

"—and be a leader," Colt would reply as he slammed the door shut.

Brad had decided he and Debra would raise Colt—and his younger brothers Chance and Case (born two and five years after Colt, respectively)—according to four godly principles:

1. They would prepare their children for the path, not the path for their children. The road is rough, narrow, and hard to find, but God had given them a roadmap—the Bible. They could prepare their children for the future by remembering Proverbs 22:6: "Train a child in the way he should go, and when he is old he will not turn from it." They couldn't overlook authority and order, a principle found in Proverbs 23:13: "Do not withhold discipline from a child; if you punish him with the rod, he will not die."

2. They would prepare their children to be the best. This is why Brad reminded Colt each morning to "do your best and be a leader." Sure, when Colt and his brothers got older, they responded with the typical *Yeah, Dad, we know*, but Brad would always lead his football teams onto the field with the chant, "Expect to win, play to win."

Parents should also aim high, not low. The applicable scripture is 1 Corinthians 9:24: "Do you not know that in a race all the runners run, but only one gets the prize? Run in such a way as to get the prize."

3. They would prepare their children to be leaders. It's not enough to be the best, but their children had to learn how to lead as well.

4. They would prepare their children for open and closed doors. Brad and Debra knew they had to trust the Lord in whatever happens in the lives of their children. Some doors will open, and some will close, but God knows what's best and has a plan for their lives.

Brad says he raised Colt and his brothers in a disciplined home. "We're fundamental," he said. "You go to bed early, get up early, and take care of your body. We're a churchgoing family. Sunday morning is Sunday morning, and we go to church. If we couldn't give back a couple of hours on the Lord's Day, then something's wrong. As they [Colt, Chance, and Case] got older, they've understood the importance of that aspect, and I think that's really strengthened them as young men."

SIDELINE PASS

One of Colt's earliest football memories was an incident that took place when he was four years old. He had been named the official water boy for one Friday night game, and he was standing on the Lovington High sidelines when one of the players ran out of bounds and squashed the pint-sized Colt, knocking him flat. Result: a horrific scream and a broken collarbone.

Colt learned to keep his eyes on the field after that.

The youngster was promoted to ball boy when he hit his elementary school years. Colt loved watching the gargantuan gladiators in helmets and pads slug it out. One time, when he was eight years old, Lovington High was mounting a drive. Colt tugged on his father's pant leg. "Dad, if you run a screen now, it'll work," said the third grader.

His father signaled in the play for a screen pass—touchdown!

"Yeah, that happened," Brad said. "Absolutely true."

By the time he was twelve, Colt was already helping his father break down game film and learning the intricacies of the game. The summer before Colt's seventh-grade year, Brad asked his son, who had already played several seasons of peewee football at the quarterback position, if he was ready to dedicate himself to something—like becoming a better football player.

As they talked about what he could do to better himself, Colt mentioned that a speaker came to his middle school and challenged the students to live healthy lifestyles. "Athletes do not drink sodas," the health speaker said. "Soda slows you down."

So father and son talked about Colt's Dr Pepper habit. Known as the "national drink of Texas," Dr Pepper's unique flavor was created in Waco in 1885 and was practically the beverage of choice in the Southwest. Colt was drinking at least a six-pack a day of the heavily sugared and carbonated soft drink, which contained 54 grams of sugar and 200 calories in each 16-ounce bottle. By drinking six bottles of Dr Pepper, Colt's young, growing body was consuming 1,200 nutritionless calories a day and enough sugar to keep a classroom of kindergartners on hyper-alert all afternoon.

"We were at On the Border by Six Flags in Arlington," Brad said. "He drank a Dr Pepper then and said, 'That's the last one of those I'm ever going to drink. I'll be a better athlete if I don't drink that stuff anymore.' "

That event happened 10 years before Colt's senior season at the University of Texas, and Colt hasn't sipped a Dr Pepper or soft drink since—which has to be difficult, especially since his friends and peers surely drink soda pop like it's coming out of a drinking fountain. But Colt hasn't wavered; he's been a water, milk, and Gatorade guy ever since. (Irony time: when Colt played at Texas, Dr Pepper was the official drink of the Big 12 Conference.)

SMALL-TOWN VALUES

During his middle school years, Colt showed every sign that he would become an excellent athlete. "A guy told me after the third game Colt played as a seventh grader that he was going to win the Heisman one day," Brad said. "I just laughed and told him he was crazy. But it was obviously noticeable that he had a lot of special characteristics."

Meanwhile, the family moved back to Texas as Brad took coaching positions at small schools in San Saba and Kermit. The coach could have moved into a big-time high school program in Dallas or Houston, but he and Debra didn't want to raise their sons in a metropolitan city or leafy suburb. They preferred one-stoplight towns in the proverbial middle of nowhere, places where everyone knew each other's name. This was the family-friendly atmosphere in which they sought to raise their sons. Hunting and fishing were their passions.

"I caught some criticism for it," Brad said, "but it's a choice I'm comfortable with. I enjoy the slow pace. I like knowing who my kids are hanging out with. It's a lifestyle that suits our family just fine."

That lifestyle included frequent trips to see family and friends around the great state of Texas. Since coaches and teachers receive the same school holidays and summer breaks as students, there was plenty of time to hunt and fish at Grandpa Burl's ranch south of Abilene, as well as vacation with their best friends—the Shipleys.

COLT McCOY, GOSPEL SINGER

In the late 1970s, Burl McCoy started an a cappella gospel group called the McCoy Family Singers. The group is comprised of Colt's grandparents (Burl and Jan), his father, Brad, and two of his father's siblings, Uncle Michael and Aunt Amy. They are the Texas version of the von Trapp family: throughout the last three decades, the McCoy Family Singers have performed in front of thousands and released 11 albums.

The group sings without instruments because, as members of the Church of Christ denomination, they hold to a doctrinal tenet that the only musical instrument God created was the human voice; man created the rest.

One of the McCoy Family Singers albums, a 2008 release named *I Will Give Thanks*, is available on iTunes. Rumor has it that Colt sang on a couple of recordings.

Bob Shipley, Brad's roommate back in their college days, was putting together a successful high school football coaching career as well. When the kids started coming along, the two families made time to go to church camp together or pitch tents at Devils River in southwest Texas, where nothing more strenuous than fishing, reading, and hanging out was on the agenda.

The Shipleys' oldest child, Jordan, was nine months older than Colt, and the two were inseparable. They were always competing: who could catch the biggest fish, bag the biggest deer, or win at H-O-R-S-E in basketball. They practiced their football skills, too. Jordan would run pass routes until his tongue hung out so Colt could fine-tune his timing and accuracy.

In the late 1990s, the two families lived within 20 miles of each other in the Big Country communities of Hamlin and Rotan, north of Abilene. Brad had taken a coaching job at Hamlin High; Bob was coaching at Rotan.

Then, during Colt's middle school years, the McCoy family moved to Tuscola (pronounced TUSS-koh-lah), a central Texas farming town in Taylor County that's located 20 miles south of Abilene and 200 miles west of Dallas. The population posted on U.S. Highway 83 coming into town was 714—Babe Ruth's career home run number—with 202 families residing within the town's limits. Brad was hired as the head football coach for Jim Ned High School in Tuscola, and he and Debra purchased a ranch house outside town. Ten acres of peace and quiet. Room for their animals to roam. No noisy neighbors. A blanket of stars each night.

Tuscola wasn't even a one-stoplight town. A blinking yellow light controlled the main intersection of U.S. 83 and Graham Street, where a convenience store/café was situated. You could find an American Legion Hall, a funeral home, a volunteer fire department, a bank, a florist shop, a restaurant, three churches, and a water tower. That's all you need, right? Well, the locals would tell you the only thing missing was a Dairy Queen.

Tuscola's major industries were cotton, wheat, cattle, and high school football, and this is where Brad came in. Jim Ned High School—named after a nineteenth-century Indian cavalry scout for the U.S. Army—educated about 330 students drawn from a school district that covered 380 square miles. The football team competed in the 2A division of Texas high school athletics and was the biggest game in town.

The move to Tuscola—actually, the McCoys lived closer to a town called Buffalo Gap, population 463—checked off a lot of boxes for Brad and Debra. They still maintained the small-town atmosphere they had enjoyed in Hamlin—although the family joked that they had to go *into* town to hunt since they lived so far from Tuscola's main drag. The move placed them closer to Burl McCoy's ranch south of Abilene. And they could worship in Abilene at the Oldham Lane Church of Christ, which had been the McCoys' denomination for several generations.

Little did the residents of Tuscola know that Colt McCoy would put this tiny Texas town on the map—or that Colt's favorite teacher at Jim Ned High, Kay Whitton, would one day attend University of Texas games carrying a homemade sign that read:

TUSCOLA, POP. 714

THE JIM NED YEARS

Vince Lavallee, the assistant football coach and vice principal at Jim Ned, remembers the time Colt jogged off the field at Coahoma High and a young fan thrust a piece of paper and a pen in front of the young quarterback.

"Can I have your autograph?" the fan asked.

The year was 2002. Colt was a sophomore in high school. No one had ever asked him for an autograph before. He turned and looked to his assistant coach for advice. "What do I do?" he asked.

"Sign it," Lavallee replied. "It'll probably be the first of many."

No one doubted—or gossiped about—Brad McCoy's decision to play his son at quarterback during his first season of high school football. Even as a sophomore, Colt overwhelmed the competition, but that's the beauty of playing at the 2A level. With such a small pool of talent to draw from, a great athlete like Colt stood out like a prize steer in a cattle herd.

Another aspect of small school football is that the superior athletes play on offense *and* defense—it's called "going both ways." Coach McCoy needed some help in the defensive backfield, so he played Colt at free safety. Late in the season, however, when 8–0 Jim Ned played Bangs High School, Bangs' 215-pound running back Jacoby Jones (who later played at Baylor University) turned the corner and ran upfield. Colt, the last line of defense, threw his body in front of the powerful runner and suffered a concussion.

Colt was held out of the next two games, which unraveled Jim Ned High School's aspirations for a state championship. His father, being the smart coach that he is, never played Colt on defense again.

But word got around about the kid with a rifle arm, and during Colt's junior year of high school, Jim Ned's stadium bleachers were filled with football fans from Ovalo, Lawn, Goldsboro, and Novice. They wanted to see what this McCoy kid was all about. He wore No. 4—the same jersey number as another quarterback putting up impressive numbers: Brett Favre of the Green Bay Packers.

Like Sam Bradford, Colt had his best—or most successful—high school season as a junior. Now that he no longer played defense, Colt helped out the team by taking on the punting duties. He had a good leg, too, averaging about 37 yards a kick (by comparison, college and pros average around 43 to 45 yards per punt).

With Colt at the reins, a pass-happy offense gobbled up yards in chunks, and Jim Ned advanced to the Texas State 2A championship game in Dallas with a perfect 14–0 record. The Indians, however, were trounced decisively by San Augustine, 28–7—the first time since Colt started playing middle school football that his team had gone down to defeat with him shouldering the quarterbacking duties.

"We got beat on a cold night in Dallas," his father said. "I remember he was at midfield sobbing, and I really felt like it was too much, so I picked him up and said I understand it was a state championship game and all. With tears rolling from his eyes, he stopped me and said, 'You don't understand. This is the first I've ever stood on a football field after a game that I've lost.' That was his mentality."

Despite Colt's suffering his first defeat, word was getting around about this phenom from the Texas prairie who was All-State at the Class 2A level. Fifty touchdowns in 15 games, 3,939 yards, and only 11 interceptions during his junior season got him on the recruiting boards.

That, however, didn't mean there was a stampede of college coaches rushing into Tuscola. Remember, Jim Ned High School was a small school competing at the 2A level, and there were three higher divisions (3A, 4A, and 5A) in Texas high school football. That's why there were questions about whether Colt could compete against players who were taller, faster, and heavier. Plus Colt was on the smallish side—probably a little over six feet and a buck seventy in weight—despite being officially "listed" at 6 feet, 2½ inches tall and weighing 188 pounds.

But Colt sure looked good on film, and his pinpoint passing earned him a second look with college coaches. Even though Tuscola was in Texas Tech territory, there's no record of Texas Tech jumping into the Colt McCoy recruiting pool. That cleared the deck for three other major college football programs in Texas—the University of Texas, Texas A&M, and the University of Houston—to ramp up their efforts in the spring of Colt's junior year. Duke, Stanford, and Kansas State said they wanted in, too.

Like the Bradfords in Oklahoma, the McCoys huddled up and decided to have Colt verbally commit to a college before his senior year of high school football. Now it was a matter of finding the right school.

In May 2004, at the end of Colt's junior year, he was running at the UIL (University Interscholastic League) State Track and Field Meet, held on the University of Texas campus in Austin. (Colt was a three-sport athlete at Jim Ned, playing basketball all four years and running the 110-meter hurdles and mile relay on the track team for three seasons.)

While Colt was in Austin, he and Brad visited with Longhorns coach Mack Brown, and they felt comfortable with him for several reasons. Like Sam, Colt had attended a college football camp between his sophomore and junior year, and he "fell in love" with the University of Texas program after attending Mack Brown's summer camp. They also liked the offensive system the Longhorn coaches had installed.

It wasn't a difficult decision; Texas wanted him, the McCoys liked Texas, so UT it would be.

"I kind of did this [committing to the Longhorns] to get it off my shoulders," Colt told Danny Reagan of the *Abilene Reporter-News*.

Brad said, "Ultimately, he decided he wanted to stay in state," which surprised no one who knew the McCoy family. "He really likes what's going on at Texas right now."

What made the decision an all-orange slam dunk was a bit of news that the McCoy family had known for a while. Jordan Shipley, Colt's close friend since their grade school days, had signed a letter of intent to play at the University of Texas back on National Signing Day a few months earlier. A grade ahead of Colt, he would be enrolling the following August.

The possibility of playing pass-and-catch with his best friend before 89,000 rabid fans at Darrell K. Royal-Texas Memorial Stadium was too exciting for Colt to contemplate.

NOTHING TO SEE HERE

After Colt committed to Texas, major newspapers sent reporters to Tuscola to snoop around. In small towns, where everyone knows each other's business, surely there was a skeleton buried in Colt's closet.

None could dig up any dirt on Colt. *Nada.*

Elderly couples described how Colt waved to passing cars while he mowed lawns for spending money. Teachers doted on the youngster who pulled down straight-A report cards. Townspeople talked about how he picked up trash by the side of the road as part of the Don't Mess with Texas program. He also delivered dinners to shut-ins with Meals on Wheels, and a couple of times a week during the school year he tutored elementary school kids with their reading. When a tornado blew through town but didn't touch down, some said that Colt lassoed the twister and rode away on it.

At Jim Ned, Colt was a student council leader, office aide, 2004 Class Favorite, Most Outstanding Male Athlete, and Mr. Jim Ned High School. He was a member of the National Honor Society with a grade-point average of 98.2 on a 100-point scale.

Colt's senior year of football was very much like his junior year, but now he had a new target to throw to—his brother Chance, a sophomore. The brother-to-brother tandem connected on 67 completions for 1,000 yards and 15 touchdowns. One can only imagine the laughter and fun the McCoy family enjoyed around the dinner table that special season.

Jim Ned breezed into the state 2A playoffs undefeated, but Canadian High, the eventual state champion, upended the Indians 32–27. This time there were no tears. Colt's high school career was in the books: a 34–2 record, more than five miles of passing (9,344 yards), and 116 touchdown passes. He was the best passer in Texas 2A football history.

Just before Colt graduated in June 2005, Brad accepted the job as head football coach at Graham High in Graham, Texas. This was a 3A school, so Chance would see an upgrade in competition. Plus, Brad and Debra had their youngest son, Case, to think about. He was entering the seventh grade and playing quarterback in youth football.

The move didn't take the McCoys much farther from Austin, though. Tuscola was just over 200 miles from Austin (about four hours one way) while Graham was 240 miles (around four and a half hours) away.

The move's dividend was that Graham was just 100 miles west of the Dallas/Fort Worth Airport. When Colt played on the road, Brad and Debra wanted to be there.

The family wasn't about to miss Game Day.

ARRIVING IN AUSTIN

Colt had one good thing going for him when he stepped on the UT campus as a student in 2005: he was the only quarterback among the 15 incoming players the Longhorns signed that recruiting season.

What he didn't have going for him—at least not at first—was a body developed well enough to play football in the Big 12 Conference. At the start of training camp, Texas offensive coordinator Greg Davis looked at the new 170-pound recruit and said, "Gosh almighty, son, get into the weight room and talk to me later."

Colt didn't fight him. He knew he looked like a "skinned squirrel"—his own words—compared with the behemoths who play NCAA Division 1 football. So Colt did three things during his 2005 redshirt season to prepare himself for the college level:

1. added 10 to 15 pounds of muscle in the weight room
2. quarterbacked the scout team against the first-team and second-team defense
3. shadowed star junior quarterback Vince Young from the practice field to team meetings to film room

Even though Colt knew he wasn't going to play his first year at Texas, he still suited up for games and was listed as third quarterback—behind Young and senior Matt Nordgren—on the Longhorn depth chart. Coach Mack Brown was careful to preserve the extra year of eligibility for Colt, however, and didn't play him a single down during the 2005 season.

Besides, the jump from 2A high school football to a major college program like Texas called for taking things slow and easy. There was no hurry to rush Colt along; Vince Young had two more years of Texas football eligibility ahead of him.

. But after Young posted a monster season in 2005, including his clutch dash to the end zone at the BCS National Championship Game, NFL scouts started drooling. With tens of millions of dollars being waved in his face, Young opted to leave early for professional football.

Texas offensive coordinator Greg Davis remembers Colt approaching him the day after Young announced he was making himself available for the NFL draft. "Colt said, 'Coach, I want to be the best quarterback that you've ever had.' At the time, Colt was about 184 pounds, and Vince Young was a massive man [6 feet, 5 inches tall and 223 pounds]. I'm thinking, *Vince is leaving and I've got Pee Wee Herman sitting across the desk from me, and he's telling me that he's going to be the best quarterback there's ever been around here.*"

As the departure of Rhett Bomar from Oklahoma paved the way for Sam Bradford, the early exit of Vince Young for the NFL created a nice opening for Colt.

And he was going to make the most of the opportunity.

A QUARTERBACK CONTROVERSY?

Colt found out in spring practice that the Longhorn upperclassmen weren't exactly welcoming him to their huddle with open arms. There were four offensive linemen on the team who would be fourth- or fifth-year seniors the following fall—and three would go on to play in the NFL. Colt said, "They were like, 'I'm not listening to you, dude. You're a freshman.'"

The Texas coaches caught the vibe, so Davis concocted a no-huddle offense with the idea that Colt, who said he could "barely spit out" plays because of nerves, couldn't be mocked by his senior linemen since there was no huddle before each play.

Colt was still a baby-faced, wide-eyed, and fairly scrawny redshirt freshman coming into summer training camp. But winning over the Neanderthals with stubble beards was the least of Colt's worries; he was in a quarterback competition with someone even *younger* than he was—Jevan Snead, a blue-chip recruit from Stephenville, Texas, who had verbally committed to the University of Florida but backed out when the Gators landed a recruit named Tim Tebow.

There was also the lingering hangover from Vince Young's departure. Coach Mack Brown said, "I thought Vince would come back, very honestly. I might have been the only one in America that did."

But Young was off to the Tennessee Titans, and Coach Brown and his staff needed to retool the Longhorn offense in a hurry. Texas was the national champion defending a 20-game winning streak, so even though the cupboard was being restocked, expectations of the fans and media for a tasty 2006 season remained high. *Sports Illustrated* ranked Texas as the No. 3 team in the country in its College Football Preview issue.

As was the case in Norman with Sam Bradford, the Texas quarterback competition would be settled in team scrimmages played under real game conditions: striped referees, a game clock, and every play being filmed for later review. Colt, the coaches and the media agreed, looked like the first-teamer all the way. His presence on the field, as well as his decision making and poised throws, proved he was ready. Colt's redshirt season had given him an extra year of college experience over Jevan Snead. There would be no quarterback controversy at Texas in 2006—unlike the one earlier in the decade featuring Major Applewhite and Chris Simms.

When Colt won the job, the sportswriters on the Longhorns beat made "Colt .45" outlaw puns or referred to him as the "the Real McCoy," a reference to Joseph McCoy, a nineteenth-century cattle baron who made good on his pledge to ship a number of Longhorn cattle from Texas to Kansas.

But still, everyone wondered if Colt could handle the pressure and perform well once the 2006 season started.

A HERO TO THE RESCUE

After his first season of spring practice in 2006, Colt drove home for Memorial Day weekend. A little less than a year earlier, his parents had moved from Tuscola to Graham, an oil town of 8,700, when Brad took the head coaching job at Graham High School. The family purchased a home on Timber Ridge Lake, a sliver of water a mile and a half long and 300 or 400 yards across. No motor boats or electric boats were allowed on the private lake, but residents could use paddle boats to get to their favorite fishing holes.

Around 9 p.m. on Memorial Day, Colt and Brad stepped outside the back of their home. It was completely dark outside—no moon—and they had fished all day long. Then they heard it: a cry of desperation traveling across the waters.

"This is Patina. Ken and I are on the dock. He's having a grand mal seizure. Call 911," the shaky voice called out in the distance.

Several minutes earlier, Patina Herrington, who lived across the lake from the McCoys, had heard Annabelle, a chocolate Labrador who lived next door, scratching on her glass doors. She grabbed a flashlight and asked, "Annabelle, what's going on?"

The excited dog ran toward the lake and quickly returned to Patina, then repeated the nervous behavior. Annabelle had never acted like this before. Patina knew something was wrong.

Then Patina remembered: Ken, her 60-year-old husband, had gone to the dock to check something out.

The Herringtons' house was perched above the lake. To reach the water, Patina followed a series of steps cut through big boulders. With Annabelle leading the way, Patina rushed to the dock with her heart in her throat. She had reason to worry; her husband had suffered numerous seizures over the years and had undergone three brain surgeries that contributed to aphasia, a speech disorder.

When Patina reached the dock, her husband was thrashing about. He was in the midst of a grand mal seizure—violent muscle contractions accompanied by a loss of consciousness.

Patina rushed to Ken's side, cradled him in her arms, and attempted to stop him from biting his tongue. As he continued to thrash about, she realized they were both in a horrible fix. The Herringtons didn't own a cell phone, and she couldn't leave him on the dock to run back to the house to call 911. If she did, Ken could twist and twitch himself into the lake and drown. But if she couldn't call 911, Ken was doomed.

"Somehow, I knew everything was going to be okay," Patina said. "I wasn't alone because God was with me."

She screamed into the darkness for help, hoping someone would hear her.

Two sets of neighbors heard her desperate plea: Sandra Boedeker, who lived directly across the lake, four doors from the McCoys, and Brad and Colt. Sandra called 911 and asked the dispatcher to send an ambulance to the Herrington residence immediately.

The McCoys didn't hesitate. Father and son sprinted for the dock, jumped into the lake, and swam toward the Herrington home like it was a 400-meter Olympic freestyle final. Neither took their shirts or shoes off before hitting the water.

Halfway across the lake, Colt, who was outpacing his father, lost both sneakers because he was kicking so furiously. He arrived first and hauled himself onto the dock. In the distance, a siren could be heard in the still night.

"How can I help?" Colt asked as he came alongside Mrs. Herrington.

"My husband's not good," she replied. "If the EMTs don't get here soon—"

"You stay here with him. I'll go tell them where we are."

Patina watched as a soaking wet and barefoot Colt raced up the boulder wall to the house. He couldn't see the path her husband had cut into the stones, but he showed no concern for his own well-being as he scampered up the boulders in bare feet. Then he raced to Timber Ridge Road so he could flag down the EMTs. The distance from the dock to the street was probably 200 yards.

Colt guided the EMTs back to the dock and helped them lower a gurney, then climbed down the boulders again and assisted them as they lifted a now-stabilized Ken into the stretcher. Colt held the IV and escorted the EMTs back to their emergency vehicle every step of the way.

"Thank goodness Colt was in *good* shape," Patina said. "Bless his heart. Ken had consecutive grand mal seizures, and doctors told us that if Colt had arrived five minutes later, my husband probably wouldn't have made it. His body was worn out."

The Herringtons became even bigger fans of Colt after his Good Samaritan gesture. "Ken graduated from UT in 1968, and I went there but never graduated, so we love the Longhorns. We never try to see Colt after a game, though. We would never intrude in that way. He gets mobbed by everybody. We prefer to say hi and hello when he's here in Graham. He and his dad have come over to the house a few times to check up on Ken, which is always appreciated."

Do they swim over?

"No," Patina laughed. "They drive a car. There's one more story. About six months after the incident, one of Colt's sneakers washed up onshore. It was a Nike. When I gave the shoe back to Colt, he laughed.

"We never found the other sneaker, though."

Colt had before him the unenviable task of following a legend—Vince Young—and he wasn't given much time to get settled in. Circled on the calendar was a home date with No. 1–ranked Ohio State on the second weekend of the season—an early showdown that would set the course of the Longhorns' season. A loss would probably scuttle any hopes Texas had of repeating as national champions.

The Longhorns opened the season by dismantling North Texas, so the matchup with Ohio State was billed as another Big, Big Game between the top two teams in the country.

Texas senator Kay Bailey Hutchison and Ohio senator Mike DeWine placed a friendly wager on the outcome: Hutchison bet a couple of half gallons of Blue Bell Ice Cream and DeWine staked some of his wife's homemade chocolate-covered peanut butter buckeye candies.

Senator Hutchison had to find some dry ice for shipping because Texas lost decisively, 24–7. The loss was pinned on the Longhorn defensive secondary, which allowed Ohio State's Troy Smith to throw for 269 yards and two touchdowns. When Texas had the ball, the coaching staff kept Colt on a short leash: lots of screen passes and underneath routes. It wasn't his fault that receiver Billy Pittman fumbled on the Texas 2-yard line and an Ohio State player picked up the ball and ran it back to midfield, silencing the record crowd of 89,422—the most to ever watch a football game in the state of Texas. The lost fumble completely turned around the momentum.

In a strange way, the loss to Ohio State was freeing for Texas. During the rest of the 2006 season, the Longhorns weren't playing to protect a No. 1 ranking or a 21-game winning streak. Instead, they ran out on the field each week to have fun . . . and to beat the opposing team into sawdust. What followed was another winning streak—eight games this time—including a Red River Rivalry victory over Oklahoma.

Why the surge? Offensive coordinator Greg Davis opened up the Texas playbook, and Colt responded by playing so spectacularly that writers began touting the redshirt freshman as a possible Heisman Trophy candidate. He managed the offense well, made great throws, picked up blitzes, and took his share of shots. He showed tremendous poise in four come-from-behind victories: over Oklahoma (in Dallas), Baylor (down 10–0 at home), Nebraska (in blowing snow in Lincoln), and Texas Tech (in Lubbock, after falling behind 21–0 in the first quarter).

The QB was clutch. For two months, Colt played way beyond anyone's expectations.

The 2006 season ended on a down note, however. A 45–42 loss to Kansas State was one that got away, and Colt had to leave late in the game with a "stinger" injury to his neck. The following week, Texas A&M upset Texas 12–7 in the Big 12 Conference Title game.

The Longhorns, however, finished with a victory over Iowa in the Alamo Bowl. The win gave the 'Horns a 10–3 season and kept intact a six-year streak of winning at least 10 games. Colt threw for 29 touchdowns, tying the NCAA single-season record for TD passes by a freshman, and his 161.8 passer rating (a formula for evaluating a quarterback based on his completion percentage, passing yardage, touchdown passes, and interceptions) ranked him eighth nationally.

Better yet, Burnt Orange fans were talking more about Colt and his future instead of lamenting what-could-have-been had Vince Young stuck around for his senior season.

One other thing happened after the 2006 season: with Colt entrenched as the starting quarterback in Austin, Jevan Snead "unhooked 'em 'Horns" and transferred to Ole Miss—the University of Mississippi.

SWIMMING UPHILL

Colt was on a lot of watch lists after his amazing freshman season, but the pressure never lets up when you're the quarterback of the University of Texas. If Colt's 2007 season could be summed up with one word, it would be this: adversity.

The Longhorn offensive line was in disarray after the graduation of four starters from the 2006 team. Six players were disciplined for alleged infractions, and another was suspended for NCAA rule violations. One of Colt's top receivers, Limas Sweed, sat out most of the season with a wrist injury. The running game was nonexistent for the first half of the season. To add a final cup of flour, running backs coach Ken Rucker announced during summer training camp that he had been diagnosed with prostate cancer and would take a leave of absence to undergo surgery.

Add it all up, and you have a recipe for one of Texas' most tumultuous seasons.

The first month started innocently enough, although a season-opening victory over Arkansas State was too close for comfort. Still, the Longhorns were ranked No. 7 going into a home tilt against Kansas State, but the Wildcat defense, using a relentless pass rush, pounded Colt into his worst game as a Texas quarterback, including four interceptions. KSU defensive end Ian Campbell ran the first pick back 41 yards for a touchdown, and Kansas State was on its way to a 41–21 beatdown. It was Mack Brown's worst home defeat in 10 years as the UT coach.

Colt had to run for his life most of the afternoon; the statistician recorded 13 "hurries" and seven tipped passes. A jarring hit just before halftime left Colt feeling woozy, and although he returned in the second half, he didn't finish the game. By game's end, he was vomiting on the sidelines, and Texas team officials later stated Colt had suffered a "mild concussion."

The following week, Colt got his first up-close look at Sam Bradford in the Red River Rivalry game. Oklahoma was ranked higher and favored, but the game was tied 21–21 early in the fourth quarter when the Sooners started a drive on their own six-yard line. All Colt could do was watch Sam make timely third-and-three and third-and-five passes to keep the winning drive alive. The Sooners won 28–21.

Texas fans thought the world had come to an end, but the Longhorns came back to win four straight games. A nationally televised day-after-Thanksgiving loss to Texas A&M, however, stuck in the craws of Longhorn fans. How could the Aggies—a .500 team at the time—beat mighty Texas 38–20?

"It's really hard," Texas defensive back Brandon Foster said. "You never enjoy losing, but losing to the Aggies is even worse."

Colt's two fumbles and an interception didn't help matters against Texas A&M, but that wasn't the only game in which he and the Longhorn offense struggled. His 18 interceptions in 2007 often thwarted the Longhorn offense. In Colt's defense, though, 10 of the picks came off tipped or deflected passes.

Texas ended the season on a bright note, taking a lopsided 52–34 Holiday Bowl victory against Arizona State. Colt won Offensive MVP honors despite fumbling four times. A second straight 10–3 season, though, didn't satisfy many Longhorn fans, players, or coaches. They wondered if UT could get over the hump and win 11, 12, or even 13 games in 2008.

If so, Colt would have to raise his quarterbacking to the elite level.

AN OUT-OF-COUNTRY EXPERIENCE

In March 2008, during spring break, Colt did something that helped him forget the uneven 2007 season and the fact that he was a Texas quarterback playing under the media microscope: he traveled to Peru on a mission trip organized by the Texas chapter of the Fellowship of Christian Athletes and T Bar M, a Texas organization that runs Christian youth sports camps.

Colt had plugged into the FCA chapter on the University of Texas campus from the get-go, but that was as natural to him as going to church on Sunday mornings. He had been involved with FCA Huddles since he was in middle school, when at the age of 14 he made a firm commitment to the Lord. His grandfather, Burl McCoy, had the honor of baptizing his grandson at his ranch south of Abilene.

Colt matured spiritually through high school, just as he was maturing into his leadership role on the football field.

Do your best and be a leader.

When it came to spiritual leadership, Colt led by example during his five years at the University of Texas. It was a rare week when he and Jordan Shipley missed a service at Westover Hills Church of Christ in Austin. Much of what Colt did on the "ministry" side while he was at Texas didn't get talked about a whole lot, which was fine with him.

He wasn't a bystander at FCA Huddle meetings on the UT campus, though. He loved hearing the speakers and hanging out with his buddies, including Jordan, kicker Hunter Lawrence, and center Chris Hall, who was a PK—a pastor's kid. There were a ton of Christians playing football, as well as other sports, for the University of Texas.

THE REAL DEAL

During Colt's senior year at Texas, he met on Thursday evenings with some teammates who were involved with FCA. The players gathered together at one of their homes for fellowship, study, and accountability.

They focused on trust, beginning with Jeremiah 17:7 ("But blessed is the man who trusts in the LORD, whose confidence is in him") and Jeremiah 29:11 (" 'For I know the plans I have for you,' declares the LORD, 'plans to prosper you and not to harm you, plans to give you hope and a future' ").The players made an agreement that when they stepped on the field, having given their lives to Christ, they had nothing to gain, nothing to lose, and nothing to prove (Colossians 3:1).

Reagan Lambert, who has been working with and discipling athletes at the University of Texas for 20 years, said Colt is the real deal. "He has a great sense of humor, and he's humble and fun to be around," Lambert said.

On many Fridays before home games, Colt joined a passel of Texas players who visited Dell Children's Medical Center in Austin, including the cancer ward. He also volunteered for The Rise School of Austin (a school that assists children with disabilities), the Children's Miracle Network Telethon, the Make-a-Wish Foundation, Caritas of Austin (which provides food for the homeless), and the Boys and Girls Club.

So it wasn't a stretch for Colt to say yes when he was asked if he wanted to go to Peru with a mission team over the 2008 spring break. The idea intrigued him, especially because he had heard his grandparents, Burl and Jan McCoy, talk about the medical mission trips they had taken to Africa.

But first, he had to clear things with Coach Brown and offensive coordinator Greg Davis. They gave their blessing, no doubt understanding the indelible impression a 10-day mission trip to South America would make on any college student athlete.

A long flight to the Peruvian capital of Lima was followed by a shorter flight to Iquitos, a city of nearly 400,000 in the Amazon rain forest that is considered the largest city in the world that cannot be reached by road. The team was bused into the jungle and the Amazon River basin, where they jumped on motorboats for transportation to tiny villages along the river. The natives lived in huts with dirt floors—or muddy floors during the rainy season. With muggy 85 percent humidity and 100-degree heat, this wasn't the Four Seasons.

The trip to the Peruvian rain forest was a wonderful, life-changing, humbling experience for Colt on many levels. First of all, the local kids had no idea who he was or what an "American football" player did—they played *futbol*, but it wasn't the same sport—so he wasn't pestered for autographs or treated any differently than the others on the trip. "Nobody had any concept of what we do in the United States," Colt said. "I'm just another guy. Nobody knows who you are. You can just be yourself for a week."

Colt's "job" was to play with the kids, distribute clothes and other necessities, and share the gospel. Every meal came with a heaping bowl of rice, but Colt detested rice. By the time he returned to Austin, he had lost 15 pounds, which Greg Davis surely noticed.

Back to the weight room.

The biggest thing Colt learned from his Peru experience was that as a young man living in America, he had nothing to complain about. The grinding poverty overwhelmed him, but the Peruvian kids' attitude of happiness amazed him. He realized he had been like most Americans: having no clue of how people outside our borders live and the conditions they survive under. He returned to Austin with a greater perspective on his circumstances and how much he had to be thankful for.

The Peruvian kids, of course, didn't know a *Yanqui* sports celebrity was in their midst. But when Colt returned to Iquitos a year later with the same mission team, the kids were excited at his return. It seems the translators had pooled their money to rent a motorcycle so one of them could ride to a neighboring village and check on the Internet to see how the 'Horns did throughout the 2008 season.

Traveling to Peru for two mission trips was just the tip of the iceberg of how Colt gave back while he was at the University of Texas. Following his peerless freshman year, the requests to speak before various high school and youth groups, as well as FCA gatherings, came by the bushel, as many as 10 a day.

At one time, Colt accepted so many invitations to share his faith and inspire others that Greg Davis called Colt's father and asked him if he could help persuade his son to slow things down a bit.

Fat chance.

Colt McCoy had never been one to run away from an incoming rush.

PLAYING FOR SOMETHING BIGGER THAN HIMSELF

Colt came back from Peru energized and eager to put his "sophomore slump"—that's what the media was calling the Longhorns' 10–3 season—behind him. "I hate that term," Colt said. "It's not a slump because I feel like I grew so much, I got better, understood the offenses, and gained a ton of experience that's going to help me this year."

The media was also calling the 2008 campaign a rebuilding season, but Coach Brown quelled that talk. There are no rebuilding years at Texas, he said.

The fact that Texas didn't lose in September or October was all Colt. The inexperience on the Longhorn interior line meant he had to absorb too many late hits or scramble for yards. Time after time, though, Colt made plays. His nimble feet allowed him to escape blitzes or turn busted plays into big gains. *Sports Illustrated*'s college beat columnist wrote, "McCoy escapes from seemingly impossible situations so often, The Watch wonders if his real surname isn't actually MacGyver."

The Red River Rivalry game of 2008 was certainly worthy of a prime-time show. The matchup pitted the undefeated and No. 5–ranked Longhorns against the top team in the country—Sam Bradford–led Oklahoma. The eyes of sporting America were on the Cotton Bowl, and rightly so.

Oklahoma took an early lead, but a Jordan Shipley 96-yard kickoff return for a touchdown in the second quarter cut into a 14–3 deficit and sparked the Longhorns. Then Colt tossed his childhood friend a short touchdown pass in the third quarter to tighten the score, 28–27, with Texas still behind. Jordan's crucial third-and-eight reception in the fourth quarter led to Texas' first lead, 38–35, and the 'Horns won going away, 45–35.

Now the Longhorns were the top dog, to mix metaphors, as well as the No. 1 team in the country.

Some rebuilding year.

An important road contest—another Big Game, as the ESPN talking heads would say—loomed in Lubbock, the home of Texas Tech. Coach Mike Leach had the sixth-ranked Red Raiders in top form, and emotions ran high on the home-field side of the ball. Texas Tech leaped to a 19–0 lead, and on a Saturday night in Lubbock, coming back from a nearly three-touchdown deficit was a tall order.

But Colt led a stunning rally, and with a little more than a minute to go, a grinding Longhorn drive resulted in a 33–32 Texas lead.

This might have been one of Colt's greatest wins, but the Longhorn defense still had to make a final stop. On the game's final play—one that would seemingly be replayed eight million times on ESPN—Tech quarterback Graham Harrell zipped a pass to receiver Michael Crabtree, who caught the ball near the sideline and somehow miraculously broke away from two Longhorn defenders and kept his balance as he tiptoed down the sideline without falling out of bounds. Crabtree stepped into the end zone with one second to play, and Texas lost a heartbreaker, 39–33.

DEDICATING A SEASON TO A FALLEN HERO

When Colt suited up during the 2008 season, he adopted a ritual: reaching into his locker for a silver crucifix on a chain and putting it around his neck. He only wore the simple cross during games.

The crucifix belonged to his cousin Grant Hinds, who was several years older than Colt. As kids, they hunted, fished, and rode four-wheelers together. Then Grant joined the Marines and went off to war. He returned from three tours of duty in Iraq and Afghanistan in one piece physically, but he battled post-traumatic stress disorder, nightmares, and depression. The member of a tank battalion, Grant had witnessed death and destruction.

Following his discharge, Grant enrolled at Kennesaw State University in Georgia, where he suffered a brain hemorrhage and died following a car accident. He was only 25 years old.

Colt dedicated his 2008 season to the cousin who had died five months earlier. "Every game I say, 'This is for Grant.' I want to play with the same heart and attitude he had with all the courage it took to fight for us," Colt said.

Colt, who didn't dedicate any other of his seasons to anyone, wore Grant's crucifix under his shoulder pads as a reminder that he was playing for someone else—the memory of a close cousin.

The bitter loss dropped Texas to No. 4 in the country, but that would be the Longhorns' only blemish of the 2008 campaign. Colt's great performances vaulted him into the Heisman race, and he traveled with his parents to New York City, where he met Sam Bradford and Tim Tebow in person.

Although he didn't win the Heisman—he finished second—Colt's 2008 season meant that when the topic of college football's top quarterbacks came up, you couldn't talk about Sam Bradford or Tim Tebow without also mentioning Colt McCoy's name.

It seemed the three of them were joined at the hips.

THE FINAL CAMPAIGN

At least the media didn't ask Mack Brown the following question when the University of Texas football team broke training camp: *Coach, your team was 12–1 in 2008 and finished as only the No. 3 team in the country. Would you call this a rebuilding year?*

That's Longhorn football for you. But everything is bigger in Texas, right? You only had to gaze at the recent opening of the palatial Cowboys Stadium to get a sense of how big—and important—football is to Texas. NFL owner Jerry Jones had spent $1.2 billion to construct the largest domed stadium in the world, including the world's largest high-definition video screen, which hung above the field from the 20-yard line to the 20-yard line.

Do you watch the game or watch the game on those huge TV screens above your seat?

The 2009 season was it for fifth-year senior quarterback Colt McCoy. Tim Tebow had already grasped two NCAA team championships, and Sam Bradford had played in the BCS National Championship Game the previous January, losing to the Tebow-led Florida Gators. Now it was Colt's turn.

Heading into the season, most everyone was saying it would be Florida, Oklahoma, or Texas fighting it out at the Rose Bowl in January. "The Top Three Quarterbacks on the Top Three Teams," declared a *SportingNews* headline.

Would Colt get his chance to win a national championship?

For that to happen, the Longhorns couldn't afford to lose. All fall, the Texas football team played like they knew the score. The Longhorns earned revenge against Texas Tech in the third game of the season, beating the Red Raiders 34–24, and they were 7–0 before the Red River Rivalry game against Oklahoma.

Sam Bradford was trying to come back from a shoulder injury and wasn't thought to be 100 percent for the game against the Longhorns. When Texas cornerback Aaron Williams hit Sam on a blitz early in the game and ended his season, it seemed inconceivable that Oklahoma could weather the loss of their Heisman Trophy–winning quarterback. The Texas offense, however, couldn't find its rhythm. The Oklahoma defense confused Colt with five blitzes he'd never seen before. At halftime, Texas trailed 6–3 and Colt was only 7-of-16 passing.

The Longhorns eked out a 16–13 lead in the fourth quarter, and Texas had the ball when disaster nearly struck. Colt threw an interception, and just when it appeared his worst nightmare would happen before his eyes—a pick leading to a game-winning touchdown against his team's greatest rival—Colt scrambled and made the game-saving tackle. The defense then did its job and held, and Colt ground out the last 3:31, punctuated by an uncharacteristic fist pump toward the Burnt Orange end of the Cotton Bowl just before he took a knee on the final play of the game.

"Good teams find a way to win," said Coach Brown after the game.

That time-honored football truism summed up the 2009 season. The Longhorns didn't overwhelm many teams, and they never looked unbeatable, but they were never outscored.

The award for Biggest Squeaker of the Year would probably go to Texas following the Big 12 Championship Game against No. 21–ranked Nebraska. A tough one the entire way: Colt was sacked nine times and threw three interceptions. Four and a half of those sacks came from Ndamukong Suh, the 6-foot, 5-inch, 305-pound defensive tackle who on one play whirlybirded Colt at least seven yards through the air.

After Nebraska had taken a 12–10 lead with 1:44 to play, an out-of-bounds kickoff put the Longhorns on their own 40-yard line. On the first play of the Texas drive, Colt found his favorite receiver, Jordan Shipley, for 19 yards; a horse-collar tackle added 15 more yards, and Texas was within field goal range on the Huskers' 26-yard line. (In case you're wondering why Jordan was still playing, since he was a grade ahead of Colt, the NCAA had granted him a sixth season of eligibility because he missed the entire 2004 and 2005 seasons due to knee and hamstring injuries.)

Seven seconds to go. Time for a quick play to get a little closer. Then Colt nearly made a mistake that could have haunted him for years. He rolled to his right, a bit casually, and threw the ball out of bounds—and the clock read 00:00! Nebraska players swarmed the field in jubilation, believing they had won, but the play was reviewed in the replay booth. A trip to the national title game hung in the balance for Texas. After a long wait, the officials decided there was enough "time" left after Colt had thrown the ball out of bounds to put one second back on the clock.

And enough time to run one more play. Hunter Lawrence nailed a 46-yard field goal, and this time it was the Texas players who flung their helmets in the air and rushed the field to celebrate an unlikely victory and an undefeated 12–0 season.

The rifle-armed Colt McCoy had dodged a bullet.

A day later, Colt and the Texas team learned they had a date in Pasadena with the Alabama Crimson Tide for the BCS National Championship Game.

"It would mean a lot [to win against Alabama]," Colt said afterward. "I think it would put an end to four great years. That's what you fight for every year."

ROSE BOWL POSTSCRIPT

After suffering the shoulder injury while playing his last game in a Texas uniform, Colt flew home to decompress and hang out with his girlfriend, Rachel Glandorf.

Colt and Rachel met while she interned at KEYE Channel 42, Austin's CBS affiliate, when she covered the team as an on-camera reporter. Rachel attended Baylor University, 90 miles north of Austin, where she ran hurdles on the Bear track team. She was nine months younger than Colt.

Rachel had been sitting next to Colt's parents at Texas games throughout the 2009 season. Colt watchers speculated on where this relationship was heading.

When ESPN's Rick Reilly wrote in October 2009 that Rachel was "hotter than shrimp vindaloo," she hit the No. 1 spot in Google Trends. (Shrimp vindaloo, in case you're wondering, is a spicy Indian dish.)

Four days after the BCS Championship Game, Colt escorted Rachel to an empty Texas Memorial Stadium and walked her to the 50-yard line, smack dab in the middle of the field. He then pointed to the stadium's giant high-def scoreboard screen, which said in big, bold letters:

Rachel,
I love you!
Will you marry me?
Colt

When she turned around, Colt was bent down on one knee in the middle of the orange Longhorn logo, holding a small jewelry box that contained an engagement ring.

If and when Colt and Rachel have any children, their quarterback-playing sons won't have to worry about reaching optimal NFL height.

That's because the statuesque Rachel stands six feet tall.

3

TIM TEBOW:
THE CHOSEN ONE

Maybe you jumped ahead to this chapter because you love Tim Tebow.

Maybe you're thinking about skipping this chapter because you can't *stand* Tim Tebow.

Or maybe you're wondering why everyone is making such a big deal out of the Incredible Hulk in eye black.

In the pantheon of quarterbacks, college and pro, Tim Tebow is a rock star. He's the most talked-about football player in America and the most discussed, dissected, and debated athlete on ESPN, the arbiter of what's important in the sports world. When he's in public, he's a compelling figure who draws stares from bystanders, screams from fans, and clicks from cell phone cameras. He's been called the NFL version of a total solar eclipse, blotting out nearly every other name or topic in the football world.

His smile melts hearts. His demeanor is humble and earnest. His attitude is respectful to elders and authority figures (like coaches), and his faith moves mountains. His work ethic is off the charts. He's so good-natured and likeable that you want to bottle him up and take him home to the family.

Admit it—you can't keep your eyes off him. The camera loves Tim Tebow. His emotions on the field run the gamut: full-throated exhortations to his teammates, fist pumps and helmet taps after big plays and touchdowns, broad smiles and gracious interviews after victories, even emotional tears in defeat.

If football was show business (and, in many ways, it's hard to separate one from the other), then Tim's charisma and poise—that special "it"—defines his uniqueness, fortitude, determination, and belief in himself. He has an amazing presence on and off the field as well as a wonderful alliterative roll to his name.

Tim Tebow is loved, hated, idolized, cheered, and booed because his outsized personality broke the mold for the quarterback position during his four-year career at the University of Florida. Things didn't change when Tim landed in the NFL. Once he plants his feet under or behind the center, he plays QB like it's his personal fiefdom. He's as relentless as Attila the Hun, as unstoppable as a Mack truck plowing through a roadblock.

His agent, Jimmy Sexton, has predicted Tim will become the most marketable athlete in history. The Davie-Brown Index, an independent marketing research firm popular with brand marketers, found Tim to be more appealing and more of a trendsetter than any other NFL quarterback. Even during his rookie season in Denver, when he wasn't playing much, Tim's No. 15 Broncos jersey led the league in jersey sales from the beginning to the end of the season.

"Nobody seems to have popped out quite like Tebow," said Darin David, account director for The Marketing Arm agency.

Nike signed Tim to a shoe and an apparel deal, and the Tim Tebow Trainer 1.2 PE was released in a limited edition. Jockey, the underwear company, is featuring Tim in catalogs and TV and print advertisements for its new "Staycool" collection. He's also done a series of ads for FRS Health Energy drinks.

IN THE BEGINNING

Timothy Richard Tebow was born August 14, 1987, in the Philippines.

In a manger.

Because his parents were told there was no room at the inn.

The part about Tim being born in the Philippines is true, but we're just having fun with his "nativity story." But this is the sort of mythmaking that happens when they start calling you "The Chosen One"—in high school.

Tim was born in Makati City, which is part of metro Manila, because his parents, Bob and Pam Tebow, were living in the Philippines as missionaries at the time. Bob and Pam met at the University of Florida in 1967, when Bob was a sophomore and Pam was a freshman. Unlike Kent Bradford and Brad McCoy, the fathers of the other two QBs, Bob Tebow wasn't on a college campus to play football, but he did see himself as an impact player. Even back then, Bob already knew his life's goal, and that was to share the message of Jesus Christ with others.

That was certainly a different goal than the one set forth by his father, whom Bob described as a workaholic who moved the family from Alabama to California to Florida as he developed a business in sales and finance. "Growing up, I knew my goal was to get a job and make a million dollars," Bob said.

That desire evaporated during a high school ski trip organized by Young Life, a ministry that reaches out to adolescents. The slopes were bare from warm weather that winter, which kept the Young Life group indoors for presentations and lectures. There, Bob heard the gospel message and became a Christian, a choice that would shape the rest of his life.

When Bob started attending the University of Florida, he and a close friend, Ander Crenshaw (who in 2001 began a career as a member of the U.S. House of Representatives, representing Florida's 4th congressional district), started a Campus Crusade for Christ chapter on the Gainesville campus.

Bob first met Pam when he was publicizing a Campus Crusade event. She was the daughter of a U.S. Army colonel who moved frequently when her father was assigned new postings, many beyond U.S. borders. She settled in Tampa during her high school years.

Bob and Pam became friends, and their first date came a year after they met, when Bob invited Pam to join him at . . . a football game between the University of Florida and the University of Georgia—a rivalry game played each year at a neutral site: Jacksonville. The Gators won, which just might have been a sign of good things to come.

Their love blossomed, and they graduated together from the University of Florida in 1971—he with a degree in health and human performance, and she with a degree from the College of Journalism and Communications. They married that summer and moved to Portland, Oregon, where Bob enrolled at Western Seminary to earn master's degrees in divinity and theology.

The extra schooling took five years. When Bob was finished, he and Pam moved back to Florida, where he became the area representative for the Fellowship of Christian Athletes (FCA) in the northeastern part of the state. Even though Bob had to raise his own support, he and Pam felt financially secure enough to start a family. After their first child, Christy, arrived in 1976, the parents spaced out Katie, Robby, Peter, and the family caboose—Tim— over the next 11 years.

Beginning in 1976, the Tebows started making major moves every three years. After a three-year stint with the FCA (1976–1979), Bob moved into church ministry at Southside Baptist Church in Jacksonville, where he was the associate pastor for three years until 1982. Then, for the next three years, he served as the pastor of Cornerstone Community Church, also in Jacksonville.

While at Cornerstone, Bob embarked on a life-changing missionary trip to the Philippines. During the trip, he received what he believed was a call in his heart and a summons he could not deny: God was calling him to become a missionary in the Philippines.

Bob and Pam believed then, as they believe now, that God had been preparing their hearts for the mission field. And even though they had been praying He would open this door, think about how difficult this undertaking must have been for the family, especially Pam. She had three children, ages eight, six, and four, as well as an infant son, Peter, who was born in 1984. To pull up stakes in Jacksonville, where her husband was a respected pastor with a bright career ahead of him, and resettle the family in a third world country must have bordered upon the unreal for her.

They would be moving 12 time zones and almost exactly halfway around the world to Southeast Asia, a 19-hour plane trip that would take her far from the creature comforts of home. The logistics had to be daunting, the heartbreak of leaving behind friends and family gut-wrenching. They would have to sell most of their personal belongings. But to her credit, Pam never blinked. Living abroad as a young girl had certainly prepared her for this time in their lives. Besides, she was convinced this was God's will for their lives, and she was fine with that.

Before their departure, Bob founded the Bob Tebow Evangelistic Association with five priorities in mind:

1. Train and employ Filipinos as full-time evangelists since the Philippine culture would naturally respond better to the gospel message when they heard it from fellow countrymen.
2. Plant churches throughout the Philippines, which is an archipelago made up of 7,107 islands and categorized broadly into three main geographical divisions: Luzon, Visayas, and Mindanao.

3. Host periodic conferences in several Asian countries to train even more pastors and local people how to talk to others in their country about their faith.

4. Organize summer mission trips to the Philippines for American young people.

5. Open an orphanage to care for the least of these.

The family settled outside Manila, the capital city of the Philippines, and the transition went as smoothly as they dared hope for. Filipinos were being trained as pastors, and countless locals were embracing the Christian faith. The Tebow kids—who had yet to reach their teenage years—acclimated well. "It wasn't always easy, but it was a wonderful time for our family," Pam said. "We learned a lot—you always learn a lot when you [live in] a third world country."

A year after their arrival, Bob was out in the mountains in Mindanao. "I was showing a film and preaching that night," he told *Sports Illustrated*. "I was weeping over the millions of babies being [aborted] in America, and I prayed, 'God, if you give me a son, if you give me Timmy, I'll raise him to be a preacher.'"

The previous sentence is taken word for word from a *Sports Illustrated* article that ran in the summer of 2009. Did you notice the editorializing? Writer Austin Murphy and/or the SI editors inserted the word "aborted" in brackets to signify that the magazine was not using the original word Bob said, or, in this case, wrote because Bob Tebow was responding to questions that had been e-mailed to him.

So what do you think Bob originally typed? Since he is ardently pro-life, you have to figure that he tapped out this sentence on his computer screen:

I was weeping over the millions of babies being killed in America . . .

That's how strongly he—and Pam—felt about abortion, which stops a beating heart and ends the life of a growing human being. Their hearts wept at the carnage of 4,000 abortions that happen every day in the United States, or 1.5 million each year.

Sports Illustrated—and the Tebows would tell you the world feels the same way—didn't like the starkness or the reality of the word *killed*. So they chose to insert *aborted* instead. More clinical. Easier to brush off, sweep under the rug.

And then Pam got pregnant with Tim, and she and Bob suddenly had to confront their beliefs about the sanctity of life and the sovereignty of Almighty God.

A CHOICE

When Pam became pregnant with Tim, she was 37 years old, living 9,000 miles from home, the mother of four energetic children, and the wife of a missionary pastor.

The pregnancy was not unexpected. In fact, she and Bob very much desired to have a fifth child. They had been praying for Timmy by name—to this day, they still call him "Timmy" and not "Tim"—before she conceived. They wanted to name their son after the young church leader named Timothy, who was the recipient of a pair of letters from the apostle Paul that now appear in the New Testament.

Just before she became pregnant, however, Pam contracted amoebic dysentery, a disease caused by bacteria transmitted through contaminated drinking water. Dysentery is common in developing and tropical countries like the Philippines and is not to be taken lightly—between 40,000 and 100,000 people die worldwide each year of amoebic dysentery, and it was the leading cause of death in the Philippines. The disease causes inflammation of the intestines and bloody, severe diarrhea.

Pam fell into a coma, and she was treated aggressively with a series of strong antimicrobial drugs. As she came out of the coma and her condition stabilized, she continued to take the powerful medications.

Then the stick turned blue when she took a pregnancy test.

Pam recalled reading a label on her prescription warning that the antimicrobial drug could cause "severe birth defects." She immediately discontinued the treatment protocol, fearing that harm had already been done to the growing life inside her. When she told her doctor what had transpired, her worst fears were confirmed when she heard that her "fetus" had been irreversibly damaged. That being the case, the doctor recommended that she "discontinue" the pregnancy—in other words, have an abortion.

Actually, "they didn't recommend," Pam said. "They didn't really give me a choice. That was the only option they gave me."

To Pam and Bob, there was a lot more than a "fetus" growing inside her womb. This was a life, not a glob of tissue or a "product" of conception. Since the Tebows believed God was the author of life—and death—there was no doubt in their minds that they would trust Him in this perilous situation for her *and* for the unborn child.

Pam and Bob's decision was set in concrete, and their determination to see this pregnancy through didn't waver when Pam's doctor told her that her placenta had detached from the uterine wall—a dangerous development known as placental abruption. Pam was a 37-year-old, high-risk patient living in the Philippine countryside, and a severe condition like this one could have easily killed her. Once again, she was counseled to have an abortion—to save her own life. Certainly she would be justified in taking this measure. But Pam wouldn't consider it.

"We were determined to trust the Lord with the children He would give us," she said in an interview with Focus on the Family president Jim Daly. "And if God called me to give up my life, then He would take care of my family."

Bottom line: Pam Tebow wasn't just *willing* to risk her life for Timmy; she actually *chose* to risk her life so that her son might live.

At the seventh month of her crisis pregnancy, Pam traveled to Manila, where she remained on bed rest and received around-the-clock care from an American-trained physician. This was a touch-and-go pregnancy the entire way, and she and Bob prayed earnestly that God would give them the chance to raise the son they would name Timmy.

On her due date of August 14, Pam gave birth to Tim—and the family learned just how serious the placental abruption had been. "There was a great big clump of blood that came out where the placenta wasn't properly attached, basically for the whole nine months," Bob said in an interview with Focus on the Family. "He was a miracle baby."

He was also skinny and long—like the malnourished newborn he was. The Tebows asked friends and family to pray that their newborn son would grow up big and strong. "It was amazing that God spared him, but we knew God had His hand on his life," Bob said. "We all, through the years, have told Timmy that."

STILL GOING STRONG

These days, Bob Tebow continues to run the Bob Tebow Evangelistic Association (BTEA) with the goal of reaching as many of the 42,000 Philippine *barangays*, or villages, as possible with the gospel through 45 Filipino pastors the ministry supports. The BTEA evangelists have preached to more than 12 million people since 2002 and founded more than 8,000 churches, but nearly two-thirds of the *barangays* have no evangelical church. BTEA's plans call for increasing the staff of national evangelists to 60.

For more information, go online and visit the BTEA website at www.btea.org.

BACK IN THE USA

When Tim was three years old, the Tebow family decided to move back to Florida to be closer to home and family. After laying down a strong foundation and sending pastors out into the fields, Bob felt he could run the Bob Tebow Evangelistic Association from a distance while continuing to make periodic trips to the western Pacific Ocean. He could also organize short-term and summer mission trips to the Philippines better while living stateside.

The family moved back to the Jacksonville area and lived on a 44-acre farm tucked between the tranquil setting of Baldwin and the city of Jacksonville. When Tim was a kindergartner, he joined his four older sisters and brothers at a special school with a limited enrollment—the Tebow Homeschool.

Homeschooling was becoming better and better known to the general public in the 1980s, thanks to pioneers like Dr. Raymond Moore and his wife, Dorothy—educators who became vocal advocates for homeschooling, particularly among Christian families. Parents purchased curriculum packages and teaching aids geared to their children's ages. The Tebows were early adopters, beginning in 1982 with Christy.

Let's face it: homeschooling was a radical idea back then, and it's still looked upon in many circles as strange. How can children learn enough to get a good education or get into college if they don't receive instruction from trained teachers in public and private school classrooms?

The Tebows had some clear ideas on how they wanted to raise their children. They were wary of worldly influences intruding upon their five offspring—outside influences that would smack them the moment they stepped on the school bus. They were also greatly concerned about the moral and cultural values conveyed in the public school classroom setting.

So Bob and Pam sought a different approach. They wanted to inspire their children to love God, live excellently, be humble, and serve their fellow man. As hands-on parents who would alone be responsible for their children's formal educations, they would be closely monitoring what came into the home and would be intentional about the lessons their children would learn.

"If I could get my kids to the age of 25 and they know God and serve God and had character qualities that pleased God, then I knew God would be happy and I would be happy," Bob said. "The only way I could do that was to do it myself, commit to God that this is my job. Traditional academics had to take a backseat to God's Word and character-building."

They started homeschooling Christy, Katie, Robby, and Peter before the family moved to the Philippines. Pam taught them the three Rs—reading, 'riting, and 'rithmetic—plus other subjects as they got older. Everything their children learned would be taught through the prism of the Bible and with an emphasis on learning how to speak in public. Bob and Pam wanted each of their children to feel comfortable and confident in communicating their beliefs.

Many of the biblical lessons Bob and Pam taught their children centered around themes of humility, honoring God, and serving others. When each child was very young, Pam chanted the words to one Bible truth in a sing-song voice. A sample teaching:

A man who walks with wise men will be wise;
A man who walks with wise men will be wise;
A man who walks with wise men will be wise;
But the companion of fools will suffer harm.

Memorizing Bible verses, as well as life lessons, was foundational to learning in the Tebow home. For instance, Proverbs 27:2 (New King James Version) taught the children not to brag on themselves:

Let another man praise you, and not your own mouth;
A stranger, and not your own lips.

Bob and Pam believed humility was one of the greatest measures of a person's character, so they constantly turned to the Bible and had their children memorize verses on humility, such as:

- "Remember how the LORD your God led you all the way in the desert these forty years, to humble you and to test you in order to know what was in your heart, whether or not you would keep his commands" (Deuteronomy 8:2).
- "You save the humble, but your eyes are on the haughty to bring them low" (2 Samuel 22:28).
- "When pride comes, then comes disgrace, but with humility comes wisdom" (Proverbs 11:2).
- "The fear of the LORD teaches a man wisdom, and humility comes before honor" (Proverbs 15:33).
- "Humility and the fear of the LORD bring wealth and honor and life" (Proverbs 22:4).

And if they wanted to see their children's eyes grow big, the parents read them the story of what happened to King Nebuchadnezzar after he took credit for what God had done. The king ended up on all fours munching grass like a cow—all because of pride.

When the children weren't memorizing Bible verses or doing their schoolwork, they learned discipline through chores like taking out the trash, vacuuming, making their beds, and washing dishes. That was just the beginning since there was always work to do on such a large property dotted with pines and grassy fields—work such as building fences, feeding the cows, and mowing the grass.

The parents turned a half-acre plot behind the house into a vegetable garden, and the children learned the value of stoop labor as they weeded with hoes and planted and cared for the vegetables that fed their family of seven year-round. They slaughtered and ate the cows they raised. Bucking fallen trees in the "back 40" was another way Bob instilled the value of physical labor in his sons.

Bob and Pam had a firm rule in the Tebow household: no complaining. That rule must have stuck, because you can't call Tim Tebow a grumbler or a whiner today. That characteristic has shown itself on the few occasions when his team has lost a football game. While Tim deeply hates losing at anything he does, he's never been one to offer excuses.

NO GRAND PLAN

It's a great quip, a superb sound bite, and something Bob Tebow loves repeating. It goes like this:

"I asked God for a preacher, and He gave me a quarterback."

There was no grand plan in the Tebow family to raise a great athlete, let alone a star quarterback who would become an NFL first-round draft pick, and this makes Tim's story very different from those of Sam Bradford and Colt McCoy.

Sam, as you read in his chapter, was the son of athletically minded parents who signed up their only child for just about every organized youth sport under the sun: football, basketball, baseball, and hockey. If he had a spare moment, he golfed with his grandfather and friends. The strategy worked: Sam became a gifted athlete with incredible hand-eye coordination.

Colt was the son of a high school football coach, so he literally grew up at the knee of a father who loved the game. From the time he could walk, Colt hung around a football field, soaking it all in. Once he was old enough to play, he developed into an excellent quarterback, thanks in large part to the tutelage of his father.

Not so in the Tebow household, where sports were more low-key. Think about it: during their five years in the Philippines, there was no such thing as Little League or AYSO soccer. The kids played outside, ran around, and did things that little kids do, but there were no "travel teams" in the Philippines.

After the Tebow family returned to Florida, Christy played some tennis, and Katie was a runner. Tim's older brothers, Robby and Peter, got into youth baseball and football. The parents kept everything in perspective; they knew getting exercise was good for the body, but they didn't want their schedules revolving around sports. But the Tebows *were* into competition. "There was no mercy in our family," Bob said. "Katie, every once in a while, would show you mercy, but everyone else would cut your throat."

The Tebow family's competitive streak extended beyond sports. Board games like Monopoly quickly deteriorated into overheated emotions when a simple roll of the dice landed one of the Tebow kids on Boardwalk or Park Place teeming with red hotels. And woe to the Risk players when their territories were captured. When Bob taught each of his children how to play chess, the sparks would fly following a checkmate.

Bob told writer Guerry Smith he never let any of the children beat him at chess—and no one can topple his king to this day. The last time he challenged anyone to take him on, there were no takers. "It's pretty dog-eat-dog around here," he said. "They know the outcome."

With that thought in mind, Bob noticed something about Tim, even when his son was a five-year-old: he had a tremendous arm and impressive hand-eye coordination—as well as the Tebow competitive streak. Tim threw left-handed, but that was his natural side, so Bob didn't try to change him.

Tim could throw a football with excellent velocity for a pint-sized tyke, and when he had a bat in his hand, he could swing and hit the ball squarely. His parents thought he'd have fun playing T-ball, the pressureless entry point for youth baseball, so they signed him up. There's no live pitching in T-ball; each batter steps up to the plate and swings at a ball placed on a plastic tee. Once the player hits the ball into fair territory, he starts running.

Many five-year-olds are clueless about how baseball is played, and some prefer to lie down in the outfield and watch the clouds roll by. Not Tim, who played second base for the White Sox. If he had another gift besides pure athleticism, it was awareness of his surroundings. He would get perturbed when the other kids didn't know what was going on, as Guerry Smith described on Rivals.com:

> Some of his teammates were picking at the ground without even paying attention. *How is that possible?* he wondered. *There's a game going on. Focus on the game.* He heard players say they were out there for the snow cone they would get when the game was over. Not Tebow. The competition was all that mattered at the moment. He heard his coach say, "You don't have to play to win. Just play to have fun," and he could not comprehend the mindset. *It's not fun if you don't win*, he said to himself. He was dumbfounded.
>
> He was also five years old.

Tim also played Pop Warner football. As one of the bigger kids on the team, he played tight end on offense and linebacker on defense. Then one day, when he was 11 years old, his coach, David Hess, watched him practice and said to himself, *This kid is such a talented athlete. He'd make a good quarterback.*

Hess asked Tim to get down on one knee and throw the ball as far as he could. The youngster heaved the ball 30 yards in the air. After that, Tim was lining up behind center. "Guess that's my claim to fame," Coach Hess said years later.

People who knew Tim during his Pop Warner days are still telling Tebow stories—like the time he lined up behind center on his team's 20-yard line and saw the tackles cheating a bit. Instead of taking the snap and tossing the ball to the tailback—the play called in the huddle—Tim ran a quarterback sneak . . . all the way into the end zone, 80 yards away.

When Tim wasn't flying past defenders, he was running over players who dared get in his way. Linebackers who searched for Tim in the open field to deliver a hit stopped searching after the first time they collided with him.

Then there was the tremendous arm strength his father first saw back on the farm. Tim was heaving the ball 50 yards in the air as a sixth grader, and everyone who saw him throw thought, *Wait until he gets to high school.*

Except Tim was homeschooled. How was he going to play high school football when he wasn't going to *go* to high school?

LEADING A HORSE TO WATER . . .

Boys don't generally love to read, and Tim Tebow was no exception. To fuel his desire to read, Pam had him read biographies of famous athletes and write reports about them. If she could relate a science lesson to sports, she tried that, too.

One time, Tim wrote a report on why athletes' bodies need more protein, which he entered in the local science fair. After winning first place, Tim convinced his mom he needed to drink protein shakes.

"She was a great teacher," Tim said of his mother. "I love listening to her talk, tell stories. She was always a very sweet teacher—it took a lot for her to get frustrated. She's continuing to teach me, even now that I'm in the NFL. She's still teaching me all the time, showing me how to do things, correcting my grammar."

LOOKING UP TO A HERO

One of the things Tim's parents encouraged him to do when he was very young was pick a hero who modeled humility and modesty. They suggested just the person for nine-year-old Tim to emulate: Danny Wuerffel, the University of Florida quarterback who would win the Heisman Trophy in 1996 and lead the Gators to a national championship the same season.

Dad and Mom both graduated from the University of Florida, so the Tebows were Gator fans who occasionally attended some of their football games. Older sister Katie was making plans to enroll there in the fall of 1997. Tim, who slept under a Gator bedspread and had a bathroom that sported a Gator shower curtain, tacked a giant color poster of Danny Wuerffel to his bedroom wall. Before the start of the 1996 season, young Tim enjoyed seeing his hero at Gators Fan Day.

Tim liked how the Florida QB was quick to give God credit and live his life to bring honor to Him. Danny loved quoting Proverbs 3:5–6 to the media: "Trust in the Lord with all your heart and lean not on your own understanding; in all your ways acknowledge him, and he will make your paths straight."

So Tim wanted to be like Danny Wuerffel—and to play quarterback like him. Would he get his chance?

The answer was yes, thanks to a new Florida law that allowed home-schooled children to take part in interscholastic sports. A homeschooling mom named Brenda Dickinson spearheaded a two-year battle in the Florida legislature that ended in 1996 with the passage of a law providing home-educated students with the opportunity to participate on athletic teams at their local schools. In other words, if a child was schooled at home, he or she had to be "accommodated" and couldn't be kept off the interscholastic playing field.

Florida became one of 16 states that allowed homeschooled kids to play varsity sports at a traditional high school. Robby and Peter Tebow took advantage of that opportunity and played high school football at Trinity Christian Academy in Jacksonville, a K–12 school with 450 high school students that was founded in 1967.

When Tim reached ninth grade, he was itching to play at Trinity Christian as well. But Tim didn't start out playing quarterback—at least not at first. The Trinity Christian coach, Verlon Dorminey, looked at Tim's broad-shouldered build and lined him up on the varsity team at tight end on offense and linebacker on defense.

That was okay for his freshman year, but Tim wanted to play quarterback. Quarterbacks were the playmakers, the center of action. If you were going to *beat* the other team, you needed a quarterback who could make plays. Tim wanted to *lead* his team to victory, not depend on someone else making a play.

Coach Dorminey was open to the idea, but he had installed a Wing-T offense that relied heavily on the run. In his system, the quarterback made a lot of handoffs or ran off the option play. Little or no passing. This run-centered offense worked for Dorminey and the team: Trinity Christian won the Florida state championship in its division in 2002.

That's not what Bob Tebow wanted for his son, though. He knew Tim had a special gift for throwing the ball and that he needed to be on a team where he could shine as quarterback. He didn't want his son typecast at tight end or linebacker—grunt positions that take size. Quarterback—the position with the ultimate skill set—was where he needed to be.

If Tim was ever going to play quarterback in high school football, he had to make his move. That's because quarterbacks establish themselves on the varsity team during their sophomore seasons. Maybe they don't get to play that much because a senior or a junior is ahead of them, but they take their place on the depth chart and learn the position on the practice field.

Since Trinity Christian didn't throw the ball—and since Tim didn't go to school there anyway—the Tebows starting shopping around. They found a public high school in nearby St. John's County where the coach, Craig Howard, ran a spread offense and liked to see the ball in the air, not on the ground.

The school was Nease High, and the football team hadn't been winning much. In fact, the Panthers were 2–8 the season before Tim arrived and 1–9 the year before that.

In other words, the perfect situation for Tim Tebow.

"We wanted to give Tim the opportunity to develop his God-given talent and to achieve his lifelong dream of playing quarterback," Bob said. "It wasn't that we were leaving an unsuccessful program to go to a successful one; it was the other way around."

There was just one hitch, though: Tim had to live in the Nease High School district, but the Tebow farm was situated in nearby Duval County.

The Tebows overcame that hurdle by renting an apartment close to Nease High in Ponte Vedra Beach. They put the family farm up for sale and signed up Tim to play football at Nease High. Pam and Tim did Bible studies and worked through his homeschool curriculum in the morning and early afternoon, and then it was off to football practice at Nease High. The family farm never sold, so the Tebows eventually ended up keeping their homestead, but as Bob said, "We were willing to make that sacrifice. We made sacrifices for all our children."

Nease High—named after Allen Duncan Nease, a pioneer of Florida's reforestation and conservation efforts in the mid-twentieth century—was a public high school of about 1,600 students that played in Florida's 4A division.

In Florida—a state that, like Texas and Oklahoma, is a hotbed of high school football talent—schools competed in one of eight classifications, all based on enrollment. The largest classification in the state was 6A, and the smallest was 1B, so there were some schools in Florida classed higher than Nease and many classed lower.

Tim's talent could not be denied nor his work ethic overlooked. Coach Howard certainly noticed. "People can always lead with words but not always with actions," he said. "Timmy was the hardest worker I've ever been around. His work ethic was uncompromising, and all of those around him were affected by it."

Like Sam and Colt, Tim won the starting quarterback role in his sophomore season. Based on their history of losing, though, the Panthers figured to be the patsy on other teams' schedules. "We had six road games my sophomore year, and we were the homecoming game for all six of them," Tim said. "Talk about embarrassing."

But the Panthers, with their sophomore quarterback making throws, bullying his way through the line, and never giving up, acquitted themselves well during Tim's first season there. Nease High finished 5–5 in 2003, a turnaround that portended better things to come.

BREAKOUT TIME

Why do you think Sam, Colt, and Tim had such big junior seasons in high school football? You could say that their maturity and confidence played a big role, but they also needed a strong cast around them to block, catch the ball, and stop the other team from scoring. In that respect, all three were in the right place at the right time as high school juniors.

But think how the situation was different for Tim. He didn't go to school with his teammates. No friendly banter between classes or hanging out in the cafeteria during lunchtime. No horseplay or kidding around while gathering for a school assembly.

Yet Tim won over his teammates with his hard work on the practice field, his unyielding determination to win, and his respectful attitude toward them and the coaches. His teammates saw him as a nice, fun-loving guy—as one of them, even though he didn't go to classes during the school day.

For Tim, all the pieces were in place for a successful 2004 season. He was big and brawny, pushing past 6 feet, 2 inches tall, and weighing in north of 215 pounds. He single-handedly, by force of will and great talent, took a nothing team and turned it into an 11–2 powerhouse that advanced to the third round of the state playoffs.

If Tim wasn't pile-driving his way through the line like a determined full-back, he was hitting receivers between the numbers and lofting bombs into the end zone. Suddenly, rival schools didn't want anything to do with Nease High on homecoming night.

Coach Howard saw that he had a thoroughbred in Tim, and he let him run—and throw and throw and throw. Before the season was over, Tim had set the state record for total yards in a season with 5,576, of which 4,304 yards came from passing (for an average of 331 yards per game). He was also responsible for 70 touchdowns in 13 games—and that's not a typo: he tossed 46 touchdown passes (more than three per game) and ran for 24 more, making himself the ultimate "dual-threat" quarterback. He threw just six interceptions all season.

NO FACE IN THE CROWD

The honors rolled in for Tim Tebow following his junior season: Florida Dairy Farmers Player of the Year, All-State, and a third-place finish in Florida's Mr. Football balloting. He rose up the college recruiting websites such as Rivals.com and SuperPrep.com like a hit song on a Top 40 chart. Scout.com even ranked him third nationally among high school quarterback prospects.

Sportswriter John Patton of the *Gainesville Sun* called Tim "the best high school football player I have ever seen"—even though he still had another season of high school ball left. Then, at the end of his junior season, *Sports Illustrated* printed his smiling mug in the magazine's "Faces in the Crowd" section.

The hype machine was pulling out of the driveway.

College coaches descended upon the Tebow family like solicitous salesmen carrying briefcases filled with their wares. Eighty schools offered him scholarships and pleaded with him to come play for State U, but the only ones the Tebows gave active consideration were the University of Miami, the University of Michigan, the University of Southern California, the University of

Alabama, and Bob and Pam's alma mater—the University of Florida.

Unlike Sam and Colt, however, the Tebow parents didn't want Tim to make a verbal commitment to any college at the end of his junior year. They weren't ready yet; they wanted to take their time.

As word got around about this Tebow kid in Florida, an ESPN producer smelled a good story and sent a camera crew from Murrah Communications to Nease High during the summer of 2005. Coach Howard gave the film crew full access throughout the 2005 season—training camp, locker room, practice field, and the sidelines during the games. The coach even allowed himself to be miked up.

This would be an ESPN *Faces in Sports* program, and the title of the hour-long documentary was *The Chosen One*. The story line was Tim's record-setting career at Nease, his senior season, and the team's drive toward a state championship. The program ended with Tim's postseason announcement in December of which school he had chosen to attend.

The Chosen One is still worth watching. (It's readily available in five segments on YouTube.) It's a chance to watch a youthful Tim—wearing a No. 5 jersey— develop not only as a player but also into a young man learning to deal with intense media scrutiny. He handled everything with aplomb. There are many amazing scenes:

- Tim and his dad sitting at the dinner table at their ranch house, sifting through a mound of recruiting letters from the nation's top college football coaches—many handwritten—informing Tim that he'd be a "welcome addition" to their program.
- Pam perched at a small table with Tim in their Ponte Vedra apartment, working through a home-school lesson together.
- Bob and Pam talking about their years in the Philippines and a clip of Tim preaching before hundreds of Filipino kids when he was only 15 years old.
- Tim in the locker room, firing up his team before a big game like it was the end of the world.
- Tim suffering a broken leg but refusing to be pulled out of the game, and later hobbling 29 yards into the end zone on sheer guts.
- Bob standing in a grassy field, reading Proverbs 22:6 from his Bible ("Train a child in the way he should go . . .").

THE NEXT BIG THING

The cameras were there when Nease High opened the 2005 season with a road game against highly regarded Hoover High in Hoover, Alabama, which aired *nationally* on ESPN. Even though Nease lost 50–29, everyone agreed that Tim put on quite a show.

The national media had now officially anointed Tim as the Next Big Thing. Tim backed that up by putting together another record-breaking season and leading Nease to its first state championship, which the Panthers took home after beating Armwood High 44–37 in the state final. Tim's stats: 237 yards and four touchdowns in the air, 153 yards and two touchdowns on the ground . . . and jokes about selling popcorn at halftime.

All that was left for Tim to do was to announce which college had won his heart. The family narrowed down the choices to Alabama or Florida, and then Bob and Pam stepped aside. *It's your decision, Son. You're the one who's going to be playing there. You pray about it and let the Lord guide your steps.*

Three days after pocketing the state championship, Tim—dressed in a dark coat, blue shirt, and white tie—took the podium at the Nease High Performing Arts Center. He stood before an auditorium packed with hundreds of screaming teenagers and Gator partisans. ESPN's cameras were there—live.

That morning, Tim and his golden Lab, Otis, had gone for a long walk into the pine trees and oaks that outlined their homestead. He sat next to a nearby lake and thought and prayed about what he should do. He and his parents liked both coaches; Urban Meyer at Florida and Mike Shula at Alabama were God-fearing men of strong character. Both schools were capable of winning the national title. This was one of those win-win decisions.

In the end, the edge went to Florida. Coach Meyer ran a spread offense, just like Coach Howard did at Nease, and the family's deep roots at the University of Florida couldn't be glossed over. Mom and Dad went there, and Pam's father had played basketball there. Tim had grown up in Gator Nation. The school was close to home, which meant his parents and siblings—Team Tebow—could watch him play at Ben Hill Griffin Stadium, a.k.a. "The Swamp."

Bob and Pam held their breath as Tim straddled the podium, looked straight into the camera, and said, "I will be playing college football next year at the University of Florida."

THE GREEN SHIRT AT GATOR NATION

How do you describe the four-year college career that launched Tebowmania and lifted Tim into the living rooms of millions of Americans?

Do you start with Tim's freshman year and his double-pump "jump pass" for a one-yard touchdown against LSU that had announcers raving about his originality? Or was it the *Braveheart* scene at Florida State—when Tim's face and white jersey were smeared in the "war paint" from the end zone? Or how about the controversy when he started inscribing Bible verses on his eye black?

When Tim announced, "I will be playing college football next year at the University of Florida," he was talking about playing the very *next* season, not kicking back and enjoying a low-stress redshirt year. In January 2006, within a few weeks of his announcement, Tim enrolled at Florida. He didn't have to wait to graduate with his high school class—he *was* the class.

Tim was eligible to enroll in college because he had completed his studies and had taken an SAT test in ninth grade. By becoming a University of Florida student, Tim made himself eligible to participate in spring football practice—the rehearsal time for the fall season.

In the college football lexicon, he was not a red shirt but a "green shirt"—green as in "go early." A green-shirt athlete is someone who graduates from high school in December of his senior year and immediately enrolls in college so he can participate in spring practice—and get a head start on learning the system and moving up the depth chart.

Chris Leak was a senior and a three-year starter for the Gators, so he was the No. 1 quarterback. But Tim wasn't willing to rock on his cleats on the Florida sidelines, helmet in hand, waiting for his chance to play. He was going to *compete* for the job, even as a true freshman.

At the annual Orange and Blue scrimmage game, which ended three weeks of spring practice, Tim looked sharp in leading his Orange team to a 24–6 victory. "Chris Leak is our quarterback, and Tim Tebow is a guy who is going to play," Coach Meyer said afterward. "There is no quarterback controversy. There are two great young men who we are going to build an offense around to be successful."

Translation: *We're going to start Chris Leak so our freshman quarterback doesn't have the pressure of being the starter, but he's going to be playing a lot.*

Tim did play a lot as a true freshman in 2006, even though Florida had arguably the toughest schedule in the nation. He scored the first time he touched the ball in a Florida uniform—on a goal-line keeper against Southern Mississippi. Coach Meyer continued to play Tim in spot situations, bringing him along slowly. But in the third game of the season, against Tennessee—in Knoxville, before 106,818 rabid Volunteer fans—Meyer threw Tim into the fire. In the fourth quarter, with the Gators trailing by six points, Florida faced a fourth-and-one inside Tennessee territory. Meyer flung Tim into the game, Tim punched out two yards to keep the drive alive, and Chris Leak took his place and led the Gators to the winning score.

Against Southeastern Conference opponents, Florida fell into a familiar pattern throughout the season—fall behind early, then claw its way back. Against LSU, Tim unveiled his first "jump pass." With Florida knocking on the door at the one-yard line, Tim took the snap five yards behind center, ran toward the pile, then suddenly leaped and lobbed a rainbow pass to his tight end, Tate Casey. Touchdown!

It was a clever play—known in the Florida playbook as Trey Left, 341 Stop Bend X Fake—that hadn't been seen since the days of Bronko Nagurski and leather helmets. With retro panache, Tim would make two more jump passes in his career at Florida. (Heads up, NFL defenses.)

After defeating LSU, Florida—now ranked No. 2 in the country—suffered its first hiccup of the season—against Auburn in a 27–17 road loss in an ESPN *GameDay* matchup. A controversial fourth-quarter fumble by Chris Leak, with Florida trailing 21–17 but driving for the potential win, sealed the Gators' fate.

That was the only smudge on an otherwise golden 2006 Florida football season. The Gators ran the table the rest of the way, beating Georgia, Florida State, and Arkansas (in the SEC Championship Game) to climb back to No. 2 in the polls and into the BCS National Championship Game—played at the new University of Phoenix Stadium in Glendale, Arizona—against top-ranked Ohio State.

Florida thrashed the Buckeyes 41–14 to win its second national football championship in school history—the other one happening in 1996 when Danny Wuerffel was the Gator quarterback. The victory also helped mark the first time in college sports history that the NCAA college basketball and football titles rested in the same trophy case—the Gator men's basketball team having won the national championship in the spring of 2006. Chris Leak played clutch football, and when Tim spelled him, he found the soft spots in the Ohio State defense with his power running, scoring one touchdown and throwing for another on college football's biggest night.

At a well-attended victory celebration at Ben Hill Griffin Stadium a few days later, a special guest was invited onstage to hand Chris Leak the Most Valuable Player trophy. Who was the surprise invitee?

Danny Wuerffel, Tim's boyhood hero.

After telling Chris they were now the only starting Gator quarterbacks in Florida football history to bear national championship rings, Danny paused for a moment and turned to the freshman quarterback standing nearby. Everyone wondered what Danny Wonderful would say.

"There's room for another one next year, Timmy Tebow," he said.

The baton had been officially passed.

IT'S TIM'S TEAM NOW

With Chris Leak graduated, the Florida Gators were now Tim Tebow's team. Everyone knew it. A FLORIDA FOLK HERO PREPARES TO FACE REALITY read a preseason headline in the *New York Times,* which knew an important story when it saw one.

The story noted that during the offseason, Tim had sung "She Thinks My Tractor's Sexy" onstage with country singer Kenny Chesney, preached in two prisons "so convincingly" that 200 hardened criminals began weeping and became Christians, and dealt with coeds camping outside his apartment—some who asked him to autograph their underwear.

Saying that Tim had a big year in 2007, after having just turned 19 years of age, would be like saying the New York Yankees and Murderer's Row had a big year in 1927. The way Tim performed in 2007 was remarkable, considering these developments:

- He played much of the season with a severely bruised shoulder.
- Some of his teammates weren't as committed, didn't play as well as the graduated seniors from the 2006 team, or got themselves into trouble off the field or in the classroom.
- Tim's roommate, Tony Joiner, was arrested for breaking into a Gainesville tow lot and attempting to retrieve his girlfriend's impounded car. Though it was a misunderstanding and the charges were later dropped, Coach Meyer stripped Joiner of his role as team captain.
- Tim's offensive coordinator, Dan Mullen, underwent an emergency appendectomy less than 24 hours before he called Florida's

offensive plays in the Gators' 20–17 loss to Auburn. (Tim called his coach a "warrior" for being at the game right after the procedure.)

- Tim fractured his right hand in a late-season game against Florida State but continued playing anyway (remember, he throws left-handed). He would wear a cast for the next three weeks.

Tim hurdled those bumps in the road like he ran over defenses—like they were just little nuisances. And the numbers he put up!

In the season opener against Western Kentucky, Tim led the Gators to touchdowns on their first four possessions. He finished his first career start by going 13-for-17 for 300 yards with three touchdown passes and one rushing touchdown in a 49–3 wipeout. Another warm-up game against Troy was also a Tebow gem.

Tim's first big test as a starter was the 2007 SEC opener against Tennessee, which was played before 90,707 hot and sticky fans at The Swamp. Tim was unstoppable, running and throwing the ball up and down the field almost at will. When he scored on a seven-yard touchdown run in the second quarter, CBS cameras caught safety and roommate Tony Joiner planting a kiss on Tim's left cheek as a reward.

The lovefest continued until Tim's first interception of the season, which resulted in a 93-yard Volunteer touchdown to pull Tennessee to within 28–20 in the third quarter. After that, though, the rout was on—31 unanswered Florida points as Tim racked up 61 yards on the ground and 299 yards through the air.

A nice Big Orange smoothie.

After the Tennessee game, the *Gainesville Sun* collected the best quotes from others about Tim Tebow:

Lou Holtz, ESPN analyst: "Florida just has so many playmakers, including that Superman who plays quarterback."

Gary Parrish, CBSSports.com: "And so his first league start was laced with such curiosity, and a national television audience turned to CBS to see what exactly this poster boy of a signal caller could do against Tennessee. Now, everybody is just wondering what he can't do. Against Tennessee or anybody else."

Stewart Mandel, SI.com: "QB Tim Tebow exceeded even the most delusional expectations in his first SEC start."

Dave Hyde, South Florida *Sun-Sentinel*: "Of all things good and great you could say about Tebow, the best is this: he is living up to the hype, the hoopla, the borderline nonsense as represented by the 'Tebow Is God' and 'Tebow for President' signs hanging Saturday from student houses by the stadium."

HE15MAN TIME

This amalgamation of Joe Montana and Jim Brown added up to two words: *Tebow hysteria*. Some zealous Florida fans created TimTebowFacts.com, where fans could contribute a list of Tim's most legendary, Paul Bunyanesque accomplishments. T-shirt makers started silkscreening "He15man" on Gator blue shirts, and the ESPN and CBS football pundits declared that Tim was the early-season favorite for the Heisman Trophy, even though they were careful to insert a "but"—*but a sophomore has never won the Heisman, Lou.* They pointed out that ex-Gator quarterback Rex Grossman didn't win one in 2001 and running back Darren McFadden of Arkansas didn't pick up the Heisman in 2006, even though both players had superb seasons, so it was likely never to happen.

Tim's legend expanded the following week against Ole Miss when he took over a road game in Oxford, Mississippi, that Florida looked destined to lose. The Gators struggled most of the game until five consecutive Tebow runs set up a short field goal that gave the Gators a 30–24 lead with less than five minutes to play. After a stop, when Florida needed to run time off the clock, Tim carried the ball six consecutive times to secure a victory and keep the No. 3 Gators undefeated for the season. In all, Tim accounted for all four Gator touchdowns and 427 of his team's 507 total yards.

But the Gators lost three of their next four games, falling to Auburn at home, LSU in Baton Rouge, and Georgia at the neutral Jacksonville site. Tim didn't do much against Georgia because of a right shoulder contusion he suffered the previous week against Kentucky. When he was in the game, the Georgia rush menaced him the entire afternoon, sacking him six times. It seemed like he was running for his life the entire game.

Tim, who had wiped tears from his face after walking off the field at LSU, had to fight back moisture in his eyes at the postgame podium as he faced the media following the tough loss to interstate rival Georgia. "I do take them [the losses] hard," he said, "but that's because I am so passionate."

Listening to the Georgia game on her computer, via the Internet, was his sister Christy. It was the middle of the night in Bangladesh, where she had recently moved with her husband, Joey, and their one-year-old daughter, Claire, to do missionary work.

After the game, Tim spoke by phone with Christy, who told him how she and her family were adjusting to life in one of the poorest countries of the world. He felt chastened. "It makes you realize that everything that happens in this game doesn't really mean that much in the grand scheme of things," Tim said. "Losing to Georgia is not the biggest thing in the world."

The Gators—and Tim—bounced back and played a perfect November, even though his shoulder bruise still bothered him. He shook off the pain and ran for five touchdowns against South Carolina, set a career-best in passing yards with 338 against Florida Atlantic, and dominated intrastate rival Florida State at The Swamp, despite suffering a displaced fracture on his nonthrowing right hand. He played 30 downs with the busted hand and laid out his final argument to win the Heisman Trophy. In the closing moments of a one-sided 45–12 victory against the Seminoles, Gator cheerleaders struck Heisman poses—carriage slightly bent, leg up, right arms thrust out to stiffarm a tackler—on the sidelines.

Florida finished the season a respectable 9–3 and earned a January 1, 2008, date with Michigan at the Citrus Bowl. But the big story in Gator Nation was whether Tim would capture the Heisman Trophy.

In the 72-year history of the award, Heisman voters—sportswriters and past winners—had never handed the award to a sophomore, reserving the honor for upperclassmen. It seemed to be one of those unwritten rules.

Wait your turn, son.

But who had played better than Tim Tebow in 2007? Some said Arkansas running back Darren McFadden deserved it after failing to strike the pose in 2006, or that University of Hawaii senior quarterback Colt Brennan should win because of his outlandish passing stats, but no one played better than Tim in 2007.

In early December, Tim and his family flew to New York City for the Heisman Trophy ceremony at the Nokia Theatre in Times Square. It turned out to be a family reunion when Christy and her family flew to New York from Bangladesh—the first time Team Tebow had been all together since the previous Christmas. The family was overjoyed.

When he heard his name announced as the winner, a beaming Tim bound up out of his chair and hugged his parents, then Gator coach Urban Meyer. Standing on the stage with all the surviving Heisman winners since 1935 was his boyhood idol, Danny Wuerffel, who greeted him with another hug.

After first thanking God for the ability to play football, Tim thanked his teammates back home, his coaches, and especially his parents: "I want to thank my dad, who taught me a work ethic every day growing up, and my mom, who instilled in me so many great characters."

It's okay, Tim. This was live TV before millions of viewers. We know what you meant: Mom instilled in you so many great characteristics.

Afterward, he told interviewers, "I think it's amazing that you're known forever as a Heisman Trophy winner. That's very special. It's overwhelming. I'm kind of at a loss for words." Football commentators agreed that being the first NCAA Division 1 quarterback ever to have a "20/20" season—22 rushing touchdowns and 29 touchdown passes—sealed the deal with Heisman voters.

Tim, the youngest Heisman winner ever at 20 years of age, accepted the trophy with a blue cast on his right hand, one year before another sophomore, Sam Bradford, would hold the same trophy with a red cast protecting his surgically repaired left thumb.

The 2007 season ended with a 41–35 loss to Michigan on New Year's Day. Tim played with a soft cast to protect his mending right hand. Although the defeat was disappointing to the Gators and their fans, they knew Tim would be returning the following season—all healed up and with a talented, more experienced team surrounding him.

A passion burned deep within Tim for a national championship ring— the one Danny Wuerffel said there was room for.

PROMISE MADE, PROMISE KEPT

In Gator lore, it's called "The Promise."

Here's the situation. Through the first three games of the 2008 season, Florida was pancaking opponents. Victories over Hawaii, Miami, and Tennessee were as lopsided as some girls' basketball games. The talk in Gator Nation was that this team could go undefeated—something never done in the history of Florida football.

Ole Miss was coming into Gainesville a decided underdog—22 points according to the odds makers. Quarterbacking the Rebels was Jevan Snead, who (1) "decommitted" to Florida after Tim announced he would become a Gator and (2) enrolled at Texas but transferred to Ole Miss after getting beat out by Colt McCoy. So you could excuse Snead if he had a bit of an inferiority complex playing in Tim Tebow's house.

But Snead was a gamer, as was the entire Rebel team. They made plays, recovered fumbles from Tim and star running back Percy Harvin, and "hung around"—football-speak for a team that should have been put away after falling behind 17-7.

The game was tied 24–24 midway through the fourth quarter when the Rebels—playing with house money since they were still in the game—got lucky (if you're a Gator fan) or made a great effort (if you're an Ole Miss fan). Snead found Shay Hodge all alone on the sideline for an 86-yard scoring play to give Ole Miss a 31–24 lead with 5:26 to play.

Tim and the Gators hitched up their pants and scored quickly when Percy Harvin scooted 15 yards for a touchdown. The extra point attempt, however, was blocked when an Ole Miss player hurdled a blocker to tip the kick—an illegal tactic in organized football. Coach Meyer argued his case but to no avail.

Disaster! Instead of being tied, Florida was down 31–30. With 3:28 left, the Florida defense needed a quick stop, which it got. Tim had the offense driving, but the Gators faced a fourth-and-one on the Ole Miss 32-yard line. Do you go for a 49-yard field goal to win the game or get the first down and try to get closer?

The Gators were going for it—but the Rebel defense stuffed Tim at the line of scrimmage.

Game over.

When Tim faced the media afterward, he was asked if he wanted to forget the loss. "I don't want to," an emotional Tim replied. "I want it to stay in our hearts and keep hurting so that we'll never let this happen again."

Then he paused and gathered his thoughts. What spilled forth was what came to be known as "The Promise":

> "I just want to say one thing" . . . *deep breath* . . . "to the fans and everybody in Gator Nation" . . . *pause, sniffle* . . . "I'm sorry. I'm extremely sorry. We were hoping for an undefeated season. That was my goal, something Florida's never done here.
>
> "I promise you one thing: a lot of good will come out of this.

You will never see any player in the entire country who will play as hard as I will play the rest of the season. You will never see someone push the rest of the team as hard as I will push everybody the rest of the season.

"You will never see a team play harder than we will the rest of the season. God bless."

With that, Tim exited the postgame podium—and Florida didn't lose another game the rest of the 2008 season.

THREE-SECOND EVANGELISM

Two weeks after the Ole Miss debacle, Tim took the field against LSU suited up like he always was for a home game: blue-jersey-and-white-pants Gator uniform, football pads, cleats, and a helmet. Underneath his eyes, on his upper cheeks, were two black rectangular patches.

Called "eye black," this dark mixture of beeswax, paraffin, and carbon is applied under the eyes to reduce glare. Sunlight or stadium lights can impair the view of an airborne ball.

Tim began wearing smudges of eye black during Florida day games, but before this important test against the defending national champion LSU Tigers, he had someone in the locker room use a white grease pencil to print **PHL** on top of the black strip underneath his right eye and **4:13** under the left eye. The idea was an out-of-the-box, genuine, and clever way to share the biblical message of Philippians 4:13—"I can do all things through Christ who strengthens me"—with millions of football viewers.

Remember, the camera loved Tim Tebow. Throughout the game, TV producers in the truck inserted as many close-up "cutaways" of Tim as they could—like when he was barking out signals in the shotgun or swallowing a spritz of Gatorade on the Florida sideline with his helmet off.

Tim wasn't the first player to write a message on his eye black. A few years earlier, USC running back Reggie Bush printed "619" on both rectangular swatches—the area code of his hometown of San Diego.

The eye-black-with-a-Bible-verse story took on a life of its own after the LSU victory, and for every game during the rest of his college career, Tim "shared" a Bible verse with his football-watching audience.

Talk about three-second evangelism. These spiritual billboards sent millions to their Bibles or to their computers to find out what the Bible verse of the week said. What Tim did with his eye black messages was share his Christian faith, jump-start a national conversation—and add to his legend.

Tim took some hits from the media, though. "There's something strange about the alliance of modern sports and religion," a columnist with *The Tennessean* opined. Others felt religion and sports should not mix. "Why must he rub it in my face?" was the sentiment of *Orlando Sentinel*'s David Whitley.

None of the potshots fazed Tim or changed the way he played throughout the rest of the 2008 season. After "The Promise," he actually accomplished what he pledged to do: grab his team by the scruff of the neck and yank them over the national championship goal line.

Look how lopsided these victories were following the Ole Miss loss:

- Arkansas, 38–7
- LSU, 51–21
- Kentucky, 63–5
- Georgia, 49–10
- Vanderbilt, 42–14
- South Carolina, 56–6
- The Citadel, 70–19
- Florida State, 45–15

The eight-game winning streak earned fourth-ranked Florida a date with No. 1–ranked Alabama for the SEC Championship. Alabama was a solid 10-point favorite for this monster matchup in Atlanta.

With star running back Percy Harvin out of the game, an even heavier offensive load fell on Tim's shoulders. The way he took over in the fourth quarter with his team down 20–17, engineering two touchdown drives, ranked right up at the top of the Tebow highlight reel. He kept the chains moving by throwing into tight spots and battering the 'Bama defense with muscular runs.

"You knew he was going to lead us to victory," said receiver Carl Moore following a 31–20 triumph that catapulted the Gators into the BCS National Championship Game against top-ranked Oklahoma. "You looked into his eyes, and you could see he was intense. We were all intense."

A HEISMAN REPEAT?

After the Alabama conquest, Tim learned he was again a finalist for the Heisman Trophy, so he and his family repeated the trip to Manhattan. This time around at the Nokia Theatre, he was the first to hug Sam Bradford after the Sooner quarterback's name was announced as college football's most outstanding player.

Tim did receive plenty of recognition for his stellar 2008 season—like the Maxwell Award and the Manning Award—but none meant more to him than taking a phone call from Danny Wuerffel, who informed Tim that he'd won the 2008 Wuerffel Trophy, presented annually to the college football player who combines exemplary community service with athletic and academic achievement.

After retiring from professional football in 2004, Danny and his family joined Desire Street Ministries in one of New Orleans' toughest and poorest neighborhoods.

"He's just an amazing young man, an amazing football player," Danny said. "It's funny how things go back and forth. Maybe one day my son will win the Tebow Trophy."

CHAMPIONSHIP GAME MOTIVATION

Florida had one month to prepare for the national championship game, which felt very much like a home game to the Gators since they would be playing the Sam Bradford–led Oklahoma Sooners at Dolphins Stadium in Miami. What made the matchup even more intriguing was that Florida and Oklahoma had *never* played each other before.

Tim didn't have to reach too deep to summon pregame motivation. The acrid smell of the September defeat to Ole Miss still singed his nostrils, and losing the Heisman Trophy vote, despite winning more first-place votes (309 to 300) than Sam Bradford, certainly smarted. And when Sooners cornerback Dominique Franks popped off that Tim would probably be the fourth-best quarterback in the Big 12 Conference—well, that was all the incentive Tim needed in his wheelhouse.

Thus, properly inspired, Tim decided to forgo **EPH 4:31** and inscribe his eye black with the most widely quoted Bible verse—and one considered the summary of the most central doctrine in Christianity—**John 3:16**: "For God so loved the world that he gave his one and only Son, that whoever believes in him shall not perish but have eternal life."

Once the BCS Championship Game started, though, Tim was out of sync—like Superman without his cape. Two interceptions came on balls he shouldn't have thrown. The Oklahoma defense swarmed the line of scrimmage and shut down Tim as well as the Gator ground game. Florida scored only one touchdown in the first half, which would normally put a team in a big hole against a team like Oklahoma, a juggernaut that averaged 50 points a game and rarely had to send their punt team onto the field. But the Gator defense was up to the challenge, and the score was tied 7–7 at halftime.

The Florida defense continued making big stops after intermission, and then Tim got into the flow, converting several big third downs by running and throwing to stake Florida to a small lead. Tim then put a cherry atop the BCS Championship sundae when he lobbed a four-yard jump pass to David Nelson with 3:07 left in the game, giving Florida a commanding 24–14 lead.

After a four-down stop, all the Florida offense had to do was run out the clock. An exuberant Tim got a bit over-the-top when he celebrated a big 13-yard rush by aiming a "Gator Chomp" at Oklahoma's Nic Harris. Tim fully extended his arms, one above the other, and then moved them together and apart to symbolize the opening and closing of an alligator's mouth. An official threw a yellow flag in the air for taunting, and Florida was penalized 15 yards.

"I was pretty excited," Tim said after the game. "Just gave it a little Gator Chomp, and it was also for the fans. I think they kind of enjoyed it." Gator fans also enjoyed how Tim made "The Promise" come true. Everyone on the Florida team believed the Ole Miss loss turned around the season.

Funny how a loss can turn out to be a blessing in more ways than one.

And on a side note, Google reported that searches for "John 3:16" totaled 93 million during and immediately after the BCS victory by Florida.

"I'M COMING BACK"

After the national championship-clinching win over Oklahoma, a plaque was affixed to the James W. "Bill" Heavener Football Complex outside The Swamp. Entitled "The Promise," the silver tablet immortalized Tim's emotional post-game speech following the Ole Miss loss.

The idea to mount Tim's heartfelt declaration came from Coach Meyer, who thought Tim's words would inspire future generations of Gators, much the same way Knute Rockne's "Win one for the Gipper" speech back in 1928 had ignited Notre Dame teams over the decades.

Quite an honor—especially for a college football player with one season left to play. Or was Tim bolting to the NFL? He was eligible to turn pro.

"Let's do it again!" he shouted to an estimated 42,000 Gator fans celebrating the team's national championship at The Swamp three days after the victory in Miami. "I'm coming back!"

A few days later, *Sports Illustrated's* cover showed Tim about to slap his palms in that infamous Gator Chomp against Oklahoma. The headline: NOT DONE YET: TWO TITLES IN THREE YEARS, AND TIM TEBOW IS COMING BACK FOR MORE.

Tim never thought seriously about passing up his senior year to go play in the NFL, but he *did* start giving a great deal of thought to what Bible verses he would inscribe on his eye black during his final season of college football. Before each game in 2009, Tim lettered a new Bible verse on his eye black, sending millions of fans to their computers to do a Google search.

Here's a list of the opponents and the verses Tim wore on his eye black:

Charleston Southern: Proverbs 3:5–6
Trust in the LORD with all your heart and lean not on your own understanding; in all your ways acknowledge him, and he will make your paths straight.

Troy: Mark 8:36
"What good is it for a man to gain the whole world, yet forfeit his soul?"

Tennessee: Romans 8:28
And we know that in all things God works for the good of those who love him, who have been called according to his purpose.

Kentucky: Isaiah 40:31
But those who hope in the LORD will renew their strength. They will soar on wings like eagles; they will run and not grow weary, they will walk and not be faint.

LSU: 1 Thessalonians 5:18
Give thanks in all circumstances, for this is God's will for you in Christ Jesus.

Arkansas: Psalm 23:1
The LORD is my shepherd, I shall not be in want.

Mississippi State: Ephesians 4:32
Be kind and compassionate to one another, forgiving each other, just as in Christ God forgave you.

Georgia: Philippians 4:6–7
Do not be anxious about anything, but in everything, by prayer and petition, with thanksgiving, present your requests to God. And the peace of God, which transcends all understanding, will guard your hearts and your minds in Christ Jesus.

Vanderbilt: Colossians 3:23
Whatever you do, work at it with all your heart, as working for the Lord, not for men.

South Carolina: Joshua 1:8–9
"Do not let this Book of the Law depart from your mouth; meditate on it day and night, so that you may be careful to do everything written in it. Then you will be prosperous and successful. Have I not commanded you? Be strong and courageous. Do not be terrified; do not be discouraged, for the LORD your God will be with you wherever you go."

Florida International: Romans 1:16
I am not ashamed of the gospel, because it is the power of God for the salvation of everyone who believes: first for the Jew, then for the Gentile.

Florida State: Hebrews 12:1–2
Therefore, since we are surrounded by such a great cloud of witnesses, let us throw off everything that hinders and the sin that so easily entangles, and let us run with perseverance the race marked out for us. Let us fix our eyes on Jesus, the author and perfecter of our faith, who for the joy set before him endured the cross, scorning its shame, and sat down at the right hand of the throne of God.

It turned out Bob Tebow got a preacher after all.

A FAREWELL AT THE SWAMP

For Tim's final home game, against Florida State—Senior Day—Gator fans were urged to wear eye black, with or without an inscribed Bible verse. After Florida whipped its intrastate rival, the Gators had a sparkling 12–0 regular season record, had been ranked No. 1 all season, and were two games away from completing the program's first-ever perfect season.

The stage was set for back-to-back national championships, but first there was some business to conduct against Alabama in the SEC Championship Game, a rematch from the year before held in Atlanta's Georgia Dome.

This time, it was all Crimson Tide. The Florida defense allowed Alabama to convert on 11 of 15 third-down opportunities, which kept the Tide rolling down the field and chewing up the game possession clock. Alabama's offense was on the field for 39 minutes, 27 seconds, nearly 20 minutes longer than Florida.

Instead of giving the Tide a hard-fought game early on, the Gators went meekly into the night, losing 32–13. Their 22-game win streak was toast, and the dream of a perfect season was rudely ended.

The enduring image from that game is Tim bent down on one knee with his team hopelessly behind by three touchdowns as the clock ticks away, the tears streaming through his eye black and down his face. He barely held it together during a postgame interview with CBS' sideline reporter, Tracy Wolfson.

"Tim Tearbow" is how some bloggers lit him up, but Tim had one game left in his college career—a January 1 date with No. 5 Cincinnati in the Sugar Bowl.

LOW THROW

If you look at Tim's performance at the 2010 Sugar Bowl, you would think he single-handedly destroyed the Bearcats. He put on a passing exhibition, completing his first 12 passes and going 20-for-23 in the first half for 320 yards and three touchdowns. When it was all over, he had torched Cincinnati for 482 passing yards and supplied the perfect ending to a storied four-year career. The 51–24 annihilation of the previously unbeaten Bearcats left Florida as the only BCS team ever to win at least 13 games in back-to-back seasons.

You'd think that Tim would be carried off the field and hailed by the media as one of the greatest college quarterbacks ever. Team Tebow, however, woke up the next day to a media drumbeat that started as a whisper but gained concussive force almost overnight: *Tim Tebow is not first-round draft material for the National Football League. In fact, he should consider a position change to tight end.*

In other words, back to the future.

Here's what happened:

With the Sugar Bowl game out of hand, the Fox commentators in the booth, Thom Brennaman and former Baltimore Ravens coach Brian Billick, tossed the topic of Tim's future into the air and batted it around between beer commercials—oops, during lulls in the action.

Does Tim have what it takes to "play at the next level" and become an NFL quarterback?

Cue up the slo-mo of Tim dropping back to pass.

Using a telestrator, Billick dissected Tim's passing motion like a high school biology teacher peeling back the innards of a frog. "You're going to have to change everything he does," the former Ravens coach declared. "He has a windup delivery. He carries the ball too low. And he needs to read his progressions. He's a helluva player, but how do you make him a first-round pick when you have to change so much?"

Billick's critique certainly made for interesting TV: a former NFL coach slicing up a legendary college player in the midst of the most dominating performance of his career. But what Billick did was bring to light the whispering campaign among NFL general managers and their coaching staffs about Tim's throwing motion—the elongated swoop of his left arm prior to releasing the ball.

The conventional wisdom among NFL cognoscenti was hardening like spackle compound. If Tim wasn't worth a first-round pick in the 2010 NFL draft, was he capable of even playing quarterback at the professional level?

4

PLENTY OF PREDRAFT DRAMA

The instant the 2010 Sugar Bowl game clock struck 00:00, Chase Heavener, who was standing on the floor of the New Orleans Superdome, turned on his Canon 5D Mark II camera—capable of shooting high-quality digital video.

Chase, the son of Bill Heavener (whom the Heavener Football Complex next to The Swamp is named after), was initializing work on a documentary about Tim's road to the NFL. Filming couldn't start until Tim's college career was officially over—to preserve his amateur status—so Chase and his small film crew patiently waited for the final seconds to tick off the Superdome scoreboard. The young filmmaker planned to produce a film about Tim's life from the end of the Sugar Bowl through his first game in the NFL.

It looked like there would be enough drama between the Sugar Bowl and the 2010 NFL draft to fill a miniseries. Tim's opening episode began with the Senior Bowl—a postseason college football exhibition game for graduating seniors played in Mobile, Alabama, in late January. With National Football League coaches and personnel monitoring a week of practices as well as the game, the Senior Bowl would be a showcase for the best prospects in the upcoming NFL draft.

Tim opted to play in the Senior Bowl because he wanted to improve his deteriorating draft standing. Following the Sugar Bowl, NFL scouts were telling reporters—anonymously—that Tim figured to go in the third round and might have to think about playing tight end or H-back, a combination tight end/fullback position. Since Tim wasn't ready to abandon his dream of playing quarterback in the NFL—a yearning of his since he was six years old—he didn't shy away from a week of Senior Bowl practices . . . or from working on his ball placement, footwork, and release.

Team Tebow was aware of the NFL's reservations about his mechanics and loopy throwing motion. In fact, he made the decision to reinvent himself *before* the Senior Bowl by attending the D1 Sports Training facility in Cool Springs, Tennessee, outside Nashville. Tim was one of 18 former college players working out with D1's coaches and trainers. Another one of those former college players was Jordan Shipley, Colt McCoy's best friend and favorite receiver at Texas.

Tim had visited several other training facilities before deciding on D1, which was co-owned by Indianapolis Colts quarterback Peyton Manning. Waiting for him were several experienced coaches: Marc Trestman, a former quarterbacks coach with Tampa Bay, Cleveland, and Minnesota; Zeke Bratkowski, a longtime NFL coach; former NFL head coach Sam Wyche; and current Arizona State University offensive coordinator Noel Mazzone.

THE ROAD TO A REALLY SUPER SUNDAY

As Chase Heavener and his small film crew patiently waited for the final seconds to tick off the Superdome scoreboard at the 2010 Sugar Bowl, there was another group of film people loitering in New Orleans that night—this one from Focus on the Family. They were in the Big Easy to discuss the latest developments regarding a 30-second commercial featuring Tim and his mother that would air during the Super Bowl.

Perhaps you heard about it.

In early 2009, Mark Waters, the head of film production at Focus on the Family—a nonprofit Christian organization that offers practical biblical advice on marriage, parenting, and life challenges—had a brainstorm. He envisioned Pam Tebow sharing the story about her son's miraculous birth in an engaging, upbeat way that would be posted as a video on the ministry's website.

Waters pitched the idea to Focus on the Family president Jim Daly, who loved what he heard. *But what about taking the concept a step further? What about involving Tim in the story and turning this into a 30-second commercial? Better yet, a commercial that would run during the Super Bowl. Not only would we generate a buzz, but we could impact the culture with a pro-life message rarely heard in the mainstream media.*

Running a commercial during the Super Bowl is the costliest "ad buy" of the year, running upwards of $3 million for 30 measly seconds— but there are 100 million sets of eyeballs looking in. The Super Bowl is probably the only televised show where viewers *don't* switch the channel during a "commercial time-out" because they know advertisers unveil their most clever and newest advertisements during breaks in football's biggest game of the year.

Phone calls were made, and a dozen supporters of the Focus on the Family ministry said they would step up and pay the $2.5 million price tag to air a 30-second ad. The next step was to see if the Tebows were on board.

Jim Daly and Ken Windebank, Focus' senior vice president of public affairs, flew to Jacksonville in the fall to float the idea past Bob and Pam. The Tebows signaled their interest and said they were open to the concept.

Back in Colorado, Mark Waters created two different mock-ups of the commercial and hired actors to play the roles of Pam and Tim Tebow. Then he, Jim Daly, and Ken Windebank traveled to New Orleans to show the Tebow family the run-throughs the day after the Sugar Bowl.

The entire Tebow family, including Tim, watched both mock-ups, transfixed by what they saw. They were emotionally moved and said they were extremely grateful that Pam's story of how she chose life for Tim could be shared in a mighty way. They were grateful to the Lord that this 30-second film would be viewed by millions watching the Super Bowl.

On Tuesday, January 12, everyone met at a soundstage at Full Sail Studios in Winter Park, Florida, just outside Orlando. Pam and Tim looked natural as they spoke their lines in front of a white seamless background. Then Bob and Pam sat in director's chairs opposite Jim Daly for a friendly chat while the video cameras whirred. They shared how they prayed for "Timmy" by name before he was conceived, what it was like to deal with a crisis pregnancy in the Philippines, and why they decided to go forward with the pregnancy—even though Pam's life was in danger and she was urged to have an abortion.

Bob passionately described his vow to God that he would raise Timmy to be a preacher if he survived this "miracle birth." He closed with an emotional plea to women contemplating an abortion: "God loves you and your baby. There are lots of people that will help you. Don't kill your baby."

The plan was to make the Tebows' long-form interview available on the Focus on the Family website after the Super Bowl spot aired. The Web address would be displayed at the end of the ad along with the tagline "Celebrate family. Celebrate life."

When the filming was completed, Focus on the Family announced in a January 15 press release that the Tebows had decided to participate in a Super Bowl ad "because the issue of life is one they feel strongly about." CBS—the broadcasting network for the upcoming February 7 Super Bowl—had approved the advertisement based on the test commercial.

With that benign statement, the Tebows tipped over a hornet's nest. Hearing the howls of protest by women's groups in favor of "choice" and "reproductive freedom," you would have thought the end of Western civilization was imminent. The National Organization of Women (NOW), the Feminist Majority, and Women's Media Center called on CBS to scrap the Tebow Super Bowl ad because it was likely to convey an anti-abortion message. NOW labeled the ad "extraordinarily offensive and demeaning." GLAAD, a gay advocacy group, accused CBS of a double standard for rejecting a gay dating site ad and accepting the Focus spot.

No one, of course, had viewed the ad, which wouldn't be shown until Super Sunday.

With the benefit of hindsight, which is always 20/20, the outrage over the Tebows' Super Bowl ad seems rather silly at this point.

In the weeks leading up to the Super Bowl, however, more than 30 women's advocacy groups pressured CBS to drop the ad—*even though none had seen the 30-second spot.* Those who *had* viewed the ad prior to Super Sunday tried to tell anyone who would listen that there was nothing political or controversial about it. "When the day arrives," said Focus on the Family spokesman Gary Schneeberger, "and you sit down and watch the game on TV, those who oppose it will be quite surprised at what the ad is all about."

Focus president Jim Daly tried to say the same thing when he appeared on the *Larry King Live* show six days before the Super Bowl. In a panel discussion, he made an offer to Terry O'Neill, president of NOW: "When you see the ad in the Super Bowl, if you don't like it, I'll buy you lunch."

It's likely that Jim Daly never heard from Terry O'Neill after the Super Bowl.

Like a brilliant fake in the open field, the Tebow ad left detractors flummoxed, flat-footed, and gasping for air. The national reaction, especially from a mainstream media that usually takes the pro-choice side, could be summed up in one sentence: *What was all the fuss about?*

The Focus ad ran in the first quarter and started with Pam, dressed in a simple black outfit, standing against a white background. Above pleasing guitar chords, she spoke in an appealing, warm manner—like she entered your living room with a cup of primrose tea in her hand.

Pam: I call him my miracle baby. He almost didn't make it into this world. I can remember so many times when I almost lost him. It was so hard. Well, he's all grown up now, and I still worry about his health. You know, with all our family's been through, you have to be tough.

Suddenly Tim plows in from stage left and tackles his mom to the floor. But she pops up, hair barely mussed, and addresses her son with a coy scold in her voice:

Pam: Timmy! I'm trying to tell our story here.

Tim: Sorry about that, Mom. You still worry about me, Mom?

Pam: Well, yeah. You're not nearly as tough as I am.

The ad closes with text telling viewers to visit the Focus on the Family website, where the interview between the Tebow parents and Jim Daly was posted.

"No mention of abortion, no recounting of the dramatic story," wrote *Politics Daily* columnist David Gibson. "No need. Without any frame of reference, the spot could have been a pitch for osteoporosis medication or the need for universal health care or a reminder not to forget Mother's Day. But everyone knew what the ad was about and the ad didn't have to say anything directly, which is the definition of the perfect advocacy ad. It was charming and disarming and went with the flow of the Super Bowl mania."

Jim Daly said afterward that the CBS network would not permit the word *abortion* to be mentioned anyway, so Focus on the Family had to play by CBS' rules. The main goal of the ad was to drive viewers to the Focus website, where they could view Bob and Pam's interview and learn more about the resources available at Focus on the Family. More than 1.5 million people viewed the Tebow interview online. Who knows how many reconsidered their view of abortion?

The D1 coaches worked Tim hard: two hours in the weight room, two hours on the field doing speed work, two hours on quarterback-specific drills, and two hours watching film and studying NFL terminology. Capturing it all was Chase

Heavener and his film crew, and the D1 staff downloaded their super-slow-motion footage into their computers and used the film to show Tim how he could improve his five-step drop, seven-step drop, and throwing motion.

After spending a week in Cool Springs working on his fundamentals, Tim flew to Mobile, where a hungry press corps was chasing the Tim-isn't-ready-for-prime-time angle. "I look at myself as a pretty self-motivated person, so I don't really need to listen to all the critics," Tim told reporters before the Senior Bowl. "But if I need a little extra motivation, they're all there. Maybe just throw them on the top to get a little extra motivation."

Sam and Colt were still mending their throwing shoulders, so they didn't come to Mobile. Tim, meanwhile, wasn't 100 percent either: he was battling strep throat, a 103-degree temperature, and a skeptical football media that smelled blood in the water.

When the Senior Bowl was over, Tim can be excused for wishing he'd never played in Mobile. What a dreary late afternoon for No. 15: two fumbles (one lost), four yards rushing on four attempts, and 50 yards passing on 12 attempts (although he did complete eight throws). Granted, he didn't play much, taking just 23 snaps as he shared playing time with two other quarterbacks on the South squad: West Virginia's Jarrett Brown and Oklahoma State's Zac Robinson. But his critics were waiting with long knives.

"It's simple," said one NFL scout. "He's just not a very good quarterback prospect." Scouts Inc. gave Tim a D+ grade, noting that he "put all his weaknesses on display in a setting that did nothing but magnify them." Todd Mc-Shay, one of ESPN's NFL draft gurus, was more muted, declaring that Tim "is just not comfortable as a pro-style quarterback."

Only one voice wasn't pessimistic—the one belonging to a feeling-under-the-weather quarterback from Florida. Tim said he improved every day in practice and that his decision to play in the Senior Bowl was proof of his willingness to work hard on his fundamentals. Yet his subpar performance was enough for many NFL coaches and GMs to sell their stock in Tebow, Inc.—despite Tim's 66 percent college career passing percentage, the dozens of passing records he had set in high school and college, and his unworldly 88–16 touchdown-to-interception ratio as a Gator quarterback.

The fact that Tim had been a winner while playing a hybrid style of running back/passing quarterback—where he punished defenses with his left shoulder as well as with his left arm—didn't count for much in the minds of NFL brass or the draft experts.

COMBINE TIME

Tim returned to Cool Springs to continue working to get rid of his swooping windup so he could pass the ball more quickly.

Was he overhauling his throwing motion? Not really, he said.

"It's more of a tweak," Tim told the press. "It's not necessarily changing my whole motion, just the way I'm holding the ball and kind of how I'm getting to where I'm throwing it. That's kind of the biggest problem we've seen, so that's what we're working on the most."

Tim practiced over and over holding the football higher—at shoulder height—after he received the snap. That movement effectively cut the loop from his throwing motion.

B-roll from Chase Heavener's film crew was released to ESPN and other media outlets showing Tim—under the gaze of his D1 coaches—dropping back seven steps with his left arm cocked high before delivering a tightly thrown pass. Even casual fans could tell his throwing motion was more compact and that he was "getting" to his releases quicker.

Between working on this throwing motion and hopping on private planes to make appearances at the Super Bowl, the Daytona 500, and the National Prayer Breakfast in Washington, D.C., Tim worked insanely hard during the month of February.

Kurt Hester, the corporate director of training at D1, said Tim's work ethic was a problem—"He just goes all-out all the time." Working around all the out-of-state appearances had been tough, Hester said, "but he won't quit. If I told him to get here at three in the morning, he'd get here at three in the morning."

Coming up during the first week of March was the National Invitational Camp, otherwise known as the NFL Combine, which was named after three scouting camps that "combined" or merged in 1985. More than 600 NFL personnel, including head coaches, general managers, and scouts, converged on Indianapolis for the camp.

The 329 players who expected to be drafted were invited to Lucas Oil Field to be weighed and measured and to participate in six measurable drills—40-yard dash, 225-pound bench press repetitions, vertical jump, broad jump, three-cone drill, and shuttle run—as well as individual drills. There would also be psychological evaluations and an IQ exam known as the Wonderlic Test administered.

The process can be dehumanizing; some call the NFL Combine the "Underwear Olympics" and compare the physicals to being poked and prodded like steers on a hoof. The extensive medical exams, which could last up to eight hours, had players clad only in undershorts, standing in a room full of NFL team doctors and scouts as they were weighed, measured, and subjected to a battery of tests—MRIs, EKGs, CT scans, X-rays, and more.

"You're investing a lot of money in some of these guys," said John Spanos, the San Diego Chargers' director of college scouting. "You really want to make sure you're not buying damaged goods."

Aspiring NFL players dare not skip the Combine, and Sam, Colt, and Tim all flew to Indianapolis to participate, even though none of the Three QBs said they would participate in individual throwing drills. All three said they would instead wait until their pro day at their respective alma maters to put their arms to the test in front of NFL evaluators.

Pro days are held at each university under conditions thought to be more favorable for the players. At their pro days, quarterbacks participate in passing drills, and position players run the 40-yard dash, make a vertical jump, do the three-cone drill, and undergo other physical tests in front of an array of NFL coaches and scouts.

The NFL Combine—an entirely different bird—is a four-day process that begins with a preliminary medical examination and orientation. During their first night in Indianapolis, Sam, Colt, and Tim went through a process called "speed dating"—where representatives of every NFL team sit at tables inside small rooms and conduct 10- to 15-minute interviews with each of the players.

"You get dizzy from it all," Sam said just before 11 p.m. after his night of speed dating. "You go from 5:30 in the morning until 11 every night, every day. You better be in good shape when you come here."

If a prospect isn't in good shape physically, the NFL has a way of finding out. The second day is reserved for four extensive medical exams—eight doctors at a time, one from each of the 32 NFL teams. If players, especially quarterbacks, had fudged on their height and weight, it was now out in the open.

Here's how the Three QBs measured up:

- Sam Bradford: 6-4¼, 236 pounds
- Colt McCoy: 6-1⅛, 216 pounds
- Tim Tebow: 6-2¾, 236 pounds

Everyone knew Sam was 6-4 and change, and Tim was usually listed at 6-3, so he wasn't too far off the mark. But Colt's height, which barely topped 6-1, was a red flag to some NFL teams because the typical pro quarterback stands at least 6-2. "I'd like to say I was six-foot-four," Colt said at the Combine, "but this is what God gave me . . . and I'm going to use it as best as I can."

When Colt was asked about being likened to Super Bowl MVP Drew Brees, who stands an even six feet tall, the Texas QB ran with the comparison. "I hope you guys can see that [comparison] because I see it," he said.

Colt participated in only two of the measurable drills—the 40-yard dash and the broad jump. He ran the fifth-fastest time in the 40 among quarterbacks with a 4.79, just behind Tim's time of 4.72. Sam did not run the 40 or participate in any of the drills.

For quarterbacks, the 40-yard dash ranks far down on the list of priorities; height, arm strength, quick release, escapability, leadership skills, and football knowledge are what matter to the NFL. Ditto for the standing broad jump, a drill where Colt excelled, vaulting nine feet, six inches, but Tim just beat him out, clearing nine feet, seven inches. Tim also wowed the scouts with his 38.5-inch vertical leap, which tied him for the Combine's all-time record for quarterbacks (held by Josh McCown). By way of comparison, Tim's leap was a half inch higher than Michael Vick's in 2001.

One test the Three QBs—or anyone else at the Combine—couldn't avoid was the Wonderlic, an exam that measures an individual's learning and problem-solving abilities. The Wonderlic Test is made up of 50 not-too-difficult SAT-like questions. The number you answer correctly in 12 minutes is your score; you can't spend more than 15 seconds on each question if you expect to finish.

The average Wonderlic score for NFL quarterbacks is 24, and Sam performed impressively, scoring a 36. Colt posted a 25, but Tim didn't do as well, scoring a 22.

It's difficult to argue that the Wonderlic Test is an accurate determiner of future success for NFL quarterbacks. San Francisco's Alex Smith and Arizona's Matt Leinart scored 40 and 35, respectively, but they haven't exactly lit it up as pros. Hall of Famers Dan Marino and Jim Kelly, however, both scored 15s, and Brett Favre scored a 22, the same as Tim.

SO HOW WOULD YOU SCORE ON THE WONDERLIC TEST?

The clock is ticking . . . and you have just 15 seconds to answer each question. Here are some sample questions from the Wonderlic Test:

1. Look at the row of numbers below. What number should come next?
   8 4 2 1 ½ ¼

2. Paper sells for 21 cents per pad. What will four pads cost?

3. The ninth month of the year is:
   a. October
   b. January
   c. June
   d. September
   e. May

4. Assume the first two statements are true. Is the final one true, false, or not certain?
   Tom greeted Beth. Beth greeted Dawn. Tom did not greet Dawn.

5. A boy is 17 years old and his sister is twice as old. When the boy is 23 years old, what will be the age of his sister?

Answers:
1. 1/8
2. 84 cents
3. September
4. not certain
5. 40 years old

Aside from the written exams, Tim also completed five of the six measurable drills, passing on the 225-pound bench press repetitions so he could protect his throwing arm.

There was one individual drill Tim performed at the NFL Combine, however, where you could say his time was a revelation: in the three-cone speed drill, Tim ran a hell-blazing 6.66 seconds, which showed he was a real speed demon.

PRO DAYS AHEAD

With so much at stake—draft position, which team would pick them, and millions of dollars—quarterbacks aspiring to an NFL career leave little to chance. Very few throw at the NFL Combine because they will be passing to unfamiliar receivers at an unfamiliar venue. NFL coaches can also dictate which passing drills they would like to see at the Combine.

As they say at golf's biggest tournaments, you can't win a major on the first day, but you sure can lose it with a poor outing.

Each of the Three QBs had excellent reasons for declining to throw at the Combine. Sam and Colt were coming off shoulder injuries—remember, Sam had missed most of the 2009 college season after undergoing ligament repair surgery, and Colt had suffered a pinched nerve in his shoulder after being rammed to the Rose Bowl turf at the national championship game.

Tim was into his second month of working to get rid of his below-the-belt throwing motion and to perfect the above-the-shoulder delivery NFL coaches like to see in their quarterbacks. The more time he had to practice and improve his new technique, the better chance he had to impress coaches and scouts when it came time to throw at his pro day.

Tim was first to fire up for pro day, and as you would expect, the March 17 event at the University of Florida was a circus. "For all the television time, Internet bandwidth, and newsprint used to discuss Tim Tebow's new throwing motion, anything short of the southpaw walking onto Florida Field and throwing right-handed was found to be a bitter disappointment," wrote *Sports Illustrated*'s Andy Staples.

More than 3,000 spectators and 100 NFL personnel were on hand at The Swamp, including five head coaches and a couple of general managers. Tim wasn't the only Gator athlete under the microscope; teammates Carlos Dunlap, Joe Haden, Aaron Hernandez, and Maurkice Pouncey—all potential first-rounders—were going through their pro day paces as well.

Tim threw for 45 minutes—outs, curls, hitches, posts, comebacks, and gos. He cocked the ball closer to his ear, released the ball much more quickly, and delivered tight spirals where they needed to be. He hit receiver David Nelson on a 45-yard post pattern—in stride. Next throw, the same 45-yard post but to the opposite side of the field, where the deep pass landed in Riley Cooper's arms in full gait.

Tim looked flat-out impressive. The backpedaling on his seven-step drops was an athletic work of art, his command of the field was sure, and his passing was on the money. The debut of his new throwing motion went off without a hitch.

Like the opening of a hit show on Broadway, Tim's new act drew raves. The consensus in the media was that he had shown "ridiculous" improvement. In less than an hour on his favorite field, Tim successfully pushed back a tide of coaching opinion that had threatened to sink his chances of ever playing quarterback in the NFL. He was once again a viable NFL quarterback prospect.

Between pro day and NFL draft day, held five weeks later, Tim scheduled private workouts with several NFL teams, including Seattle, Washington, and New England.

Tim also hoped to get a closer look from the Denver Broncos. During one of the "speed dates" at the NFL Combine, he had sat in a meeting room just a few feet apart from Josh McDaniels, the boyish-looking 33-year-old head coach of the Broncos. They were talking football, and the energy level rose as their eyes locked and their ideas spilled forth. In a word, they *clicked*.

The 15 minutes passed by way too quickly. Tim felt jacked as he left the room. He had met someone with the same passion for football that he had himself. Coach McDaniels was just as intense, just as juiced about finding a way to win in the NFL. He understood where Tim was coming from.

Tim stood up and shook hands with the Broncos coach, and he left the meeting not wanting to visit with another team.

SHOULDERS ARE OKAY

Because they had suffered injuries during their final seasons in college, Sam Bradford and Colt McCoy both had to submit to magnetic resonance imaging (MRI) exams on their right shoulders. No NFL general manager wanted to buy a pig in a poke, and both QBs knew they'd have to prove their previously injured shoulders were sound.

Their MRIs checked out fine; NFL medical personnel found nothing else wrong with their shoulders. Sam's repaired shoulder ligaments were as good as new, and Colt's nerve injury had healed just fine. Those in Sam's and Colt's camps breathed easier.

The rehabilitation process hadn't been easy for either player. Following the loss to Alabama at the Rose Bowl, Colt flew to Birmingham, Alabama, to meet with Dr. James Andrews, who told him he didn't need surgery and that he should be as good as new following rehab. Colt then returned to Southern California— after asking Rachel Glandorf to marry him and presenting her with a ring he had designed—and devoted nearly a month to getting his shoulder back in shape.

The road back had been longer for Sam. A few weeks after the skilled hands of Dr. Andrews surgically repaired his shoulder with an absorbable synthetic braid, Sam embarked on a nine-week rehabilitation program at the affiliated Andrews Institute for Orthopaedics and Sports Medicine in Gulf Breeze, Florida. Located on the same campus was Athletes' Performance, Inc., perhaps the premiere training program for elite athletes. The NFL's previous four No. 1 draft picks (Matthew Stafford, 2009; Jake Long, 2008; JaMarcus Russell, 2007; and Mario Williams, 2006) had trained with Athletes' Performance before their NFL Combine and pro day workouts.

Still, the question remained: would Sam be the fifth straight No. 1 pick? No one was sure, and his situation was dicey in many ways. He had no idea if he'd be able to throw over mountains again. When Sam moved to the Pensacola area of the Florida panhandle to train with Athletes' Performance, he lived alone for the first time in his life and set his nose toward getting back in shape. To combat homesickness, he sent text messages to his family and friends.

Terry Shea, a former college and NFL coach, oversaw Sam's workout program. The first order of business was his footwork. Sam's coaches at Oklahoma had taught him that poor footwork led to poor throws, so he knew it was paramount to set the right foundation before he threw the ball. Also, poor footwork following shoulder surgery could put even more pressure on Sam's tender shoulder, so Shea and Sam worked day after day on tedious footwork drills.

He wouldn't throw a ball for three months.

The 10-hour days in Florida included *beaucoup* hours in the gym—band exercises, BOSU ball, weight training, and free weights. He worked his derriere off, and as his shoulder strengthened, he gradually added more weight plates.

Sam started throwing in late January, keeping things short and easy before progressing to 30-yard throws. The magic in his arm was still there. "They were ropes," Sam said.

Sam grew stronger—and heavier. The time well spent in the weight room had added 13 precious pounds of muscle to his 6-foot, 4¼-inch frame. He hoped the extra weight would help him withstand the poundings of an NFL pass rush.

NFL evaluators at the Combine immediately noticed that Sam had gained muscle mass in his upper body, and the confidence and ease he displayed during his one-on-one meetings in Indianapolis also left a strong impression. His Wonderlic Test results were head and shoulders above his quarterback competition.

A low rumble came out of the Combine and would build into a roar: Sam Bradford was the guy who would go No. 1 to the St. Louis Rams. The only thing standing in his way was his performance at the pro day at the University of Oklahoma on March 29.

At Sam's pro day, dozens of expressionless football men ringed the sidelines of the Everest Training Center, the Oklahoma football team's indoor training facility. At least 21 NFL teams were represented, and the St. Louis Rams sent four members to observe Sam.

Kent Bradford watched his son complete 13 stationary warm-up passes before Sam threw to moving receivers. Dad kept glancing sideways at the poker-faced NFL coaches and front office personnel, each of them wearing a frozen expression, and he wondered what they were thinking.

Sam began a 50-pass "script" to five different receivers, utilizing a variety of three-step, five-step, and seven-step drops and rollouts. His full virtuosity was on display—from dump-down screens and 10-yard stick routes to a 65-yard bomb that nearly hit the rafters before settling into the arms of his receiver. His teammates and workout partners whooped it up, while the NFL folks murmured (they don't clap at pro days).

After Sam had finished his 49-of-50 workout—there was one drop—Seattle Seahawks coach Pete Carroll tapped out a tweet on his Twitter account: "He lit it up."

NFL überscout Gil Brandt said Sam's workout "almost left me speechless" and was the best workout he'd seen since he watched Troy Aikman, a future Dallas Cowboy quarterbacking great, back in 1988. He had another effusive description for Sam's 30-minute throwing session: "It was a Picasso out there."

The gelling consensus was that Sam's pro day performance had sewn up his spot as the No. 1 pick in the NFL draft. A little more than a week later, the Rams telegraphed their intentions when they released veteran quarterback Marc Bulger . . . on his 33rd birthday.

Bulger, who had played nine seasons for the Rams, saw the handwriting— SAM'S COMING!—on the wall, and he asked St. Louis to let him go so he could hook up with a team looking for a backup quarterback.

Some birthday present.

55 FOR 55

Two days after Sam Bradford's brilliant workout, many of the same NFL executives ringed the sidelines of "The Bubble"—the University of Texas indoor practice facility—to watch Colt go through his pro day paces.

Like Sam, a calm and focused Colt threw with something to prove: that he belonged in the same discussion with Sam, Tim, and Notre Dame's Jimmy Clausen. If they were first-round material, then he was, too.

According to Texas offensive coordinator Greg Davis, who scripted the workout, Colt threw 55 passes. Only two were slightly off the mark; his old roommate Jordan Shipley made a diving catch on one ball to save Colt's perfect 55-for-55 performance.

Colt showed off his healed shoulder and excellent form. His eagerness showed in his quick movement and quick strikes. Green Bay Packers coach Mike McCarthy came away suitably impressed, saying Colt's workout was even better than Sam's.

"I like this workout better. . . . I thought Colt was challenged more in his workout as far as the type of throws," McCarthy said.

Colt said his favorite throw was off a play-action when he went deep to hit Jordan for 50 yards. He also thought he proved his arm strength with wide-field comebacks and digs to the weak side.

"They wanted to see my footwork underneath center," Colt said afterward. "They [the scouts] told me it was excellent. They wanted to see some play-action, and I felt like I did great at that. They wanted to see my accuracy, and my quick release and what I did on the deep ball. When you go 100 percent, there's really not much you do wrong. I felt like today was really good."

Colt said he enjoyed his "pitch and catch" with Jordan and former Texas receivers Quan Cosby, who was playing for the Cincinnati Bengals, and Nate Jones.

"I can't wait to see where I end up," Colt said.

Without a doubt, the other two QBs were saying the same thing.

5

THE 2010 NFL DRAFT

It used to be that character didn't count for much in the National Football League.

As long as you could deliver blistering hits in the open field, create a hole in the line, make a catch in traffic, or run the two-minute offense, you pretty much got a free pass.

Back in the day, fans were amused by the antics of Broadway Joe Namath—he of the white llama rugs and "bachelor pad" fame who entitled a chapter in his 1970 autobiography "I Like My Girls Blonde and My Johnny Walker Red."

Those relatively innocent days are as long gone as love beads and incense sticks.

Between January 2000 and the spring of 2010, arrests, citations, and drunk-driving charges involving NFL players piled up—495 according to an investigative article in the *San Diego Union-Tribune*. It seems like there's a report every week about an NFL player arrested for public intoxication, driving under the influence, brandishing a weapon, battering a girlfriend, getting caught in a bar fight, or being charged with sexual assault.

One of the most scandalous affairs was an alleged sex party early in the 2005 season involving prostitutes and 17 Minnesota Vikings football players—including the team's starting quarterback—aboard a pair of chartered boats on Lake Minnetonka.

Another example involved the disturbing revelations about Pittsburgh Steelers quarterback Ben Roethlisberger, accused of sexual assault by a 20-year-old college student who claimed the Steelers QB forced himself on her in a bar restroom. Although Roethlisberger wasn't formally charged with a crime due to a lack of evidence, NFL commissioner Roger Goodell handed "Big Ben" a six-game suspension—which was later reduced to four games—for the 2010 season.

For years, some NFL teams have closed one eye to character issues in their evaluation of draft prospects. The St. Louis Rams drafted running back Lawrence Phillips in 1996 despite the fact that he received a six-game suspension during his senior year at the University of Nebraska for dragging his girlfriend by her hair down a flight of stairs. The Rams believed the on-the-field reward of playing Phillips in the backfield outweighed any off-the-field risk. Bad call. Phillips was arrested three times in two seasons before the Rams released him . . . for insubordination.

When quarterbacks Peyton Manning and Ryan Leaf were in the running to be selected first in the 1998 NFL draft, Indianapolis Colts president Bill Polian made appointments to meet with both at the NFL Combine. Manning showed up on time, groomed and mature, while Leaf blew off the appointment.

Small actions make big impressions, and the Colts took Manning as the No. 1 pick. The Chargers followed with Ryan Leaf, who quickly unimpressed his teammates and coaches with a lousy work ethic, surly attitude, and profane outbursts at members of the media. Leaf was one of the more remarkable flameouts in NFL history, and many point to his character, or lack of it, as the main reason why.

Then came a disturbing period between April 2006 and April 2007, when the NFL realized it had a serious problem with players of poor conduct and character. At least 79 incidents, including a series of high-profile arrests involving Tennessee Titans cornerback Adam "Pacman" Jones and Cincinnati Bengals wide receiver Chris Henry, prompted Commissioner Goodell to decree a tough personal conduct policy.

When it seemed like NFL rookies stood a better chance of making the police blotter than making the team that drafted them, Goodell and the league had to look at a different way of doing things. The commissioner's personal conduct policy spurred NFL front office personnel to rethink the criteria they used when looking at a professional football player.

THREE "CHARACTER GUYS"

In recent years, the new buzzword in NFL draft war rooms—thank goodness—has been *character*. These days, you're apt to hear GMs say, "He's a character guy," for someone on their draft board, or "He had character issues," for a player they passed on.

Character is one of those intangibles that may be hard to define but is easy to recognize. As someone once pointed out, character means having the inward motivation to do what's right even when nobody is looking. Character means practicing self-restraint regardless of the circumstances. In light of that, it might be a good idea for every football player to memorize this observation from nineteenth-century American newspaper editor Horace Greeley: "Fame is a vapor, popularity an accident, riches take wing, but only character endures."

Going into the 2010 NFL draft, coaches and team personnel were paying attention to character more than ever in making their player evaluations. That's part of why many teams thought so highly of Sam, Colt, and Tim. While there were internal debates about Sam's right shoulder, Colt's height, or Tim's throwing motion, there was a league-wide consensus that the Three QBs were "character guys"—upstanding young men with a strong moral compass.

When the 2010 NFL draft arrived, it turned out that character played a huge role for Sam, Colt, and Tim. Their attitude, work ethic, disposition, and respect for authority were the determining factors in where the Three QBs landed during the draft.

And character issues apparently sank the hopes of another highly touted quarterback.

SAM'S DRAFT DAY

The evolution of the NFL draft from a modest gathering of team officials in smoke-filled rooms at a downtown hotel into a prime-time, made-for-ESPN extravaganza mirrors the growth of football into America's most popular game.

The inaugural NFL draft was held in 1936 at Philadelphia's Ritz-Carlton Hotel and consisted of nine rounds—one for each team in professional football at the time. The number of rounds later ballooned to 30 before receding to today's seven rounds. The doormat of the 1935 NFL football season, the Philadelphia Eagles, chose swivel-hips running back Jay Berwanger from the University of Chicago as their No. 1 pick.

Berwanger was in the news because he had just won the first-ever Downtown Athletic Club Trophy as the most outstanding college football player. The award would be renamed the following year after John Heisman, a trailblazing, turn-of-the-century coach who pioneered the forward pass and originated the use of the word *hike* to start plays. Heisman was also chairman of the Downtown Athletic Club.

The Eagles offered Berwanger $150 a game, a good salary in those Depression-era days. When Berwanger declined, the Eagles traded him to the Chicago Bears—"hometown boy coming back to the Windy City" was how they billed it. When Bears head coach and owner George Halas asked him what he wanted, Berwanger said the figure he had in mind was $25,000 for a two-year contract. Otherwise, he'd put his college education to better use.

Papa Bear Halas smiled and extended his hand, then told Berwanger the Bears couldn't afford such an astronomical amount. Halas wished him the best, and the running back walked away from professional football and never played a down. Berwanger became a foam-rubber salesman and gave the first Heisman Trophy to his aunt Gussie, who used the 25-pound bronze statue as a doorstop in her home.

It's doubtful Sam's Heisman Trophy is being used as a doorstop at the Bradford house these days, just as it's highly improbable that Sam and his agent asked for a two-year contract worth $25,000 following the 2010 NFL draft. Try *two thousand times* that amount. Sam signed the richest contract in NFL history, becoming the league's first $50 million man. (Technically, he signed a six-year, $78 million contract, of which $50 million was guaranteed.)

After Sam's Picasso-like performance at pro day, when all the doubts regarding his rehabilitated shoulder were put to rest, the die was cast: it was looking more and more like Sam's year to go No. 1.

Holding the top pick were the St. Louis Rams, the worst team in pro football with a 1–15 record in 2009. Drafting Sam wasn't a slam dunk, though; the Rams needed help on both sides of the ball, so they could have traded their No. 1 pick—Sam—for a garden variety of draft picks to help them rebuild a dismal team that had won just six games and lost 42 since 2007.

From the Rams' point of view, there was also the risky business of drafting a quarterback with the No. 1 pick. Since 1970, 17 quarterbacks had gone

No. 1. There were booms and busts, but most went on to have so-so careers. The diamonds included Troy Aikman, who went to the Dallas Cowboys and won three Super Bowls for America's Team. Other No. 1–pick quarterbacks who worked out fabulously were Peyton Manning of the Indianapolis Colts, Peyton's brother Eli with the New York Giants, John Elway of the Denver Broncos, Jim Plunkett of the Oakland Raiders, and Terry Bradshaw of the Pittsburgh Steelers—all of whom won Super Bowl rings.

But there were some famous busts like Jeff George and Tim Couch. Ja-Marcus Russell, the No. 1 pick in 2007, struggled mightily with the Oakland Raiders, who unceremoniously dumped him following the 2010 NFL draft.

With so much at stake, the Rams would be counted upon to do their due diligence. Head coach Steve Spagnuolo came away impressed with Sam after their 15-minute "speed date" at the NFL Combine. "Everything you hear about him, that's said, it's legit," Spagnuolo said. "He walks into a room, you can see he's a quarterback. That was impressive to me."

Ten Rams officials, including general manager Billy Devaney, were in the crowded Combine meeting room with Sam and Coach Spagnuolo; the room was lit with floodlights because the Rams were taping the interview.

"There were a lot of bodies in there, in kind of a small room," Spagnuolo said. "It was a little intimidating, or it could've been for a 22-year-old guy. And yet, he walked in and did not seem . . . rattled at all."

What Spagnuolo and the Rams were looking for in Sam, besides zip in his arm, were the intangibles—leadership, body language, presence, and how he interacted with coaches. He apparently passed the interview with flying colors.

After the Combine, Devaney and offensive coordinator Pat Shurmur traveled to Florida to meet with Sam at Athletes' Performance, the world-class training facility, and witness for themselves how Sam's rehabilitation was going. They sat down with Sam and talked football, and they also met with Dr. James Andrews, who performed Sam's surgery, to discuss the quarterback's progress in rehab.

Devaney couldn't be blamed for treading cautiously. He was the San Diego Chargers director of player personnel back in 1998 when the Bolts drafted Ryan Leaf, so he knew how first-round picks could turn sour. Although Chargers general manager Bobby Beathard ran the show and made the call on Leaf, Devaney learned a valuable lesson when it came to drafting quarterbacks. Things won't work out "if you don't have the intangibles to play that position," he said. "There's so much that goes into being a quarterback in the NFL. The work ethic you have to have. The leadership. The time that you put in. The media scrutiny. If you can't handle all that stuff, you're going to have a hard time performing on the field."

The 2010 NFL draft would be done a bit differently than in the past. For many years, the draft was a weekend staple, beginning at noon Eastern Time with three rounds on Saturday and finishing up on Sunday. But the 75th draft was the first to kick off in prime time, starting at 7:30 p.m. EST on Thursday, April 22—a move Commissioner Goodell said would make the draft "more accessible to fans." (He obviously wasn't thinking about those on the West Coast who were still at their work cubicles at 4:30 in the afternoon.) ESPN and the NFL Network planned wall-to-wall coverage of the three-day draftapalooza, which would be held at the venerable Radio City Music Hall in Manhattan.

Sam was among the 18 draft prospects invited to New York City for two days of promotion—posing for pictures atop the marquee of Radio City Music Hall, ringing the closing bell at the New York Stock Exchange, and visiting pediatric patients at Kravis Children's Hospital—before hanging out backstage at Radio City Music Hall and waiting for their names to be called—in the first round, they all hoped.

The invitation is quite an honor but can be a two-edged sword because if you're *not* drafted in the first round—or No. 1 when everyone expects you to go as the first pick—your anguish is on full display for the whole world to see from inside the Radio City Music Hall green room.

Sam wasn't sure he wanted to go to New York and step into the hurricane of media attention, but he realized his absence would have cast a shadow over one of pro football's signature events and raised even more questions. "It's a once-in-a-lifetime thing," he said after he arrived in New York the day before the draft. "I figured I didn't want to look back and have any regrets about not going. Everyone said that all the guys who have ever come just really enjoyed their time here, so that's one of the reasons I decided to make the trip."

Nobody expected Sam to wait very long for his name to be called. On the day before the draft, the latest *Sports Illustrated* issue hit the newsstands with Sam on the cover, clad in a crimson Nike Dri-FIT collarless shirt and dark shorts, looking resolute as he dropped back to pass with a football clutched between his hands. CALL TO ARMS: FRANCHISE QBS ARE THERE FOR THE TAKING—AND OKLAHOMA'S SAM BRADFORD TOPS THE LIST was the cover headline.

Would the *Sports Illustrated* cover jinx knock Sam off the No. 1 perch?

Even Sam wasn't sure. Billy Devaney didn't call Sam in advance of the draft to let him know it was a done deal, so the Oklahoma QB was still in the dark at 7:30 p.m. that night when Goodell officially put the St. Louis Rams "on the clock," meaning the club had 10 minutes to either announce its selection or trade the draft choice to another team seeking to "move up."

Four minutes later, Sam's cell phone chirped. Billy Devaney was on the line with the good news: Sam was a Ram—St. Louis' franchise quarterback—and would be forever known as an NFL No. 1 draft pick. The news was relayed to Commissioner Goodell, who strode to the podium:

With the first pick in the 2010 NFL Draft, the St. Louis Rams select Sam Bradford, quarterback, Oklahoma . . .

Watching on a monitor backstage, a relieved Sam gave his father, Kent, a soul shake and a hug, then embraced his mother, Martha, before gamboling to the stage and posing for pictures with the commissioner while wearing a Rams cap and holding a Rams No.1 jersey.

In a conference call with St. Louis reporters a few minutes after his

selection, a getting-giddier-by-the-minute Sam talked about the Rams selecting him as the No. 1 pick. "You have no idea how excited I am, just to have the
opportunity to come to St. Louis and start my NFL career," he said. "It's just a
blessing, and I can't wait to get there and get to work."

"We didn't see any negatives," Devaney said in his remarks afterward.
"Rare size. Accuracy off the charts. . . . He's a much better athlete than I'd
given him credit for early on in this process. Extremely intelligent. Character.
I think he's a classy kid. All those things. I happen to think he's the whole
package."

So did a lot of people who'd known Sam for a long time.

TIM TEBOW: THE FIRST-ROUND SHOCKER

Tim Tebow was in New York City, too, but not for the NFL draft. He traveled to Manhattan a couple of days earlier to promote *NCAA Football 11*, EA
Sports' new college football video game. After making an appearance at an
upscale restaurant on lower Broadway and playing his brother Robby in the
football video game—Tim was Virginia Tech and Robby was Florida—Tim
announced he would be flying back to Jacksonville to be with his family for
the draft, even though he was one of the 18 players the NFL had invited to be
in attendance.

"It would have been exciting to be here, to hold your jersey up with the
commissioner. That's always something every athlete wants to do," Tim told
NFL Network's Charles Davis the day before the draft. "But it's going to be
special being at home. Being with my family, my friends, my best friends, my
high school teammates, people like that that I know couldn't make their way
up here, that I wanted to be able to spend this moment with. That's what it's
truly about for me."

The prospect of sitting in the Radio City Music Hall green room—with
TV cameras recording every nose twitch—until his name was called under-
standably lacked appeal in the Tebow camp. Who wants to squirm on national
TV as the pressure mounts when you're passed over?

Tim and his parents had no idea whether Tim would be picked in the first
round or drop ingloriously to the second, third, or—gasp!—fourth round.
From the going-out-on-top Sugar Bowl victory to the Senior Bowl washout
to the raves he received for his revamped throwing motion at pro day, Tim's
stock among NFL teams fluctuated like the Dow Jones average.

Throughout the spring of 2010—swirling through March Madness, the
first pitch of the Major League Baseball season, and Tiger's return to golf—one
of the biggest stories in sports remained: *Where will Tim Tebow be drafted?* If
an NFL player or coach wanted to get some face time with the media, all he had
to do was venture an opinion on Tim's draft day prospects.

Tim's former teammate at Florida, Cincinnati Bengals wide receiver Andre Caldwell, said the right spot to draft the Gator quarterback would be "late
second round," adding that the former Heisman winner would need significant time to adjust to life in the NFL. Following Tim's pro day, Miami Dolphins

quarterback Chad Henne bluntly told WQAM radio in Miami, "My judgment is that he's not an NFL quarterback. I'll leave it at that."

That's precisely what draftnik Mel Kiper Jr. had been saying since the end of Tim's junior year, when he began ringing the town bell and proclaiming that Tim wasn't NFL quarterback material—and would be better suited to playing professional football as a tight end or H-back. The helmet-haired analyst dissed everything about Tim's quarterbacking skills.

To his credit, Tim did an interview on ESPN Radio with host Freddie Coleman and Kiper at the end of his junior season. The Florida quarterback showed he could think on his feet just as quickly as he could move them after a snap count. "You tell me this," Tim said during his radio exchange with Kiper. "What do you think I need to do to be an NFL quarterback? You tell me that."

Kiper backpedaled like an All-Pro cornerback and mumbled something about the NFL being a "flip of the coin" and that Peyton Manning had his detractors when he came into the league. "You're too good with the ball in your hands not to think, *Could he be Frank Wycheck? Could he be Chris Cooley?* That's why," Kiper said. "You're too good, doing what you do, Tim, running with the football."

Wycheck and Cooley were NFL tight ends, but in this context, the comment was a thinly veiled insult since Tim's peers were quarterbacks like Sam and Colt, not journeymen tight ends.

After hearing Kiper out, the Florida quarterback replied, "The quarterback has the ball in his hands every play."

Touché, Tim. . . .

In the weeks leading up to the 2010 NFL draft, Tim's name was nowhere to be found on Kiper's "Big Board" of Top 25 picks, but "he's the story of the draft, like him or not," said Peter King of *Sports Illustrated*. For every Tebow doubter, though, there was a Tebow booster. Perhaps the biggest voice in his corner was former Tampa Bay coach Jon Gruden, who had worked out Tim as part of *Gruden's QB Camp* specials that ran on ESPN leading up to draft day. Gruden told anyone who would listen that Tim could very well crack the first round.

"If you want Tim to be on your football team, if you want him bad enough, you're going to have him in the first round or the second," Gruden said. "If you want Tim in your locker room, on your football team, and you can see a little down the road, a team like that is going to take him earlier than some people expect. I'm very confident in this guy."

Preceding the draft, five NFL teams requested private individual workouts with Tim. They were as follows:

- The New England Patriots, whose coach, Bill Belichick, loved the way Tim played and loved that his good friend, Urban Meyer, had coached him. The thinking in Beantown was that All-Universe QB Tom Brady could mentor Tim or that a creative football mind like Belichick could find a spot role for Tim as a tight end/H-back.

- The Seattle Seahawks, whose new coach, former USC head man Pete Carroll, was rebuilding a team with 34-year-old veteran Matt Hasselbeck under center. Carroll's interest in Tim cooled considerably, though, after he traded Seattle's second-round draft pick and cash to San Diego for third-string quarterback Charlie Whitehurst in March.

- The Buffalo Bills, whose former quarterback Hall of Famer Jim Kelly was in Tim's corner. The quarterback position in Buffalo had been a revolving door since Kelly retired; the Bills had started nine different QBs during a decade-long playoff drought. "Whether it's Tim Tebow . . . you look for a guy with good character, good leadership ability, and good arm strength," Kelly said.

- The Minnesota Vikings, who might have had an opening at quarterback if Brett Favre didn't return—or if the soon-to-be-41-year-old NFL legend did come back, Tim could learn from one of the best. The Vikings had the 30th pick in the first round, too.

- The Denver Broncos, whose young head coach, Josh McDaniels, was said to be intrigued with Tim, even though the club had recently traded for Cleveland's Brady Quinn, a third-year pro out of Notre Dame. In the week preceding the draft, the Broncos visited and worked out Tim twice in a five-day span.

Several other teams were rumored to have been flirting with the idea of taking Tim, including the Jacksonville Jaguars, who had the No. 10 pick. The thinking was that Jacksonville wasn't selling out its games, and drafting a local hero like Tim would put fannies in the seats. *Tebowmania stays in Florida!* Throughout the spring, though, the Jags hadn't shown the slightest interest in Tim. Was it a head feint? A move not to tip their hand?

Or maybe something really wild would happen—like Pittsburgh trading bad boy Ben Roethlisberger and bringing in Boy Scout Tim Tebow, but that was held to be as unlikely as Mel Kiper getting a Mohawk haircut.

Kiper and his ESPN sidekick, Todd McShay, stuck to their guns regarding Tim's draft prospects. "I think Tim has got to develop into a starting quarterback to be worth being a second-round choice," said Kiper, showing his belief that the first round was beyond the realm of reason for Tebow. "I don't think he can be. Others do. We'll see. . . . I'll root for Tim to prove me wrong on that one."

McShay called Tim a "project" and said he'd be surprised if any team parted with a cherished first-round pick for him. "I would not draft Tebow in the first two rounds. My philosophy is you draft people who have a legitimate shot to be starter right away."

Through it all, Tim's faith and confidence never wavered. On the morning of the NFL draft, he told *USA Today*, "I believe I'll be drafted as a quarterback and used as a quarterback."

After the St. Louis Rams tabbed Sam as the No. 1 pick, the NFL draft proceeded down a fairly expected avenue, although the San Diego Chargers gambled by trading up to No. 12 and drafting a much-needed running back,

Ryan Mathews of Fresno State, to replace LaDainian Tomlinson.

Two highly regarded Florida Gator teammates were drafted ahead of Tim: the Cleveland Browns took cornerback Joe Haden with the seventh pick, and the Pittsburgh Steelers selected center Maurkice Pouncey—who did a great job protecting Tim at Florida—with the 18th pick. It turned out Ben Roethlisberger wasn't going anywhere after all.

Tim watched the draft unfold at a private residence at Jacksonville's Glen Kernan Country Club, surrounded by two or three dozen family members, close friends, and others in the Tebow camp, including his agent, Jimmy Sexton. Sitting in the corner of the living room was a cardboard box stuffed with Denver Broncos hats.

They knew.

A few—*very* few—put two and two together before the draft. On draft day eve, Mike Klis, a sports columnist for the *Denver Post*, wrote that, yes, he could see the Broncos taking Tim Tebow. The way he envisioned things, the Broncos would trade back their No. 11 pick and get an extra second-round selection, and then offer a team a package of second-round picks to grab Tim somewhere in the first round—between No. 20 and No. 30. Klis then offered these reasons:

1. If Coach McDaniels was bold enough to trade away talented quarterback Jay Cutler and All-Pro receiver Brandon Marshall, then he'd have the steel nerve to draft Tim Tebow.
2. McDaniels liked proven winners with good height standing in the pocket. Tim met both requirements.
3. McDaniels was big on all his players, quarterbacks or otherwise, being men of good character and football smarts.
4. McDaniels' brother, Ben, was the Broncos quarterback coach, and they saw themselves as just the right team to bring Tim along.
5. While Tim developed and watched starting Broncos quarterback Kyle Orton, he could come in for four or five plays a game as a "Wildcat QB" and make those tough third-and-two and fourth-and-one conversions for first downs. *Shades of his freshman year at Florida.*

Mike Klis called it; the Broncos indeed took Tim in the first round. But you need a flow chart to follow the Broncos' crazy route to using the No. 25 pick to select Tim Tebow.

•   First, the Broncos traded their No. 11 pick to the San Francisco 49ers for the Niners' first-round pick (No. 13) and a fourth-round pick.

•   Next, the Broncos sent the No. 13 pick to Philadelphia in exchange for the Eagles' first-round pick (No. 24) and two third-rounders.

•   Then the Broncos traded the No. 24 pick (as well as a fourth-round choice) to New England for the Patriots' first-round pick (No. 22), which they used to draft *not* Tim Tebow but Georgia

Tech receiver Demaryius Thomas.

- Three picks later, the Broncos grabbed the No. 25 pick from Baltimore in exchange for Denver's second-, third-, and fourth-round picks. The Broncos also received the No. 119 pick in the deal.

All this shuffling momentarily confused the ESPN talking heads. Could it be that Denver . . . ?

And that's when Tim's cell phone rang with a 303 area code.

"Should I answer it?" he asked his agent, Jimmy Sexton.

Of course, Tim.

Coach McDaniels was on the line, but he didn't seem at all in a hurry to get down to business. He made small talk and asked Tim if he was enjoying the night. *Oh, and by the way, we're going to trade up and take you.*

The electrifying news swept through the living room just as an ESPN camera cut away to the joyful scene of Tim hugging his family and friends. Then Team Tebow brought out the Broncos hats, and Tim, wearing an ear-to-ear grin, slipped one on.

At 10:09 p.m., in the midst of the pandemonium, Commissioner Goodell's official announcement came that Tim Tebow was a first-round draft choice of the Denver Broncos. The proclamation sent shock waves through Radio City Music Hall and caused Mel Kiper Jr. to blanche like he'd just swallowed a dose of cod liver oil.

"I just think I showed them [the Broncos] I was willing to do whatever it took," Tim told ESPN. "I want to thank everyone in the organization. Over the last few weeks, we really hit it off. I was hoping and praying that was where I could play."

Tim said his private workout three days earlier with the Denver coaching staff raised his hopes that Denver would be the team that would take him. "It was awesome," he said of his day in Denver. "It was a day full of ball. We talked ball, watched film. We watched so much stuff. . . . It was the best day I've had. I enjoyed it. Their coaches are awesome. It was great. Their coaches are just likes the coaches I have at Florida. I'm just excited to be a Bronco."

The Denver media reported that the Broncos knocked the NFL on its insignia ears by selecting Tim, and headlines around the country called Denver's drafting of Tim "shocking" and "surprising."

There was electricity in the rarefied Colorado air, but there were also some interesting dynamics regarding the pick. The Centennial State is really the tale of two cities: Denver, the state capital, and Colorado Springs, 60 miles to the south, along the Front Range corridor. Denver (and nearby Boulder) is uniformly more liberal, while Colorado Springs, which is home to dozens of Christian ministries, including Focus on the Family, is more conservative.

Would Tim be a polarizing figure in such an environment?

"Tim Tebow is a lightning rod," said Bill McCartney, the former University of Colorado football coach and founder of the Promise Keepers men's ministry, adding, "There is an anointing on Tim and his family. He's one of those guys who comes along who has God's handprints all over him." McCartney predicted that Tim, who's heavily involved in philanthropic efforts through his Tim Tebow Foundation, would make a difference for Denver's poor and oppressed.

Perhaps that's why *Denver Post* columnist Woody Paige—a regular panelist on the ESPN sports-talk program *Around the Horn* who is not known for any conservative views—preached tolerance shortly after Tim was drafted. The headline on his sympathetic column: IT'S NOT FAIR TO RIP TEBOW FOR HIS FAITH.

COLT McCOY: STAYING IN ORANGE

Colt McCoy wasn't drafted on the first night of the 2010 NFL draft, but then again, he wasn't expected to go in the first round.

Nearly every NFL draftnik with a platform declared that Colt was no better than the fourth-best quarterback in the draft anyway, lodged behind Sam, Tim, and Notre Dame quarterback Jimmy Clausen. For months, Mel Kiper had said that the most "pro-ready quarterback" in the 2010 draft was not Sam or Tim or Colt but Jimmy Clausen.

As was the case with Tim, the NFL didn't believe Kiper's siren call about Clausen, and there was a reason why—those pesky "intangibles."

A couple of NFL scouts, speaking anonymously, told CBS Sports the reason Clausen dropped all the way to the No. 48 pick—23 spots behind Tim—was due to his personality, not his mechanics and capabilities on the field. "With what I was listening to, I thought I was hearing Ryan Leaf all over again," said one scout. "He has a sense and a degree of entitlement that's off the charts." Another scout added, "I heard horror stories about the guy off the field to the point where I wasn't interested."

Jimmy Clausen suffered a precipitous fall in the NFL draft. Colt McCoy did not, even though the Cleveland Browns eventually drafted him with the 85th pick. In fact, Colt wound up with a team that's a great match for his dogged style of playing quarterback—an appropriate metaphor since the Browns' zealous fans, known as the Dawg Pound, take up residence behind the east end zone of Cleveland Browns Stadium.

You see, the reason Colt was picked late in the third round was the NFL's fixation with height and heft. Since Colt was "only" 6-1 and 216 pounds—the measureables—there was concern that his body could not hold up to the pounding he could expect while slinging passes from an NFL pocket. The intangibles, though, were no problem; Colt had checked out as a "character guy." Cleveland Browns first-year president Mike Holmgren—a proven winner in the NFL following coaching stints at Green Bay and Seattle—wanted Colt all along, but on his terms, meaning the third round.

There was some symmetry working. Holmgren had been the quarterbacks coach with the San Francisco 49ers in the 1980s when the West Coast team drafted a relatively unheralded quarterback from Notre Dame—also in the third round. At 6-2 and 205 pounds, Joe Montana wasn't a player of "NFL prototype" size, but he still managed to cobble together a 15-year career that left him with four Super Bowl rings on his fingers and a Hall of Fame career in his back pocket.

Holmgren had brought Colt to Cleveland for a private workout a couple of weeks before the draft. The quarterback hopeful also spent time with Coach Eric Mangini and practiced with Browns quarterbacks Jake Delhomme and Seneca Wallace. Similar to the bond that quickly developed between Denver coach Josh McDaniels and Tim Tebow, Colt felt something click with the Browns' Mike Holmgren. His sure, experienced hand with producing quality quarterbacks felt assuring to Colt.

The Cleveland Browns weren't the only team taking a close look at Colt. Exactly two weeks before the draft, he had an hour-long private workout in Austin for the St. Louis Rams in front of Billy Devaney, Steve Spagnuolo, and quarterbacks coach Dick Curl. Devaney said afterward that Colt was extremely impressive and showed "all the stuff that you look for in a great quarterback."

Let the guessing game begin . . . *if the Rams pass on Sam Bradford and draft top defensive tackle Ndamukong Suh instead, they could take Colt in the second round.* . . .

Colt worked out for several other teams, including the New England Patriots and the Washington Redskins. Leading up to the draft, he was like dozens, if not hundreds, of other hopefuls: he had no idea where he'd end up.

Colt and his family, along with his fiancée, Rachel Glandorf, gathered with friends at a spacious Austin home for the first round and returned the following night for rounds two and three. As the second evening played out and his name wasn't called, he spoke with his old coach at Texas, Mack Brown, who was at Radio City Music Hall as a guest commentator for the NFL Network.

"Don't worry, son, you're in a great place," said his old coach. "You hang in there."

"Coach, I've been through this my whole life," Colt said. "I just want to go to a team that wants me, and I'm going to prove it again."

Then two of the most wonderful omens appeared. The first was the announcement of the No. 84 pick by the Cincinnati Bengals, who selected wide receiver Jordan Shipley, Colt's childhood buddy and teammate from the Texas team.

Then, a minute later, someone new walked to the podium at Radio City Music Hall. It wasn't Commissioner Goodell but Coach Brown holding a card. Fans sitting in the mezzanine took up a chant: "Colt, Colt, Colt . . ."

Wait . . . could it be?

"With the 85th pick in the 2010 NFL draft, the Cleveland Browns select Colt McCoy, quarterback, Texas," announced his old coach.

Back in Austin, Colt hugged his parents, accepted a kiss on the cheek from Rachel, and became a Cleveland Brown.

Mike Holmgren had looked past Colt's measureables, just like Mack Brown had six years earlier when he offered a scholarship to a high school junior from a tiny 2A high school in Tuscola, Texas.

"Nobody expected Colt to have the career that he had at Texas because he came from a small school, and he's a little bit shorter, a little thin—all the things they still say about him," Brown said after the draft. "My expectation is that he'll do a great job in the NFL."

TIM AND THE NATIONAL PRAYER BREAKFAST

Back in early February 2010, shortly after the horrible earthquake that struck Haiti, Tim Tebow was asked to wrap up the National Prayer Breakfast. It's quite an honor to be asked to close such an august event, held annually in Washington, D.C., and attended by the president of the United States, U.S. senators, and members of Congress. Around 3,000 people were on hand for the 2010 gathering, including Vice President Joe Biden and Secretary of State Hillary Clinton.

President Barack Obama, who had addressed the audience earlier, had left by the time Senator Johnny Isakson of Georgia took the podium to introduce Tim. Calling him a "role model for the youth of America," Isakson joked that he found it funny that a fan of University of Georgia football would invite a former member of the Florida Gators to present a closing prayer.

The audience enjoyed a chuckle, and as Tim accepted the microphone, he quipped, "It is rather incredible that a Georgia Bulldog invited a Florida Gator, so you can see the hand of God here."

Tim bowed his head and delivered a wonderful prayer that included the eye black verses worn in the Senior Bowl game:

Dear Jesus, thank You for this day. Thank You for bringing together so many people that have a platform to influence people for You.

Lord, as we disperse today, let us be united in love, hope, and peace. Lord, let us come together as one and break down all the barriers in between us that separate us. Lord, You came to seek and save that which is lost, and we thank You for that. Lord, we don't know what the future holds, but we know who holds the future, and in that there is peace, and in that there is comfort, and in that there is hope.

Lord, we pray for the people all over the world who are hurting right now, Lord. The verse that comes to mind is James 1:2–4, "Consider it all joy, my brethren, whenever you encounter various trials, knowing that the testing of your faith produces endurance. And let endurance have its perfect result, that you may be perfect and complete, lacking in nothing."

And we pray for the people in Haiti right now, Lord, that You make them perfect and complete because You love them and have a plan for their lives, just as You do with our lives now.

So my prayer, as we leave today, is that we are united as one because of You. We love You and thank You. In Jesus' name, amen.

MOVING TO THE NEXT LEVEL

Going into the 2010 season, everyone was asking what would happen to these three special NFL rookies.

Neither Sam, Colt, nor Tim could have predicted how their rookie seasons would play out.

6

THEIR FIRST TWO NFL SEASONS

Being an NFL rookie quarterback is a tough gig.

From their first snap, first-year signal callers discover that the pro game is played at a much faster pace than in college. They are pitted against more athletic defenses, and they must perform under a new spotlight. Because NFL players are paid for their services, home-field fans feel freer to vent their displeasure after the latest interception or three-and-out series. The local media, which are often friendly boosters in college towns, delight in carving up pro players like a Thanksgiving turkey—proving the adage that the pen is mightier than the sword.

It generally takes a few seasons for a young quarterback to mature and feel comfortable in the National Football League. That's why Drew Brees caddied for Doug Flutie during his rookie year with the San Diego Chargers in 2001, playing in just one game. When Philip Rivers was drafted behind Brees in 2004, he threw only three passes as a third-string rookie.

Those who *do* play a lot during their first season in the pros take their lumps while adapting to a faster and tougher professional game. For nearly every hotshot collegian entering the league, it's *normal* to struggle in the rookie season. Learning an NFL offense is like learning a new language, and with speedy 250-pound linebackers shooting through the gaps, it's easy to see why rookie quarterbacks are often overwhelmed when they line up behind center.

Looking at today's ranks of premier quarterbacks, only one held his own in his first year of pro ball:

- **Peyton Manning** of the Indianapolis Colts set five different NFL rookie records, including most touchdown passes in a season, but he also threw a league-high 28 interceptions for a team that struggled to a 3–13 record.
- **Tom Brady**, drafted almost as an afterthought by the New England Patriots in the sixth round, started the 2000 season as the fourth-string quarterback. He threw just three passes his rookie year, completing one.
- **Michael Vick**, the No. 1 draft choice in 2001, was brought along slowly by Atlanta Falcons head coach Dan Reeves. He played in eight games, starting two, while experiencing marginal success for a team that finished 7–9.
- **Aaron Rodgers** arrived in Green Bay in 2005 where Brett Favre was only in his 15th season. Rodgers saw limited action in three games.
- **Ben Roethlisberger**, thrust into a starting role early due to injuries, turned in the best season ever for a rookie QB in 2004, going 13–0 as a starter and leading the Pittsburgh Steelers to the AFC Championship Game.

Fourteen quarterbacks were selected in the 2010 NFL draft, but none had Big Ben–like results in their rookie seasons. As for the Three QBs, there was a certain beginning, middle, and ending symmetry to their first season of professional football:

- Sam got his chance early and played every down.
- Colt got his chance in the middle of the season when he suddenly zoomed from third string to starter.
- Tim—who looked like he would be relegated to spot appearances in second-and-goal "packages" all year long—created an end-of-the-season buzz when he got a chance to close out Denver's dismal schedule. Tim started the Broncos' last three games.

Let's take a closer look at how all three did.

SAM BRADFORD: ROOKIE OF THE YEAR

As the player stamped with "No. 1 Draft Pick" on the back of his jersey, Sam Bradford carried the biggest expectations going into the 2010 season, even though he was drafted by a franchise that won three games in 2007, two games in 2008, and just one game in 2009.

But Sam wasn't going to get the starting job just because he was the first draft pick to shake Roger Goodell's hand. At the start of training camp, St. Louis coach Steve Spagnuolo tabbed 33-year-old journeyman A. J. Feeley as his starter, repeating a familiar refrain to reporters: "Just like I stated all spring, if we played today, A. J. would be the guy. Maybe I should put that on tape."

Maybe "Spags" was thinking of an old eight-track tape that nobody could play anymore—because everyone knew that Sam would get a strong shot to compete for the job, given Feeley's spotty résumé and Sam's megamillion-dollar contract. Besides, the Oklahoma standout had never been the type to stand contentedly on the sidelines, signaling plays in a spotless uniform. Remember how Sam hated receiving his red shirt when he arrived on the Norman campus? Knowing Sam's competitive nature, he wouldn't be content waiting his turn. That wasn't going to happen—even in the pros.

So Sam set his mind to learning a new offense, memorizing the playbook, improving his reads, and practicing his throws into the "tighter spaces" of NFL secondaries. When Spagnuolo put a 40-second clock into play during offensive drills, Sam responded by getting the team to the line of scrimmage and delivering crisp throws while working under the gun.

Sam performed well in the first two preseason games. Then Feeley sprained the thumb on his throwing hand in the next-to-last exhibition game, giving Sam even more snaps in practice and the final two preseason games. The door suddenly flew wide open. When Sam looked great against the Baltimore Ravens in the preseason finale, no one was terribly surprised when Spagnuolo announced Bradford as starting quarterback for the season opener against the Arizona Cardinals.

The Rams lost narrowly at home to Arizona, 17–13, but Sam's arm nearly engineered a last-second win. In that game, he set his first NFL record—most throws by a rookie in his first game (55). But when the Rams traveled the following week to the "Black Hole"—Oakland-Alameda County Coliseum, home of the Oakland Raiders—they lost again. Suddenly, Sam's team was 0–2 and Rams fans had a sinking feeling of déjà vu.

Sam helped right the ship. He led St. Louis to wins over the Washington Redskins and Seattle Seahawks, and from that point, the Rams would win one, lose one—or so it seemed—the rest of the way. One of the more interesting matchups was a Week 12 tussle with the Broncos. Playing in Denver, Sam threw for three touchdowns and had his first 300-yard game while Tim Tebow watched from the sideline and didn't play a down. The win over the Broncos lifted St. Louis to a 5–6 record—identical to the first-place Seattle Seahawks in the National Football Conference West division—and raised hopes among Rams fans that the team could return to the NFL playoffs as a divisional winner.

As the season wore on, everything came down to the final game of the 2010 season—the St. Louis Rams versus the Seattle Seahawks. The winner would advance to the NFL playoffs, and the loser would go home.

Even though the Rams were 7–8 and the Seahawks were 6–9 (Seattle would win the tiebreaker if the Seahawks were victorious), NBC picked this game for their Sunday flex and showed it in national prime time, Sunday night, January 2, 2011.

ESPN reporter Anna McDonald reported that Sam was still reading the story of David and Goliath before every game. "It reassures me every Sunday that when I go out on the field that I'm not going out alone," he said. "God is with me in everything I do, just like he was with David. I think that just really gives me comfort. It really gives me strength."

Sam would need comfort because the Rams lost 16–6 on a frustrating evening: several of Sam's passes were batted down at the line of scrimmage, several passes were dropped, and the Rams could only muster 47 yards on the ground. "I think one of the reasons [we lost] is we never got in a rhythm," Sam said afterward. "We never came close to getting in a rhythm. We put together one drive early in the game, and then after that, it seemed like it was three-and-out or we might make one decent play."

The loss in Seattle meant Sam's rookie season was over, but he could hold his helmet high. In 2010, Sam put up one of the more impressive rookie years in NFL history. He passed for 3,512 yards, connected for 18 touchdowns, had 15 interceptions, and left the field with a 60 percent completion rate—all this while throwing to a depleted receiver corps over an offensive line that leaked oil throughout the season.

Sam broke Peyton Manning's rookie year mark for completions, and he also set a rookie record for most attempts without an interception, going 169 passes between picks at one point in the season. For these accomplishments, Sam was named Offensive Rookie of the Year by the Associated Press, breezing past wideout Mike Williams of Tampa Bay and stalwart Pittsburgh center Maurkice Pouncey. Once again Sam overwhelmed the competition by capturing 44 of the 50 votes cast by a nationwide panel of media members who regularly cover the NFL.

The biggest accomplishment for Sam, however, didn't show up on the stat sheet—and that was his durability. Though some of the draftniks said his shoulder would be suspect or that one good hit would knock him out for the season again, Sam proved them wrong. Despite taking big-time shots, Sam pulled himself up and took every Ram snap in 2010. Even in the season-ending loss to Seattle, he hung in there despite some horrific blows when the Rams were playing from behind and being forced to throw the ball.

"I take a lot [of pride] in that," Sam told the *St. Louis Post-Dispatch*. "Especially coming off the shoulder injury last year [in college] and knowing that there were a lot of questions about my durability, about my ability to take hits in this league. So the fact that I was able to take every snap with this offense, I do take a lot of pride in that."

COLT McCOY: SURPRISING EVERYONE

The biggest pressure Colt McCoy faced before the start of his rookie season was keeping a straight face at his wedding to Rachel on July 17, 2010.

At the wedding reception, lifelong friend Jordan Shipley and country musician Aaron Watson cooked up a tribute to him in a country western song entitled "When I Grow Up, I Want to Be Just Like Colt McCoy."

You had to be there to enjoy it. But, wait a minute, you can be—thanks to the magic of YouTube. (Just type in "Colt McCoy wedding song.")

In front of a country band picking out a honky-tonk tune, Shipley and Watson brought the house down with these lyrics:

Some say he's a ninja, rumor has it he's Superman.
He's got the heart of a lion, still he's as gentle as old Peter Pan.
All you Hatfields better beware, I heard he's stronger than a Kodiak bear.
He's your real deal, he's no decoy, he's still his mama's little pride and joy . . .
Hey, when I grow up I wanna be just like Colt McCoy.
He's the true gun-slinging inspiration to every small town country boy.
Having cool friends like Jordan Shipley
(well, ain't no singers singin' songs about me).
Well, when I grow up, I wanna be just like Colt McCoy.

The wedding party was loving every second of the song when the following lyric earned an uproarious response:

Now he's gettin' sick and tired of people getting fired up for rubbing elbows
with Tim Tebow . . .

The reference was an in-joke referring to criticism Colt received from die-hard Texas fans for being friendly with the dark prince from the University of Florida. But if you watch the video, you'll see that lyric earned the loudest laughter at Colt's wedding reception.

After a short honeymoon, Colt reported for the Cleveland Browns training camp, firmly ensconced as third-string quarterback on the depth chart. Unlike Sam Bradford, Colt was never going to be given a chance to compete for the starting role. All along, president Mike Holmgren said the Browns brought him in to learn behind veteran Jake Delhomme, 35, and Seneca Wallace, 30, picked up in a trade with Seattle. "Things could change, but I don't expect him to play this year," Holmgren said at the start of camp.

As part of his transition from college to pros, Colt had to learn a new offensive system that was much different than what he played under at Texas. Growing pains surfaced early on. In a brown-white scrimmage and a preseason outing against Green Bay, Colt didn't look very good. He continued to struggle, and beat reporters dished out rumors that Colt could be cut from the Browns' 53-man squad. Then in the Browns' final preseason game, Colt came alive and went 13-for-13 passing.

He was still sent back to the bench to sit and learn—but Colt didn't look at it that way. Even though he was third-string, he prepared for each game like he was the starter. Coaches call it "keeping your head in the game."

Two games into the season, Jake Delhomme went down with a high-ankle sprain. Seneca Wallace was handed the reins, and three games later, *he* went down with a similar high-ankle sprain. Week 5, with the Browns record at 1–4, Colt was the last man standing in the O.K. Corral.

Okay, Colt. Here's the deal: your first NFL action will be against the Super Bowl–contending Pittsburgh Steelers—at Heinz Field. Oh, you should also know that this road game will be Steelers quarterback Ben Roethlisberger's emotional return from his four-game suspension for violating the NFL personal conduct policy.

At the Saturday night team meeting, Colt addressed his teammates. He told them that they didn't have to worry about him; he was ready and he was going to play a good game. "The hay is in the barn," he said, which drew more than a few quizzical looks from teammates who had never visited a working farm in their lives.

Feeling a translation was necessary, Colt explained that the preparation was done and it was time to go out and do the job.

After taking the field against the blitz-happy Steelers, no one could blame Colt for feeling like a Christian thrown to the Coliseum lions. But what he did in three hours probably changed the arc of his career.

So let's set the scene: a fall-like October afternoon at Heinz Field, a loud, foreboding crowd waving Terrible Towels, and a boisterous reception for Big Ben, their Prodigal Son. Against the 3–1 Steelers, Colt and his teammates had a pretty low expectations bar from the football pundits. The Browns were heavy underdogs.

On his first series, Colt made several completions and moved the team down the field, but then a tipped pass resulted in an interception. Not an auspicious beginning.

But Colt showed no panic—in fact, just the opposite. He displayed more poise, toughness, and promise the rest of the way. He *looked* like an NFL quarterback as he moved the ball down the field, and even though the Browns lost 28–10, he impressed his teammates and the Browns organization with his heady play, pinpoint passing, and on-the-field leadership.

"You can tell that he is a natural-born leader," Browns guard Eric Steinbach said after the game. "It is good to have him in the huddle. A lot of rookies can't come in right away. They want to be a leader, but they don't have that 'it.' "

Colt completed 23 of 33 passes for 281 yards, added 22 rushing yards—and won himself another start. But coming up was the Super Bowl championship team, the New Orleans Saints, and their ace quarterback, Drew Brees.

The Browns shocked the football world by knocking off the Saints 30–17—on the road. Two pick-6 interceptions by linebacker David Bowens were the difference, but Colt won praise for managing the game and completing 9 of 16 passes.

Then the *really* unlikely happened in the following game—a 34–14 thrashing of the New England Patriots, led by All-Universe quarterback Tom Brady, before a delirious home crowd. Colt, 14 for 19 with no interceptions, was now 2–1 as a starter, and Browns fans were crediting Colt with changing the losing culture in the Dawg Pound.

But wait—there was *another* great team waiting in the wings—the New York Jets. Talk about a Murderer's Row to start your professional career. As NFL baptisms go, it's difficult to see how things could get any tougher for a rookie quarterback.

Unfortunately, they did. The Browns lost in overtime to the Jets, despite a late fourth-quarter game-tying touchdown drive by Colt that was a thing of beauty. In following games, Cleveland continued to struggle to hold leads, and then in Week 11, Colt injured his ankle and missed three weeks before returning for the last three games of the season.

Even though the Browns lost all three contests, Colt acquitted himself well, establishing himself as the Cleveland starter going into the 2011 season.

TIM TEBOW: THE MILE HIGH MESSIAH

Tim Tebow arrived in Denver supremely happy that he was picked in the first round by the Broncos. The local media swooned over the Florida quarterback, even admitting they were seduced by his charismatic charm and his aw-shucks, Jack Armstrong, all-American attitude. Many fans warmed to the idea that Tim could take hold of the franchise like Hall of Famer John Elway did in the 1980s.

If Tim had worked hard in the months leading up the NFL draft (retooling his throwing motion and footwork), he doubled down during training camp. Tim told reporters that he had a saying on his bedroom wall at home: "Hard work beats talent when talent doesn't work hard."

His presence drew a record 3,100 fans to the first day of training camp, and Tim worked his way past Brady Quinn on the depth chart to establish himself as the No. 2 quarterback behind starter Kyle Orton. In the middle of summer camp, Tim showed that he wasn't a prima donna by readily submitting to a ridiculous "Friar Tuck" haircut—a humongous bald spot on top of his dome surrounded by a ring of hair. Looking like he stepped out of a Robin Hood and Sheriff of Nottingham movie, the monk haircut was part of a rookie hazing ceremony. Tim said he went along with the gag to build team chemistry.

For most of the 2010 season, as the team kept losing and losing, the Broncos' team chemistry wasn't very good. Sure, head coach Josh McDaniels—who made it no secret that Tim was his pet project—featured him in the team's "Wild Horse" packages on third-and-short and goal-line situations early in the season, but Tim was kept on the shortest leash possible. He didn't throw his first pass until the middle of November—a mini three-yard touchdown toss.

By then, the Bronco season was already in tatters, but the worst was yet to come. During the last week of October, the Broncos had flown to London, England, to play the San Francisco 49ers as part of the NFL's "International Series" outreach. Steve Scarnecchia, the team's director of video operations, videotaped the 49ers' walkthrough practice at Wembley Stadium—and was caught doing so. The practice is strictly forbidden.

The media dubbed it "Spygate II" because what transpired was reminiscent of the New England Patriots' Spygate scandal of 2007–08. Since McDaniels was a Patriots assistant coach at the time and a Bill Belichick acolyte . . . well, you can connect the dots.

McDaniels was fired in early December for his role in Spygate II as well as the Broncos' 3–9 belly flop. With the disastrous season going nowhere and starting quarterback Kyle Orton out with injured ribs, Orange Nation—and the Denver media—clamored for *something* to cheer about.

Give Tebow the rock!

With three games left on the schedule, interim head coach Eric Studesville decided it was Tebow Time, naming Tim the starter for a road game against the Oakland Raiders. With Silver and Black fans screaming, "Tebow Bust! Tebow Bust!" Tim electrified his teammates by galloping for a 40-yard touchdown up the gut—and later endeared himself to his fans when he admitted after the game that he was supposed to hand the ball to running back Correll Buckhalter. In other words, he scored on a busted play.

Although Denver lost to Oakland, Tim infused an energy into the Broncos players and showed leadership and determination. He also had the dirtiest Denver uniform when the clock ran out.

The following game, against the Houston Texans, became the first installment of the Tebow legend in Denver. Playing before a boisterous sellout crowd with only 5,717 no-shows, the Broncos fell behind 17–0 at halftime—which was par for how their season was going. A Tebow interception in the end zone didn't help their cause.

Then, after intermission, something special happened. Tim unleashed a 50-yard bomb to receiver Jabar Gaffney on the opening drive of the second half that led to a touchdown. The next two drives resulted in a field goal and another touchdown. With the Broncos defense suddenly developing a spine,

Denver was down just 23–17 with 7:42 remaining.

A clutch third-and-10 dump-off pass netted 22 yards. Then Tim lasered a 15-yard strike, followed by an 11-yard scramble. Down at the 6-yard line, Tim took the ball in the shotgun, shook off a sack, and had the football sense to pivot to his left, where there was plenty of green grass and no white Houston Texans uniforms in the vicinity. Tim won the footrace to the pylon, and Denver's comeback was complete, 24–23.

If you can't chuck it, then tuck it.

Orange Nation rejoiced that the Broncos had snapped a five-game losing streak, and some fans believed a star was born that afternoon against Houston. Time will tell if Tim becomes a modern-day Moses who leads the Broncos out of the wilderness to the Promised Land of the NFL playoffs.

Tim's three-game audition probably raised as many questions as answers about his future as an NFL quarterback. He certainly proved that he belonged behind center and could lead his team down the field, seemingly by force of will. But being an NFL quarterback is a lot more than a seven-step drop and flinging the ball down the field, as Tim has been learning.

Bronco legend John Elway, who was named executive vice president of football operations following the disastrous 2010 season, said Tim needs to work on the fundamentals of being a pocket passer and anticipating throws. "We all agree on one thing," Elway said. "Tim Tebow is a darn good football player. What we have to make him is a darn good quarterback, and that is what we have to figure out."

THEIR SOPHOMORE SEASONS

The 2011 NFL campaign was a mixed bag for the Three QBs—although Tim Tebow was the story of the year for any quarterback. Remember how tebowing became part of pop culture? We'll recap Tim's season first.

Though Tim had acquitted himself well at the end of the 2010 season, there were too many doubting Thomases in the Broncos' brain trust. Denver's new head coach, John Fox, reinstalled Kyle Orton as the starting quarterback during training camp. Tim was again on the outside looking in.

Rumors circulated that Denver would release Tim because Brady Quinn had beaten him out for the backup spot. ESPN columnist Rick Reilly wrote Tim's epitaph, saying he was a "nice kid, sincere as a first kiss, but he's not ready yet, might never be ready. Somebody alert the Filipino missionaries. If he doesn't improve, he might be among them sooner than we thought."

But hold that plane ticket to Manila—Tim had the support of Denver fans, who recognized the leadership and intangibles he brought to the team. When the Broncos won only one game in the first month of the season, the natives got restless. Denver supporters chanted, "Tebow! Tebow!" after every three-and-out—and the pressure mounted on Coach Fox to see what Tim could do.

In the season's fifth game, the Broncos were down 23–10—at home, at halftime—to conference rival San Diego. With a lusty chorus of "Tebow!

Tebow!" filling Invesco Field, Tim was handed the reins to the Bronco offense. He shone against the Chargers, nearly delivering an improbable come-from-behind victory. Tim's stellar play earned him a start against Miami.

Unfortunately, Tim did little of note for the first 55 minutes of the Dolphins game. With five minutes to play, he was looking down the barrel of a 15–0 deficit.

Those who witnessed the Miami game are still wondering how Tim found a way to complete an amazing comeback. As soon as the Broncos' winning field goal sailed through the uprights, cameras caught Tim taking a knee and bowing his head in a prayer of thanksgiving. As fast as you can say "social networking," the verb *tebowing* became part of the popular culture.

In the fall of 2011, a six-game winning streak had football pundits labeling Tim the "Mile High Messiah." His miraculous play was the talk of ESPN SportsCenter and every football pundit on the pregame shows—but those same commentators gave Tim and the Broncos no chance against mighty Pittsburgh in the NFL playoffs.

But the Broncos took the Steelers to overtime—and on the first play of the extra period, Tim whistled a clean pass to a streaking Demaryius Thomas, who won a footrace to the end zone. The sporting world was astounded by yet another David-and-Goliath upset.

A stronger, deeper, and supremely talented New England Patriots team was waiting for Tim and the Broncos in the next round, however—and that's when their storybook season ended. Disappointing, to be sure, but you had to figure the Broncos had found their quarterback of the future.

Not so fast, said John Elway, when the Indianapolis Colts released future Hall of Fame quarterback Peyton Manning shortly after Super Bowl XLVI. Suddenly, one of the best signal-callers since . . . well, John Elway . . . was a free agent. Sure, he had a creaky neck and hadn't played a down in 2011. But he was still only 36 years old and hadn't lost his pinpoint passing touch.

Manning visited several teams, but it was clear that the Broncos were galloping to the front of the Peyton parade. When Manning agreed to a $96 million, five-year contract, Tim's days in Denver were clearly numbered. Within two weeks, a trade was arranged with the New York Jets—and one of history's most celebrated Christian athletes was thrust into the center of the media universe.

So here we go again. New York already has a quarterback—Mark Sanchez—but the third-year pro struggled in 2011. When the highly regarded Jets failed to make the playoffs, the media and fans cast about for a scapegoat—and painted a hunter green bull's-eye on the back of Sanchez's jersey.

What will happen during the 2012 season? Who will quarterback the Jets? No one knows, but one thing is sure: football fans everywhere—east, west, north, and south of the Hudson River—will tune in for the next installment of *As the Jets' World Turns*.

Starring Tim Tebow.

UP IN THE AIR

Following the 2011 season, the Cleveland Browns fired a shot across the bow of Colt McCoy's career as well.

To the surprise of more than a few draftniks, Browns president Mike Holmgren and his coaching staff pulled the trigger on Oklahoma State quarterback Brandon Weeden in the first round of the 2012 NFL draft, making him the 22nd pick overall. Weeden was an impressive passer at OSU, setting all kinds of records. He could really throw the ball—not surprising, because Weeden was a hotshot pitcher coming out of high school. That was way back in 2002, and the New York Yankees took him in the second round of the Major League draft. Weeden never made it to the big leagues, bouncing around the minors for five years, foiled by injuries and a high earned run average. When he enrolled at Oklahoma State in 2007, he was hoping to remake himself as a college quarterback.

Credit to Brandon: the gamble worked, and many expect him to supplant Colt as the Browns quarterback in 2012. As Yogi Berra would say, Weeden's the youngest 29-year-old rookie in the NFL.

So once again, Colt is being told that he lacks the arm, isn't good enough, doesn't have what it takes—you pick the reason—to be a starting quarterback in professional football.

But, as with Tim Tebow, you count out Colt at your own peril. Sure, he started 21 games in his two seasons at Cleveland, winning only six—but he was playing behind a depleted offensive line and running for his life. The Browns had no running attack. The receiving corps wasn't good enough. Talk about taking a knife to a gunfight.

The outlook looks better in 2012 with the addition of power running back Trent Richardson, the first-round draft pick (third overall) from the University of Alabama. Expect to see a few new faces on the O-line and among those catching the ball.

The reason the Browns felt compelled to enter the quarterback sweepstakes is the way the 2011 season played out. Things looked good early, after Colt won the starting QB position in training camp and led Cleveland to early season victories over the Indianapolis Colts and Miami Dolphins. At 2–1, Browns fans thought the team might be good enough to finish with a winning record and claim a playoff spot.

Running back Peyton Hillis, after a breakout season in 2010, was a shell of himself in 2011, however. Off-field drama and injuries caused him to miss six games—and when he did play, he lacked the production of the previous season. With a pop-gun running attack, Colt was forced to the airwaves. Defenses adjusted accordingly, sending waves of blitzes.

Colt was never more of a sitting duck than when he roamed out of the pocket against the Pittsburgh Steelers late in the 2011 season. The Browns were down 7–3 late in the fourth quarter, driving in Pittsburgh territory for the potential game-winning score.

Unprotected in the flat, though, Colt was nearly decapitated by Steelers linebacker James Harrison after making a pass to Montario Hardesty. The devastating helmet-to-helmet hit flattened Colt, who lay on his back, occasionally flailing his arms and legs. One had to wonder how scrambled his brains were.

Enough for a major concussion, as it turns out. Harrison was flagged for a personal foul (and later suspended for a game), but the damage—brain damage—had been done. Colt lay on the field a long time before being helped to his feet.

Here's where the story gets more interesting: when Colt came off the field, he didn't specifically complain of concussion issues, so he wasn't given the standard SCAT2 concussion test. He was only checked for a hand injury he mentioned.

Given a pass on the hand, Colt jogged back on field less than four minutes after being poleaxed by Harrison. On his first play from scrimmage, Colt forced a throw into end zone coverage and was picked off. Game over.

But the controversy continued. When medical personnel checked Colt after the game, they determined he'd been concussed. He remembers nothing of the vicious hit—which might actually be a blessing. Ultimately, Colt's 2011 season was over, as he didn't play a down in the Browns' final three games of a dismal 4–12 campaign.

That may be when the Browns' coaching staff and management began thinking Colt was not their guy. By April 26, 2012, they were gambling a first-round pick on Brandon Weeden.

It will be fascinating to see how this bold move plays out for Cleveland.

A FORGETTABLE SEASON

Sam Bradford seems like the forgotten man among the Three QBs. After a good rookie year, he missed six games in 2011 to injury. Hobbled by a high-ankle sprain, Sam returned ahead of schedule to play even though there were times he could hardly move out of the pocket.

Unlike Tim and Colt, Sam's job appears secure with new head coach Jeff Fisher, formerly with the Tennessee Titans. After a horrible 2–14 season filled with injuries and too many losses, the Rams' owner, Stan Kroenke, fired head coach Steve Spagnuolo and general manager Billy Devaney and began rebuilding.

Sam is still the quarterback of the Rams' future.

He'll have to up his game, though. Football analysts say Sam did not look like the same confident pocket quarterback he was during his first season in the pros. That's when he won the NFL Offensive Rookie of the Year award, setting three records:

- most consecutive passes without an interception by a rookie quarterback (169),
- most attempts by a rookie quarterback (590), and
- most completions by a rookie quarterback (354).

All of the Three QBs are entering Year 3 of their NFL careers, that time when elite quarterbacks are expected to "make the leap" and show they can win games. No doubt there will be some great stories to follow in 2012, making this season a great one to watch:

- Will Tim get a chance to play quarterback for the Jets—and have something magical, unexpected, unprecedented happen in Gotham City?
- Will there be a quarterback battle in Cleveland between Colt and Brandon Weeden? Who will shine when given the keys to the offense?
- Will Sam be able to lift the St. Louis Rams from the slag heap again, like he did in his rookie season?

Whatever happens, we can appreciate how all of the Three QBs have remained true to their faith on and off the field. Let's pray that Tim, Colt, and Sam remain humble and strong, free from injuries, and bold witnesses for Christ.

Thanks, guys, for playing with purpose.

AFTERWORD

BY TRENT DILFER, SUPER BOWL–WINNING QUARTERBACK AND NFL ANALYST FOR ESPN

Author's note: When Fresno State quarterback Trent Dilfer was the sixth player taken in the first round of the 1994 draft by the Tampa Bay Buccaneers, expectations ran high that Trent would turn around a franchise that had lost at least 10 games a season for the previous 11 years.

He struggled early on but blossomed in his fourth year with Tampa Bay, putting together a solid season that catapulted the Bucs into the playoffs and earned Trent a Pro Bowl appearance. After six up-and-down seasons with Tampa Bay, though, he signed with the Baltimore Ravens as a free agent to back up highly touted quarterback Tony Banks. Trent accepted that role, but when Banks faltered, Trent got his chance and led the Ravens to 11 straight victories, including a clutch performance in Super Bowl XXXV—ironically played in Tampa—where the Ravens spanked the New York Giants, 34–7.

"Redemption" was the word often associated with Trent's name following the Super Bowl win, but he had experienced a better kind of redemption when he attended a Fellowship of Christian Athletes camp during his junior year of college and finally understood what it meant to be a Christian. One thing he learned was that following Christ meant paying attention to others, not getting everyone else to pay attention to him.

That focus on Someone greater than him would be what he and his wife, Cassandra, would rely on when they lost their five-year-old son, Trevin, to a heart condition in 2003. Trent's faith sustained him during this trying ordeal, and he said that heaven got a lot more real when he realized that he would have a child waiting for him. One day, they would be reunited.

Trent retired from professional football after the 2007 season and joined ESPN as an NFL analyst for a variety of ESPN programs, including NFL Live, NFL PrimeTime, Monday Night Countdown, and SportsCenter. After playing 14 seasons as an NFL quarterback as well as being recognized for his solid commitment to Christianity—Trent won the Bart Starr Award given to the NFL player who best exemplifies character and leadership—he is just the right person to say a few words to Sam, Colt, and Tim as we close this book.

Please note that Trent's afterword was written before their rookie seasons, but as you'll see, his insights about what Sam, Colt, and Tim would face in their first year of pro football were uncanny and spot-on.

As a former NFL quarterback who gets paid to offer his opinions about pro football, I'm really looking forward to the arrival of Sam Bradford, Colt McCoy, and Tim Tebow into the National Football League. This is going to be fun.

I've never met Sam, I have met Tim briefly, and I know Colt pretty well. After Colt's career at Texas ended at the Rose Bowl, he signed with sports agent David Dunn, who happens to be my agent. David asked me if I would help Colt—as well as a couple of other just-out-of-college quarterbacks—get ready for the NFL Combine and upcoming NFL draft in early 2010. I was glad to help out, and I wasn't compensated for my efforts.

At Mission Viejo High School in Southern California's Orange County, I worked with Colt and quarterbacks Sean Canfield and Zac Robinson, giving them my two cents on what they needed to work on to impress NFL scouts. Colt was inquisitive and asked good questions. It was clear that he had high expectations for himself. He wanted to know how he could get better and what he needed to work on. I appreciated that attitude and constantly pushed him to improve his skill set at the quarterback position.

Without getting too technical, I helped Colt refine his throwing motion to make him even more efficient. I'm a big believer that quarterbacks have to be more "compact" in everything they do in the NFL, meaning they have to play in tight spaces. In college, Colt, Sam, and Tim usually threw to open receivers who were easy to find because of good separation.

In the pros, however, there is almost *always* tight coverage. They'll have a split second to get the ball in there, and they'll have to learn to throw the ball very accurately into tighter windows as well as make throws from what I call "cluttered quarters." To do that, they'll have to be more compact in their footwork as well as their upper body mechanics.

I told Colt that I thought he used a lot of arm and not enough body to throw the ball, which I identified through film and through watching him in action. He really was only using 60 to 70 percent of his strength when he threw the ball, so that tells me he has a lot more in the tank than he's ever shown. I was just helping him unleash more of his talent when he throws the football, which was something I had to do when I got drafted. I wish I had worked harder on my mechanics earlier in my career.

I haven't worked with Sam or Tim, but if the Three QBs were sitting in my living room, the best advice I would share about entering the NFL is this: *Understand the magnitude of the position.* While many agree with me that the quarterback plays the most important position in sports, I would also argue that playing quarterback is the most *influential* position in all of sports.

Think about it. The way you play and approach the position impacts so many people beyond your immediate sphere of influence—your teammates, your coaches, and your family. The way you play can affect an entire city and even several states, sending shock waves across the country—but the way you play also affects people you never think about. Maybe it's the secretary in the team's front office, the single-parent mom with two kids. If you don't play well and the general manager gets fired, she's going to lose her job, too. That's a small example, but understanding the magnitude of the quarterback position will heighten your awareness and propel you to properly handle your business.

I must also remind you that there are very few things that translate from the college game to the NFL when playing the quarterback position. You will have to relearn a lot of things from a fundamental standpoint, from a technical standpoint, and even from a leadership standpoint with the older athletes—some in their 30s—in your locker room.

You're young rookie players who need to focus on the education of the position and learning what successful quarterbacks do. You'll have to improve. You'll have to do a lot of work to get better while keeping that constant motivation, so think of every day as an opportunity to get better. When I came into the NFL, I thought this was a talent-driven league. It's not. It's a craft-driven league. You have to maximize your talent by honing your craft, and for a quarterback, that means working on your mechanics all the time.

Sam, you're in a unique position as the No. 1 draft pick in the 2010 NFL draft. I would find a big Post-It note and write the following words: *Earn it.* Then I'd stick that note on a mirror in your bedroom or bathroom.

When Peyton Manning signed a seven-year contract worth $98 million in 2004, he was asked at a press conference, "What are you going to do with the money?"

Peyton glared back at the reporter with the same icy determination he displays with a fourth-and-two call. "I'm going to earn it," he announced, adding that is how he has always felt about the money he makes as an athlete.

That's the perspective you need to have as the No. 1 draft pick with a big contract—a constant motivation to earn your salary, earn the respect of your teammates, and earn victories. Keep working at your craft, and keep getting better and better every day. *Earn it.*

Tim, I'll start by saying that I'm rooting for you as much as anybody. You are a unique individual with leadership skills that are God-given and not from man. I know you've been working hard on your fundamentals and focusing on improving your throwing motion. Continue to educate yourself about what successful quarterbacks do and retrain your quarterbacking instincts.

Colt, as I told you in Southern California, it's not how you start but how you finish. Where you got drafted has very few ramifications for your long-term success. I think you went to a great spot with the Cleveland Browns. You'll be developed. You'll be handled properly. You won't be rushed into playing.

Congratulations on your marriage to Rachel just before the start of your first season with the Browns. I was married my rookie year, so I think it's a good thing. One of the challenges you will have as a young player in this league, and this goes for all three of you, is that you'll be on an emotional roller coaster. It's easy to say that you're not going to listen to all the outside voices, especially from the media and bloggers, but it's hard not to do. Because of that, it's hard to stay on an even keel emotionally.

I think being married and embracing your marriage relationship and trusting Rachel as your best friend will be very helpful because there will be some dark moments. It's comforting to share those dark moments with someone you know intimately, and obviously Rachel is that person for you.

Finally, I know all three of you are aware of this, but I would urge you to get hooked up spiritually with like-minded people. Iron sharpens iron. Growing in your faith is ultimately more important than growing as a player.

Anyone who tells you that growing spiritually will translate into on-the-field success isn't telling you the truth. That's not what the Bible teaches. God doesn't say, *If you follow Me, you're going to be successful on the football field.*

Instead, we're all called to grow in our faith, to mature in God's grace, no matter what our profession or calling is—NFL quarterback, corporate executive, department store cashier, parking lot attendant, student . . . whatever.

Sam, Colt, and Tim, I'm sure you'll do great. I can't wait to watch what unfolds from my chair inside the ESPN studios.

ACKNOWLEDGMENTS

I have to admit I didn't know that much about Sam Bradford, Colt McCoy, and Tim Tebow when I started writing *Playing with Purpose*. That's because I live in San Diego, and while I love college football—during the 2009 season, I witnessed games in South Bend, Indiana (Notre Dame versus Michigan State); Corvallis, Oregon (Oregon State versus Arizona); Berkeley, California (Oregon State versus Cal); and Los Angeles (Oregon State versus USC) *and* the 2010 Rose Bowl (Oregon versus Ohio State)—I think you can understand why I view myself as a Pac-10 guy. After all, I've lived much of my life on the West Coast, graduated from the University of Oregon, and like following the Oregon State Beavers because head coach Mike Riley used to coach my hometown NFL team, the San Diego Chargers. His wife, Dee Riley, is great friends with my wife, Nicole, and we were in a couples' Bible study with the Rileys.

As I began researching and talking to people acquainted with the Three QBs, I quickly realized that those who have known these three young men since their high school and college days had wide grins on their faces. The phrase I kept hearing and reading about each of them was, "He's the real deal." They all know the Three QBs as young men who have "run with perseverance the race marked out for [them]," as Hebrews 12:1–2 says, fixing their eyes on "Jesus, the author and perfecter of [their] faith."

David Wheaton, author of *University of Destruction*, said research shows that 50 percent of young Christians who go to college end up losing their faith—or at least make it a low priority—by the time they graduate. Not so with these three young men. In fact, if anything, they became bolder about proclaiming their faith while they were on their college campuses.

Check out the terrific *I Am Second* videos Sam and Colt have posted on the Internet (just type "I Am Second" into your Web browser); they are very moving and well produced. Tim Tebow has been standing up before audiences and preaching since he was a teenager, and that boldness carried right through his college career. Don't be surprised if, when his football career is over, Tim begins sharing the gospel message in stadiums, schools, and prisons here in the United States and around the world.

So the first people I want to acknowledge are Kent and Martha Bradford, Brad and Debra McCoy, and Bob and Pam Tebow. Your boys wouldn't be where they are today without your guiding hands, measured discipline, and instillation of godly values.

Well done, good and faithful servants.

The idea for *Playing with Purpose* came from my literary agent, Greg Johnson of WordServe Literary Group in Denver, Colorado—which is ironic since he now has a front-row seat for Tebowmania in the Rockies. Throughout the winter of 2010, Greg kept pitching to me the idea of writing a book about these three young quarterbacks. I hesitated at first, but then something clicked, and after I put together a proposal, Greg found Barbour Books within a week. My editing team at Barbour, Paul K. Muckley and Tracy M. Sumner, were great to work with. Thanks for the partnership!

Writing this book was like running the two-minute offense without any time-outs—I didn't have much time and the clock was running. Jill Ewert, editor of *Sharing the Victory* magazine, gave me her insights. Kent Bowles and Reagan Lambert of Fellowship for Christian Athletes at Oklahoma and Texas, respectively, pointed me in the right direction. Patina Herrington, whose husband suffered a grand mal seizure and was rescued by Colt, told me their story and read chapters as I finished them.

And finally, I'd like to thank my wife, Nicole, who did tape transcriptions and edited chapters as I wrote them. For someone who grew up in Switzerland and doesn't know an onside kick from a field goal, she did an awfully good job helping me out on a football book.

PLAYING

WITH

PURPOSE

Inside the Lives and Faith
of Top NBA Stars—
Including Jeremy Lin, Kevin Durant,
Kyle Korver, and more!

MIKE YORKEY

CONTENTS

FOREWORD

BY ERNIE JOHNSON,
HOST OF TNT'S *INSIDE THE NBA*

Back during the 1990s, the New York Knicks and Indiana Pacers were perennial playoff teams that developed quite a rivalry. Who can forget the feud between Pacers guard Reggie Miller and Knicks fan Spike Lee, who, from his courtside seat, gave Miller the business and then some?

The two teams grew to really dislike each other, and our TNT analysts, Charles Barkley and Kenny Smith, certainly had enough to talk about whenever the Knicks and Pacers squared off in the playoffs. With no love lost between two teams fighting over the same bone, their playoff series made for great television.

One time, either in 1999 or 2000, the Knicks and the Pacers were battling it out in the Eastern Conference finals. There was a day off between games, and the Knicks were staying in the same hotel as the TNT crew. I ran into Knicks guard Allan Houston in the lobby, and we were talking about some of the crazy things happening on the court when he casually mentioned, "A few of us are going to get together and have a little Bible study and get into the Word."

"Wow," I said. "Can I get in there, too?"

You see, a couple of years before, I had realized something major was missing in my life—a relationship with Jesus Christ. For forty-one years, my life had been all about me. Everything was in place: I had a great wife, Cheryl, four happy kids who gave me great joy, and a TV career in full ascendancy. I was living a performance-driven life as studio host for TNT Sports, quarterbacking coverage of the NBA, NFL, and Wimbledon tennis. My identity was tied up in what I did. You might as well have stamped a red TNT logo on my forehead—or "E.J."

But since everything was always about me, I was growing weary.

At a critical time in my life, a good friend came alongside me and explained that everything *doesn't* revolve around my existence—that there was more to life. He talked about God having a plan for me and how much He loves me. I had never really explored a personal relationship with Jesus Christ, so this was a revolutionary idea for me. I mean, I always knew God was there, and I knew Jesus Christ was there—but I had never put the two together.

When I heard that Jesus was holding out His hand, saying, "Come to Me, all you who are weary and burdened, and I will give you rest," I grasped that hand. Oh, how I needed rest. Oh, how I needed that peace.

So when Allan Houston mentioned a Bible study during that off day, I invited myself in a New York minute.

Allan smiled and answered, "Sure, you can join us."

A couple of hours later, Allan, two or three other Knicks players, and a couple of people from the New York front office got together in one of the team's meeting rooms. We circled up the chairs and dove into God's Word, and we had an awesome time.

Impromptu Bible studies like that built my faith, and I certainly needed that spiritual foundation when I faced a personal crisis a few years later. In 2003, I was diagnosed with non-Hodgkin's lymphoma, a low-grade and treatable cancer. My oncologist recommended that we "watch and wait," meaning we would monitor my condition with checkups every four months with the option to begin treatment if and when I began showing symptoms of the illness.

Then, in late 2005, a lymph node near my left ear began swelling. That became noticeable to TNT viewers and prompted questions about my health. Now it was time to take more aggressive treatment measures. Beginning in June 2006, I skipped my usual summer responsibilities and submitted to six chemotherapy treatments. In my official press release, I noted that my family and I "continue, as we always have, in both good times and bad, to place our faith in Jesus Christ, and to trust God . . . period."

One of the good things about the chemotherapy treatments, besides the fact that they saved my life, was that I became just as bald as Sir Charles and Kenny the Jet. Then the cancer went into remission and my hair and eyebrows grew back.

When people ask me, "How did you get through that?" I repeat what I said in my press release: "Trust God . . . period," not "Trust God if this next test comes back the way I want it to . . . period."

I'm thanking God I'm still here. The 2012–13 NBA season will be my twenty-third on TNT. People often ask me how the professional game has changed over the years, and I like to quip that there are still five guys to a side and whoever scores the most points still wins. The game of basketball still captivates, still stirs our passions.

We have some wonderful Christian players, coaches, and front-office people in the NBA today, and you're going to read about some of them in this book. I think it takes a special guy to make a decision for Christ and continue to live for Him as an NBA player. That's because these professional athletes face so many temptations. Most professional basketball players are in their twenties, and the best advice I can give them—based on my long experience with life and the NBA—is to ask themselves, *How did I get here?*

I would advise them to look at the talents they have and ask these questions: Where did your talents come from? Who gave you the opportunity to develop them? Who gave you the ability to jump up and touch the top of the backboard? Were special people put into your life at just the right time to mold you, shape you, and lift your game to the NBA level?

Those kinds of questions are important no matter who you are or what you do. Who gave you your business acumen? Who gave you the ability to communicate? Who gave you the ability to lead others? And who gave you the ability to complete a variety of different tasks on time and on budget?

I understand that it's God who has given me the talent to broadcast live sporting events and host studio shows that require me to think on my feet, provide thoughtful analysis, ask interesting questions, and move in and out of commercials. And it's always live TV, where slip-ups aren't tolerated.

I know who gave me the talent to do what I do—the Lord. I've seen time and time again how He uses me in ways I never thought possible. One example took place during the 2007 NBA All-Star weekend in Las Vegas, Nevada. It was just a few months after I returned to the air following my chemotherapy treatments, and I was asked to emcee an Athletes in Action All-Star breakfast. The organizers asked me to deliver a speech, and I woke up the morning of the breakfast really wrestling with what I should say. I mapped my talk with a few notes in my hotel room, but as the start of the program neared, I still wasn't sure what I would share with those in attendance.

After I was introduced, I welcomed the guests and thanked them for making time that morning to be with us for such a worthy cause. But in the back of my mind, I was thinking, *Where am I going to go now?* When I opened my mouth, though, God gave me the right words to say.

"Has your life been touched by cancer?" I began. "Has your family's life been touched by cancer? You have a Friend. This is my cancer story."

I've heard from hundreds of people that my eight-minute talk was powerful and from the heart. (You can watch it on YouTube by typing in "Ernie Johnson cancer.") It was like God put His hand on my shoulder and said, "Stick with Me, kid. I'll get you through this."

God, through His Son, Jesus Christ, is the One who created us and gave each of us unique gifts that make us part of the body of believers. If you keep that in mind, it keeps you centered and balanced. It keeps you from thinking about what a great guy or great gal you are. Instead, it keeps you—and me—focused on God and leaves you with this thought: *Wow, what a great God I have who has given me all these talents.*

The players and other people you are going to read about know exactly where their talent came from, which is why they are "playing with purpose."

INTRODUCTION

IT'S NOT AN EASY GIG, PLAYING IN THE NBA

The year was 1993, and I (Mike Yorkey) was in my seventh year as editor of *Focus on the Family* magazine, the monthly periodical published by the Christian ministry founded by Dr. James Dobson.

The early '90s were great years to be the editor of a national magazine with a circulation in the millions. Something called the "Internet" was still the province of nerds on college campuses, so the terms *e-mail*, *websites*, *Google search*, and especially *LOL* were still unknown in the culture. When two and a half million copies of *Focus on the Family* magazine landed in people's homes every month, they got read—as long as that month's issue included compelling stories, helpful how-to articles, and emotional heart-tuggers.

In early 1993, I had a brainstorm for what I thought was a great idea: feature three young men in their twenties who were "willing to wait"—wait until marriage to have sex, that is. I wanted to explore how these guys were able to hold themselves back from the super-strong urge to get physical in a permissive society where the barriers to premarital sex were practically nonexistent. Why were they *not* doing it when probably everyone they knew *was*? What safeguards did they equip themselves with to prevent their motors from overheating?

I discussed my idea with the editorial team, and I received nothing but thumbs up. Now came the hard part: finding three good-looking, cool, hip men in their twenties willing to tell five million readers they were virgins. And I wanted to give the story some added cachet, so I decided one of the three had to be a celebrity, someone in the public eye.

At Focus on the Family, we generally worked on our articles two to three months in advance of the magazine's release. This planning session took place toward the end of February, which meant our story wouldn't be published until June at the earliest.

June . . . that's baseball season. *Our celebrity could be a baseball player*, I thought. I figured there had to be someone in Major League Baseball who followed God's Word regarding premarital sexual behavior. And with twenty-eight major league teams (this was before the Tampa Bay Rays and Arizona Diamondbacks joined the game) each sporting a twenty-five-man roster, I had a pool of seven hundred players to contact. I figured that if even half were married, there had to be at least one virgin among the never-married players who'd be willing to make a public stand.

I worked my Rolodex—yes, we still had those desktop rotary card indexes in those pre-smartphone days—and started dialing my contacts. After a week of putting out feelers, I came up with zilch. "Forget it," said one contact. "There are no virgins in Major League Baseball."

Maybe, maybe not, I thought. But as each lead proved fruitless, I had a sinking feeling I wouldn't find that special person I was looking for.

One day, I discussed my problem with Gary Lydic, a colleague at Focus on the Family. I explained who I was looking for—a Christian athlete who'd be willing to tell the world he was willing to wait. The sport didn't matter.

Among his other duties, Gary ran the annual Focus on the Family summer basketball camps. I had played in early morning pickup games with Gary and Dr. Dobson—more on that later—back when the ministry was headquartered in Arcadia, California. Gary was crazy about basketball as well as a great shooter with a velvet touch. I was sure he'd have some ideas for me.

Gary asked me if he could think about it, and the next day he called. "A.C. Green is your guy," he said. "He's the one you want to speak to."

I knew who A.C. Green was. I had grown up in Southern California and been a lifelong Lakers fan, starting with the Jerry West and Elgin Baylor days to the championship teams of Wilt Chamberlain and Magic Johnson. A.C. Green, who played on three Lakers championship teams, was one of those solid players every team needs—not a superstar but a star performer who plays defense and sweeps the boards. He was a power forward who played both ends of the court.

"How do I get hold of him?" I asked Gary.

"Call the Lakers and ask for the media relations department," he said. That meant dialing 411 for information, then calling the Lakers. I figured that if I got to talk to a live voice, I'd probably get shuffled around.

I was looking at the local newspaper over lunchtime when I noticed that the Lakers would be in Denver the *very next night* to play the Nuggets. I was in luck, since the Lakers came to Denver only twice a year. Colorado Springs, by then the home of Focus on the Family headquarters, was only seventy miles south of Denver, a straight shot north on Interstate 25.

When I called the Nuggets front office, I was immediately put through to the media relations department. I explained who I was and why I was requesting a press pass, which would allow me access to the Lakers locker room after the game. "No problem, sir," said the young man helping me. "Your media pass will be waiting for you at Will Call."

I couldn't remember who won this unremarkable midseason game between two sub-.500 teams, but thanks to the Internet, I found out that the Nuggets had beaten the Lakers 127–115 on March 2, 1993.

When the Lakers locker room was opened to the media after the game, just one reporter and I walked into a tomb-like space. The locker room was quiet because the Lakers had lost but also because Magic Johnson was gone. I still remember where I was on November 7, 1991—riding in my car in downtown Colorado Springs—when I heard the announcement over the radio that Magic had been diagnosed HIV-positive and was retiring from pro basketball. He was the first sports superstar to announce that he was HIV-positive, and that created quite a stir and remained a big story throughout the early 1990s.

Magic said that he had contracted the virus as a result of having multiple sex partners over the years, adding that he didn't know from whom he contracted the virus or how long he had been infected.

As I moved about the locker room, I saw the Lakers' biggest star, James Worthy, lying buck naked on a trainer's table, getting rubbed down, while players like Vlade Divac and Byron Scott filtered in and out of the shower. We were still a few years away from the Kobe and Shaq era.

I approached my quarry, A.C. Green, as he was toweling off after his post-game shower. After introducing myself and holding up a recent copy of *Focus on the Family* magazine, I held up a mini-cassette recorder—A.C. was 6 feet, 9 inches tall—and asked him if he knew of Dr. Dobson.

A.C. looked at me warily. This wasn't the sort of question he usually received during post-game interviews.

"Yeah, I've heard of him," A.C. answered.

"Well, we're doing a story on guys who are willing to wait—willing to wait until marriage to have sex."

A.C.'s eyebrows peaked. I had his attention now.

"Is that something important to you—abstinence?" I asked.

"Oh yes, that's something I talk about to kids all the time."

I had heard that A.C., who didn't hide his Christian faith under a bushel basket, hoped to become a preacher or a speaker when his playing days were over.

"But what does abstinence mean to *you*?" I probed.

"Oh, it's really important. I tell kids that abstinence works every time it's tried. Condoms aren't as successful as many would have you believe. Putting a condom on won't make you as secure as Fort Knox. Condoms have a hard enough time just stopping a woman from getting pregnant, let alone blocking the HIV virus. It's like water going through a net."

The way A.C. warmed to the subject matter told me that he had spoken a few times on this topic.

"But what does abstinence mean to *you*—in your life?" I wanted A.C. to talk about abstinence in personal terms, not just as something good and healthy for kids to practice.

A.C. skirted the question again and talked about how abstinence prevents unwanted pregnancy and helps stop the cycle of single-parent poverty.

When he was done, I made a show of clicking off the tape recorder and lowering my arm. "Sorry, A.C., but I kind of need to know something."

"What's that?"

"I need to know whether you're a virgin or not for this story."

A.C. looked me in the eyes and shrugged his shoulders. "Yeah, I am," he said matter-of-factly.

"Would you be willing to say that in *Focus on the Family* magazine?"

"Sure." This time A.C. didn't hesitate.

I explained how the process would work. I would interview him a little longer, and then I would write a story for him in the first person—as if *he* was the one who had written the article. Then I'd send him the article so he could make sure everything was expressed the way he wanted.

"Sounds great to me," A.C. said.

The Lakers forward gave me a great interview, and I returned to Colorado Springs and began writing right away. A few days later, I faxed a thousand-word story to the Lakers' team hotel in Philadelphia. When A.C. called me later, he made very few changes.

Here's an excerpt of what he had to say:

> *As a professional athlete, I have to deal with groupies in many cities. It seems as though my teammates and I are often confronted by young women wanting to meet us from the time we arrive to the time we depart. They hang out everywhere—airports, hotel lobbies, restaurants, and sports arenas—always trying to catch our eyes.*
>
> *Not many resist their advances. I don't know how many virgins there are in the NBA, but you can probably count them on one hand. Pro basketball players have this larger-than-life image, and it doesn't help when a former player such as a Wilt Chamberlain boasts about bedding twenty thousand women in his lifetime.*
>
> *While I've remained sexually pure, I still hear the locker room talk about the latest sexual conquests. But I don't let that weaken my resolve because I have chosen to follow God's standard. I've communicated my stand to my teammates. Some—in a humorous vein—have threatened to set me up with women who would make themselves available to me. "Let's see how strong you really are," they joke.*

We put a warm, engaging, close-up picture of A.C. hugging a leather NBA basketball on the cover of the June 1993 issue, and we got great responses to the story. In fact, the A.C.-Green-is-a-virgin story seemed to grow legs of its own, as other national magazines and big-city newspapers published their own articles about A.C.'s amazing decision.

Imagine that—being an NBA player, single to boot, and choosing not to have sex!

In 1999, after fifteen seasons in the NBA, A.C. received another shot of publicity as he neared the record for playing the most professional basketball games without a miss—1,041, set by Ron Boone, who established the record playing in the American Basketball Association and the NBA. He was about to become the Cal Ripken of his sport.

But as *Sports Illustrated*'s Rick Reilly pointed out, there was a much more impressive streak that A.C. had put together—remaining a virgin for thirty-six years.

"The NBA Player Who Never Scored" was the title of Reilly's column, and it was very complimentary and in good fun, which was nice to see in a national magazine. Here are some hilarious quips from a clever writer:

- "He's still as pure as a baby's sneeze."
- "He has lugged his morals in and out of every Hyatt from Sodom to Gomorrah."
- "Not only is Green perhaps the only adult virgin in the Los Angeles Basin, but he's kept his virginity while working in the NBA—the world's oldest permanent floating orgy! I mean, if you were trying to lose weight, would you spend fifteen years working at Häagen-Dazs? If you were an alcoholic, would you marry a Seagram's heir?"

A.C. played one more season in the NBA, extending his league record for consecutive games played to 1,192 before he retired following the 2000–01 season. He left behind a wonderful legacy.

When *Sports Illustrated* published its once-a-year "Where Are They Now?" issue in the summer of 2008, an article about him stated that when people heard the name A.C. Green, the word that sprung to mind most often, seven years after his retirement, was one not often associated with pro athletes: *virgin*.

"I love that people remember me for that," A.C. said. "I took a stand, and I was a voice for a generation. I'm proud of that."

MAKING A DIFFERENCE

A.C. Green's days as an NBA basketball player have been over for more than a decade, but his boldness in speaking up for biblical values means he was playing with purpose during all those years he chased loose balls and grabbed rebounds. Today, there are dozens of NBA players following in A.C.'s footsteps—trying to make a difference in the lives of those around them and in the lives of the fans looking on.

I'll be telling you about some of those players (and some other important people in the NBA) in *Playing with Purpose: Basketball*. They've agreed to share their stories because, like A.C. Green, they want their playing careers to count for something more than championship rings, individual awards, and hefty paychecks.

It's not an easy gig, playing in the NBA. The 82-game regular season schedule has players bouncing from city to city like a pinball. The physical strain of playing on back-to-back nights in different cities fatigues the legs and zaps the desire to perform at the highest level. Even the best-conditioned athletes find they must pace themselves during the season—even during games—so they have something in reserve for a fourth-quarter rally.

I would argue that Christian hoopsters have it even tougher in the NBA because of temptations that bombard them daily. They are regularly presented with every opportunity to turn *away* from Christ and *toward* themselves and the world.

These NBA players who follow Christ face challenges and temptations most of us can't even begin to understand. They have money and lots of free time on their hands . . . and they have flocks of women hoping to catch their eyes in hotel lobbies, restaurants, and bars.

The women are attractive and dressed provocatively, and they flirt like schoolgirls as they give the players their "come-hither" gazes. Some, unfortunately, are just looking to get pregnant by an NBA player. They see having an NBA star's child out of wedlock as a fast-track ticket to child-support payments that begin in the five figures and can rise to sums of $75,000 *a month*. The number of children NBA players father outside of marriage is staggering—and commonplace in other professional sports, too. Child-support payments are some athletes' single biggest expense.

One of the players featured in this book told me the NBA has sent representatives out to talk to players about how to be "careful."

"They basically told us how to cheat and get away with it," he said. "It was pretty crazy. They told us to get a prepaid cell phone not registered in our name and not to leave any phone or text messages. They reminded us that if you have unprotected sex and knock up a girl, there are consequences, especially in New York City, where the state of New York will hit you with an alimony bill of $75,000 a month if you make the league average of $5 million. They reminded us that there are girls out for your money, so take precautions."

"Most people forget that we're talking about kids in their early twenties," said Jeff Ryan, the chaplain for the Orlando Magic. "If you can remember your early twenties, and I can remember mine, you don't always make the right choices. I was fortunate that I didn't have the temptations that these guys have. Remember, they are targeted. Some handle it well, and some don't. Unfortunately, there are plenty of guys who get caught up in the women thing and get their heads turned. They come into the league with the best of intentions, wanting to be faithful, wanting to be strong, but they give in to temptation. It's like my doctor telling me what I shouldn't eat. Once in a while I'm going to have it anyway. I think that's what happens to a lot of these guys. They know they shouldn't, but they give in."

Despite the threat of paternity suits, sexually transmitted diseases, and the emptiness associated with love-'em-and-leave-'em one-night stands, the easy availability of women sends many NBA players down a path "like an ox going to the slaughter, like a deer stepping into a noose," as Solomon, the wisest man who ever lived, wrote in Proverbs 7:22. We need to pray for those in the NBA who are staying strong—the A.C. Greens of today—as well as for those who know or have heard the Truth but are now living prodigal lives.

That's why I've written this book. Sure, I want to give you—the reader—interesting stories about some of the people in the NBA who are "playing with purpose" (or helping others to play with purpose). But I also want to give you the opportunity to support these talented athletes as they work to make their NBA careers a platform for taking the message of Jesus Christ to their teammates and the world around them.

Because as big and strong as they are on the basketball court, they need to be even *stronger* off the court.

1

DR. JAMES NAISMITH:
INVENTING WITH PURPOSE

The man who invented the game of basketball embraced Jesus Christ.

That's right. Dr. James Naismith, basketball's founder, was also a Christian theologian who invented the game more than a century ago as a way to reconcile his love of sports with Christian integrity.

Dr. Naismith had an amazing backstory that shows the hand of God directing his path. Born in 1861 near Almonte, Ontario, in Canada, James was the eldest son of Scottish immigrants John and Margaret Naismith. At the age of eight, James moved with his family to Grand-Calumet, Quebec, where his father began working as a sawhand at a lumber mill. The young boy would discover tragedy a year later when his parents both contracted typhoid fever. They died within three weeks of each other, leaving James and three younger siblings as orphans.

The reeling children were taken in by a godly grandmother who lived in the east Ontario village of Bennies Corners, but then *she* died two years later. A bachelor uncle, Peter Young, gave them a home, but he was an authoritarian type who kept James busy around the farm and working in the woods. Young taught the boy how to chop trees, saw logs, and drive horses. His stern uncle put great stock in reliability and self-reliance, and he raised James and his siblings in God's Word.

James attended grade school in a one-room schoolhouse. The walk from the farm to school was five miles—and yes, the Canadian lad walked through snowdrifts in winter. James wasn't a great student but showed excellent hand-eye coordination and athletic skill. During the winter, his favorite activities were snowshoeing, skating, ice hockey, and tobogganing.

After the snow melted, James loved playing a simple children's game known as "duck on a rock." Players formed a line at a distance of fifteen to twenty feet from a base stone. Atop the stone was placed a smaller drake stone—otherwise known as the "duck." Each player would toss a fist-sized stone toward the "duck," attempting to knock the rock from its perch. Players found that the best way to play "duck on a rock" was to lob a soft shot rather than making a straight, hard throw. That's because if they missed, they had to retrieve their rock to stay in the game. So players found it better to throw their stones in an arc, a discovery that later proved essential in James' invention of basketball.

James attended Ontario's Almonte High School for two years but dropped out to work as a logger in a lumber camp so he could help support his younger siblings. Life as a lumberjack meant hard—and dangerous—work. Then, at nineteen years of age, a random exchange altered the course of James' life. Here's the story:

James walked into a crowded bar and ordered a whiskey from the barkeep. A man standing at the bar, cap pulled low over his eyes, spoke to the young man without turning his head.

"Ye're Margaret Young's son, aren't ye?" he asked, using James' mother's maiden name.

"Aye," Naismith replied, reaching for his tumbler of whiskey.

"She'd turn over in her grave to see ye."

Naismith set the whiskey down—never to drink again. The story goes that he made a vow that night never again to do anything he knew would make his mother ashamed of him.

James realized that education was his only way out of a life of backbreaking, dangerous manual labor. He returned to high school, where a teacher named Thomas B. Caswell took an interest in his welfare and tutored him in reading, writing, arithmetic, Latin, and other subjects.

Naismith turned out to be a late bloomer academically, graduating from high school when he was twenty-one years old. After graduation, he immediately enrolled at McGill University in Montreal, where he was a rare four-sport athlete, competing in football, lacrosse, gymnastics, and rugby. James was a tough and durable athlete who rarely missed a game, match, or meet.

Naismith planned to go into the ministry, based upon his ideal for Christian service and honoring the memory of his mother. But many of his fellow students openly wondered how a future "man of the cloth" could justify his participation on football and rugby teams that attracted such bullies and brutes. Rugby and football—especially in those pre-Leatherheads days—were rough-and-tumble sports. Think *Gladiator* without the swords.

In the 1880s, many Christians believed that athletics were not only a waste of time but also a "tool of the devil." A group of James' friends—as well as his sister Annie—even met to pray for his soul. When Annie confronted her brother about his involvement in athletics, she cited Luke 9:62 ("Jesus replied, 'No one who puts a hand to the plow and looks back is fit for service in the kingdom of God' ") as biblical proof that James should be in the pulpit, not the play yard.

Naismith didn't see things that way, though. In fact, this offspring of Scottish parents was a forerunner of Eric Liddell, the early twentieth-century Scottish athlete featured in the movie *Chariots of Fire*. Liddell said he could feel God's pleasure when he was sprinting because he was truly using the gifts God had given him. (By the way, Liddell also played the "brutish" game of rugby and later served as a Christian missionary to China.)

Naismith viewed athletics as a ministry and a way to impact others for Christ, a position that was strengthened after a telling incident involving a teammate on the rugby team. One time at practice, the teammate blurted a curse word in frustration. He looked up and noticed James had been within earshot. He knew of James' faith in Christ, and he immediately apologized to him.

"Sorry about that, Jim," said the offending player. "Forgot you were here."

Naismith had heard much worse language when he worked in the lumber camps, but on that day he realized that a righteous man could have an incredible impact on the athletic field, which, in those days, was mainly populated by ruffians.

After earning his bachelor's degree in physical education, Naismith stayed at McGill University and enrolled at Presbyterian College, McGill's theological school on the university campus, to earn his divinity degree. He kept playing on the football and rugby teams, which prompted more mumbling from Annie and from his theology professors. They must have really gotten their knickers in a knot after Naismith showed up in the student pulpit one Sunday morning sporting two black eyes earned in a particularly rough rugby match against Ottawa.

Naismith could not understand why so many people believed that his studying to be a minister disqualified him from playing and enjoying athletic competition. His belief was reinforced when a man from Yale University, an American named Amos Alonzo Stagg, appeared at McGill to deliver a lecture that said, in part, that it took many of the same qualities to become a good athlete as it did to become a good Christian, including enthusiasm, perseverance, and hard work.

It all came together for Naismith. He persevered and earned his divinity degree in 1890 from Presbyterian College and then moved to the United States, where he became both a graduate student and a PE instructor at the International YMCA Training School in Springfield, Massachusetts. The YMCA, as in the Young Men's Christian Association.

The "Gay Nineties" of the late nineteenth century was a time when the C in YMCA meant something more than just another letter in a Village People song. The Young Men's *Christian* Association was founded in 1844 in London, England, by a twenty-three-year-old fellow named George Williams.

Williams was concerned about the lack of healthy activities in major cities for young men like himself, many of whom were drawn from rural areas to factory work in London during the height of the Industrial Revolution. They worked ten to twelve hours a day, six days a week in a bleak landscape of noisy factories, overcrowded tenement housing, and dangerous influences. Taverns and brothels were their only entertainment options.

Williams and eleven friends organized the first YMCA meeting as a refuge of Bible study and fellowship for young men seeking escape from the hazards of life on the London streets. The YMCA offered something unique for its time, and its openness to anyone and everyone dissipated the rigid lines separating English social classes. The goal of putting Christian principles into practice, Williams said, was achieved through developing "a healthy spirit, mind, and body." The YMCA system became known as "muscular Christianity" because it promoted the idea that a healthy body leads to a healthy Christian mind.

The YCMA concept quickly traveled across the Atlantic Ocean to North

America, and the first YMCAs were established in the United States prior to the Civil War. The local Ys broke down social barriers and brought together different church denominations in the United States. It's noteworthy that in the patriarchal society of the nineteenth century, women and children were also invited to take part in the YMCA's popular programs as well as their physical fitness classes.

It was this milieu that James Naismith became part of when he first arrived at the YMCA Training School, where he continued his athletic career by playing on the school's first football team, which was under the direction of none other than Amos Alonzo Stagg.

As a graduate student teacher, Naismith was given a group of restless college students who were taking a regular PE class during the winter quarter—presumably to burn off some energy and stay in shape until the spring lacrosse season. All students at the YMCA Training School were required to exercise for one hour a day—in keeping with the YMCA ideal—but there wasn't much for them to do during the winter other than march around the gym, perform jumping jacks, count off pushups, and do more monotonous calisthenics. These unpopular calorie-burning activities were pale substitutes for intramural football in the fall and lacrosse games in the spring.

Naismith did the best he could to keep enthusiasm high inside the school's gym that first winter. The following fall, he returned for his second year of graduate school, studying under Dr. Luther Halsey Gulick, the superintendent of physical education at the college. In one class called the Psychology of Play, Gulick stressed the need for a new indoor game that could be played during the winter months—a game that would be interesting to play and easy to learn.

As the fall semester came to a close, no one in Naismith's class had followed up on Gulick's challenge to invent such a game. Dr. Gulick pulled Naismith off to the side. He reminded James that football season was ending soon and that the young men at the YMCA Training School faced another dull winter of boring jumping jacks, uninspiring push-ups, and silly lines of leapfrog inside the gym.

"Naismith, I want you to see what you can do with those students," the superintendent said. "They need something that will appeal to their play instincts."

With those marching orders, Naismith went to work and came up with a checklist. Since the new game would be played in the winter, it had to be designed for the indoors. It also had to involve a large number of players and provide plenty of lung-burning exercise. Finally, since the game would be played in a confined space on a hardwood floor, it would have to forgo the roughness found in football, soccer, and rugby.

James also decided the sport could not be fundamentally elitist, like golf and tennis were at the time, nor could it require money for joining a country club or the purchase of expensive equipment. At its very heart, it must be a simple game—one for the masses, not just for the well-to-do.

Over the course of a couple of weeks, Naismith took a little bit of this and a little bit of that from games already in existence:

- passing—from American rugby
- the jump ball—from English rugby
- the use of a goal—from lacrosse
- the size and shape of the ball—from soccer
- and the "shooting" of the ball toward a target—from his child-hood game "duck on a rock"

Naismith approached the school janitor to ask if he could provide two eighteen-inch-square boxes to use as goals in the new game. The janitor rummaged around the storage room and found two peach baskets instead. Naismith nailed the half-bushel baskets to the lower rail of the gymnasium balcony, one at each end. The height of that lower balcony happened to be ten feet, which is where we get our ten-foot basket today. (Good thing the lower balcony wasn't *twelve* feet off the ground, or we wouldn't have the NBA Slam Dunk Contest every year.)

A man was stationed at each end of the balcony to pick the ball from the basket and put it back into play after a score. (It wasn't until a few years later that someone came up with the idea of cutting off the bottom of the peach baskets.) Naismith used a soccer ball for the game, and play involved running and passing to teammates—including the "bounce pass"—but no tackling. Dribbling was not part of the original game, but leather balls at that time weren't very symmetrical anyway, so they probably wouldn't have bounced consistently. The game's objective was for players to get the ball close enough to their elevated goal to toss it into the peach basket—and to prevent their opponents from doing the same to *their* goal.

Dr. Gulick was impressed with Naismith's new game, and he underlined the game's noble origins of fair play and no hard contact, lest a "foul" be called. He told Naismith, "The game must be kept clean. It is a perfect outrage for an institution that stands for Christian work in the community to tolerate not merely ungentlemanly treatment of guests, but slugging and that which violates the elementary principles of morals . . . therefore excuse for the rest of the year any player who is not clean in his play."

Naismith drew up thirteen original rules (see sidebar, below) and published them on January 14, 1892, in the YMCA Training School newspaper, *The Triangle*.

THE 13 RULES OF BASKETBALL by James Naismith

Author's note: This list of rules is the sturdy foundation that the game of basketball was laid upon 120 years ago. Of course, dozens of rules have been added to the game since then.

1. The ball may be thrown in any direction with one or both hands.

2. The ball may be batted in any direction with one or both hands, but never with the fist.

3. A player cannot run with the ball. The player must throw it from

the spot on which he catches it, allowance to be made for a man running at good speed.

4. The ball must be held by the hands. The arms or body must not be used for holding it.

5. No shouldering, holding, pushing, striking or tripping in any way of an opponent. The first infringement of this rule by any person shall count as a foul; the second shall disqualify him until the next goal is made or, if there was evident intent to injure the person, for the whole of the game. No substitution shall be allowed.

6. A foul is striking at the ball with the fist, violations of Rules 3 and 4 and such as described in Rule 5.

7. If either side makes three consecutive fouls, it shall count as a goal for the opponents (consecutive means without the opponents in the meantime making a foul).

8. A goal shall be made when the ball is thrown or batted from the grounds into the basket and stays there, providing those defending the goal do not touch or disturb the goal. If the ball rests on the edges, and the opponent moves the basket, it shall count as a goal.

9. When the ball goes out of bounds, it shall be thrown into the field and played by the first person touching it. In case of dispute, the umpire shall throw it straight into the field. The thrower-in is allowed five seconds. If he holds it longer, it shall go to the opponent. If any side persists in delaying the game, the umpire shall call a foul on them.

10. The umpire shall be the judge of the men and shall note the fouls and notify the referee when three consecutive fouls have been made. He shall have power to disqualify men according to Rule 5.

11. The referee shall be the judge of the ball and shall decide when the ball is in play, in bounds, to which side it belongs, and shall keep the time. He shall decide when a goal has been made and keep account of the goals, with any other duties that are usually performed by a referee.

12. The time shall be two fifteen-minute halves, with five minutes' rest between.

13. The side making the most goals in that time shall be declared the winner.

And that's how Dr. James Naismith invented basketball.

The first game was played on January 20, 1892, at the YMCA Training School between two nine-player teams. The final score was 1–0; only one goal was made, a 25-foot shot that nestled inside the peach basket. You could say the players hadn't honed their shooting touch yet.

Despite the lack of scoring, the new game was an instant success. "Basket Ball" spread across the nation like wildfire as students who learned the game from Naismith took it across the country . . . and even around the world on Christian mission trips. Dozens of YMCAs and colleges around the country jumped on the basketball bandwagon and organized teams.

One of Naismith's protégés formed the first college team at Geneva College in Beaver Falls, Pennsylvania. On April 8, 1893, Geneva defeated the New Brighton YMCA 3–0 in its first game. The first women's game was played at Smith College later that year. To this day, Geneva College is considered the birthplace of college basketball.

But this was all just the beginning. Over the coming decades, *basketball*, as the game came to be known, would change, grow, and expand into a game played all over the world and as a multi-billion-dollar enterprise.

DR. NAISMITH'S LEGACY: PLAYING THE GAME WITH PURPOSE

If you could travel back in time to January 20, 1892, and see the world's first basketball game, you'd probably see a sport that bears only a faint resemblance to the game as it is played today. On the other hand, if Dr. James Naismith could somehow appear at an NBA arena today—or even a high school or college gymnasium—he would probably have a hard time making a connection between the simple game he invented and the modern game of basketball.

There's no way Dr. Naismith could have envisioned the game of basketball as we know it today. He had no idea that the game would evolve into what it has become, just as he had no idea what kind of ball-handling, passing, and shooting skills players would develop over many decades.

It's impossible to say with certainty what parts of today's game would please Dr. Naismith and what parts would send him running to the exits. He would probably enjoy the teamwork and fundamentals, but it's probably safe to say he would have no use for the hot-dogging and showboating so many players have made a part of their game.

But we can also assume Dr. Naismith would recognize that there are young men and women today who use the game of basketball not just to enjoy the team atmosphere and the athletic competition it provides—or, in rare cases, to make a king's ransom for playing a kid's game—but also to use it as a platform to share their faith in Jesus Christ and to make a difference in the world today.

In other words, Dr. Naismith would see that there are young athletes today who really are *playing with purpose*.

And, as a man of faith in and devotion to Jesus Christ, he'd be very pleased.

2

KYLE KORVER:
THE KNOCK-DOWN SHOOTER

You probably didn't know that Kyle Korver started a fashion trend in the NBA—wearing his socks long and high.

Kyle isn't going retro and bringing back the calf-high tube socks popular in the 1970s—the big-hair days when long-limbed players wore short, tight, bun-hugging shorts that showed a lot of leg. What Kyle wears are extra-long socks that cover his *entire* lower leg, all the way up to the knee, where they meet up with his baggy shorts. Lately, though, he's been showing a little knee.

Kyle, traded to the Atlanta Hawks during the summer of 2012, was a come-off-the-bench-and-light-it-up scoring machine when he played for the Chicago Bulls from 2010 to 2012. He started pulling his socks up to his kneecaps back in college. He has kept his socks up—as well as his long-range shooting skills—throughout a solid nine-year NBA career.

Blessed with the good looks of a Hollywood leading man, Kyle has disappointed a few female fans who'd like to see his gams. One time when he was playing for the Utah Jazz, two girls brought a homemade sign to the arena that said: HEY KORVER, SHOW US SOME LEG.

So how did the socks-to-the-knees fashion statement happen?

"When I was playing at Creighton University my sophomore year, a teammate said, 'Let's wear long socks tonight,' and I was, 'Okay, let's do it,'" Kyle explained. "And then I played a good game, so I wore long socks the next time we played, tucking the top underneath my knee pads. I had another good game, so I kept wearing them. It's become such a habit that if I play basketball *without* my long socks, I feel kind of naked.

"I take a lot of grief for wearing them, however, especially on the road. Fans ride me all game long, yelling things like 'Take your tights off!' or 'Give your girlfriend her socks back!' Between that and 'Ashton Kutcher,' I hear stuff like that all game long. But it's all in good fun. I learned to block it all out a long time ago."

Since you brought up Ashton Kutcher . . .

Do you see a resemblance between Kyle's facial features—the shock of tousled brown hair falling down his forehead, the high cheekbones, and the winning smile—and the Hollywood actor best known for marrying Demi Moore, fifteen years his senior, for replacing Charlie Sheen on *Two and a Half Men*, and for hosting the MTV hidden camera/practical joke series *Punk'd*? Many do, although Kyle doesn't see much of a resemblance. The only thing he and Ashton

Kutcher have in common, he says, is that they both grew up in Iowa.

The celebrity look-alike thing is a cross Kyle must bear. He's given up telling kids on the street that he's not the Hollywood star they think he is, but if the teeny-boppers insist on the actor's autograph, he scribbles a signature on a piece of paper so they can walk away happy. "I've been called Ashton Kutcher so many times that I've stopped counting," he said. "It's not that I have anything against him, but when you hear someone yell, 'Ashton!' or 'You got punk'd!' for the fortieth game in the row, it gets pretty old."

What hasn't gotten old is seeing a high-arc jumper from beyond the three-point line whistle through the net. Kyle gets to see that a lot because he is one of the best spot-up, long-range shooters in the game today. "Shooting is what I do best," he said. "It'll always be what I do best."

Good thing, because filling up the basket is a great skill for an NBA player to have. His father, Kevin Korver, always told him, "If you can shoot, some team will need you."

As a potent perimeter threat throughout his NBA career, Kyle has made 41 percent of his three-point tries from beyond the 23-foot, 9-inch arc (22 feet from the corner sidelines) and 88 percent of his free throws. He holds the NBA season record for highest three-point shooting percentage with an amazing 53.6, set during the 2009–10 season with the Utah Jazz. He has also led the league in free throw shooting during the 2006–07 season with 91.4 percent.

Kyle was a sixth man for the Bulls—the player expected to come in cold off the bench, spell the starters, and keep the offense going. At 6 feet, 7 inches tall, he usually plays the position of shooting guard—of course—but he can also play small forward.

The key to being a great role player is knowing what your job is and not trying to be the star—a supporting role that suits Kyle well. Not only does he play tough defense, dive for loose balls, and find the open man, but he can be counted on to make the clutch shots in crunch time—which is why he's often left in the game late in the fourth quarter.

Kyle plays unselfishly and has great chemistry with his teammates, and he's one of the reasons the Chicago Bulls had such a great 2010–11 season.

There's another reason Kyle plays unselfishly, as you'll soon learn.

SPECIAL K'S

If you want a quick description of what Kyle's life was like growing up, try this: it was pretty much church and basketball. His father was a pastor, just like *his* father before him, so Kyle almost literally grew up in the church. As for the basketball side, both his parents are crazy about the game and played it at the collegiate level.

Kevin Korver was quite a player, making a name for himself in the mid-1970s at Central College in Pella, Iowa, where he twice won the Mentink Award for leadership, sportsmanship, and inspiration. His mother, Laine, was no slouch on the hardwood, either. She once scored 74 points in a high school game, and if you're wondering how that's possible in a thirty-two-minute contest, here's the explanation:

When Laine grew up in Iowa, high school girls' teams played six-on-six basketball.

Six-on-six?

"In six-on-six basketball, you don't get to cross the half-court line, so there are three players on defense and three on offense," Kyle said. "The whole goal of six-on-six basketball was to pick up the pace of the game. Mom played on the offensive side of the court, so it was three-on-three basketball. She was their main scorer, averaging something like 43 or 44 points a game her junior year. She used to put up some pretty big numbers."

Kevin and Laine met at Central College's admissions office, where they both worked. They fell in love and eventually married. Following graduation, Kevin, no doubt influenced by the career path of his father, Harold Korver, who was a minister in the Reformed Church of America, felt the Lord calling him into the ministry.

Kyle's grandfather grew up as one of eight kids on an Iowa farm during the Great Depression of the 1930s. There wasn't much food on the table during those Dust Bowl days, but somehow Harold and his family survived. Their hardscrabble existence—the family lived without electricity and indoor plumbing—shaped Harold's character. As a young man, he decided that he wanted to labor in the fields for a different kind of harvest—souls for the Kingdom. He became a church pastor in Iowa, but in 1971 he accepted the pastorate of Emmanuel Reformed Church and moved his family of five sons (Kevin was the oldest) to Paramount, California, a Los Angeles suburb.

Paramount is south of downtown Los Angeles—as in south-central LA. Back in the 1970s, Paramount was a tough, blue-collar community cut from the same tattered cloth as nearby Bellflower, Compton, Lakewood, and Lynwood. Kevin attended Paramount High School, where he was a basketball standout. Following his graduation from high school, he returned to his Iowa roots by playing for Central College, a Christian college affiliated with the Reformed Church of America. Harold Korver had graduated from Central College in 1952.

Shortly after Kevin married Laine, his father asked him to come back to Paramount to help him minister to families in a community ravaged by drugs and hopelessness. The young couple readily agreed to start their lives together in Southern California. Kevin joined his brother Ken as an assistant pastor at Emmanuel.

Kyle, the oldest of four sons, was born in 1981 in Paramount. (His brothers are named Klayton, Kaleb, and Kirk . . . as you'll see throughout this chapter, the Korver family has this *K* thing going.) The family lived in a parsonage, a church-provided home where pastors and their families live to offset the high cost of housing. "I doubt anyone knows what a parsonage is today," Kyle said, "but that was our home."

One day when Kyle was four or five years old, he watched his uncle Kris play in a high school basketball game. (Kris was fifteen years younger than his brother Kevin.) "I remember sitting in the stands, looking down on the court and thinking, *Wow, how cool would that be to be on that court in front of all these people who've come to watch me play,"* Kyle said. "I loved all the cheering, excitement, and competition. I couldn't grasp it all at that age, but there was something about basketball that made me think, *I want to be on that court someday.*"

Kyle started playing hoops at the church playground, where basketball rims and backboards had been erected over an asphalt playing surface. There were always kids to play with after school and on weekends. Kyle would practice for hours on that court, pretending he was Magic Johnson and hearing Lakers' radio announcer Chick Hearn in his mind:

Rebound from Kareem to Magic. It's a three-on-two. Magic into the middle. He's still going. Looking left . . . great fake . . . lays it up and in!

Magic yo-yoing with the ball, puts McHale into the popcorn machine, dribble drive, hangs Bird out to dry—alley-oop is good!

Magic's "Showtime" with the Lakers was in full bloom when Kyle entered elementary school. "I watched the Lakers a lot on TV during the basketball season," Kyle said. "We did not have a whole lot of money growing up, so we could never afford to go to a Lakers game. But we would watch the Lakers on TV every chance we got."

Kyle joined a basketball league in the third grade that played on Saturday mornings. Sundays were reserved for church, but that didn't mean he couldn't go out and play after the services let out. There were times when Kyle and his friends would head out to the asphalt court and play in their Sunday best, trying not to get their nice clothes dirty.

One time, Kyle was shooting baskets with two hands when his uncle Kris dropped by. "That's pretty good, but you have to pick a hand to shoot with—right or left," the elder Korver said.

Kyle was right-handed, but for some reason, he could shoot the ball farther with his left hand. After the word of advice from Uncle Kris, he started shooting with his left hand. This went on for a good year until his uncle saw him shooting jumper after jumper with his *left* hand. When Uncle Kris asked him why he was shooting left-handed, Kyle answered, "You told me to pick a hand, so I picked my left."

"Well, you're right-handed, so you should use your other hand," Uncle Kris said, knowing that Kyle would be more coordinated—and more accurate—using his dominant hand. So that's what Kyle did. But all that practicing with his left hand helped him develop greater ball-handling skills. "Even today when I pass the ball, I'm apt to do it with my left hand and not my right," he said.

Since the family lived across the street from the church, they had planted themselves into the heart of a struggling community. In 1980, Paramount residents were shocked when their community was named the fourth-worst U.S. city (with a population under fifty thousand) to live in. The negative publicity prompted the Korver pastors to launch an Emmanuel Reformed Church campaign called "Let's Get Paramount's Neighborhoods Looking Good Again."

During the campaign, every other Saturday, the church would supply a couple of hundred volunteers, and the city would provide the supplies and public works supervisors to guide the small army of workers. Together they would clean up trash, landscape yards, haul away overgrowth, and paint over graffiti. Kyle, just eight years old at the time, found out that he could be handy with a paintbrush and could also make himself useful by picking up trash.

"We transformed the entire city that summer and fall," he said. "I can remember painting over the graffiti on those walls, though, and then coming back two weeks later and seeing graffiti there again. We would paint over it a second or a third or a fourth time. Eventually, the taggers got tired of doing the graffiti because they knew we would paint over it again. People took pride in themselves and how their neighborhood looked. We saw an overall attitude change. Gangs were no longer welcome, and crime rates dropped. Sure, our helping hands, some paint, and a positive attitude helped, but it really was about love. Our church received a Point of Light Award from President Bush."

Helping out the Paramount community on Saturday mornings taught Kyle a valuable lesson: "The whole concept of serving others was ingrained into my head at a young age. I was taught by my parents that it's just what you do."

CHANGES AHEAD

While Kyle was learning about what it meant to serve others, a couple of things happened to shake up his orderly world. They both occurred when he was in the fifth grade, although at that age he wasn't able to really understand the full context of what was going on in the adult world around him.

The first incident happened on a weekday in November 1991, and Kyle remembers like it was yesterday.

"I came home from school, and Mom met me at the door," Kyle said. "She was crying. I asked what was wrong, and she explained that Magic had AIDS and couldn't play basketball anymore. I was so sad. I did not totally understand what AIDS or HIV was, but I just knew that he was really sick and would never play basketball again."

The other incident affected the community Kyle and his family lived in far more seriously. In the spring of 1992, a bystander videotaped the beating of a black motorist named Rodney King, who had been stopped following a high-speed pursuit. When an all-white jury acquitted four white police officers, the verdict provoked fury in the predominantly black neighborhoods of south-central Los Angeles. Over a six-day period, widespread looting, assault, arson, and murder erupted in the gritty urban areas that surrounded Paramount.

Kyle remembers seeing, from his bedroom window, flames and smoke rise into the sky. Storefronts were burning in Compton, which bordered Paramount, and looters ransacked retail outlets. At one point, a mob dragged a white truck driver from his vehicle and beat him severely as news helicopters circled above, recording the incident.

Soon after the riots, Kyle's father did a preaching series on the book of Jonah to encourage the congregation to be a people of faith who were willing to enter into a city that seemed to be disintegrating.

"Shortly after I preached on that topic, we received a phone call from

Iowa," Kevin said. "The Third Reformed Church in Pella asked me to become their pastor. This was totally out of the blue and threw me for such a loop that my back gave out. The anticipation all along was that we would become the senior pastor family of Emmanuel Reformed Church. Our congregation in Paramount seemed to be affirming it. This is what I knew and was trained for—inner-city ministry. And yet we were being asked to move to small, rural, and white Iowa."

Kevin and Laine were the parents of four boys, all under the age of eleven. *Is this where God wants us to move the family?* they wondered. They were happy in Paramount and committed to staying for as long as God wanted them there. But as they prayed for direction and talked to family members, they sensed the Lord leading them to Third Reformed Church in Pella, where Kevin had lived before the move to California in 1971.

"When my parents told me that we were moving, I cried for a good month," Kyle said. "I did not want to leave. I was a California kid all the way. I liked the sunshine. I liked the beach. I liked being able to shoot baskets outside year-round. I didn't even have a pair of jeans at the time. I wore shorts to school every day and took pride in that. There were a lot of reasons why we moved, but I think my dad being obedient to the Lord's leading was the main reason."

In the mid-nineteenth century, about eight hundred Dutch immigrants founded Pella, now a small city of ninety-eight hundred in central Iowa. An annual Tulip Time Festival celebrates the town's Dutch heritage, but it is better known throughout the United States as the manufacturing home of the popular Pella windows, a company a Dutch couple founded in 1925.

Is everything starting to come together here? Korver is a Dutch name, and Kyle's family heritage could be traced to the immigrants who settled in Pella in the 1800s. Pella was home to them. The Reformed Church of America, their denomination, dated back to the Dutch colonists who settled New Amsterdam—later known as New York City—in the early 1600s. Third Reformed in Pella was a megachurch with twenty-five hundred members—this in a town of barely ten thousand people.

The Korvers would go from being small fish in the big pond of Paramount to a fishbowl existence in Pella.

"We were a big part of the community in Pella, as you can imagine," Kyle said. "When we moved back just before my teenage years, I definitely found out that there is a spotlight that comes with being a PK—a preacher's kid. Everyone was watching me, and I felt like I was supposed to act in a certain way. With a lot of pressure and a lot of eyes on me, I think my family did a good job of not forcing their faith on me or saying, *You have to be this way, you have to do that, you have to uphold the standard that makes us look good.* They were never that way with me or my brothers."

Kyle said his parents were smart in the way they raised him and his brothers. Since they were at church whenever the doors were open, they knew it would be easy to burn out their kids with youth group on Wednesday nights, Sunday school, church services on Sunday morning and Sunday evening, plus the special events that find their way onto the church calendar.

"If we had been in church for five nights in a row, for example, my parents would tell us on Sunday morning, 'We'll skip Sunday school this morning and just go to church,' or 'We won't go to Sunday night service.' There would be Sundays when my father wasn't preaching, and we would all stay home and not go to church. Maybe Dad would go through a Bible story with us at breakfast or talk a little longer at lunch, but he'd let us know that we were taking a break."

One of the first things Kevin and Laine did when they moved the family back to Pella was install a basketball court in the backyard of their new home. Bringing in dirt, laying down a concrete slab, putting in a basketball standard, and erecting lights cost two thousand dollars—not a trifling sum.

Kyle's father announced at dinner one night that if the family was going to spend that much on a basketball court, they should match the amount with a gift to charity. In other words, forget about going to Disney World next summer. His parents already had the same idea in place for Christmas—whatever they spent on gifts for themselves, they gave the same amount away so that the focus wasn't all about *getting*.

The boys didn't bat an eye. "That was the mind-set in which I was raised," Kyle said. "Everything was all about supporting the Lord's work and trusting God for your future."

During his middle school years, Kyle played for a team his uncle Karl coached. Uncle Karl schooled Kyle—the former California kid who tossed no-look passes and flipped scoop shots toward the rim—on meat-and-potatoes Midwest basketball fundamentals. No Showtime in Pella.

Kyle learned how to set and use screens, break a press, and run an offense from the point guard position. Wraparound, behind-the-back passes were out; chest-high two-handed passes were in. Kyle's passing game, jump shot, and fundamentals improved quickly and raised his game several notches, which helped him make the Pella High School varsity as a sophomore. Even though he was a great player in high school—the Dutch retired his No. 25 in 2006—he wasn't heavily recruited to play college basketball.

The best basketball school that recruited Kyle was Creighton University, a Catholic institution in Omaha, Nebraska, which was just 180 miles west of Pella. Being close enough to go home on weekends to see the family and enjoy Mom's cooking was a huge draw for Kyle. Plus, his parents and brothers could come to his home games. Kyle also liked the Midwest feel of Omaha, showing that his days as a California beach boy were finally behind him. (He still streaked his hair with blond surfer-dude highlights, though.)

As for the basketball side, Creighton may not have been a big-time program like Duke or North Carolina—but it was still Division I ball in the highly competitive Missouri Valley Conference, which gave flight to Larry Bird, by the way. Larry had played at Indiana State.

Kyle played a big part in bringing Creighton back to national prominence, leading the Bluejays into the NCAA Tournament—March Madness—all four of his seasons.

The highlight was the 2002–03 season, Kyle's senior year, when the Blue-jays won 29 regular-season games. Creighton was consistently ranked in the Top 20 that season, and Kyle earned Missouri Valley Conference Most Valuable Player honors and was named an Associated Press Second Team All-American.

College basketball's three-point line was 19 feet, 9 inches from the basket when Kyle played for Creighton, and he made mincemeat of that standard. (The NCAA extended the three-point distance to 20 feet, 9 inches in 2007.) He made 371 career three-pointers at Creighton, which tied him for sixth in NCAA history, and shot 45.3 percent from long distance. In one game against Xavier, his shooting stroke accounted for *eight* three-pointers, and he hit seven in games against Notre Dame and Fresno State. Kyle was also invited to the Three-Point Shootout during the Final Four weekend, where he finished second out of eight competitors.

NBA scouts were there, notepads in hand.

As his father said, teams could always use another shooter.

A COLD DRINK AND A BOX OF DONUTS

Unlike the NFL, which constantly replenishes its teams with untested rookies drafted out of college, the NBA is more of a closed shop. It's not often that players taken after the first round of the NBA draft catch on with an NBA team. Teams can have up to fifteen players signed and practicing with them, but only twelve can suit up for games.

Kyle was an underrated player from what is considered a lesser conference going into the 2003 NBA draft. Would he go in the first round? After the end of Kyle's senior year, thirty guys crowded into his dorm room at Creighton to watch the draft unfold, ready to cheer when Kyle's name was called.

Kyle wasn't drafted in the first round, which put a damper on the party. As the second round progressed and his name was still not called, his dorm room resembled a tomb. With three draft picks left in the second round, ESPN cut to a commercial break. When NBA draft coverage resumed, Kyle's name was part of the "crawl" along the bottom of the screen. Cheers erupted! The New Jersey Nets had taken a flier on him in the second round, making him the fifty-first player picked.

Kyle began thinking how he'd get a chance to fulfill a dream that began on the asphalt courts back in Paramount, but then he learned the stunning news: after drafting him, the Nets immediately traded him to the Philadelphia 76ers—for "a cold drink and a box of donuts," he quipped.

Kyle caught on with the 76ers and showed he wasn't afraid to shoot the trey in the NBA. Early in the season, he came off the bench to connect on five-of-five three-pointers against Boston and started receiving more PT, or playing time. He was making it in the NBA. He was achieving his lifelong goal of playing before big crowds, traveling in style, staying in the best hotels, and receiving a handsome salary.

During Kyle's NBA rookie year, he was the only white player on the 76ers, so his teammates called him "Sunshine," the nickname of the long-haired white quarterback in the movie *Remember the Titans*. And as he continued to pour in jump shots from near the 76er bench, his teammates added another nickname: *Sniper*. "That was my street name, my street cred," Kyle said.

And yet, despite his acceptance, Kyle was unsettled. Something didn't feel right.

Near the end of his rookie season, Kyle woke up one morning feeling sick to his stomach. Why?

"Because I felt like I had totally missed the boat," he said. "I was like, *I am here, in the NBA. I can walk down the street and people want my autograph. I can walk into a mall, and if I see a hat or a shirt that I like, I can buy it because I have enough money. I don't have to look at the price tag.*

"These were the things that you think will make you happy. You have fame, people recognize you, people like you, people cheer for you, and I was sitting there at that moment feeling sick to my stomach. I felt that I had nothing in my life. I was wondering, *What is going on?*"

Kyle trudged from his bed to his shower. He lived in a huge apartment complex where the hot water never ran out. He stood in the shower for forty-five minutes, letting the water cascade over him as he grappled with heavy thoughts about the meaning of life and about his faith in Christ.

His faith, he knew in his gut, had been primarily based on keeping the rules, on staying within the boundaries. As long as he stayed inside the lines, he believed, he was right with God. At least that was how he had been living his life. But as he examined his soul, Kyle knew he wasn't fooling anybody. Sure, he wasn't a bad person and he wasn't doing anything illegal or crazy, but he wasn't pursuing his faith in the Lord. He had fallen into the trap of thinking that being a "good" person was enough. But it wasn't enough. God wanted his heart, soul, and mind—not his good works and his keeping a bunch of rules.

Kyle thought about how he had tried to find a good church. So far in Philadelphia, he hadn't had any luck. He quickly learned that the NBA doesn't base its weekly schedule around church and that he was much more likely to have a Sunday game (often a road game) than have Sunday off.

One Sunday, though, Kyle didn't have a game, so he decided to check out a Reformed Church that was on a list his father gave him. It was only four blocks from his apartment. One of his good friends from high school, Adam Bruckner, was living with Kyle, so off they went.

When the two young men walked into the church, the first thing Kyle saw was a huge map of Korea. Then he looked around, and all he saw were Koreans. He and Adam had walked into a Korean church! Kyle remembers how everyone welcomed him and Adam and insisted that they take a seat right up front. "I was by far the tallest man in church that day," he said. "I must have blocked people's vision for five rows behind me."

Okay, so the Korean church wasn't the right fit for him. His other attempts to find Christian fellowship in Philly had been air balls, too.

Kyle lowered himself to the shower floor as the warm water continued to wash over him. He poured out his heart to God: "Lord, I know there is more to life than this. I have seen it in my family. I have seen purpose in their lives, but basketball is not doing it for me. I need to get back on track. I may have been there at one time, but I'm not there now. I don't want this anymore. I want You to change my heart."

Then Kyle had a question burning within.

"God, why haven't You given me a church that I can regularly attend?"

Kyle sat there and cried as the water poured over his body, and then he heard a voice in the quiet of his heart.

Because you haven't asked Me.

Kyle stopped. It was true. He hadn't asked the Lord specifically for a church. So he closed his eyes and whispered this prayer: "Lord, I need a church. I need a community. I need people. I need worship. I need all these things. Please help me find a church."

And then the hot water finally ran out.

"Kind of a crazy story," Kyle said.

So what happened?

"A few days later, my roommate wanted to meet up with these girls at this bar, but I did not want to go there for a whole lot of reasons," Kyle said. "He said, 'I met this girl, and she was really cute. I need somebody to go with me.'

"'Dude, I don't want to come. I have a game tomorrow. I don't want to sit in a smoky bar.' But eventually he talked me into it. So I go, and I'm sitting in the corner watching SportsCenter when these girls walk in. The girl wasn't cute and her friends weren't cute either. They sat and immediately lit up cigarettes, which I hated. Then I saw these two guys waving me over, so I excused myself to go over and talk to them."

The three made small talk, and the two men asked Kyle where he was from. "I told them my dad was a pastor, and they said, 'We're Christians, too.' So we started sharing our faith, and we ended up praying together in that bar. Then they said I had to come to their church. It was ten miles away with about seven hundred people our age. I said, 'You have to be kidding me.' "

And that's how God answered Kyle's prayer to find a church: Calvary Fellowship in Downingtown, Pennsylvania. The church held a Sunday night service called "The Bridge," and Kyle got himself plugged in right away.

"That was huge for me," he said. "After that prayer, it was like *wham!* I had community, church, spiritual leadership, accountability—all those things. I learned that you have to ask God for the desires of your heart and that God won't give you what you don't need. He will give you what you need if you just ask for it."

COAT DRIVE

A couple of good things happened after Kyle got plugged into a new church during his second season in the NBA:

1. He won a starting position with the 76ers.
2. He collected tons of coats on behalf of something called "Operation Warm."

Operation Warm provided new winter coats to children in need. The 76ers and the NBA hosted coat drives to collect the much-needed winter clothing. Early in his second year with the 76ers, the front office asked Kyle if he wanted to be part of Operation Warm and lead the coat drive—be the public face, if you will.

"At first, I didn't want to because the player who did it the previous year went through the locker room hitting up teammates for money. He was like, 'Yo, rookie, give me two hundred bucks. I gotta buy coats for the kids.' I wanted to do more than ask my teammates for money, so I took a different approach. I had several coat drives before games and announced that anyone who brought a coat to the game could meet me, get an autograph, or have a picture taken with me. The coat drive ended up being a huge success and a really cool thing." When he was playing in Philadelphia, more than twenty-eight hundred coats were collected and given to needy families.

Operation Warm whetted Kyle's appetite to do more with his rising visibility as an NBA player. He started his own foundation—the Kyle Korver Foundation—and became its biggest donor.

Then another opportunity for ministry came his way. Here's how that happened:

"I was living downtown, and Adam and I were driving to Cavalry Fellowship, our church out in Downingtown. The trip could be an hour to three hours to get there, depending on whether there had been an Eagles game that day.

"One Sunday evening, we happened to start driving for Downingtown right after the end of an Eagles game. We were stuck in traffic for close to three hours. We were late for church, miserable, and asking ourselves, *Why are we driving to Downingtown when we live in downtown Philadelphia? How come there isn't a church we like closer to where we live?*

"So we kicked around the idea, *Why don't we start a church?* We knew what we wanted it to look like. We gave the idea some serious thought and prayer. We had a pretty strong sense from the Lord that something was going to happen.

"We talked to a bunch of people and got a small group together, and my friend Adam had run a homeless meal ministry downtown on Mondays for the last seven years. The place where he cooked his meals was called the Helping Hands Mission in North Philly. It wasn't a real good neighborhood, but that was the only place we could find to meet.

"So we started meeting there on Tuesday nights, just like a Bible study. We were sitting on the front steps of the mission one night, a bunch of us white people. The neighborhood kids came out. There was an apple tree close by, so they chucked a bunch of apples at us.

"We were trying to be good Christian people. I said, 'You guys are funny, but you better not throw any more apples in case we fire back.' I said it with a friendly smile that defused the situation. A couple of weeks later, some guys in our group were throwing around a football when the neighborhood kids came running over and wanted to play. We started playing with them, and they talked some trash and we talked some trash back, and everyone had a good time. We had such a good time that when we came back the following week an hour early, the kids wanted to come out and play football with us.

"We started to come an hour early every single week. We learned their names, talked with them, and got to know them. We cleared it with the mission to bring the kids inside, where we did crafts and shared Bible stories."

That was the modest beginning of an after-school program, which Adam runs to this day, that mentors kids, puts on basketball camps, and tutors kids with their homework—all funded through the Kyle Korver Foundation.

"We've put up some really nice goal-centered hoops with fiberglass backboards that can be cranked up from six feet to ten feet," Kyle said. "There are eighteen of them put up all over the neighborhood. We have over a hundred kids coming every week, including Muslims. It's something great to be a part of."

BASKETBALL WITHOUT BORDERS

Kyle settled nicely into a starting role with Philadelphia, but in the middle of his fifth season in the league, he was traded to the Utah Jazz. Adam Bruckner remained in Philadelphia to run the inner-city after-school program.

After learning that Kyle was a God-fearing guy with a charitable heart, the fans in Salt Lake City embraced him, but they also appreciated how the team improved after his arrival. The Jazz had a so-so 16–16 record before Kyle joined the team in late 2007, but his silky-smooth shooting helped lift the Utah Jazz from ninth place to fourth in the NBA Western Conference standings as the Jazz won 38 of its last 50 games.

The "Korver Effect," as the media called it, carried over to the young women attending the sold-out games. Masha Kirilenko, the wife of Andrei Kirilenko, one of Kyle's new teammates, owned a boutique called *Fleur de Lis*, and she made a mint selling pink "Mrs. Korver" T-shirts to smitten female fans.

Kyle took it all in stride and looked for new ways to contribute off the court. He came up with an out-of-the-box idea: support a nonprofit construction company that could build handicap ramps for people in need. He asked his brother Klayton to give him a hand with the foundation work and to oversee an initiative to build wheelchair ramps as well as perform roof repairs and landscaping. "We've built almost forty ramps in 2011, but all this stuff obviously costs money," Kyle said.

Kyle donates plenty of his own money to his foundation work, but the need is great.

"We do fund-raisers, fun things like dodgeball and kickball tournaments, but we came up with an idea for a T-shirt line to raise money for the foundation," Kyle said. "A guy hooked us up with Hurley and other companies to get us going. We came up with sixteen T-shirts with really cool designs. They have a theme to them: Strength-Love, Strength-Courage, Strength-Courage-Honor, Peace, Respect, and Knowledge. What is Strength? Strength is not being the bully of the block. It's an inner strength and an inner confidence.

"We called our company 'Seer Clothing' because a seer in the Bible is a visionary or a prophet. Our website is SeerClothing.com, and everything we make after expenses goes straight into our foundation and our causes."

Finally, there's one more Kyle Korver story that needs to be mentioned, and it's his involvement with Basketball Without Borders, a joint effort of the NBA and the International Basketball Federation (FIBA) to promote the sport and encourage positive social change in the areas of education, health, and wellness in local communities.

During the first four off-seasons of his career, Kyle has volunteered to fly to China, Brazil, South Africa, and India to promote the game by working at a basketball camp in the morning with top junior players from each country and then doing some type of community project in the afternoon.

His last trip was to India during the summer of 2008 when he joined fellow NBA players Ronny Turiaf, Pat Garrity, Linton Johnson, and a team of NBA coaches for the league's first outreach event in India.

"I love to see the world because it gives me an incredible perspective on how life is outside the United States," Kyle said. "India was an incredible experience. I saw people bathing in front of fire hydrants, eating food with flies all over it, and renting out space on sidewalks so they could sleep at night. I had seen that stuff on *National Geographic* shows before I went, but when you go there and actually talk to people in the streets, it gives you a whole new perspective on life, especially for guys in the NBA.

"I mean, we are so fortunate. It's easy to take everything for granted, but life in many parts of the world is not like it is here in the United States. Going on the Basketball Without Borders trips helps keep my heart right."

That's great to hear, but Kyle's heart has been in the right place for a long time.

2012 update: Kyle continued to pour in buckets coming off the bench for the Chicago Bulls during the lockout-shortened 2011–12 NBA season. The Bulls won 50 of 66 games, which tied Chicago with San Antonio for the league's best record. MVP winner Derrick Rose, however, suffered five injuries during the regular season plus a season-ending ACL tear just before the playoffs.

"My grandpa has a saying: 'God does His best work in life's graveyards,' " Kyle said before the playoffs. Alas, the Bulls dug themselves too deep a hole against the Philadelphia 76ers and were bounced out in the first round. Then the Bulls made a surprise move after the season by trading Kyle to the Atlanta Hawks, where he'll continue knocking down the three. He'll be joined in Atlanta by his wife, Juliet Richardson, a professional singer-songwriter whom he married in 2011.

3

ANTHONY PARKER:
TAKING HIS GAME WHERE JESUS WALKED

Like every American old enough to remember that day, Anthony Parker (not to be confused with Tony Parker, the French basketball player who plays for the San Antonio Spurs) will never forget where he was when he learned that terrorists had flown two passenger jets into the World Trade Center on September 11, 2001.

Anthony was in Tel Aviv, Israel, preparing for his second season with Maccabi Tel Aviv, one of the premier teams in European professional basketball. Around four o'clock in the afternoon (Israel is seven hours ahead of the Eastern Time Zone), Anthony was meeting his agent in Israel at a restaurant when he asked Anthony if he had heard the news about a plane hitting the World Trade Center in Manhattan.

"No, I haven't heard anything," Anthony replied. He imagined a small private plane clipping one of the Twin Towers. His mind couldn't envision anything larger than that.

Anthony returned to his Tel Aviv apartment and flicked on CNN International. As he and his wife, Tamaris, watched the events of that day live, they were horrified by the incredible sight of the mighty Twin Towers collapsing one after another into a mountainous pile of rubble, dust, and debris. What Anthony witnessed that day shook his confidence—and tangibly reminded him that he was living in a Middle Eastern country where acts of terrorism happened often and occurred without warning.

He wondered if he had done the right thing by taking his game overseas. Since America had been hit by a massive terrorist attack, was Israel next? The question rolled around in Anthony's mind, and in those first few uncertain hours after four planes were hijacked in the United States, anything seemed possible. There were anxious moments that day and evening as he and Tamy tried to call loved ones back home in the United States but found their efforts fruitless because of the jammed telephone lines.

So how did this American basketball player find himself in Tel Aviv on that fateful day?

Anthony's story begins with his father, Larry, who was a good basketball player at the University of Iowa. Larry got to know his future wife, Sara, when she played on the intramural basketball team he coached. After they fell in love and married, the young couple went into the commercial insurance business and settled in Naperville, Illinois.

A few years ago, *Money* magazine ranked Naperville, a bucolic municipality of a hundred thousand, as the second-best small city in America.

Naperville's close proximity to Chicago and its popular Riverwalk brick path, which follows the DuPage River's course through downtown, makes this upper-middle-class community a great place to raise a family.

Anthony, Larry and Sara Parker's first child, was born in 1975. Dad practically put a Nerf basketball in his hands while he was still in his crib. Before he started elementary school, young Anthony was practicing in the backyard on a Nerf basketball hoop with a picture of Julius Erving (Dr. J) on the backboard.

"My father was my main basketball influence and showed me how to play the game," Anthony said. "Dad played in men's leagues while I was growing up, and my earliest memories were going to his games, where I would run out onto the floor during halftime and try to throw the ball at the rim."

Anthony's parents were keen on his education, and the excellent Naperville school district was one reason why families flocked to live within its borders. Anthony grew like a tree sapling between his freshman and sophomore years at Naperville Central High, vaulting from 5 feet, 8 inches to 6 feet, 2 inches tall. His game also jumped by leaps and bounds, and he continued growing, reaching 6 feet, 5 inches by his senior year. He added another inch in college.

Though he was quite a player, Anthony's high school years weren't all basketball. Schoolwork and education were also important—more important than even his rising basketball skills. He excelled academically in math and science classes.

But Anthony worked hard on his game. You'd think that as a young man growing up in the Chicago area in the mid-1990s, Anthony would have idolized Michael Jordan, but he wasn't swept up by MJ fever. He was intent on honing his passing and shooting skills and becoming the *first* Anthony Parker, not the second coming of His Airness.

Anthony had the good grades and the basketball chops to play at many colleges, but he wanted to commit to a program early so that he wouldn't have to worry about losing a full-ride offer due to injury. He chose a private institution, Bradley University, because of its strong academic reputation, solid basketball tradition, and close proximity to home. Located in Peoria, Illinois, Bradley was just 150 miles from Naperville, meaning his parents would be close enough to attend most of his home games.

Larry and Sara Parker deserve a lot of credit for raising three children of accomplishment. Anthony's younger brother, Marcus, is a radiologist who graduated from Washington University in St. Louis and went on to medical school at Johns Hopkins University, where he also completed his residency. He's married and lives with his two little girls fifteen minutes from Anthony's permanent residence in Tampa, Florida.

And you may have heard of Anthony's youngest sibling, Candace. She happens to be one of the best female basketball players in the world.

BROTHER-SISTER ACT: ANTHONY AND CANDACE PARKER

She's the first Women's National Basketball Association (WNBA) player to win the Most Valuable Player crown and Rookie of the Year award in the same season. She's also the first woman to dunk in an NCAA tournament game, which she did when she was a key member of the University of Tennessee's Lady Volunteers basketball team—winner of the 2007 and 2008 NCAA championships. She's also the second woman to dunk in a WNBA game.

We're talking about Candace Parker, Anthony's little sister—although at an eye-popping 6 feet, 4 inches tall, she's not that little. Candace dominates the game in a way few women have. On any night, she can be the best scorer, best passer, best guard, best forward, best post player, and best rebounder on the floor.

She's also a great mom. Candace married Shelden Williams, a college basketball star for Duke University who has played several seasons in the NBA, and the couple welcomed a girl, Lailaa Nicole Williams, into the world in 2009. Candace took maternity leave for the entire season, but now she's back playing for the Los Angeles Sparks in the WNBA as well as a Russian team, UMMC Ekaterinburg. She can afford a nanny: the Russian team pays her a reported $1.2 million annually.

So Anthony, was there any sibling rivalry between brother and sister growing up? Did you and Candace go at each other in cutthroat one-on-one games in the family driveway?

"No, because there's an eleven-year age gap between us," he said. When Anthony left home to play for Bradley University, Candace was going into the second grade. She was still in elementary school when Anthony was a rookie with the Philadelphia 76ers.

One day Candace, who was a standout soccer and basketball player, asked her mother, "How can I live up to Anthony and Marcus? Anthony is this great basketball player, and Marcus is studying to become a doctor."

Sara smiled. "Don't worry. You can do anything you want—become a basketball player or become a doctor."

Candace chose basketball, and the rest is history.

The only brother-sister combination that compares to Team Parker is Reggie and Cheryl Miller. Some say Cheryl is the best female basketball player of all time, and Reggie was no slouch, either, playing in some memorable games with the Indiana Pacers during his storied eighteen-year pro career. Today, he works as an NBA commentator on TNT.

Which begs an intriguing question: since Anthony and Candace are ten to twenty years younger than Reggie and Cheryl Miller, how many baskets would they have to spot them in a two-on-two matchup?

FILLING A VOID

Away from home for the first time, Anthony went through a time of transition during his freshman year of college. His coach at Bradley, Jim Molinari, was a Christian, and he'd invite the team chaplain to share a devotional thought after pregame meals. Players could stay and attend, or they were free to leave. The chaplain program was part of a Campus Crusade for Christ ministry.

Anthony was intrigued enough to stick around to listen to the chaplain. He hadn't gone to church much growing up . . . his parents were Christmas-and-Easter churchgoers, so his exposure to the Gospel was limited. But Anthony felt a void in his heart, like something was missing in his life.

Sure, he was a good person who came from a good family. Sure, he had never been a problem to his parents or gone through a rebellious stage. Sure, he was respectful to his coaches and showed a willingness to work hard on the basketball floor as well as on his academic studies. The adults in his life called him a model kid.

But Anthony knew in his heart that he wasn't perfect—and that only one person who ever lived fit that description: Jesus Christ.

Anthony continued to attend team chapels and developed a friendship with the chaplain, Dick Belsley, who invited him to drop by his office so they could talk about questions he had about Christianity. They had long discussions about how God desired to have a personal relationship with Anthony, and about how believing and accepting the truth of the death and resurrection of Jesus Christ was the only way he could enter into a personal relationship with the Lord of the universe and begin his walk with God.

Eventually Anthony said yes to Jesus Christ. He didn't understand a lot about what it meant to be a Christian, but if the Lord was willing to meet him where he was, then Anthony was willing to take His hand.

Meanwhile, Anthony excelled on and off the basketball court at Bradley. While fashioning a fine four-year playing career at Bradley, which is part of the Missouri Valley Conference, he majored in chemistry his first three years before switching to liberal arts and sciences his senior year. Anthony was never an All-American player or even talked about much outside the conference, but he had an explosive first step, slashed well to the hoop, and was an efficient shooter with great mechanics. His best year was his junior season, when he averaged nearly 19 points a game and was named the Missouri Valley Conference MVP.

Even though Anthony was an excellent player, he played in a "mid-major" conference that didn't send a lot of players to the NBA. Several NBA scouts, however, saw something special in him. They liked the unselfish way he played the game, how he exhibited good court vision, and how he made everyone around him play better.

Even though he was well regarded, the Bradley product still raised a few eyebrows when the New Jersey Nets selected him with the twenty-first pick in the 1997 NBA draft. The Nets promptly traded him to the Philadelphia 76ers in a multiplayer deal. (Does this story sound familiar? That's exactly what happened to Kyle Korver, who also played for a Missouri Valley school—Creighton University—and was also drafted by the Nets, who immediately traded him to Philly.)

Although Anthony was regarded highly enough to be a first-round draft pick, he wasn't regarded highly enough to play much his first year in the NBA. He was typecast as a tenth or eleventh man who came off the bench for a few spot minutes or who got in late in the game when the outcome was decided (that's called "garbage time" in the NBA).

Anthony languished on the 76ers bench throughout his rookie season, appearing in only thirty-nine regular season contests and averaging just five minutes a game. But then again, the guy playing ahead of him—a fellow named Allen Iverson—had a way of not only sucking up all the oxygen in the room but also taking all the playing time.

Iverson, whose cornrows, tattoos, arm sleeves, and headband represented the hip-hop culture in the NBA, was the same age as Anthony but was already in his fourth season in the league when Anthony arrived. He had turned pro after his freshman year—called a "one and done"—at Georgetown University and become an NBA star overnight. Despite his diminutive size (he stands only 6 feet tall), the blazing-quick point guard scored at will and ran the show in Philadelphia.

In Philly, Allen Iverson was known as "The Answer." Anthony, on the other hand, was "The Question," as in "Would he catch on with the team?"

The answer: not for long.

Injuries and the fact that he didn't fit into the offensive scheme with Iverson around conspired against him. At 6 foot, 6 inches tall and weighing 215 pounds, Anthony had the prototypical size for an NBA shooting guard. He was a good scorer from the perimeter, which can accompany any threats the team may have had inside the paint. The scouting report on him was that he was not an elite run-and-jump athlete like Iverson, although he could be deceptively quick and very fluid with the ball in his hands. On the defensive side of the ball, he made some plays but was not known for having a lot of lateral quickness.

Ankle injuries kept Anthony on the bench during his first two seasons in the league, and at one point he was put on the injured reserve list with a broken foot. With one year left on his three-year rookie contract, Philadelphia shipped him off to the Orlando Magic, where he also didn't last long, playing in only sixteen games. The Magic waived him—meaning he was released—and no other NBA team picked him up.

Needing a basketball job—and to gain some confidence—Anthony dropped down to the minor league Continental Basketball Association (CBA) and finished the season with the Quad City Thunder in Iowa. He hoped a strong summer league showing with the Toronto Raptors would fast-track him back into the NBA, but he got hurt again, which doused any hopes of landing with another NBA team anytime soon.

If Anthony was going to resurrect his career, he would have to play overseas.

THE ROAD TO ISRAEL

Anthony's agent shopped him around to various teams in Europe and Asia. The most interest came from Maccabi Tel Aviv, who said they'd take a flier on him.

"Maccabi Tel Aviv was really the only team I considered," Anthony said. "For me, it just felt like this is where the Lord was telling me to go. Maccabi was a high-level team coming off a strong season, losing the final of the Euroleague championships, so it was a great situation for me. As an American playing basketball, Israel is one of the best countries I could go to because a lot of people speak English and a lot of Americans live there. But I didn't know that before I agreed to come."

Just like that, Anthony Parker, who had never been outside North America, was moving to Israel with his wife of one year, Tamy. Talk about a major adjustment. Whereas Anthony's first three years of professional basketball could be likened to the Hebrews wandering in the wilderness—meaning he wasn't getting anywhere—now he was confident God had set a path for him. Since that path was taking him and his wife to Israel, they followed that course in faith. Little did he know that saying yes to Maccabi Tel Aviv would lead to a five-year stint in the *real* Promised Land and pave the way back to the NBA.

Maccabi Tel Aviv, Israel's top professional basketball team, usually qualified to play in the Euroleague, which is the highest level and most important professional basketball competition in Europe. Teams from up to eighteen different countries compete. (Geographically, Israel is actually part of Asia but is a member of FIBA Europe, the federation that governs European basketball.)

European basketball is a lot like Premier League soccer in Europe in that a team must beat out regional and national competition to qualify for the Euroleague. Twenty-four teams qualify for Euroleague competition, which starts every fall with games eventually feeding into playoff rounds, just like in the NBA. A "Final Four" tournament, featuring the winners of four quarterfinal series, play each other in one-off knockout games held at a predetermined site. The semifinal winners vie for the European championship; the semifinal losers play for third place.

Maccabi Tel Aviv, originally founded in 1906 as the Maccabi Tel Aviv Sports Club, was the biggest and most successful sports team in Israel. It's hard to explain to Americans how big a deal Maccabi is in Israel, but try to think of the Boston Celtics, New York Yankees, and Pittsburgh Steelers all rolled into one. Maccabi plays in the modern Nokia Arena, which is located in the Yad Eliyahu area of Tel Aviv—Israel's capital city.

Maccabi plays a brand of basketball that's just a notch under the level played in the NBA. For more than twenty-five years, NBA teams have either traveled to Europe or invited Euroleague teams to come to the United States for a series of preseason games. The NBA teams win more than nine times out of ten, but these exhibition contests are close and hard-fought. The Euro teams have some very talented players, and when they step on a basketball court with an NBA team, they play as if they have something to prove.

The gap between the NBA and Euroleague teams is narrowing, although it must be noted that Europe's best players are now playing in the NBA. In the past two years, the Euroleague has changed its rules to make them more like the rules in the NBA. For example, the Euroleague altered the size of its three-second key, also known as the "paint." The awkward trapezoid lane was changed to a good old-fashioned rectangle, and the three-point line was extended to almost match the NBA's.

Historically, Maccabi had shown Yankees-like dominance of Israeli basketball by winning every Israeli League title since 1970, except in 1992–93. Seen around the world as the face of Jewish sports, the team was held in high esteem as Israel's national sporting representative. With a sizable budget to sign players, Maccabi's team usually included four to six Israelis, a couple of Americans, and a pair of dual-nationality players like Derrick Sharp and David Sternlight, who were Americans with Israeli citizenship because of marriage or ancestry.

This was the situation Anthony was getting into when he agreed to play for Maccabi and move to Israel—and the first few weeks in Tel Aviv were an eye-opener for him.

Anthony and Tamy had no sooner landed and moved into their apartment when an event called the "Second Intifada"—or uprising—broke out on September 28, 2000. The conflict started after Israel's then-opposition leader, Ariel Sharon, visited the Temple Mount in Jerusalem. Since the site is sacred to both the Islamic and Jewish religions, the question of sovereignty remained a thorny issue between Israel and the Palestinians.

To protest their displeasure at Sharon's visit to the Temple Mount, Palestinian demonstrators threw stones at Jewish worshippers at the Wailing Wall, which prompted Israeli security forces to fire rubber-coated metal bullets and live ammunition at the crowd. Five Palestinians were killed, setting off another vicious cycle of violence.

Violence escalated rapidly, going from rock throwing to machine-gun and mortar fire to suicide bombings and lethal road ambushes. Over the next five years of insurrection, Palestinians killed more than a thousand Israelis, and Israeli security forces killed nearly five thousand Palestinians in retaliatory raids.

This was the backdrop as Anthony joined the biggest symbol of Israeli sports—the Maccabi Tel Aviv basketball team.

"It was tough," Anthony said, putting it mildly. "This was the first time I left my country, and suddenly there was a war forty-five minutes from my doorsteps. CNN was covering it in a big way. My family back in the States watched what was happening in the Middle East, so they were calling me and wanting me to come home. Tamy was hearing the same from her family. Initially, we stayed in our apartment as much as we could, but then we started venturing out. When I went out into the streets, I saw that life was normal. I saw kids going to school and people shopping in malls. The buses were running and restaurants were open. Everything was normal, or what passes for 'normal' in the Middle East."

Part of that "normal" was the way security became a second way of life. Anytime Anthony or his wife went out in Israel, they had to be prepared to open her purse or backpack before entering any public building or even private establishments. "Everywhere you go in public, the security forces can and will open your purse or wand you," Anthony said. "If you are driving into an underground parking lot, they will look in your backseat and make you open your car trunk."

Security was especially intense around the Maccabi basketball team, which was a target-rich environment since the team was a national treasure. "We always had beefed-up security with Maccabi," he said. "We'd have armed men with us at the hotels and on the bus. We had police escorts everywhere we went. For us, that was all part of playing basketball for an Israeli team."

Even games played *outside* Israel reminded Anthony that he could never really escape what was happening back in the Middle East. Energized fans in European cities like Paris, Rome, and Berlin waved Palestinian flags and chanted emotional slogans Anthony couldn't understand. Some rallying calls he *could* understand, like the fans in Barcelona who chanted, "Boycott Israel, Viva Palestine."

How did he cope?

By doing what his Israeli teammates had learned to do long ago: he got used to it.

"I lived in a culture of people who had developed a thick skin to what was going on around them," he explained. "When we first moved there, a bomb would go off in Jerusalem or one of the cities nearby and kill some people. Tamy and I would say, 'Whoa! They're killing people out there!' But my teammates and coaches would tell us, 'Don't worry about it. It's thirty minutes away.' Slowly but surely, we got desensitized to the violence happening around us."

Fans attending games at the Nokia Arena had to pass through airport-like screening, including stepping through metal detectors and being subjected to searches. What authorities *did* allow into the basketball arena surprised Anthony. "Fans could bring in flares and horns, which they don't allow in the States," he said. "They could also bring in flags, drums, and trumpets, just like they could for soccer games. So fans over there were very passionate and used to making a lot of noise.

"But as I like to tell people, I felt safer in Tel Aviv than in most cities back in the U.S. It seems like the Israelis are in a perpetual state of war, and often in times of war, the crimes inside that country go down. There's just so much nationalistic pride that you don't have a whole lot of rape cases and murders and things like that. Sure, you can be in a situation where you are in the wrong place at the wrong time, but overall, I felt safe when I lived in Israel. I did not feel like my life was in danger from anyone around me."

One thing Anthony and his wife refused to do, however, was ride a bus—a popular target of suicide bombers willing to unleash their murderous mayhem. And he learned to keep his eyes open his first year in Tel Aviv, something that becomes second nature to anyone living in that region of the world.

And then the events of September 11 took place, and Anthony and Tamy were far from home. They clung to each other and got through it. "What I remember is how supportive the world was of America after 9/11," he said. "I talked to friends and people I knew in Israel, and everybody took it the same way as Americans did. For a time, it seemed that the world was united against such a horrific terrorist attack, but unfortunately, that did not last."

Not long after the Twin Towers went down, Palestinians set off a week-long wave of bombings in and around Jerusalem and Tel Aviv. "That was the closest we came to leaving," Anthony said. "My wife was pregnant at the time, and the medical facility where she got her ultrasounds done was around the corner from a bombing attack, so that was close.

"But we were forming relationships with people and the community, and we felt like we just couldn't leave them. We used to do things as a team where we would go to the hospitals and see kids and families who had gotten injured by mortar or missile attacks. It's a lot different when you meet these people in person. It used to be that I would see footage on CNN and hear the announcer say, 'Five people killed and ten injured,' and I didn't know what that really meant until I went into those hospitals and saw how these attacks affected families and their lives."

Anthony and Tamy became good friends with a family whose daughter had paid a heavy price just for being in the wrong place at the wrong time. She was hanging out with some friends in a pizza restaurant when a young Palestinian male walked in with a backpack, which he placed on the table. Then he announced to everyone in the restaurant, "See you on the other side." He detonated the explosives in the backpack, which was also filled with nails and screws. The suicide bomber died instantly, believing he would be rewarded for killing "infidels."

Several people were killed in the attack, but Anthony's friends' daughter somehow survived. "This girl had a whole lot of complications as a result of that suicide mission," Anthony said. "Developing a relationship with the family and seeing how their lives were affected by that physically and psychologically gave me a whole different perspective on these kinds of events happening around the world."

RETRACING JESUS' STEPS

The violence and threats of violence were the downside of living in Israel during a tumultuous time in history that continues today. But there was an upside for Anthony, and that was a once-in-a-lifetime opportunity to live in the Holy Land.

Anthony was staying in the land God gave His chosen people, the Israelites, after He delivered them from slavery under the pharaoh of Egypt. This was Canaan, the land of milk and honey that was also known as the "Promised Land." Jerusalem became the political and spiritual center of the ancient Jewish kingdom, the city where David reigned and where his son Solomon constructed the Temple. A small portion of the historical Temple, the Western Wall—also known as the Wailing Wall—still stands in a part of Jerusalem called the Temple Mount, which, as Anthony quickly learned after his arrival in Tel Aviv, is perhaps the most hotly contested area in the Holy Land.

"My faith grew so much, going to Israel and being a Christian," Anthony said. "I saw places that I read about in the Old Testament. I took a couple of tours, like to the Jordan River and the Sea of Galilee, where Jesus walked on water. I saw a lot of the country during my five years there, but there were areas that were off-limits, like the West Bank. But I went to the Negev in the south, the wilderness area where the Hebrews wandered for forty years. Just seeing all this history and being part of it grew my faith. I also observed a lot of the traditions that were talked about in the Old Testament that the Israelis still observe today," he said.

"Being a Christian and reading the Bible and being able to see the different cities and different landmarks discussed in the Bible was amazing. My time there was something I wish everyone could experience. I couldn't put a price tag on it."

Over the next few years, Anthony's friends and family would come to Israel to visit him and his wife. They would arrive in Israel at Tel Aviv's Ben Gurion International Airport with one mind-set and then depart with a whole new way of looking at the nation. "I just wish more people would go over there and experience the things I did," he said.

Even though ambling through streets Jesus and the apostles likely walked on nearly two thousand years ago was awe-inspiring as well as inspirational to Anthony's faith, he knew that he was being paid a lot of shekels to play basketball for Maccabi—and the team expected a good return on its investment.

You could say Maccabi invested wisely.

Anthony had an unbelievable five-year career with Maccabi, plus two short stints with an Italian team, Pallacanestro Virtus Roma. In fact, he went from being a forgotten man in the NBA to someone the league scouting website Draftexpress .com called "hands down the best player in the world outside of the NBA."

So how did that happen?

After settling into Tel Aviv during the Second Intifada, Anthony—by now healed of his injuries—knew he would have to make some adjustments in his game. Sure, the fundamentals of European basketball were the same as those in the NBA: pass, dribble, shoot, defend, rebound, screen, play hard, and play together. But there were important differences, starting with the basketball court, which was three feet shorter from end to end with a trapezoid-shaped lane that was wider on the baseline but narrower at the free throw line. This meant post players tended to set up position higher in the lane, which impacted the offensive flow. Americans playing the guard position, like Anthony, often felt like there was nowhere to drive toward the basket.

In addition, there was no defensive three-second rule in European basketball (in the NBA, players aren't allowed to stand in the lane without guarding someone for more than three seconds), which clogged the lane and also reduced spacing between players. Also, the three-point line in European basketball was nearly two feet closer than it is in the NBA, which meant shooters were *looking* for the three-point opportunity and expected to launch—and make—plenty of three-point shots.

Another important difference was that European games were forty minutes long, matching the length of American college games but shorter than the NBA's forty-eight minutes. A shorter game impacted substitutions, rotations, and effort levels since players didn't have to pace themselves as much as they did in the NBA.

And then there was the officiating. In European basketball, it's not uncommon to have three officials from three different countries—all with different interpretations on what constituted traveling, a foul, or a legal screen. European officials, he discovered, loved to call offensive charges, so there was a lot of "flopping" by 7-foot centers when much-smaller point guards bumped into them on drives to the basket.

But the biggest difference, Anthony found, was the team aspect that permeated the culture of European basketball. Teams didn't "clear out" one side of the court to let their best player—their Kobe or LeBron—go one-on-one. There was more willingness to involve everyone in the offense and pass the ball around.

Anthony learned that the "extra pass" was the norm rather than the exception in the European game. Case in point: penetrating the lane with the dribble is a big part of the international and NBA game, but a European player usually looks to pass rather than score—unless he has a clear lay-in.

"The way the rules are in the NBA, you can be more one-on-one and get to the basket, and teams put a premium on that in the U.S.," Anthony explained, "while in Europe, you're almost forced by the rules to move the ball around and play in more of a team setting."

Though European teams don't play as many games—usually between sixty and seventy per season—as NBA clubs, it's still a long season that starts with training camp in August and ends in late May with the Euroleague championships. With fewer games on the schedule, Anthony and his teammates practiced more, which turned out to be to his benefit because it helped him to improve his game while he was in Europe.

Maccabi had signed Anthony to fill a void at shooting guard left by Doron Sheffer's retirement. Sheffer, an Israeli who grew up in a kibbutz, had played guard for the University of Connecticut back in the mid-1990s. He was good enough that the Los Angeles Clippers drafted him in the second round of the 1996 NBA draft, but he chose to sign with Maccabi. After four productive seasons, however, the twenty-eight-year-old Israeli was staggered to learn that he had cancer. He retired suddenly to undergo treatments and to travel around the world to places like India, South America, and Costa Rica, where he could escape the public eye.

News of Sheffer's cancer and travels dominated coverage on Israeli sports pages, and Anthony can be excused for feeling like Babe Dahlgren, the first baseman who replaced ailing New York Yankee Lou Gehrig in 1939. Sheffer was held up as one of Israel's greatest basketball players, and now Anthony was being called in to pick up the slack while Sheffer fought a cancerous tumor.

Anthony did more than that—he grabbed the reins of leadership on Maccabi by becoming both a scorer and a playmaker for the team during his "rookie" season, when he helped the Tel Aviv team win its first Euroleague championship in *twenty* years. He had a captivating style of play that made it impossible for fans to take their eyes off of him. The Israeli fans, ecstatic to be cheering a winner again, accepted him as one of their own.

Anthony loved playing in Israel, and although Maccabi didn't repeat as European champions in 2001–02, he had firmly established himself as a fan favorite. But then Tamy became pregnant, and that complicated matters. As the birth of Tamy's first child approached, and as certain hormones began kicking in, she understandably began feeling the need to be back home in the United States. Anthony comprehended his wife's desire to be near hearth and family, so he agreed to take a six-month sabbatical from the game, meaning he wouldn't be returning to Maccabi for the start of his third season with the team.

Anthony and Tamy returned to Florida, where she gave birth in late 2002 to a son they named Alonso. Once mother and son were feeling settled, Anthony needed to get back to work. He took a short gig with a prominent Italian team, Pallacanestro Virtus Roma, and played the last half of the 2002–03 season in Rome.

Anthony could have stayed in Italy, but all along he wanted to return to Israel, a country he and Tamy had grown to love. Maccabi wanted him back, and so did the Israeli fans, who held high hopes for the coming season. Maccabi had lured former head coach Pini Gershon out of a two-year retirement because there was a strong feeling that the team had the horses to go back to the Final Four and win the Euroleague championship—which would be played in Tel Aviv!

So imagine the excitement among Israeli fans when Maccabi won the Israeli domestic championship and the Israeli National Cup to qualify for the Euroleague playoffs. But once again—as in 2000 with the Second Intifada and 9/11—the real world intruded onto the playing court. Not only was the Second Intifada still in the news (a truce wouldn't be called until 2005), but President George W. Bush commenced Operation Iraqi Freedom on March 20, 2003. Many Israelis feared that Saddam Hussein would retaliate by firing Scud missiles toward Israel's major cities—a tactic he used in the first Gulf War, when he launched forty-seven Scuds toward Israel.

Would Saddam launch missiles toward Israel again?

The answer was no, but that didn't mean that the Israeli populace wasn't unconcerned or unprepared. Israel had an impressive civil defense system in place. Since 1951, all Israeli homes, residential buildings, and industrial buildings were required to have bomb shelters, which people were supposed to enter after hearing a warning siren. Anthony and Tamy even had gas masks at the ready, but the attacks from Iraq never materialized.

The Euroleague Final Four, scheduled for late April in Tel Aviv, nearly didn't come off because of Israel's support of the United States. This led to a huge controversy, and other Euroleague teams tried to move the Euroleague Final Four out of Tel Aviv. But in the end, the Final Four stayed in Israel, and Maccabi gave the citizenry something to cheer about during another time of apprehension and uncertainty. Even better, the home team lifted the country's spirits by defeating CSKA Moscow in the semifinals and then annihilating Skipper Bologna 118–74 in the finals to win the Euroleague championship.

Anthony was named as the Final Four MVP, which only further cemented his status as a sports hero in Israel. The following season (2004–05), Anthony and his teammates backed up their Euroleague championship by winning it again. That season, the Final Four was played in Moscow, and Maccabi Tel Aviv defeated TAU Cerámica, a Spanish team, in the final. Anthony wasn't named as the Final Four MVP this time, but he walked away with something better—the Euroleague Most Valuable Player trophy.

Anthony was now a big deal in Israel, and his handsome face graced billboards around Tel Aviv with advertisements for Nissan Pathfinders. He was also featured in the TV ad campaign for the car.

Some commentators believed Anthony was the most complete swingman (a player who can play guard or forward) in the history of European basketball. The way his game blossomed since he first traveled overseas to play astounded the basketball experts. They all agreed that he was not the same player he was when he joined Maccabi back in 2000.

THE JUMP SHOT THAT BROUGHT ANTHONY PARKER HOME

The first exhibition game between an NBA team and a European team was played in 1978 between the Washington Bullets and Maccabi Tel Aviv. The Bullets (renamed the Wizards in 1997) were the defending NBA champions when they traveled to Israel for this historic game. They probably wished they hadn't boarded the charter jet: the Washington Bullets lost in a shocker, 98–97.

It would be another six years before another NBA team ventured to Europe. In August of 1984, the New Jersey Nets and the Phoenix Suns journeyed to Yad Eliyahu Arena in Tel Aviv. Both teams lost to Maccabi on consecutive nights.

Maccabi played six more exhibitions against NBA teams over the next twenty years but lost them all. After Maccabi Tel Aviv won back-to-back European championships in 2004 and 2005, though, the basketball world took notice. The Maccabi team was invited to play the Toronto Raptors in a preseason game in Toronto. For the first time in five years, Anthony would play against NBA competition.

For Anthony and his Maccabi teammates, this was Game 7 of the NBA Finals. Just days before the start of the 2005–06 NBA season, a sellout crowd of 17,281 fans filled Air Canada Centre for the mid-October game. NBA commissioner David Stern was there, along with the consular general for Israel in

Toronto and a huge contingent of Jewish fans eager to see their sports heroes.

They were treated to quite a game. The game was tied 103–103 with 11 seconds left. Maccabi had the ball, and after a time-out the ball was put into Anthony's hands. This time, his teammates uncharacteristically cleared out the right side of the court for Anthony, who was isolated with Morris Peterson guarding him. He made a move on Peterson and then pulled up for a twenty-footer that swished the net with .8 second on the clock.

After Toronto's desperate three-point attempt at the final buzzer missed, giving Maccabi the win, Anthony's clutch jumper was the talk of the basketball world. This was the first time since 1988 that an NBA team had lost a sanctioned international game and only the second such defeat in the past twenty-eight games. Anthony's winning jumper impressed the Toronto Raptors coaching staff, who filed that information away. The following July, when the Raptors were in the midst of overhauling the team, they asked Anthony to come back to the NBA after a six-year hiatus.

Anthony didn't have to be asked twice. He signed with the Raptors and quickly established himself as the team's starting shooting guard and as a player who could handle the three-point shooting duties. He finished fourth in the NBA in three-point shooting during his first season back and was credited with helping the Raptors clinch their first-ever division title in the 2006–07 season and their first NBA playoff berth in five years.

Anthony was in his early thirties, and he was making the most of his second chance in the NBA. He played three seasons with Toronto before signing a two-year deal with the LeBron James–led Cleveland Cavaliers in 2009.

Before the 2010–11 season, however, LeBron left the Cavaliers after a much-ballyhooed signing with Miami that allowed him to join Dwyane Wade and Chris Bosh with the Heat. Without the player many considered the best in the NBA to lead them, the Cavaliers floundered in the 2010–11 season, winning just 19 games and losing 63. The Cavs' lowlight that season was when they set a dubious NBA record by losing twenty-six games in a row.

Anthony's contract with the Cleveland Cavaliers expired at the end of the 2010–11 season. With Cleveland doing some housecleaning during the season, coupled with the expiration of the NBA's collective bargaining agreement during the summer of 2011 and a possible lockout or shortened season in 2011–12, Anthony is not sure when or where he'll play next.

Who knows?

Maybe the Lord is calling him back to Israel—to Maccabi Tel Aviv.

2012 update: Anthony re-signed with the Cavaliers after the lockout ended, lending his shooting touch in a backup role and mentoring youngsters like Kyrie Irvin and Tristan Thompson. Back problems, however, plagued him throughout a forgettable season in which the Cavs finished with a 21–45 record.

He waited until the NBA playoffs were over to announce his retirement, saying, "I'm at peace with it and excited for whatever the future has for me." That future may include a front office job or getting into broadcasting.

4

CHRIS KAMAN:
GETTING OFF THE MEDS

"Did you take your pill this morning?"

Chris Kaman says he heard that question about ten times a day from the adults in his life while growing up in the Grand Rapids, Michigan, area. What his parents, schoolteachers, school nurses, and administrators were *really* asking was this: *Did you take your Ritalin with breakfast?*

They had good reason to ask.

Chris had been a little monster since his toddler days, when his parents, Leroy and Pam, began wondering what to do with the whirling dervish of misbehavior on their hands. Their rambunctious son would do anything or say anything that came to mind. One time, he whacked his sleeping father with an Etch A Sketch, bloodying his nose. He threw toys against walls and kicked over Lego creations. He was always testing boundaries and coming up with creative ways to cause trouble, sending Pam to the local library to read all the books she could about raising children.

"I'd tell him to brush his teeth, and he'd put up a fight," Pam said. "I'd tell him to put on his pajamas, and we'd fight. Go to bed, and another fight. I tell people that it was much worse than anybody could have dreamed of. We couldn't go to an amusement park or to a movie together. He couldn't stay still. He couldn't concentrate. He was all over the place."

Pam ultimately became so exasperated at Chris' antics that after church one day she tearfully confessed to her pastor, M. Wayne Benson, that she wanted to give Chris away to someone who could do a better job raising him. She loved Chris dearly, but her young son was driving her crazy.

Pastor Benson comforted Pam. "Just be patient," he said. "You won't always feel this way. Things will get better."

Meanwhile, four or five babysitters quit on Pam because they had grown so exasperated trying to handle Chris. The babysitters who didn't quit had to be ready for anything.

One high school girl, Amy Farrell, was asked to look after Chris, then two and a half, and his older brother, Michael (who was seven years old), while the parents attended a wedding rehearsal and dinner for Chris' aunt Carole.

Just before dark, Michael bounded down the steps to the backyard to feed Shadow, the Kamans' black Labrador puppy. When Michael had trouble freeing Shadow from a chain around his neck, he called out for help. Amy stepped outside to assist Michael, then looked back just in time to see Chris slam the back door shut, which automatically locked the door. She and Michael immediately shouted for Chris to open up, but he refused.

Christopher Zane Kaman, not yet three years old, was ruler of the house now. Ignoring the loud banging on the door, he set a chair next to the stove and put a frying pan atop one of the burners. Then he poured some Pringles potato chips into the pan and squeezed ketchup over the chips. He wanted to do some cooking, and what better way than to prepare a snack out of two of his favorite foods?

A boy in his terrible twos, a hot stove, and no parents around . . . this was getting serious. Michael ran to a nearby neighbor for help. Together, they found an open window and took the screen off to gain access back into the home—and save everyone from disaster.

Stuff like that happened all the time during Chris' childhood, but don't get the idea that Chris was born to permissive parents who lost control of a son they doted on. His father and mother were traditional, God-fearing parents who believed that sparing the rod would spoil the child. They were on board with Dr. Dobson's *Dare to Discipline* and attempted to instill godly values by the seat of the pants—meaning they weren't averse to giving Chris a couple of good whacks on his bottom when his behavior warranted it.

They were also salt-of-the-earth parents: Leroy was a city employee for Wyoming, a suburb of Grand Rapids. He plowed streets, fixed potholes and water main breaks, and painted fire hydrants, while Pam worked in the Wyoming Police Department, the senior citizen center, and the accounting office for the municipality.

Leroy and Pam wanted to raise their children in the admonition of the Lord, and if they could get Chris to sit still long enough, they read him books with Bible lessons and took him to church on Sundays.

When Chris started school and his younger siste, Jessica, came along, Pam quit working for the city and ran a day care out of her home. She also cleaned houses to help cover tuition at Tri-Unity Christian School because she and her husband believed strongly in Christian education. *Whatever it takes to keep them in a Christian school* was their motto.

Even though Pam and Leroy spanked Chris, put him in time-outs, and regularly scolded him for his willful misbehavior, nothing worked during those early childhood years. Even before the locking-out-the-babysitter incident, Pam came to believe that the situation was serious enough to talk to her family doctor about Chris' behavior. But the doctor just patted Pam on the shoulder and told her Chris was going through a phase and would turn out just fine. "He'll grow out of it," he said.

Except that he didn't. In fact, as he grew older, his behavior became more unruly than ever. They visited a new family doctor, Dr. Janet Talmo, and she referred them to the Ken-O-Sha Diagnostic Center in Grand Rapids, which offered testing for off-the-wall kids like Chris. For half a day, Ken-O-Sha evaluators watched from behind a one-way mirror as Chris, then around two and a half, played with puzzles and interacted with other kids.

A week later, Leroy and Pam received the bad news: their son had been diagnosed with Attention-Deficit Hyperactivity Disorder, or ADHD. The recommendation: give the boy the antihistamine Benadryl (for sedation purposes) and enroll him in a Pre-Primary Impaired program (PPI) at Eastern Elementary School, which was part of the Grand Rapids Public School system.

The Ken-O-Sha evaluators told Pam her son wouldn't be ready for kindergarten until he attended the PPI pre-kindergarten program to work out his behavioral kinks. That meant having Chris board a yellow school bus—the "short bus" for handicapped or special-needs children—each morning so he could be transported across Grand Rapids.

It wasn't Chris' fault that he had to take the little yellow bus. In those pre-kindergarten days, he could no more sit still or take an afternoon nap on the classroom carpet than he could dunk a basketball.

Whenever he got into trouble at the PPI school—which seemed to happen every five minutes—his teacher would tell him, "Time to go in the barrel." In Chris' classroom was a wooden barrel lying on its side that had enough room inside for a misbehaving student to crawl into for a short period of time-out. After several minutes inside the barrel, Chris would rejoin the class, but it wasn't long before he'd forget about the punishment and start throwing plush toys at the other kids or taking off his belt and swinging it above his head. Then it was another crawl into the wooden barrel for yet another cooling-off period.

Even as a preschooler, Chris was big for his age, so he looked a lot older. Shortly after starting the PPI program, the teacher asked Chris if he knew his birthday.

"Apprul twenty-eight," he replied.

"How old are you?"

Chris held up two fingers.

"No, you're three years old," corrected the teacher.

Chris wouldn't back down. "I'm two!" he said, holding up two fingers.

No wonder the teacher thought Chris should be further down the maturity road—because of his size, she was convinced he was a year older than he really was!

When Chris was about three and a half years old, the PPI administrators strongly recommended that he be put on Ritalin, a potent anti-depressant, to manage his ADHD.

Leroy and Pam figured the school authorities knew what was best and agreed to give the drug a try.

"We trusted the professionals and put Chris on Ritalin," Pam said. "They also told us he would eventually grow out of it. I remember one doctor saying, 'You don't see adults bouncing off a couch.' At the same time, though, Chris' ADHD diagnosis was based on a few forms filled out by a couple of teachers back during the half day of testing at Ken-O-Sha Diagnostic Center. The school psychologist reviewed them in a matter of minutes and made a judgment that would impact Chris for the rest of his life."

When Chris reached elementary school age, Leroy and Pam enrolled him in Tri-Unity Christian School, which was about a half hour from their home.

Even though Chris took Ritalin during the school day—he didn't have to take his "medicine" during the weekends—he was still a handful during his early elementary school years.

Chris didn't misbehave just at school either. He'd take other kids' bikes and dump them on the railroad tracks or climb on neighborhood roofs—just for the heck of it. One time, Pam was sitting on her front porch, visiting with her sister-in-law, when she looked up at the neighbor's house across the street. There was Chris, eight years old, moving around on the roof. She got up, feeling her heart in her throat, and calmly walked across the street. She didn't want to yell at him and cause him to make a fast move—and slip off the roof.

Chris wasn't mean-spirited toward other children or a bully—just out of control and goofy. He was also very impressionable. His older brother, Michael, said he and other kids in the neighborhood often dared Chris to do crazy stunts. He was too immature to say no.

You're daring me? Then watch this . . .

Chris' rowdy behavior even when he was on Ritalin prompted head scratching from his parents as well as his doctor. Ritalin was supposed to mellow him out—make him docile and obedient—but that wasn't happening. That's why people at school often asked him whether he had taken his medication that morning.

"I hated being asked all the time to take a pill to make myself regular," he said. "That drove me just as crazy."

Chris was always scheduled to take his second pill of the day in the nurse's office during morning recess. The school nurse would hand him a pill and a glass of water. The ritual was repeated in the afternoon, too.

Chris didn't know it at the time, and neither did his parents, but he was a pawn in a system where health care professionals, school administrators, and teachers make snap judgments about boys who have continual ants in their pants. (Boys get tagged with attention-deficit disorder three to six times as often as girls.) Once a child has been diagnosed with ADHD, doctors and psychologists hand the parents a prescription for Ritalin . . . and that's when the ADHD train leaves the station.

The Drug Enforcement Agency has classified Ritalin as a Schedule II drug—a designation reserved for the most addictive and dangerous drugs that can be legally prescribed. For nearly fifteen years, Chris took Ritalin or another anti-depressant called Adderall. He was among the six million kids under the age of eighteen who take these drugs daily. Some of these kids are given these drugs as freely as kids who are given Flintstone Chewable Vitamins to start their day.

Ritalin's side effects include decreased appetite, trouble sleeping, headache, irritability, stomachache, mood swings, and nausea—and Chris experienced them all. Ritalin's main side effect on Chris was to depress his appetite, but it didn't make him any easier to manage. For most of his early school years, Chris was forced to sit next to his teacher lest he disrupt the class again.

GROWING LIKE A BEANPOLE

Looking back, Chris knew he was a handful for his teachers and for his parents.

"My dad is very old school and traditional," he said. "His father was in the military, and he served in the military. When I'd done something wrong, I got either the belt or the paddle from him, but it was usually this handball paddle with a person's face on it. My brother and I called him 'Harry.' So when I heard Dad or Mom say, 'Go get the paddle,' that meant doing the dreaded paddle walk. Then I'd get one or two good whacks from Harry."

Chris also received spankings at Tri-Unity Christian School. At the beginning of the school year, the Tri-Unity principal would send letters to the parents asking for permission to spank their children under certain circumstances—and with witnesses present for everyone's protection. Up until the sixth grade, Chris heard his teachers utter the dreaded command several times a year: *That's enough, young man. Go report to the principal's office.*

"Whenever I got sent to the principal's office, I'd walk in where the principal and another teacher would be waiting for me. Then I'd have to put my hands on the principal's desk, and she would say, 'Butt out.' Then she'd give me a couple of good whacks. Early on I cried, but as I got older, say around the fifth grade, I had trouble keeping a straight face. One time I laughed, which got me into more trouble. I was suspended for that episode."

The parent-approved spankings eventually stopped in middle school, but the attempts to keep Chris in check continued. Poor classroom behavior resulted in "early birds"—going to school before first period and writing lines in a notebook— or losing rights and privileges at home. He was often grounded from playing with friends, playing video games, or enjoying other fun activities.

There were times, though, when Chris would surprise his parents by coming home with a gold-colored "Godly Character" award his teacher had given him after he had done something noteworthy in class. One time, his teacher praised him by writing, "Chris was such a good helper today. He helped me clean out my marker drawer." Another time, Chris found money on the playground and gave it to his teacher so she could find the rightful owner. The amount: eleven cents. The money was later taped to a "Godly Character" award and presented to Chris. Pam still has that award as a keepsake.

Meanwhile, Chris was growing like a beanpole and showing impressive athletic talent on the soccer field and the basketball court. His favorite sport early on was soccer, and he was an excellent goalie, defenseman, and striker. "I liked the running part about soccer," he said. "I could run forever, and I had good footwork. My feet were pretty coordinated for a big guy."

Chris was also a good baseball player, but everyone could see he was cut out to play basketball. Tall for his age (he stood head and shoulders above his classmates), he was well coordinated, able to move well, had a deft touch as a shooter, and was very skilled around the basketball hoop.

DEALING WITH A REPUTATION

By the time Chris started high school as a freshman at Tri-Unity Christian, he had grown to 6 feet, 2 inches tall. He enjoyed athletics, but he hated everything else about school. He barely earned passing grades: his grade point average his freshman and sophomore years hovered between 1.4 and 1.6. "I did not care about schoolwork," he said. "I was at the point where I was going down and down and down."

And he was still getting into trouble for doing dumb, immature stuff in the classroom: talking out of turn, making jokes about his teachers when he thought they weren't within earshot, and flicking paper wads from his desk. At times, he felt his teachers had it out for him, based on his reputation as one of the "Ritalin kids."

"It wasn't like I was beating kids up," he said, "I wasn't doing drugs. I wasn't out there having sex. It was nothing like that. It was just dumb stuff."

What Chris and his family didn't know was that the Ritalin acted in his body like a stimulant . . . much like caffeine. In other words, the anti-ADHD pills were making him even *more* hyper.

"Basically, when a kid has ADHD, he's not paying attention. His brain is going too slow, so it's turning off a lot more than it should," Chris explained. "He has a hard time keeping attention. He doesn't focus on what he's supposed to be doing. So doctors give him a stimulant, thinking that will bring him back to normal. But in my case, I was misdiagnosed. I did *not* have ADHD, although I wouldn't discover that for a long time. But when I was taking my pills, I was basically receiving speed when I was already speeding. No wonder I was having so many behavioral problems. I was crawling out of my own skin, basically."

Chris had more and more skin to crawl out of, too. By his sophomore year, he had sprouted to 6 feet, 8 inches tall, but was as thin as a rail post at 170 pounds. During the summer before his junior year, he shot up to 6 feet, 11 inches tall.

That same year, Chris attended a big man's basketball camp at Western Michigan University, where he played and practiced under the appraising eyes of college coaches. He must have made a strong impression at the summer camp because shortly after he got home, he received more than thirty letters from college basketball coaches expressing an interest in him playing for their teams.

But Chris knew his 1.6 grade point average would probably sink any hopes he had for playing college basketball—at least for a four-year school. So he decided to do two things:

1. Stop taking his medicine whenever he thought he could get away with it.
2. Start applying himself to his schoolwork like never before.

If his mother was watching him take his pill with breakfast, he gulped one down. But if he could fool his mom and get away without taking the pill, he'd go that route.

Chris was supposed to take his second pill of the day after third period, when students received a fifteen-minute break. He knew the drill: report to the school office, where the secretary would be waiting with his pill and cup of water. Like he did at home, when he thought he could get away with it, he'd pretend to take the Ritalin pill and then stuff it into his pants pocket. Then he'd toss the medicine into the trash can. Ditto for the afternoon pill.

Did his behavior or demeanor change?

Chris wasn't sure, but the person who knew him best at Tri-Unity was Mark Keeler, his varsity basketball coach and math teacher, and he noticed something was different about Chris—though he couldn't quite put his finger on what it was.

One day, Mr. Keeler asked Chris point-blank if he had been taking his pills.

Chris didn't want to lie, not to a coach and teacher he trusted.

"No, I haven't been taking them," he confessed.

Coach Keeler suggested a parent-teacher conference to discuss what to do. When he met with Chris' parents, they decided Chris should see a psychologist.

"When I saw this guy," Chris related, "he told me in less than ten minutes, 'You are ADHD for sure. We're going to put you on Ritalin.' But I told him I'd been on Ritalin since I was three. I hated it."

"Then let's try Adderall," replied the expert.

Adderall is a powerful stimulant that has been compared to methamphetamine. Because of this, Adderall has a relatively high potential for abuse and addiction.

As far as Chris was concerned, it was another round of *Here we go again*.

"When I started taking Adderall at the end of my sophomore year, I tried my best to deal with it," Chris said. "Meanwhile, I knew I had to get my grades up to play college basketball, which was a great incentive. I applied myself like never before and saw a lot of improvement in my test scores and book reports. I did this through one-on-one tutoring with Coach Keeler, who really helped me. I discovered I was a hands-on learner, so if I was in a regular class where I was expected to take notes, that wasn't going to do anything for me. I'd sit in class and have five lines of notes written down after an hour, while some girl next to me would have a page and a half of notes. I just wasn't good at learning that way. But having someone sit down with me and go through the lesson material—like geometry and algebra—made all the difference."

Chris was a kinetic learner, meaning he learned best by carrying out certain physical activities. In other words, he learned by doing, which could happen when he worked one-on-one with Coach Keeler. The two other learning styles—visual learning and auditory learning, which involve learning by what you see or what you hear—did not work for Chris.

Armed with a better understanding of how he learned best, Chris made rapid progress in the classroom. During his junior and senior years, he earned a 3.7 to 3.8 grade point average, which lifted his four-year average to a 2.4 or 2.6 overall—good enough to play ball at a quality four-year college.

College basketball coaches liked the fact that Chris was ambidextrous on the court, meaning he could shoot equally well with the right or left hand.

Perhaps he inherited genes for this proficiency—his mom was a lefty and his father was right-handed—but don't discount the hard work he put into the game. "I was a gym rat growing up," he said. "I did the extra shooting, played pickup games all the time, but God blessed me with good hands and solid mobility."

GETTING OFF THE MEDS

Between his sophomore and junior year of high school, when Chris grew to 6 feet, 11 inches tall, he was still very thin. He couldn't gain weight, even though he drank protein shakes like they were going out of style. That was because the Ritalin and Adderall sped up his metabolism so much that everything he ate was consumed in the burning furnace of his stomach.

Another problem was what the drugs did to his appetite. When he was on his meds, Chris just wasn't very hungry. Breakfast was a bowl of cereal and a glass of juice, and lunch would be a small sandwich and an apple and chips. But watch out when dinnertime rolled around and the pills wore off. "My dinners were huge, man," he said. "My mom was a good cook who would serve us meat and potatoes Midwest style—steak, hamburgers, goulash, macaroni and cheese with tuna, lasagna, spaghetti—anything you could think of."

Despite the suppertime pig-outs, Chris could barely keep body and soul together, and he weighed just 200 pounds.

He was a standout on the high school basketball court, but he had a hard time getting the bigger college programs to notice him because he played for a small high school of around 150 students. Playing against some much bigger schools in Grand Rapids—and beating them—helped his cause, though. After leading his team to a 24–2 record and the state quarterfinals his senior year, Chris received a handful of scholarship offers, including one from Azusa Pacific University, a Christian college in Southern California.

Chris wanted to play close to home, so he accepted a full-ride offer from Central Michigan University in Mount Pleasant. A Division I school, CMU had a strong basketball program and was just seventy-five miles from his home. Over the next three years, his parents not only wouldn't miss a home game, but would also cheer him on at nearly all his road games.

Before leaving home to enroll at Central Michigan, however, Chris made a major decision that would change the arc of his life—he stopped taking his Adderall. It was his choice.

"In the summer of 2000, I was done taking my medicine," he said. "I didn't need my parents' permission because I was eighteen. When I told my parents what I wanted to do, they asked me to stay on my medicine. I explained I didn't want to do that. We got into a scuffle, but ultimately it was my choice."

After getting off the Adderall, Chris immediately began putting on some much-needed weight. During his freshman year in college, he quickly leaped to 214 pounds. His weight gain continued, and he steadily moved up to 225 pounds his sophomore year and tipped the scales at 237 pounds going into his junior year. By the time he started playing in the NBA, he was up to 255 pounds. No longer could heavier, more muscular centers push him around in the paint.

Chris' breakout season at Central Michigan came during his junior year, when he doubled his point-per-game average to 22.4 and averaged 12 rebounds per game. During the 2002–03 season, he carried the Chippewas' hopes on his tall shoulders. An early season win at the University of Michigan raised eyebrows in the Great Lakes State. Chris scored 30 points and secured 21 rebounds in the victory at Ann Arbor.

Basketball was rocking again in Mount Pleasant. The student section in the east end zone—known as the Rose Rowdies because the Chippewas played in the Rose Arena—loved Chris, who led CMU to the NCAA Tournament for the first time since 1987.

Playing as an eleventh seed, Central Michigan stunned sixth-seeded Creighton in the first round of the West Regional played in Salt Lake City. The Chippewas had to hold off a furious second-half Creighton rally led by Kyle Korver, who scored 14 points in the second half to cut a 26-point lead to 2 late in the game.

Waiting in the second round was Duke University and Coach K—Mike Krzyzewski—whose Blue Devils were always one of the top teams in the country. Alas, Central Michigan was no match, losing 86–60. Chris played well, though, scoring 25 points and impressing Coach K.

"He can use both hands, and he can run the floor," Coach Krzyzewski said about Chris after the game. "If he gets fouled, he can hit free throws. He's going to be a pro; there's no doubt about it."

Since mobile, athletic 7-foot centers who can shoot don't come around too often, NBA scouts told Chris he should skip his senior season and turn pro because he was a certain first-round draft pick.

But was it the right time to leave Central Michigan to play in the NBA? His coach, Jay Smith, wanted Chris to come back for his senior year, but as Chris and his parents discussed their options, they felt the time was right to turn pro. "I have to do it now," Chris told his parents. "If Central Michigan doesn't do as well next year, the NBA will forget about me."

Chris decided to turn pro and was the sixth player taken in the 2003 NBA draft. The perennial doormat of the NBA—the Los Angeles Clippers—selected Chris, making him the highest draft pick of any athlete in any sport to come from Grand Rapids.

WESTWARD HO

And now Chris was in the NBA.

Playing at the next level presented its own challenges, not the least of which was leaving his home state and moving to Los Angeles. Chris made a good decision when he asked Ben Chamberlain, his older brother, Michael's, best friend at Tri-Unity, to be his personal assistant and keep his life in order. Ben was like a big brother to Chris.

Later in Chris' rookie season, Ben's younger brother, Caleb, as well as Jeremy Scully, a friend of Michael's, also moved from Grand Rapids to LA to live with Chris and Ben. Jeremy, who had earned a degree at a culinary school, was put in charge of cooking for everyone at the home Chris purchased in Redondo Beach.

"They were all Christian guys who thought the same way I do," Chris said. "They were good people to surround myself with. They lived with me the whole time until I got married in 2010, but I had them around for two reasons: one was to make sure that I had people I knew and felt comfortable to hang out with. And two, I wanted them to be a barrier between me and anybody who wanted to befriend me to get to my money."

Before Ben was on board, Chris had been overly generous with his newfound riches. His first fifty thousand dollars was gone in a week and a half; he handed out hundred-dollar bills or wrote checks to friends and family members like he was passing out Monopoly money at a game table. After that, he voluntarily gave up his checkbook and restricted himself to a bank card that had a preset spending limit each day.

It helped that Chris had no desire to sample LA's nightlife, and having a three-man posse to hang out with—and keep him accountable—helped him avoid temptations with the ladies.

"I liked my teammates, but I couldn't see myself doing some of the things they did," Chris said. "The hardest part about joining an NBA team was staying positive in my faith when people all around me were talking about stuff I didn't need to hear. Bad company robs good spirit, and I wanted to surround myself with good company."

Besides, with Jeremy's great food, tons of video games to play, and a pet Rottweiler at home, what more could four guys in their twenties living in LA's beach-centric west side want or need?

Chris and his buddies held Bible studies and went to church together. Ben sent two or three Bible verses a day to Chris' BlackBerry whenever he was on a road trip. Chris upped the ante by being vocal about his faith and telling reporters that he didn't consider himself a religious person but someone who wanted to be a good person who loved God.

Chris got a lot of media attention in Los Angeles when he won the Clippers' starting center position during his first training camp. He performed well his first few years in the NBA, although Clippers coach Mike Dunleavy wanted him to be more selfish with the ball. Chris would get the ball in the low post and have a close-in shot, but he'd pass off to a teammate who would take a long-range jumper—and that player usually wasn't half the shooter Chris was.

Then Chris always seemed to be fighting ankle sprains and other nagging injuries—and a reputation that he wasn't all together during games. There were times when Coach Dunleavy would call time out and draw up a play for the next possession, and Chris would walk out of the huddle as the horn sounded. A second later, he'd turn around in a half panic and ask, "Coach, what play are we running again? I forgot already."

Not good, especially when you're down by one point with ten seconds left in the game.

The occasional bouts of forgetfulness led to whispers around the league that Chris was a flake—a space cadet on the court. His brain was still moving too fast, and he was missing stuff.

In 2007, after five up-and-down years in the league, Chris' uncle, Mike Palmitier, heard about a new company in Grand Rapids called Neurocore. Psychologist Dr. Tim Royer and his associate, Dr. Brad Oostindie, started Neurocore, which helped people find long-term, non-invasive, non-drug solutions to behavioral issues. Uncle Mike's teenage daughter Torrie had used the program to improve her grades as well as her attitude around the home.

Chris was initially dubious when Uncle Mike told him about Neurocore, but he decided to check the company out. Neurocore technicians attached twenty-one electrodes to Chris' head so they could assess his brainwave activity. Using a system of neurofeedback, they were able to identify ways Chris could sharpen his focus, reduce stress, and make positive changes in the way his brain operates.

They also discovered that Chris *didn't* suffer from ADHD, despite what other doctors had told him and his parents.

"I was real skeptical about Neurocore," Chris said. "After being hooked up and having my brainwave activity assessed, they told me that I wasn't ADHD at all. What I had was high anxiety, and taking Ritalin made my high anxiety worse for all those years. That's why I always felt like I was crawling out of my skin and forgetting plays and coverages in my games."

In other words, Chris had been misdiagnosed since he was two and a half years old! Dr. Royer at Neurocore suggested that Chris undergo Neurocore's Autonomic Nervous System Regulation (ANSR) program, which he did. The results were nothing short of amazing.

Since Chris completed the ANSR program, his game has really picked up. His best season was the 2009–10 season, when he averaged a career-high 18.5 points and 9.3 rebounds a game. A sprained ankle early in the 2010–11 season, however, limited him to 32 games, but he remained a huge advocate of Neurocore. "I've noticed a big difference in the way I play," he said. "I'm not so impulsive, and I can stay on task longer."

For the past few summers, Chris has traveled around the country giving talks before parents or doing teleconferences from Los Angeles and Grand Rapids on how Neurocore helped him understand what he was really up against and how Neurocore's technology showed him once and for all that he was *not* ADHD.

"When a kid is told he has ADHD, that usually comes after a doctor visit seven to ten minutes long," he said. "During that short amount of time, the doctor prescribes a strong medication that can change your life forever. This is why I'm out there talking to parents, saying, 'Don't be so quick to put your kids on medication. Maybe there is an alternative way to do it. Maybe your kid is not really ADHD.' "

How has that message been received?

"Sometimes it's good, and sometimes the parents are tired of battling their kid, so they say, 'Yeah, the doctor must be right.' But as I point out, doctors get paid money to put kids on medications. They get a bonus when they write scripts. So what I tell everybody is check out Neurocore first. What's it going to hurt?"

SPRECHEN SIE DEUTSCH?

Six months before the 2008 Olympics in Beijing, China, Chris Kaman and his buddy Dallas Mavericks star Dirk Nowitzki talked about the upcoming Summer Games. Dirk, also a 7-footer, was born and raised in Würzburg, Germany, and was planning to play on Germany's Olympic basketball team. The pair discussed what kind of chance Germany had against a strong American team that was heavily favored to win the gold medal.

Chris, who was invited to try out for Team USA but wasn't selected, actually has some German blood running through his veins. He told Dirk that his great-grandparents immigrated to the United States from Germany just before the start of World War I.

As the two kept talking, they hatched a plan: based on his heritage, could Chris qualify for a German passport and play for Germany?

Chris was available.

"I was asked to be on the U.S. practice squad and scrimmage against the guys going to Beijing, but that wasn't the same as playing in the Olympics," Chris said. "The more I talked to Dirk about playing for Germany, the more I decided to just go for it. My dad's grandparents came over from Germany, and that was enough to get me a German passport."

The paperwork proved more daunting than expected. His application wasn't approved until June, just days before the qualifying games started.

He wasn't the only American-born NBA player on the German national team: Demond Greene, a 6-foot, 1-inch guard from Killeen, Texas, was also on the team. Demond qualified because he was the son of a U.S. serviceman who met his future wife, a German local, while stationed in Germany. Demond was the offspring of their union.

Chris knew what people were thinking when news got out that he would be playing for the Germans: *traitor.*

"I was an American, playing for Germany, so 'traitor' is the first thing that comes to your mind," Chris said. "I didn't care. I wanted to enjoy the entire Olympic experience, and I did. It was a once-in-a-lifetime thing, walking into the Bird's Nest for the opening ceremonies. Dirk held up the German flag, and I tried to take it all in. Walking around the track was unbelievable. I remember that it was so hot; it must have been 90 degrees and the humidity must have been 80 percent. All my clothes were drenched. When I walked by those 2,008 guys beating the drums, I wondered if this was really happening. It was just a cool opportunity, and I'm glad I got to play, even if it was for Germany."

If you're wondering how Chris—whose German vocabulary isn't much more than *ja* and *nein*—communicated with his teammates, he had no problems. All but two of the players spoke perfect English.

The German team won only one game out of five in Group B, defeating Angola. The United States defeated Spain in the gold medal game.

Will Chris play for Germany in the 2012 Olympics in London?

"If Dirk is ready to play, I'm ready to play," Chris said.

WEDDING BELLS

Chris met his future wife, Emilie, back at Central Michigan University, but they were not close in college and never dated.

One day in 2007, Chris was looking at his MySpace page—the social networking website in which he introduces himself by saying, "I love Jesus and basketball"—and noticed that Emilie had posted a hello.

Chris responded with his own message: "Hey, what's going on? What have you been up to?"

He learned that Emilie was in Phoenix, and they kept messaging back and forth. One time, when Emilie was in LA, they had lunch together, and things progressed from there.

Did any of Chris' teammates find out he was seeing Emilie?

"I kind of kept it on the down low because I wasn't sure if it was going to work out or not. I had been real skeptical of girls in the past—skeptical that nothing ever worked out before. A lot of girls you don't know about because you don't know them," he said, sounding like he was doing his best imitation of Yogi Berra. "But if you know someone from before, you feel more comfortable with her."

He even kept their budding love story secret from his family for a while.

Chris and Emilie dated for three years before Chris asked her to marry him in 2010. They had a wonderful wedding in Kauai in June, where they also honeymooned.

But what happened to his posse after Chris and Emilie returned from their Hawaii honeymoon? After all, two's a couple and three (or more) is a crowd.

"Ben and Caleb Chamberlain moved back to Michigan, and Jeremy Scully is now my personal assistant/chef/business manager. He's renting an apartment near our home in Manhattan Beach. Now we have this huge house just for Emilie and me, and that feels kind of weird," Chris said.

"Maybe we'll fill up the house with kids someday."

HE'S A WILD AND CRAZY GUY

Chris Kaman has always marched to the beat of a different drummer. When he turned pro and signed a multi-million-dollar deal, he treated himself to a car—a '72 Chevelle. He drove that heap for many years before buying a used Mercedes that allows him to stretch his feet.

Chris, who hunted a lot growing up in Michigan, is also an avid collector of guns and knives. One summer a few years ago, back home in

Michigan, he purchased a junkyard '88 Ford Taurus for fifty dollars and had it hauled to his parents' property. (One of the first things Chris did after signing with the Clippers was build his parents a new home on twenty-four acres outside Grand Rapids.)

Then he and his buddies spent a summer afternoon firing .50-caliber shells from a semi-automatic Barrett rifle. Each round was bigger than a giant-sized Tootsie Roll and cost five dollars. "We shot five clips that day—fifty shots."

Just type in "Chris Kaman and guns" into a YouTube search, and you can watch Chris and buddies take out the defenseless Taurus.

2012 update: What a wild 2011–12 season for Chris, who was traded from the Clippers to the New Orleans Hornets as part of the Chris Paul transaction. At one point, the Hornets told Chris to stay home, even though he was still part of the team—because they wanted to trade him. Chris expected to be shipped to another team looking for a big man during their playoff run, but nothing materialized.

So come on back, Chris! The Hornets decided they wanted Chris to play after all, and he responded by performing very well in the low post. When the season ended, Chris became an unrestricted free agent, able to sign with any team looking for a veteran seven-footer. Several teams stepped up, including his old team in New Orleans, but Chris decided to play with his old friend and former Olympic teammate Dirk Nowitzki when he signed a one year, $8 million contract with the Dallas Mavericks.

5

JEREMY LIN:
WELCOME TO THE SHOW

He's been called "Lincredible," a balm of "Liniment" for the NBA, and the architect of "Linsanity." For a few weeks in the spring of 2012, he was one the most talked-about athletes on the planet.

Of course, we're talking about Jeremy Lin, the twenty-four-year-old Asian-American point guard who moved from anonymity to stardom—even pop icon status—faster than an outlet pass off a clean rebound.

In early February 2012, he was the last man coming off the Knicks' bench during garbage time; by Valentine's Day, his dribble drive through five Los Angeles Lakers graced the cover of *Sports Illustrated*, basketball pundits on ESPN SportsCenter had run out of superlatives to describe him, and his No. 17 Knicks jersey was the NBA's top seller—telling touch points of stardom reminiscent of another professional athlete who had recently seized the public's imagination: Tim Tebow.

Think about it: the professional version of Tebowmania dominated the national conversation in the late fall and early winter months of 2011, continuing into the NFL playoffs. Everyone talked about Tebow's quick slant pass to Demaryius Thomas on the first play of overtime and the thrilling footrace to the end zone. The mighty Pittsburgh Steelers were slain, and the legend of Tim Tebow was writ even larger.

And then, barely a month later, Jeremy Lin leaped into our living rooms. In one short week—in just a handful of games in a consolidated, lockout-shortened season—Jeremy progressed from anonymous benchwarmer to the toast of the Big Apple as the Knicks' leading scorer, playmaker, and spiritual leader.

West of the Hudson River, he galvanized our attention in a fragmented media universe. The reason why is simple: everyone loves an underdog story, and Jeremy's improbable journey has all the ingredients of a Hollywood fairy tale.

I watched all this develop with great interest since I had been following Jeremy Lin for more than a year. I had interviewed him twice after he finished his rookie season with the Golden State Warriors and was enraptured by how this son of Taiwanese immigrants overcame preconceived ideas of who can and can't play basketball at the highest levels of the game.

I shared those thoughts in an earlier version of this book, *Playing with Purpose: Inside the Lives and Faith of Top NBA Stars*, which released in November 2011. We chose to put Jeremy's picture on the cover because we believed in him—his "upside" as they like to say in sportspeak. Quite frankly, though, we were taking a chance with Jeremy. Nobody knew what the future held. The jury was out on whether he'd stick with the NBA.

During his rookie season with the Golden State Warriors, Jeremy played in nearly as many games (20) for the club's D-League team, the Reno Bighorns, as he did with the Warriors (29). When he was part of the parent club, he rode the Golden State bench. Many nights, "DNP" appeared next to his name in the box score. When he did see action, he averaged 9.8 minutes and scored just 2.6 points per game for a sub-.500 team that failed to make the playoffs.

Nobody was saying that Jeremy was the next Jerry West, but I was fine with that. The fact that Jeremy even made it onto an NBA roster was noteworthy for several reasons:

1. At 6 feet, 3 inches, he wasn't tall for a game dominated by humongous athletes who could have played on Goliath's team back in the day.
2. He came from an Ivy League school, Harvard University, which last sent a player to the NBA in 1953—the year before the league adopted a 24-second shot clock.
3. He was the first American-born player of Chinese or Taiwanese descent to play in the NBA.

These against-the-grain characteristics caused us to put Jeremy on the cover of *Playing with Purpose*, but none of us knew about the breathtaking odyssey awaiting him in 2012. We'll get to that, but first you need to read about his remarkable backstory: where Jeremy came from, how he was raised, and how this undrafted prospect beat the odds to play in the NBA.

WHERE IT ALL BEGAN

There are plenty of entry points for Jeremy's story, but a good place to start would be by painting a picture of China in the late 1940s, when civil war ripped apart the world's most populous country. Chinese Nationalist forces led by General Chiang Kai-shek fought the People's Liberation Army—led by Chinese Communist Party leader Mao Zedong—for control of China, which, at that time, was a feudal society where a small elite class lived well and hundreds of millions barely survived. In 1949, after three years of bloody conflict, the Communist forces won, and Chiang Kai-shek and approximately two million Nationalist Chinese fled for their lives to the island of Taiwan off the coast of mainland China.

Among those refugees were Jeremy's grandparents on his mother's side. Shirley Lin ("Shirley" is actually an anglicized version of her Chinese first name) was born to a mother who was one of Taiwan's first prominent female physicians. One time during the 1970s, a contingent of American doctors visited Taiwan to study the advances Taiwanese physicians were making in health care. As Shirley's mother made contacts with those in the American medical community, the seed was planted to immigrate to the United States, where the family could pursue a better life. In 1978, just after Shirley graduated from high school in Taiwan, she and the family moved to the United States.

Shirley worked hard learning English and later enrolled at Old Dominion University, a college in Norfolk, Virginia. Her major was computer science, a discipline with a bright future. Many felt the computer revolution would explode in the 1980s. A newfangled invention called the PC, or personal computer, was starting to find its way into American homes.

There weren't too many Asians (or second-generation Asian-Americans, for that matter) at Old Dominion, and those who spoke Mandarin could be counted on two hands. The dozen or so Chinese-speaking students formed a small Asian support group for fun and fellowship, and one of those who joined was a graduate student from Taiwan—a handsome young man named Gie-Ming Lin, who'd come to the United States to work on his doctorate in computer engineering. His ancestors had lived in Taiwan since the nineteenth century, long before Communist oppression began on the mainland in the late 1940s and early 1950s.

Sharing the same cultural background and a common language brought Gie-Ming and Shirley together, and they began dating. It wasn't long before their love blossomed. When Gie-Ming told her that his plan was to finish his doctorate at Purdue University in West Lafayette, Indiana, they decided to move together to Purdue, where Shirley would continue her undergraduate classes in computer science while Gie-Ming worked on his Ph.D.

Don't get the idea that these two foreign-born students had plenty of time to linger over coffees at the student union, attend a concert at the Elliott Hall of Music, or go sledding down Slayter Hill after the first snowfall of winter. Gie-Ming and Shirley's parents didn't have the financial resources to contribute to their education, so they both had to work to pay their own tuition and living expenses. Shirley took shifts waitressing and bartending, while Gie-Ming moonlighted in his chosen field of computer engineering.

While at Purdue, Shirley was introduced to a Christian fellowship group, and she heard the Gospel presented for the first time. Curious about who Jesus was, she began exploring and learning about the Lord of the universe and how He came to this earth to die for her sins. She fell in love with Christ and got saved. When she told Gie-Ming what she had done, he investigated the Gospel and became a Christian as well. They soon plugged into a Chinese-speaking church and began their walk with Christ.

Gie-Ming and Shirley married while they were still in school. They liked living in the United States and became two of the many millions of immigrants chasing the American dream.

They certainly weren't afraid to work hard—or live frugally. Early on, Gie-Ming and Shirley would go fishing on the weekend at a nearby reservoir. Behind the dam was a lake teeming with bluegill, shad, crappie, and huge bass. Gie-Ming, who loved fishing and was quite good at it, would catch his limit and then bring home his haul in a galvanized bucket. They ate some of the fish that night and tossed the rest into the freezer.

And that's how the young couple would feed themselves all week long—from the fish Gie-Ming caught on weekends.

One evening, Gie-Ming flipped on the television to relax, and he came across a basketball game. The Lakers were playing the Celtics during one of their great 1980s NBA Finals battles, and the sight of Bird and Magic doing wondrous things on the Boston Garden parquet floor mesmerized Gie-Ming. He was smitten by the athleticism of these larger-than-life figures who made the basketball court look small. Gie-Ming started watching NBA basketball every chance he had, but that wasn't often since his studies and part-time work took up much of his free time.

Wait! Wasn't there a new technology arriving in people's homes back then? Yes, it was called the VHS recorder, and this then-state-of-the-art electromechanical device could record television broadcasts on cassettes that contained magnetic tape. Suddenly, the images and sound of TV shows and sporting events could be played back at a more convenient time—or replayed over and over for the viewer's enjoyment. The advent of the VHS tape in the 1980s revolutionized the way Gie-Ming—and millions of Americans—watched TV.

Gie-Ming started taping NBA games, and he loved watching Kareem's sky hook, Dr. J's gravity-defying dunks, and Magic leading the fast break and handling the ball like it was on the end of a string. It wasn't long before Gie-Ming was a certifiable basketball junkie. He studied those tapes with the same fervor as when he studied for his Ph.D. He couldn't tell friends why he loved basketball, but he just did.

Gie-Ming also started playing a bit of basketball himself. He taught himself how to dribble and how to shoot by practicing jump shot after jump shot at a nearby playground. He was too shy to join a basketball league, but he could be coaxed into playing the occasional pickup game. He loved breaking a sweat on the basketball court, and playing the game became his favorite form of exercise.

When Gie-Ming and Shirley completed their schooling at Purdue, they moved to Los Angeles, where Gie-Ming worked for a company that designed microchips. Shirley jumped on the mommy track and gave birth to their first child, a son they named Joshua. Two years later, on August 23, 1988, ten years to the day after Kobe Bryant entered the world in Philadelphia, Jeremy Shu-How Lin was born.

A WESTWARD MOVE

A job offer moved the Lin family to Florida for two years, but then Silicon Valley lured Jeremy's parents, Gie-Ming and Shirley, to Northern California in the early 1990s. Gie-Ming's expertise became computer chip design, while Shirley—who had given birth to her third son, Joseph—returned to work in her specialty: quality control, which meant making sure new computer programs were bug-free when they were released.

The Lins settled in Palo Alto, a community of sixty thousand residents that bordered Stanford University. Gie-Ming, who wanted to introduce his favorite game—basketball—to his three sons, signed up for a family membership at the local YMCA. (You can be sure that James Naismith would have been very pleased.) When firstborn Joshua was five years old, Gie-Ming introduced him to the fundamentals of basketball by using the passing, dribbling, and shooting drills he'd studied on his VHS tapes. Jeremy received the same instruction when he started kindergarten, and so would Joseph when he reached that age.

When Jeremy entered first grade, his parents signed him up for a youth basketball league. But at that young age, Jeremy wasn't very interested in the action around him. He was like those kids in T-ball who lie down on the outfield grass and watch the clouds pass by instead of what the next batter is going to do. Most of the time, Jeremy stood at half-court and sucked his thumb while the ball went up and down the floor. Since he couldn't be bothered to try harder, his mom stopped coming to his games.

As Jeremy grew and matured, he eventually became more interested in basketball, especially after he grew big enough to launch an effective shot toward the rim and watch it swish through the net. As shot after shot poured through the hoop, he was hooked. He asked his mother if she would come back and watch him play, but she wanted to know if he was actually going to try before she committed to returning to his games.

"You watch," he promised. "I'm going to play, and I'm going to score."

He scored all right. Sometimes Jeremy scored the maximum amount of points one player was allowed to under biddy basketball rules.

For the rest of Jeremy's elementary school years, his parents regularly took him and his brothers to the gym to practice or play in pickup games. They also enrolled him in youth soccer, but basketball was the game he wanted to play.

As the demands of schoolwork grew, Jeremy and his brothers would do their homework after school, wait for their father to come home for dinner, and then everyone would head over to the Y at eight o'clock for ninety minutes of shooting and pickup games. Gie-Ming continued to stress the fundamentals because he wanted the game's basic moves to become second nature to Jeremy.

As Jeremy improved, he couldn't get enough hoops action. On many nights, he and his family practiced and played right up until the time they closed the doors at the Palo Alto Family YMCA at 9:45 p.m.

While basketball turned out to be a fun family sport for the Lins, they weren't going to sacrifice academics or church on the altar of basketball. Academics were important to Gie-Ming and Shirley because they had seen firsthand how education could give them a better life. Church was even more important because they knew what a relationship with Christ meant to them and to the spiritual well-being of their sons.

Wherever they lived, the Lins gravitated toward a Chinese Christian church. When they moved to Palo Alto, they found a church they immediately liked: the Chinese Church in Christ in nearby Mountain View. This place of worship was really two churches in one. There were two services every Sunday at 11 a.m.—one in Mandarin and the other in English—in separate fellowship halls. Usually two hundred or so attended the Mandarin-speaking service, while around a hundred attended the worship service presented in English.

The strong demand for a church service in Mandarin was reflective of the demographics of the San Francisco Bay Area, home to the nation's highest concentration of Asian-Americans. At one time, the U.S. Census revealed that 27 percent of the people living in Pala Alto were Asian-Americans—racially identifying themselves as Chinese-American, Filipino-American, Korean-American, Japanese-American, or Vietnamese-American. There was a large Taiwanese-American community in nearby Cupertino (24 percent of the population), while other bedroom communities like Millbrae, Foster City, Piedmont, and Albany had Asian populations of 10 percent or greater.

Stephen Chen, pastor of the Chinese Church in Christ, remembers the first time he met Jeremy a little more than ten years ago, when Chen was the youth counselor. "Jeremy was around thirteen when I first ran into him," he said. "We were having a church cleaning day, and he was running around with his friends and being rambunctious. I remember scolding him, saying, 'Hey, we're trying to clean things up, and you're making things more messy.' "

Feeling chastised, Jeremy went home and told his parents he didn't want to go to that church anymore because the youth guy had been so mean to him. His parents didn't take his side, however, and the incident soon blew over.

Stephen Chen, looking for things to do with the youth in the church, discovered that Jeremy and his older brother, Josh, were avid basketball players. Josh was starting to play high school basketball, and Jeremy was living and breathing the game in middle school.

"I hadn't played a lick of basketball before that time," Stephen said. "But I wanted to connect with the Lin brothers, so I asked them if we could do a little exchange: I would teach them about the Bible and they would teach me how to play basketball."

Josh and Jeremy readily accepted. After youth group was over, they'd go to a nearby basketball court, where the Lin brothers taught Stephen how to do a layup, properly shoot the ball, and box out on rebounds. Then they would get the youth group together, choose up sides, and play basketball games.

"Jeremy would pass me the ball, even when the game was on the line," Stephen said. "He wasn't afraid that I'd lose the game for him. If we did lose, his older brother would get upset, but Jeremy would even console his brother. Even at that young age, Jeremy was hospitable, eager to get along with different types of people. He was also a natural leader, and kids listened to him."

Before entering high school, Jeremy wanted to get baptized as a public statement that he believed in Jesus Christ as his Lord and Savior. Stephen was pleased to hear of that desire. The Chinese Church in Christ had a baptismal inside the church sanctuary, and Jeremy was dunked during a Sunday morning service. Not long after that, Stephen asked him if he'd become part of the youth ministry's leadership team.

Jeremy was willing. The church had been renting out a local high school gym on Sunday evenings so the kids in the youth group could play basketball and invite their friends to join them. "Jeremy would always be the one who would ask other kids to come out and play basketball with us," Stephen said.

"And they would come. Jeremy wanted everyone to feel at home. That was just another way how he extended kindness to others."

The gym had two full courts across the main court. Many dads saw how much fun their kids were having, so they would play, too—fathers on one court and their sons on the other. Moms would visit with each other during the games of roundball.

All this basketball playing—after school, on weekends, and on Sunday nights—helped Jeremy to become quite a player, even though he was a shrimp on the court. As he entered his freshman year of high school, Jeremy topped out at 5 feet, 3 inches tall and weighed 125 pounds. Jeremy had set his sights on playing high school basketball, but he knew that if he didn't grow a lot in the next couple of years, he wasn't going to get a chance to play, no matter how talented he was.

One day, Jeremy told Stephen, "I want to be at least six feet tall."

Stephen looked at Jeremy. He knew that Asians were stereotyped as a short people, and there was some truth to that. The average male height in the U.S. is 5 feet, 10 inches, while in China, the average male height is 5 feet, 7 inches. Unfortunately for Jeremy, his parents weren't tall either. Both stood 5 feet, 6 inches, so he didn't have a great gene pool working for him.

"So how are you going to become six feet tall?" Stephen asked.

"I'm going to drink milk every day," the young Jeremy replied.

For the next few years, Shirley was constantly running to the local supermarket to buy milk by the gallon. He drank the dairy product like it was . . . water. Jeremy had a glass of milk with his breakfast cereal, drank milk at lunch, and always had a couple more glasses of milk with dinner.

"I drank so much milk because I was obsessed with my height," Jeremy said. "I'd wake up in the morning and measure myself every day because I heard that you're always taller in the morning, at least when you're growing. I wanted to see if I had grown overnight."

Jeremy's great wish was to be taller than his older brother, Josh, who was in the midst of a growth spurt that would take him to 5 feet, 10 inches during high school. Desperate to will his body to grow taller, Jeremy even climbed on monkey bars at school and let himself hang upside down, thinking that would expand his spinal column and make him taller.

Jeremy understood that he couldn't "force" his body to grow, but he also believed that to be competitive in the game of basketball, he had to grow to at least six feet tall.

MIRACLE-GRO

Jeremy enrolled at Palo Alto High School, where he made a big impression on his freshman basketball coach—even though he was one of the smallest players on the team. Years of playing in youth basketball leagues at the Y had honed his skills. His freshman coach stood up at the team's end-of-the-season banquet and declared, "Jeremy has a better skill set than anyone I've seen at his age."

And then something miraculous happened.

Jeremy grew.

And grew.

And grew.

By Jeremy's junior year, he had sprouted nine inches to reach the magic number—six feet of height. But he wasn't done. Jeremy would go on to add two more inches by his senior year and another inch or inch and a half in college to reach his present height, which is a tad over 6 feet, 3 inches. He also added bulk: his body filled out to a solid 200 pounds.

Not only did Jeremy grow like a beanstalk during his freshman and sophomore years, but he also showed Palo Alto High opponents that he could run the offense, shoot lights-out, and make the player he was guarding work extra hard. His position was point guard, which is perhaps the most specialized role in basketball. The point guard is expected to lead the team's half-court offense, run the fast break, make the right pass at the right time, work the pick-and-roll, and penetrate the defense, which creates open team-mates when he gets double-teamed.

When Jeremy dribbled the ball into the front court, he played like a quarterback who approached the line of scrimmage and scanned the defense to determine its vulnerabilities as well as its capabilities. Jeremy's mind quickly determined how an opponent's defense was set up and where the weak spots were. His quickness and mobility were assets.

During his sophomore season, Jeremy was not only good enough to win the point guard starting role, but his fantastic play also earned him the first of three first-team All–Santa Clara Valley Athletic League awards. During his junior season, he was the driving force behind Palo Alto High, helping the team set a school record for victories by posting a 32–2 record.

It was during Jeremy's senior year that he was the motor that propelled his team to the Division II California state championship. Going into the championship game, Palo Alto was a huge underdog against perennial power-house Mater Dei, a Catholic high school from Santa Ana in Southern California. No team had won more state basketball titles than Mater Dei, and the Monarchs, who had a 32–2 record, came into the game ranked among the nation's top teams.

Talk about a David-versus-Goliath matchup. Mater Dei was loaded with Division I recruits and had eight players 6 feet, 7 inches or taller, while Palo Alto had no one over 6 feet, 6 inches. Playing at Arco Arena, home of the Sacramento Kings, Jeremy was all over the court and personally engineered the plucky and undersized Palo Alto team to a two-point lead with two minutes to play. Could the Vikings hang on?

Jeremy brought the offense up the floor, trying to eat up as much clock as possible. Suddenly, there were just seconds left on the 35-second shot clock. Jeremy was above the top of the key when he launched a rainbow toward the rim to beat the shot clock buzzer. The ball banked in, giving Palo Alto a five-point lead.

Mater Dei wasn't finished yet, and neither was Jeremy. The Monarchs cut the lead to two points with 30 seconds to go, and then Jeremy dribbled the ball into the front court. Mater Dei didn't want to foul him because the Monarchs knew he was an excellent free throw shooter, so they waited for him to dish off to a teammate. Jeremy, however, sensed an opening and drove to the basket in a flash, taking on Mater Dei's star player, 6-foot, 8-inch Taylor King, in the paint. Jeremy went up and over King for a layup that gave him a total of 17 points in the game and iced the state championship in the 51–47 win.

You'd think that with all the college scouts in the stands for a state championship game, Jeremy would have to go into the Federal Witness Protection Program just to get a moment's respite. But the recruiting interest had been underwhelming all season long and stayed that way after the win over Mater Dei. It wasn't like Jeremy played for a tumbleweed-strewn high school in the middle of the Nevada desert. He was part of a respected program at Palo Alto High, and his coach, Peter Diepenbrock, was well-known to college coaches.

And Jeremy was highly regarded in Northern California high school basketball circles. He was named first-team All-State and Northern California's Division II Scholar Athlete of the Year. The *San Francisco Chronicle* newspaper named him Boys Player of the Year, as did the San Jose *Mercury News* and the Palo Alto *Daily News*.

Despite all the great ink and the bushel basket of post-season awards, despite sending out a DVD of highlights a friend at church had prepared, and despite Coach Diepenbrock's lobbying efforts with college coaches, Jeremy did not receive any scholarship offers to play at a Division I school. That MIA list included Stanford University, which was located literally across the street from Palo Alto High. (A wide boulevard named El Camino Real separates the two schools.)

It's perplexing why Stanford didn't offer Jeremy a scholarship. After all, Jeremy checked off a lot of boxes for the Cardinal:

- great high school basketball résumé
- local product
- strong academic record
- Asian-American

Regarding the last bullet point, almost 20 percent of the undergrad Stanford student body was Asian-American, and, as you read earlier, the school was located in a part of the country with a strong Asian population. But the Stanford basketball program took a pass. Some Stanford boosters interceded for Jeremy, telling the coaches that they had to give this Lin kid a look. But the best response the family received was that Jeremy could always try to make the team as a walk-on.

The Lins' eyes turned across the bay toward Berkeley, but the University of California coaching staff said the same thing: You can try to walk on, but no guarantees. During one recruiting visit, a Cal coach called Jeremy "Ron."

The disrespect continued at Jeremy's dream school—UCLA, where Josh was enrolled. Jeremy would have loved to have played for the storied Bruin program, and he was the kind of upstanding young man legendary Bruin coach John Wooden would have loved to recruit back in the 1960s and 1970s.

But the message from UCLA coaches was the same: You'll have to make the team as a walk-on.

Jeremy knew that few walk-ons—non-scholarship players invited to try out for the team—ever stick on the Division I basketball roster. He would never say it himself, but some basketball observers thought the fact that Jeremy was Asian-American cost him a Division I scholarship. Recruiters couldn't look past his ethnicity, couldn't imagine an Asian-looking kid having the game to compete against the very best players in the country. For whatever reason, they couldn't picture him playing basketball at the Pac-10 level.

RUNNING UP AGAINST A WALL

Jeremy had run into a "system" that blocked his path like two Shaqs in the paint. College coaches, who are the decision makers, look for something quantifiable in a high school player—like how tall he is or how high he can jump or how many points per game he scores. Jeremy's greatest strengths didn't show up in a box score. His game was running the show, leading the offense, and setting up teammates. He had an incredible feel for the game, a Magic-like peripheral vision, and a take-charge attitude that coaches love to see in their point guards.

"He knew exactly what needed to be done at every point in the basketball game," said his high school coach, Peter Diepenbrock. "He was able to exert his will on basketball games in ways you would not expect. It was just hard to quantify his fearlessness."

The problem likely stemmed from the fact that major college coaches had never recruited a standout Asian player before, so they didn't know what to do with Jeremy. Asian-American gym rats like him were a novelty in college basketball; only one out of every two hundred Division I basketball players came from Asian-American households. In many coaches' minds, college basketball stars had a different skin complexion or looked different than Jeremy.

The family had some options, however, thanks to Gie-Ming's and Shirley's insistence that their sons study and perform just as well in the classroom as they did on the basketball court. Jeremy carried a 4.2 grade point average (in the grade point system, an A is worth 4 points, but AP or Advanced Placement classes were weighted heavier because of their difficulty) at Palo Alto High, where he had scored a perfect 800 on his SAT II Math 2C during his freshman year. Jeremy's parents felt that if Pac-10 and other Division I teams didn't want their son, then maybe he could play for a top-ranked academic college—like Harvard.

The Lins looked east—toward the eight Ivy League schools, which are the most selective (and therefore most elite) universities in the country. Harvard and Brown each stepped up; both coaches said they'd guarantee him a roster spot. Each made the case that they really wanted him to play for their basketball programs.

In the Lin family, there was no discussion. If Harvard—the assumed No. 1

school in the country in nearly everyone's eyes—wanted him, then he was going to play basketball for Harvard, even if that meant his parents would pay for his schooling out of their own pockets. Harvard, like Yale, Princeton, Columbia, and the rest of the Ivy League schools, didn't offer athletic scholarships.

This was no small consideration for Jeremy's parents. In round numbers, a year of undergraduate studies at Harvard costs fifty thousand dollars, which covers tuition, room and board, books, fees, and the like. The Lins were already shelling out for Josh's education at UCLA.

"The tuition is nuts," Jeremy said. "My parents did everything they could to get me through school. I received some financial aid from Harvard and took some loans out."

It turned out to be a great investment on the academic as well as the athletic side.

DEALING WITH THE YAHOOS

Harvard basketball dates back to 1900, when John Kirkland Clark, a Harvard Law School student, introduced the game to the school. Basketball at Harvard, and at other colleges around the country, changed during the next century, and one telling example is the student section. You don't have to be studying to become a rocket scientist to know that college basketball crowds can be brutal.

So it should come as no surprise that the sight of a prominent, all-over-the-floor Asian-American basketball player personally beating their team would prompt a few immature—and likely drunk—members of student sections to taunt Jeremy during his four-year playing career at Harvard.

Some yelled really stupid (and racist) stuff, like "Hey, sweet and sour pork" or "wonton soup" from the stands. "Go back to China" and "The orchestra is on the other side of campus" were some of the other dim-witted taunts. One time at Georgetown, Jeremy heard terribly unkind remarks aimed in his direction, including the racial slurs "chink" and "slant eyes."

Jeremy just showed God's grace and gave his tormentors the other cheek. But he also played harder. Granted, the taunts bothered him at first, but he decided to let his game speak for itself. In the process, he helped make Harvard relevant again in college basketball and revived a dormant program.

During his junior and senior years, he was the only NCAA Division I men's basketball player who ranked in the top 10 in his conference for scoring, rebounding, assists, steals, blocked shots, field goal percentage, free throw percentage, and three-point shooting percentage.

Was anything missing? Well, he was co-leader of a campus Bible study group, so maybe there was a "souls saved" category that didn't get counted.

Many college-age Christians lose interest in their faith, even live prodigal lives when they go off to college. Jeremy, though, grew spiritually because he connected with the Harvard-Radcliffe Asian American Christian Fellowship (HRAACF). Although his involvement with the group was limited by the demands of class work and playing basketball, he met regularly with Adrian

Tam, an HRAACF campus staffer. Adrian became a spiritual mentor to Jeremy as they studied the Bible together and read books like *Too Busy Not to Pray*. "He loved his roommates, spending lots of intense one-on-one time with them, leading investigative Bible studies with them, and just plain hanging out with them," Adrian said.

What Tam remembers most about Jeremy, from their very first meeting, was his humility. "Even though he was more accomplished, smarter, and just plain bigger than I was, he always treated me with respect and honor," Tam says. "He was real with me, earnestly desiring to follow God in all things. He had a quiet ambition—not only to be the best basketball player he could be, but also to be the best Christ-follower he could be."

That quiet ambition was fully displayed on the basketball court, where Jeremy was a hit, pure and simple. He was such an exciting player that Harvard fans wore crimson red T-shirts with the words "Welcome to the Jeremy Lin Show" silkscreened across the front. He achieved such notoriety that Santa Clara University, which is located fifteen miles from Palo Alto, invited the Harvard team to the West Coast for a "homecoming" game during Jeremy's senior year and sold out its 4,700-seat arena.

The East Coast media heard of the Jeremy Lin Show and sent reporters from New York and Boston to check him out. Some of the more memorable quotes:

- "Jeremy Lin is probably one of the best players in the country you don't know about" (ESPN's Rece Davis).
- "He is a joy to watch. He's smooth, smart, unselfish, and sees the floor like no one else on it sees" (*Boston Herald* columnist Len Megliola).
- "Keep an eye on Harvard's Jeremy Lin. The fact that he's an Asian-American guard playing at Harvard has probably kept him off the NBA radar too long. But as scouts are hunting everywhere for point guards, more and more are coming back and acknowledging that Lin is a legit prospect" (ESPN NBA draft analyst Chad Ford).

Jeremy's stock rose during his senior year when Harvard played then No. 12–ranked University of Connecticut, a traditional college basketball powerhouse, on the road. He dissected and bisected UConn for 30 points and nine rebounds and threw a scare into one of the top teams in the country. Harvard lost 79–73.

When Jeremy's playing career at Harvard was over, he had high hopes that an NBA team would draft him and give him a clean shot at making the roster. But then . . . God had another plan, because the way Jeremy made it to the NBA only could have happened in God's economy. In other words, it was a miracle.

Let's review what happened.

After pre-draft workouts with eight teams, including his hometown Golden State Warriors, Jeremy was passed over through two rounds and sixty players chosen in the 2010 NBA draft. Playing at an Ivy League school probably had a lot to do with that—the last Harvard player to wear an NBA jersey was Ed Smith, who played all of eleven games in his one-season career back in 1953–54. The conventional wisdom among pro scouts was that Harvard players never pan out in the NBA.

After the draft, Dallas general manager Donnie Nelson invited Jeremy to play on the Mavericks' Summer League team. NBA Summer League games are played at a frenetic pace, and they can be a bit sloppy, but for rookies, or other non-roster players like Jeremy, Summer League provides a fleeting chance—perhaps a last chance—to pit their skills against NBA-level players and make an impression. The eight-day Summer League season was held in Las Vegas in July 2010.

Jeremy wasn't a starter for the Maverick Summer League team, not by a long shot. He sat behind an electrifying point guard named Rodrigue Beaubois, whom Dallas coaches were appraising for a roster spot. In the first four Summer League games, Jeremy was a spot substitute who averaged just 17 minutes and eight points a game.

In Summer League's final game, Jeremy's team was playing the Washington Wizards Summer League team, which featured John Wall, the No. 1 overall draft pick in the 2010 NBA draft.

Jeremy's teammate, Rodrigue Beaubois, twisted an ankle and had a poor outing in the first half. When Jeremy took his place, he outplayed, outhustled, outdrove, and outshined John Wall while leading his team to a big comeback—drawing *oohs* and *aahs* from the crowd with several fearless drives to the rim.

After that single half of brilliant play, several NBA teams looked at Jeremy in a new light. The Mavericks, the Los Angeles Lakers, and the Golden State Warriors all saw something in the kid. They thought that with the right seasoning, he could develop into an NBA player. Their thinking was that Jeremy could play a season in the NBA's Development League—known as D-League—and see where that took him.

And then Joe Lacob entered the picture.

Who is Joe Lacob?

During the summer of 2010, Lacob was in the midst of purchasing the Golden State Warriors with Peter Guber, the former chairman of Sony Pictures. Together, they put a $450 million tender to buy the team.

So how did this affect Jeremy?

Well, it turns out that Joe Lacob had coached his son's youth basketball team, which played against Jeremy when he was a pipsqueak. This fascinating interview between Lacob and San Jose *Mercury News* columnist Tim Kawakami explains things:

> Let's just confirm that you made the call to sign Jeremy Lin.
> *Lacob:* It was my call.
> Why Lin?
> *Lacob:* Well, that's a special situation.

Your son played with Lin? Against Lin?

Lacob: There were probably three guys that were pretty much the best point guards in high school in this area at that time, and Jeremy Lin was probably the best of them. And my son, Kirk, was right there with him. I've watched them play against each other, and I've coached against him since he was this high.

So I know him from [the time he was] a little kid. Also at Palo Alto I watched him win the state championship over a superior team, and he dominated Mater Dei. And he has heart, he has a lot of talent, he's athletic, which a lot of people don't understand. He's pretty long.

He has a game that translates to the NBA. He can drive, he's a slasher. He needs to shoot better, obviously. He needs to be a better outside shooter.

It's funny, people don't know his game. They say, oh, he's a shooter but he doesn't have these other skills. No, that's not true, it's the opposite.

Jeremy Lin, I think, can play. He didn't sign because he's Asian-American. That was a nice feature, like anything else. And I think it's great for that community and for the Warriors. But he got signed because he can play.

And that's how Jeremy Lin got his chance to play in the NBA. Two weeks after Summer League, he signed a two-year contract with the Warriors, and the news of his signing sent a shockwave through the San Francisco Bay Area—especially the Asian-American community. Then, through hustle and grit in training camp, he won a spot on the Warriors roster.

Undrafted, given up, and forgotten, Jeremy had somehow beaten the incredible odds to put on an NBA jersey.

Even better, his hometown team wanted him—and so did the hometown fans.

HIS ROOKIE YEAR

Jeremy made his debut in Golden State's second game of the 2010–11 season—on "Asian Heritage Night"—before a crowd of 17,408 fans that exploded with cheers when he was inserted into the game with two and a half minutes to go. Jeremy had the honor of dribbling out the final seconds of a hometown victory over the Los Angeles Clippers.

Jeremy Lin had made history. Not only did he become the first Chinese/Taiwanese-American basketball player in the NBA, but he was the first American-born player of Chinese descent to step onto an NBA court.

His parents had some advice for him when the season started. "They said, 'Be smart. There are going to be girls throwing themselves at you, so be smart.' Typical parent stuff," Jeremy said. "They also reminded me to make sure that I took care of my relationship with God first."

"So was it difficult or easy being a Christian in the NBA?" I asked.

"I don't want to say it was easy, but it wasn't as bad as I thought it would be. It helped that I had a couple of teammates who were strong Christians—Stephen Curry and Reggie Williams. We would go to chapel together before the games, and we would occasionally have Christian conversations, so that was definitely helpful. I had a lot of accountability in terms of a small group at home. And I was at home playing for the Warriors, so I went to my home church whenever I could. I had my pastor, Stephen Chen, and then I had my small group."

After signing with the Warriors, Jeremy got his own place in Hayward, located roughly midway between his parents' home in Palo Alto and the Oracle Arena in Oakland, where the Warriors play.

Having his family nearby made the transition into the pros a lot easier, Jeremy said, but the difficult part was not having any type of rhythm.

"You know, church is really tough to attend, and the schedule is so crazy. I had to listen to sermons on my computer on a lot of Sundays. The sermons would not always be from my home church but from a variety of places. My dad burned a bunch of sermons for me onto a CD, so I would carry a little case of all the sermons. Devotionals were a big part of my walk this year—just quiet times in my hotel rooms."

I asked Jeremy about those stretches in hotel rooms, since there's a lot of downtime in the NBA during long road trips that can stretch from five to eight days.

"Yeah, I had more spare time this year and more time to spend with God this year than I have ever had," he said. "That was one of the parts that made it easier versus in college, where you wake up, go to class, practice, then do your homework and go to sleep. I had a lot more free time, since I was no longer in school."

"And what about the temptations?" I asked. "I imagine one of the difficulties about playing in the NBA is all the women hanging around the hotel rooms and all the people trying to talk to you and that type of thing."

"Yes, I think that's definitely true, but it wasn't really an issue for me because I didn't go out very much. And then there were guys on my team that I hung out with, and we had a different lifestyle, so it wasn't a huge issue. But it's definitely out there if you want it, but I chose to take it out of play. Once you take a stand for something at the beginning, everybody respects that and they don't bother you about it."

While at Golden State, Jeremy wore No. 7—the biblical number that denotes completeness or perfection—and local fans loved cheering for their native son. But all the attention created an intense spotlight that followed him everywhere, and it became apparent that he was and would be a work in progress as a basketball player.

In late December 2010, the Warriors reassigned Jeremy—who had been averaging 17 minutes a game—to their D-League affiliate, the Reno Bighorns. It was hard for him not to see the move as a demotion.

"It was a shock because I did not realize how different the two leagues were," he said. "It was also humbling because the locker rooms, facilities, attendance at games, the travel—it was all very different. Playing in Reno gave me a whole new perspective on everything. In the NBA, it was easy to complain about this or about that, but after being in D-League, I gained a greater sense of gratitude."

The Warriors coaching staff sent him down to give him playing time, and for the rest of the season, he bounced back and forth between Reno and Oakland. By the end of his rookie season, he had played in only twenty-nine games for a struggling Golden State team that finished 36–46.

So how did he take all those difficulties?

"It was really hard," he confessed. "People don't believe me when I say my rookie season was the toughest year of my life, but it was. I had a lot of long nights and struggles. I had to really learn how to submit my will to God and learn to trust Him while going through difficult situations that I thought were maybe unfair at times or things that I had wished would have gone in a different way.

"What I learned was to lean on God in those situations, and to make my relationship more intimate by spending more time with Him every day. I did a lot of reading and I did a lot of praying. More praying than I had ever done. I just learned a ton."

Jeremy had signed a two-year contract with Golden State, so there was every expectation that the team would bring him along, give him more playing time, and help him become the best player he could be.

Funny how things worked out.

THE LOCKOUT

The 2011 NBA lockout was the fourth in the league's history and nearly cost the NBA the 2011–12 season. As it was, the 161-day work stoppage began on July 1, 2011, and ended on December 8, 2011. The lockout delayed the start of the regular season from November 1 to Christmas Day, and reduced the regular season from eighty-two to sixty-six games.

During the lockout, Jeremy could not step inside the Warriors' gleaming training facility in downtown Oakland. Nor was he allowed any contact with the coaches, trainers, or staff. It was up to Jeremy to stay in shape, but he didn't lack in motivation. He worked harder than ever to be ready when the NBA started up again.

His schedule was Navy SEAL Team 6 material:

- 10–11 a.m.: agility training
- 11–noon: weight training
- 1–2 p.m.: shooting work with a private coach
- 2–4 p.m.: individual work

He posted YouTube videos of his maniacal workouts on the court and in the weight room while keeping an eye on the latest news of the contract negotiations. As each "deadline" passed without an agreement, both sides inched closer to the unthinkable—losing the entire season.

At the eleventh hour, the two sides reached an agreement on November 25, 2011. NBA commissioner David Stern announced that the first practice would be Friday, December 9, with the official season beginning on Christmas Day.

Jeremy arrived at the Oakland facility for the first day of practice and suited up. He had just met his new coach, Mark Jackson, who had never seen him play. Undoubtedly, Jeremy felt mounting pressure to prove himself all over again.

He was loosening up when he was told that general manager Larry Riley wanted to see him. The Warriors hadn't even started their layup drills.

If you've seen the Brad Pitt movie *Moneyball*, you know it's never good news when the GM asks to see you. This occasion was no exception.

Jeremy, the Warriors organization has decided to put you on waivers. We think you'll clear the waiver wire so that we'll get you back.

No matter how much perfume Riley sprayed into the air, the pronouncement stunk. Jeremy was being let go, cut from the team, categorically released. For all he knew, his short-lived NBA career was over.

This is where the "business" side of professional basketball can snap a player's dream in a heartbeat. What happened is that the Golden State management made a calculated decision to go after Los Angeles Clippers center DeAndre Jordan, a restricted free agent, to shore up a big hole in their low court. But to make Jordan an offer he couldn't refuse, the Warriors had to create room under their salary cap. That meant moving a few pieces around the chessboard: cut Jeremy loose, use their amnesty clause on veteran guard Charlie Bell, and delay the signing of two rookies they liked—Klay Thompson and Jeremy Tyler. Then, under salary cap rules, the team would have enough money to bring in the center they desperately needed.

Once Jordan was signed, sealed, and delivered, the Warriors could bring back Jeremy—if no other team claimed him.

On the same day—December 9—something important to Jeremy's story was happening in New York. The Knicks waived veteran point guard Chauncey Billups and signed center Tyson Chandler, leaving the team out of cap space and without a true point guard.

Three days later, the Houston Rockets picked up Jeremy, so he *couldn't* go back to his childhood team. To add insult to injury, Clippers owner Donald Sterling—a notorious skinflint—matched Golden State's overly generous four-year, $43 million offer for DeAndre Jordan, which meant the bruising center was staying in Los Angeles.

Talk about collateral damage. Golden State's gamble had blown up in their faces, and Jeremy was starting all over with a new team in Houston.

Jeremy arrived in Space City to discover he'd have to take a number and wait his turn to make an impression on the coaches. The Rockets were overstocked with point guards, and Jeremy had a hard time getting reps in practice. In two preseason games with the Rockets, he got on the floor for only eight minutes in each.

"At the time, I was thinking if this doesn't work out, I maybe needed to take a break from basketball," Jeremy told Marcus Thompson II with the Silicon Valley *Mercury News.* "I put in four months of training. I felt like I worked harder than anyone else. And now I was fighting for my chance to practice. I was questioning everything."

Then, on Christmas Eve, Jeremy woke up to find a lump of coal under his tree: he was being waived—let go—by Houston. This time GM Daryl Morey was the bearer of bad news, and he didn't salve the wound by saying that he hoped Jeremy would be back. His explanation was that the Rockets needed cap room to sign Haitian center Samuel Dalembert.

Merry Christmas, kid. Best of luck to you.

This could have been the end of the line. Yet Jeremy knew that faith is the assurance of things hoped for, the conviction of things not yet seen (Hebrews 11:1), and this latest zigzag was not the time to doubt that God was still in control. It was the time to double down on his commitment to the Lord.

"As he headed back to the Bay Area, he gave up trying to control everything," Thompson wrote. "He gave up worrying. Or at least he tried like crazy."

The day after Christmas, Jeremy woke up at his parents' place and did a devotional before heading to the gym to stay in shape. During his shoot-around, each time anxiety about the future crept in, he whispered Romans 8:28 to himself:

And we know that in all things God works for the good of those who love him, who have been called according to his purpose.

Something good was about to happen, he was sure of it. But Jeremy had no idea that more trials were ahead of him.

NEW YORK, NEW YORK

The New York Knicks had a guard problem.

When the lockout was over, the club signed thirty-two-year-old Baron Davis to be their point guard, even though he had a back injury that would keep him out until the end of February. Until Davis could join the team, the Knicks would forge ahead with veteran guards Mike Bibby and Toney Douglas at point and Iman Shumpert as a shooting guard. Bill Walker (6 feet, 6 inches) and Landry Fields (6 feet, 7 inches) were small forwards who could play in the backcourt, too.

Then in the Christmas Day season opener against the Boston Celtics, Iman Shumpert got tangled up in the paint and injured his right knee. After the game, the team medical staff called the injury a sprained medial collateral ligament and said Shumpert would need two to four weeks to heal.

The Knicks were down to two guards.

The front office searched the waiver wire for a body—and Jeremy Lin was available. On December 27, the team claimed Jeremy, prompting Knick head coach Mike D'Antoni to say, "Yeah, we picked up Jeremy Lin off of waivers [as] a backup point [guard] in case. We've always liked him as a player, so we'll see where we go with it."

Reaction among the New York media was more muted. "The Knicks offense didn't get a huge boost Tuesday, but their collective GPA sure did," sniffed *New York Daily News* beat writer Sean Brennan, referring to the new

Ivy Leaguer in their midst.

Jeremy didn't see it that way. He hit his Twitter account and sent out this message: "Thankful to God for the opportunity to be a New York Knick!! Time to find my winter coats from college lol!"

He was back in the NBA, but his contract wasn't guaranteed. He could be cut any day, so there was no reason to shop for a Fifth Avenue penthouse.

Fortunately, by this time his big brother, Josh, was living in the Big Apple, attending New York University as a dental student. Josh had married and set up housekeeping in a one-bedroom apartment in the Lower East Side, so if Jeremy didn't mind sleeping on the couch . . .

At Madison Square Garden, Jeremy was parked at the end of the bench like there was a wheel clamp strapped to his Nikes. D'Antoni rarely called his number, which was No. 17. His favorite, No. 7, wasn't available because the team's marquee player, Carmelo Anthony, wore it. We can surmise that Jeremy added a 1 before the 7—1 being the numeral that symbolizes unity and primacy, as God is one, although in three persons. (At least that's *my* interpretation for Jeremy wearing No. 17.)

From December 28 to January 16, Jeremy played sixteen minutes in twelve games, scoring a total of nine points. I didn't see his name pop up very often in the box scores, but I was thankful he was still in the NBA. He was, after all, still on the cover of *Playing with Purpose*, though driving to the hoop in a navy blue Golden State jersey.

The Knicks were losing more than they were winning. And there was no way Jeremy could get into the offensive flow at the end of the game when the outcome had been decided and the play was chaotic and unrehearsed. He couldn't learn D'Antoni's system because there were very few practice days in the contracted season.

On January 17, Jeremy was demoted to D-League—the Erie BayHawks, the Knicks' developmental team affiliate.

Not again!

"I had no opportunity to prove myself," he said. "There was definitely a little bit of 'What's going on?' in my prayers. My flesh was constantly pulling at me. Whine. Complain. Whine. Complain. But the other side of me was thinking, *My God is all powerful . . . why do I even doubt God?* At the same time, it's a growing process."

And at least he'd get to play ball. In his BayHawks debut against the Maine Red Claws on January 20, Jeremy laid down a triple double: 28 points, 12 assists, and 11 rebounds. He played forty-five of the forty-eight minutes and repeatedly beat defenders with an extremely quick first step.

The Knicks scouts were impressed, as they should have been. Jeremy was immediately recalled to New York, where the season was going nowhere fast. Throughout the rest of January and early February, losses piled up like snowdrifts. Six losses in a row. Win a game. Three losses in a row.

Mike Bibby and Toney Douglas were playing horribly. Baron Davis was still out. Iman Shumpert showed little aptitude for the point guard position.

Then Carmelo Anthony, the team's leading scorer, suffered a groin injury in mid-January and looked to be out for six weeks. There was no clear ball handler or offensive catalyst on the Knicks team. Jeremy was still the forgotten man on the bench.

On Saturday, February 4, at halftime of a home game against the New Jersey Nets, the injured star Carmelo Anthony—dressed in street clothes—pulled Coach D'Antoni aside in the locker room. He suggested that he play Jeremy more. See what the kid could do. What was there to lose? The Knicks had been beaten in five of their previous six games and were on a 2–11 losing jag.

Jeremy played like he was back with the Erie BayHawks—aggressive, like he belonged in the NBA. D'Antoni left him in, and Jeremy grabbed the reins of leadership. He scored 25 points, snared five rebounds, and dished out seven assists—all career highs—leading the Knicks to a 99–92 victory.

D'Antoni liked what he saw—a real point guard running the offensive show. "You're starting Monday night," he told the second-year player.

Linsanity was about to be unleashed on an unsuspecting public.

THE MIRACLE NEAR 34TH STREET

On the morning of Jeremy's first NBA start against the Utah Jazz on Monday, February 6, the Knicks webmaster made some changes to the team's website: the smiling face of youthful Jeremy Lin greeted eyeballs on the splash page. The marketing department sent out an e-blast with "Lisanity!" in the subject line.

The Knicks were shorthanded without Amar'e Stoudemire, who was granted bereavement leave after his older brother Hazell was killed in a car crash in Florida. Carmelo Anthony tried to play but had to leave the game after six minutes because of a strained right groin.

Time to step up.

Jeremy set the tempo again with dazzling dribbling and sweet drives to the basket. A nifty midair hand change for a reverse layup prompted the Knicks home crowd to chant "MVP! MVP!" They were obviously still in a celebratory mood after cheering their beloved New York Giants to a come-from-behind victory over the New England Patriots a day before in Super Bowl XLVI.

Jeremy scored a career-high 28 points, showing that his 25-point performance against the New Jersey Nets was no fluke. The fact that Jeremy orchestrated a win against a decent team attracted some notice around the league. But this was going to be a busy week for the Knicks. On Wednesday, they had a quick road trip to play the Washington Wizards, then a return home to host the Kobe-led Lakers on Friday night, followed by another road trip to Minnesota to play the T-Wolves on Saturday night.

Awaiting Jeremy in the nation's capital was John Wall. Remember him? He was the No. 1 pick in the 2010 draft—and Jeremy's foil in the final game of Summer League, the game where Jeremy played flawlessly and earned a roster spot with the Golden State Warriors.

On this evening, Jeremy was guarded closely by Wall when he employed a crossover dribble and blew past his defender like his sneakers were nailed to the floor. The lane opened up like the parting of the Red Sea. Instead of kissing the ball off the glass with a lay-in, Jeremy elevated and slammed a one-handed dunk that electrified even the home crowd.

"I think they messed up their coverage," Jeremy said after the game.

Chalk up Jeremy's first double-double: 23 points and 10 assists in a 107–93 victory.

A tsunami was building. It wouldn't crest yet—that would happen two days later when Kobe and the Lakers came to the Garden. But for now, "the fluke no longer looks so flukey," wrote Howard Beck in the *New York Times*. "The aberration is not fading away. Jeremy Lin is not regressing to the mean, whatever that mean is supposed to be."

Surely he'd be put in his place by the great Kobe Bryant. Surely the thirty-three-year-old star had taken notice of the hoopla and would show this young buck a thing or two. Surely Jeremy wasn't still sleeping on his brother's couch.

Actually, he wasn't. Now he was sleeping on the couch of his teammate Landry Fields. The night before his breakout game against the New Jersey Nets, Jeremy found himself homeless. The comfy sofa where he laid his head at his brother's pad in the Lower East Side was reserved for friends who were coming over for a party.

Landry heard about Jeremy's plight and said he could crash at his place in White Plains, New York, which was close to the Knicks' training facility. Landry had a nice large brown couch in the living room. A flat-screen TV, refrigerator, and bathroom were steps away. What more did a bachelor need?

There was no way that Jeremy or Landry was going to change a winning routine. Jeremy was sleeping on that couch whether he wanted to or not.

A date loomed with Kobe Bryant—the player he shared a birthday with—in the heart of downtown Manhattan. It's hard to describe how the American and global media apparatus had trained its lens on Madison Square Garden that evening, but they had. A galaxy of celebrities was on hand, including filmmaker and Knicks superfan Spike Lee, actor Ben Stiller, erstwhile wrestler and actor Dwayne "The Rock" Johnson, and New York Giants receiving hero Justin Tuck.

A lot—really a lot—was riding on the sinewy shoulders of Jeremy Shu-How Lin. He had everything to gain and much to lose, which is why you have to love what he did that night. All the pressure, all the hype, all the microphones, all the cameras examining every muscle twitch—and he didn't flinch.

I mean, laying down 38 points on Kobe and the Lakers was ridiculous. He made everything, including scoring nine of the team's first 13 points to help the Knicks build a large lead. Analysts like to call that "making a statement." He nailed short jumpers, put a deft spin move on Derek Fisher to beat him to the hoop, and flung in a three-pointer from the left baseline. Kobe nearly matched him, scoring 24 of his 34 points in the second half—but Bryant left the Garden on the wrong side of a 92–85 Knicks victory.

There was a telling moment when the torch of popularity may have been passed.

Derek Fisher had been manning him, but on this possession, Kobe and Jeremy were running down the court together. Kobe reached out and put his hand on Jeremy's body. This was a subtle yet effective way for Kobe to establish defensive dominance and put Jeremy in a subservient position.

Jeremy, without hesitation, quickly but firmly pushed the hand away, as if to say, *There's a new sheriff in town.*

Jeremy proved he was no one-week wonder in outplaying Kobe Bryant and the Lakers team. He was being called the "Taiwanese Tebow" for the way he impacted his teammates and lifted their games—and for the forthright and earnest way he spoke about his faith afterward.

The hype surrounding Jeremy would only grow. He was legit. He had four straight games with at least 20 points and seven assists. In the history of the NBA—since the 1976 NBA/ABA merger—no player had scored more points in his first four starts.

More importantly, he had embraced the challenge of beating one of the league's top franchises in his first nationally televised game.

A LIFE OF ITS OWN

The Knicks had a tall order following the Lakers win: hop on the team plane and fly to Minneapolis for a road game the following night. Prior to tip-off, Jeremy and his new "roommate" Landry Fields enacted a rather unique pre-game ritual that they first tried out against the Washington Wizards four days earlier.

Facing each other in front of the Knicks' bench, Jeremy pretended to flip through an imaginary book that Landry was holding in his hands. Then the pair pretended to take off their reading glasses, which they placed into imaginary pocket protectors. The routine ended with both players simultaneously pointing to the sky.

Okay, so it's not as dramatic as LeBron James throwing talcum powder into the air, but it was pretty cute. More than a few bloggers figured it was some sort of nerdy, bookworm faux handshake involving a Harvard grad with a former Stanford student-athlete. Actually, there was a lot more significance than that.

Landry Fields said that after Jeremy's first start, they had to come up with something since everyone was talking about the Harvard/Stanford connection between the two. "So we wanted to go out there and do something that was lighthearted and not too serious," he said.

The book is not a college textbook, Landry said, but God's Word. "It's a Bible because at the end of the day, that's what we're playing for. And that's why we point up toward the sky at the end."

The Jeremy Lin Show, meanwhile, played well off Broadway. Jeremy scored 20 points, reaching the 20-point plateau for the fifth time in a row, and his free throw with 4.9 seconds left (after missing the first) gave the Knicks a 99–98 lead and capped a furious fourth-quarter 12–4 comeback.

Jeremy and the Knicks team knew they stole one in Minnesota. After starting off hot in the first half with 15 points, the man guarding him, Ricky Rubio, showed why he was the league leader in steals. He forced Jeremy into making multiple turnovers, and Rubio even swatted away one of his layup attempts.

But just like there are no ugly babies, there's no such thing as an ugly win. The Knicks had now captured their fifth in a row without Carmelo Anthony and Amar'e Stoudemire, who was burying his brother in Florida.

From my home in Southern California, I was doing my best to keep up with Linsanity. The Knicks, I noticed, were finally getting a breather—two glorious days—before their next game in Toronto against the Raptors.

The game wasn't on any of my 500 channels, so I did the next best thing: I turned to *NBA Gametime Live.*

"Here's what's going on in Toronto," host Ernie Johnson said, who then showed a clip of Jeremy driving into the maw of the Raptor defense. Jeremy was met there by Raptor Amir Johnson. A collision ensued, and on the continuation, Jeremy double-pumped a feathery four-footer into the hole. Three-point play!

Jeremy's fearless drive to the rack capped a 17-point rally to tie the game. A minute and five seconds was left to play.

Great, I thought. *I'm just in time to see a thrilling ending.*

"We cannot take you live to that game because of contractual restrictions," Ernie said, as if he was reading my mind. "But we will keep you up to speed. It's eighty-seven apiece in Toronto."

Ernie attempted to make small talk with analysts Greg Anthony and Chris Webber, but Anthony stared off into the distance, no doubt watching the live feed on an off-camera monitor.

Ten or fifteen seconds passed when Ernie interrupted the patter to announce an update from Toronto that they *could* show. The visual is still imprinted on my brain: Jeremy, yo-yoing the ball above the top of the key, letting the clock run down. The crowd of twenty thousand on its feet. A quick feint, and Jeremy pulls up for a beyond-the-arc, high-flying rainbow that sails cleanly through the net to give the Knicks a 90–87 lead with .05 seconds to go.

"Are you kidding me?" EJ exclaimed. "Are you kidding me? This story gets crazier and crazier every night the Knicks play."

He had done it again.

AN UNEXPECTED TURN

Just as quickly as Jeremy became a household name, he fell off the radar. Just weeks after the launch of Linsanity, he suffered a serious knee injury. When an MRI revealed a small chronic meniscus tear on his left side, the decision was made to go straight to the operating room in early April 2012. Team officials expressed an initial hope that Jeremy could return in six weeks for a playoff run, but that turned out to be too much to ask.

Jeremy became a restricted free agent after the 2011–12 season ended, meaning the Knicks could match any offer and keep him. You'd think many teams would pursue this uncommon young man with extraordinary leadership and athletic skills. But only the Houston Rockets—the team that let him go to New York—put an offer sheet of $25.1 million before him.

The Knicks, with a week to think about it, said thanks but no thanks. So Jeremy is now hooping it in Houston, which in some ways must feel like a return to sanity for the player who electrified New York fans with his passion and versatile play.

6

LUKE RIDNOUR:
HEIR TO PISTOL PETE

Luke Ridnour was in fourth grade when his schoolteacher announced a big assignment she wanted Luke and his classmates to complete in two weeks.

The task?

Write a three-page paper on a person of their choosing.

Luke shifted eagerly in his seat. He knew exactly whom he wanted to write about.

When school let out, Luke gathered his backpack and sprinted from the rear of Blaine Primary School, past the green tennis courts, to the Blaine High gymnasium. The elementary school, middle school, and high school were located on the same campus, so the distance was only a hundred yards. Luke knew his father—a PE teacher and the high school's head basketball coach—would be in his office preparing for practice.

The Ridnour family lived in Blaine, Washington, a small town of four thousand situated in the very northwest corner of the continental United States. The border town is the terminus point for Interstate 5, the West Coast highway that links the Canadian border with the boundary of Mexico, 1,381 miles to the south. Blaine's colorful past dates back to the Fraser River gold rush of 1858, which brought an influx of eager prospectors into the region.

When Luke bounced into Rob Ridnour's office that afternoon, he told his dad about the assignment he had received that day.

"Who are you going to write about?" his father asked.

"Pistol Pete."

Of course, Rob thought.

Ten-year-old Luke knew about Pistol Pete because he and the family had recently watched *The Pistol: The Birth of a Legend*, a video that had been released a few months earlier. The slice-of-life movie told the story about Pete Maravich's eighth-grade year when he played on the varsity basketball team at Daniel High School in Central, South Carolina, despite being too young to attend the school.

Set in 1961, the film recounted how Pete's teammates ostracized him because of his young age and because of his unworldly talent for shooting and whipping behind-the-back passes. *The Pistol* also explored the supportive father-son relationship between Pete and his father, Press Maravich, who was a former pro player and Clemson University coach.

"Well, you'll have to do some research on Pistol Pete before you write your paper," said Luke's father, who knew the entire Maravich story. Rob was a middle-schooler in the late 1960s when Pete's sleight-of-hand artistry left crowds gasping and sportswriters crooning about the new sensation from Louisiana State University. (You'll read a lot more about Pete Maravich in the last chapter.)

Over the next couple of weeks, Luke read Maravich's autobiography, *Heir to a Dream*, and also watched *Pistol Pete's Homework Basketball* training videos, which mesmerized him. Luke had been dribbling a basketball since age three and was a very skilled player for his age, but Pete could make the basketball do things he'd never seen before. Pete's effortless demonstration of ball-handling prowess captivated Luke's young imagination.

Luke emulated everything Pistol Pete did on the *Homework Basketball* videos—from ball-handling exercises like the Square V dribble, the crossover dribble, and the through-the-legs dribble, to positioning his wrist properly so as to impart backspin and thus more control on the jump shot. Luke even taught himself to twirl the ball on his right index finger like a spinning top.

Since Pete had said he took a basketball everywhere with him when he was a youngster, Luke started doing the same thing. He started carrying a basketball into Blaine Primary School and dribbling in the hallway on his way to class, though he sometimes got into trouble for being disruptive. After the final bell, he would dribble from the elementary school to his father's office inside the gym, where he'd hang out for a bit before leaving to shoot baskets with the high school players.

"I emulated everything I saw Pete do because I wanted to handle the basketball just like he did," Luke said. "I tried dribbling from a car while my dad drove down the street, and I dribbled on a railroad rail, but that was pretty difficult."

Luke even slept with his basketball, just like Pete.

There was another reason Rob Ridnour and his wife, Muriel, supported Luke's desire to write a paper on Pete Maravich. You see, Pistol was very outspoken about the transformation he had experienced after accepting Jesus Christ as his Lord and Savior following his retirement from pro basketball. That part of Pete's story was the focal point of *Heir to a Dream*, which was published a few months prior to his death from a sudden heart attack at age forty.

Rob and Muriel had Luke listen to a *Focus on the Family* broadcast in which Dr. James Dobson talked about the dramatic morning when Maravich collapsed and died after playing in a pickup basketball game with the *Focus on the Family* radio host and members of his staff. "I learned that Pistol Pete, toward the end of his life, was sold out for Jesus," Luke said. "That was the big thing that stands out in my memory, more than the basketball stuff. Yes, Pete was passionate about basketball, but when he found Jesus, that became his main passion."

Luke's parents were familiar with Dr. Dobson because they listened to Christian radio programs like *Focus on the Family* on Praise 106.5 FM while riding in the car. In addition, they raised Luke and his older sister, Heather, in the Christian faith and took them to church every Sunday morning and Wednesday night.

A COMMITMENT TO THE GAME

While working on his Pistol Pete paper, Luke saw the commitment Pete had made to the game at a young age—and he was inspired to do the same. Beginning in the fifth grade, he would get up at five every morning, rain or shine, to start his training regimen.

Blaine, since it lies so far north, can be a chilly, damp place in winter. The average highs in December and January are barely above 40 degrees, and it's not unusual for the lows to dip into the 20s. Rain is a constant. That never stopped Luke from his workouts, though. "He would religiously get up and do those drills *every* morning," Rob said. "Rain, snow . . . it didn't matter. He was out there every day from the fifth grade through his senior year of high school, even in winter and the pre-dawn darkness."

One Saturday, Luke had set a goal of making fifteen hundred free throws. Even though there was a driving snowstorm in Blaine that day, Luke stayed outside, his numb fingers stiff from the freezing cold, until he made his fifteen hundred free throws.

Rob had installed a basketball rim in the backyard patio, and that's where Luke practiced every morning before school. He began his training with a jump rope routine to warm up, and then he'd move into the "Maravich drills" he'd seen in the videos or that his father used in his summer basketball camps.

On one occasion, Luke asked his father how he could increase his quickness. "Now we're talking about a fifth-grader asking that question, which shows you how determined he was to improve every facet of his game," Rob said. "I told him boxers always had good body balance, good footwork, and improved quickness from jumping rope. So he decided to try rope jumping, and Luke became very good at it. I think jumping all that rope really helped his career. He's always had good feet and good body balance."

All that hard work—day after day, week after week—helped Luke make big leaps in his game. While he was still in elementary school, he would get the local parents clapping and cheering at his father's games at Blaine High when he put on dribbling demonstrations during halftime. Luke, whose specialty was simultaneously dribbling two balls at the same time, could dribble circles around anyone.

After seeing his halftime shows, friends of Luke's parents lavished praise on him, and some started calling him "Cool Hand Luke"—after the famous 1960s film starring Paul Newman.

By the sixth grade, Luke had outgrown his middle school competition in Whatcom County, so his parents had him try out for an elite travel team from Seattle. When he was accepted, it necessitated some huge sacrifices on his parents' part. They had to drive Luke 220 miles round-trip to the big city three times a week for practices and games.

COURT HUSTLER

When Luke Ridnour was in middle school, he'd often challenge the high school players on his father's team to three-point shooting contests before they started practice. The stakes: a bottle of Gatorade from the vending machine.

It wasn't long before the upperclassmen discovered that shooting treys against Luke was a losing bet.

So one time Luke said he'd shoot his three-pointers left-handed. This time he got some takers.

Big mistake.

They all had to pay up.

Luke was one of the youngest kids on the Seattle travel team—and the only white player. His black teammates called him "Casper," but that didn't bother Luke—in fact, he had fun with it. His team played in numerous AAU tournaments up and down the West Coast, which necessitated expensive road trips but also boosted Luke's basketball experience and abilities. His Central Area Youth Association (CAYA) team qualified for a national tournament in Lexington, Kentucky, and played in Florida.

All that tournament experience helped Luke make great strides in his game, and that was a big help when he started playing for his father during his freshman year of high school. Luke would become a dominant high school player and would help guide the Blaine Borderites (don't you love that mascot name?) to the Washington Class 2A state championship during his junior season. The grateful townspeople threw a huge parade down H Street for their favorite son and favorite team.

As Luke headed into his senior year, everyone could see that the 6-foot, 2-inch point guard was an awesome talent. All the 5:00 a.m. workouts, all the after-dinner shooting in the Blaine High gym, and all the out-of-state competition paid off as college scholarship offers began rolling in. College coaches could see he was a natural in the way he created separation with the dribble, pumped the perfect pass to his teammates, displayed his silky stroke at the free throw line, and showed leadership on the floor.

Luke was the prototypical point guard the top-flight college basketball programs desired. Kentucky and Utah wanted him. So did Gonzaga University, an up-and-coming program in Spokane, located in the eastern part of Washington. In the Pac-10, the University of Washington was waiting to roll out the purple carpet in Seattle. Farther south, Oregon and Oregon State both wanted Luke, but he couldn't visit both schools because he only had one recruiting trip left. The NCAA limits high school players to five out-of-town recruiting trips.

Luke flipped a coin to see which Oregon school he would visit. The University of Oregon won, and during his weekend visit in Eugene, he called his parents to tell him how much fun he was having.

Luke liked what he saw during his recruiting trip. I'm sure McArthur Court—the field house known as "The Pit" because of the way the crazy fans sit in bleachers almost directly on top of the players and shake the building from its wooden rafters to its hardwood floor—made a huge impression on him. Built in 1926, Mac Court's electric atmosphere was the consummate stage for college basketball.

Luke committed to Oregon before the start of his senior year, but he didn't put his game into cruise control. The way he played during his final season made him the talk of high school basketball in the state of Washington. Luke and his teammates at Blaine High netted another state championship, and McDonald's and *Parade* magazine named Luke a high school All-American.

During his four seasons of high school varsity basketball, Luke led the Blaine Borderites to a 97–11 record.

GO, DUCKS, GO!

Eugene, Oregon's second-largest city, is a college town, pure and simple. Humorist Dave Barry once said that Eugene is "approximately 278 billion miles from anything," but that's not really true. Eugene is a happening place—and the birthplace of Nike—that evokes a retro vibe that comes from a high concentration of hippies and vegetarian restaurants. While the Emerald City promotes its natural beauty and recreational opportunities—with a focus on the arts, alternative lifestyles, and a live-and-let-live culture—at the end of the day, Eugene is a small city that revolves around the twenty-three thousand students attending the University of Oregon.

Sure, Eugene is also a liberal enclave, where protests against "Big Oil" are clothing optional and people pass the tofu pâté around a campfire of hemp. But once you get beyond the red flannel shirts and the Birkenstocks, people are people. Not many are Christians, though. Eugene is the least-churched city in the least-churched state in the country. No one would ever confuse the Willamette Valley with the Bible Belt.

Yet Luke will tell you that it was a divine appointment for him to play his college career in Eugene for the Oregon Ducks, and much of the reason is because he met an ex-marine who mentored him during this three-year career at the school.

That ex-marine was Keith Jenkins, pastor of Jubilee World Outreach Church, which grew from a congregation of seventeen persons in 1996 to nearly a thousand while Luke was in Eugene.

"Pastor Keith," as the Oregon athletes called him, was a volunteer chaplain for the University of Oregon sports teams who forged deep bonds with Duck athletes. In Luke, Pastor Keith saw a young man from the uppermost corner of Washington who needed a place of refuge, a Christian community he could plug into.

It helped that Luke's coach at Oregon, Ernie Kent, encouraged his players to foster relationships with their team chaplain. Luke didn't have to be asked twice. He and Pastor Keith met for Bible studies, and those times of reading God's Word deepened Luke's faith immeasurably. Sure, he had believed in Jesus since he started playing biddy basketball, but the things Pastor Keith taught him about God kicked things up a notch. "Really, when I started reading the Word with my chaplain, everything changed—the way I thought, the way I acted, and my attitude," Luke said. "It was like I was being washed by the Word."

Luke had a frustrating freshman year at Oregon, averaging 7 points a game and shooting 33 percent from the field for a Duck team that was expected to do better. Oregon won half its games, finishing 14–14, but posted a dismal 5–13 record in the Pac-10 Conference. Still, Luke attracted notice for his play and was voted to the Pac-10 All-Freshman team.

Luke, who wanted to have a better sophomore year, went back to work during the off-season. It was hard to keep him out of Mac Court. Thanks to his father, Luke was used to having his own key to the gym, but at Mac Court, he had to be more creative. He made his way in during off hours by sticking athletic tape over the strike plate of one of the broad doors leading to the locker room so it wouldn't lock.

During Luke's sophomore season, the Duck basketball program won a lot of games because of him and *another* Luke on the team—Luke Jackson, a left-handed 6-foot, 7-inch small forward with a sweet jump shot and athletic in-the-paint moves. The two collaborated on a rip-and-run style that often saw Luke Ridnour accept an outlet pass, run the floor on the fast break, and hit the streaking Luke Jackson for a lay-in or dunk. Coach Ernie Kent preached up-tempo basketball—the equivalent of a no-huddle, two-minute offense in football—and that was the two Lukes' kind of game. Defenses chased Luke & Luke all game long.

As the Ducks piled up wins during the 2001–02 season, sportswriters began proclaiming Luke Ridnour the best point guard in the country—someone who could play in the NBA. Glowing stories about Luke called him an "old school" player who could have stepped off the set of the movie *Hoosiers*, the 1986 film about a small-town Indiana high school basketball team that won the state championship in 1952, at a time when all high schools in Indiana, regardless of size, competed in one state championship tournament. Sportswriters compared him to Jimmy Chitwood, the shy, reserved player who made the last-second shot to win the title for Hickory High.

Luke also showed spiritual leadership on a team that included a half dozen Christians—including Luke Jackson—by helping organize voluntary pregame chapels and by asking the entire team to recite the Lord's Prayer in the locker room before tip-off. These "kumbaya" moments translated to the court, too: the Ducks were ranked in the top five in the country for eleven different offensive categories during the 2001–02 season, including No. 1 in points per possession and true shooting percentage.

These Ducks liked to pass the ball around, and most of the assists came from Luke Ridnour, who showed an uncanny ability to penetrate and dish as well as work the pick-and-roll with his teammate and friend, Luke Jackson. Coach Kent summed up his point guard's contribution this way: "He gives himself up for his teammates."

The Luke & Luke Show helped the Ducks capture their first Pac-10 championship since 1945 and advance to the Elite Eight in the NCAA Tournament. Their title dreams ended with a loss to the No. 1 overall seed Kansas, however.

Back to sneaking into Mac Court through one of the taped-up back doors during the off-season.

ONE MORE COLLEGE SEASON . . . THEN ON TO THE NBA

The fall before his junior year at Oregon, Luke was named to *Playboy* magazine's preseason All-American team. As far as Luke was concerned, however, that was a non-starter. He politely turned down *Playboy*, saying, "My mom wouldn't be too happy about it, and I didn't feel I should do it. It's a great accomplishment and all that, but it was a beliefs thing for me."

Interesting how God honored that stand. Not too long after Luke passed on *Playboy*, Nike announced it was commissioning a 50-by-170-foot billboard of Luke as a candidate for the Wooden Award, one of college basketball's top individual honors. The seventeen-story portrait of Luke, with ball on hip, was erected on a skyscraper near New York City's Times Square.

Luke didn't win the Wooden Award during his junior year at Oregon, but he cemented his status as one of the elite players in college basketball. He won plenty of other awards, including Pac-10 Conference Player of the Year after averaging 19.7 points a game.

The iron was hot, and it was time to strike and turn pro, although the Mac Court fans chanted, "One more year!" so loudly during Luke's last home game that play had to be stopped as he walked off the court.

Luke made himself available for the 2003 NBA draft, and lo and behold, his hometown team, the Seattle SuperSonics, took him as the fourteenth pick. It many ways, it was a dream come true for Luke and his family: he would be playing NBA basketball within driving distance of his hometown of Blaine, meaning his parents could come to a lot of his games. Also, the Sonics needed a talented point guard prospect to replace aging Gary Payton, who was traded to Milwaukee.

Prior to his rookie season, Luke underwent surgery on his abdomen and groin, which forced him to miss nearly the entire slate of preseason games. Once he was healthy, he played in spurts—sometimes ten minutes a night, sometimes twenty-five. His rookie season was marked by ups and downs, which were reflected in the team's season. Seattle floundered and missed the playoffs with a 37–45 record.

Luke had a breakout season during his second year in the league. He won a starting position in training camp, and with Luke quarterbacking the offense from his point guard position and sharpshooter Ray Allen scoring from the shooting guard slot, the Sonics turned things around. Seattle was the surprise of the NBA early in the 2004–05 season, winning 23 of its first 29 games. The Sonics climbed to the heady heights of 40–16 in early March before slumping the last six weeks of the season. After finishing 52–30, their quest for a championship was dashed with a loss to the San Antonio Spurs in the second round of the NBA playoffs.

SETTLING IN AND SETTLING DOWN

Luke's sophomore season showed that he belonged in the NBA, and since then, he has settled into a good pro basketball career. Off the court, he decided to settle down, too. In August 2005, he married Kate Reome, whom he had been dating for three years.

Luke and Kate first met during the state basketball tournament in his senior year of high school. They had both been asked to appear at a Rotary Club luncheon honoring the best high school basketball players in the state. Luke represented Blaine High, while Kate was invited on behalf of Lakeside High in Spokane.

Luke and Kate sat next to each other at the luncheon. Kate knew about Luke because all the girls on her team had a crush on this cute boy with tight blond curls. Kate wasn't completely impressed, though, because she thought Luke looked like a slacker. He was dressed in his standard uniform—faded T-shirt, beige cargo shorts, and backwards hat—while everyone else, including herself, had dressed nicely for the occasion.

Luke went off to the University of Oregon, while Kate had another year of high school before moving on to Central Washington University in Ellensburg, where she had earned a scholarship to play volleyball. You would think that would be the last time Luke and Kate would ever see each other. But you'd be wrong.

Luke and Kate's opportunity to "reconnect" started when she visited a guy friend who happened to be an acquaintance of the Ridnours. She needed to get this fellow's e-mail address—as well as the e-mails of any of their common friends—because she had lost her contact list.

As her friend scrolled through his smartphone, his voice rose an octave. "Oh, here's Luke's e-mail! Do you remember him?"

Sure, she remembered Luke Ridnour. He was practically famous in Washington sports circles. But she didn't think it was a good idea to send Luke a "Hi, howya doing?" e-mail out of the blue; after all, it had been two years since their one meeting at the Rotary luncheon. She thought that if she e-mailed him, he'd probably think she was some eighth-grade teenybopper.

Kate changed her mind, though, and sent Luke a friendly e-mail reminding him of how they sat at the same table at the Rotary luncheon. The e-mail went out during March Madness in 2002, the year the Ducks were in the national championship hunt.

To her everlasting surprise, Luke quickly responded and said, "Of course, I remember you."

As they got to know each other through phone calls and e-mail messages, Luke learned that he and Kate were in sync spiritually. Back in high school, she had become interested in Christianity while attending Young Life events. Then several of her girlfriends invited her to a Wednesday night service. That night, the speaker said if anyone at the service hadn't made a decision to accept Jesus into their life, now would be a great time to do it. Kate knew she didn't understand everything about Christianity, but something in her heart prompted her to move forward and start down the road of life . . . with Jesus Christ holding her hand every step of the way.

Luke and Kate's long-distance relationship grew slowly. After three years, their love blossomed. When she walked down the aisle in a wedding dress, on the arm of her father, she was ready to marry a young man she was crazy in love with.

Here's how Kate described her courtship to Jill Ewert, editor of *Sharing the Victory* magazine:

You must have made a big impression on him then.

Kate Ridnour: You know, I guess so. He told me later on that after we met at that Rotary Club, he went home and tried to get my phone number from my high school. I kidded him that he was a stalker.

But I look back on that day when I went over to my friend's place to get those e-mail addresses. It was such a God thing because it was windy out. I was like, *I don't want to go anywhere.* But then I decided to go see this guy so that I could keep in touch with friends. Funny how things panned out.

You can see how you almost didn't go, right?

Kate: Oh, yeah! Looking back you can see how it was just scripted, you know? God was like, *Okay, go here. Go there. Okay, e-mail. Talk. Now you're together.*

It's funny. It's almost a boring story because we weren't high school sweethearts. But it's neat because I did know him before he was in the league. I knew him before he was the big Luke Ridnour from the Seattle SuperSonics. I knew the little, scrawny white guy.

Is that how you still think about him?

Kate: Oh, no! He's so much bigger. He's strong and manly! But you know, he is just a boy. There are things that he does and in how he acts. He's just a boy in a big man's world.

Believe me, Kate was not in any way putting down her husband. For the longest time, Luke was content to drive around an old beat-up truck, but his sensible wife pointed out to him that he was being penny-wise but pound-foolish—if the truck broke down when he was on his way to practice and he was late, the fine would be five thousand dollars.

The couple lived in a waterfront home on Lake Washington that Luke had purchased after the Sonics drafted him. Following their marriage, they settled into the NBA lifestyle—but not the lifestyle many associate with professional basketball players. Luke was a devoted husband who had no interest in straying. Being separated from Kate during long road trips wasn't easy for him, so Luke took advantage of advances in modern technology. He and Kate got into Skype, a software application that allows users to make voice calls over the Internet and to see each other via webcams on their computers. As soon as he arrived at the team hotel—as long as it wasn't late at night or in the wee hours—Luke would call his wife for a chat.

I asked Luke how he handled it when the team bus pulled up to the player hotel at 3:00 a.m., following a plane flight, and he saw all sorts of women hanging out in the lobby. Since he always walked straight to his room without passing Go or collecting two hundred dollars, as they say, how did he protect himself from temptation?

By wearing the full armor of God, he told me.

Luke says that Ephesians 6:11—"Put on the full armor of God so that you can take your stand against the devil's schemes"—is a reminder that Satan will always try to come at him but that the Lord always prevails in the lives of those who "armor up."

BENDS IN THE ROAD

Three years into their marriage, life threw Luke and Kate a pair of curves—on the same day. They weren't *bad* curves . . . just new bends in the road for them to navigate.

The 2007–08 season, Luke's fifth in the league, was filled with turmoil for the SuperSonics. The team had been sold in 2006 to a group of investors from Oklahoma City that included Clay Bennett. The handwriting was on the wall: Bennett threatened to move the team to Oklahoma if a deal for a new lease at KeyArena couldn't be worked out between the franchise and the city of Seattle. The Sonics were looking like a lame duck team to their fans.

Then, in August 2008, a blockbuster trade involving three teams and six players was announced, and it included Luke, who was being shipped to the Milwaukee Bucks.

Trades happen in the NBA.

On the same day that Luke heard he would be playing for Milwaukee, he and Kate learned she was pregnant with their first child. That was a double-barrel blast of family news.

Kate always liked the name Trey, but after Luke got *traded*, she started playing around with that verb and came up with "Tradon"—pronounced TRAY-don.

"I think it's a pretty unique name," Luke said.

Tradon Lukas Ridnour was born on April 13, 2009.

Luke played two seasons with the Bucks, averaging 10.9 points, 4.9 assists, and 2.2 rebounds per game. He became a free agent after the 2009–10 season and signed a four-year, $16 million contract with the Minnesota Timberwolves.

Luke's veteran presence on the floor was an asset, but the T-wolves fell on hard times during the 2010–11 season, compiling the NBA's worst record at 17–65. As the losses piled up like snowdrifts, Kate learned she was expecting again. Ultrasounds revealed that the Ridnours would become parents of twin boys in early February 2011.

When Beckett and Kyson Ridnour were born, Luke and Kate were stunned to learn that Kyson suffered from life-threatening complications in the esophageal area. Though Kyson's condition has made for difficult times in the Ridnour household, Luke and Kate hold fast to their faith in God.

And they're praying for a miracle.

"I don't want to get into the details of what's going on, but Kate and I believe that one day there will be an amazing testimony that we'll be able to share with thousands and thousands of people about the miracle that God has done," Luke said.

Luke and Kate have received emotional support from friends and from the pastor of their home church in Seattle, who flew into Minneapolis to pray and lay hands on Kyson. (The Ridnours maintain a permanent home near Seattle during the off-season.) Their home church, Eastridge Church in Issaquah, sent out prayer chain updates regarding the family's difficult situation.

"It's been a tough go for the family," said Rob, "an emotional time for Luke, but he's holding on to his faith and praying for God's healing."

It hasn't been easy, but Luke says he has an extreme amount of peace about what will happen with Kyson as the family perseveres through this tough time.

"We believe miracles still happen."

2012 update: The 149-day NBA lockout in 2011 turned out to be a blessing for Luke and his family, giving them a couple of extra months to stay at the beside of their infant son, Kyson, in a Seattle hospital. The youngster was released before the lockout ended and continues to make progress for the gap in his esophagus.

Despite the distractions on the home front, Luke saw lots of playing time during the strike-shortened season, averaging 33 minutes in 53 games and scoring 12.1 points per game from the perimeter. A late-season injury limited his effectiveness, but he is expected to return to the Timberwolves' lineup for the 2012–13 season.

7

THEY'RE PLAYING WITH PURPOSE, TOO

Here's an interesting starting five to take the floor for an NBA game: Luke Ridnour and Jeremy Lin at guard, Anthony Parker and Kyle Korver at forward, and Chris Kaman at center.

But as Ernie Johnson pointed out in this book's foreword, there are other NBA players trying to live out their faith as well as play great basketball for their teams. Here are a half dozen other players—as well as an NBA chaplain, coach, and general manager to watch out for.

STEPHEN CURRY—GOLDEN STATE WARRIORS

Twenty-four-year-old Stephen Curry has some impressive genes working for him.

Stephen, the son of former NBA sharpshooter Dell Curry and former Virginia Tech volleyball standout Sonya Curry, is the face of the Golden State Warriors franchise after just three seasons with the team. Though ankle sprains limited him to 26 games in the 2011–12 season, he's the established team leader at point guard. When healthy, he's capable of putting up big numbers—like the 18.6 points and 5.8 assists per game he put up during the 2010–11 season.

Stephen became a Christian in fifth grade when he responded to an altar call at Central Church of God in Charlotte, North Carolina. His parents thought it was important that he attend a Christian high school, so he played prep ball at Charlotte Christian School, where he scored more than 1,400 points to become the school's all-time leading scorer.

Stephen's father played for Virginia Tech back in the day, so he naturally wanted to follow in his father's footsteps. But when the Hokies didn't offer him a scholarship, he chose a school close to home—Davidson College in Davidson, North Carolina—that played a Division I schedule and occasionally qualified to play in the NCAA tournament.

One time before a preseason practice heading into his freshman season at Davidson, Stephen opened a cardboard box containing a new pair of sneakers. He then took a Sharpie pen with silver ink and wrote "Romans 8:28" on each toe as a reminder of his mother's favorite verse. That became something he did with all his basketball shoes.

It was during Stephen's sophomore year at Davidson that he first attracted national attention. During the 2008 NCAA tournament, he led tiny Davidson all the way to the Elite Eight. The Wildcats registered upset victories over Gonzaga, Georgetown, and Wisconsin before the Kansas Jayhawks, the eventual national champions, ended their Cinderella run with a 58–57 win in front of seventy thousand fans at Ford Field in Detroit.

During the 2008 March Madness tournament, Stephen averaged 34 points a game (including 30 in the *second half* against Gonzaga), prompting reporters to ask him about the meaning behind a different silver inscription on his sneakers that read: "I can do all things." Was he exhibiting the "look at me" mentality that's often seen today, or was it a simple case of an overblown ego?

"Oh, that," Stephen replied. "That's Philippians 4:13: 'I can do all things through him who strengthens me,'" he told reporters. "It's always been one of my favorite Bible verses [because it helps me] realize that what I do on the floor isn't a measure of my own strength. Having that there keeps me focused on the game, a constant reminder of who I'm playing for."

Stephen upped his scoring production during his junior year to 28.6 points per game—the best in the nation. As a consensus All-American getting a lot of ink, he decided to skip his senior season and turn pro. The Golden State Warriors took him with the seventh pick in the first round of the 2009 NBA draft.

Stephen had a good rookie season in 2009–10, and he finished second in the Rookie of the Year voting. He then backed up his solid first year with an outstanding second season with the Warriors. His future is bright as he plays to bring glory to God through basketball.

Keep an eye on Stephen, just like his headmaster at Charlotte Christian School, Dr. Leo Orsino, has been doing for the last half dozen years. It turns out that Dr. Orsino is a blogger, and he had this to say about his former student:

> On behalf of the faculty, staff, and Board of Trustees, we want to congratulate Stephen Curry and his family. We are extremely proud of him and blessed by his character and accomplishments.
>
> Can you imagine being on national television? Can you imagine handling all of the pressure both on and off the court? Everyone who knows Stephen is not surprised by his success of Christ-honoring character. We experienced the same "humble superstar spirit" both on and off the court while he was a student at Charlotte Christian School. There is no doubt that there is something very special about Stephen Curry. We already know what makes him special. He loves Jesus Christ and knows the Truth of God.

NENÊ—DENVER NUGGETS

Nenê (the circumflex is often dropped in favor of an un-accented *e* when printed in the United States) is the legal name of Maybyner Rodney Hilário, the power forward/center for the Washington Wizards.

Nenê, a native of Brazil, is the latest in a long line of Brazilian sports stars who have changed their legal names to a single word. Think Pelé, Ronaldo, Kaká, and Ronaldinho.

These one-word names have cropped up over the years because Brazilian full names tend to be rather long (for example, Pelé, the great soccer star of the

1960s and '70s, was christened Edson Arantes do Nascimento, which is a handful to pronounce). But the greater reason is because Brazilians value individuality and flair on the field, so going to a one-word moniker fosters a more intimate, romantic relationship with the fans. And probably more media attention as well, which is the name of the game when it comes to "branding" yourself and getting endorsement deals.

Enter Nenê, a 6-foot, 11-inch, 250-pound powerhouse who played with the Denver Nuggets for most of ten seasons before being traded to the Wizards in the midst of the 2011–12 campaign. Such a massive man taking the name Nenê—which means "baby" in Portuguese, the official language of Brazil—is filled with irony. Nenê is the only player in the NBA to go with only one name, and that makes him truly unique among professional basketball players.

Nenê's a late bloomer in the game of basketball. After playing soccer for most of his childhood and learning that sport was probably not in his future professionally, he took up basketball at the relatively late age of fourteen. He improved quickly, though, and turned pro at age sixteen, playing for a Brazilian team known as Vasco da Gama. He got his big break after an NBA pre-draft camp in 2002, when the New York Knicks drafted him but promptly traded him to Denver.

Moving to the United States at the age of nineteen presented challenges for Nenê. Not only did he have a lot to learn about playing in the NBA, but he also had to learn a new language, adjust to the different foods here in the States (no *frango com quiabo*, or chicken with okra), and live in a cold city (the Mile High city of Denver). He has adapted well, and he now speaks fantastic English and connects with fans. On the court, he has performed admirably for the Nuggets, showing that he is a player who can dominate the offensive end of the court. His critics, however, say he lacks aggression and is soft on defense.

Nenê said he is seriously thinking of retiring by 2016 to work in ministry at his church in Brazil, known as God Is the Answer.

"I have like a deal for my pastor," he told one interviewer. "I want to get involved with the church right here in Brazil. If my financial situation is stable, why am I going to [want to] have more money? I'm not crazy for money. I think the best I can do is with the church. . . . I can help with things with my testimony."

Nenê will be thirty-three at the start of the 2015–16 season, and athletes are notorious for changing their minds about retirement (and who can blame them, since jobs that pay several million dollars—even tens of millions of dollars—come to few individuals who inhabit this planet). But Nenê has shown that his heart is in the right place as he looks at his future beyond the boundaries of the basketball court.

Perhaps facing his mortality several years ago helped him see things in a different light.

In early 2008, Nenê took a leave of absence from the Nuggets after he learned why he hadn't been feeling well: at the age of twenty-four, he had testicular cancer. Several other high-profile athletes have dealt with this serious, life-threatening disease, including bicyclist Lance Armstrong, ice skater Scott Hamilton, and baseball player/ESPN commentator John Kruk.

In January 2008, Nenê submitted to surgery to have his right testicle and a malignant tumor removed. "It was scary, but I believe in God," Nenê told the *Denver Post* when he went public with his story in the spring of 2008. "And now I'm a survivor."

So far, it looks like Nenê's doctors detected and treated the cancer early enough, and he's been symptom-free for several years. Now he's starting all over with a bottom-rung team in Washington, though there are hopes that the Wizard organization is assembling a better cast around him.

But the Wizard front office had better work quickly.

There's a church in Brazil waiting for Nenê to arrive and lend a hand in ministry.

REGGIE WILLIAMS—GOLDEN STATE WARRIORS
You'd think that leading the NCAA in scoring for two consecutive seasons would make a player a lock to play in the NBA.

But things didn't happen that way for Reggie Williams, the shooting guard from Virginia Military Institute (or VMI) who quarterbacked a run-and-gun offense that regularly scored more than 100 points per game—not an easy task in a forty-minute game.

When Reggie wasn't selected in the 2008 NBA draft, he kept a great attitude. He didn't lash out in anger or complain but said that being passed over "definitely made me humble myself." Sure that God had a different plan for his life, Reggie took his game overseas—like Anthony Parker did—and played for a French team in Dijon, France.

Reggie put enough *moutarde* on his jump shot in Dijon to earn a spot the following season with the Sioux Falls Skyforce of the NBA Development League—the Triple A level of professional basketball. This was actually something of a step back for Reggie. He didn't have a car in frigid South Dakota and was paid a scant $19,000 for the season, but the way he saw it, playing in Sioux Falls was his best chance to get a shot in the NBA. He played great in Sioux Falls and, finally, the phone rang. The Golden State Warriors were on the line, and they offered Reggie a ten-day "take-a-look" contract toward the end of the 2009–10 season.

Reggie showed enough moxie and game that Golden State signed him for the 2010–11 season. Reggie joined Jeremy Lin as another rookie guard trying to make an impression with the Warriors. He also got a salary bump to $762,195 for the season.

Though he and Jeremy came from different backgrounds and college experiences, they were brothers in Christ. The pair fell in with each other for morale and support.

Reggie performed well alongside Jeremy Lin and Stephen Curry but, like Jeremy, was released by the Warriors in December 2011 to make cap space for an offer to Los Angeles Clipper DeAndre Jordan. As an unrestricted free agent, Reggie signed a two-year deal with the Charlotte Bobcats. He played about half the time for a team that set a dubious record: an NBA-worst 7–59 win-loss record.

Reggie will be back for the 2012–13 season. He has a knack for making buckets, whether he's taking awkward but athletic shots 10 to 15 feet from the basket, or drilling spot-up jumpers from beyond the three-point line. He's always found ways to score within the flow of the game, showing that he's the type of player who can "quietly" score 20 points in a game.

Finally, we have this anecdote to share about Reggie and his days as a Golden State Warrior:

When Reggie mentioned to the media that he was looking for a church to attend, Pastor Ryan Nash of Union Baptist Church in nearby Oakland went to a Facebook page dedicated to Reggie (though not Reggie's personal page) to invite him to drop by. "Please feel free to come by anytime, no pressure to join," the pastor wrote. "I just want to offer a place where you could worship. Please forgive this form of communication as I had no other way to reach you."

When Reggie put himself out there and told reporters covering the Warriors that he was looking for a church, he sent a signal about who he was and what was important to him.

And that's cool to see from an NBA player.

Let's pray that Reggie is plugged into a great church in Charlotte, which happens to be home of the Billy Graham Evangelistic Association.

NICK COLLISON—OKLAHOMA CITY THUNDER

Maybe Nick Collison should change his name to Nick *Collision*.

The 6-foot, 10-inch power forward with the Oklahoma City Thunder is known for planting his feet in the lane and letting the LeBrons and the Carmelos of the league plow into him so that he can draw the offensive foul.

It's called "taking a charge."

Charges taken is not an official NBA statistic, but if it were, Nick would probably rank among the league leaders. What he does is the spiritual equivalent of giving his body up for his teammates—something the apostle Paul wrote about: "No, I strike a blow to my body and make it my slave so that after I have preached to others, I myself will not be disqualified for the prize" (1 Corinthians 9:27).

Here's how Nick "strikes a blow" to his body. When a bulky and well-built behemoth charges toward the rim—only to find Nick blocking his path—what happens next isn't pretty. The crash usually sends both players to the floor—and it's almost always Nick who gets the worst of it. Even a collision with a diminutive point guard can hurt since he's coming at full speed and often sticks his pointy knees into Nick's chest.

Those who follow Oklahoma City closely say Nick takes three times as many charging fouls as anyone on the Thunder roster. "It's a good play for our defense," he said. "It's better than a blocked shot, because you get the ball back, and you get a foul on someone on the other team. On a block, you might get the ball back, and you might not. And you don't draw a foul."

Nick is also one of the league's most underrated defenders—a "glue guy" who usually takes on the other team's best forward. His top-notch defensive skills are why he's paid in the $11 million a year range—which is close to All-Star numbers. A native Iowan who helped Kansas University reach two consecutive Final Fours (2002 and 2003), Nick has been called the ultimate hard-hat player.

Nick and his wife, Robbie, have hosted several charity events in Oklahoma City, most notably an annual Passion for Fashion benefit for AIDS foundations in the area. He became interested in helping fight AIDS after traveling to Johannesburg, South Africa, with Basketball Without Borders, which partnered with Habitat for Humanity and the Sky Foundation, which helps people with the HIV virus.

While in Johannesburg, Nick and Robbie, a microbiology major in college, witnessed firsthand how AIDS has ravaged families in South Africa and left so many children orphaned. The visit to South Africa inspired them to organize a fashion show benefit and silent auction, which has become a big hit in Oklahoma City since the first one in 2009.

But don't ask Nick to walk down the runway in a smart suit.

"Luckily, I've got the excuse that they've got no clothes that fit me," he said. "There's no big-and-tall line [in the fashion world]. There's nothing for me to model."

Actually, Nick is modeling Christ to those attending the annual charity event on behalf of orphaned children.

KEVIN DURANT—OKLAHOMA CITY THUNDER

While Nick Collison is the blue-collar, in-the-trenches player every team needs, Kevin Durant, Nick's teammate with the Oklahoma City Thunder, is the go-to guy at crunch time, the big-time player who understands the responsibility of being "the guy" to carry the team. As one of the NBA's established stars, he accepts the spotlight and the accolades, but as a young Christian man of faith, he doesn't seek the fame and attention.

It's hard to escape fame and attention, though, when you're a three-time NBA scoring leader. His game is smooth and seamless, a mixture of grace, class, and force. He's the face of the Oklahoma City Thunder franchise—and part of the NBA firmament that includes LeBron James, Kobe Bryant, and Blake Griffin.

In short, Kevin Durant is endorsement gold right now because he's unstoppable with the ball in his hand, humble off the court, and quick with a smile.

During the 2010–11 playoffs, Kevin showed up at postgame news conferences wearing a Nike backpack that will be part of his KD III line that's coming out during the 2011–12 season. Eventually, the inevitable question came from the back: "Hey, Kevin, what's in your backpack?"

Well, I've got my iPad, my earphones, my phone chargers—and my Bible.

Actually, the Bible was a recent addition to his backpack, but more on that later.

Kevin was raised in a Maryland suburb of Washington, D.C. His mother and grandmother cared for him and his older brother, Tony, after their father left the family when Kevin was eight months old. As Kevin was growing up, he was always the tallest person in his class, but his grandmother Barbara consoled him, saying that his height would be a blessing—just wait and see.

He didn't have to wait long.

Kevin was a phenomenal basketball player from a young age, and when he was in middle school, he joined an AAU team. His AAU coach, Taras "Stink" Brown, laid down several rules, and Rule No. 1 was "no pickup games"—because his coach thought they engendered bad habits. Instead, Coach Brown gave Kevin a set of drills to perform. During his summer breaks, Kevin was often in the gym eight hours a day.

Kevin played his freshman and sophomore years at Montrose Christian High in Rockville, Maryland, where he was so good that his older teammates threatened to stop passing the ball to him because they didn't want Kevin to show them up. He later transferred to Oak Hill Academy in Mouth of Wilson, Virginia, where he played well enough to be named a McDonald's All-American. His shooting and driving skills were unmatched among prep players.

The University of Texas won the recruiting war for Kevin. As an eighteen-year-old freshman, Kevin controlled the flow of the game—and there was never a reason to call for a set play when he was on the floor. He posted twenty 30-point games, was named the Associated Press College Player of the Year, and won the Naismith and Wooden awards.

And promptly declared himself eligible for the 2007 NBA draft after one college season.

The Seattle SuperSonics (who would become the Oklahoma City Thunder) took Kevin with the second overall pick in the draft. He would become the NBA Rookie of the Year.

For a 6-foot, 9-inch player, Kevin has an usually long wingspan of 7 feet, 5 inches. Think about what impressive wingspan means to his game: with his arms outstretched on defense, he is eight inches *wider* than he is tall, which gives him the appearance of a windmill with four blades. As for the offensive side of the court, his long arms and quick first step make him a nearly unstoppable force. Whether he's pulling up for a jumper or slashing through the lane, he makes it look easy—as most scoring champions do.

Some people believe Kevin could break Kareem Abdul-Jabbar's all-time NBA scoring record of 38,387 points. Kevin has one advantage that could help him break Abdul-Jabbar's record. Kareem stayed at UCLA for four years, so the great center didn't turn pro until he was twenty-two years old. Kevin will be twenty-four years old at the start of his sixth NBA season, giving him a three-season leg up on Abdul-Jabbar.

Through his first five seasons, Kevin had a lifetime scoring average of 26.3 points per game, and he could up his point-per-game average in coming years. Since Abdul-Jabbar averaged 24.3 points per game over a twenty-year career,

Kevin would have to . . . well, the mathematic permutations are numerous.

But back to how the black leather Bible with his name engraved on the front cover got into his Nike backpack.

Kevin's strong faith comes from how his mother and grandmother brought him up. He says he went to church a lot when he was young, but as year-round basketball took up so much time in his adolescence, he attended church less. When he arrived in the NBA, a Christian teammate named Kevin Ollie took him under his wing and helped him feel more comfortable about talking about his faith, about praying for others out loud, and about attending chapels before games. It has helped that there were a half dozen players on the Thunder who took their faith seriously and were walking with the Lord.

Kevin comes across as a down-to-earth humble player, a guy you won't catch pounding his chest and getting in the grills of opponents. When he was asked how he appeared to stay humble while living and working in a world where it's easy to get caught up in the hype of fame and fortune that defines the NBA, Kevin said, "It's tough, man. I can't lie about that. But I always kind of pinch myself and say that any day this can be done. In the Bible, [it says] the Lord exalts humility, and that's one thing I try to be all the time. When I'm talking in front of people or when people tell me I'm great, I [remind myself that I] can always be better. I've just got to be thankful to the Lord for the gifts He's given me. My gift back to Him is to always be humble and to always try to work as hard as I can."

Kevin started toting his Bible around in the spring of 2011 after making a commitment to read Scripture passages at his locker before games. He told reporters that he wants to grow spiritually with the Lord, especially after a Thunder team chaplain stressed the difference reading the Bible each day can make in one's life.

"I'm keeping strong at it, just trying to make my walk with faith a little better," he said. "That's making me a better person, opening my eyes to things. I'm also maturing as a person. I'm just trying to grow."

Growing spiritually, growing into one of the elite basketball players in the world, Kevin Durant is someone to keep your eyes on—and pray for.

GREIVIS VASQUEZ—MEMPHIS GRIZZLIES

When Greivis Vasquez attends the NBA chapels before every game, he enjoys praying with opposing players because he enjoys being with other believers so much.

"I've got Jesus in my heart," he told Bill Sorrell, a Memphis-based sportswriter. "I put everything in his hands. I live out of grace."

Greivis grew up playing street basketball in the barrios of Caracas, Venezuela. He and his family lived in a downtrodden neighborhood known as El Coche, where the young boys would huddle up and watch basketball on televisions so small that they could barely make out the players running up and down the court.

Greivis was such a flashy dribbler that his friends called him *Callejero*, or street-baller. Seeing how big and tall Greivis was growing during adolescence, Venezuelan sports ministers plucked him out of the barrios and put him into the national development program.

As Greivis' skills progressed, his family made the tough decision to send him to the United States so he could further his basketball skills. They enrolled him at Montrose Christian Academy in Rockville, Maryland—a private high school known for its basketball prowess. "Your potential is God's gift to you," begins the program's motto. "How you choose to use your potential is your gift to God."

When Greivis arrived in the United States, he didn't know how to speak English or anything about a personal relationship with Jesus Christ. He quickly picked up English, and he was introduced to a personal relationship with Christ, which left Greivis a changed young man.

Greivis went on to play college ball at the University of Maryland, where the 6-foot, 6-inch point guard became the first-ever Atlantic Coast Conference player to score at least 2,000 points (2,171), ring up 750 assists (772), and grab 600 rebounds (647). In 2010, he won the Bob Cousy Award as the nation's best point guard.

The Memphis Grizzlies drafted Greivis in the first round of the 2010 NBA draft, and his rookie year went well for him. He received more and more minutes as the season wore on, especially in the playoffs, where Memphis went much further than anyone expected before losing to Oklahoma City and Greivis' former teammate from Montrose Christian High, Kevin Durant.

During the 2011 off-season, Greivis traveled to his Venezuelan homeland where he staged basketball clinics for youngsters as part of a US State Department–sponsored trip. At the start of the lockout-shortened 2011–12 season, he was traded to the New Orleans Hornets and came off the bench in the first 22 games. But an injury to point guard Jarrett Jack left an opening for starter minutes, and Greivis shined. He improved his assist-to-turnover ratio and dished out ten or more assists for the second-lowest scoring team in the NBA. Greivis nearly doubled his minutes of play from his rookie year, which allowed him time to make major strides in his game.

Greivis is the third Venezuelan to play in the NBA, but his countrymen—Carl Herrera and Oscar Torres—were journeymen players who didn't see much action during their short two-year careers. After becoming a more effective floor general with New Orleans, he has a strong shot at becoming the first impact player from his country. He's known for his instinctive nature on the court and ability to make things happen.

Maybe God has bigger plans for Greivis. In the interviews he's given, he certainly hasn't shown any reluctance to talk about being a Christian. He likes to recite Philippians 4:13 before every free throw: "I can do all things through him who strengthens me." Greivis has memorized Scripture, too—the entire eighth chapter of Romans.

Asked how his Christian faith has helped him in the NBA, Greivis replied, "It helps me in every aspect of my life. I have a sense of peace because

I know God has blessed me so much. I thank Jesus every day, no matter what happens, good or bad. My faith is what got me to where I am today."

Greivis is active on Twitter, where he routinely talks about his faith in Spanish or English—sometime in both languages—like the time he tapped out the following message: Easy with that bro. Jesus es un caballo!" (*Caballo* means "rider" or "horseman," but in this context, the phrase is Venezuelan slang meaning "He's a big guy.")

Other tweets are more straightforward, like this one: "On my way to church. Thank you God for another day."

At last count, thirty-five thousand people were following Greivis on Twitter.

Maybe a few of them went to church that Sunday after reading his tweet.

JEFF RYAN—CHAPLAIN OF THE ORLANDO MAGIC

Jeff Ryan is part of an NBA program that places a chaplain with every team in the league. Many fans don't realize that a chapel service is held one hour before every NBA game—regular season and playoffs—and that players from *both* teams are welcome to attend.

This open invitation makes pro basketball different from other major sports, where players from opposing teams are kept separate during chapel services. NFL players have the option of attending a chapel service—just for their team—on the night before their games. Major League Baseball chapels are held in each team's locker room on Sunday mornings. Ditto for the NHL.

But in the NBA, one hour before tip-off, players from each team are invited to meet near the home and visitor locker rooms. It could be in an extra locker room or even the dressing room of the team mascot. Attendance is voluntary.

The home-team chaplain greets the players and might lead an a cappella song. Then he speaks for ten to fifteen minutes, teaching from the Bible. Topics range from overcoming life's challenges to a reprise of the Gospel message, but the basic goal is to equip players to live lives that glorify God—especially by encouraging them to remain strong in the face of temptation.

At the end of the chapel, players might share a prayer request or ask a question about the message. Discussions must move quickly: whatever direction the chaplain takes, the mini-service must end promptly since players must be on court shortly to warm up for the game.

After they loosen up, players approach midcourt for the opening tip-off. And once the referee tosses the ball in the air, players from both teams—some of whom were seated in the same room discussing God's love less than an hour earlier—try to outrace, outhustle, and generally outshine their opponents—which is one of the beauties of competition.

Jeff said he's never had any issues with players from two teams meeting together before game time. They understand that professional rivalries don't matter in chapel, because that's a time allotted for God.

"As much as these guys are competitors, they realize that there are only four hundred professional basketball players in the NBA," Jeff said. "Playing is a privilege, not a birthright. They worked hard to get into that room. They know they are paid to perform, and they are going to play hard."

NBA chaplains like Jeff are volunteers, not part of the front office staff. They're usually pastors or involved in some form of full-time Christian ministry. One is even a former player: Andrew Lang, the Atlanta Hawks chaplain, who played twelve NBA seasons as a solid, consistent force in the low post. Whatever their background, chaplains present the Word of God to players with love and grace. They plant the seed, but God makes it grow. They see their ministry as sharing the Gospel, trying to encourage players and keep them strong.

"It's a great ministry, but it's also a humbling ministry," Jeff said. "I think the most important thing about being a chaplain is that it's about the message and not the messenger. As a chaplain, as a pastor, I'm irrelevant—but the message of God is relevant. That's what we're called to do—share the Good News. For some guys, we're just planting that one seed that will grow sometime down the road. For those guys who really embrace Christ, and live for Christ, our hope and prayer is that we will be good ministers for them."

MONTY WILLIAMS—HEAD COACH OF THE NEW ORLEANS HORNETS

When thirty-eight-year-old Monty Williams was hired in the summer of 2010 to coach the New Orleans Hornets, he became the youngest head coach in the NBA. But for someone so young, Monty Williams is close friends with his mortality—and Jesus Christ.

Tavares Montgomery "Monty" Williams was a nineteen-year-old sophomore at Notre Dame and a starter on the Fighting Irish basketball team. At the start of preseason practice in 1990, he underwent a routine physical. The doctor frowned when he listened to Monty's heartbeat. Something didn't sound right.

The doctor sent Monty to a cardiologist, who determined that he suffered from hypertrophic cardiomyopathy (HCM), a structural defect resulting in the heart muscle being bigger than it's supposed to be. Intense physical activity—like running up and down a basketball court—can trigger a heart attack, perhaps a fatal one, in people with HCM.

In the fall of 1990, the basketball world was still in shock after watching Hank Gathers, an All-American forward for Loyola Marymount University, collapse on the basketball court on March 4 of that year.

During the first half of a West Coast Conference tournament game against the University of Portland, Gathers ran the court in LMU's fast-break attack, taking a long lob pass in midair and slamming the basketball through the hoop. The home crowd cheered the athletic play, and Gathers dropped back on defense. Suddenly, he collapsed at midcourt with a thud. The crowd gasped.

Gathers' body started going into convulsions, and when the team doctor and coaches rushed onto the court, it was apparent that something was terribly wrong. The sight of Gathers' bewildered look about what was happening to him—all captured by cameras that night—was a sad spectacle.

Gathers was later declared dead on arrival at a Los Angeles hospital. The autopsy revealed that he had suffered from hypertrophic cardiomyopathy.

Notre Dame officials weren't going to take any chances with their star 6-foot, 8-inch forward from Forest Heights, Maryland. "Heart Condition Ends Notre Dame Player's Career," read the headline in the *Los Angeles Times* on September 29, 1990. Monty was quoted in the story as saying he was grateful his condition was diagnosed, even though that meant he would never play basketball again.

"I'm lucky to get a second chance," he said. "I wasn't on the court and died like Hank Gathers did."

But that gratefulness turned to bitterness and frustration as the reality of losing his basketball career overwhelmed him. Monty's mother had raised him in a Christian home, and he was a believer at the time of his diagnosis—but he was still crushed.

Friends quickly jumped off the Monty Williams bandwagon in South Bend, Indiana. Nobody wanted to hang out with a has-been—except for his girlfriend, Ingrid Lacy, the daughter of a preacher.

During that dark time, Monty rededicated his life to Christ. He and Ingrid spent hours walking around the Notre Dame campus in introspective prayer—begging the Lord for a miracle.

Meanwhile, Monty continued to play in pickup games at the Knute Rockne Memorial Gym on campus, telling friends that if he were to die, then at least it would be on a basketball court. He'd just wake up in heaven, that's all.

Two years passed, and Monty couldn't feel any ill effects from his heart condition. Then he heard that the National Institutes of Health (NIH) in Bethesda, Maryland, was studying the risk posed to athletes with HCM. He contacted NIH and asked if he could participate in the study, which meant enduring three days of exhaustive medical and stress tests. The results stunned the doctors. They couldn't find anything wrong with his heart.

When Monty heard the news, he dropped to his knees, praying and crying. "To this day, the doctors can't understand what happened," he said. "But God healed my heart. Medicine has its place in the world. Faith has its place, too. And faith overrides medicine."

In 1993, Monty resumed his basketball career at Notre Dame and averaged 22.4 points per game as the only star on a lousy Fighting Irish team. He could have played another year of college ball but elected to turn pro. Several teams passed him over because of his medical history, but the New York Knicks selected him with the twenty-fourth pick of the 1994 NBA draft.

The Knicks organization, no doubt spooked by the death of Boston Celtics player Reggie Lewis a year earlier, after he collapsed and died of HCM while playing basketball, told Monty he would have to pass another round of cardiological tests before they'd sign him.

Monty passed his physical with flying colors and went on to play nine years in the NBA for five different teams before a knee injury sent him to the bench permanently. One of his coaches, Gregg Popovich of the San Antonio Spurs, always thought of Monty as one of those coachable players who understood the game and had the correct don't-get-too-high-or-too-low demeanor. Coach Popovich hired Monty as a bench coach, and he made a smooth transition into coaching and mentoring players.

Monty later moved on to Portland, where he worked as an assistant coach for the Trail Blazers, and in the summer of 2010, he was named the head coach for the floundering New Orleans Hornets. New Orleans promptly made a big turnaround during the 2010–11 season. The Hornets finished the regular season with a 46–36 record and returned to the playoffs, where they put a scare into the defending champion Los Angeles Lakers before bowing out in six games. The 2011–12 season was tough sledding, however, as the team regressed to 21–45, tied with Cleveland for third-worst in the NBA. Monty kept his job because the front office recognized that the loss of guard Chris Paul meant the team was put into a rebuilding mode.

With the visibility of being an NBA head coach, Monty welcomed questions about what was really important in his life, which gave him a platform to talk about his faith and act it out on the court. For instance, he doesn't use bad language when yelling at referees—or when trying to get a player's attention. He told interviewers he reads his Bible every day and that the Word was as much a part of his existence as his wife, Ingrid—whom he married in 1995—and their five children.

He and Ingrid, along with youth pastor Dave Bullis and his wife, Kaci, wrote a devotional called *Look Again 52: One Scripture, Every Day, Each Week, for One Year*, which was released in the fall of 2010.

"We came up with a tool that will help people take certain verses and chew on them for a week," Monty said. "The book came out of a problem. I struggled, and we felt like the Lord gave us this idea to come up with a tool. It cost me a bunch of money to do the book because we self-published it, but being in the NBA, I'd blow that much money on a car and a dog, so it wasn't a big deal to do it."

Monty has run into people who have read *Look Again 52* and told him the book ministered to them. "It puts it in perspective that God could use a jerk like me, with all my shortcomings and blemishes, to do something that helps somebody that I would never meet," Monty said.

PAT WILLIAMS—GENERAL MANAGER OF THE ORLANDO MAGIC

Not only are there players playing with purpose in the NBA, as well as coaches coaching with purpose (like Monty Williams, Avery Johnson of the New Jersey Nets, and Paul Westphal of the Sacramento Kings), but there are also front office personnel of faith working behind the scenes to put the best possible team on the floor.

One of those Christian executives is Pat Williams, the senior vice president of the Orlando Magic. Nobody wrings more out of a day than Pat—and that is no hyperbole. Consider what this seventy-one-year-old Renaissance man has accomplished since he came into the NBA in 1968. He's:

- been the general manager of four NBA teams: the Chicago

Bulls, the Atlanta Hawks, the Philadelphia 76ers, and the Orlando Magic, which he co-founded in 1987.

- brought professional basketball to Orlando—a medium-sized city filled with amusement parks and a transient population. He was ridiculed for trying to sell basketball in a football fanatical state, but it was Pat who had the last laugh.

- written seventy-five books in the past four decades, mainly on the topics of leadership, teamwork, good business practices, being a better parent, and living a successful and rewarding life.

- carved out a successful career as one of America's top motivational and inspirational speakers, speaking 150 times a year to Fortune 500 companies like Allstate, American Express, Disney, Nike, and Tyson Foods, as well as to nonprofit organizations.

- raised nineteen children—and that is not a typographical error. He and his first wife, Jill, had four children on their own and adopted fourteen—from four foreign countries—during the 1970s and 1980s. His second wife, Ruth, brought one child into their marriage. At one point, sixteen of his kids were teenagers living under his roof at the same time, and Pat was single-parenting them. "That's when I understood why some animals eat their young," he quipped.

- run in fifty-eight marathons, including the Boston Marathon and the New York Marathon. At the time of this writing, his most recent was the Walt Disney Marathon in Orlando in early 2011—his third in four months.

Two days before the Disney Marathon, Pat visited his doctor for his annual physical. Blood was drawn and tests were done. Then he jogged 26.2 miles on a course that ran through all four theme parks inside the Magic Kingdom. But when he woke up a few days later, he felt a lot more than the usual soreness. His back was on fire.

During a return visit to see his doctor, Pat was told that abnormalities had shown up in his blood work. Further results revealed that he had multiple myeloma, a cancer of the plasma cells in his bone marrow. One of the symptoms of multiple myeloma is extreme back pain.

Pat was referred to Dr. Robert Reynolds, a leading oncologist in Orlando, who told him he was confident that Pat's multiple myeloma—also known as MM—had been detected in its early stages and could be treated. Dr. Reynolds told him that while multiple myeloma could be treated but not cured, he had a 70 to 75 percent chance of remission.

With that information as a background, Pat asked if he could tell his own story, and that seemed like an easy request to agree to:

PAT WILLIAMS IN HIS OWN WORDS

It's funny that this is a basketball book, yet my opening topic is baseball. But baseball was my prime sport when I was growing up in a sports-minded home in Wilmington, Delaware. Baseball, to paraphrase Sammy Sosa, was very, very good to me. Baseball got me through Wake Forest University, where I played catcher. Upon my graduation, I signed a contract with the Philadelphia Phillies and spent two years catching in their farm system, during the 1962 and 1963 seasons.

When I saw the handwriting on the wall—that I wasn't destined for the Major Leagues—I sought out other opportunities in the Phillies minor league system. I spent four years as the general manager of their farm club in Spartanburg, South Carolina. We had enormous success in Spartanburg during the mid-1960s, setting attendance records and winning national honors in minor league baseball.

I loved coming up with promotions that would pack Duncan Park with lots of baseball fans. One season, the Phillies sent us two pitchers out of spring training—guys named John Parker and John Penn. Well, back then Parker Pens were a big deal, so I conjured up Parker-Penn night where everyone in attendance would get a free pen.

Anything to have a little fun at the ballpark in those carefree days.

I was in my mid-twenties and searching and seeking to get to the top of my profession, yet with all the success I was enjoying, there was this certain emptiness as well. I surely relished all the honors and all the success, but there was soul-searching and questioning on my part.

There has got to be more than what I am experiencing here, I thought to myself. As I was pondering those larger-than-life thoughts, different people came into my life—like the "King of Squat," Olympic weightlifting champion Paul Anderson, and former Major League Baseball players Bobby Malkmus and Bobby Richardson, the great Yankee second baseman. They all talked to me about Christianity, and what they said appealed to me.

Just prior to my twenty-eighth birthday, I made a decision: *I want to get into this Christian thing*. I accepted Christ into my life. It was a radical transformation for me and changed my life totally and immediately. Anybody who says there can't be instant conversion, well, I tell them that's not true. One day I was walking one path, and fifteen minutes later I was heading in a whole different direction.

I obviously had a huge transformation in my life. I had been pushing and maneuvering, but trying to get to the top on my own wasn't working out the way I thought it would. When I accepted Christ, I said, "Lord, You do what You want with my life. I'm just going to surrender it. I am going to take my hands off the wheel, and You take over from here."

With that mind-set, I walked into the ballpark one day in July 1968 and found out there was a message for me to return a phone call to a man named Jack Ramsay. I recognized the name. He had been the longtime basketball coach at St. Joseph's in Philadelphia before becoming the general manager of the 76ers.

What could Jack Ramsay want? I wondered. I knew *of* him, but I certainly didn't *know* him. When I returned the phone call, Jack explained to me that he was taking over the coaching duties for the 76ers in the fall of

1968, in addition to his GM job. He needed somebody to run his front office while he concentrated on coaching the team. Would I be interested?

I gulped and thought, *Me?* I was twenty-eight years old, running a minor league baseball team in South Carolina. What did I know about NBA basketball? But Jack had checked me out, and after bringing me to Philadelphia for two interviews, he offered me the job as business manager, which was basically running the front office.

It was a huge jump from minor league baseball to running an NBA basketball operation day to day. But I learned a great deal and had a wonderful experience. Twelve months later, another door opened. This time, the owners of the Chicago Bulls contacted me and said they needed a general manager to run their team. Was I interested?

Jack Ramsay let me out of my contract with Philadelphia, and in the late summer of 1969, I moved to Chicago and took over the GM duties for the Bulls. I later moved on to the Atlanta Hawks and the Philadelphia 76ers again before finally landing in Orlando, where I helped launch an NBA expansion franchise in 1986 and bring professional basketball to central Florida.

Along the way, I have been responsible for the day-to-day general manager duties, which have entailed everything from contract negotiations to the draft, team trades, halftime shows, promotions, and even the exhibition schedule.

During my forty-three-year soirée through the National Basketball Association, I have witnessed the sport grow and become a worldwide entity. I have seen the influx of foreign-born players into the NBA. I have seen the league office in New York City grow from four full-time employees to about twenty-five hundred employees worldwide. Basketball has become a huge global sporting endeavor, and being part of that for four and a half decades has been staggering but rewarding in many ways.

Throughout these years I have been very fortunate to develop a side career. When I initially arrived in Orlando twenty-five years ago to help start the Magic expansion franchise, Orlando was just beginning to grow as a convention city and as a destination resort. Speaking opportunities seemed to pop up for me from the corporate world. I started speaking on leadership, teamwork, quality of life, living to your full potential, and what it takes to be a winner.

I speak probably 150 times a year to different groups in Orlando and around the country—and in some cases other countries. The Magic ownership, starting with Rich DeVos and his family, has been supportive and given me the freedom to do that.

Probably the highlight has been speaking at two Billy Graham Crusades—one in Chicago and one in Syracuse, New York, back in the 1970s and 1980s. I'll never forget seeing Dr. Graham in his heyday, as well as Cliff Barrows and George Beverly Shea. Feeling the Lord's presence as I walked into each evening session—with the four-thousand-voice choirs and forty thousand people sitting there—oh boy, I'm not sure that I'll ever experience anything like that again this side of heaven.

As my speaking career grew, it led to opportunities to write books. My seventieth book was released in early 2011, and I have more books I want to write. My speaking and writing careers have allowed me to meet fascinating people in corporate America and provided me enough money to get my children through college—not an easy task when there were nineteen of them. Now that all my children are adults and marrying and forming families of their own, my focus is on getting my grandchildren through high school and college, which I have committed to do for them.

Yes, the ending of my first marriage in the mid-1990s was very difficult for me and very difficult for our eighteen children. My ex-wife just didn't want to continue the marriage, and there was nothing I could do about it. We had written about marriage and had been very visible in the Christian community, so it was an embarrassing and difficult time in my life when we separated and divorced.

I ended up single-parenting eighteen children for a few years, but I was sinking fast. Then Ruth, who would become my second wife, came along and basically saved my bacon. I refer to her now as "St. Ruth," and she remains St. Ruth today—with nineteen adult children and eight grandchildren, dealing with daily issues I could never deal with on my own. She has been a lifesaver for all us.

Those years in the mid-1990s were times of adversity for me and my family, which has given me a forum to talk about how we can deal with adversity and use it to develop strength. When winners experience setbacks, disappointments, or failures, they don't waste those difficult times. Instead, they learn and grow and take advantage of those experiences to become smarter, wiser, and more capable of going through the tough times the next time around.

Even though I had been speaking on adversity for many years, little did I realize that I would be given an opportunity to live out my own words in front of the world beginning in 2011.

It all started when I visited my doctor for my yearly physical two days before the Disney Marathon. When my blood work results came back, my doctor said, "There is something that needs further checking. I would encourage you to get on it right away."

Over the next few weeks, I saw a series of specialists, including Dr. Robert Reynolds, an oncologist here in the Orlando area. After reviewing my results, he sat me down and explained that I had an illness called multiple myeloma.

"I have never heard of that," I said. "What is it?"

Dr. Reynolds explained that multiple myeloma is a cancerous condition of the bone marrow and not a common illness (which was interesting to hear now that I've heard from every MM patient in America!).

Dr. Reynolds started me on chemotherapy treatment immediately, and then I had to make a huge decision. What do I do about informing my children? The Magic organization? And the public? I knew that sooner or later the story would start leaking and hit the newspapers. In February 2011, I decided to get it all out in front of people.

The Magic organization called a press conference for me, and I stood at the podium, with Dr. Reynolds by my side, and announced that I was dealing with multiple myeloma. I remember saying that I have been talking for years to audiences about dealing with adversity and tough times, but now I would get a chance to live it out. I also talked a great deal about my faith and the importance of living for the Lord. I said that when I received the news of my cancer diagnosis, I could have shook my fist in the Lord's face and turned angrily away from Him. You know—*Why me? How could You do this to me?* Instead, I decided to make a flying leap into His lap and hug Him around the neck and never let go.

In many ways, I'm grateful for this news about my cancer diagnosis and its timing. We caught it early. It's certainly nothing I would have planned or wanted, but learning I have cancer has certainly drawn me closer to the Lord and given me a closer walk with Him.

In addition, I feel I have been called to a ministry of encouraging and uplifting other people. Every day I get a phone call or an e-mail from someone dealing with cancer or other health-related issues. I try to respond to all of them with an optimistic, upbeat attitude, to pray with them, and to help give them a spark to keep fighting hard to regain their health. I am also convinced that every family in America has been touched in some form or fashion by cancer. I feel the Lord wants me to be a cheerleader for as many cancer patients as I can.

I made good progress throughout 2011 after submitting to several months of chemo treatments. One of the nurses at the clinic really encouraged me, saying, "Listen, these chemo treatments take about an hour each time, twice a week, and that's it. The rest of the week is yours. So don't sit on the sidelines. You may not feel 100 percent, but go out there at 80 percent and go on with your life."

I have been feeling more energetic with each week as I seek to live a normal life. I resumed traveling and flying here and there to do my talks, and I have several books on the docket to write. I may not feel perfect, but I'm going out and playing at the level God has given me. Obviously, I am grateful for the enormous amount of prayer support around the country, from friends and strangers alike who have reached out to encourage me.

Once I began chemotherapy, I started keeping a journal. Who knows? I've heard that people are already anticipating a book about this whole experience, so I'll keep good notes and see where this leads.

When I'm out speaking and young people hear my story, they often ask me, "What is the key to having a good life?" I tell them to figure out what they love to do more than anything in the world and then come up with a way to get paid every two weeks for doing it. When you max out every day of your life, you'll have life by the throat.

Another question I'm often asked is, "What makes a good GM?"

Well, you're never off duty. You are working 24/7. Your stomach is churning every day when things are going well *and* when they are not going well. It's fortunate that I became a Christian before I became a general manager;

otherwise I could not have functioned in this world. The pressures are too intense, the tension is too nerve-racking.

But the Lord has given me a certain peace and a certain calmness through it all. It helps that I view my work as a ministry. Sure, winning is important. I would not still be in this business after forty-three years if the teams I worked for hadn't won a whole lot more games than they lost. But I always viewed my position as an opportunity to impact people through the power of sports. Having that thought in the back of my mind gives me a different perspective. I want to win as badly as anybody, and I'm willing to work hard, but I've always felt this has been the Lord's work.

Part of that work involves evaluating talent—who you bring to play on your team. You have to draft well. You have to trade well. You have to make good decisions in free agency. You have to have good people around you, and you have to listen to them, trust them, and give them the freedom to be good decision-makers on your behalf.

You must have talent, but character counts enormously. When you get caught up with talented players who are deficient in the character department, you end up spending all your time putting out fires that are due to character issues. That takes time, and inevitably you end up neglecting your good-character guys, which diverts from everything you're trying to do.

At the Orlando Magic, we do everything in our power to draft talent *with* character, and when you get those two in combination, you know you are going to have wonderful success. It's not easy to discover a player's character, however, which is why we must do an enormous amount of research. We have a whole lot more scouts than we used to. We had one scout when I started out with Chicago, Atlanta, and Philly. We probably have eight or ten scouts on the Magic payroll now.

We go back and try to check into each player's youth and spend as much time as we can around his college campus. We talk to the people who have coached that player when he was a young person. It helps if we can do psychological testing, too. It's not a perfect formula, but we spend as much time as we can evaluating and digging deep into a youngster's past.

With the Internet, that's much easier these days. It seems like we can find out everything about everybody in the world. If a player spilled a cup of coffee in a Starbucks a few months ago, we probably have a report on that. When something more serious has happened in a player's past—such as a DUI or an assault arrest—we have to make a decision: was it youthful peccadilloes, was it a maturity issue, or was this part of a pattern?

The danger for scouts and general managers is that we are tempted by talent. I've sat in meetings where people say, "Well, I can overcome the character stuff." At the end of the day, though, a kid's character is pretty well formed by the time he is a teenager. You have to be very careful, especially now that the game has become a worldwide sport. We have players coming from all over the world. How can we determine a player's character when he's grown up in France, Germany, or Turkey? That's why we have to be scouting on every continent, but it also comes down to asking the Lord for guidance.

I don't know where my life would be without that resource from above. I am convinced that everything that has happened on and off the basketball court started with the decision I made in February 1968 to turn my life over to Christ and let Him run with it and control it, which He has been doing very, very well for these many years.

I'm deeply thankful I was drafted onto His team.

2012 update: Pat says he's doing "wonderful" and winning his battle against multiple myeloma. He also noted that June 2012 marked "fifty straight years that I've been getting a paycheck from a pro sports team"—the first one coming from the Philadelphia Phillies when he tried to make it as a catcher in their minor league system.

Pat's still an Energizer bunny—writing books (his latest is Leadership Excellence*), speaking before groups, doing radio interviews, and being involved with the Magic.*

OVERTIME

PISTOL PETE MARAVICH, THE PRODIGAL WHO PLAYED WITH PURPOSE

I (Mike Yorkey) loved playing basketball growing up in La Jolla, California, a seaside community about twenty minutes north of downtown San Diego.

In the Mediterranean climate and bucolic setting of La Jolla, the neighborhood gang and I could play outdoors year-round, although basketball was generally a Thanksgiving-to-Lent sport sandwiched between baseball and beach time. When I was in the fifth grade, my father constructed a freestanding wooden basketball standard that was low enough for us to dunk on. Playing on low rims didn't help my jump shot, but it was sure fun to stuff like Wilt "The Stilt" Chamberlain.

The low rim was strictly for horsing around. I made sure I played plenty of hoops on ten-foot rims because that was *real* basketball. I haven't forgotten how much joy I received from seeing my jump shots spring from my fingertips, suspend in midair for the longest time, and swish through the basket.

In the late 1960s, as I entered my teen years, the NBA awarded an expansion franchise to San Diego. The team was named the Rockets because Atlas rockets were made in San Diego, and since these massive liquid-fuel space launch vehicles blasted American astronauts into space, there was a lot of local pride. (If you're a younger reader, rockets were a big deal in the 1960s because of the "Space Race" to get a man on the moon before the Russians.) The Rockets would play only four seasons in San Diego, from 1967 to 1971, before moving to Houston.

The Rockets were horrible during their inaugural year, finishing with a 15–67 record, which, at that time, was the worst in NBA history. The team was populated with castoffs and journeymen like Art "Hambone" Williams and bald-as-a-billiard-ball Toby Kimball—although an interesting rookie guard with shaggy hair, big sideburns, and a Fu Manchu mustache, Pat Riley, was making some noise.

But not enough noise to win many games. With such a lousy team, professional basketball was greeted with yawns in laid-back San Diego, a place of surf, sun, and sand. Most people decided they had better things to do than go see a professional basketball game.

One Saturday night during the Rockets' first season in San Diego, my father and I decided at the last minute to go check out the team. The Cincinnati Royals, led by the Big O (Oscar Robertson), were in town. I was in junior high at the time.

My father and I walked right up to the ticket window to buy tickets—there was no line—and asked what was available.

"We have two seats on the floor," said the ticket seller.

"How much?" my father asked.

"Five bucks each."

Considering that actor Jack Nicholson pays $5,500 for a pair of courtside tickets at a Lakers game these days, ten bucks was a bargain, even in 1967 terms.

We took them. That was the first time—and the last—that I ever sat courtside for an NBA game. Listening to the Big O direct traffic and tell his guys where to go was a real treat. (With just a few thousand fans inside the San Diego Sports Arena, crowd noise was minimal.) He moved players around like they were pawns on a chessboard. I loved the way these amazing athletes flicked snap passes, played above the rim, and routinely made difficult shots look easy. That evening cemented my love for NBA basketball.

Meanwhile, I kept honing my game to where I was good enough to play on the La Jolla High varsity team. But I was one of those undersized and undertalented players who wasn't going anywhere. I knew I had no future in basketball—tennis would become my sport anyway—but that didn't diminish my ardor for the game.

I pretty much quit playing basketball after high school—until I started working for Focus on the Family in 1986. I was hired as the editor of *Focus on the Family* magazine, which had a monthly circulation of well over a million readers.

Focus on the Family is a nonprofit Christian organization founded in 1977 by Dr. James Dobson, the author of bestselling books such as *Dare to Discipline* and *The Strong-Willed Child*. The main focus of the ministry was Dr. Dobson's daily radio show, which featured him and a guest talking about parenting and family issues. The ministry, which employed around 350 people at the time, was based in Dr. Dobson's hometown of Arcadia, California, an upscale community thirteen miles northeast of downtown Los Angeles and sitting on the border of Pasadena.

I soon learned that Dr. Dobson, fifty years old at the time, was also a basketball nut. He was crazy about the game, so much so that the job description for Gary Lydic, Focus' human resources director at the time, included the heavy responsibility of making sure enough players showed up before work to play five-on-five half-court games three mornings a week. The venue was a nice, well-appointed gymnasium on the grounds of First Church of the Nazarene of Pasadena, where Dr. Dobson's first cousin, H. B. London, served as pastor.

"Let me tell you, it was an incredible responsibility to have players organized for those games three times a week," Gary said. "When I had my list made up, I'd call everyone the day before and say, 'Guys, you know how important this is to the Doctor to be there tomorrow morning. There is no way you cannot be there, unless you're playing on one leg.' It wasn't so easy to get to everyone in those days before cell phones, but if somebody didn't show up, it was my fault. I hated to get those early morning phone calls from Dr. Dobson saying that not enough players had showed up to play."

Shortly after Focus hired me, I was put on Gary's call list. (I think I mentioned to Dr. Dobson that I had played some high school basketball and would love the opportunity to scrape off the rust and play again.) I learned quickly that when Dr. Dobson invited you to play basketball, you had better be ready to play at 6:30 a.m. at "First Naz Paz."

What followed was an hour and fifteen minutes of quick-burst five-on-five half-court games. There were usually enough players to field four teams, so we had two half courts going. First team to score ten baskets won the game. Winners would play winners and losers would play losers.

I actually preferred half-court basketball, as did Dr. Dobson. I felt that keeping both teams on the same side of the court—but having to take the ball back beyond the top of the key following each change of possession—made for a better game. Often when amateurs and weekend warriors play full-court basketball, the game degenerates into a series of two-on-one fast breaks, which are no fun.

With half-court basketball, though, it was always five-on-five with screens and movement and open jump shots—and no "cherry pickers" taking off for the other rim and an unmolested layup. I'm sure I worked up *more* of a sweat playing half-court hoops, and the competitive games certainly satisfied my craving to play basketball. I also liked the "winners out" rule, where your team kept the ball after scoring. That way, any team could make a late charge.

Dr. Dobson was a good player, especially for someone his age. Give him an uncontested jump shot near the free throw line, and he was money. Even though most guys in his pickup games were fifteen or twenty years younger than Dr. Dobson, he more than held his own. He used his height and size to his physical advantage to jostle for rebounds and score easy baskets.

Another thing I remember about those early morning games was that Dr. Dobson was very big on players calling fouls on themselves. There was kind of an "honor system" we all had to adhere to, meaning that if one of us made contact with an opponent who was taking a shot, then we'd better raise our hands and acknowledge the foul.

Dr. Dobson is 6 feet, 3 inches, so he was more of a forward, while I, at my 5-foot, 9-inch height, was more of a guard. Sometimes, though, he'd break free and it would be up to me to contest his shot. If I hacked him or even gave him a little bump, I'd immediately raise my hand if and when the shot clanged off the rim so his team could retain possession. Hey, I called fouls on myself because I wanted to stay on the invite list!

There was one time, though, when I wasn't invited to play early morning basketball with Dr. Dobson and the rest of the guys. The date was January 5, 1988, the day when Pete Maravich was in town to tape a *Focus on the Family* radio program with Dr. Dobson. Pistol Pete had agreed to play a little pickup ball with Dr. Dobson and the guys at First Church of the Nazarene before going to the studio.

I was perfectly fine with not being invited to play that day—I knew my place. But if I had shown up at Parker Gym, I would have witnessed something I never would have forgotten—the sight of Pete Maravich, one of the most talented players ever to play the game, dying in Dr. Dobson's arms.

HEIR TO A DREAM

Pete Maravich wasn't the first player to dribble behind his back or make deft passes between his legs. But when the ball was in his hands, Pete was a mesmerizing showman.

Pistol Pete played basketball like no one before him, although some believe he paid a terrible price for putting his playground moves, circus shots, and hotdog passes on display. Many basketball purists felt he was more style than substance. In Pete's mind, though, if he could get you the ball with a chest pass or a behind-the-back bounce pass, why did it matter how he delivered the ball?

"If I have a chance to do the show or throw a straight pass, and we're going to get the basket either way," he once said, "I'm going to do the show."

Paul Westphal, who played in the NBA with Maravich before embarking on a long coaching career, compared Pete to an artist: "His canvas was the basketball floor, and his brush was his basketball."

Pete cultivated a freewheeling image that matched the tenor of the turbulent late '60s and early '70s. Even his dribbling wizardry—the double clutch and flip flap jack—was considered outrageous for his era. Yet with his Beatlesesque mop top of brown hair, trademark floppy socks, and a dead-eye shot that earned him the nickname "Pistol," he would become one of basketball's enigmatic icons. He *averaged* 44 points a game throughout his storied three-year career at Louisiana State University, but that could have easily been 50-plus points a game if there had been a three-point shot in college basketball when he played.

Peter Press Maravich was born June 22, 1947, the son of Serbian immigrants living in the steel town of Aliquippa, Pennsylvania. His father, Press, had grown up dirt poor at a time when he was expected to eke out a living in one of the huge gray steel mills that belched thick black smoke and polluted the upper Ohio River Valley.

Press viewed sports as his ticket out of the steel mills, and he threw himself into a game that was gaining popularity in the 1940s—basketball. After flying dozens of dangerous missions in the South Pacific as a U.S. naval pilot during World War II, he came home and played professional basketball with the Youngstown Bears of the National Basketball League (1945–46) and the Pittsburgh Ironmen of the Basketball Association of America (1946–47). These were the pre-NBA days, when salaries were miniscule.

Following marriage and the birth of Pete, Press needed something more secure than playing pro basketball to earn a few bucks. He turned to coaching and quickly reached the college ranks, but bubbling underneath the surface was a dream of what basketball and basketball players could become one day. His son, Pete Maravich, would become the embodiment of that dream, the realization of that vision. That's why Pete titled his 1987 autobiography *Heir to a Dream*.

Pete was a normal kid growing up, and he usually had some sort of ball in his hands. One day when Pete was seven years old, Press was shooting baskets in his yard in Clemson, South Carolina, where he worked as the head basketball coach at Clemson University. Pete came out and took a shot. He missed.

He was hooked. "Daddy, let me try again," he pleaded.

His father looked at him. "Pete, if you will let me teach you basketball, maybe one day you will play on the professional level like I did. Maybe you will be on a team that wins the world championship, and they will give you a big ring."

Pete's eyes lit up. He wanted that ring more than anything. He wanted to play basketball and earn fame and fortune.

Press had a willing subject to teach the fundamentals of basketball to. They went to work. Pete must have repeated his father's shooting mantra thousands of times: "fingertip control, backspin, and follow-through." The Clemson field house became the laboratory where Pete mastered the creative ball-handling drills his father had devised. Most were dribbling exercises with names like "scrambled egg" and "space clap." On weekends, young Pete dribbled and shot baskets eight to ten hours a day . . . until his fingertips were raw. He played games of three-on-three until he nearly dropped from hunger pangs.

The leather basketball almost became a natural extension of Pete's body. Everywhere Pete went, he took his basketball with him, bouncing it like a yo-yo.

"Whenever I went to the movies, I'd take my ball with me and be sure to get an end seat so I could dribble in the aisle while the movies were on," Pete wrote in a first-person article that appeared in *Sports Illustrated* in 1969, during his final season at LSU. "There were only a few people in the theater then. Clemson, South Carolina, wasn't the biggest metropolis in the world, you know. Those people in the theater were old and tired, and they looked like they'd been sitting there for three years. They didn't mind my dribbling—the floor was carpeted and I had a rubber ball—and I never got thrown out for it or anything.

"Later, about the fourth or fifth grade, I was still timid and shy around people—like a lot of kids my age—and I would practice in the gym all by myself. When you're in the gym alone, you know, you can do anything you want because nobody is there to stop you. I began finagling with the ball in there, fooling around with it and doing funny things. I would get bored with just shooting straight to the basket or dribbling around in circles.

"So I practiced different stuff with ball handling and dribbling, stuff that was exciting to me and much more fun. I would throw it off the wall and try to make a basket. I'd bounce it off the floor and up to the rim. I'd throw it over the rafters and try to bank it, stuff like that. Then I'd try passing against the wall, first throwing the ball behind my back, then through my legs and around my neck, aiming for a spot on the wall. Usually I made all kinds of difficult shots that seemed impossible to the rest of the kids when I would tell them about them."

Pete took his basketball to bed with him and practiced his shooting form before fatigue lulled him to sleep. After he got a bike for Christmas one year, he began learning to dribble while pedaling.

One time, his father took him for a car ride and drove at varying speeds while Pete leaned out the passenger window, trying to dribble the ball from the moving car. He also dribbled along sidewalks blindfolded and dribbled on railroad tracks, keeping the bouncing ball in the center of the three-inch-wide strips of iron rail. (Not easy to do, as Luke Ridnour would one day discover.)

Pete became so good at spinning the ball on his fingers that he once took a five-dollar bet that he could spin the ball on his fingers for one hour without stopping. After ten minutes of spinning the basketball on his index finger, the digit turned raw and started to bleed. He moved the spinning ball to the other fingers on his right hand—then his left. When all his fingertips became too tender to continue much further, he switched to his knuckles and thumbs to keep the spinning ball aloft—and collected his five bucks.

For much of his childhood and adolescence, Pete was devoted to dribbling, practicing his passes, and honing his jump shot along with the one-hand push, the set shot, and the hook. He became a student of the game, sitting beside his father in dozens of different college field houses, watching him chew on a white towel and periodically blow up at the referees.

Pete's stunning basketball skills earned him a spot on the high school team when he was in the eighth grade, a development his older teammates didn't take well. Remember, this was the early 1960s, and his style of "show time" basketball had never been seen before. Pete became the target of ridicule and was socially ostracized by his teammates, which was very difficult for him to take.

It wasn't until Pete's junior and senior years in high school that he gained acceptance from his teammates. As he poured in jump shots from every spot on the court, "Pistol Pete," as the local sportswriters tabbed him, became a blue-chip college basketball recruit. He was in the midst of a growth spurt that would take him to 6 feet, 5 inches tall—the perfect height for a playmaking, shooting guard.

Lots of schools wanted him, but there was a complication: during Pete's senior year of high school, his father had finagled a job offer to coach at Louisiana State University—a football school if ever there was one. There was an implicit *quid pro quo* between Press and LSU: *If you want this job, you'd better bring Pete with you.*

Pete wasn't thrilled to learn that. He didn't want to play for some doggone football school where the field house smelled like a barn. He wanted to play for the University of West Virginia, where Jerry West—"Mr. Clutch" for the Los Angeles Lakers—had sharpened his game.

Press delivered an ultimatum to his son: *If you don't come play for me at LSU, don't ever come home again.*

Pete caved, and that's how he landed at Louisiana State. Despite taking his game to bayou country, he captured the nation's attention, very much like John, Paul, George, and Ringo had when they stepped off a plane at John F. Kennedy Airport in 1964. He was a great scorer who entertained crowds with between-the-legs passes and flashy dribbles that left bug-eyed defenders playing like someone had bound their ankles with rope. The 3,667 points he scored during his collegiate career is still a Division I record—and that despite the fact that he played only three years at LSU due to an NCAA rule at the time that prevented college freshmen from playing varsity basketball. That rule was changed in 1972.

When Pete's amazing college career was over, he signed what was then the largest pro contract in history with the Atlanta Hawks—$1.9 million. Pete sat at a press conference with famed sportscaster Howard Cosell and forty-two microphones and announced to the world, "I've arrived. Now all I need is that ring. Then I'll be happy for the rest of my days on earth."

THINGS DIDN'T WORK OUT AS EXPECTED
Pete Maravich never got his NBA championship ring.

For all his personal achievements and all the flair he put on display during his ten-year NBA career, Pete was never a big winner in the pros. Sure, he led the league in scoring one season, played in five NBA All-Star games, and averaged 24 points a game over his career, but Pistol Pete could never escape the perception that he played mostly for himself, that the team was secondary.

A former teammate, "Sweet Lou" Hudson, summed it up this way: "This man has been quicker than Jerry West or Oscar Robertson. He gets the ball up the floor better. He shoots as well. Raw talent–wise, he's the greatest who ever played. The difference comes down to style. He will be a loser, always, no matter what he does. That's his legacy. It never looked easy being Pete Maravich."

With his game underappreciated, his teams losing more than they were winning, Pete was miserable. Basketball had always been his god, his religion—the most important thing in his life. But he wasn't finding salvation on the basketball court.

Pete tried all the things the world said would make him happy: alcohol, women, and buying stuff like the latest muscle cars coming out of Detroit. But nothing gave more than fleeting satisfaction. Although he played well enough at Atlanta (the Hawks always suffered early exits from the playoffs, however), Pete found out he was dispensable when the team traded him to the New Orleans Jazz, an NBA expansion team looking for a marquee player. Sending Pete to New Orleans (the media dubbed the trade the "Louisiana Purchase") was like sending a thoroughbred to a stable filled with nags destined for the glue factory.

Pete could be excused for not remembering the names of the aging veterans, journeymen, and unproven talent who passed through New Orleans that first season. After all, twenty-two different players wore Jazz colors during the team's inaugural year. The Jazz' 23–59 record was the worst in the league.

Flashy moves seemed pointless when the team was down 20 points late in the first half, so Pete cut down on the show and started shooting more. He led the NBA in scoring with 31.1 points per game in the 1976–77 season with the Jazz, but then his body began betraying him. His physical downward slide began in January 1978, when he tore up his right knee in classic Maravich style: instead of throwing a routine outlet pass during one game, he jumped into the air and tried to whip a between-the-legs pass down the court. He landed awkwardly, badly injured his knee, and would never again play with his old joy and abandon.

Pete's knee problems were too much to overcome, and the last few seasons of Pete's NBA career were a steady descent to mediocrity. He wore the same kind of two-pound brace on his right knee that New York Jet quarterback Joe Namath did for much of his career—and suffered recurring problems in his lower back. Playing basketball with a heavy knee brace was like trying to run the court with a ball and chain. His once-quick pirouettes turned into slow-motion spinouts.

Pete's final stop in the NBA was a short-lived stint with the Boston Celtics, where he was a role player expected to drain long three-point jumpers. (The NBA had finally adopted the three-point shot at the start of the 1979–80 season.) Even though he was 10 of 15 shooting the trey during his final season, Pete couldn't defeat Father Time or his injuries. Pete walked away from the game at thirty-three years of age.

He flew home to New Orleans, where his wife, Jackie, and two-year-old son, Jaeson, were waiting for him. He made a clean break from basketball, packing his trophies and memorabilia into boxes. Anything that reminded him of the game was purged from his life—either packed away in storage or given away.

"For two years, I remained in seclusion, trying to wean myself from the effects of basketball," he wrote in *Heir to a Dream*. "At first, quitting seemed an easy proposition, but I soon discovered that leaving basketball cold turkey was the most difficult thing I had ever done. I envisioned my retirement as lazy afternoons sipping cold drinks poolside; instead I found myself wrapped in depression and self-pity, wondering what to do with all the time on my hands."

Perhaps Pete would have found happiness and peace of mind if he had become Husband of the Year to Jackie and Father of the Year to Jaeson. But it didn't work out that way. Being a loving husband and attentive dad didn't satisfy him the way he hoped it would. Plus, Jaeson was a toddler and unable to do a lot of things on his own.

Maybe putting together some great investments and increasing his net wealth would give him a sense of self-worth. But maintaining a watchful eye on the commodities and stocks he purchased caused him nothing but gut-wrenching anguish.

Maybe living longer would make life meaningful. Pete got into nutrition, thinking it would help him live to 150 years of age—and this was long before the popularity of health food stores. He tried vegetarianism for a while and filled a refrigerator with dozens of bottles of expensive vitamins and natural foods. Then he read survivalist tracts about the coming Apocalypse and toyed with the idea of building a bomb shelter where he and his family could ride out a nuclear attack. The bomb shelter was never built.

Meanwhile, Jackie remained extremely patient with each jag that her getting-weirder-by-the-day husband chased after. His obsessive-compulsive personality pushed him into a "neat freak" stage that saw him constantly scrubbing tiles and washing dishes. Then he turned to bouts of fasting to "detox" his body of wastes and toxins. (He once fasted for twenty-five days.) Next he tried Transcendental Meditation, which was popular at the time after Maharishi Mahesh Yogi introduced TM to the Western world—via the Beatles—in the late 1960s. Pete's TM technique was a combination of teachings from Krishna, Buddha, and Shankara.

After Pete found Transcendental Meditation wanting, he turned his spiritual search toward the extraterrestrial: astrology and UFOs—unidentified flying objects. Pete even painted a message on the roof of his house to welcome any UFOs passing through the stratosphere. "Take me," the message said. Celestial exploration was another distraction from reality.

"I found nothing to hang on to that would last forever," he later wrote. "Even my greatest records would someday be broken. The trophies were collecting dust in the closet. And one day, no one would remember or even care about a floppy-socked basketball player named Pistol Pete Maravich."

But then Pete found the peace he was looking for.

One November night in 1982—two years into his hermit-like existence, which was marked by moodiness and silence—Pete couldn't fall asleep. Jackie lay dozing next to him in their bed.

The sins of Pete's youth paraded through his mind for hours. His conscience bothered him as never before. He couldn't find peace. No matter how hard he tried, he couldn't rid his mind of the guilt-inducing memories.

As early morning approached, Pete knew he had to make things right with Jesus Christ. Back when he was at LSU, he had heard the Gospel message from Bill Bright, the founder of Campus Crusade for Christ. He had seen hundreds of young people go forward, including a close friend who jumped out of his seat with tears in his eyes to give his life to Christ.

Thinking back to that event, Pete had to admit a sad truth: he had rejected Christ that day in Baton Rouge. Back then, to his way of thinking, he was going to get his championship ring in basketball, and then he'd have time for God.

But Pete never got that ring, and the acclaim he received and the cheers he heard became distant memories. As the first hints of dawn approached, he realized that his life had amounted to *nothing*.

At 5:40 a.m.—Pete remembers the time because he looked at his alarm clock—he pulled himself out of bed and got on his knees. He cried out to the Lord, saying, "I've cursed you and I've spit on you. I've mocked you and used your name in vain. I've kicked, punched, and laughed at you. Oh, God, can you forgive me? Please save me, please. I've had it with this life of mine. I've had it with all the world's answers for happiness."

An overwhelming silence filled the room, and tears flowed down the cheeks of a spiritually broken man. What Pete later remembered as an audible voice spoke to him: "Be strong. Lift thine own heart."

The words were loud and clear to him. He woke up Jackie and said, "Did you hear that? Did you hear God?"

Jackie told him that he had finally gone completely crazy, flopped her head back on the pillow, and fell back asleep.

But Pete couldn't rest. The power of God had touched him and completely changed him. From that day forward, he would give himself to serving God with all the intensity he had ever shown on a basketball court.

THE CLOCK WINDING DOWN

People who knew Pete Maravich during the last five years of his life say he couldn't go five minutes without talking about Jesus Christ.

If he was sitting in a taxi, he'd ask the cabbie if he was saved. If a total stranger was sitting next to him on a plane flight, he'd steer the friendly patter toward the topic he really wanted to talk about: Jesus Christ.

Heir to a Dream was released in October 1987 to coincide with the start of a new basketball season. The book's coda was Pete's testimony, which has been condensed for this chapter.

Having a book out gave Pete a newfound platform to share his story as well as his faith, and he gave dozens of interviews to support the launch of the book. His publisher, Thomas Nelson Publishers of Nashville, contacted Focus on the Family and asked if Dr. Dobson would be interested in interviewing Pete about his book for the daily radio program, which was heard by millions.

Focus on the Family's broadcast department forwarded the request to Dr. Dobson's office. Knowing the doctor's rabid love for basketball, I would imagine that interview request was approved faster than you could say, "Pistol Pete."

And then Dr. Dobson had another idea: invite Pete to play basketball with him and the boys at First Church of the Nazarene. Might as well take advantage of the opportunity to play with a legend.

Audacious?

Sure. This would be like asking Willie Mays to drop by your church softball team practice or asking Arnold Palmer to show up at your men's group choose-up at the local muni.

Gary Lydic, the Focus HR director who organized the early morning games, picks up the story from here:

> I'll never forget when Dr. Dobson called me on the morning of January 4, 1988. I was in my office at Focus on the Family. He said, "Gary, you are not going to believe this. Pistol Pete Maravich is coming in tomorrow to do a broadcast, but he has also agreed to play basketball with us. I want you to get the guys together. He'll have his friend Frank Schroeder with him. Frank is the producer of the new film *Pistol*."
>
> Dr. Dobson asked me to pick up Pete and Frank at the San Dimas Inn and drive them to the First Church of the Nazarene in Pasadena—about a forty-five-minute drive in morning rush hour

traffic. "Be sure to pick them up early enough so we can get started right on time," he said.

"No problem, Doctor." As soon as I hung up the phone, I started calling the guys. The next day was a Tuesday, and we normally played on Mondays, Wednesdays, and Fridays. Did you think I had any trouble getting together a Tuesday game? No way! I got nothing but yeses, and they were thrilled to learn that they were going to play basketball with Pete Maravich.

For the rest of the day, I stayed in my office and shuffled papers. I got nothing done. I kept thinking, *I get to play with Pistol Pete Maravich tomorrow! I get to pick him up!*

Back in those days, you didn't get to see the great players play like you do today. Cable TV was in its infancy, so there weren't zillions of NBA games available on ESPN or TNT. I may have seen Pete play once or twice on TV, but I certainly knew all about him from reading the newspaper and magazine stories about him.

When I got home that night, I couldn't stop talking about Pete Maravich with my bride, Debbie, and our two young sons, Trevor and Brent. I tried my best to explain what a big deal it was for me to play basketball with the famous Pistol Pete.

When I went to bed, I couldn't sleep. At two or two thirty in the morning, I got up, grabbed my Bible, and went out to the living room. For the next few hours, I spent time with the Lord, reading and praying. I had this feeling inside me that this was going to be an incredible day.

I can't tell you how excited I was—like a kid on Christmas morning. I kept praying that this would be a wonderful opportunity, not only for those of us who'd get a chance to play with Pete but also for Pete's chance to do the broadcast with Dr. Dobson and reach millions with his amazing testimony.

I went back to bed, but I didn't sleep a wink. I got up shortly after 5:00 a.m. to get ready for the drive to the San Dimas Inn. I was scheduled to pick up Pete and Frank at 5:30 a.m. It was pitch dark on that chilly January morning.

I pulled up to the San Dimas Inn and walked into the lobby, where I used the house phone to call Pete's room. When Pete picked up, my heart skipped a beat. "This is Gary," I said. "I'm here to pick you up."

"I'll be right down," he said. I stood in the lobby, about to meet one the best players who ever played basketball, and my knees were shaking. I had to sit down because I was so excited.

When Pete walked into the lobby, followed by Frank, he thrust out his hand. "This must be the man," he said. Introductions were made, and then we headed out to my car. Almost immediately, Pete started talking about Jesus Christ.

As we merged onto Interstate 210 into Pasadena, Pete continued talking about what Christ had been doing in his life. Even at that early time of the morning, the rush hour traffic was horrible. As we slowed into bumper-to-bumper congestion, Pete continued to describe the adventure that God had sent him on. It became apparent to me that this guy was sold out to Christ.

The longer we were stuck in traffic, though, the more I worried that we were going to be late. I decided we'd be better getting off the 210 and onto surface streets, which wouldn't be so choked with cars.

I was starting to change lanes when a car roared past and nearly clipped us. I pulled back into my lane and shot up a quick prayer: *Lord, not now, not with Pistol Pete in the car . . . any other time, but not now.*

Then, for just a moment, a thought flashed through my mind: *Maybe, just maybe, you're not supposed to be there today.* But that thought left me just as quickly as it came. I managed to get us off the freeway and onto Foothill Boulevard, but we were still twenty minutes late when we pulled into the parking lot of the First Church of the Nazarene.

When we walked inside the gym, I could see that Dr. Dobson and the guys were already playing a half-court game.

Pete, Frank, and I took the free basket on the other end of the gym and started warming up. Pete talked to me about his dad's death from cancer the previous spring. He said he took his father all over the world in private planes, trying to find a cure for him. "Gary, sometimes I took him off the plane and wasn't sure if he was still breathing or not," he said.

Pete said his dad had accepted Jesus Christ as his personal Savior before his death, and he talked about how much that meant to him. (I later learned that Pete whispered, "I'll see you soon," to his father after he took his final breath. He also told an interviewer in 1974, when talking about how his pro basketball career wasn't turning out the way he dreamt it, "I don't want to play ten years in the NBA and then die of a heart attack when I'm forty.")

I was quite moved by Pete's stories of how he cared for his father right up until the end. I looked at him, and with great emotion I said, "Pete, my dad lies in a hospital in Dayton, Ohio, and he has bone cancer."

Pete came alongside me and put an arm around my shoulders. "Gary, I've been there, and I want to walk through this with you."

I was thanking Pete when I heard Dr. Dobson's voice saying, "Come on over, guys."

We headed over to the main court, where I introduced Pete and Frank to Dr. Dobson and the rest of the guys.

Dr. Dobson was in a great mood. "Why don't you go ahead and

pick the teams, Gary," he said.

Well, I've never been a very bright guy, but I decided that Pistol Pete should be on Dr. Dobson's team, and then I made sure I was part of that five-man team as well. I put our ringer, 7-foot, 2-inch Ralph Drollinger, on the other team to make things even.

Ralph had played for John Wooden at UCLA. Following graduation, he chose to play with Athletes in Action, an amateur team that toured the world playing basketball and preaching the Gospel at halftime of their games. After three seasons with Athletes in Action, Ralph played one season with the Dallas Mavericks before retiring with a lingering knee injury.

We started playing our half-court game, and what unfolded was just wonderful. Whenever one of us passed the ball to Pete, we stood around and watched him effortlessly dribble through his legs and make one beautiful shot after another. He took it easy, playing probably at one-third of his normal speed. He didn't have to play very hard because his competition was a bunch of out-of-shape guys in their thirties and forties huffing and puffing to keep up.

But we were all having fun, laughing, and horsing around. We played three games to ten baskets. I don't think I need to tell you who won those three games, but I happened to be on the winning team with you-know-who. Well, after the third game, we took a short break. Some of the guys went outside to get some fresh air, and some went into the hallway to get a drink from the water fountain. Before I knew it, it was just Pete, Dr. Dobson, and myself on the court.

Pete bounced a basketball near the top of the key with Dr. Dobson while taking a few shots at the basket. I stood underneath to receive the ball as it swished through the net and pump the ball back to Pete for the next shot.

Dr. Dobson asked him when he had played basketball last. Pete said he hadn't played basketball in over a year, except for an appearance at the NBA Legends game during the All-Star break the previous spring.

"Pete, how could you ever give this game up?" Dr. Dobson asked. "You love it so much, and it's so much a part of your life."

Pete replied, "You know, I didn't really realize until today how much I miss this game. I am really enjoying this, being out here with you guys."

He flexed his legs and flung another shot toward the rim. "Two weeks ago I couldn't lift my right arm up past my shoulder because I had neuritis in my right arm, and it was very, very painful."

"How do you feel today?" Dr. Dobson asked.

"I have never felt better," Pete responded. He flipped another shot toward the rim. I gathered the rebound and was starting a two-handed chest pass back to Pete when—boom . . . he fell backward like a statue, his head hitting the floor with a sickening thud.

Surely my eyes were betraying me. Dr. Dobson took a step toward him, and I did as well. Pete had a great sense of humor, and I thought that at any moment he would jump to his feet with a "gotcha" grin on his face.

But when I got to him, I saw his eyes rolling back and color draining from his face. I immediately knew he was in big trouble. Right away, Dr. Dobson lowered himself to Pete's side and started CPR chest compressions.

I ran to the doors. "Guys! Get in here! Something happened to Pete!"

Their faces were masked with concern, and I ran to the closest church office to call 911. There were no cell phones in 1988.

After I reached 911, I went to the parking lot and waited for the paramedics to arrive. The minutes ticked by like hours. It seemed like it took forever for the ambulance to arrive, but when paramedics finally arrived on the scene, I rushed them into the gym.

Dr. Dobson was still working on Pete. He pulled back as the paramedics placed defibrillation paddles on Pete's chest to restart his heart.

Dr. Dobson, the other players, and I formed a circle and began begging the Lord out loud in prayer. We were crying out, "No, not now, Lord! He just has accepted You, and all he cares about is sharing the love of Christ with everyone!"

In just an hour or two with Pete, I could see that he wanted to spend the rest of his life talking about Jesus Christ. He wanted to share with as many as he could what God had done for him—how he had tried everything that the world had to offer but was left with a huge void in his heart. When Pete found Christ, there was a total, 180-degree transformation of his life.

"Please, Lord, don't take him now," we prayed out loud. "He is sharing You with everyone. He has such a strong testimony of what You have done for him."

Meanwhile, the paramedics continued to work on him, but his body was still and unresponsive. He was dead and had been since he hit the floor. The decision was made to put him on a stretcher and take him to St. Luke Hospital in Pasadena.

I remember helping the paramedics lift and place Pete's body onto the stretcher as one of them continued to perform chest compressions. We watched as his body was loaded into the back of the ambulance. Dr. Dobson, Ralph Drollinger, and I hopped into Dr. Dobson's car to follow.

We pulled onto Sierra Madre Boulevard, but there were no sirens or red flashing lights. And the ambulance wasn't going very fast, either.

Tears poured down my face. The reality slammed into me like a crushing wave. Pete Maravich, one of the greatest basketball players ever, wasn't alive anymore.

When we got to the emergency room, the three of us sat down in the waiting room. We weren't there very long when a doctor came out and said: "Guys, I'm sorry, but Pete has died."

Hearing that statement from a medical authority, though expected, still hit me hard. The doctor invited us into the room where Pete's body lay. Never before and never since have I ever seen a more peaceful face in death. Dr. Dobson, Ralph, and I held hands around Pete's body and thanked the Lord for his life. We all knew he had gone home to be with Jesus.

But we also knew that a very difficult phone call had to be made to Pete's precious wife, Jackie Maravich, and their two little boys. Dr. Dobson left to go make that phone call. When he returned, he said, "Gary, when we get back to Focus on the Family, I want you to handle all the phone calls and all the media that is going to come in the rest of the day."

Dr. Dobson and I both knew the most important thing to Pete was not the acclaim or scoring records, or even his notoriety, but his relationship with Jesus Christ. When I got back to the office, the phone *did* start ringing off the hook. I could not believe how quickly news of Pete's death spread. I received calls from all over the country—New York, Chicago, Atlanta, Dallas, and San Francisco—as well as calls from all around the world, including Germany, Guatemala, and Spain. The reporters and producers calling in all wanted to hear the story of what happened that morning.

By and large, the stories about Pete's death that day included a description of how he was a changed man the last five years after becoming a "born-again Christian," as the media described it. In the aftermath of Pete's passing, this was gratifying to see.

Dr. Dobson was asked to go to Baton Rouge to speak at Pete's memorial service. I was grateful that he asked me to join him. I remember reading Pete's book, *Heir to a Dream*, on the plane flight to Louisiana and meeting many of the same people that Pete wrote about in the book. These sports figures all wanted to hear about Pete's last moments on earth, and I recounted the story as I have told it here. At the memorial service, Dr. Dobson said, "Basketball at one time was his greatest love. But his greatest passion was the love of the Lord he served."

A few days after we returned to Southern California, the autopsy results came back, and they were shocking. Pete had died of a congenital heart malformation he never knew he had. In layman's terms, he was born without one of the two artery systems that supply the heart with blood. The news stunned cardiologists and other heart experts.

They said most people with this condition don't live past the age of twenty—especially those who sprint up and down a basketball court for much of their lives.

In other words, Pete's heart was a ticking time bomb, and he never should have lived beyond his sophomore year at LSU.

Two weeks after Pete's death, Dr. Dobson and I met in his office. We asked each other, *Why was Pete with us when this happened?* There had to be a reason for it. And since there was a reason, what did God want us to do?

During those two weeks, I learned that Pistol Pete had his own summer basketball camps in St. Augustine, Florida. I said to Dr. Dobson: "You know, we both have been praying about what God wants us to do. We both know how Pete shared the fundamentals of the game as well as his love for Christ at his camps. What if we did a basketball camp in memory of Pistol Pete? We could share about his life and the importance of the relationship he had with the King of kings and Lord of lords. I think a basketball camp would be the most important thing that we could possibly do in his memory."

Dr. Dobson said, "Okay, run with it." So that summer at nearby Claremont-McKenna College, we held our first basketball camp in memory of Pete Maravich. But we had a stipulation for those who wanted to come: they had to be from a single-parent family or the inner city.

That was the start of eight years of basketball camps, and what a great run we had. We traveled all over the country putting on these summer basketball camps at various colleges and universities, and we also did girls' camps.

On the morning of his last hour on earth, Pete Maravich was wearing a T-shirt that read, LOOKING UNTO JESUS.

Those words come from Hebrews 12:2, which in the King James Version starts like this:

> *Looking unto Jesus the author and finisher of our faith; who for the joy that was set before him endured the cross, despising the shame, and is set down at the right hand of the throne of God.*

What a bold witness for Christ, Pete Maravich! We will never know why the Lord took Pete so suddenly and prematurely, but that is part of the sovereignty of God.

But what happened that morning at Parker Gym changed my life, and I know Pete's life and death continue to impact people nearly twenty-five years later.

A PLOT TWIST THAT HOLLYWOOD COULDN'T SCRIPT

Wasn't that quite a story from Gary Lydic?

But the narrative doesn't quite end there.

In August 1990, Dr. Dobson was playing one of his usual early morning basketball games at the First Church of the Nazarene, on the same floor where Pete Maravich had died two and a half years earlier.

Dr. Dobson did not bring his best game to the gym that morning, however. In basketball lingo, he shot bricks at the glass backboard and let players drive by him like his feet were nailed to the polished hardwood floor. After blowing an easy lay-in, a sharp pain hit Dr. Dobson in the center of his chest.

As he caught his breath, he immediately knew something was not right. When his chest pains failed to diminish, he picked up his car keys and waved good-bye. "Sorry, guys, gotta go," he said as he strolled out.

It wasn't like him to quit playing basketball before 8:00 a.m. One of the players ran after Dr. Dobson, asking him if he was feeling all right. "I think I'm okay," he said, but something told Dr. Dobson that he wasn't 100 percent.

Instead of going home to shower, Dr. Dobson drove himself to the same hospital, St. Luke's of Pasadena, where paramedics had taken Pete Maravich's body. Dr. Dobson parked the car and gathered his thoughts. To march into an emergency room and announce that he was suffering chest pains would blow a huge hole in his hyper-busy schedule: meetings with the executive staff, broadcast tapings, and responding to the dozens of phone messages his personal assistants had fielded.

Dr. Dobson sat in his car for nearly thirty minutes, weighing the consequences of stepping through the emergency room doors. "What do You want me to do, Lord?" he prayed. "I'm fifty-four years old, and I'm having chest pains."

It's a good thing Dr. Dobson admitted himself at St. Luke's that morning because tests revealed that he had suffered a mild to moderate heart attack. Apparently, one of the five coronary arteries supplying his heart with blood had become blocked. Thanks to quick intervention, Dr. Dobson received the medical care he needed to stay alive.

Even though that was the last time Dr. Dobson would ever play competitive basketball, he survived a heart attack that allowed him to continue writing books, recording new broadcasts, speaking out on the issues important to families, and directing a worldwide ministry to millions of parents and children for many more years.

You have to wonder if Dr. Dobson would have ignored those chest pains if Pete Maravich hadn't died in his arms.

PLAYING

WITH

PURPOSE

INSIDE THE LIVES AND FAITH
OF THE MAJOR LEAGUES'
TOP PLAYERS—

INCLUDING MARIANO RIVERA,
ALBERT PUJOLS, AND JOSH HAMILTON

MIKE YORKEY

WITH JESSE FLOREA AND JOSHUA COOLEY

CONTENTS

INTRODUCTION

Baseball has been called, among many other things, timeless—which is an interesting statement when you consider that this great game is the only major sport in America contested without a time clock.

Beginning at the moment the umpire shouts, "Play ball!" baseball moves to its own distinct rhythms. The leadoff batter steps into the box, and the pitcher fidgets on the mound before hurling his first pitch—and then the game proceeds at its own pace. Throw the ball. Swing the bat. Three strikes and you're out. Four balls and take your base. Touch home plate and score a run. Nine innings make a game. The permutations of the game's outcome are seemingly as infinite as the stars in the heavens or the particles of sand on a seashore.

Baseball actually follows the patterns of nature. After a gloomy winter, baseball season begins in the spring with its promise of hope and sunnier times. The hot summer months are a proving ground, a time when greatness is forged in the crucible of the regular season. Fall is reserved for the final and decisive moments of baseball's playoffs, after which another dreary winter sets in.

Baseball may not be America's oldest sport—there's evidence that Native Americans played a game that resembled modern-day lacrosse in the seventeenth century—but nearly everyone agrees that baseball seeped into the national consciousness earlier than any other sport. The history of baseball dates back to the Revolutionary War, when George Washington's troops at Valley Forge batted balls and ran bases in a game that resembled cricket, a British pastime that played a role in the evolution of baseball. Lewis and Clark played catch during their exploration to the Pacific Ocean. Robin Carver's *Book of Sports*, first published in 1834, described how an American version of "rounders" rivaled cricket in popularity.

According to American folklore, Abner Doubleday invented baseball in 1839. But baseball historians, after reading Doubleday's diary, have discovered that he was never in Cooperstown, New York, when the first game was supposedly played . . . or any time after that. Instead, he was a cadet at West Point and never even mentioned baseball in numerous letters and papers found after he passed away in 1893.

Alexander Cartwright, a New York bookseller, is now generally credited with inventing the modern form of baseball. In 1845, he formed a committee that drew up rules for baseball—like limiting the number of outfielders to three and tagging the runner instead of throwing the ball at him. The new rules were widely adopted.

Cartwright founded the New York Knickerbockers Base Ball Club, and it wasn't long before other teams formed and new leagues banded together. By the turn of the twentieth century, "major league" baseball was played in the biggest cities in the Northeast, particularly New York City, as well as farther west in Cincinnati and Chicago.

The game of bats and balls captured the hearts of the working class. Granted, there wasn't much competition in an era that predates radio, movies, and television. But it's irrefutable that baseball became woven tightly within the fabric of American culture, thanks in large part to the emergence of sports pages in daily newspapers and to the country's rapid industrialization and urbanization. Baseball provided an escape and a refuge from the pressures of daily life. The lush greenness of the baseball field in the middle of a gritty tenement-strewn city heralded a return to nature's simple and pure roots.

The first twenty years of the twentieth century saw an unprecedented rise in the popularity of baseball. Commodious new ballparks—New York's Ebbets Field and the Polo Grounds, Boston's Fenway Park, Chicago's Wrigley Field and Comiskey Park, and Tiger Stadium in Detroit—filled their box seats with prosperous businessmen and their bleachers with working-class Italian, Polish, and Jewish immigrants. *Philadelphia Inquirer* reporter Edgar F. Wolfe argued that the ballpark was a common meeting ground for Americans of *all* classes and backgrounds. The game suited the national temperament and enraptured presidents and paupers alike.

A decision in 1919 to strictly enforce new rules governing the size, shape, and construction of the baseball ushered in a golden era for the game. With the demise of the "dead ball" and the emergence of home run hitter Babe Ruth, baseball fever swept over the country. For the next fifty years, America's love affair with baseball was both singular and satisfying. Baseball even became a shibboleth during World War II—a cultural reference that only a true-blue American would know about. The question "Who won the 1943 World Series?" posed to Nazi spies was thought to reveal their true identity, because every red-blooded GI knew that the New York Yankees beat the St. Louis Cardinals in the Fall Classic.

Just a generation later, though, the merger of the NFL and AFL pro football leagues in 1970 and the marketing of the Super Bowl into a quasi-religious festival along the lines of Rome's bread-and-circuses knocked baseball off its lofty perch. But the Grand Old Game refused to get off the field. In the past four decades, there have been dynamic changes in American society and culture, but one of the few constants has been baseball. Broadcaster Bob Costas had it right when he said, "So many things in our country have changed drastically, as they must, over the years and over the decades, and although baseball has changed, its essence remains the same. It's one of the enduring institutions in our country, and I think we take some comfort in that."

During today's uncertain times, with global upheaval, natural disasters, and terrorist mayhem in the forefront of people's minds, baseball's constancy is part of its allure, a sign of its strength. Sure, there's been a tweaking of rules over the years, like the shrinking of the strike zone and lowering of the pitcher's mound in 1969 as well as limited instant replay on home run calls starting in 2008. But, by and large, modern-day baseball is the same game Rogers Hornsby, Babe Ruth, Lou Gehrig, Mickey Mantle, and Willie Mays played.

Baseball is a team sport—and an individual sport—that harkens back to a simpler time when life was more manageable, understandable, and fair. It's the only major professional sport (NFL football, NBA basketball, and NHL hockey being the others) where the winning team can't run out the clock. The pitcher has to throw the ball over the plate and give his opponent a chance. Until the team that's ahead records twenty-seven outs in the scorebook, anything can happen.

There's no doubt that the passion for baseball is passed down from generation to generation. This is a strength but also a weakness of the sport because many fear that today's young fathers—many who grew up playing video games or taking part in action sports like skateboarding, paintballing, snowboarding, BMX biking, and rock climbing—won't bother to introduce their sons and daughters to a fuddy-duddy game like baseball.

That wasn't the case when I (Mike Yorkey) was growing up in La Jolla, California, a beach community a few miles north of San Diego. My father *and* my mother loved baseball. Mom was a die-hard Willie Mays fan who, if she tilted her Philco wooden radio just right and rapped her knuckles against the left side, could manage to pull in KSFO's staticky signal from five hundred miles away to listen in as Russ Hodges and Lon Simmons regaled listeners with the play-by-play of Willie's latest exploits.

After the San Diego Padres joined the National League in 1969 as an expansion team, Mom and Dad took me to the first major league game ever played in America's Finest City. (I even remember the score without going to Google—a 2–1 home team victory over the Houston Astros.) The following season, my folks became season ticket holders who shared four seats in the second row behind home plate at San Diego Stadium (today known as Qualcomm Stadium).

Mom and Dad remain season ticket holders to this day at Petco Park, the Padres' handsome downtown ballpark that opened during the 2004 season. My wife, Nicole, and I attend a few games each year with my parents or our adult children and their spouses. And yes, we've kept the same second-row-behind-home-plate vantage point. I will admit that I'm a spoiled baseball fan.

My father was also my Little League coach, which is why the 1989 baseball movie *Field of Dreams* resonated with me. I wasn't so much taken with the way farmer Ray Kinsella plowed under part of his corn crop to build a baseball diamond in the middle of an Iowa farm field, thus fulfilling the voice in his head telling him, "If you build it, he will come." What caused a lump in my throat was a moment during the film's denouement, when a catcher on the field removed his mask. Ray recognized that the catcher was his father as a young man. He gathered enough courage to ask his father a simple question: "Hey, Dad. You wanna have a catch?"

If you've ever played catch with your father—or your son—the emotions connected with the simple tossing of a baseball back and forth are timeless and never forgotten. I can still remember asking my father if he would play catch with me after dinner back in my elementary school years. Even though he was pretty well spent after a day of hand-sawing two-by-fours and pounding nails at the construction site, he'd get into a catcher's crouch and let me pitch to him. When I outgrew our small backyard, he brought in dirt and built a mound in the front yard so I could continue practicing my curveball during my Little League days. (I was known as a "junk ball" pitcher back then.)

I continued that father-and-son tradition as soon as my son Patrick could hold a mitt. We started with a soft, light ball and graduated to hardballs in our games of backyard catch. Then I coached his Little League team—just like my father did for me. Except this time we weren't living in sunny San Diego but in weather-volatile Colorado Springs, Colorado, where the start of Little League season—March—happened to be the snowiest month on the calendar. I can remember pitching batting practice while huge, wet snowflakes danced in the air before evaporating when they hit the no-longer-frozen ground. I wasn't happy pitching with fingers numb from the sleet, but no one would get me off that mound while my son was on the team.

Now, in 2012, Patrick is a young father with a son, Joshua, celebrating his first season of life. Since the passion for baseball seems to be passed from parent to child, I expect Joshua to be our family's next big fan. There's a real and tangible emotional element in baseball—a tie that is often directly connected to the game's history in our own lives.

It will be interesting to see what the game of baseball is like when Joshua grows up. Nineteenth-century poet Walt Whitman once deemed baseball as the "hurrah game of the republic" because of its "snap, go, and fling of the American atmosphere." But baseball has since relinquished its crown as the national pastime to football. Baseball attendance has steadily dropped the past four years, and though the hurting economy may be the culprit, few can deny that baseball has lost some of its appeal, especially with the younger generation gravitating to other pastimes or used to texting, watching TV, and surfing the Web—all at the same time.

Today's younger audiences demand entertainment that asks them to do little more than sit back and be amazed. Baseball, however, is a strategic and cerebral game. Full enjoyment of baseball requires more than surface-level observation. Once you begin to understand the nuances—the batting order, the pitcher's count, the timing of the bunt, the positioning of the infielders, the hit-and-run, the pitch-out, the intentional walk, the pinch hitter, and playing for the double play—the game becomes fascinating. The variables reset between batters, supplying the mind with many more contingencies to consider. Because of this, baseball demands considerable attention while offering a unique capacity for numerical analysis, thanks to a treasure trove of statistics that would fill the Library of Congress.

Baseball is probably the only game in which statistics are discussed, dissected, debated, and treasured. Batters are remembered—and paid accordingly—for their batting average, number of hits, doubles, triples, home runs, bases on balls, intentional walks, stolen bases, and runs batted in. Pitchers are judged by their win-loss records, earned run averages, strikeouts, walks, and innings pitched, to name a few measurements.

Some of those numbers have a way of sticking with you. Anyone with a modicum of sports knowledge knows that Babe Ruth hit 714 home runs before Hank Aaron passed him up as baseball's all-time leader with 755 round-trippers. Even casual fans are aware that Joe DiMaggio once hit safely in 56 straight games, that Roger Maris smacked 61 homers in 1961, and that Ty Cobb stole 96 bases back in 1915.

Even players' contracts are memorable. Alex Rodriguez's ten-year, $252 million contract, signed before the 2001 season, was the most lucrative contract in sports history at the time and was worth $63 million more than the second-richest baseball deal. A-Rod was heralded everywhere as the "252-million-dollar man."

When Rodriguez signed a new ten-year, $275 million contract with the New York Yankees on December 13, 2007—the newest "biggest contract ever"—baseball fans barely noticed for two reasons. One, because such mega-deals were becoming more commonplace and seemed beyond the scope of reality to the average fan, and two, because the explosive Mitchell Report was released the *very same day*. The 311-page report—an independent investigation into the illegal use of steroids and other performance-enhancing substances by major league ballplayers—blew the lid off a scandal that had been brewing for nearly a decade.

It all started innocently enough during the 1998 season when St. Louis Cardinals slugger Mark McGwire was running neck and neck with the Chicago Cubs' Sammy Sosa in a chase to break Roger Maris' single-season record of 61 home runs. Their home run derby treated the nation to a summer of stroke and counterstroke, of packed houses and adoring media attention.

Then, during a game at Shea Stadium in New York, baseball writer Steve Wilstein noticed a small brown bottle sitting on the top shelf of Mark Mc Gwire's locker. The bottle's label said "Androstenedione."

Wilstein did some checking around and learned that "andro" was an anabolic steroid precursor that converted to strength-building testosterone in the body. At first, McGwire denied using the drug but later admitted that he'd been taking "andro" for a year. "Everybody I know in the game of baseball is using the same stuff I use," McGwire said.

Baseball fans shrugged their collective shoulders. Androstenedione was legal at the time, and baseball didn't have a drug-testing policy in force. Besides, who wanted to rain on McGwire's home run parade during that magic summer of 1998?

Then Barry Bonds—jealous of the attention heaped upon McGwire and Sosa—transformed his body seemingly overnight into the Incredible Hulk. He obliterated McGwire's home run record with another number that has earned milestone status: 73 home runs during the 2001 season.

The cracks started forming in the baseball's facade in 2003, however, when a San Francisco grand jury investigated the machinations of the Bay Area Laboratory Cooperative (BALCO), owned and operated by Victor Conte, who had discovered a way to distribute then-undetectable steroids. And Conte knew Bonds through his trainer, Greg Anderson, which led to *a lot* of speculation that Bonds' swollen head and bloated physique was the result of pharmacology.

Two influential books built the case that there was trouble in River City. *Game of Shadows* by Lance Williams and Mark Fainaru-Wada, a pair of *San Francisco Chronicle* reporters privy to BALCO transcripts and court documents, outlined the entire BALCO scandal and led readers to a path that deposited them at Bonds' front door. Then former big-leaguer Jose Canseco's "tell all" book, *Juiced: Wild Times, Rampant 'Roids, Smash Hits, and How Baseball Got Big*, unabashedly championed steroids as a means to greater home run production as well as a fountain of youth. Canseco matter-of-factly described his steroid use and how he injected teammates Mark McGwire, Jason Giambi, Rafael Palmeiro, and Juan Gonzalez.

Pressure was mounting to do something about steroid use in baseball, and in the spring of 2005, several players were subpoenaed to appear before a U.S. congressional committee. By all accounts, McGwire's appearance was disastrous to his credibility and likely wrecked his chances of ever being elected to the Baseball Hall of Fame. Under the hot glare of scrutiny and pointed questioning about steroid use, he repeatedly told several U.S. congressmen that he was "not here to talk about the past."

But the past had caught up with McGwire—and with the rest of baseball. The final nail in the coffin representing baseball's steroid era occurred just before the start of the 2009 season when *Sports Illustrated* reported that Alex Rodriguez had tested positive for two anabolic steroids during the 2003 season. The test results were supposed to remain anonymous, but a coded master list of 104 names was leaked to the press.

Citing an "enormous pressure to perform" after signing his whopper $252 million contract, Rodriguez admitted to using anabolic steroids and other performance-enhancing drugs from 2001 to 2003. Mark McGwire fessed up as well, finally admitting before the 2010 season that he had been taking steroids all along. "Looking back, I wish I had never played during the steroid era," he said.

Say it ain't so, Joe.

But it was so. Even though baseball's dalliance with performance-enhancing drugs (PEDs) will leave a lingering smell on the game for a long time to come, there is some good news to report. Today, it's harder to cheat—*a lot* harder—thanks to random and more sophisticated tests. And there are players who have chosen to fashion careers without performance-enhancing drugs, choosing instead to place their faith in their God-given abilities to play this great game straight up, the way it was meant to be played.

Exhibit One is Albert Pujols, who understands that people are watching his every move. "At the end of the day, as long as I glorify God and those forty-five thousand people know who I represent out there every time I step out on the field, that's what it's all about," he said. "It's about representing God."

I believe Albert hasn't taken PEDs. I believe that because I know he's a mature Christian who's playing with purpose. He understands how much damage there would be to the Kingdom if he *were* juicing. That's why I don't think we'll see a young kid, ball cap on his head, approaching the Los Angeles Angels star on the street and saying, "Say it ain't so, Mr. Pujols."

But we still need to pray for Christian ballplayers like Albert Pujols and Josh Hamilton—who *did* take steroids during his prodigal years—to stay strong in the face of the temptation to gain an edge on the ball field. They are truly playing with purpose, and it's their stories, as well as those of Adrian Gonzalez, Mark Teixeira, Ben Zobrist, Brian Roberts, Carlos Beltran, and pitchers Matt Capps, Clayton Kershaw, and Mariano Rivera, that you will read about in *Playing with Purpose: Baseball*.

So my co-authors, Jesse Florea and Joshua Cooley, and I invite you to sit back, grab a box of Cracker Jack, and enjoy our baseball version of *Playing with Purpose*. As you'll learn in the following chapters, these players are something special, and it's for reasons that go far beyond balls and strikes.

1

CLAYTON KERSHAW:
STANDING ON THE PRECIPICE OF GREATNESS

You are God's field.
1 CORINTHIANS 3:9

In the gloaming, the curious children came.

Their little heads bobbed up and down in the tall, weed-infested field like inquisitive prairie dogs. They came from their hillside village—a shantytown, really—where ramshackle homes populate the landscape and hope remains a street urchin.

In the distance, the sun was setting over this forgotten corner of the world, casting long shadows over the village. Shadows are nothing new in Zambia. Moral decay, poverty, and deadly disease have veiled this small, south-central African nation in spiritual darkness for many years. The bleakness, visitors say, is palpable.

Past the field, the children gathered on both sides of a skinny dirt road. Their clothes were tattered and their feet were dusty, but their smiles were radiant.

They came to marvel at the stranger.

"Musungu!" some of them exclaimed. Others didn't know what to say. They had never seen a white man before.

Standing 6 feet, 3 inches tall and weighing 215 pounds, the Texan towered over the children as he and another foreigner threw an odd white spheroid with red stitches back and forth. Soon the *musungu* handed a glove to one of the boys, backed up a few feet, and played underhanded catch. He did the same for every child. The youngsters giggled with delight. No language barrier could conceal the fact that everyone was having the time of their lives.

But the *musungu* hadn't traveled across ten time zones to promote baseball. He had come to pierce the oppressive shadows with the light of Jesus Christ.

Five months later, on a beautiful Southern California morning, the screaming children came.

Their energetic legs churned as they sprinted across the manicured fields of Pasadena Memorial Park like excited puppies. Here, in the prosperous shadows of the City of Angels, hope and opportunity soar upward like the lush mountain peak of Mount Wilson to the north and the skyscrapers of Los Angeles to the south.

The children came to marvel at their sports hero.

"It's Clayton Kershaw!" they cried incredulously.

The children surrounded—accosted, really—Clayton, his wife, Ellen, and two of the Kershaws' childhood friends as the adults were coming back from breakfast. In a region known for its celebrity sightings, the kids had hit the jackpot. Lacking paper or baseball cards, several boys thrust out their arms for Clayton to autograph their flesh. One boy lifted his shirt.

"Whoa, whoa, whoa!" Clayton said, smiling as he stymied the impromptu tattoo session. Ellen got some paper from their car nearby, and he obliged every child.

Somewhere, between these two disparate fields of dreams, you can find Clayton Kershaw. The Los Angeles Dodgers' budding young superstar lives at the intersection of Christianity and Growing Fame. It's a tricky junction, with plenty of distracting, and often dangerous, traffic coming at him from all directions. Some terrible wrecks have happened there.

But Clayton seems different. He has a strong faith, a great support network of friends and loved ones, and a humility that is as striking as his vast career potential, which portends multiple Cy Young Awards.

Consider this: At the callow age of twenty-two, he became the staff ace on one of baseball's most historic franchises in America's second-most populous city, just a long fly ball away from the glitter of Hollywood. Yet when his sublime abilities are the subject of conversation, he squirms—seems even a bit repulsed.

How many professional athletes do you know like *that*?

"It's never about him," said longtime friend John Dickenson. "It's humility at its best."

THE NATURAL

Clayton didn't always live at this complicated intersection. Life used to be much different.

Born on March 19, 1988, Clayton grew up as an only child on Shenandoah Drive in Highland Park, a posh northern suburb of Dallas known as "The Bubble" for its insular qualities. Highland Park is a white-collar town of fortysomething professionals with a median household income hovering around $150,000—more than three times the national average. Houses are huge, crime is low, schools are great, and people are nice. It's Pleasantville.

The Kershaws were typical suburbanites. Clayton's dad wrote TV commercial jingles, and his mom was a graphic designer. The only reason they stuck out in Highland Park is because they didn't live in one of the town's ubiquitous mansions.

Fame? That was a foreign concept. Well, Clayton *was* the great-nephew of Clyde Tombaugh, the man who discovered Pluto. But Great-Uncle Clyde died before Clayton was born and, heck, poor Pluto's not even considered a planet anymore. So that probably doesn't count.

Young Clayton was always on the move. As a child, his favorite toy was a life-sized Flintstones car with a hole for his feet to touch the floor, so he could scoot around just like Fred and Barney.

That *yabba-dabba-doo* energy was quickly parlayed into athletic prowess. Clayton learned to walk at seven months, and his first word was "ball." Before he lost all his baby teeth, he earned the nickname "The Brick Wall" for his soccer goaltending skills in a local select league.

Losing his baby fat was another matter. When he was in high school, Clayton stood about 5 feet, 10 inches tall, but his waistline housed a few too many burritos from Qdoba's, a local Mexican restaurant where he loved hanging out with his buddies.

"Growing up," Dickenson said, "he was always a chubby puffball." It's nice to have pals, eh?

It also must be nice to have natural athleticism oozing from your pores. Clayton excelled at virtually any sport he played—basketball, football, tennis . . . you name it. Even Ping-Pong. His long arms and great hand-eye coordination meant his childhood buddies were no match for him. In fact, they still aren't.

"He's an amazing Ping-Pong player," Dickenson said. "If he could, he'd give up baseball to do that."

About the only sport Clayton isn't good at is golf. "We played golf the day before his wedding," said Josh Meredith, Clayton's best friend. "He hit one [drive] from the tee box that ricocheted off a tree and landed fifty yards from where he hit it. I laughed pretty hard at that."

By ninth grade, Clayton's athleticism had landed him on the varsity football and baseball teams at Highland Park High School, a rarity for a freshman. During the fall, he played center, snapping to a quarterback whose name you might recognize: Matthew Stafford, the Detroit Lions' number one overall draft pick of 2009.

But Clayton's true love was baseball. That spring, he earned the number two spot in the varsity rotation and soon became one of the most ballyhooed prep pitching prospects ever in Texas, which has produced its fair share of future stars (see "Ryan, Nolan," "Clemens, Roger," "Pettitte, Andy," et al.). With colleges banging down his door, Clayton signed with Texas A&M University, largely because that's where Ellen Melson, his girlfriend and future wife, was going.

Clayton's sublime senior season in high school had the whiff of legend, like a real-life pitching version of *The Natural*. Highland Park, like most of Texas, is batty for high school football, but on days Clayton pitched, the Scots' modestly sized baseball stadium became a hub of interest. Folks wanted to witness the tall, powerful lefty with the mid-90s fastball and sweeping curve do something amazing—which happened often.

Scouts, too, came out in droves. Like a conductor's baton cueing orchestral instruments, dozens of radar guns would pop into position behind home plate whenever Clayton started his windup.

The whole scene was surreal, especially for those who remembered Clayton's freshman physique.

"Early on, he was baby-faced, almost roly-poly," said Lew Kennedy, his former Highland Park coach. "Pretty soon, he lost all that baby fat and turned into a monster. At times, he was virtually untouchable. Batters were happy just to foul one off."

That's not hyperbole. Clayton's statistics as a senior prompt a double-take: in 64 innings, he posted a 13–0 record, 0.77 ERA, and 139 strikeouts. No typo there.

Clayton appeared mortal in the Scots' regular-season finale after a strained oblique muscle sidelined him for several weeks. But when he returned to action against Justin Northwest High in the regional playoffs, he one-upped himself with the rarest of gems—a perfect game in which he struck out *all fifteen batters* in a five-inning, mercy-rule-shortened contest.

True to form, as his teammates celebrated around him, he calmly walked off the field with a satisfied smile. To each teammate who showered him with praise, he simply replied, "Thanks, man." Nothing more.

"He was so soft-spoken," Kennedy said. "Very humble. He was one of the guys. He didn't lord it over anybody. Everybody looked up to him."

After the season, the accolades came rolling in, none more prestigious than the Gatorade high school national baseball player of the year award. He entered the 2006 draft ranked as *Baseball America*'s top prep pitching prospect and the sixth-best prospect overall.

The fun was just about to begin.

FAITH IN THE HEART OF TEXAS

On America's extra-large Bible Belt, Dallas is the big ol' shiny brass buckle. On any given Sunday, you can find a church as easily as a Cowboys jersey. Same for the Highland Park bubble. Everywhere you went, people called themselves Christians.

So Clayton did, too.

He grew up in a Bible-believing home, got confirmed at Highland Park United Methodist in sixth grade, and, because of the company he kept, thought his ticket to heaven was punched. Badda-bing.

But life in a fallen world isn't that easy, as Clayton quickly learned. When he was ten, his parents divorced and his dad moved out. It was an emotional hand grenade in his young life. To this day, he prefers not to discuss it publicly.

Clayton's mom, Marianne, sacrificed much for her son. Their house was a two-bedroom shoe box compared to some of the old-money mansions in Highland Park, but Clayton was never in want. Marianne began working from home so she could be there when Clayton returned from school, and they continued attending church.

Spiritually speaking, though, Clayton was on autopilot. Presented with a Bible trivia game, he could've fared well, but his faith was, well, trivial. Then the Holy Spirit began prodding him. He started considering deep spiritual questions that shook him out of cruise control: *Is the Bible really the inspired, inerrant Word of God? Was Jesus Christ really who He said He was? How can Christianity be true and all other religions false?*

By his senior year, Clayton understood his desperate need for a Savior. The deep, life-altering words of Ephesians 2:8–9 became truth to him: salvation is by grace and faith alone, not by works. None of his upbringing, church attendance, or good deeds merited God's eternal favor. Only Jesus Christ could provide that.

"When you grow up in [Christianity], you assume it's the only way—'Oh, everybody is this,'" he said. "But when you get a little older and a little smarter, you hear about other religions and beliefs, and you start thinking, 'Why do I believe this?' That's when you make your faith personal."

Clayton already had a solid group of friends, so the transition to his new faith wasn't hard. Around age sixteen, he and seven other Christian buddies made an agreement: they didn't need alcohol to have a good time.

While other kids were sleeping off weekend benders on Sunday mornings, Clayton's crew was worshipping. One of his buddies, Robert Shannon, would drive through the neighborhoods and fill up his big Chevy Suburban with half a dozen guys. With Third Eye Blind cranking on the sound system, they'd all head to Park Cities Presbyterian Church in Dallas and then head out for lunch together. Holy rollers indeed.

"We all got very lucky with our group of friends," Meredith said. "It made it easy for us to live the right way at such a young age. A lot of people at our high school were doing their partying on weekends. All of us, we were doing our partying without the alcohol or whatever else was there."

PRINCESS ELLEN

Clayton spent plenty of time with the fellas in high school. But he always made time for someone else.

Life, it seems, has never been without Ellen, even though they didn't meet until their freshman year. Theirs is a true high school sweetheart story, with all the cute, funny, and awkward moments that usually accompany that sort of thing.

At the beginning, it was heavy on the awkward. In the Courtroom of Clumsy Teenage Love, Clayton was guilty as charged:

• **Exhibit A: The first meeting**

Before they started dating, Clayton and Ellen had never spoken to each other. Ellen, a short, pretty girl on the school's dance team, had no clue that Clayton played baseball. She just knew him as a "goofy kid" with "a ton of friends." One day, between school periods during their freshman year, Clayton stopped her in the hallway and mumbled something about going steady. She said yes.

And after that?

"We didn't speak for the first year of our relationship except at our locker and in large groups at lunch," Ellen said.

• **Exhibit B: The first hangout away from school**

"We played basketball at a park," Clayton recalled, laughing. "I tried to teach her how, and she wasn't too interested." It was the start of a good-natured yet unsuccessful attempt to turn Ellen into an athlete. Clayton hasn't given up yet.

"It still doesn't work out so well," Ellen admitted. "I've always been a dancer, and he's always wanted me to be more athletic. One year, he bought me a pink baseball glove just to give me an incentive to help him throw over the summer." But aren't dancers athletic in their own right? "I don't know if he buys that," Ellen said with a chuckle. "I don't think he thinks it's a sport."

• **Exhibit C: The first time he met his future in-laws**

Imagine you are the loving parent of four children. You are trying to raise them well and instill proper values. Your second youngest, a girl, has an infectious smile and soft heart. Then, at the impressionable age of fourteen, she brings home a football player who has "55," his jersey number, shaved into the back of his head, thanks to a hazing ritual by his upperclassmen teammates. Now, ask yourself: what would *you* do?

"My parents were like, 'Who are you dating?' " Ellen said.

• **Exhibit D: The first kiss**

The epic moment happened at Caruth Park, a popular local hangout just north of Highland Park. Who better than Clayton's best buddy to provide the scoop? "The first time they kissed," Meredith said, "Ellen had some trouble breathing."

Ellen doesn't deny it, but she provides a bit of context: "Clayton and I were each other's first kiss," she said, laughing. "We were fourteen years old. Neither of us had experience." Fair enough.

Clayton and Ellen just seemed *right* together, despite the fact that they are polar opposites. She is 5 feet, 5 inches tall; he stands 6 feet, 3 inches. She likes watching girly TV shows; he likes video games and anything involving competition. She eats like a bird; he consumes like a hyena.

"Their No. 1 date spot was a Chili's [restaurant]," Dickenson recalled. "Ellen, she doesn't eat that much. She's tiny. She'd always get mac and cheese, and he'd get a huge platter. She'd eat two bites, and he'd finish it. Even with his buddies, he'd wait for us to finish, and then he's eyeing everybody's meals. The guy can eat."

The couple's memorable dating stories are as plentiful as young Clayton's food intake. Once, early in the relationship, Ellen and some girlfriends were watching *The O.C.*, one of their favorite TV shows, at her house. Suddenly, Clayton and his buddies barged in, screaming and throwing a football around. They were wearing nothing but shorts and football shoulder pads. For whatever reason, Mr. and Mrs. Melson didn't install perimeter fencing that night.

Another time, the guys invaded the girls' *Friends*-watching party, turned off the TV, and pillaged their cake. Annoyed, the girls hatched a plan to lure the guys out of Shannon's house, where they often played "Halo" for entire days, to steal their Xbox.

On the day of the Great Video Game Heist, the girls drove into the neighborhood, parked the car down the street from Shannon's house, and turned off the car. Ellen called Clayton's cell phone. "Clayton," she said, feigning excitement, "Jennifer Aniston is in Highland Park giving autographs!" Seconds later, the door flew open. Scientists are still investigating claims that this group of teenage boys broke the cheetah's land-speed record.

At the car, the guys practically dove feet-first through the windows, à la

Dukes of Hazzard, fired the engine, and raced down the street, past Ellen and her giggling friends. The girls' plan seemed to be working perfectly . . . until they saw brake lights. Down the road, the guys' car was turning around. The jig was up.

The girls had made one crucial error: they didn't factor in one of Clayton's strangest abilities. As the boys were whizzing past, Clayton had recognized the plates on the girls' car. Somehow, he can remember the license plate numbers of friends' cars after only one glance.

"It's one of the weirdest things," Ellen said.

All things considered, Ellen didn't mind the failed plan. It was another chance to see "my Clayton," as she's fond of calling him.

The affection is a two-way street. Clayton has always been smitten with Ellen, too. Take, for instance, the alert on his cell phone. Whenever she calls, the screen reads "Princess Ellen."

"When he wakes up every day, he just treats her like that—like his little Princess Ellen," Meredith said. "That's just the way it's always been."

In 2006, the Dodgers drafted Clayton out of high school and quickly shipped him to their Gulf Coast League rookie affiliate in Vero Beach, Florida. Ellen enrolled at Texas A&M. The distance was tough on the couple, but the time was "some of the best years of our lives," Ellen said.

By 2009, Ellen was ready to tie the knot—but to stay sane, she convinced herself it might not happen soon. Clayton, meanwhile, was planning and scheming. He knew Christmastime was Ellen's favorite part of the year, not only for the holidays but also because it was one of the few months when the couple was back together in Highland Park.

Clayton went all-out for the proposal. This is a man who gets ragged on by richly garbed teammates for rolling into the Dodgers' clubhouse every day in cargo shorts and a T-shirt. But he showed up to Ellen's house in a new suit—and a white limo. The couple ate in downtown Dallas at Wolfgang Puck's Five Sixty, a skyscraper restaurant that offers a stunning vista of the city from the fiftieth floor. He even shaved for the first time in years.

"That," Ellen said, "was a point of contention for years—his dadgum chinstrap [beard]."

After dinner, Clayton took Ellen to his new town house, which he had decked out as a winter wonderland, complete with music playing and rose petals strewn about the living room. There, he gave Ellen a box with a little Santa figurine holding a green velvet ring box before dropping to his knee and proposing.

After their heartbeats leveled off, they went to Ellen's parents' house for a prearranged engagement party. Not bad for the once-awkward freshman.

Clayton and Ellen were married on December 4, 2010, at Highland Park Presbyterian Church. At the reception, they picked a humdinger of a first dance. No slow jam for this couple. Instead, they performed a choreographed dance to Usher's hit, "DJ's Got Us Falling in Love Again." Ellen, it should be noted, achieved lieutenant status on the high school drill team. Clayton . . . well, he tried hard.

In front of five hundred people, Clayton sauntered onto the dance floor wearing shades and neon Nikes along with his tuxedo and tried to keep up with his bride. Those who witnessed their first dance will never forget it.

Someone uploaded the dance video to YouTube, and the Kershaws initially left it there so loved ones who weren't at the wedding could see it. By the time they removed the video a month later, however, it had attracted twelve thousand hits.

"Ellen was a dancer in high school, so she nailed it," Meredith said. "Clayton was lost."

"MIGHT AS WELL GO BY ZEUS"

It's not that Clayton is some sort of attention-allergic hermit. Clearly, the wedding dance antics prove otherwise. But he's never felt entirely comfortable with all the acclaim his bestowed-by-heaven talents have invited. Hullabaloo has always been the obnoxious kid brother he can't shake.

When Los Angeles drafted Clayton seventh overall, the hype machine revved into action. Dodgers scouting director Logan White compared Clayton to Dave Righetti, a sixteen-year big leaguer who won the 1981 American League Rookie of the Year award, played in two All-Star games, and was once the best closer in baseball. Clayton had just turned eighteen.

Two weeks later, Clayton officially signed with the Dodgers for $2.3 million (no need to scavenge other people's mac and cheese anymore) and headed to Vero Beach, where he dazzled coaches and players. Still, he needed some seasoning. In 2007, he started with the Dodgers' Class A affiliate in Midland, Michigan—the Great Lakes Loons. Welcome to baseball's boondocks.

Clayton lived in a duplex—four players on one side and four on the other. The furniture in Clayton's unit consisted of two beanbags, a TV resting on a folding chair, and a card table with a few other chairs for dining. All the guys slept on air mattresses. Road trips consisted of twelve-hour bus rides and sharing hotel rooms with a half dozen other guys.

"He loved it," Ellen said. "He had no other responsibility but to show up at the field and play baseball."

The décor was lacking those years, but Clayton's burgeoning legend wasn't. After another strong season, he entered 2008 with high hopes—he and every Dodgers fan on planet Earth.

During a spring training game against Boston, he struck out three-time All-Star Sean Casey on an 0–2 curveball so nasty that Hall of Fame broadcaster Vin Scully proclaimed it "Public Enemy No. 1." Two days later, Dodgers legend Sandy Koufax, whom some would call the greatest left-handed pitcher of all time, watched Clayton throw a bullpen session and predicted that he'd be called up to L.A. soon. As endorsements go, those are hard to beat.

After thirteen games at Double-A Jacksonville (Florida) to start the season, he had a 1.91 ERA. The hype machine's RPMs were redlining. A *Yahoo! Sports* article trumpeted his curveball as "probably the best in the world." The Dodgers could no longer justify keeping him in the minors.

On May 25, 2008, after only 48 minor league games, Clayton made his big league debut. Chavez Ravine was electric. The Dodgers beat St. Louis 4–3, but Clayton got a no-decision despite a stellar effort: two earned runs on five hits and one walk with seven strikeouts in six innings.

The reviews were overwhelmingly positive. The following day, a *Yahoo! Sports* story said Clayton "might as well go by Zeus for all the mythology that accompanies him."

The dam of self-restraint had officially been breached. Praise flooded in from every direction.

"These guys don't come along often," Dodgers pitching coach Rick Honeycutt gushed in the same article. "There's been other guys—Doc Gooden comes to mind—who get it at this early an age."

Amid towering expectations, the rest of the season didn't go as smoothly. Clayton finished 2008 with a pedestrian 5–5 record and 4.26 ERA in 22 games. The following year, he was even-steven again with an 8–8 record, although he pitched appreciably better, sporting a 2.79 ERA and 185 strikeouts.

Those who had been around baseball a long time saw nothing but upside. By 2010, the hype machine was running full-throttle again, spewing out hyperbole at a rapid-fire rate. "Ceiling? There is no ceiling," Honeycutt said of his then-twenty-one-year-old protégé in spring training.

No pressure, Clayton. Honest . . .

If he felt any pressure, he sure didn't show it—not with a 2.91 ERA and 212 strikeouts in his second full big league season. His 13–10 record would have been more impressive if the Dodgers, who finished a middling 80–82, would have scored more than 17 total runs in his 10 losses.

Clayton's standout year, at age twenty-two, elevated him into rarified air within one of baseball's most venerable franchises. For perspective, consider how some of the all-time Dodgers greats fared at the same tender age:

- Among the Dodgers' Hall of Famers, Dazzy Vance went 11–14 for the Superior Brickmakers in the old Nebraska State League (1913). In his second year with the Dodgers, Don Sutton had a losing record (11–15) and finished with an ERA barely under 4.00 (1967). And even Koufax was mortal at age twenty-two, finishing his fourth year with the Dodgers with a .500 record and a 4.48 ERA (1958).
- Orel Hershiser was still three years away from cracking the Dodgers' rotation with a lackluster 4.68 ERA at Double-A San Antonio (1981).
- Future 27-game-winner Don Newcombe was still trying to make it out of Triple-A Montreal (1948).

Did we mention that Koufax didn't have a sub-3.00 ERA until his eighth season, at age twenty-six? Clayton has had *three* such seasons by age twenty-three.

No pressure, Clayton. We're just sayin' . . . .

Before the 2011 season, Honeycutt went so far as to compare the excitement buildup around Clayton to "Fernandomania," the hysteria that surrounded Fernando Valenzuela, the pudgy, look-to-the-sky Mexican sensation who won the National League Cy Young and Rookie of the Year awards and led the Dodgers to a World Series title in 1981—at age twenty.

"I was there when Fernando [played in L.A.]," said Honeycutt, a Valenzuela teammate from 1983 to 1987. "It's getting to be kind of like that hype. The fans are putting their hopes and dreams on this guy [Clayton] leading the team back to greatness and the World Series."

In February 2011, Dodgers manager Don Mattingly officially named Clayton the team's Opening Day starter. The move made Clayton, at twenty-three, the Dodgers' youngest such pitcher since, well, Valenzuela in 1983.

Clayton opened the season by throwing seven shutout innings in a 2–1 win over San Francisco, the defending World Series champion. The pitcher he outdueled? None other than Tim Lincecum, the two-time Cy Young Award winner.

If only the rest of the season had been so rosy. Clayton's season-opening gem was barely in the books when at least two men attacked and severely beat a Giants fan, Bryan Stow, in the Dodger Stadium parking lot, sending him into a coma.

The vicious assault only underscored the chaos plaguing the franchise in recent years under Dodgers owner Frank McCourt. Among the tabloid fodder:

- A bitter divorce court battle between McCourt and his ex-wife, Jamie, over control of the team dragged through the 2011 season.
- The revelation from court documents that the McCourts had borrowed more than $100 million from Dodgers-related business to fund a profligate lifestyle.
- Major League Baseball's assumption of team control in April 2011 and its ensuing rejection of a new, multi-billion-dollar TV deal between FOX and the Dodgers, forcing the troubled franchise to file for bankruptcy protection in August.
- McCourt's agreement on November 1, 2011, to sell the team, Dodger Stadium, and the surrounding parking lots in cooperation with Major League Baseball through a court-supervised process.

In the midst of the mayhem, Clayton was magnificent. He won the National League's "Triple Crown" of pitching with a 21–5 record, a major league–best 2.28 ERA, and league-leading 248 strikeouts to earn his first All-Star appearance and win the NL Cy Young Award. He even claimed his first Gold Glove Award for good measure.

(Note to the curator of the sizable Dodgers pitching pantheon: time to create another wing. Clayton became the franchise's first Cy Young recipient since closer Eric Gagne in 2003 and the first Dodgers starter to win the award since Hershiser in 1988.)

Clayton's twentieth win, which came in a dominant 2–1 victory over the rival Giants in his penultimate start of 2011, made him the first Dodgers pitcher to go 5–0 against the Giants in a season since Vic Lombardi in 1946. And four of those victories came against none other than Lincecum.

Dodger fans love a Giant slayer.

Then there's this telling nugget: only one lefty in Dodgers history has recorded more strikeouts in a season—Koufax.

"There's no reason to really set limits on him as far as how much better he's going to get," Mattingly said, "because he's still young and he works awful hard."

No pressure, Clayton . . . aww, who are we kidding?

"FOR HIS GLORY"

How do you respond when fans, media, former All-Stars, and front office cognoscenti are all tripping over themselves to adequately describe your abilities? Clayton simply shrugs it off.

"I've got a really, really, really long way to go," he said.

This is not false modesty. This is Spirit-led Clayton modesty. And it sticks out like a sore thumb in Tinseltown, where the twin gods of fame and riches are worshipped religiously.

Clayton is so *un*-Hollywood. The red carpets, velvet ropes, glittering marquees, screaming fans, and insatiable paparazzi of his six-month home are foreign to him. He's one of the best pitchers in the world, yet he and Ellen still get a touristy kick out of the area's palm-tree-lined roads, the Hollywood Walk of Fame, and the mansions of Beverly Hills.

"I have my own version of the celebrity stars tour," Ellen said. "I could be a certified stalker if I took people over there anymore."

Clayton has shot the breeze with Koufax, learned to bunt from Maury Wills, and achieved rapid renown in starry-eyed L.A. Yet you'd never know his day job if you saw him strolling hand in hand with Ellen in Malibu. At heart, he is just a big kid from Texas with a Lone Star lilt and a wide, toothy smile.

He honestly doesn't understand what all the fuss is about. Like the crush of autograph seekers leaning over the railing after games. Or the trash bags filled with fan mail that started piling up in 2010.

"He couldn't even get his head around it," Ellen said.

Those closest to him say he's the humblest person they know. C.S. Lewis once said, "Humility is not thinking less of yourself, but thinking of yourself less." It's a vertical-relationship thing, and Clayton seems to get it.

"Clayton doesn't lie about his abilities," Dodgers chaplain Brandon Cash explained. "He knows how good he is. But he realizes that no matter how good of a baseball player he is, it doesn't mean anything when he'll stand before God."

Said Clayton, "You have to understand what this platform is for."

Never was Clayton's humility more on display than during the 2010–2011 off-season. Less than a month after getting married, as their loved ones were clinking glasses and singing "Auld Lang Syne" in the States, Clayton and Ellen were half a world away, toiling in a bleak, oppressed land. With sweat-soaked shirts clinging to their backs, they rang in the new year in Zambia.

The trip marked Ellen's fifth visit, and Clayton's first, to the small, south-central African nation. Ellen had tried to prepare Clayton for what to expect, but no prior warning can fully assuage the culture shock.

Disease, destitution, hunger, moral neglect, and religious syncretism are like gloomy shrouds veiling the country in darkness. Zambia is one of the poorest nations in the world. Many people live on a dollar a day. Homes are often plastic tarps or tents with earthen floors. Affluence means your one-room home is made of cinder blocks or concrete and features an outdoor stovetop to cook on. Dishes and babies are washed in the same tub. A child's wardrobe is what he's wearing. Trash and raw sewage are everywhere.

So, too, are the orphans. Thanks to a widespread HIV/AIDS epidemic, nearly 47 percent of Zambia's population is zero to fourteen years old, and the median age is 16.5 years, according to 2011 U.S. government figures. It's a place where kids are raising kids—where unmarried mothers abandon their children, like an endangered ship purging jetsam, to seek a different life in another province.

"It's an overwhelming task because you can't get to every kid," Clayton said. "It's hard. Some people don't go because you think, 'It's just one person.' But one kid you do help is one life affected."

The Kershaws affected plenty. During a nine-day mission trip with a non-profit organization called Arise Africa, Clayton, Ellen, and other Christians visited various "compounds," or slums, on the outskirts of Lusaka, the capital city.

The group delivered two thousand pounds of supplies to two schools that double as orphanages, constructed a four-room building for one of them, hosted a Bible camp for two hundred children, and cared for impoverished families. Clayton also got to meet twenty young orphan girls Ellen has spiritually invested in over the years.

To stay in baseball shape, Clayton ran and threw each day. The local children flocked to him, and he played catch with them every night. Using his God-given talents, he reached across a broad cultural chasm to shine the light of Christ. It was Matthew 19:14 in action.

"He has a heart of gold," said Alissa Hollimon, a college friend of Ellen's who started Arise Africa. "He jumped right in to whatever we were doing. I think he liked seeing Ellen in her element."

The trip said much about Clayton's priorities. Pitchers of his caliber don't just happen. It takes an extraordinary amount of work, especially in the off-season. Winters are also crucial downtime for athletes consumed by their profession from February through September.

Clayton could have just supported Ellen's passion project from a distance, by cutting a check and keeping his golden arm comfortably within American borders. Instead, he chose to travel to an ignored back alley of the world and open compassionate arms to those enslaved in darkness. For such a quiet man, this spoke volumes.

"He's characterized by humility," Cash said.

It's a humility that seeks to serve others wherever he is. Despite being one of the youngest players on the roster, he is the Dodgers' Baseball Chapel representative—the guy Cash looks to for getting guys in Sunday morning chapels and midweek Bible studies. He does charity work in greater L.A.

through the team, and he speaks to the Fellowship of Christian Athletes group at his old high school each off-season.

Most of all, he and Ellen are looking forward to continuing their work in Zambia each off-season. Inspired by their trip, the couple started Kershaw's Challenge, an effort to raise $70,000 to build an orphanage outside Lusaka called Hope's Home, named after an eleven-year-old, HIV-positive orphan they'd met. Before the 2011 season, Clayton pledged to donate a hundred dollars for every strikeout he threw, which resulted in a $24,800 donation based on his career-high 248 punch-outs.

Think God was at work there?

THE PARABLE OF THE TALENTS

Yes, the children will continue to come. They will travel across fields of indigence and affluence, through the forsaken slums of Africa and the shiny turnstiles of Chavez Ravine, all to see the meek wunderkind. Heck, plenty of adults will come, too. People are always attracted to greatness, and that's the precipice upon which Clayton stands.

This, of course, creates a lot of racket. The quiet, lanky Texan is still getting used to all the attention. His immense gifts, for some, might be the object of regular worship on *SportsCenter*, but he sees them through the lens of Jesus' parable in Matthew 25.

"I think it's for His glory, to make people aware that it's not something where I was lucky to throw baseball," Clayton said. "In Matthew, it says God gives everyone at least one talent. One guy hides his talent and gives it back, and God says, 'Cursed are you.' He doesn't want us to hide our talents; He wants us to put them in the spotlight and glorify Him.

"That's a pretty cool thing."

2

BEN ZOBRIST:
THE PK WHO'S A ZORILLA ON THE FIELD

It's called "entrance music"—a snippet of a song that's played loudly over the stadium speakers whenever the hometown hitter walks from the on-deck circle to home plate. Relief pitchers also get their own "walk-up" song when they jog in from the bullpen to save the day for the local nine.

The choice of music provides players with a rare opportunity to inject their personality into the game or reveal their musical tastes, which vary from hip-hop tunes and unvarnished rock 'n' roll to, well, Justin Bieber. (Colorado Rockies shortstop Troy Tulowitzki stepped into the batter's box during the 2011 season with the sound of J-Bieb's "Baby" swooning the teen-girl set.)

Most of the time, though, the entrance music makes a strong and raucous statement. When slugger Mark McGwire stepped up to home plate in St. Louis, "Welcome to the Jungle" by Guns N' Roses pumped up the crowd for a home run hitter who was already pumped up with something else. Trevor Hoffman, the great San Diego Padres closer, intimidated visiting teams with the ominous gong of his entrance anthem, "Hell's Bells" by the heavy metal band AC/DC. Mariano Rivera, one of the players featured in this book, has said that he's tired of the Metallica dirge "Enter Sandman," which plays whenever he takes the mound in a save situation, but Yankee fans would give him the Bronx cheer if he tried to change tunes now.

If you go to Major League Baseball's website (mlb.com), you'll find a list of the walk-up or entrance songs for every player on every team, but only one batter strides to the plate hearing a song sung by his *wife*—and that's Tampa Bay Rays second baseman Ben Zobrist.

During the 2011 season, Ben's walk-up track was "Only You," sung by Julianna Zobrist, who's cut a CD of Christian-themed electronic pop/rock songs. Saying she was influenced by Plumb and Imogen Heap as well as childhood favorites like the Beach Boys and Gloria Estefan, Julianna sings an emotional *I want You and only You and no one else will ever do* as Ben digs in for his at-bat. " 'Only You' is about desiring God above anything else in your life," Ben said.

Ben first attracted notice for playing his wife's music during the 2009 and 2010 seasons when he chose Julianna's "The Tree" as his walk-up song. Julianna says "The Tree" speaks to the fact that "we are deserving of the wrath of the Almighty God, and He, out of His mere good pleasure, delivered us from the way of thinking that our own 'goodness' could justify us before Him."

Isn't that great? Julianna Zobrist uses her God-given gift for music to impact others, while her husband, Ben, uses his God-given athletic skills on the baseball diamond. Together, they make a pretty good team each time he steps to the plate at Tropicana Field. (Julianna also sang the National Anthem at one of Ben's playoff games in 2010.)

The big stage they find themselves on today is light-years away from the humble beginnings of this pair of PKs—pastors' kids—from the nation's heartland. She's from Iowa City, Iowa, and Ben hails from the checkerboard farmlands of central Illinois, having grown up in Eureka, a small town of five thousand people once known as the "pumpkin capital of the world" back in the 1950s. Eureka is also the home of Eureka College, whose most illustrious alumnus is President Ronald Reagan, a 1932 graduate.

Zobrist—pronounced ZOH-brist—is a Swiss name. Ben's great-great-grandfather—Jakob Zobrist—immigrated from Switzerland's Alpine meadows in 1867 as a nine-year-old boy. His family settled in Illinois' verdant flatlands to farm and milk cows in the Morton area. Jakob begat a son named Noah, who begat a son named Alpha, who begat Tom, who begat Ben in 1981. Ben is the second of five children, with an older sister, a younger sister, and two younger brothers.

Tom, Ben's father, is a pastor with a love for baseball inherited from his father, Alpha, who was a St. Louis Cardinals fan. The Gateway City is just three hours away from Eureka, so every summer the Zobrist clan—aunts, uncles, and cousins—would travel to St. Louis to take in a major league baseball game.

"That was our big treat for the year, our big vacation," Ben said. "We didn't really travel much except to one baseball game a year in St. Louis."

Tom has been ministering at Liberty Bible Church, which has a congregation of two hundred, since 1988. He and his wife, Cindi, raised their five children in a farming community with two stoplights, a courthouse, a small downtown, a private college, and abundant parks. It was Tom who put a slender yellow plastic bat into Ben's hands when he was a three-year-old tyke and underhanded a perforated plastic Wiffle ball to him in the living room. It wasn't long before Tom and Ben had to move batting practice to the backyard.

Wiffle ball was a big deal in the Zobrist family. There were Sunday-afternoon tournaments with the extended family in their backyard, and little Ben was always begging to take his cuts. By the time he was in elementary school, he was playing baseball in organized leagues and neighborhood pickup games.

"I played a lot of sandlot ball growing up," Ben said. "There was a lot across the street from one of my friend's houses, and a bunch of us kids would play with a metal bat and a tennis ball. We liked playing with a tennis ball because it would fly a lot farther and make us feel like we were hitting long home runs. During the school year, Sunday afternoons were the big times because we'd play after church. We'd just go to the sandlot and play."

This was *unorganized* baseball—just Ben and his buddies choosing up sides and inventing different games. No umpires, no coaches, just kids going out and having fun swinging a bat and hitting a ball. He and the neighborhood kids would play for countless hours during the summer.

It was playing sandlot ball that got Ben—a natural righty—learning to switch-hit. Since there were usually just enough players to play one side of the field, if Ben announced that he was batting left-handed, then all the players would move to the right side of the field. "I liked batting left-handed because the fence was closer. I liked hitting a line drive into the backyard and getting a home run."

There was another benefit to playing with a tennis ball—no broken windows.

Ben played other sports growing up—youth football, AYSO soccer, and junior basketball—and he even ran track when he was in middle school, posting a 5:01 mile in the seventh grade that remained a school record seventeen years later.

But Ben came from a baseball family, and he wanted baseball to be his sport when he got to high school. He had designs on playing varsity ball at Eureka High during his freshman year, but there was a problem—Ben was a small kid. "I was about 5 feet, 5 inches tall and 112 pounds, but somehow I played varsity my freshman year," he said. "I added about two inches and fifteen pounds my sophomore year, but then I hit my growth spurt in my junior year. I shot up to 6 feet, 1 inch, but I only weighed 150 pounds or so. I was eating frozen pizza and applesauce since we were always on the run with different extracurricular activities. We had school stuff, church activities, and sports. It was a busy time."

One summer before his junior year of high school, Ben built his own "Field of Dreams"—a Wiffle ball diamond in his backyard. He used white spray paint for the foul lines, lined the outfield with two-foot-high rabbit fencing, dug holes in the grass for each base and home plate, and planted a flag beyond the center-field fence.

"Alpha Memorial Field"—named after Ben's grandfather—was the home of the Ben Zobrist Wiffle Ball League. There were four teams with five guys on a team, and they even played night games. His dad helped him illuminate the field by going to Home Depot and finding a pair of twenty-foot poles that they topped with bright lights. All they had to do was run an extension cord from the house, and they had the only night Wiffle ball field in Illinois . . . maybe in the entire country.

Sometimes Ben and one of his best friends, Jason Miller, would pitch batting practice to each other using a sponge ball that traveled a little farther than a Wiffle ball, but most of the time, the Ben Zobrist Wiffle Ball League adhered to its regularly scheduled games. Some Wiffle ball games lasted past midnight before Dad said, "It's time to go home, boys."

As any parent of energetic teens will tell you, when you put ten testosterone-laden teen boys into a small backyard and set out the plastic bats and Wiffle ball, you can expect the fur to fly. One evening, Ben was pitching—one of the rules of Wiffle Ball League was that pitches had to be tossed "friendly" toward home plate, not "burned" in there—to a friend named Ryan. The pitch sailed over the plate. Ryan flicked his wrists and homered over the left-field rabbit fencing.

As Ryan rounded the bases, he chortled and gave Ben the business. Ben was wearing a cheap plastic helmet—the type that he had received at the Cardinals' "Helmet Day"—when Ryan veered toward Ben and whacked him on the back of the head, striking his plastic helmet with his hand. The action stung a bit, so Ben unfurled a few choice comments at his friend.

Just as Ryan was crossing home plate, Ben yelled out, "I dare you to step over this line."

Challenged before their mutual friends, Ryan couldn't back down. He charged the mound, and the next thing Ben knew, he was in the midst of an old-fashioned, bench-clearing baseball brawl. Ryan tackled him to the ground, but in typical baseball brawl fashion, no punches were thrown. They wrestled with each other in the grass as the other players dove in. It was one big dog pile!

"Ryan and I were the guys running the league," Ben said. "It didn't bother our friendship, but when Ryan said, 'I don't want to play Wiffle ball anymore,' things kind of disbanded after that."

BASEBALL AFTER HIGH SCHOOL

When spring came around, Ben set his sights on hardball again. He says he was maybe a better-than-average high school ballplayer—a solid pitcher and sure-handed infielder who could hit for average—but he didn't win any All-Conference awards until his senior year. Despite playing well, and despite being thought of as one of the top high school players in his region, Ben wasn't on any college coaches' radar throughout his last season of high school baseball.

Ben saw a spiritual component to what was happening. Sure, he was apprehensive about the future—where he'd go to college and if he'd get to play ball—but he felt like the Lord wanted him to trust Him for his future, so that's what he did. Ben got on his knees and said, "Lord, my life is yours, and I'm not going to be in charge. As for baseball, You can have that, too."

And that's how it went—God was in control. If baseball wasn't in his future, that was okay. If that's the way it turned out, Ben knew it was God's will for his life.

Still not sure where he wanted to go or what he wanted to study, he settled on Calvary Bible College in Kansas City, Missouri, the school his dad attended when Ben was a preschooler. His older sister Jessica was attending Calvary Bible at the time, so the family's thinking was that his big sister could ease Ben's transition into college life.

Calvary Bible College didn't have a baseball team, but they did have a basketball team, so Ben figured he could play hoops in college. Again, this would be fine with him. In many ways, Ben was a seasonal athlete whose favorite sport was the one he was playing at the time. As high school graduation loomed, he assumed he had played his last game of organized baseball and would be done with the sport forever.

Then the high school coach at Brimfield—thirty-five miles west of Eureka—

called not long after graduation. He said a dozen college coaches were holding an open tryout at Brimfield High because they were looking to fill holes on their rosters. He thought Ben had a good chance of playing college baseball somewhere. "You never know what might happen," said the Brimfield coach.

Ben thought about the request for a moment. "Are they going to have guns there?" he asked, referring to radar guns that measure how fast a pitcher throws the ball. He had never thrown for a radar gun.

Told yes, Ben said he wanted to come. In his mind, this was a chance to learn how fast he threw. But there was just one minor detail—the Brimfield coach said the open tryout cost fifty dollars.

When Ben talked to his father about the tryout, Tom said, "I'm not paying the fifty dollars. If you want to go, you'll have to pay for it."

Tom wasn't being obstinate—just realistic. For the pastor of a small church with five children to care for and two in college, fifty bucks wasn't small pumpkins, er, make that small potatoes.

"You think about it and pray about it," he told his son.

Ben was a teenage kid just out of high school, without much money. The next day, after giving the matter some prayer, Ben said he wanted to take his birthday present money from his grandparents and go to the tryout.

This one decision changed his life. Because Ben paid the fifty dollars his grandparents had given him and then showed up at that ball field in Brimfield, he is playing Major League Baseball today.

On Friday, the morning of the tryout, however, rain poured from the skies. The tryout was postponed until Monday.

That complicated matters. There was another open tryout—this was being held by the Atlanta Braves—on Monday as well. This tryout was in Normal, Illinois, about twenty-five miles southeast of Eureka. Even though the tryout was free, the odds of signing with the Braves organization were astronomically low.

There was also another moving part—the start of a weeklong Bible conference that Ben's youth group was participating in. It began Monday night and was being held a little farther east than Normal.

When Ben's Friday tryout at Brimfield High was washed out, Tom said, "Son, you're going to have to blow off Brimfield. I don't see how you can do it."

Tom said this because Brimfield was a good forty minutes *west* of Eureka, and the youth Bible conference was eastward a couple of hours away.

Tom and Ben called the Brimfield coach and explained the situation—and asked if the fifty dollars was refundable. It wasn't.

"Mr. Zobrist, I don't want to tell you what to do," the coach said, "but I guarantee you that Ben will get some money for college if he comes."

Tom turned to his son.

"I sorta would like to go," Ben said.

Tom relented, even though that meant a lot of extra driving for Ben.

Ben arrived to find dozens of players yearning for a chance to make a good impression before the watchful eyes of a dozen college coaches. After running the 60-yard dash, each player took six ground balls at shortstop, which they were to field and throw hard to first base. Next was the batting portion—twelve swings per player. Ben was a switch-hitter, so that meant six hacks on each side of the dish. Ben didn't go yard or put on a Josh Hamilton–like home run jag, but he lined several ropes into the outfield.

Then Ben finished with six pitches from the mound, which were timed by the radar gun. He topped out at 84 miles per hour, which Ben was happy with. Now he knew how fast he threw.

And that was it. Ben was gathering up his stuff and getting ready to head out when one of the coaches caught up with him.

"Hey, my name is Elliot Johnson, and I'm from Olivet Nazarene University," he said, sticking out his hand to shake Ben's.

"Pleased to meet you," Ben replied.

"I heard that you are a Christian," he continued. "I'm a Christian, too, and I heard that you might be going to Calvary Bible."

"That's the plan," Ben said.

"Well, we're a Christian school near Chicago with a good baseball program, and I'm just letting you know that I might give you a call to come take a visit up in Olivet some time. But believe me, I don't want to take you away from God's will for your life."

And that's how Coach Johnson left it.

Ben thought their interaction was interesting, but he didn't give their conversation any more thought because he had to get on the road and drive several hours to the youth Bible conference. That night, he learned that the theme of the week was to be open to what God wants to do in your life. "I was like, *I'm cool with that idea,*" Ben said.

Meanwhile, the phone was ringing off the hook back home. By Tuesday night, Jessica, the Zobrists' oldest daughter, had taken five calls from five different college coaches, all of whom wanted Ben to come play for their school.

Tom and Cindi came home a day or two later to do some things while Ben stayed with his youth group at the conference. The sudden interest in Ben's ball-playing abilities surprised them. When they spoke on the phone with Coach Johnson, he explained that he was looking for one more pitcher to round out his staff, and he thought Ben would be perfect for the Olivet Nazarene team. Everyone agreed that the next step was for Ben to come look at the campus.

The following week, Ben drove with his high school coach, Bob Gold, to Olivet Nazarene University in Bourbonnais, Illinois, two hours away. Tom and Cindi had a commitment that day and couldn't accompany their son. Coach Gold, who was the FCA Huddle leader for Eureka High School, had always encouraged Ben to follow God's will through sports.

Upon their arrival, Ben heard Coach Johnson explain that his goal for the team was to bring in Christian players who would have a positive influence on the non-Christian team members and represent the school *and* Christ well. (About half the players were not believers.)

"That's why I would like to offer you a full-ride scholarship to play baseball at Olivet Nazarene," the coach said, adding that he saw Ben as the type of player who would pitch and play some shortstop for the team. But he was recruiting Ben primarily to be a pitcher.

Ben was stunned to hear the out-of-left-field offer, which came as a result of fielding six ground balls, taking twelve swings, and throwing a half dozen pitches. But he was pleased as well. The only thing that concerned him was that he thought he was a better hitter and position player than a pitcher . . . but at least he would be playing baseball again.

When Ben got home and talked with his parents about the scholarship offer, Tom and Cindi were pleasantly surprised. They had figured Ben's baseball-playing days were over. But here was a Christian coach offering their son a college athletic scholarship—which would certainly help the tight Zobrist family budget—to play baseball at a Christian college. Olivet Nazarene was a nice school with nice facilities, a nice coach, and a nice offer of free tuition and room and board. Other than the pitching situation, what was there not to like?

But Tom and Cindi weren't immediately sold on the scholarship offer. They told Ben they wanted to pray about where God was leading him and then meet with the coach to discuss the situation. An appointment with Coach Johnson in Bourbonnais was quickly made.

After sitting down and exchanging pleasantries, Cindi asked a pointed question: "Coach Johnson, you've never seen Ben pitch or play in a game. How do you know he's worth this much money?"

"Ma'am, I've coached baseball for many years," Coach Johnson replied. "I've seen Ben's curveball, and I know he can get college players out with it. I also see your son's desire to glorify God with whatever he does."

Tom asked if the family could have an hour to discuss the situation. Told yes, they drove over to a Cracker Barrel restaurant near campus to get something to eat. Remember, all this was transpiring in late June, a month after high school graduation.

Cindi was upset by this sudden turn of events. She felt like Ben was supposed to go to Calvary Bible College—and now this. Through tears, she said the opportunity to play baseball at Olivet Nazarene was happening too fast for her.

Tom listened and turned to his son. "Ben, you've been praying about this. You're a young man now, and you need to decide what you believe God wants you to do. I can't make this decision for you."

"I'll do anything you want me to do, Dad," Ben replied. "If you believe it's right for me to go to Calvary, then I'll go to Calvary. I trust your judgment."

Hearing Ben say that—and seeing how he was willing to submit to his authority—told Tom that his son was mature enough to make this decision on his own. "Ben, this needs to be your decision," he said.

Ben took in a deep breath. "I believe I'm not done playing baseball. I want to see what God has in store for me."

Tom looked at Cindi, who nodded her assent. "Okay, let's do it," his father said. "You'll be only two hours from home, so that means we could come watch you play."

The family returned to the Olivet Nazarene campus, where a smiling Ben informed Coach Johnson that he wanted to play ball for him.

Olivet Nazarene was not an NCAA division school, however. The Olivet Nazarene athletic teams played in the NAIA, which had different eligibility requirements. When Ben turned out for fall ball his freshman year, Dan Heefner—a senior who was the team's leading home run hitter and had a batting average of .402—took Ben under his wing. "He was kind of *the* guy," Ben said. "He was the big MVP and team leader who led Bible studies. Dan discipled me and put me on the right path."

Ben needed some steadying because when the season started, Coach Johnson—as promised—had him work on pitcher-conditioning drills and not take infield or batting practice. When the team took its annual spring break to Daytona Beach, Florida, to open the season, Ben was part of the five-man pitching staff. He was a curveball artist who wasn't afraid to throw the yakker on a full count.

When the season opened, the Olivet Nazarene shortstop booted a few ground balls that cost them a couple of games. He was replaced by another shortstop who also struggled in the field. Needing to plug a gaping hole in the infield, Coach Johnson turned to one of his pitchers—Ben Zobrist.

Once in the lineup, Ben played like a younger Derek Jeter, vacuuming up every ground ball hit his way and making the throws. He also got his fair share of hits (he batted .330 his freshman year) even though he was still called upon to pitch every fourth or fifth game.

"By the end of the season, my arm was about to fall off, but doing both—pitching and playing shortstop—turned out to be a very successful year for me," Ben said.

So why did he perform so well, especially early on when he didn't take infield or batting practice?

"Guys like Dan Heefner told me that I had to take extra batting practice *after* practice if I wanted to get better," Ben said. "So whenever I had free time, I would go to the batting cage and set up the hitting tee and hit the ball into the back of the net. I worked on trying to control my swing because I wanted to be ready if I got the opportunity." He also asked teammates to hit him ground balls after practice so he could get in some glove work. He was always the last one to leave the ball field and the locker room.

There was something else that Ben learned from watching guys like Dan Heefner—take your walks. "When I was in high school, I would hack at the ball and didn't walk much. Then when I got to college, I saw that the better hitters were walking more. Before they got two strikes, they were looking for one pitch in a specific zone, and if the pitch wasn't there, they weren't going to swing. That's when I started to learn 'plate discipline' and the importance of looking for that one pitch."

After his freshman year was over, Ben wanted to play summer ball, but the college leagues around the country didn't have any room on their rosters for freshman players. When no offer came, Ben heard about an opportunity from Coach Johnson to play on a baseball "mission trip" with Athletes in Action, a ministry of Campus Crusade for Christ International (known today as Cru). During a six-week tour, the Athletes in Action team would travel to Mexico and Nicaragua, playing local teams and sharing the gospel after the final out was made.

Just one problem—Ben had to raise his own support, which was a couple of thousand dollars. But with the backing of his dad's church and all the Zobrist next-of-kin chipping in, Ben got enough money to pay for the mission trip.

This was the first time Ben had been out of the country, and taking buses around the Mexican and Nicaraguan countryside was an experience he wouldn't soon forget. Sometimes they pulled into tiny villages where a ragtag team of gray-hairs and grandkids were waiting for them. Other times they competed in small cities against local All-Star teams who could play some serious ball.

Whether they had to take their foot off the gas or play hard, each game ended with one of the AIA players sharing his testimony—through an interpreter who followed the team—of how he came to know Jesus Christ as his personal Lord and Savior. Then a second speaker would share the Four Spiritual Laws—the Christian message of salvation contained in the Bible. "It was definitely more a ministry summer baseball experience than a pure baseball experience, but that was fine with me," Ben said. "I had an awesome time."

Playing in Mexico and Nicaragua raised Ben's game more than he thought. He had a sensational sophomore year at Olivet Nazarene, and Coach Johnson lightened his pitching load, just bringing him in to throw in relief situations.

When his sophomore season was over, Ben didn't have a summer league team to play on, so he took a job at the Christian Center, a multi-use recreational center with ball fields in Peoria, Illinois, about twenty miles west of Eureka. His uncle, Matt Zobrist, hired Ben to mow the grass, rake the infield dirt, and line the fields.

An old youth baseball coach named Dave Rodgers ran the sandlot program that encouraged kids to show up and play pickup games with no parents, coaches, or umpires involved. He asked Ben to give him a hand with the sandlot program as well.

Coach Rodgers had been around the horn and even coached New York Yankee catching great Joe Girardi (who's presently the Yankees skipper) back when he was a Little Leaguer growing up in East Peoria. The longtime coach had seen Ben play, knew all about him, and was concerned that Ben wasn't playing that summer.

Coach Rodgers took it upon himself to call the manager of the Twin City Stars, part of the Central Illinois Collegiate League, and tell him that he needed to have Ben on his team. "This boy is too good," said the old coach. "He needs to be playing somewhere."

The Twin City Stars played in Bloomington, Illinois, less than thirty miles from Eureka. Their coach was reluctant, saying he had enough guys, but Coach Rodgers pressed his case.

"Okay, I'll give him a one-week tryout," the Twin City Stars coach said.

Ben's tryout lasted one night. He went 5 for 5—3 for 3 batting left-handed and 2 for 2 batting right-handed. "You're on the team," the coach said after the game.

That summer, Ben joined a Christian Center bus trip to go see a Cardinals game in St. Louis with dozens of kids in the sandlot program. His father and uncle Matt came along as chaperones. The large group sat in Busch Stadium's upper deck—the "Bob Uecker" seats. During the middle innings, Ben snuck down behind home plate to get a closer look at big league pitching.

When he returned, his father asked him where he had been.

"Checking out the pitchers," he said. "Dad, I think I can hit these guys. I think I can play in the major leagues."

Tom didn't see how that was possible, but he didn't want to discourage his son. "We'll see where it goes from here," he said. "Maybe you'll end up playing in the majors someday."

At the start of Ben's junior season, Coach Johnson moved him over to second base, saying he wanted to save Ben's arm from the long throws from deep in the hole.

The move felt like a demotion, however. Friends and family members said moving him to second base didn't make sense, but Ben's attitude was that it was the coach's decision to make. "I just went with it," he said. (His flexibility at the time has served him well because today he's one of the best utility players in the majors.)

That attitude was typical of Ben, who was exhibiting spiritual growth off the field as well. He was the leader of the campus Fellowship of Christian Athletes Huddles, the weekly Bible studies for sports-minded students. Teammates and friends were impressed at how Ben invested in their spiritual lives and helped make everyone around him spiritually stronger—as "iron sharpens iron."

Ben also showed leadership on the field, where he hit .409, made nine appearances on the mound, going 3–0 with two saves, and was named Player of the Year in the Chicagoland Collegiate Athletic Conference, an NAIA All-American, and an NAIA Scholar-Athlete.

Ben had become a skilled baseball player in a few short years. And now that he had filled out to 6 feet, 3 inches, and 185 pounds, he was on the scouts' radar screen.

Ben had seen other NAIA All-Americans drafted, and scouts told him that he could find himself signing with a major league team. But nothing happened in the 2003 June draft, held shortly after the end of his junior season.

God is in control, right?

Time for summer ball, and this time Ben chose to play in the Northwoods League, a sixteen-team association that plays in small towns and cities in Wisconsin, Minnesota, and Iowa. Ben joined the Wisconsin Woodchucks of Wausau, Wisconsin.

His manager was Steve Foster, who played for the Cincinnati Reds and scouted for the Florida Marlins. He told Ben, "I have no idea why you're here. You should have been drafted and be in pro ball now."

Coach Foster set Ben up for a meeting with a scout that summer, but the middle infielder never received an offer good enough to leave school, where he had a full scholarship. Still, the episode boosted Ben's confidence that he could play professional baseball at a high level. "I know what these guys are like, and you can play," Coach Foster said.

Playing in the Northwoods League turned out to be a great experience for Ben. "Learning how to play almost every night in front of decent crowds of two or three thousand people was a big deal for college players," Ben said, "and good for my baseball abilities."

The team randomly assigned roommates, and Ben was thrown together with Jeff Gilmore. Here's where Ben's story gets even more interesting: Jeff Gilmore was a fine ballplayer at Dallas Baptist University who knew Dan Heefner well—very well.

Why?

Because Jeff's older sister Liz had married Dan Heefner back when Dan was leading the team at Olivet Nazarene.

With that in common, Ben and Jeff hit it off. They swapped stories about their college ball experiences, with Jeff telling him that Dallas Baptist was moving up to play NCAA Division I baseball the next season. That meant the team would be playing a lot of Big 12 schools like the University of Texas and Oklahoma State.

"Oh, and there's one more thing," Jeff said. "We need a shortstop."

Shortstop? My old position?

The wheels started turning in Ben's mind. The higher level of competition in Division I would bolster his chances to play pro ball. He had one year left, so if he was going to make a move, it was now or never.

Ben talked to Coach Johnson about the idea, but his coach wasn't thrilled with the prospect of losing one of his star players. Nonetheless, Olivet Nazarene released Ben from his scholarship so he could transfer. At Dallas Baptist, Ben moved right into the starting shortstop role. His days as a pitcher were over.

A QUICK TRIP TO THE BIG LEAGUES

Ben had a great senior season at Dallas Baptist, which earned him a closer look from major league scouts. This time around, the Houston Astros made him a sixth-round pick in the 2004 draft.

"I was obviously very excited to go play," he said. "To me, coming from Eureka, where no other athlete had played anything in professional sports, was definitely huge. It was like God was saying, *Look what I can do if you commit your work to Me and you just follow Me where I want you to go. I can do some things that you don't think are even possible.*"

Ben was assigned to the bottom rung of the ladder—the Class A Tri-City ValleyCats in the New York–Pennsylvania League (NYPL). The night before Ben left for his assignment in New York, his parents threw him a going-away party filled with family, friends, and old coaches. After everyone left, Ben and his father found themselves alone in Ben's bedroom.

"Dad, this is more important to others than it is to me," he said. "The way I look at it, I'm a missionary but I don't have to raise support. Instead, I'm going to reach people for Christ, whether it's my teammates, fans, or whatever."

His father looked at him. "Here's what is important to me. I don't care what you do for a living as long as you live for God."

Ben led the NYPL with a .339 batting average, which earned him a promotion to the South Atlantic League. His All-Star play and .333 batting average got him selected to Team USA, which played in the World Cup, held in the Netherlands. The international experience was invaluable.

It's amazing that Ben played so well because he was head over baseball cleats for a young woman named Julianna. She was studying music at Belmont University in Nashville, Tennessee, and she'd set her sights on a career in Christian music.

"She was just this awesome, godly woman who I put on a pedestal," Ben said. "I just decided to put myself out there and see if she had any interest."

Julianna said she had been praying intentionally about the person God wanted her to marry. "When Ben had felt this urgency to know if I felt anything for him, I was like, *Okay, Lord, I get it*. We started dating that night."

After more than two years of courtship, the Zobrists were married on December 17, 2005—the same anniversary date as Ben's parents. (Ben and Julianna asked if that would be okay, and of course Tom and Cindi were thrilled.) Ben's old roommate and teammate at Dallas Baptist, Jeff Gilmore, was at the wedding as well, which seemed only right to Ben.

You see, Jeff was Julianna's brother. And Liz Heefner was Julianna's older sister.

Meanwhile, Ben continued his meteoric rise from the minors to the majors. Houston assigned him to their Double-A team in Corpus Christi, Texas. During a road trip to play the Springfield Cardinals in Springfield, Missouri, Ben's parents took a week off to see him play in the southern Missouri city.

At 8:30 in the morning, Ben received a phone call from the Astros organization informing him that he had been traded to the Tampa Bay Rays. His new club would be assigning him to their Triple-A club in North Carolina—the Durham Bulls. If possible, his new team wanted him in Durham that night.

Ben was shocked at the trade because he was playing really well for Corpus Christi. He had yet to learn that in the baseball world, sometimes you get traded because you're good, not because you're bad.

The trade set off some momentary pandemonium. The decision was made that Ben would fly immediately to Corpus Christi, where he and Julianna would pack up their belongings and drive nearly four hours to Houston. Julianna would drop Ben off at Houston Bush International Airport so he could catch a flight to the East Coast and wait for her father-in-law to fly in from Springfield. Upon Tom's arrival, they would drive together to Durham—a twenty-hour one-way trip.

"When you hear about guys getting traded, you don't think about all the things these guys have to go through with their wives and their families and their cars," Tom said. "They don't make a lot of money yet, so they can't hire people and companies to help them move or take their cars somewhere."

Ben wasn't in Durham long, though, because the parent club called him up on July 31, 2006. This time, the move to Tampa Bay was a lot easier, and the family back home in Eureka was ecstatic. His father had always said, "Ben, if you make it to the big leagues, I'll be there."

The next day, August 1, was the twelfth birthday of Ben's youngest brother, Noah. What a way to celebrate. Noah, brother Peter, and Tom and Cindi bought plane tickets that morning to Tampa Bay and arrived in time to see Ben take the field against the Detroit Tigers. He went hitless that night, but they were in the stands a couple of days later when Ben notched his first major league hit—off Boston Red Sox ace Curt Schilling. Ben finished the 2006 season playing 52 games and batting .224.

Ben's 2007 and 2008 seasons were *interesting*, to say the least. He slumped early in the 2007 season, which resulted in a demotion back to Durham. He bounced back and forth between Tampa Bay and Durham but stuck with the team during the Rays' magical run to the 2008 World Series. Even though Tampa Bay lost to the Philadelphia Phillies, Ben got to start two games—and his parents were there in person to watch their son play on baseball's biggest stage.

It was during Ben's breakout season in 2009 that he became known as "Zorilla" for his monster home runs and ability to play anywhere at any time. Ben played seven positions during the 2009 season—all three outfield positions and all four infield positions. He batted everywhere in the lineup except ninth, and his approach to batting—swing mechanic Jaime Cevallos and old teammate and now brother-in-law Dan Heefner had helped him overhaul his stroke during the off-season—changed from being an OBP-oriented gap hitter to a major league slugger. His 27 home runs, .297 batting average (he was over .300 for much of the season before tailing off near the end), 91 RBIs, and .543 slugging average raised eyebrows around the league and earned him a handsome long-term contract.

How handsome? Try going from $438,100 a year to $4,500,000 in a single season. And Tampa Bay has a $7 million option for 2014 and 2015, if Ben keeps producing. Fortunately, the 2011 season was a good one: a solid .269 batting average, a third-best 46 doubles, and 20 home runs.

Ben was also part of a special team that won the AL wild card spot on the season's final day, coming back from a late-inning seven-run deficit to beat the New York Yankees 8–7 and pass the Boston Red Sox, who blew a nine-game wild card lead in September. The Rays then lost in the ALCS to the Texas Rangers.

Sure, being part of a Cinderella team and winning big games in dramatic fashion was a lot of fun, but when I (Mike Yorkey) interviewed Ben, he told me that his mind-set was, *How can I be a better player today than I was yesterday?* He was quick to add that he took the same approach with his spiritual walk.

How can I grow closer to the Lord?

How can I not become complacent?

How can I join up with people who are really loving God and seeking after God?

It's not the easiest situation when you're a major league baseball player living away from home and playing six games a week. He takes advantage of Baseball Chapel, an organization that provides a weekly church service on Sundays before games as well as Bible studies during the week that players can tap into. Today's technology makes it easy for Ben to listen to podcast sermons from his pastor, Byron Yawn of Community Bible Church in Nashville, Tennessee.

Ben and Julianna make their home in Music City so she can pursue her singing career while being a mom to their son, Zion, who came into their lives on February 1, 2009, and their daughter, Kruse, born September 19, 2011. (Kruse is the maiden name of one of Ben's grandmothers.) Ben has received permission from the Tampa Bay organization to fly home on his off days, so he tries to get home every chance he can during the regular season.

Each time Ben steps into the front door of his home, he hears a different type of "walk-up music"—the sound of home life.

3

ALBERT PUJOLS:
A HOME RUN HITTER WITH
A HEART FOR OTHERS

Every time All-Star first baseman Albert Pujols steps into the batter's box, the crowd buzzes in anticipation. They know something amazing *might* happen.

Albert has a lifetime batting average over .325, so the odds are pretty good that something remarkable *will* happen. No player in the history of baseball has amassed the kind of statistics Albert has put together during his first eleven years in the sport.

Not Babe Ruth.

Not Joe DiMaggio.

Not Ted Williams.

Not Barry Bonds.

Nobody.

And on this fall afternoon in 2010, Albert was about to give the crowd a treat.

The slugger walked confidently into the box and took his iconic stance. Feet wide apart. Hands held high. Legs crouched like a linebacker ready to explode into a tackle. When the ball left the pitcher's hand, one thing was certain—that piece of cowhide was about to get whacked.

That's because Albert doesn't hit a ball; he punishes it.

As the ball neared the plate, Albert's powerful swing was already in motion. His hands ripped through the hitting zone and sent a towering home run well over the left field fence.

The crowd leapt to its feet cheering. Albert's teammates emptied out of their dugout. Even the opposing players spilled onto the field to embrace Albert at home plate.

After all, this wasn't a major league contest before a full house. This was an exhibition softball game at a baseball field the Pujols Family Foundation helped build in Albert's hometown of Santo Domingo in the Dominican Republic.

Everybody was excited to be there and to see Albert do what he does better than anyone else: swing a bat. They also knew they had nearly missed the opportunity of watching their hometown hero in action. That's because a hurricane had skirted the country the previous day, leaving the field a muddy mess. A grounds crew had worked feverishly to get the field ready, even using gasoline to burn off the puddles. With the water semi-evaporated, the game went on as planned, and Albert provided the memorable moment.

Every year, Albert returns to his home country to help the people in his old *batey*, what the shantytown neighborhoods are called in the Dominican

Republic. The Pujols Foundation works year-round to provide the people there with medical care, food, clothing, and other necessities. It has even given new mattresses to families whose kids had doubled or tripled up on worn, lumpy beds.

Conditions in the *batey* aren't great, but some things are much better than when Albert was growing up in the D.R. in the 1980s. For one thing, he didn't have a nice baseball field to play on back then.

Albert developed his love of the sport using a stick for a bat, a milk carton for a glove, and a lime as a ball.

Today, though, children in Batey Aleman can play on a field where Albert's and several other players' pictures are painted on the outfield wall. The kids practice on Tuesdays and Thursdays and play games against each other on Saturdays all day long.

"That was me twenty-five years ago. I was one of those little boys with no hope and just a dream," Albert said in a *60 Minutes* interview in 2011 as he watched some kids he had been helping in his old neighborhood. "This is not so I can be looked at as 'Mr. Nice Guy.' I don't care less about that."

Albert helps out in the D.R. for one reason: he feels God has called him to give back. And Albert wants to honor God in every area of his life.

"Believe it or not, baseball is not the chief ambition of my life," Albert writes on his foundation's website. "Becoming a great baseball player is important to me, but it is not my primary focus because I know the Hall of Fame is not my ultimate, final destination. My life's goal is to bring glory to Jesus."

That's saying a lot, considering those words are coming from the best player in baseball during the first decade of the twenty-first century.

From the time Albert broke into the majors with the St. Louis Cardinals in 2001, he's put up monster numbers and been recognized for his talent. He won the National League Rookie of the Year his first season. From 2001 to 2010, he won three Most Valuable Player awards, six Silver Sluggers (given to the best offensive player at each position in both leagues), two Gold Gloves, and was named to nine All-Star games.

Between the 2001 and 2010 seasons, he became the only player in major league history to hit better than .300, hammer more than 30 home runs, and drive in at least 100 RBIs every season during his first ten years in the big leagues. No player had posted similar numbers in his first *two* years in the league, let alone ten. Unfortunately, that streak ended in 2011 when he came within a whisker—a home run?—of doing it for the eleventh season in a row when he batted .299 and had 99 RBIs to go along with his 37 home runs.

No matter. Albert's body of work would be phenomenal for any player, but it's especially impressive for someone who was selected 402nd in the Major League Baseball draft.

401 MOTIVATIONS

Coming out of high school, Albert wasn't on many professional scouts' radars. He'd lived in the United States for just a few years after his family emigrated from the Dominican Republic in 1996.

He ended up settling in Independence, Missouri, because his uncle already lived there. Not many Spanish speakers lived in Independence, but the town did have baseball. And on the diamond, there was no language barrier for Albert to overcome.

Baseball had always been a constant for Albert, even when nothing much else remained the same.

He was born José Alberto Pujols Alcántara on January 16, 1980. His mom and dad divorced three months later. His father, Bienvenido, had played baseball and was known as a good pitcher. Despite the divorce, Bienvenido stayed involved in Albert's life and was there for him and his mother.

But nobody was a bigger part of his life than his grandmother, America. (Yes, that's her real name.) She took on a lot of the duties raising Albert. His ten aunts and uncles were also around to provide guidance and a helping hand.

By United States standards, Albert grew up dirt poor. But he never saw it that way. He says he didn't feel poor because he ate breakfast, lunch, and dinner every day. Many of the kids around him were fortunate if they got just *one* meal. In his mind, *those* were the poor kids.

Living in the *batey*, Albert spent most of his time playing baseball. Before he was a teenager, he realized that his skills were ahead of those of his peers and that he might have the ability to make it to the big leagues.

"Growing up in the Dominican Republic, that's pretty much all I did is play baseball," Albert said. "That's pretty much everybody's dream, to play professional baseball."

When Albert moved to Missouri at age sixteen, one of the first things he did was walk into Fort Osage High School and say through an interpreter that he wanted to play baseball.

In his first season, Albert played shortstop and helped the Indians win the Class 4A state championship. His hitting totals were especially impressive: a .471 batting average with 11 home runs and 32 RBIs. *USA Today* recognized him as an "honorable mention" in its All-USA baseball rankings.

Albert stayed hot in summer ball. Playing 60 games for an American Legion team, he blasted 29 home runs and had 119 RBIs.

The seventeen-year-old returned to Fort Osage in the fall and asked if he could repeat his junior year. Although he had cousins at the school who could translate for him, he struggled to pick up English. Albert really wanted to master the language and earn his high school diploma. The school and the Missouri State High School Activities Association agreed, giving Albert an extra year of high school eligibility.

During the 1998 season, Albert was a force for the Indians, hitting .660. The problem was, he couldn't sneak up on teams anymore. Everybody knew who he was and didn't want to give him a good pitch to hit. Albert drew a record-setting 26 walks that season, 18 of them intentional.

In the summer Albert's stature grew even more as he broke his own home run record by bashing 35 round-trippers, including one that caught the attention of *Independence Examiner* writer Dick Puhr, who described one of Albert's grand slams as a "blast down the left-field line [that] was higher than the light standards and sailed, not only over the fence, but the railroad tracks and landed in a mulberry bush."

His summer coach, Gary Stone, said, "It's the farthest and hardest I've seen a baseball hit."

Of course, Stone was already a big fan of Albert's. During a tournament the previous summer in which all the players had to use wooden bats instead of aluminum, Stone noted that Albert would "have power even if he used a toothpick."

While Albert's talents on a baseball field were obvious to everybody who saw him play, he didn't attract the praise of many scouts. They didn't like Albert's footwork at shortstop and said that he lacked control on his throws.

Albert came back for his senior year in 1998 but earned enough credits to graduate early. He enrolled at Maple Woods Community College in Kansas City in January and started playing for the college team that spring.

Immediately, Albert proved he had the ability to play at the next level.

In his first game for the Monarchs, Albert turned an unassisted triple play at shortstop and hit a grand slam off Mark Buehrle (now a four-time major league All-Star who's thrown a no-hitter and a perfect game).

For the season, Albert hit .461 with 22 home runs and 80 RBIs.

When baseball's 1999 draft rolled around on June 2, Albert watched in anticipation. He knew his dream of making it to the pros was about to come true.

The Tampa Bay Devil Rays (now just the "Rays") selected Josh Hamilton first overall. Josh Beckett went second to the Florida Marlins. Nearly everybody close to baseball believed those two players would go right away. Albert figured he'd probably go in the first few rounds. The *Examiner* agreed, writing that he'd be drafted in the top three rounds. Other experts had him pegged to go anywhere from the fifth to eighth round. Scouts still didn't like Albert's throwing motion and worried because he'd gained a little weight in junior college.

After the first day of the draft was over, Albert's name was still on the board.

He had to wait until the morning of June 3 to hear that St. Louis had drafted him in the *thirteenth* round with the 402nd pick.

Albert was devastated. His girlfriend at the time, Deidre Corona, said he cried like a baby. He even talked about quitting baseball.

Deidre persuaded him not to give up on his dream.

When St. Louis offered Albert a $10,000 signing bonus (Hamilton had been given $3.96 million), he turned it down because he felt like he was worth more.

To prove his worth, Albert went to the Jayhawk League, where college-aged players showcased their talent over the summer. In 55 games, Albert led the team in home runs and batting average. St. Louis came back and offered him $60,000. He took the deal and joined the team.

But the sting of being drafted in the thirteenth round didn't go away.

Albert knew he had the talent and work ethic to make it in the pros, and he wanted to show his detractors they were wrong about him.

Albert had lived with doubters. But when coaches worked with him and saw his daily dedication, they often became his biggest fans.

"He's the best hitter I've coached or seen," said Marty Kilgore, Albert's coach at Maple Woods Community College. "But what impresses me most about Albert is his work ethic. A lot of coaches in the area told me he didn't have good work habits and that he was moody. I've seen just the opposite. He's the first player at practice, the last to leave, and when practice is over, he's heading over to the batting cage to take some more swings."

Albert developed his swing during his younger years and continued to hone it with countless repetitions. These days, he estimates that he takes between fifteen and twenty thousand practice swings a year in the batting cage. He works so hard to get his mechanics exactly right that it's no wonder he's earned the nickname "The Machine."

As it turns out, it was the scouts who didn't get a whole lot right in the 1999 draft. Only twenty-three of the fifty-one players drafted in the first round ever made it to the big leagues. Carl Crawford and Justin Morneau went in the second round. Shane Victorino was selected with the 194th pick, and amazingly, Jake Peavy, a future Cy Young winner, was picked *after* Albert at the 472nd spot.

Being slighted in the draft has been a driving force for Albert—even to this day.

"I'll never, never get over it," he said.

With 401 reasons fueling his drive to succeed, Albert played just one year in the minor leagues. During that same time, he worked more on his physique, turning his body into a muscular 6-foot, 3-inch, 230-pound baseball-bashing machine.

Albert started the 2000 season with the Class A Peoria Chiefs in Illinois. After playing third base and being named the league's Most Valuable Player, Albert had a brief stay at Double-A before jumping up to the Triple-A Memphis Redbirds.

The Redbirds were preparing to enter the Pacific Coast League playoffs. In Albert's first seven games, he hit .367 with two home runs. Then he helped lead Memphis past the Albuquerque Dukes and into the championship series against Salt Lake City. On September 15, 2000, the twenty-year-old showed no signs of nerves as he hit a walk-off home run in the thirteenth inning of Game 4 to give the Redbirds their first-ever PCL championship. For his efforts, Albert earned the league's Most Valuable Player award in the postseason.

In 2001, Albert entered spring training with the hopes of gaining a spot on the Cardinals' twenty-five-man roster. Most people close to the team figured Albert would spend another year with the Redbirds before he'd be ready for the majors. Albert wanted to prove them wrong. He took extra fielding practice to learn how to play first base and outfield, and he always looked strong at third.

When the Opening Day lineup was announced, Albert found himself playing left field against the Colorado Rockies.

FIRM FOUNDATION

While Albert's baseball career was taking off, his personal life was doing the same.

In the summer of 1998, the teen went salsa dancing at a club in Kansas City, where he met a young woman named Deidre. It wasn't love at first sight, but the two became dancing buddies.

After several weeks, Albert worked up the courage to ask Deidre on a date. When they were out together, he admitted to lying to her about his age. He had told her that he was twenty-one when he was really only eighteen years old. Deidre also had a confession to make: she had just given birth to a baby girl with Down syndrome.

Instead of running away from the relationship, Albert wanted to meet Deidre's daughter. When Albert met Isabella for the first time, he didn't see her as a child with Down syndrome. Instead, he just looked at her as a beautiful little girl.

Albert continued to date Deidre and to act as Isabella's occasional babysitter. Deidre had recently rededicated her life to Jesus Christ and encouraged Albert to attend church with her. She also explained the existence of heaven and hell to him and said the only way to heaven was through a personal relationship with Jesus Christ.

"I went to church every once in a while growing up," Albert said. "At that time, I didn't realize how important it was to go to church and have a relationship with Christ."

His grandmother had raised Albert to have good morals and to be a good person. He didn't drink, smoke, or have any tattoos. But he also didn't know God or have a relationship with His Son.

Albert began attending church every week and learning more about Jesus. Once Albert understood the truth of the gospel, he walked down the aisle and prayed to give his life to Christ on November 13, 1998.

"I wouldn't say it was easy and that the Lord started turning things around [right away]," Albert said. "There were still challenges and still some tough times in my life, but the Lord was preparing me for the big things."

That included getting married and being successful in baseball.

Albert and Deidre were married on New Year's Day—January 1, 2000. When Albert was assigned to play in Peoria, Deidre and Isabella accompanied him.

Albert made around $125 a week playing baseball in the spring of 2000 (these days, his on-the-field salary is more than $280,000 a week, which doesn't include endorsement income). This wasn't enough money for a young family with a special-needs child. The couple barely had enough money to pay rent or buy furniture. Albert remembers going to Walmart and purchasing a cheap card table and folding chairs so they could have a seating area.

When Albert made the jump to the majors in 2001, that all changed. His salary shot up to $200,000 for the year. And after Albert won NL Rookie of the Year honors by batting .329 with 37 home runs and 130 RBIs, his salary tripled to $600,000 the following year.

As Albert's statistics grew and his consistency became obvious—he was no one-season wonder!—the Cardinals kept rewarding him with larger contracts.

In 2005, his annual salary reached eight digits . . . $11 million to be exact. That was also the year that he and Deidre started the Pujols Family Foundation.

"I had been praying for God to be able to use Albert to share Jesus and wanted it to be bigger," Deidre said. "Todd Perry had been calling and presenting us with an idea [for the foundation]. It took about a year to get everybody in the same place. Our mission is faith, family, and others."

The Pujols Family Foundation helps families and children who live with Down syndrome and also works in the Dominican Republic to improve the quality of life of needy children. Perry has worked as the executive director from the beginning. Albert and Deidre don't just write a check and help raise money; they get physically involved with the people their organization touches.

One of the highlights of Albert's year is hosting a formal dance for teenagers with Down syndrome. The kids show up at this gala event in fancy dresses and tuxedoes, walk the red carpet, and enjoy the prom-like atmosphere. And, of course, all the girls want to dance with Albert.

At the end of the 2010 celebration, Albert dripped with sweat but had a huge smile on his face.

"It must've been the highlight of the year for them," the *60 Minutes* reporter said to Albert during his interview.

"And for me, too," Albert quickly responded. "Every time I'm around them, I enjoy it and have a great time."

As the Pujols Family Foundation got going, Albert's own family was growing. Isabella got a little brother when Albert Jr. (known as A.J.) was born a couple of years after Albert and Deidre married. In 2005, Sophia came along, and more recently, Ezra was born.

"One thing I have learned is that it's not about me; it's about serving the Lord Jesus Christ," Albert said. "His plan was bigger than what I ever thought. I have a beautiful family and four beautiful kids."

Albert doesn't only want to be a role model to his own children; he hopes to positively influence other kids. During a recent season, the slugger had the opportunity to meet two young men who made an especially big impact on him.

One of them was Jacob Trammell, a fifteen-year-old who had been diagnosed with a cancerous tumor and had gone through chemotherapy and radiation. Through the Make-A-Wish Foundation, Jacob got to hang out with his idol. Albert showed Jacob around the Cardinals' clubhouse and took batting practice with him at Busch Stadium. ESPN recorded the events for its show *My Wish*.

"He's like the best baseball player in baseball now," Jacob said about Albert. "He's a good Christian man. He's my role model because my dad had left."

The teenager, a good baseball player in his own right, dreamed of playing in the majors and got some hitting tips from Albert. With a few tweaks of his swing—such as keeping his hands high and swinging in one fluid motion—Jacob was smacking line drives all over the indoor hitting facility at Busch Stadium.

"That's the stroke I've been looking for all year," Albert quipped after Jacob stroked a streak of solid hits.

According to Jacob's mom, Debbie, it was the high point of Jacob's year.

"Albert is such a great player," she said. "Jacob likes his morals and the way he uses his Christian background, giving all the glory to God. Jacob is kind of like that, too."

A few weeks later, during the 2010 season, Albert lashed his 400th major league home run, making him the third-youngest player to accomplish that feat. Only Alex Rodriguez and Ken Griffey Jr. reached that benchmark at a younger age.

Four days after reaching that milestone, Albert took the bat that hammered the historic home run and gave it to Brandon Johnson, a thirteen-year-old battling a malignant brain tumor at Texas Children's Hospital. Albert didn't go with a lot of fanfare or television cameras. He just quietly slipped away after the game with the Houston Astros, went to the hospital, prayed with Brandon, and stayed for about an hour.

Faith, family, and others. It's not just the mission of Albert's foundation—it's the foundation of his life.

MAKING HISTORY

While many of the best athletes in the world make headlines with little indiscretions or poor decisions, Albert makes headlines with the good he does—on and off the field. With a bat in his hands, he's put up numbers that are unparalleled in the long, storied history of baseball.

In his first eleven years in the big leagues, he hit more than 40 home runs and drove in better than 120 RBIs six times. He's won the National League's Most Valuable Player award three times (2005, 2008, and 2009). He led St. Louis to the World Series three times. The Cardinals lost to Boston in 2004, but the Redbirds came back two years later to beat Detroit. And during the recent 2011 campaign, Albert was at the front of the charge as St. Louis won its National League–leading eleventh World Series title.

The seven-game victory over Texas will be remembered as one of the most unlikely championships in baseball history. St. Louis was 10½ games back in the NL wild card race at the end of August when the Redbirds went on a tear in September. Albert hit .355 that month with five homers and 20 RBIs as St. Louis clinched the wild card spot on the final day of the regular season.

The underdog Cardinals defeated mighty Philadelphia in five games in the National League Divisional Series. Then they got past Milwaukee to set up the finale against the Rangers.

Albert had a slow start in the World Series but then erupted for one of the best games ever by hitting three home runs and knocking in six RBIs in a 16–7 victory in Game 4. Albert's 14 total bases stand as a World Series record, and it marked the first time since 1977 that a player had hit three dingers in the Fall Classic. Only Reggie Jackson and Babe Ruth had accomplished the feat before.

"I'm glad it was him," the Hall of Famer Jackson said of Albert tying his record. "He's a fabulous representative of the game. . . . I told him I admire the way he went about his business. I know he has a charity; I know he's a good, Christian man, a good team guy. He's got great focus."

Albert displayed that laser-like focus in the 2011 postseason by batting over .350 with five home runs and 16 RBIs.

"I think the last month of the season, that's where it started," Albert said. "Different guys were coming huge, getting big hits, and we carried that into the postseason and here we are, world champions."

Fans, sportswriters, opponents—even his manager—marvel at what Albert accomplishes on the diamond.

"Enjoy it. Respect it. Appreciate it," said longtime Cardinals manager Tony La Russa, who retired following the 2011 World Series victory. "I'm left with just watching him. And if you watch him, he'll do something to show you how great he is."

Now American League fans will get a chance to witness that greatness. In December 2011, Albert signed a ten-year, $254 million contract with the Los Angeles Angels that broke the hearts of Redbird fans.

Albert was one of the most highly prized free agents ever. After ten years in the sport, he'd won six Silver Slugger awards at three different positions— third base, outfield, and first base. He was also a two-time Gold Glove winner (2006 and 2010) at first base, proving that his fielding, throwing, and catching were also among the league's best.

But perhaps nothing showed Albert's ability better than an illustration that FOX Sports put on TV screens during one of Albert's World Series games. When a batter came to the plate, a graphic would flash on the screen to show where pitchers could throw the ball to get him out. When Albert's graphic came up, there were no spots that pitchers could pitch to. He was capable of hitting any pitch at any count and making his opponents pay.

"Albert has no glaring weaknesses, and he doesn't chase many bad pitches," Hall of Famer Tony Gwynn said.

It's not just the hundreds of thousands of practice swings that have made Albert a great hitter. He has studied the game and worked on his weaknesses. He's spent hours talking with Cardinal pitchers about how they work certain batters and vary their pitches. This helps Albert get into the mind of a pitcher, so that he'll know what to expect in different situations.

All of his efforts have paid off. Albert hits for average, hits for power, and is known for coming through in the clutch. No Cardinal has hit more grand slams than No. 5.

As of the end of the 2011 season, Albert had tallied 11 grand slams. He's nearly automatic with the bases loaded; in 2009 alone, he came to the plate with the bases full eight times and hit a home run on four occasions.

And his bat doesn't disappear during the postseason, when the pitching is better and the pressure ratchets up. Through the 2011 season, he's hit .330 in the playoffs with 18 home runs and 52 RBIs.

"He's the face of baseball," said ESPN baseball analyst Peter Gammons. "When we're looking at history, he's an icon. And we should appreciate him because he's never done anything that's stained his reputation."

During an era where baseball's best power hitters have been embroiled in steroid rumors, Albert has stayed above the fray. Despite his prolific numbers and prodigious physique, he's never failed a drug test and never been accused of using any kind of performance-enhancing drug. It gets his dander up, though, when people voice suspicions about his Hall-of-Fame-worthy statistics.

"I would never do any of that," Albert said about taking performance-enhancing drugs. "You think I'm going to ruin my relationship with God just because I want to get better in this game? You think I'm going to ruin everything because of steroids? . . . I want to be the person who represents God, represents my family, and represents the Cardinals the right way."

On many occasions, Albert has invited baseball to test him every day. He has nothing to hide and wants people to know that he walks his talk.

In fact, Albert looks for ways to tell people about what God has done in his life. He's often said that God doesn't need him, but he needs God to live a successful life.

Since the early 1990s, the Cardinals have hosted a Christian Family Day when players share their testimonies with the fans at Busch Stadium after the conclusion of the game. From the time Albert joined the team, he and Deidre have become regulars at this event and others like it around the country.

The Christian Family Day organization also created a special testimony card for Albert and other members of the team. It looks like a baseball card, but instead of statistics on the back, it's packed with a player's personal story of accepting Jesus and a prayer that people can pray to invite Christ into their lives.

Albert signs the cards, and he and Deidre look for opportunities to pass them out to young fans.

Deidre has said that she sometimes feels like she's hitting a home run when she gives the card to people and sees the look on their faces. But when it comes to hitting balls out of major league parks, the former softball player leaves that up to her husband.

Even in 2011, when an early season slump and fractured forearm hurt Albert's statistics, he managed to hit more than 30 home runs for the eleventh consecutive year.

Not surprisingly, no player in Cardinals history has put together more multiple home run games than Albert. During the 2011 season, he hit two or more home runs in 42 games—breaking Stan Musial's record of 37. Mark McGwire was third on the list at 28 games. Albert has five career three-homer games (the most of any active player), and some say his record-setting 465-foot blast in Busch Stadium during the 2011 season still hasn't come down to earth.

Albert's fans often can't decide what's their favorite thing about a Pujols home run. Is it gawking at a towering drive as it leaves the yard for some distant destination? Or is it seeing him glide around the bases until he approaches home plate, where he does his trademark shuffle step as he looks up and points to heaven?

Albert doesn't point to the sky to disrespect his opponents. He does it to show his respect to his Savior.

Many experts have tried to dissect Albert's swing and figure out the secret to his success. But Albert already knows the answer.

"I don't believe in all that science stuff," Albert said. "I believe in Jesus Christ, who gave me the strength and power and talent to honor Him. You can always try to figure it out and be scientific and look for success. Not me. It's dedication, hard work, practice, and God."

The All-Star's plan for moving forward is simple: he'll keep working hard, keep swinging the way God created him to, and keep pointing to heaven.

Because in playing for the Los Angeles Angels, Albert has even higher places to go.

4

CARLOS BELTRAN:
PRAYING ALL THE WAY TO THE BALLPARK

The choice wasn't momentous.

It wasn't like it would determine the fate of Carlos Beltran's eternal soul or anything like that. Still, what happened was significant because of what it said about his priorities.

Carlos was in his second or third year as the New York Mets' much-ballyhooed center fielder. Young, telegenic, ridiculously talented, and filthy rich, he was the type of five-tool star who graces the top of every major league team's wish list. In January 2005, he had signed a whopping seven-year, $119 million contract with the Mets. Gotham was his personal playground.

Carlos was also a faithful chapel attendee, so when he missed the pre-game service one day at Shea Stadium, chaplain Cali Magallanes went looking for him. Carlos was finishing a clubhouse interview with a media outlet from his native Puerto Rico. He asked Magallanes if they could go pray together, so the two men searched for a private room.

Just then, Jay Horwitz, the Mets' media relations director, tapped Carlos on the shoulder. "The governor of Puerto Rico is here," Horwitz said. "He'd like to speak to you."

So much for prayer, Magallanes thought. When you make nearly $21,000 every time you step into the batter's box, as Carlos did at that time, everybody wants your time. Even high-ranking politicians.

But then the unexpected happened. Without hesitation, Carlos told Horwitz, "Tell him I'll be right out. I have something more important to do."

Magallanes was pleasantly surprised.

"That really impacted me," Magallanes said, adding that he was impressed the Met outfielder didn't want to be distracted—even by the governor of Puerto Rico—until he had finished praying.

Prayer has been a vital part of Carlos' life ever since he placed his faith in Christ in 2001 during a postgame Bible study with former teammate Luis Alicea. He prays every morning and on his drive to the ballpark. During games, he often prays while patrolling the outfield.

"Some people might think I'm crazy, but I try to do that," he says.

No, Carlos isn't crazy. He's just healthily dependent on God. Prayer always comes in handy, even—and sometimes *especially*—for guys making a fortune.

Carlos' humble beginnings portended none of the life he now knows. He was born on April 24, 1977, in Manatí, Puerto Rico, a modest-sized town near the island's north-central shoreline. His father, Wilfredo, worked hard at a pharmaceutical warehouse so Carlos' mother could stay home with their four children.

By the time he could spell *plantain*, Carlos had fallen in love with baseball. It's easy to do in his home country. For every banana this U.S. territory exports, Puerto Rico seems to produce a baseball star, too.

In 1942, Hiram Bithorn became the first Puerto Rican major leaguer, and there have been more than two hundred since, including Hall of Famers like Roberto Alomar, Orlando Cepeda, and, of course, the great Roberto Clemente.

Wilfredo encouraged young Carlos to work hard at baseball, just like everything else. "Anything worth having is worth working for," Wilfredo would say. So Carlos worked hard at baseball, modeling his game after another Puerto Rican great, Bernie Williams, the New York Yankees' five-time All-Star center fielder.

In June 1995, the Kansas City Royals drafted eighteen-year-old Carlos in the second round out of Fernando Callejos High School, and by 1999, the franchise had anointed him as its starting center fielder and leadoff hitter. He responded by hitting .293 with 22 home runs, 108 RBIs, and 112 runs scored, marking the first time a rookie had totaled 100 RBIs and 100 runs in the same season since Fred Lynn performed that feat in 1975. That fall, Carlos got married and found out on his honeymoon that he had won the American League Rookie of the Year award. Not a bad year, eh?

At that moment, Vegas was probably giving good odds on Carlos reaching the Hall of Fame. He was a Puerto Rican Picasso, and baseball diamonds were his canvas.

But now, in the twilight of his career, what are we to make of Carlos' body of work? Much has happened in between that clouds the perspective. He became a star in Kansas City, a postseason legend in Houston, a hero/goat in New York (depending on whom you speak to), and a rent-a-bat acquisition for San Francisco at the 2011 trade deadline.

This much is obvious: plenty of players would envy Carlos' career. Through 2011, he had earned six All-Star appearances, three Gold Gloves, and two Silver Slugger awards. He had reached the 100-RBI plateau eight times and eclipsed the 300-home-run mark for his career. He swiped 42 bases in 2004 and smashed 41 homers in 2006. But his career will always be dogged by that most haunting of sports questions: *What if?*

When the New York Mets signed Carlos before the 2005 season, he was the hottest free agent on the market, coming off one of the greatest postseasons in history. The previous fall, after a midseason trade from Kansas City to Houston, he had helped the Astros come within one win of reaching the World Series, hitting .435 with eight homers, 14 RBIs, 21 runs, and 6 stolen bases in 12 playoff games.

Carlos' mega-contract with the Mets made him only the tenth player in major league history at the time to land a $100 million deal. That's a ton of money . . . and a ton of expectations. Carlos took everything in a spiritual stride.

"It's good to have a big house and a nice car, but it's better when you have Jesus Christ in your heart," he said. "He's more important than anything."

New Yorkers, though, are a demanding bunch. Carlos' arrival, along with that of pitching ace Pedro Martinez, had plenty of Mets fans planning for the franchise's first World Series championship since 1986. But the team's grand visions of annual National League East dominance quickly morphed into maddening mediocrity. While the Mets finished above .500 in four of Carlos' six full seasons in New York, the team made just one playoff appearance (2006).

For his part, though, Carlos mostly dazzled when he played. In six and a half years in New York, he amassed 149 home runs, 208 doubles, 100 stolen bases, and 559 RBIs.

But the trick was keeping him on the field. From 2003 to 2010—during the age span of twenty-six to thirty-three, the prime of his career—Carlos missed an average of 32 games per season. There were oblique strains in 2003 and 2007, a scary outfield collision with teammate Mike Cameron in 2005 (resulting in a facial fracture and a concussion), and a myriad of debilitating knee issues. Thanks to his arthritic joints, he played in just 81 games in 2009 and 64 in 2010.

Fair or not, perhaps the most indelible memory of the Carlos Beltran era for Mets fans came in Game 7 of the 2006 National League Championship Series against St. Louis. Facing a 3–1 deficit with two outs in the bottom of the ninth, Carlos came to the plate with the bases loaded. A single would tie the game. A home run would win it and send the Big Apple into juicy delirium and the Mets to the World Series. But Cardinals closer Adam Wainwright froze Carlos with an 0–2 curveball. Game over.

In 2011, during the final year of Carlos' contract, the struggling Mets shipped him to San Francisco at the trade deadline. After finishing the season with the Giants, Carlos was a free agent. He signed a two-year, $26 million deal with the St. Louis Cardinals, who had lost Albert Pujols to the Los Angeles Angels.

How does Carlos respond to life's big changes? He gets on his knees.

"I pray every day when I wake up and while I'm driving to the ballpark," he says. "Before I go out and play, I try to read the Bible and memorize it and think about it the whole game."

All things considered, the highs have far outnumbered the lows in Carlos' career. He will go down as one of the greatest all-around players in Mets history. And in 2011, healthy for the first time in three years, he played in 142 games between New York and San Francisco and hit an even .300 with 22 home runs.

Through everything, Carlos sees God's fingerprints all over his life . . . which, of course, is something he prays about.

"He's going to put you in different situations to see how you deal with it and what path you're going to take," Carlos says. "I pray for every decision in my life. I can see everything to a point, but God can see farther. I know every decision God makes is perfect. I'm not perfect, but He is."

5

ADRIAN GONZALEZ:
GONZO FOR GOD

Excitedly, the boys scattered the baseball cards across their bedroom floor without regard for the merchandise's future value on the trading market.

Crease marks? Fuzzy corners? *Who cares!* This was no time to worry about a mint-condition collection. There were bedroom baseball lineups to be picked, for Pete's sake!

Speaking of Pete, he was available on the carpet. You could do a lot worse than Pete Rose, baseball's all-time hit king. But young Adrian Gonzalez always reached for someone else first: Tony Gwynn. As a San Diego area native and a left-hander, Adrian adored Gwynn, another lefty whose .338 lifetime batting average for the hometown Padres punched his ticket into both Cooperstown's and Adrian's hearts.

Usually, Will Clark was drafted next. My, oh my, Will the Thrill sure had a sweet stroke. Then another lefty: Darryl Strawberry. With his pre-pitch bat waggle, exaggerated leg kick, and powerfully loopy swing, the Straw Man was always a favorite.

On and on it went until Adrian and his two older brothers, David Jr. and Edgar, finished their lineups. Each team had to reflect all nine defensive positions. (Stacking the lineup with Mike Schmidt *and* Wade Boggs—two third basemen—was strictly taboo.)

Out came the plastic bat. Next, the ball—usually a wad of tape or balled-up socks. Finally, the bases . . .

Uh, let's see. How about the bed, the closet door, and that pile of dirty clothes? What about home plate? Aw, heck, let's get started. Just throw something down on the floor.

And batter up!

Once bedroom baseball started, the boys tried to mimic each player's real-life swing. Every square inch of the room was demarcated for the type of hit it produced. The top of the far wall was a home run. There were plenty of those.

Adrian and Edgar's battles, in particular, were epic.

"When I got back from school, they were already playing," recalled David Jr., who is eight years older than Adrian and four years older than Edgar. "Whoever won, they were the champions of the world. When Adrian won, he'd be shouting it all over the house. Edgar would get mad and want to play again. Same thing the other way."

Adrian has come a long way from those halcyon childhood days, bathed as they were in baseball, simplicity, and the SoCal sun. He is now the Boston Red Sox' newly minted superstar, a $154 million slugger who is quickly etching his name into franchise history with his gorgeous swing. After the magnificent season he fashioned in 2011—a .338 batting average that was second best in the major leagues and 213 hits that tied him with Michael Young of Texas for the most in the majors—Adrian is generally acclaimed as one of this generation's greatest hitters.

Just don't expect any of this to faze him. All the hubbub in Hub City elicits little more than a shoulder shrug from this twenty-nine-year-old batsman who's in the prime of his career. Don't let his nonchalance fool you, though. Adrian's levelheaded outlook has as much to do with his deep Christian faith as it does with his mellow personality. He mixes his *SportsCenter*-highlight abilities with genuine Christlike humility as well as anyone in the game today. For Adrian, the dichotomy fits like a well-oiled mitt.

"I don't want to be remembered in baseball," he said. "I want to be remembered as a good witness for Christ."

At this point, Adrian is destined for both.

ALL IN THE FAMILY

Born on May 8, 1982, in San Diego, Adrian always dreamed big. If he wasn't imitating his favorite baseball hero's swing, he was imagining himself as a music star. In one classic family photo, he sported a heavily gelled Mohawk while using a tennis racquet like a Jimi Hendrix Stratocaster. (To this day, family members are still puzzled at what the ski gloves and boots were for.)

Alas, musical stardom never panned out for Adrian. But boy, the kid sure rocked it on the diamond.

Adrian's love for baseball comes from his father, David Sr., who grew up dirt-poor in Ciudad Obregón, a large city in Mexico's arid Sonoran Desert region, where he sold popsicles and ice cream sandwiches to anyone with a parched tongue and a few *pesos*. When he grew older and was asked to help support his family, David Sr. dropped out of high school and started working for an air-conditioning company. He was always a good handyman.

But he could also play *béisbol*. He was a big, strong first baseman with huge wrists that required custom-made watches. Maybe that's what happens when you lug AC units up and down stairs all day long.

While those Popeye forearms produced plenty of pop, he was also stealthily fast on the base paths, enough to earn the nickname *El Correcamino*—"The Roadrunner."

David Sr.'s skills are part of Gonzalez family lore. In the days before the San Diego Padres' inaugural major league season in 1969, as the story goes, a Padres scout saw the Gonzalez clan playing baseball during a family reunion in the San Diego area and set up a scrimmage. After Team Gonzalez beat the pro squad, the Padres extended tryout offers to David Sr. and his cousin, Robert Guerra. David Sr. declined for financial reasons, but his passion for the game never waned.

He played for the Mexican national team in the late 1960s and early 1970s and attracted other professional offers. But by then, his business was making more money than Mexican baseball paid.

The family immigrated to Chula Vista, a San Diego suburb a few miles north of the border, prior to Adrian's birth and moved to Tijuana when Adrian was a year old. But the air-conditioning business was doing so well that the Gonzalezes could afford to keep a home in both cities. Oftentimes, the family would spend their weekends in Tijuana—Adrian played in elite leagues in Mexico growing up—but would return to their Chula Vista home on Sunday nights since the boys had school in the morning. The consistent border crossings aided Adrian's baseball and bilingual abilities.

As each son came along, David Sr. baptized him into baseball. From his earliest memory, Adrian recalls throwing a tennis ball against the side of his house, glove in hand, eagerly awaiting his older brothers' return from school to play with him.

David Sr. would often take his sons to a nearby field for infield practice—David Jr. at shortstop, Edgar at second, and Adrian at first. Even as an ankle-biter, Adrian wouldn't stand for any patronizing lobs.

"I can catch it!" he'd squeal in protest.

"No you can't," his brothers retorted, laughing.

But sure enough, little Adrian showed a preternatural ability to catch bullets and dig out bouncers.

"He always wanted to be a part of us," David Jr. recalled. "He was always above his age group. We didn't baby him."

As David Sr.'s business took off, he was able to provide his sons with opportunities that he never had growing up. He built an enormous backyard batting cage at their Chula Vista home. That was really cool until one day . . . *crash!* The boys had used the cage so much that a hole had formed in the protective netting. The poor window in the neighbor's house never saw it coming.

For the good of all houses within range, the brothers took up Wiffle ball. But this wasn't just any ol' casual game. When it came to competition, the Gonzalez brothers didn't *do* casual. This was no-holds-barred Wiffle.

At first, Edgar seemed to have the upper hand. So Adrian bought a book on how to throw Wiffle pitches—yes, that's correct; he actually purchased a book specifically designed to improve one's Wiffle pitch arsenal—and developed a wicked curve that Edgar couldn't solve.

"He was always looking for an edge to win," Edgar said.

Baseball was like oxygen for the Gonzalez brothers. When they weren't swinging in the bedroom or the backyard cage, they were playing baseball games on Atari and Nintendo. On vacations, the family would bring bats, balls, and gloves so the boys could practice on the closest field or beach.

Even religion took a backseat to baseball. The Gonzalezes were practicing Catholics, but weekend tournaments often trumped Mass. "God will forgive us if we don't go to church," David Sr. told his boys, "as long as we're playing baseball." Dubious theology, yes, but you catch the drift.

Each brother became a star in his own right. David Jr. was good enough to spark college interest from the University of California Riverside and San

Diego State. The Montreal Expos even offered to sign him as an undrafted free agent. He ended up at Point Loma Nazarene University, an NAIA program in San Diego, where he led the team in runs scored (38) as a junior in 1996, played every position during one game as a senior, and graduated with an engineering degree.

Edgar, meanwhile, starred at San Diego State before Tampa Bay drafted him in the thirtieth round in 2000. In 2011, he completed his twelfth professional season with the Fresno Grizzlies, the San Francisco Giants' Triple-A affiliate, where he hit .315 with career highs in home runs (14) and RBIs (82). Even if he never gets back to the majors, Edgar can always say that he played alongside Adrian at Petco Park, appearing in 193 games for the Padres between the 2008 and 2009 seasons.

The best of the Gonzalez bunch, though, was the baby brother. A power-hitting first baseman, Adrian destroyed opposing pitching as a prep star, batting .559 in his final two seasons at Eastlake High School in Chula Vista. As a senior, he hit .645 with 13 home runs and earned Player of the Year honors from the California Interscholastic Federation and the *San Diego Union-Tribune* newspaper.

Later that year, the Florida Marlins drafted him No. 1 overall, making him the first high school infielder since Alex Rodriguez in 1993 to be the top pick. Before Adrian, the only other first baseman selected first since the draft started in 1965 was Ron Blomberg (Yankees) in 1967.

One day after being drafted—only twenty-nine days after his eighteenth birthday—Adrian signed with Florida for $3 million. He splurged on a Cadillac Escalade, but, always the sensible kid, he invested most of his remaining bonus.

Stardom seemed inevitable. But it didn't come easily.

DESTINED FOR GREATNESS

Things started well enough. The Marlins quickly assigned Adrian to their Gulf Coast League rookie affiliate in Melbourne, Florida, where he hit .295 in 53 games and showed a deep hunger to improve.

At night, the Marlins' prized bonus baby would sneak into town to take extra batting practice at a local cage, feeding quarters into the machines like an eager Little Leaguer. When manager Kevin Boles found out, he quickly put the kibosh on it. No overexertion for this future star, thank you.

"I still have my reports on him from back then," Boles said. "I put down 'Franchise-type first baseman. Offensive force. Multiple Gold Glove winner.' "

Call Boles prescient. In 2001, Adrian exploded, hitting .312 with 17 home runs and 103 RBIs in 127 games for the Class A Kane County Cougars in Geneva, Illinois. He won the Midwest League's MVP honors and the Marlins' Organizational Player of the Year award. He continued his power surge in 2002 with 17 homers and 96 RBIs at Double-A Portland (Maine). But that August, he suffered a wrist injury that required off-season surgery and sapped most of his pop the following season, when he hit just .269 with five home runs and 51 RBIs at two different minor league levels.

Worried about Adrian's future power and desperate to make a second-half playoff push, the Marlins packaged him in a July 2003 trade to the Texas Rangers for reliever Ugueth Urbina, who eventually helped wild card Florida shock the mighty 101-win New York Yankees in the World Series that fall.

Suddenly, Adrian had become expendable trade bait—a still-valuable commodity bubble-wrapped in question marks. It was a terribly frustrating year for the twenty-one-year-old.

"There were a lot of times of doubt and wondering what was going to happen," he said.

Ironically, as Adrian's career suddenly entered a stage of whitewater rapids, his love life was enjoying smooth sailing. In January 2003, he married Betsy Perez, his teenage sweetheart. Adrian and Betsy had met at Bonita Vista Middle School in Chula Vista, but it certainly wasn't love at first sight.

"At the beginning, Adrian was always trying to go out with her," Edgar Gonzalez recalled. "She had a boyfriend and was always standoffish."

Eventually, the Gonzalez charm won out. Adrian and Betsy became an item, even though they attended separate high schools. For Betsy's graduation ceremony, Adrian spent some of his signing bonus on a plane that flew overhead towing the message: "I love you, Betsy. . . . Congratulations."

"He was pretty romantic," Edgar said.

Early in the 2003 season, newly married and facing a professional crisis as he struggled at Triple-A Albuquerque, Adrian felt an uneasy emptiness in his heart. He had been attending Baseball Chapel services for a while, but faith in Jesus Christ hadn't yet sprouted in his heart.

Betsy was a believer, though, and the couple's desire to build their marriage on a strong spiritual foundation spurred Adrian. They began attending Bible studies outside the ballpark. Baseball Chapel sermons started penetrating his soul. And in April 2003, he repented and turned to Christ.

"It's been a blessing since," he said.

Adrian's spiritual rebirth didn't immediately resolve his baseball struggles. He made his major league debut with the Rangers on April 18, 2004, but with Mark Teixeira firmly entrenched at first base, Adrian shuttled back and forth between the parent club and the minors three times before Texas shipped him to his beloved Padres in a six-player deal in January 2006.

Adrian finally caught his big break later that year when Ryan Klesko, San Diego's incumbent first baseman, suffered an early season shoulder injury. Adrian grabbed opportunity by the throat, hitting .304 with 24 home runs and 82 RBIs in his first full regular season. The Padres made the playoffs in 2006, and Adrian's slashing swings flummoxed St. Louis pitching at a .357 clip during a four-game National League Division Series loss. Just like that, the Padres had a hometown hero.

"Now, looking back, I'm grateful for everything that happened because it made me a stronger person and made me understand you have to leave it all up to Christ and His path for you," Adrian explained. "If everything would've been gravy and you breeze right through the minor leagues and make it to the big leagues, you don't see the need for God. It really allowed me to see that, no matter what, my focus has to be on God."

In hindsight, the trade that sent Adrian from Texas to San Diego goes down as one of the best in Padres history. With 161 home runs, 501 RBIs, three All-Star selections, and two Gold Gloves in five seasons, he became arguably one of the three greatest position players in franchise history, alongside Hall of Famers Tony Gwynn and Dave Winfield.

Aside from his baseball prowess, Adrian was marketing gold—a well-respected Latino playing in a diverse metropolis just across the Mexican border.

"He was very popular," longtime Padres chaplain Doug Sutherland remembered. "Being Hispanic and [the team being] close to the border, he was a great influence among the people who are Latin. Everybody had a Gonzalez jersey. He was highly thought of in the community."

One of the greatest thrills of Gonzalez's career was playing on the same team as Edgar. "That was a lot of fun," Adrian said of competing with his brother. "It was a dream come true playing in San Diego."

Inevitably, the dream had to end. Baseball economics aren't sympathetic to small-market teams like San Diego, which often can't afford to retain their young stars once they become eligible for free agency. So rather than watch Adrian walk away after the 2011 season and get nothing in return, the Padres traded him to Boston for a trio of highly regarded prospects.

"You don't make a trade like that without knowing pretty much what you're going to get," former Boston manager Terry Francona said. "We gave up a lot of good players for one really good player, but it is nice to see it in person. You read all the scouting reports and certainly you know about him, but when you see him every day, it's pretty exciting."

Welcome to Beantown, Adrian.

FAME, FORTUNE, AND THE FISHBOWL

The proud old building at 4 Yawkey Way in downtown Boston is not exactly holy ground. But for baseball nuts, it might as well be. This is where the pilgrims sojourn.

Awash in green paint and vivid memories, Fenway Park opened its doors on April 20, 1912—five days after the *Titanic* sank. The revered baseball shrine drips with history like a brimming bowl of clam *chowdah*. Here is where the Sultan of Swat—Babe Ruth—launched his first moon shots, where Lefty Grove added to his trove of pitching victories, and where the double-play combination of Joe Cronin and Bobby Doerr was magic up the middle. It's where the Splendid Splinter—Ted Williams—hit .406 in 1941, where Carl Yastrzemski was Triple Crowned in 1967, and where Carlton Fisk waved it fair in 1975.

The stories this creaky New England cathedral has generated have tiptoed between reality and mythology for generations. From Bridgeport to Bangor, young and old alike tell its tales each year at bars, on fishing piers, and in living rooms. Venerable Fenway, the oldest stadium in the majors, is the nerve center of Red Sox Nation.

And now it's Adrian's personal playground.

Playing in Boston is a far cry from anything Adrian was used to before. Despite his sublime stretch in San Diego, he never achieved top billing on Major League Baseball's marquee. Not even the great Tony Gwynn, his childhood idol, could do that. A mediocre franchise history, small-market budget, near-perfect weather, and too much surf and sand all conspire to keep the Padres in baseball's roadside motel.

Boston, meanwhile, enjoys the penthouse suite. Thanks to the New England Sports Network, a regional cable company that is partially owned by the Red Sox and reaches four million homes in the six-state New England area, the team is flush with cash. Consider: In 2011, the Padres' payroll was a skosh below $46 million. Boston's was $161 million.

On April 15, 2011, Adrian officially tapped into those riches, signing a massive seven-year contract extension that will pay him $21 million a year starting in 2012. That's a lot of beans, even for Beantown.

"Remember," Edgar told his little brother after the deal was completed, "that the money is not yours. It's God's. He gave it to you. It's a bigger stage for you to glorify Him."

"Yeah, I know," Adrian said. His tone wasn't haughty. It simply reflected a heart that was already prepared for such bounty.

"At the end of the day, you're not taking any of that with you," Adrian acknowledged. "When you pass away, God's not going to say, *Oh, that's a great contract you acquired.* He's going to say, *Because of Me, you had that contract, so what did you do with it?* There's nothing I've obtained or done that hasn't been because of Christ."

Still, all that money brings expectations by the truckload. In breezy San Diego, baseball is often an afterthought. In Boston, Red Sox fanaticism borders on clinical. This, after all, is a place that blamed eighty-six years of playoff futility on the fabled curse of a barrel-chested slugger with pipe-stem legs nicknamed "The Bambino."

When Red Sox Nation pays a superstar that much coinage, it expects results. Everything about Boston's amiable "Next Big Thing" will be scrutinized like never before. Fair or not, Adrian was expected to slay the Yankees single-handedly and ensure Boston's third ticker-tape parade since 2004. But hey, no pressure, right?

"There is *no* pressure," Adrian said, straight-faced. "I've said all along, people talk about pressure, but who are you trying to satisfy? If you're trying to make the writers or the front office or certain people happy, then you can put pressure on yourself. But for me, it's being good for Christ, so my statistics don't matter."

Fair enough. But they matter to everyone else in Boston.

Entering the 2011 season, the city was abuzz with talk of what Adrian could do with Fenway's cozy corners: *If he posted great numbers in cavernous*

Petco Park, just think what he could do to the Green Monster!

Can you blame them? Adrian is a 6-foot, 2-inch, 225-pound hitting marvel who uses his lovely-as-a-Monet stroke to spray the ball to all fields.

Adrian's new teammates got caught up in wide-eyed curiosity, too. Early in the season, they would often stop and stare at the novelty and beauty of his pregame batting-practice swings.

"He's so fun to watch," Red Sox catcher Jarrod Saltalamacchia exclaimed. "He's so smooth. It's just a beautiful swing. Number one is obviously still Griffey," he said, referring to Ken Griffey Jr. "Griffey's swing was the most beautiful swing ever made, but Gonzo's is right there, man."

Still, considering the fact that Adrian underwent right shoulder surgery in October 2010, only extreme optimists would have predicted what actually transpired in 2011. By the All-Star break, he was unquestionably the best hitter in baseball, leading the majors with a .354 batting average, 77 RBIs, 29 doubles, and 214 total bases. His 128 hits at that point were the most by any player in Red Sox history—more than Jimmie Foxx, Nomar Garciaparra, Manny Ramirez, Jim Rice, Carl Yastrzemski, and, yes, even the great Ted Williams.

"He can ruin your day really quick," said San Francisco reliever Jeremy Affeldt, who faced Adrian when the latter played for San Diego.

While Gonzalez has always possessed power, it was his first-half batting average that induced awe. At the break, it was a whopping 70 points higher than his career average and 50 points higher than his single-season best of .304 in 2006.

You can attribute that to "smaller ballparks" like Fenway, as Adrian modestly does. Or you can say he benefited from hitting in a lineup that featured names like Ellsbury, Ortiz, Pedroia, and Youkilis. But the fact is, Adrian is maturing as a hitter, too, and the great ones perform on the game's biggest stages. They don't call him A-Gone for nothing.

"He uses the whole field," Francona said. "A lot of power hitters, like David Ortiz [Boston's designated hitter], they're going to take some of the field away from him. That's okay because that's the way [David] hits. Gonzo can manipulate the bat. You don't see that with power hitters that much. He can loft the ball to left field. Sometimes, it looks like a right-handed hitter, which is impressive."

The fireworks continued at the All-Star Game in Phoenix, Adrian's fourth straight Midsummer Classic. In the Home Run Derby, he launched 30 bombs and finished second to the Yankees' Robinson Cano. In the All-Star Game itself, his blast to right-center off Phillies star Cliff Lee accounted for the American League's lone run in a 5–1 loss.

Adrian tailed off a bit in the second half of the season, losing the batting title in the last week of the season to Miguel Cabrera. He finished 2011 batting .338, despite being one of the few lefties in the game today who warrant a defensive shift from opposing teams. Even though the Red Sox swooned in September and lost a nine-game lead in the AL wild card race to Tampa Bay, Adrian's long-term deal gives BoSox fans hope for another run at the Yankees.

"Everybody was just going crazy over him in Boston," said Dennis Eckersley, the Hall of Fame closer turned Red Sox TV analyst on the New England Sports Network.

While fame and fortune have kicked down Adrian's front door, his Christian faith has steadied him. He challenges himself by reading C.S. Lewis and fights pride by studying C.J. Mahaney's book *Humility: True Greatness*.

"He's really unimpressed with fame," said Doug Sutherland, the Padres' chaplain. "He shies away from it. He doesn't like to talk about it. If you try to talk about something, he'll change the subject. He knows where it belongs."

Adrian knows scripture and even injects biblical reminders into his at-bats. Every so often, he steps out of the batter's box and eyes his bat, a 35-inch, 32.5-ounce piece of lumber from the Trinity Bat Company. It's more than a between-pitches habit. His bat is inscribed with "PS27:1," a reference to his favorite Bible verse, Psalm 27:1: "The LORD is my light and my salvation—whom shall I fear? The LORD is the stronghold of my life—of whom shall I be afraid?"

Adrian is the antithesis of the stereotypical, modern-day superstar. He is quiet and unassuming. He looks you in the eye when speaking to you. And he's a bit of a homebody. Nightlife isn't his thing. He and Betsy "just like to hang out at home, hang out with our dogs, and maybe cook up a meal," he said.

"He's very easygoing, almost a little bit of a disarming figure," Red Sox chaplain Bland Mason commented. "You expect to have this giant personality with his skills, but he's pretty laid-back."

Fishbowl, schmishbowl.

A LIGHT IN BOSTON

"Watch this."

Adrian's eyes dance with mischievousness. It's July 2011, and Boston is in Baltimore for a three-game weekend series against its AL East foe. Game time is still three hours away, and Adrian wants to display a fun little clubhouse ritual he has.

"Jacoby!" he yells.

His teammate, All-Star center fielder Jacoby Ellsbury, doesn't respond. He's talking to a team public relations assistant.

Adrian tries again: "Jake!"

Ellsbury looks over.

"Say it loud and proud," Adrian says noisily. "Who's the man?"

"Je-*SUS*!" Jacoby bellows.

Adrian grins, satisfied. He explains that Miles McPherson, his pastor at San Diego's Rock Church, near his off-season home in La Jolla, does the same thing with the congregation during sermons.

"So I had Jacoby listen to it, and he loves it," Adrian says. "So now he'll yell it at me, and I'll yell it at him."

Baseball clubhouses aren't exactly church choir lofts. Foul language, raunchy humor, and lewd music are often the soundtrack *du jour* of locker rooms. In this dark environment, Adrian winsomely shines the light of Jesus.

His teammates, by all accounts, have responded at every stop. In San Diego, he once used his bilingual abilities to encourage a Spanish-speaking teammate to attend chapel ("If Adrian hadn't brought him, I don't think he'd be coming," Sutherland said), and he also helped save another teammate's marriage by pointing him to Sutherland for counseling.

"From that, this couple became Christians and have a great walk with the Lord," Sutherland said. "That's the kind of influence Adrian has. He's watching. He'll get guys to come to chapel and get counsel and encourage them. He's an influencer in that way. He's not aggressive in the sense of making people uncomfortable with Christianity. With his success, people listen, but they also listen because of his character."

After Adrian met Mason during his first Red Sox spring training in 2011, he immediately asked the Boston chaplain what his spiritual vision for the team was and offered to lead Bible studies on road trips. During the first half of the season, he led his new Christian teammates in a book study of Mahaney's *Sex, Romance, and the Glory of God.* (The previous year in San Diego, he led a book study of Jerry Bridges' *The Pursuit of Holiness.*)

During the 2011 season, he also helped organize Boston's first Faith Night in at least thirty years. Adrian, Saltalamacchia, outfielder J.D. Drew, and reliever Daniel Bard all shared their testimonies with the crowd after a game.

Adrian's presence has been "a big uplift," Saltalamacchia said. "That's kind of where we struggled as a team [before]. We've had some guys who have been in the faith, but Bible studies have been four guys or three guys. When he came in, we talked about it, and . . . he's delivered every bit of it. He's getting Bible studies on the road, he's getting Bible studies at home, and he's getting Faith Night in Boston. He's different, man—he's different than anybody else."

"He's done more than any other player that I've been around," Mason added. "He's earned instant credibility, and he's just a consistent guy. He doesn't shove Christ down people's throats, but he wants to share with all his teammates. He's a leader in the clubhouse, both as a player and a Christian."

Adrian is active in the community, too. In August 2008, he launched the Adrian & Betsy Gonzalez Foundation, which helps underprivileged youth. And in 2011, he donated a thousand dollars to Habitat for Humanity for every home run he hit. He has been involved with several other San Diego area charities, and he's planning to expand his generosity into New England.

AN EXAMPLE TO FOLLOW

Who knows . . . right now, somewhere in Boston, a trio of fun-loving brothers could be playing bedroom baseball with Adrian Gonzalez trading cards. If so, here's a tip, kids: Don't worry about bending those card corners. Just mimic this man—both his swing and his faith. He is greatly blessed by God and greatly blessing others.

"God has put me in a situation where I have a big platform to profess Christ to people, so I've got to take advantage," Adrian said. "He's given me abilities to play this game, and I'm grateful for that. I do the best I can with them, and in return, try to be the best disciple I can for Him."

6

JOSH HAMILTON:
BASEBALL'S BAT MAN COMES
BACK FROM THE BRINK

Yankee Stadium in New York City has witnessed its share of historic events.

Babe Ruth hit the first home run in the ballpark on Opening Day in 1923. Lou Gehrig, after playing 2,130 consecutive games and being diagnosed with a deadly illness, delivered his "Luckiest Man on the Face of the Earth" speech in 1939. Pitcher Don Larsen threw a perfect game during the 1956 World Series. Roger Maris hit his sixty-first home run to break Ruth's record for most dingers in a season. One-handed pitcher Jim Abbott tossed a no-hitter in these fabled confines in 1993.

But perhaps no performance was more awe-producing than when Texas Rangers slugger Josh Hamilton stepped into the batter's box for the 2008 Home Run Derby. On baseball's biggest stage, the first-year All-Star came up big. No, make that huge.

From his first swing, the people packed into the stadium knew they were witnessing something special.

"Are you getting this?" a fan asked his buddy, who was videotaping the action on his cell phone.

"I am," his friend shouted back. "This is big-time."

The rules for the Home Run Derby are simple. A player doesn't have to swing at every pitch. But if he does swing, the ball had better leave the yard. Any swing that doesn't produce a home run counts as an out. Ten outs and the round is over.

Some of baseball's most powerful hitters have left the batter's box with a goose egg. That wasn't the case for Josh.

Bending his knees a couple of times and breathing deep to relax, Josh sent ball after ball into the dark New York sky.

One, two.

Teammate Ian Kinsler ran over to wipe Josh's face with a towel after he crushed his second home run at 502 feet. The two shared a laugh before Josh got back to work.

Three, four, five, six, seven, eight.

Almost immediately, New York's fickle-yet-intelligent fans started chanting his name.

"Ham-il-ton, Ham-il-ton, Ham-il-ton!"

The bat became a blur in his hands. *Nine, ten, eleven.*

With every swing of his arms and snap of his wrists, Josh hammered another ball into the stratosphere. Low pitch. *Smack.* A towering home run into the second deck of right field. *Number twelve.* High pitch. *Crack.* A line drive home run that zoomed over the fence into a fan's glove. *Number thirteen.*

Josh smiled at his pitcher. Being an All-Star and hitting in Yankee Stadium may have been new to him, but seventy-one-year-old Clay Council was a familiar face. Council often threw batting practice for Josh during summer baseball when he was a teen in North Carolina. Now Council was watching Josh live up to all the promise he saw in the youngster years before.

Fourteen, fifteen, sixteen. Pretty soon Josh's opponents turned into cheerleaders. David "Big Papi" Ortiz laughed and pointed as yet another ball jetted over the fence. *Seventeen, eighteen, nineteen.*

Ridiculous. Like guided missiles, every ball found its target in the right field bleachers. Pretty soon Josh started laughing. Nobody had ever hit like this before. *Twenty, twenty-one, twenty-two.*

"What's the record?" a fan said.

"I have no idea," his friend answered.

The answer was 24. Bobby Abreu set that mark in the first round of 2005's Home Run Derby in Detroit's Comerica Park.

But it wasn't just Josh's total that amazed. It was the magnitude of his drives. Three of his home runs sailed over 500 feet—the longest estimated at a massive 518 feet.

Yankee Stadium started feeling like a party. Fans sensed history was taking place. Competitors shook their heads and smiled. Would it ever end? At one point, Josh hit thirteen home runs in a row. *Twenty-three, twenty-four, twenty-five!*

Rangers teammate Milton Bradley ran up and gave the slugger a little back massage. Josh was hot. Incredibly hot. Fans began bowing down to Josh in mock worship.

He still had two outs left. *Twenty-six, twenty-seven, twenty-eight.* Finally, his last two hits fell short of the fence. Fellow All-Star Michael Young gave Josh a hug. Sportswriters started saying fans had just witnessed twenty of the most exciting minutes in the history of baseball.

Before walking into Yankee Stadium on July 14, 2008, Josh was a relatively unknown center fielder for the Rangers playing in his first full major league season. Stepping out of the batter's box, Josh effectively introduced himself to the baseball world. Actually, maybe it's better to say he *reintroduced* himself to baseball.

A long battle with drug and alcohol addiction had nearly erased Josh from baseball's memory. With twenty-eight swings, Josh announced he was back.

But more important to Josh than the media attention was the opportunity to talk about the difference Jesus Christ had made in his life. Before, his life had been all about baseball. Now it focused on Jesus.

ONE GOAL

Just nine years before this historic night, baseball was abuzz with talk about Josh. As a 6-foot, 4-inch, 205-pound senior at Athens Drive High School in

North Carolina, Josh was a can't-miss prospect. A five-tool player.

He could play outfield, first base, or pitch. He hit for power and still had a stunning batting average. And his arm in the outfield made opposing coaches think twice before trying to score a runner from second base.

During his senior year, Josh hit .529 with 13 home runs and 35 RBIs in 25 games. He struck out just seven times all year, while drawing 26 walks. His speed in the outfield allowed him to track down would-be base hits in the gap. He also stole 20 bases.

And pitching? His 95-mph fastball baffled hitters and amazed professional scouts. Josh tallied a 7–1 record his senior year with 91 strikeouts in just 56 innings.

At some games, more than fifty scouts would crowd together to watch the two-time North Carolina Player of the Year show off his talents on the diamond.

Not that Josh was a showoff. Sure, he knew he was the best player on the field every time his size-19 cleats stepped onto the turf. But he stayed humble and didn't mock the opposing team.

It was Josh's humility that most impressed Dan Jennings, the Tampa Bay Devil Rays' director of scouting in 1999. That spring, Jennings traveled to Raleigh to watch Josh play in a home game for Athens Drive. Nearly sixty scouts watched wide-eyed as Josh crushed a home run well over four hundred feet.

"But that wasn't the amazing thing," Jennings said. "After [Hamilton] returns to the dugout, he comes back out and serves as the batboy for his teammates. And there was this mentally challenged kid [on the team], and Josh was treating him like his best friend."

Josh and Ashley Pittman were friends. Pittman had Down syndrome. At first, a high school baseball star and special education student might have seemed an unlikely pair. But both shared a love for baseball. Pittman worked as the team batboy, and Josh was impressed with his dedication to the game. Pittman rarely missed a practice, never missed a game, and always came looking professional in his team uniform.

The two often ate lunch together. Pittman called Josh by his nickname, "Hambone," and Josh referred to his friend as "Big Ash."

Big Ash was devastated when Athens Drive lost in the state semifinals during Josh's senior year, but the Jaguars' coach had a surprise at the year-end banquet. He was starting a special award to honor the player who best showed what the qualities of compassion and sportsmanship are all about.

The first winner of the Ashley Pittman Award was . . . of course, Josh Hamilton.

"I've gotten a lot of trophies over the years, but the Ashley Pittman Memorial Award is special to me," Josh wrote in his autobiography, *Beyond Belief*. "It's still prominently displayed in a case at my parents' house. More than any other trophy or newspaper clipping, it reminds me of who I was and how I lived at that point in my life."

Talent. Statistics. Size. Character. It was no surprise that Tampa Bay chose Josh with the first overall pick in the 1999 draft.

More than fifty family members, friends, and reporters were gathered at the Hamiltons' home on June 2 when Josh got the call from Jennings. With his selection, Josh became the first high school player to go number one since Alex Rodriguez went first in 1993.

"We've watched him for a long time," Tampa Bay general manager Chuck LaMar said. "Josh Hamilton withstood every test that we gave him, whether it be his performance on the field or questions we asked. . . . We feel like he's the number-one player in this draft."

Josh felt like he was the top player, too. It wasn't pride. Josh had worked hard to get the most out of his God-given abilities, and he was ready to make his mark on the major leagues.

After learning he was the first selection, he hugged his mom and dad. His father, Tony, had coached him from before he could attend school. His parents had rarely missed a game, often driving hundreds of miles to make it for the first pitch.

Then the giddy eighteen-year-old walked into his front yard for his first press conference. When asked how he envisioned his career, Josh replied: "I'm thinking three years in the minors, then fifteen years in the big leagues." Josh paused for a moment before adding, "Then I'll have to wait five years to get into the Hall of Fame."

Everyone laughed, but Josh really wasn't kidding. He'd always felt special on a baseball field. He'd always had one goal—being a baseball All-Star.

People recognized Josh's talent when he was very young. He was just six when a scout came to watch him for the first time. Okay, maybe the word *scout* isn't quite right.

Josh was practicing with his brother Jason's eleven- and twelve-year-old team. Despite being half their age, Josh kept up with and often surpassed the older players with his baseball skills. The president of the Tar Heel League needed to decide what to do with the precocious elementary student who played like a middle schooler.

Playing with kids his own age certainly wasn't a challenge. Josh could hit farther and throw faster than any of his teammates. His skills were so advanced that other parents asked if Josh could be moved up because they were worried their sons could be hurt by one of Josh's hits or throws.

"Their fears became real in our first game," Josh wrote in *Beyond Belief.* "I fielded a ball at shortstop and threw it across the infield as hard as I could to get the runner. There was a problem, though—the first baseman either never saw the ball or didn't react fast enough to catch it. He stood there with his glove turned the wrong way as the ball smacked into his chest. He went down like a sniper got him. . . . I felt terrible."

Shortly after, Josh was promoted to his brother's team. He turned seven on May 21, 1988, making him five years younger than his opponents.

But his talent bridged the gap. Batting ninth, Josh made his presence felt on the Hamilton Machine Little League team by hitting his first real home run. Just two weeks after Josh turned seven, a twelve-year-old pitcher learned an important lesson: Don't throw Josh a fastball over the plate. The youngster cracked it over the left-center field fence.

It was the first of many home runs to come.

ON THE RIGHT PATH

When Josh hits a baseball, it just sounds different. The speed of his swing combined with the impact of the bat draws *oohs* and *aahs* from onlookers.

After Josh's post-draft celebration, he jumped into the car with Jason and went to the high school field to hit some baseballs.

A family with two young boys lived in a house beyond center field. They often watched Josh play games or take batting practice. On that evening, the father and his two boys walked up to the backstop.

"I didn't expect you'd be out here tonight," the dad said. "But I can always tell when you're hitting. It just sounds different inside my house when your bat hits the ball. From the first crack of the bat today, my boys said, 'Josh is hitting.' "

Josh's hitting impressed the Devil Rays as well. They signed him to a contract that included a $3.96 million signing bonus—a record at the time for a No. 1 pick. And despite the fact that Josh had a fastball that nearly reached triple digits, Tampa Bay wanted him to play outfield so he could hit every day.

With the major league season already under way, Josh was assigned to Tampa Bay's Class A Rookie League team in Princeton, West Virginia.

Josh had just turned eighteen, so he hopped in the car with his parents and drove to Princeton. In his first game, on June 19, 1999, Josh hit his first professional home run.

With his mom making sure her son had clean clothes and remained well fed, and his dad talking through at-bats and situations, Josh stayed fully focused on baseball.

Sure, the other rookies didn't have their parents traveling with them. But the other players probably weren't as close to their families and didn't have the means (i.e., nearly $4 million) that allowed them to come along.

Josh lived up to his hype in Princeton. In 56 games, he hit .347 with 10 home runs, 48 RBIs, and 49 runs scored.

Tampa Bay bumped Josh up to Class A Hudson Valley in New York in August. Instead of playing against rookies, he now faced second- and third-year professionals.

Hudson Valley was in the middle of a playoff race, and Josh was placed in the middle of its lineup. After struggling at first, he turned things around and helped the Renegades win the New York–Penn League championship by hitting .429 with two home runs and eight RBIs in the playoffs.

His rookie year had been a success. But during the season and back at home, he felt something was missing in his life. He had occasionally attended church with his aunt and uncle growing up, so he knew something about God. When he returned to North Carolina, he visited his aunt and uncle's house to discuss some spiritual issues that he was wrestling with. He ended up praying to accept Jesus Christ into his life.

"I got saved when I was eighteen years old," Josh said. "I accepted Christ in my aunt and uncle's living room. But I didn't know how to grow spiritually. I didn't know how to get in the Word. I didn't know how to pray like I needed to. I didn't know how to fellowship with other people. I tell people that Satan comes after you a lot harder when you're a child of God."

Everything seemed to be going according to Josh's plan professionally when he reported to Tampa Bay for spring training in 2000. He had a strong spring and was assigned to the Class A Charleston RiverDogs in the South Atlantic League. Many of these players were more experienced, with three or four years of minor league baseball under their belts.

Again, Josh's parents came with him. They were at every home game, even showing up early to watch batting practice. They traveled with the team for road games, staying in the team's hotel. And Josh continued to flourish. Surrounded by people he loved and playing the game he loved, he was named co-MVP of the South Atlantic League. He was also honored as the Player of the Year in Class A baseball, and the Devil Rays named him their Minor League Player of the Year. Check out his stats: a .301 batting average, 13 home runs, 61 RBIs, and 62 runs scored.

Going into the 2001 campaign, Josh appeared to be ready to make the leap to the Big Show. If he wasn't going to be with the big league club to start the season, he certainly seemed destined to join the Devil Rays soon. But in a split second, everything changed.

ACCIDENTS AND BAD DECISIONS

On March 3, 2001, Josh and his parents were driving to their home in Bradenton, Florida, following an exhibition game. His mom, Linda, was behind the wheel of the family's Chevy Silverado, while Josh half-dozed in the front seat and his dad sat in the back. As the family drove through the intersection of Victory Road and U.S. 301, a dump truck ran a red light and barreled into the driver's side of the pickup.

Josh saw the whole thing about to happen and reached over to pull his mom to him. The impact sent the Hamiltons spinning in their truck for about a hundred feet.

The family was rushed to Memorial Hospital. Linda had neck pain. Tony was treated for a skull fracture. Josh had some pain in his back but was untreated and went back to spring training the next morning.

Over the next few days, however, the pain got worse. Doctors were baffled. They performed MRIs and CAT scans to diagnose the problem. Prescription painkillers didn't help much. Physically, everything looked fine, but Josh felt anything but okay.

With his parents recovering in North Carolina and playing baseball not an option, Josh started hanging out in a tattoo parlor.

He had shown up that spring with six tattoos. His first ink featured his nickname "Hambone" in all capital letters around his right bicep. Soon the word "Hammer" graced his other arm. He didn't have many friends in

Florida, and without baseball, he didn't have anything to do, so pretty soon Kevin and Bill in the tattoo parlor became his "friends."

Josh would show up at the tattoo parlor and spend hours in the chair—sometimes getting two or three tattoos in a day.

The nineteen-year-old had six tattoos when his parents went to North Carolina. When they returned a few weeks later, he had twenty-one.

With doctors not finding a cause for his pain, Josh felt pressure to play. He was sent to Double-A Orlando to start the season, but he struggled. In 23 games, his stats were the worst of his professional career. He hit just .180 with no home runs and only four RBIs.

To make things worse, Josh tore his hamstring muscle running to first base in the first month of the season and was sent down to Charleston for an injury-rehabilitation assignment.

Josh's leg healed, but his back never felt right, so Tampa had him see a specialist in California. After doing an MRI, the doctor pointed to a white spot near the spine. It was a pocket of fluid pushing against a nerve. The doctor gave Josh a cortisone shot on the exact spot.

"He plunged the needle into my spine till it felt like it was grinding on bone," Josh said. "But as soon as the needle was removed, the pain was gone. I've never thanked a man so many times in my life."

Sporting a healthy back and renewed optimism, Josh headed into the 2002 season with something to prove. According to his timeline, this was the year he was supposed to break into the majors. Shortly after Christmas, he went to Florida to start training. He knew he had to make up for a disappointing year in 2001.

But one afternoon, he injured his back while training. The next morning he could barely get out of bed. Spring training was less than two weeks away. Depressed and disappointed, Josh returned to the comfort of the tattoo parlor.

His collection of ink continued to grow. Soon, he had a total of twenty-six tattoos. After hanging at the parlor one afternoon, Kevin and Bill asked Josh if he wanted to go out when the shop closed. Without thinking, he immediately said yes.

They took him to a strip club and ordered Josh a beer. He was still too young to legally drink and had never consumed alcohol before, but he downed that beer and a few more. Later, the trio went to Kevin's house, where Josh was offered some cocaine.

A little drunk and not thinking straight, Josh inhaled the drug.

"I had a lot of 'firsts' that night," Josh said. "[The cocaine] gave the adrenaline rush that I wasn't getting by playing baseball."

At first, when Josh was playing baseball, he didn't do drugs. But as in so many cases, soon the drugs took over. For the next three and a half years, drugs and alcohol ruled Josh's life.

Despite being plunged into a personal darkness, the light of his talent shined through from time to time.

Playing Class A ball for Bakersfield, California, during 2002, Josh produced a few highlights that have become things of legend. One evening, he hit an opposite-field home run in Sam Lynn Ballpark that smashed a digital display so hard that it stopped working—kind of like in the movie *The Natural*. Years later, the display still hadn't been fixed and was covered by a banner that promoted the team's website.

Josh also described a mammoth home run he hit that traveled 549 feet and landed in the Kern River. And another time, Josh showed his arm was still a weapon when he caught a fly ball on the warning track and threw to home plate, nailing a runner who had tagged up at third and tried to score.

But Bakersfield was also the first place Josh used drugs during the season. After 56 games, his numbers weren't bad—he hit .301 with 9 home runs, 44 RBIs, and 23 runs scored. Elbow pain caused Josh's season to end early. Surgery in Alabama and rest in North Carolina cured the elbow pain, but not the drug problem.

Josh was using cocaine nearly every day while rehabilitating his injury with the Triple-A Durham Bulls. He knew there was a possibility of being randomly drug tested, but even when he was asked to do one, he remained in denial. The test came back positive, and Josh was suspended from baseball for the first time.

Subsequent failed tests led to even longer suspensions until on March 19, 2004, Josh was suspended from baseball for one year for failing to comply with the MLB drug policy. Another failed drug test in August led to additional penalties.

In all, Josh played no professional baseball from the end of the 2002 season through most of 2006. Instead, he fell deeper into the darkness of drug addiction.

Not that everything was bleak in his life. During streaks of sobriety, he struck up a relationship with former high school classmate Katie Chadwick.

"Everybody knew who Josh was in high school," Katie said. "Everybody had a lot of respect for him, because he never did anything wrong."

Three years after graduating from high school, Josh was doing plenty of things wrong, but he called her out of the blue. She agreed to let him come to her house, and they ended up dating for three months. They broke things off but got back together in July 2004. Five months later, they were married.

Josh was attending Alcoholics Anonymous meetings and had convinced himself and Katie that his addictions were behind them. He had a slipup in January, but then on his twenty-fourth birthday, Josh went on a bender that led to a series of relapses.

Josh pulled himself together when the couple's first daughter, Sierra, was born on August 22, 2005. (Katie had another daughter from a previous relationship.) But three days later, Josh went to Walgreens to pick up his wife's prescription and ended up at a bar instead.

Over the next six weeks, he spent more than $100,000 on drugs.

By this time, Josh had turned to crack cocaine to get the high he used to get from the powder form of the drug. But while the highs were higher, the lows were lower.

Numerous times, Josh felt as if he might die—like his heart might thump its way out of his chest. He was never violent with Katie, but his erratic behavior caused her to get a restraining order against him. Trips to the emergency room weren't uncommon. Almost all of his nearly $4 million signing bonus was gone.

His life spiraled down until one night Josh found himself high, out of gas, and walking down a two-lane road.

"I was a shell of a human, a soulless being," Josh said. "I had stripped myself of self-respect and lost my ability to feel love or hope or joy or even pain."

On October 1, 2005, Josh showed up at his grandmother Mary Holt's house . . . at around two in the morning. He weighed 180 pounds and was almost unrecognizable.

"I was a wreck—dirty, twitchy, and barely coherent," Josh said. Granny's house had always been a place of refuge for Josh growing up. He'd even kissed Granny, as Josh affectionately called her, on the cheek before playing every baseball game growing up. Now, when he had nowhere else to turn, he went to his grandmother's. She fed him and tucked him into bed.

Within a couple of days, Josh was using crack again—this time in Granny's house. After just five days under her roof, the seventy-two-year-old had seen enough. She confronted Josh in the hall.

Of course, Josh had seen and heard it all. He'd been in and out of eight rehabilitation centers, spent days on counselors' couches, and talked for hours with his father, mother, and wife. But there was something in the way that Granny looked at him with a mixture of sorrow and anger that pierced Josh's heart.

"I went back in the room where I'd just been using drugs, grabbed a Bible, and the first verse I read was James 4:7," Josh said, referring to the verse that says: "Humble yourselves before God. Resist the devil, and he will flee from you" (NLT).

At that moment, Josh recommitted his life to Christ. Unlike the first time he prayed to accept Christ, this time he followed through with action. His life began to change as he started reading his Bible, praying, and going to church with his aunt and uncle. Then a few weeks later, on the advice of her pastor, Katie called Josh and told him she forgave him.

BEING SECOND

After more than twenty-four years of putting himself first in his life, Josh had put someone new on the throne: Jesus Christ.

Josh started living and eating right. And God began restoring everything that Josh had nearly destroyed. He quickly gained back the fifty pounds of muscle he'd lost. His family rallied to his side. He reconciled with his wife. He started working—good, honest work with his brother's tree service.

Then on June 20, 2006, Josh got the call reinstating him to Major League Baseball.

Amazingly, after abusing his body for years, his skills hadn't diminished. He played 15 games for Hudson Valley that summer—the same Class A team he'd played for in 1999—with solid results. He hit .260 and scored seven runs.

One day that December, when he was trimming trees for his brother, Josh learned that the Cincinnati Reds had acquired him through the Rule 5 draft.

Instead of languishing in the minor leagues like he probably would've done with the Rays, guidelines in the Rule 5 draft required the Reds to give him the opportunity to make the big league club. And Josh wasn't about to ruin his second chance.

Josh became one of the Reds' best hitters in spring training. He batted .403 and made Cincinnati's roster as the fourth outfielder behind Adam Dunn, Ken Griffey Jr., and Ryan Freel.

On Opening Day, Josh received nearly as big an ovation as Griffey. The fans were immediately drawn to him and his story of overcoming addiction. Josh has said many times that standing on a major league field again—with his family, his parents, and his wife's family in the stands and everybody on their feet—nearly brought him to tears.

But he wanted to be a professional, so he fought back the lump in his throat. Like Tom Hanks said in the movie *A League of Their Own*, "There's no crying in baseball."

A week into the season, Josh got his first start and rewarded the Reds with his first major league hit—a home run. By the end of the month, Josh was named National League Rookie of the Month.

"Baseball is third in my life right now, behind my relationship with God and my family," Josh said at the time. "Without the first two, baseball isn't even in the picture. Believe me, I know."

The twenty-six-year-old rookie hit nearly .300 in his first season. He did end up on the disabled list twice during the year, once for a stomach ailment and once for a sprained wrist. He played eleven games at Triple-A Louisville, but he stayed clean the whole time—much in part due to Cincinnati manager Jerry Narron's brother, Johnny.

Johnny had coached Josh when he was a teenager in North Carolina. The Reds hired the faithful man of God as their video coordinator and gave him the extra responsibility of keeping Josh accountable on the road.

Proving he could play at the big league level, Josh ended the 2007 season with a .290 batting average, 19 home runs, 47 RBIs, and 25 runs scored.

That off-season, though, Cincinnati traded Josh to Texas. The Rangers needed power in the outfield, and Cincinnati needed pitching. Johnny Narron came along, too, as an assistant hitting coach.

Texas fans and his new teammates immediately embraced Josh. He responded with monster numbers. Batting third for the Rangers, just ahead of Milton Bradley, Josh had 95 RBIs by the 2008 All-Star break.

In his first full major league season, Josh was voted onto the All-Star team and made history at the Home Run Derby.

Before the derby, Katie prayed that Josh would hit at least one home run. He did much better than that. A lot of people were praying that night, including Josh and Council, who knelt down and prayed for God to be with them before stepping on the field for the first round.

And God answered big-time. All people remember from that July night in Yankee Stadium were Josh's 28 bombs in the first round. They don't remember that Justin Morneau beat Josh 5–3 in the finals. But Josh didn't care about losing—he'd already won because his story was being told on TV screens around the world.

"God has given me such a platform to share what He's done in my life," Josh said. While he was in one of the darkest, most drug-riddled parts of his life, he said, "My wife was telling me that God was going to allow me to get back into baseball. But it wasn't going to be about baseball. It was going to be about sharing how He brought me through the storm."

Josh stayed healthy the entire season, notching some impressive statistics. He hit .304 with 32 home runs, 130 RBIs, and 98 runs scored.

In the off-season, Josh wanted to prepare for an even better season in 2009. He went to Arizona to work out a month before spring training. But on January 21, 2009, he fell into old habits. Josh went into a restaurant that had a bar and ordered a drink.

"I was out there for three weeks and stopped praying, stopped doing my devotions, stopped reading the Word, stopped fellowshipping with my accountability partner," Josh said. "Doing all those things that had got me to where I was. I thought I could have one drink. And that thought doesn't work out too well with me. One leads to about twenty, and I don't remember half the stuff I do. . . . Immediately, it hit my heart why I'd done those things, and it's because I took God out of first position."

Josh woke up the next morning and immediately called his wife and told her what happened. He called the Texas Rangers. He called Major League Baseball.

News of Josh's escapade didn't surface for seven months, but when it did, the revelations included several rather risqué photos of him and three young women in the bar. Josh didn't shy away from the controversy of being an outspoken Christian who had just shown up in some compromising photos. He addressed it head-on.

"I'm embarrassed about it for my wife, Katie, for my kids, and for the organization," Josh wrote in a press release. "I'm not perfect. It's an ongoing struggle, and it's real. It's amazing how these things can creep back in. But I am human, and I have struggles."

Josh flew home right after the incident in January to get things right with his wife and with God. For her part, Katie knew things would be okay the moment Josh came in the house.

"When he walked in the door, and I [saw] how broken and repentant and remorseful he was, and how he was so upset at himself for the sin and for hurting me, I was just encouraged because I was looking at a transformed man," she said. "It just made it so easy to extend that grace to him again."

In the past when Josh had relapsed, his attitude was, *Oh well, I might as well keep doing it.* But now Josh was different. He was committed to God, to his family, and to staying clean.

He redoubled his efforts to keep Christ first in his life through a multilayered support system that was described by the *Dallas Morning News* as "rooted in his Christian beliefs and his rigorous daily devotions. Its primary components are his wife, his parents, and a host of 'accountability partners' that includes a Texas Rangers coach, pastors from three churches, his Christian sports agent, and his father-in-law."

Josh knew he was weak when he counted on his own strength, but he found power in the Holy Spirit to live according to God's commands.

The 2009 season proved to be forgettable for Josh, although the Rangers showed improvement by posting an 87–75 record. Injures limited him to just 89 games, and his statistics suffered accordingly. His batting average dropped to .260, and he hit just 10 home runs and drove in only 45 runs.

Despite his subpar year, Josh had an All-Star off-season. He and Katie made more than thirty appearances around the country, speaking about redemption and forgiveness through their foundation, Triple Play Ministries. Their ministry also hosted Christian sports camps, did community outreach, and helped support an orphanage in Uganda.

Early in the 2010 season, it was obvious that the Rangers and Josh were going to have a special year. In June, the team posted a 21–6 record—its best month in the franchise's fifty-year history.

By August, Josh had distinguished himself as the definitive choice for American League Most Valuable Player. He led the league in batting average at .362, slugging percentage (.634), and hits with 161. Tom Verducci pointed out on SI.com that the last three players to bat over .360 with a slugging percentage of more than .600 while playing center field were Mickey Mantle, Stan Musial, and Joe DiMaggio. That's not bad company.

Verducci went on to describe a mid-August performance by Josh: "Just another night in the life of the best player in baseball went something like this: smash four hits all over the park; a single to left, a 440-foot bomb to center, a single and double to right; score from third base on a pop fly to deep shortstop/short left; score from second base on a ground ball to second; make a diving catch on the warning track and a leaping catch against the center field wall; cause the third-base coach to halt a runner from scoring from second on an otherwise routine run-scoring single to center field."

Being called the "best player in baseball" certainly felt better than being labeled one of the most disappointing No. 1 draft picks of all time. Josh was finally living up to his potential.

Despite missing nearly all of the final month of the regular season with broken ribs, Josh helped Texas reach the playoffs with a 90–72 record. His gaudy 2010 statistics looked like this: a .359 batting average to go with 32 home runs and 100 RBIs.

Things were going great for Josh and the Rangers. But late in the season, on one of the best nights in team history, Josh was noticeably absent. It was September 25, 2010, and Texas had just clinched its first American League

West title in more than a decade with a 4–3 win over Oakland. But instead of celebrating with his teammates, Josh chose to be alone.

It's a long-standing baseball tradition for teammates to spray each other with champagne after making it to the playoffs. Josh didn't want any part of the alcohol. He didn't even want it to touch his skin—it had caused that much pain in his life.

A few weeks later, on October 12, after Texas defeated Tampa 5–1 to advance to the American League Championship Series, Josh's teammates made sure he was part of the festivities. They grabbed him, gave him some eye goggles, and walked him into the clubhouse.

"Everybody yelled 'Ginger ale!' and I just jumped in the middle of the pile and they doused me with it," Josh said. "It was the coolest thing for my teammates to understand why I can't be a part of the celebration, and for them to adapt it for me to be a part of it says a lot about my teammates."

The Rangers faced the Yankees in the next round for the right to play in the World Series. Right away, Josh showed the Yankees that things would be different this time. He hit a three-run home run to open up the series.

When Texas won the second game 7–2, it broke a ten-game losing streak against New York in the playoffs. The Rangers eventually defeated the Yankees in the series, four games to two, to advance to the World Series for the first time in team history.

In the Fall Classic, the Texas offense struggled against San Francisco pitching, and the Giants claimed the title in five games.

About a month later, Josh won the American League Most Valuable Player Award. His 22 first-place votes and 358 points easily outdistanced Detroit's Miguel Cabrera's 262 points.

In February 2011, Josh was rewarded with a two-year, $24 million contract that included a $3 million signing bonus. He backed it up by hitting .298, knocking 25 home runs, and driving home 94 runners during the 2011 season, when the Rangers advanced to the World Series for the second straight year.

Josh nearly proved to be the hero of the Fall Classic when his two-run, tenth-inning home run in Game 6 put Texas just three outs away from its first world championship. The St. Louis Cardinals, however, rallied to tie the game in the tenth and win it in the eleventh on David Freese's dramatic walk-off home run. Even though the Redbirds went on to win the title in seven games, the Rangers proved they were among the game's elite teams.

In a similar fashion, Josh has made it to the top of the major leagues. His path hasn't been straight—as with the Israelites wandering through the desert, it took him awhile to find the Promised Land. But Josh has said many times that he wouldn't change his past.

"Could I have reached people being that clean-cut kid coming out of high school?" Josh asked rhetorically during an interview. "Probably so. How many more people can I reach having tattoos, having an addiction problem? I've been through that. . . . And I've come back."

His comeback has inspired countless people who are fighting their own demons to give their lives to God. Josh's message to them is simple: *Put God first.*

"One thing I can't live without is, obviously, Jesus," Josh said. "When I don't put Him first, my decisions don't work out too well for me."

The Hall of Fame may still be well into the future, but with Jesus first and his priorities firmly in place, Josh Hamilton is finally on his way.

7

STEPHEN DREW:
GOOD THINGS COME IN THREES

Countless boys across America dream of being major league stars one day. But not many actually feel *pressure* to become one.

Welcome to Stephen Drew's world.

When you're a prep star whose two older brothers were both drafted in the first round, pressure to reach The Show is inevitable. Stephen, the Arizona Diamondbacks' shortstop, was fourteen years old when Cleveland selected his middle brother, Tim, out of high school with the twenty-eighth overall pick in 1997. One year later, St. Louis chose Stephen's older brother, J.D., out of Florida State at No. 5.

"I always got compared," Stephen said.

Stephen was born on March 16, 1983—four and a half years behind Tim and seven and a half years behind J.D.—in Hahira, Georgia, a nondescript nook off I-75 near the Florida border. Never heard of it? Well, scan the map for neighboring towns like Adel, Barney, and Cecil, and you can't miss it. Honest.

With a population of roughly sixteen hundred during Stephen's youth, Hahira had one stoplight, a Main Street, and an old-time city hall. It's the type of place where the town barber knows your name, honeybee festivals draw a big crowd, and the collective twang in conversations sounds like competing steel guitars.

"It's growing a little," Stephen said in his sleepy Southern drawl. "Now we've got some eating restaurants—you know, the kind of little hole-in-the-wall places."

Like most brotherly trios, the Drew boys were a rough-and-tumble bunch. Sports and skinned knees ruled the days. The boys enjoyed baseball, basketball, football, hunting, and fishing. As long as the activity was outdoors, it made the cut.

But baseball was king. J.D., the quiet brother, a 6-foot, 1-inch lefty, was a power-hitting monster who became a two-time consensus All-American and the national Player of the Year in 1997 at Florida State University. Tim, the outspoken one, was a 6-foot, 1-inch righty with a blazing fastball who landed a professional contract without stepping foot in college.

As baseball mentors go, Stephen couldn't have asked for much more.

"Tim could throw the fire out of a ball," said Stephen, whose personality is a mixture of his brothers. "He was always a pitcher. It helped us out. He always threw harder than what I could hit. [J.D.] is the one who taught me to hit left-handed."

Stephen followed J.D. to Florida State, where he starred for three years after turning down a $1 million offer from Pittsburgh out of high school. He earned *Baseball America*'s college Freshman of the Year award in 2002 and *Collegiate Baseball*'s second-team All-America honors in 2004. When Arizona took him fifteenth overall in 2004, the Drews became the first sibling trio in major league history to be drafted in the first round.

"[Stephen] saw all that with us and continued to work hard," Tim said. "For him, he was never awestruck by anything because he's like, 'All right, I belong.' That's a God thing. God prepared him for something special."

God had been preparing Stephen's heart for a long time. His parents, David and Libby, raised their sons at Bethany Baptist Church, a dirt-road mile from the Drews' five-acre property. The family was at church every Sunday morning and Wednesday night.

By age nine, Stephen started realizing that good morals and his family's faith weren't good enough to appease a holy God. One night in bed, as he lay awake staring at the ceiling, all those Sunday school lessons and meaning-of-life questions started really percolating:

Did God really create the universe?

Why am I here?

Are heaven and hell real?

Was Jesus really who He says He was?

That night, he submitted himself to Christ.

"God speaks in different ways," Stephen said, "and that's how He spoke to me."

His faith came in quite handy after he was drafted. With hard-line negotiator Scott Boras as his agent, Stephen sat idle through yearlong contract talks. By April 2005, eager to play ball somewhere—*anywhere*—Stephen signed with the Camden (New Jersey) Riversharks of the independent Atlantic League.

Six weeks later, just minutes before a signing deadline would have sent him into the next draft, he finally agreed to terms with Arizona. Boras hailed him as the next coming of Alex Rodriguez. Talk about pressure.

But if Stephen felt any, it didn't show. He spent the next year feasting on minor league pitching before an injury to Arizona's starting shortstop, Craig Counsell, prompted his big league call-up in July 2006. For the rest of the season, Stephen looked like a seasoned veteran, hitting .316 in 59 games. A star had been born.

"Talent-wise, he's the most talented [of the Drew brothers]," Tim said in 2006.

But baseball, like life in general, can be a bumpy ride. After undergoing LASIK surgery that November, Stephen suffered through a season-long sophomore slump in 2007 (.238 batting average in 150 games) before exploding in the playoffs (.387) as the Diamondbacks reached the National League Championship Series. He rebounded in 2008 to hit .291 with 21 home runs and 67 RBIs in 152 games, but he has struggled to reach that level since.

The 2011 season looked like it could finally be the year everyone had been expecting from the youngest Drew. By the end of April, he was hitting

.321 and appeared to be on track for his first All-Star Game appearance. But he slumped miserably over the next two and a half months.

Then disaster struck.

In a game against Milwaukee on July 20, Stephen suffered a gruesome, season-ending ankle fracture. As he slid into Brewers catcher Jonathan Lucroy at home plate, Stephen's right foot appeared to catch underneath him and twist violently, contorting about 100 degrees from its normal position. The video replays were enough to make even Gumby cringe.

Stephen had surgery the next day. While he finished the year with a cool .252 average, Arizona caught fire and won the NL West crown. The unwanted midseason vacation, though, allowed him to be there for his wife, Laura, during the birth of their second son, Nolan.

"Stephen is disappointed that he can't be out there to be helping the team make the drive to the playoffs, but at the same time he understands that the Lord is the one who directs his steps, like it says in Proverbs 16:9," Diamondbacks chaplain Brian Hommel said following the injury. "Stephen doesn't know why he got hurt, but he is okay with that because it has put his faith to the test, and a faith untested cannot be trusted."

Overall, Stephen's career has been solid, if unspectacular. Judged against his brothers, he currently falls ahead of Tim and behind J.D. on the scale of major league success.

Tim played eleven pro seasons overall, including parts of five in the major leagues, compiling an unsightly 7.02 ERA in 35 games with Cleveland, Montreal, and Atlanta from 2000 to 2004. He underwent surgery for a torn labrum in his right shoulder in January 2006 and retired at age twenty-nine after a failed comeback attempt with two independent league teams during the 2007 and 2008 seasons.

J.D., meanwhile, has struggled to live up to the billing of a top-five draft pick. Yet the oft-injured outfielder has still enjoyed an enviable career. Through 2011, he had played in fourteen big league seasons with four teams, hitting 242 career homers. He finished sixth in NL MVP voting in 2004, made an All-Star appearance in 2008, and has been to the playoffs eight times. In 2007, his first-inning grand slam in Game 6 of the AL Championship Series against Cleveland was a pivotal moment in Boston's drive to its second World Series title in four years.

Stephen would love to experience playoff euphoria like that. But whatever happens in his career, he finds great comfort in his faith.

"Things don't always go your way," he said. "People sometimes get a wrong perspective of Christians—like it's always easy [for us]. It can be the total opposite. But with Jesus sitting there with you, He can hold your hand through things. He's there with you. You might not be able to see it now, but you can look back and see He's got His hand on you the whole time. He's with me every day."

Stephen's value is perhaps seen best off the field. He has become a spiritual leader in the Diamondbacks' clubhouse—a guy who isn't shy about telling his teammates like it is. But his unique relational skills help temper his boldness.

"He's not afraid to call guys out a little bit," Hommel said. "It's often in a fun way, but he wants guys to move in their journey and become closer to Jesus. He's never been ashamed of that, but now he has more say in the clubhouse, and he doesn't jam it down anybody's throat."

Maybe one day the former first-round draft pick will become an All-Star, or win a Gold Glove, or reach the World Series. For Stephen, though, life isn't about living up to other people's expectations. It's about loving God.

More than anything, the youngest of Hahira's talented baseball brothers is taking his cues from Jesus' exhortation in Matthew 5.

"It's my job to be a witness," Stephen said, "and to be salt and light to the earth."

8

JEREMY AFFELDT:
SOLUS CHRISTUS—BY CHRIST ALONE

Sitting in his office, David Batstone stared at his computer screen in disbelief.

This is a hoax, he thought. *One of my staffers is pulling my leg. There's no way a major leaguer really sent me an unsolicited e-mail.*

Still . . . what if? Batstone, an avid San Francisco Giants fan, couldn't help the initial surge of excitement as he read the message. It was late November 2008, and twenty-one months had passed since he had cofounded Not For Sale (NFS), a San Francisco Bay Area nonprofit that aggressively fights worldwide human trafficking and slavery. Public awareness of his project was growing slowly, but its gritty subject matter didn't exactly attract your average, charity-minded major leaguer.

Then again, Jeremy Affeldt is not—in any way—your average major leaguer. So there it was, an e-mail from Jeremy—or whoever was posing as him—sitting in Batstone's inbox only days after the veteran reliever signed a two-year, $8 million contract with the Giants. The e-mail expressed interest in meeting with Batstone in person and learning more about NFS.

Being a business professor at the University of San Francisco and a man of reason, Batstone scanned the e-mail again, scrutinizing the typed message for any signs of trickery. Then he checked with his NFS staff: *Okay, who's the jokester?*

But it was no joke. The e-mail was real.

The two men met in San Francisco soon thereafter. Before leaving, Jeremy cut a $10,000 check for an NFS-created medical clinic/rescue center in Thailand that cares for former child slaves. He also pledged a hundred dollars to NFS for every strikeout he recorded during the 2009 season. (He finished with 55.)

Just like that, Batstone had a celebrity advocate that most charitable organizations only dream of. "It shocked me that he had some sort of awareness about what we do," Batstone said.

In today's age of wealthy, prima donna professional athletes, Jeremy is indeed unique. At first glance, he appears to be just like any other modern star. He blogs and tweets. He sports body art, frosted surfer hair, sideburns down to his earlobes, and a long, vertical strip of hipster chin hair.

But there's plenty of substance with the style. If he had pitched seventy or eighty years ago, during the Depression era, one could envision young newsboys heralding his stark distinctiveness on busy street corners:

"Extra! Extra! Read all about it: Professional Athlete with a Soul

Patch, Tattoo, and No College Education Is an Intelligent, Articulate, Well-Read, and Theologically Grounded Force for Worldwide Gospel Proclamation and Social Reform!"

The "dumb jock" label dies hard. But Jeremy breaks—no, pulverizes—stereotypes with a faith-in-action sledgehammer. He crosses the often-great divides between elite athleticism, strong theology, and Christlike activism with a rare combination of grace, knowledge, and vision.

His public ministries of choice are revealing, too. Lots of pro athletes do charity. But few wade into the filthiest depths of humanity to shine the light of Jesus Christ like Jeremy does.

Put it this way: How many other pro athletes zealously work to stop forced child labor in Peru? Or the child sex slave industry in Asia? Or the use of the mentally handicapped for pornography in Romania?

How many sports celebrities fund the construction of orphanages in Uganda? Or get emotional when they hear the sound of running water from an African well they helped construct? Or seek to ignite the humanitarian flames of an entire next generation? Jeremy is a walking, talking embodiment of James 1:27 and 2:26, which speak of the faith-empowered good works Christians are to embrace.

Oh, and by the way, he's a mighty good pitcher, too.

"God is showing me how justice is a big deal to Him," Jeremy said. "He's all about righteousness and justice. Jesus said, 'I came to set the captives free.'"

REBELLION AND TRANSFORMATION

So how exactly does one become a Jeremy Affeldt? Were there any "Road to Damascus" moments? Any angelic visions at night or heavenly voices in the wilderness?

Not really. There was just a bunch of spiritual confusion, a bad apocalyptic movie, and a discerning basketball coach.

Okay, so that's a bit of a sweeping generalization. Let's rewind a bit and fill in the gaps.

Jeremy was born on June 6, 1979, the younger of two kids in a military family. David Affeldt, Jeremy's father, was an Air Force captain whose job kept the family bouncing around to Arizona, Minnesota, various parts of California, and Guam before finally settling in Spokane, Washington, during Jeremy's high school years.

All that moving exposed the Affeldts to a lot of different types of churches—Baptist, Evangelical Free, and non-denominational, to name a few.Jeremy's mom, Charlotte, grew up Southern Baptist, and David grew up Lutheran. It was quite a religious stew for a young man to digest.

Jeremy uttered the Sinner's Prayer at age five but admits he didn't understand what he was doing. At age twelve, he "re-upped" after being spiritually rattled by a 1970s movie about the end times.

"It had a guillotine," Jeremy recalled. "It tried to scare you to death—[like religion was] a fire insurance policy deal." His theological waters were getting muddy.

By the time he was an upperclassman at Northwest Christian School in Colbert, Washington, Jeremy was a confused kid with a rebellious streak.

One day during his junior year, he started teasing a girl before English class. Another classmate, Larisa Walker, a particularly spunky gal with sandy blond hair, had grown tired of Jeremy's antics. In front of everyone, she stood up and shouted, "I'll never marry a guy like you!"

(Insert the sound of crickets chirping in an otherwise awkwardly silent room.)

Jeremy's bad attitude worsened. During basketball season, his head coach suspended him from a Christmas tournament after he drew a technical foul for mouthing off at a referee. One more tech, his coach said, and he'd be thrown off the team.

While Jeremy watched the next game in street clothes, an assistant coach, Jim Orr, took a seat beside him. "We need to talk," Coach Orr said.

Coach Orr gave Jeremy a few books and met with him frequently, helping him work through his anger and connect the spiritual dots.

Initially, Jeremy's motive for personal growth was simply to stay on the team. But God's Spirit was at work. Soon, Jeremy came to a true awareness of the gospel and his need for a Savior. He repented and placed his faith in Christ. His understanding of God and Christianity changed. So did his life.

Spiritual fruit immediately began to blossom. Jeremy apologized to girls at school whom he had offended. Those thudding sounds echoing through the Northwest Christian hallways were classmates' jaws hitting the floor.

One girl who noticed the change was Larisa Walker. Yes, *that* Larisa Walker. As first impressions go, Jeremy hadn't exactly wowed her. But now he was different. Where before she saw pride, anger, and sarcasm, she now saw humility, kindness, and empathy.

One day, Jeremy and Larisa were walking through the school gymnasium at the same time. It was chapel day, so they were both dressed up. No one else was around.

"You look really nice today," Jeremy said.

Larisa was stunned. "Oh," she stammered, "you do, too."

Seeing daylight, Jeremy took a chance: "We should go out sometime," he said. She dismissed the suggestion with a laugh, but Jeremy was undeterred. He persisted until she said yes—despite the advice of a close friend who, like Ananias with the recently converted apostle Paul in Acts 9, was skeptical of the authenticity of Jeremy's transformation.

On their first date, Jeremy and Larisa went to a local park, sat on a blanket, and talked for hours. By the time they were seniors, the two were having great conversations, especially about religion. Jeremy's family, despite playing church hopscotch, was conservative. Larisa, meanwhile, came from a charismatic background.

"We were seventeen years old and debating theology," Larisa recalls. "I don't know if he would've asked those questions if he hadn't started dating me. It made us both grow through the years."

As Jeremy was maturing spiritually, he was dominating athletically. He enjoyed basketball, but baseball was clearly his future. He could do things on a pitching mound that opponents were powerless against. So in 1997, three days before his eighteenth birthday, the Kansas City Royals drafted him out of high school in the third round.

The Royals immediately shipped Jeremy to their Gulf Coast League rookie team in Fort Myers, Florida. He was barely old enough to vote, a relatively new believer, and marooned nearly three thousand miles from home in a very worldly environment. It was a recipe for spiritual disaster.

Yet God protected Jeremy. He found a good church, started reading a chapter of the Bible a day, and marveled at how God revealed Himself in powerful ways. In some ways, it mirrored Paul's post-conversion trip to Arabia (Galatians 1)—a time of spiritual strengthening before public ministry.

"It's amazing how God became alive to me," Jeremy said. "I chose to become a professional athlete, and He ordered my steps."

MARRIAGE AND THE MINORS

Distance—that demanding proving ground for all romantic relationships—only strengthened Jeremy and Larisa's bond. While he toiled in the minors, she completed a two-year interior design degree at two community colleges in Washington. But he missed her, and she missed him. When he came home for the off-season, the time together never felt long enough.

In February 1999, Jeremy took Larisa to a basketball game at their alma mater. The Northwest Christian gym was buzzing with fans. The fact that many of the couple's family members and closest friends were there didn't register with Larisa.

At halftime, the public address announcer encouraged the crowd to stay seated for a blindfolded three-point shooting contest. The winner, he said, would take home a big-screen TV. Four contestants were called onto the floor. Larisa was the last.

After she finished shooting, she removed her blindfold to see Jeremy on one knee, holding a ring and a big sign that said, "Larisa, will you marry me?" The brash girl who once publicly announced, "I'll never marry a guy like you!" was now shouting, "Yes!" before hundreds of onlookers. Nine months later, they got married.

"He always jokes that it was a challenge, that he'd make sure I'd have to take it back," Larisa said of that day in English class.

The following spring, reality broadsided newlywed bliss. Entering his fourth pro season, Jeremy was assigned out of spring training to the Royals' Class A affiliate in Wilmington, North Carolina. It was a tough season for someone who expected to be playing in a higher league. Jeremy went 5–15 on the mound. Money was tight on a minor league salary, so Larisa got a job as the director of a children's equestrian camp. The couple shared a three-bedroom apartment with two other players.

"That was interesting," Larisa recalled.

Despite his poor stats, Jeremy was moved up to the Royals' Double-A club in Wichita, Kansas, for the 2001 season to see what he could do. This time, he and Larisa rented their own apartment, but the place was a dump. When Larisa first saw it, she cried. For furniture, they had a bed, a sofa, and some plastic furniture. They watched TV on a nine-inch screen.

To make ends meet, they both worked off-season jobs at a chain of furniture stores owned by Larisa's father in the Spokane area. It certainly wasn't the stereotypical glamour lifestyle of pro baseball, but the couple was enjoying life together. "This is fun," they would often tell each other, for reassurance. "It's just the two of us. This is an adventure."

Adventures are all well and good—for a time.

The fact is, Jeremy's faith was being tested acutely. By 2002, he was still just a middling prospect. His first five minor league seasons had been so nondescript that his 2001 season at Wichita (10–6 record, 3.90 ERA in 25 starts) qualified as his best year. He asked God hard questions and struggled for faith.

Then, like manna from heaven, success rained on him. That spring training, Jeremy had a fantastic outing during a game in Bradenton, Florida. The Royals' brass took note. So did *Kansas City Star* columnist Joe Posnanski, now a senior writer at *Sports Illustrated*.

Posnanski immediately started waving the Affeldt banner in his articles for the *Kansas City Star*. Here's how Posnanski described it years later, in a *Sports Illustrated* story on October 24, 2010, a day after Jeremy and the Giants clinched the National League pennant in Philadelphia:

> *Jeremy Affeldt.*
>
> *We go way back.*
>
> *We go back to a day in Bradenton, Fla., this had to be 2002, a boring spring training game, nothing happening, when suddenly the Kansas City Royals put in this kid, this mediocre prospect named Jeremy Affeldt.*
>
> *Nobody knew anything about him. He'd put up only decent numbers in Double A. The scouts yawned. I yawned. And then . . . he started pitching. And jaws dropped. Ninety-five mph fastball. Electric Barry Zito-like curveball. What the heck was this?*
>
> *Suddenly the scouts stood up straight. The Royals general manager at the time, Allard Baird, started leaning forward, and leaning forward more, until he was practically on the shoulder of the guy in front of him. Affeldt threw two innings. He struck out five. The other batter fouled out.*
>
> *As a scout said: The kid ain't Koufax. But for two innings in Bradenton, Koufax couldn't have been any better.*
>
> *So, I was hooked. I became the biggest Jeremy Affeldt fan around. Affeldt is convinced that my columns in the Kansas City Star got him his big-league job, and because of this he credits me with his career.*

Said Jeremy: "In 2002, I wasn't even supposed to make the big leagues. Joe Posnanski wrote a story that sent all of Kansas City into a buzz. Every time I pitched, he wrote a great story [about me]. Even my wife said, 'I always like reading what he writes about you.' Those stories out of spring training put more and more pressure on the front office. I always tell him thanks."

Jeremy made the Royals' 2002 opening day roster and debuted on April 6. With five seasons on the farm that felt like ten, the 6-foot, 4-inch, 230-pound lefty was still only twenty-two years old.

He had finally arrived in the major leagues—out of nowhere.

MAJOR RELIEF

Jeremy's four and a half years in Kansas City had all the noteworthiness of a rain delay. The Royals were mostly atrocious during that time, posting 100-loss seasons in 2002, 2004, and 2006 to mark their worst five-year stretch since the franchise debuted in 1969. In 2005 alone, the team had three managers—Tony Pena (fired after starting the season 8–25), Bob Schaefer (replaced 17 games later), and Buddy Bell.

Personally, Jeremy battled a rash of injuries and never fully established himself as a starter or closer in K.C. At the 2006 trade deadline, the Royals shipped him and his 4.77 career ERA to Colorado in a four-player swap. It was a breath of fresh, Rocky Mountain air.

"Getting traded was something I prayed for every day in Kansas City," he admitted. "I didn't hate it, but I just needed a change."

The Rockies converted Jeremy to full-time relief duty and worked with him to correct several mechanical flaws in his delivery. In 2007, he enjoyed the finest year of his career to that point, posting a 3.51 ERA, including a miniscule 1.74 ERA at hitter-friendly Coors Field. But the best was yet to come.

On September 15, during the stretch run of the 2007 season, the Rockies were 76–72 and six and a half games behind National League West leader Arizona. Their postseason chances seemed to be slipping away. Then they went on one of the hottest streaks in major league history, winning 21 of their next 22 games as they snatched the NL wild card, swept Philadelphia and Arizona in the playoffs, and reached the franchise's first World Series.

Jeremy was crucial to Colorado's success. After allowing a home run to Phillies slugger Ryan Howard in Game 2 of the NL Division Series, he settled down and finished the playoffs with six scoreless appearances. Alas, mighty Boston swept Colorado in four games in the World Series. Still, it was an underdog story for the ages.

"We were a Cinderella team—one of those runs they think will never happen again," Jeremy said.

Cashing in on his success, Jeremy signed a one-year, $3 million deal with Cincinnati, where his role mostly frustrated him and he never really warmed to the city. But God continued to bless him. Jeremy threw a bunch of innings (78), set a new personal best with a 3.33 ERA, and caught the eye of the Giants, who handed him a sweet two-year deal in the off-season.

In 2009, Jeremy enjoyed a career year, earning MLB.com's Setup Man of the Year Award with a 1.73 ERA in 74 games. He credits much of his success to former Reds teammate David Weathers, who helped transform Jeremy from a four-seam to a two-seam pitcher by teaching him a nasty sinker.

"It gets me out of a lot of jams," Jeremy said. "If I was there in Cincinnati just to learn my pitch, that's my journey. Now I'm a ground ball pitcher, and I've been pretty effective with it since."

The 2010 season, however, was tough for him. Jeremy missed 23 games with a left oblique tear, battled a nagging hamstring injury, and disagreed with manager Bruce Bochy about his bullpen role. His ERA ballooned to 4.14, and he posted his highest WHIP (walks plus hits per innings pitched) since 2006 at 1.60.

But by November 3, when ticker tape was showering Jeremy and his teammates as they paraded through downtown San Francisco as the 2010 World Series champions, that all felt like ancient history. Thanks to a late-season collapse by San Diego, the Giants and their well-named "torture" offense had overcome a six-and-a-half-game deficit in late August to win the NL West division title.

In Game 6 of the NL Championship Series against Philadelphia, Jeremy faced the biggest outing of his career. With San Francisco leading the series three games to two, Jeremy relieved starter Jonathan Sanchez in the third inning with two men on and no outs in a 2–2 game. Antacid tablet, anyone?

Not for Jeremy, thank you. He shook off a season's worth of difficulty by shutting out the Phillies for two innings in the series-clinching 3–2 win. Nine days later, the Giants claimed their first World Series championship since 1954 with a five-game win over Texas.

"It was amazing," Jeremy said with a grin.

The 2011 Giants missed the playoffs, but Jeremy enjoyed great personal success. He posted a 1.15 WHIP (the lowest of his career) and a 2.63 ERA (the second-lowest of his career), and he held opponents to a .207 batting average. His ERA after the All-Star break (1.21) was visible only by magnifying glass.

But the good times were cut short . . . literally. On September 8, 2011, a Thursday off-day, Jeremy was grilling in the backyard with Larisa and their two young sons when he badly lacerated his right (non-throwing) hand with a paring knife while trying to separate frozen burger patties. His pinkie suffered nerve damage that required season-ending surgery.

Jeremy could've wallowed in bitterness or self-pity. Instead, he chose to celebrate God's kindness and protection, especially the fact that the knife didn't damage any tendons and missed his throwing hand altogether.

And then there was this: The severed nerve was directly underneath a main artery. It was almost like the artery had miraculously moved out of the knife's path. Jeremy's hand surgeon said he had never seen anything like it.

"I don't know what you believe in," the doctor told Jeremy, "but keep believing in it."

In the days that followed, Jeremy purposefully pressed in spiritually to see what God wanted to teach him through the ordeal.

"God sees and He knows," Jeremy said shortly after the injury. "We choose our course, but He orders my steps. He's already seen the end of my life. He already knows. He knows how to heal my body.

"Now it's like, *What do You want from me right now? Do you want me to be more of a family man? Do You want me to spend more time with my team-mates in a different scenario?* I'm constantly asking and learning and believing. When these things happen, do you have enough trust in Almighty God to believe He knows why it happens? Where do you grow? How do you increase in maturity in Christ through these things?"

"THIS IS MY PATH"

In Luke 4, we read the story of Jesus entering a synagogue on a Sabbath in His hometown of Nazareth. Before a rapt audience of devout Jews, He opened a sacred Old Testament scroll and read from the book of Isaiah:

> *"The Spirit of the Lord is on me, because he has anointed me to proclaim good news to the poor. He has sent me to proclaim freedom for the prisoners and recovery of sight for the blind, to set the oppressed free."* (LUKE 4:18)

These words resonate with Jeremy—perhaps more deeply than with most folks. But why?

Why does Jeremy's heart beat so urgently for victims of sex trafficking and child slavery in remote corners of the globe where he's never been? There are a gaggle of other worthwhile charity options out there that aren't so, well, depressing. Yet here he is, diving into the cesspools of a sin-stained world with a life preserver, hoping to rescue flailing souls from the black waters of despair.

"It's really connected to his spirituality and faith in Jesus, for starters," David Batstone of Not For Sale said. "He sees that as part of Jesus' life, not an add-on to the story. That's just who Jesus was. It's not a social gospel distinct from personal faith. It's really linked in a way that's profound theologically."

Or, as Jeremy summarizes: "God has just shown me that this is my path." It's that simple.

The more Jeremy reads scripture, the more he sees how the Savior's heart broke for the lost, the downtrodden, and the helpless. Jesus dined with outcasts and befriended traitors. He touched lepers and forgave harlots. The Son of God loved the world's riffraff.

This affects Jeremy. It rattles him out of self-absorption. His compassionate pursuits are more than just feel-good philanthropy or a box to cross off on the "Public Relations Checklist of a Multi-Millionaire Athlete."

His motivation is intrinsically connected to a keen understanding of the gospel. In conversation, he uses words like *redemption* and *restoration* a lot. The doctrine of vicarious atonement propels him into action. Mercy and grace have changed his life, and he wants others to be liberated as well.

This, of course, all comes from an extensive knowledge of scripture. He quotes the Bible like well-known movie lines. His bookshelves include titles by Tim Keller and other reformed, socially minded Christian authors.

"He's always reading a new book," Larisa marveled. "He's not someone who's going to get stuck in life. He's always going to learn and read and put it into practice. I don't know if I've ever met someone who is so willing to improve himself."

Check out Jeremy's online presence sometime. His blog, entitled "To Stir a Movement: Christian Social Justice," includes mini-treatises on topics like modern-day abolitionism, faith-driven fatherhood, and licentiousness versus legalism. You know, typical blog fare.

His Twitter page, too, is far from the usual tripe. You won't find any entries like "*Stuck in traffic . . . listening to Rihanna*" here. He's a serial tweeter of pithy quotes from the likes of C.S. Lewis, Aristotle, Napoleon Bonaparte, Benjamin Franklin, General George S. Patton, and Winston Churchill. He even sprinkled in a little Steve Jobs before his death.

You could describe Jeremy as a modern-day Renaissance Man, although that would probably be a slight since church theology was pretty screwed up during the Renaissance period. Oh, did we mention that Jeremy is a student of church history, too? He can easily hold his own in conversations about Luther and Calvin.

For proof, check out his left forearm. In May 2011, he got a tattoo that reads *Solus Christus*, a Latin phrase that means "by Christ alone" and represents one of the Five Solas of the sixteenth-century Protestant Reformation. Shortly afterward, he wrote a four-part blog series, totaling 2,086 words, on the meaning of his first tattoo. Nothing in Jeremy's life, not even body art, is done willy-nilly.

"It's like a crest for me—in Christ, I can do the impossible," he said of his forearm ink. "That crest, I put my family under, my children under, and I compete under—everything I do. It made so much sense."

With NFS, which is active on five continents, Jeremy found a worthy vehicle in which to pour all of his faith-fueled intellect and passions. He first heard about NFS through Mike King, the president of Youthfront, a large Christian youth ministry in the greater Kansas City area, during his time with the Royals. Alarmed to learn that human trafficking and slavery exist in the United States, Jeremy wanted to get involved. That's why he jumped at the chance to meet with Batstone when he signed with the Giants.

The two men quickly became fellow soldiers in heady spiritual warfare. In February 2011, Batstone included Jeremy in his inaugural "Montara Circle," an ambitious, two-day think tank of fifty-three business, academic, and non-profit leaders who met in Montara, California, to address various global issues like poverty, HIV/AIDS, water scarcity, and human trafficking. The guest list was teeming with influential movers and shakers, including three billionaires. The invitation spoke volumes about Jeremy.

On day two, the attendees split into smaller focus groups and brainstormed solutions for the rampant human exploitation in a Peruvian area of the Amazon rain forest where NFS runs a children's shelter. Participants then voted on the best idea.

The winning idea was to launch an iced tea company, Smart Tea, that would harvest the drink's unique ingredients from a plant indigenous to the troubled area of Peru, thereby creating local jobs and providing residents with an alternative to selling themselves (or their children) into slavery. Profits from drink sales would then be injected back into the region to boost the economy and infrastructure.

As of the fall of 2011, Smart Tea's investment group, board of directors, and business plan were all being finalized. Guess who helped hatch the winning idea? Yep . . . Jeremy.

"He plays that card—'I'm just a dumb ballplayer here'—but he's totally engaged with world leaders," Batstone said.

Jeremy speaks with his wallet, too. In 2010, he donated more than $20,000 total to NFS. And in 2011, he upped his pledge from $100 for every strikeout to $250, including another $250 for every lead he held. He also got Cardinals slugger Matt Holliday, a former teammate in Colorado, to agree to donate $500 every time he homered in 2011.

That's not all. Thanks to Jeremy's influence, the Giants' home game against Minnesota on June 21, 2011, featured two NFS public service announcements by Jeremy on the stadium video screen at AT&T Park. He also advocates for NFS during the off-season at his home church in Spokane and local colleges. And he is the main spokesperson for NFS' Free2Play initiative, which encourages sports fans to make NFS pledges related to their favorite team.

"Even during the season, he's writing me asking what's going on in Romania," Batstone said. "He's more than just your typical baseball player. He realizes that he has financial and celebrity resources to make this [our work] more effective. The more I've interviewed with major media, the more they say, 'You realize how amazing of a guy you've got there, don't you?'"

Baseball's unofficial ambassador of social justice is certainly fighting the good fight. But he knows the next generation is infinitely more influential than one man. So he created the Jeremy Affeldt Foundation and Generation Alive. His foundation seeks to spread the gospel to youth through camps and mission trips. Generation Alive, meanwhile, is a movement he started to inspire kids and young adults to start changing the world in tangible ways.

In 2011 alone, Generation Alive teamed up several times with Youthfront's "Something to Eat" campaign to host weekend events where young volunteers packaged more than three hundred thousand meals to ship to Africa. Jeremy sees it as a great, practical way to heed the call of Matthew 25:34–40 while inspiring the next generation to action.

"I don't want a program," Jeremy says. "I don't want a youth rally. I want a movement. I want something like Martin Luther King Jr. I want to see a movement of young people who stand up for the kingdom of Jesus Christ, but do it right."

Jeremy also sees Generation Alive as a powerful witnessing tool to socially conscious unbelievers who want to aid a charitable cause but aren't necessarily ready to sit through a church sermon. It's the Pauline principle of 1 Corinthians 9:22: "I have become all things to all people so that by all possible means I might save some."

"They've heard, 'Jesus loves you,' and they usually run from it," Jeremy said. "Jesus loved on people first. He gained a voice in their lives, and when they asked for His view, He gave it to them. He didn't soapbox it right out of the gate. That's my deal with kids. I want to empower them."

Jeremy's bold faith and winsome personality affect the entire Giants organization, too. He is the key organizer of the team's annual Fellowship Day, where church groups are encouraged to attend a game and hear Christian players' testimonies afterward.

In April 2011, when the Dodgers came to town eleven days after the well-publicized assault on Giants' fan Bryan Stow following the teams' Opening Day game in Los Angeles, Jeremy gave a live, impassioned pregame speech to the crowd, imploring them to respect others. It was so powerful that talk radio shows in the Bay Area were talking about it for days, according to Giants chaplain Jeff Iorg.

Within the clubhouse, Jeremy is a chapel leader and a proactive gospel witness among his teammates.

"Jeremy is very approachable, and he has an ongoing relationship with some players who are investigating the Christian faith," Iorg said. "There's really no other shoe to fall. He's a really committed, passionate Christian. He's really living out his faith in the game. There's no *but*."

No, there's no *but*. Just plenty of work to be done to advance God's kingdom in a lost, dying world. So Jeremy rolls up his sleeves—revealing *Solus Christus*, his mantra—and gets to it . . . one pitch, one water well, one orphan, and one slave at a time.

"Jesus came to bring the kingdom of God to earth, because in heaven, there's nothing wrong," Jeremy said. "He came to restore things. He expects us to carry on the restoration process. We have the same spirit in us, but obviously He has a little more pop. But we are image bearers.

"So what can I do? I can help restore life. For me, it's restoration— bringing justice to where injustice is because that's the love that Jesus displayed."

9

MATT CAPPS:
OPENING A ONCE-CLOSED FIST TO GOD

The phone call came just before midnight.

Surprised, Matt Capps picked up. It was his younger brother, Chris.

That's strange, Matt thought. *Chris normally doesn't call this late.*

Chris' voice was different. The news he carried would change the brothers' lives forever.

"Dad fell."

Time stood still. The hands on the clock froze in perpetuity. At least, that's the way it felt to Matt. Like a boxer driven to the canvas by a jarring blow, he struggled to comprehend what just happened.

Matt's father, Mike, had endured plenty of health challenges before. For years, his body had run like a banged-up jalopy, sputtering along life's highway as best it could but needing frequent tune-ups.

This, however, was no tune-up situation. It was the real deal. So Matt and his wife made the nine-hour drive from their off-season home in Sarasota, Florida, to Matt's hometown of Douglasville, Georgia. In the hospital Matt found his father lying in bed, unresponsive.

None of Mike's prior health scares had fully prepared Matt for this. Everything felt surreal. And Matt felt utterly helpless.

Mike wasn't just Matt's father. He was his chief mentor, closest confidant, and best friend. Mike had once coached his son's Little League team. He had pushed his son, sometimes to tears, to achieve the levels of baseball success that Matt couldn't have envisioned. He watched all his son's games—every one—and then waited for the late-night phone call whenever Matt pitched. The two would dissect Matt's performance into the wee hours of the night. Mike was a steadying rudder for his son amid the unpredictable swells of life as a major league reliever.

Then, suddenly, he was gone.

THE GOOD OL' DAYS

Douglasville sure has changed.

For that, the locals can thank the ever-expanding urban sprawl from Atlanta, about twenty miles to the east. Credit also goes to Arbor Place, a four-million-square-foot regional mall that opened in 1999.

But when Matt was born there—on September 3, 1983—Douglasville had a cozy, small-town feel, stemming from its roots as a nineteenth-century railroad town. During Matt's childhood, the downtown district, with its quaint, two-story brick buildings from the turn of the century, felt less touristy and more like home.

Life back then held simple pleasures, like Krispy Kreme doughnut fund-raisers, which Matt's Little League All-Star team held at the local Kmart. Or Friday night family dinners at either PoFolks, the local country kitchen, or Hudson's Hickory House, where six bucks got you some mighty fine barbeque. Halcyon days never tasted so good.

Matt and Chris frolicked away their days outside with a close-knit group of neighborhood buddies. If it wasn't football in their aunt's big backyard, it was baseball in the front. There were plenty of driveway basketball and sandlot baseball games, too. On quieter afternoons, they'd head to the local fishing hole.

"It was sports all the time," Matt recalls. "I don't know about this generation. It's all video games."

In high school, Matt was a stereotypical jock. He played baseball, football, and even ran cross-country as a freshman—not what you would expect from a man now listed at 6 feet, 2 inches and 245 pounds.

But baseball was his favorite. As his skills grew in Little League, so did some gnawing spiritual concerns. Provoked by the example of a Christian coach, young Matt started asking his parents deep questions—the kind that non-churchgoing folks have a tough time answering.

Mike and Kathy Capps were trying hard. Their sons knew the difference between right and wrong, and the boys recited bedtime prayers each night at their parents' behest. But Matt's questions trumped Mom and Dad's theological understanding.

So the Capps family started attending First Baptist Church of Douglasville, where Matt's coach went. At age ten, Matt prayed the Sinner's Prayer and got baptized.

In high school, though, Christianity became like a rosin bag to Matt. He'd pick it up occasionally, whenever the palms of life got sweaty, but he inevitably dropped it to the dirt again. Eventually, his church attendance stopped. By the time he reached the minor leagues, his passions were worldly, and his faith was a wreck.

STEADY RISE TO THE BIG LEAGUES
Matt was always good at baseball.

He starred at Alexander High School in Douglasville and helped Team Georgia win the 2001 Sun Belt Classic, a prestigious prep All-Star tournament in Oklahoma where he played alongside fellow future big leaguers Brian McCann and Jeff Francoeur. Matt signed a National Letter of Intent to play at Louisiana State, but he quickly chose a professional career after the Pittsburgh Pirates drafted him in the seventh round in 2002.

His first stop was Bradenton, Florida, home of Pittsburgh's Gulf Coast League (GCL) affiliate, where he blew away opposing hitters with a 0.69 ERA in 13 innings out of the bullpen. In 2003, he converted to a starter, and the good times kept rolling. Between the GCL Pirates and Class A Lynchburg (Virginia), he finished with a 5–1 record and a 2.13 ERA in 11 starts. He was looking more and more like a seventh-round steal.

Then came 2004.

In his first two months with Class A Hickory (North Carolina), he failed miserably as a starter and didn't do much better in relief—so the Pirates demoted him and his 10.07 ERA to short-season Class A Williamsport (Pennsylvania). He returned to the rotation but continued to struggle, posting a 4.85 ERA in 11 games.

It was Matt's first taste of prolonged failure in baseball. Dejection was a constant teammate. But as bad as life was professionally, it was worse spiritually.

Starting in late 2003, Matt had developed a taste for nightlife. He never did drugs, but he drank . . . a lot. And he now admits his relationships with women weren't biblical.

"It was so empty," he said of his life at the time. "It was not fulfilling."

Church was not on the radar. Neither was scripture or prayer. When his team's chapel leader would enter the room, Matt would bolt in the other direction. Everyone could see straight through his spiritual duplicity—or at least, that's the way it felt to Matt. He was ashamed of his spiraling morals but felt powerless to halt the descent.

It wasn't that Matt had renounced his beliefs or questioned scripture's claims. He just wasn't living like the "new creation" the apostle Paul wrote about in 2 Corinthians 5:17. He was running away from God, looking for a ship to take him to Tarshish. But as Jonah learned, you can't outrun the Almighty.

That off-season, the Holy Spirit started stirring in Matt's heart. By the time he arrived in Florida for 2005 spring training, the pistons of conviction were firing full-bore. The Pirates assigned the twenty-one-year-old to Hickory again to start the season. That's when Matt met David Daly.

David, a longtime minister in the area, was in his first year as the Crawdads' chaplain. David saw a spiritual hunger in Matt, and he took an immediate liking to the young man. Matt felt comfortable around David, too. One Sunday morning early in the season, Matt confided in his new mentor.

"David," Matt said, "I've done a lot of things I shouldn't. Honestly, I've been enjoying them physically, but I know they're not right. I'm not setting a good example for others."

Matt exhaled. It felt so good to confess that to someone! Still, he braced for the hammer of condemnation from David.

Instead, David nodded. He lovingly exhorted Matt to embrace his role as an earthly ambassador of Christ. He told Matt that baseball was a platform for ministry, with nothing less than God's glory at stake.

Matt was all ears. Soon, David asked Matt to become the team's chapel representative. Matt enthusiastically said yes.

But there was much work still to be done. As spiritual warfare raged inside Matt, guilt had entrenched itself deeply in the furrows of his soul. *How,* he wondered, *could God accept a rebel like me? Look at my spiritual rap sheet. My lifestyle has been a complete affront to God's standards. Why should I expect love and forgiveness when my offenses are stacked so high?*

Matt didn't yet grasp divine mercy and grace. So David explained it. He helped Matt see that God sent His perfect Son, Jesus Christ, to cover the overwhelming debt that Matt could not pay. He showed Matt that God's forgiveness was not based on human merit, but rather on the finished work of Calvary.

Matt listened, read scripture, and asked deep questions. Slowly, his myopic view broadened into big-picture understanding. One night following the 2005 season, he was sitting in his bedroom, and—*wham!*—the liberating truth of the gospel hit him.

"That was the first time, really, when I asked Jesus to completely take over my heart," he said. "I had done it at church as a younger kid because I knew it was the right thing to do, but I wasn't sure what I was doing."

David, meanwhile, was enjoying a front-row seat to Matt's transformation.

"He began to take seriously who God had made him to be—a reflection of Christ, not a reflection of Matt," David said. "I don't think that's any small part of his meteoric rise from A ball to the majors."

WELCOME TO THE SHOW

Considering how Matt's 2004 season ended, dreaming of a big league call-up the following year would have been audacious, to say the least. In spring training, the Pirates' organization converted him into a reliever. Matt didn't particularly like the move, but something clicked.

After a virtually unhittable stint at Hickory to start the season, Matt earned an August promotion to Double-A Altoona (Pennsylvania), where he continued his mastery on the mound. In September, he joined Triple-A Indianapolis for the International League Championship Series and threw two scoreless innings in Game 1.

Three days later, barely past his twenty-second birthday, he heard the words every minor leaguer dreams of hearing: "You're going to the big leagues, son." He was headed to Pittsburgh.

The Pirates were in disarray. Ten days earlier, they had fired manager Lloyd McClendon and replaced him with bench coach Pete Mackanin as they spiraled toward a 67–95 record and their thirteenth straight losing season. But Matt didn't care. He had made The Show.

That day—and all its craziness—will forever be etched on Matt's mind. After learning of his promotion at 1:00 a.m., he boarded a plane the next morning for a 9:30 flight to Pittsburgh, where the Pirates were hosting Cincinnati in a doubleheader, starting at 5:06. But as his plane was preparing to taxi, the flight was canceled due to engine problems.

Matt languished in the airport terminal for five hours before boarding another plane, which landed in Pittsburgh twenty minutes before the start of the first game. He arrived at PNC Park by cab in the third inning. Once there, he had to wait at the players' entrance because his credentials hadn't arrived and the security guards didn't recognize him. Finally, by the top of the sixth, a frazzled Matt reached the bullpen.

Two innings later—yikes!—he entered the game with the Pirates trailing

3–0 in an eventual 8–2 loss. On Matt's first pitch, Reds outfielder Chris De-norfia, who had made his own major league debut just nine days earlier, smacked a liner to right-center. Denorfia stole second, but Matt buckled down. He struck out a pair of Pirates, but just when he thought he was going out of the jam, a single drove Denorfia home. Welcome to the big leagues, kid. Matt got pitcher Brandon Claussen to line out to end the inning.

He made three other appearances that season and finished with a 4.50 ERA in four innings. His talent was raw, but the kid showed promise.

"That was a fun season for me," he says. "I started the season not even on the radar, and then I ended up in Pittsburgh."

The following season, Matt proved he belonged by going 9–1 with a 3.79 ERA and allowing only 12 walks in a whopping 85 innings of middle relief. The Pirates loved the way the burly right-hander pounded the strike zone with mid-nineties fastballs while keeping hitters off-balance with a wicked slider and an occasional changeup.

After starting 2007 as the Pirates' setup man, Matt replaced the struggling Salomon Torres as the closer on June 1. He responded by converting his first nine save opportunities and finished with 18 total and a 2.28 ERA.

The hard-throwing kid from Douglasville was on his way up. But even at that new elevation in life, he couldn't foresee the gathering storm clouds in the distance.

LOVE ENTERS THE GAME

"I could marry that girl tomorrow."

Brett Campbell laughed at Matt's hasty comment. This, after all, was coming from the guy who'd initially balked at the idea of meeting Jenn Martin in the first place.

"You are an idiot," Brett said.

Brett's crack didn't even register. "I don't know," Matt said dreamily. "I've just never felt this way before."

Brett started his car, and the two friends drove off. It was late 2006, shortly after Matt's rookie season with the Pirates, and the buddies had just finished a blind double date at a Texas Roadhouse in Douglasville.

Neither Matt nor Jenn entered the evening with many expectations. The whole thing was the idea of Matt's agent's daughter-in-law, who worked with Jenn. Matt wasn't a big fan of blind dates. Jenn was just coming out of another relationship and didn't want to date a baseball player.

Other than that, what could go wrong?

The evening went harmlessly enough. Matt didn't say much. Jenn wasn't repulsed, but she wasn't exactly smitten, either. Brett had every reason for skepticism.

Matt called Jenn several times over the next two weeks, but she didn't respond. Her silence seemed awfully loud. Then, the day before he left for a vacation, she called. Matt floated the idea of another date. Jenn's tepid response didn't exactly inspire confidence, but they eventually went out again.

The ensuing courtship was slower than a Tim Wakefield knuckleball. After a couple more dates, Matt had to leave for spring training in Florida. Surviving the distance gauntlet was no guarantee.

Still, there was hope. Matt and Jenn talked on the phone almost every day, and Jenn agreed to attend the Pirates' second regular-season series in Cincinnati that April since she had family in the area.

Matt had a fairly uneventful weekend, appearing in only the Sunday finale and throwing one and a third scoreless innings. But off the field, he was falling hard for Jenn. By mid-July, he knew he wanted to marry her.

During a Pittsburgh home stand that month, Jenn flew into town to see him, and the couple went out to dinner after a day game. Had anyone had the audacity to lift up Matt's pant leg, he would have noticed a large bulge in his sock. Matt had hidden an engagement ring there.

Call it cautiousness bordering on fear. A man's mind processes a thousand thoughts when he's about to propose, and most of them explore the countless ways his romantic magnum opus can crumble into epic failure.

The site Matt had chosen to pop the question was Pittsburgh's charming Mount Washington neighborhood, which sits six hundred feet above downtown and is accessible by two historic incline railcars. At night, Mount Washington provides a stunning view of Pittsburgh's glittering skyline and the convergence of the Allegheny, Monongahela, and Ohio rivers. *USA Today Weekend Magazine*, in fact, ranked Mount Washington's nighttime view second on its list of the ten most beautiful places in America in 2003.

The moment had arrived. Matt swallowed hard. The butterflies that had been flitting about in his stomach all evening were now like fighter planes engaging in a World War II dogfight.

Then, from out of nowhere, a female voice broke the tension: "Oh my gosh, you're Matt Capps!" A local Pirates fan, enamored at her good fortune to run into the team's newly minted closer, ran up to greet Matt.

Talk about a mood-killer.

All was not lost, though. While at the lookout, Matt had noticed that the Point State Park fountain—a civic treasure in Pittsburgh for its central water plume that blasts one hundred feet high and its scenic location on the bank of the Ohio River—was finally working. It hadn't worked all season.

Coincidence? Perhaps. But Matt saw it as serendipity.

"What are we doing?" Jenn asked as they boarded a descending railcar.

"Let's go for a walk," Matt coyly responded.

At the fountain, Matt handed her a penny. "Make a wish," he said. They both threw their pennies into the water, and Matt playfully asked what she wished for.

"I can't tell you if I want it to come true," Jenn replied, smiling. By the time she asked Matt about his wish, he was down on one knee.

"Shut up! Shut up! Shut up!" Jenn screamed in raw excitement. Then, thankfully, she said yes. In November 2008, the couple got married.

"She loves the Lord and loves him," David Daly says of Jenn. "He's blessed to have her and he knows it. Her family is very kind to him."

Matt and Jenn recently bought a house on a five-acre spread in Roswell, Georgia, just north of greater Atlanta, to be close to their friends and family. In February 2012, they had their first child.

Through it all, Matt has discovered what he savors most about marriage.

"My favorite part," he said, "is knowing that every time I come home from the field, she's there waiting for me. It could be a good day, bad day or a nothing day, and I get to spend the rest of the day or night with her. It makes me a better person."

FATHER KNOWS BEST

In 2008, Matt enjoyed another solid season, posting 21 saves and a 3.02 ERA despite missing almost two months with bursitis in his right shoulder. All signs pointed to a breakout 2009. But baseball has a funny way of taking "all signs" and throwing them into a meat grinder.

Matt saved 27 games in 2009, then a career high, but otherwise it was a disastrous season. Opposing hitters batted .324 against him, almost like he was lobbing a softball underhanded. His ERA ballooned to 5.80.

"It was a pretty rough year," Matt says. "Baseball is one of those games that, as long as the season is, you've got to find a way to put the last game behind you. You can't worry about last night or the next. You have to worry about today."

After the 2009 season finale—a listless 6–0 loss to the Reds on October 4 that dropped the Pirates to 62–99, their worst record in eight years—Matt was ready for a mental break. But it never came.

Sixteen days later, Matt's father fell in his carport and hit his head on the concrete floor. When Kathy found Mike a few minutes later, he was breathing but unconscious, bleeding badly, and had significant brain damage. By the time the paramedics arrived, Mike had gone into cardiac arrest.

It was the final blow to a weary body that had endured five heart attacks, lung surgery, and more than two dozen kidney operations.

Matt and Jenn made it to the hospital to see Mike one last time. But in essence, he was gone. On October 22, 2009, two days after Mike's fall, the family took him off life support. He was sixty-one.

The loss was devastating to Matt. His father meant the world to him.

Mike was a rough-edged, no-frills kind of man. For most of Matt's life, Mike had been a real estate appraiser. But he had held other jobs, too—like working in a hospital or running a food joint called the Wiener Stand. Whatever it took to provide for his family.

The Capps family wasn't well-off, but Mike loved giving his sons opportunities. Ironically, a Little League experience was the one thing Mike initially didn't want Matt to have. He was suspicious of the local league's politics and good-ol'-boy network. But one of the Capps' neighbors, who also coached a team, persuaded Mike to let Matt join.

Mike never did anything halfway. So before you could say "Batter up!" he had purchased a baseball rulebook to learn the game's intricacies and had become the vice president of the local league's board of directors. Anytime Matt was on the field, even at practices, Mike seemed to be there, too.

In 1990, Mike made a friendly wager with Matt, only seven years old at the time, on the Cincinnati-Oakland World Series. Mike won by picking the Reds. The former Little League naysayer had transformed into a bona fide seamhead.

Father and son bonded over Atlanta Braves games at the old Atlanta-Fulton County Stadium. Young Matt would gawk in wide-eyed wonder as stars like Dale Murphy and Chipper Jones launched bombs into the bleachers.

"Man, that's got to be cool to be a major leaguer," Matt would say.

Without hesitation, Mike replied, "Someone has to be the best. Why not you?"

The words resonated in Matt like a motivational soundtrack:

Someone has to be . . .
Someone has to be . . .
Someone has to be . . .

For Mike, baseball became a teaching tool about life. He wasn't always a gentle instructor, but he was effective. He dispensed tough love, sometimes breaching his son's emotional dam. But Matt never doubted Mike's affection. *That's just the way Dad pushes me*, Matt told himself.

Even in Little League, Matt quickly learned that a bad day on the field meant a long car ride home. If he struck out or committed an error, he'd try to sneak into his mom's car. It never worked.

"C'mon, let's go," Mike would say, with a firm voice and an equally firm hand on Matt's shoulder.

In the best game of his high school career, Matt enjoyed a sublime day at the plate: three for four with a home run and two doubles. Only one problem: He didn't go four for four. The lone blemish was a strikeout.

"That's all I heard about for two weeks," Matt says. "He'd say, 'You don't know the strike zone! How are you going to go to college or play professionally?' Once I got drafted, there was more encouragement. He'd try to pick me up more than break me down. And he *did* a few times—he did break me down. But I think he knew it. I think he knew that would drive me."

Once Matt reached the majors, he started calling his father after every outing so he could scrutinize his performance, whether good or bad. Imagine: a major leaguer taking advice from a guy who hardly ever played baseball growing up! But that was Matt and his dad.

In 2008, Matt noticed a change in Mike's attitude during their late-night chats. After one game, Mike said, "I think I'm going to stop telling you things about baseball. You're smarter than me about it." Just like that, the adviser became a listener. Matt will never forget that night.

Something else peculiar: Earlier on the day he fell, Mike had called Matt to chat. The two always ended their conversations with "Love ya."

But on this day, Mike said, "I love you, son." It was a small variance, but one that stuck with Matt. Later that night, Chris called with the horrible news.

To this day, Mike's insights still reverberate in Matt. On the underside of his game hat, Matt writes: *Someone has to be*. But the most important lesson Mike taught Matt was often unspoken—and it extended far beyond baseball.

"The most important thing is impacting others," Matt said. "My dad touched a lot of lives. Every time I go home, [people] talk about the imprint that he left on their lives. It's hard for me to imagine that anything I do on a baseball field means more than what I can do off it."

MOVING ON

If Mike's death was a punch that sent Matt reeling, the next blow was a kick to the gut while he was down. Seven weeks after Mike passed away, Pittsburgh, the only team Matt had known in his first eight professional seasons, released him after a contract dispute. Matt made $2.4 million in 2009 and, despite his off year, likely would have received a raise in arbitration, a process that often favors the players. Pittsburgh decided to move on.

On January 6, 2010, Matt signed a one-year, $3.5 million deal with the Washington Nationals, who were desperately looking to shore up their bullpen after a 59–103 train wreck in 2009.

In D.C., the 2010 season could best be summed up in one word: Strasburg. The local—and national—media went gaga that summer for Stephen Strasburg, and rightfully so. The flame-throwing prodigy and No. 1 overall draft pick from 2009 captivated a slack-jawed national audience with a dazzling twelve-game rookie debut before suffering a season-ending arm injury in August.

Lost in the hullabaloo was a great career renaissance story of a quiet, down-to-earth, country-music-loving Georgian whose best fastballs weren't far off Strasburgian levels. In fact, on the same night that Strasburg made his breathlessly awaited debut on June 8, 2010, Matt earned his nineteenth save with a ten-pitch ninth inning.

"The night that Strasburg pitched, which everybody seems to forget that [Capps] pitched in, he hit 97 miles per hour," Nationals pitching coach Steve McCatty recalled.

With *Someone has to be* etched onto his cap, Matt conjured up magic fireballs from his fingertips once more in 2010, earning baseball's top relief pitcher award in April and his first All-Star selection. In the All-Star game, he struck out his only batter, Boston slugger David Ortiz, in the bottom of the sixth, then earned the win when the National League, which trailed 1–0 when he entered the game, scored three runs in the top of the seventh for an eventual 3–1 victory. Not a bad night.

The game of baseball, though, is nothing if not ironic. Matt's stock was so high that summer he became trade bait for contenders. Two weeks later, Washington dealt him to Minnesota, which eventually won the American League Central Division crown, thanks in no small part to Matt's arrival.

With Minnesota, he was even more dominant (2.00 ERA, 1.19 WHIP) than he had been with Washington (2.74 ERA, 1.30 WHIP). Matt's first trip to the playoffs ended with a first-round exit, but he finished the year with a career-best 42 saves and a 2.47 ERA.

"It was a whirlwind of a season," Matt said.

The winds of change continued in 2011. After starting the season as Minnesota closer Joe Nathan's setup man, Matt assumed ninth-inning duties in mid-April at the suggestion of Nathan, who was struggling to regain his consistency following elbow surgery. But by July 16, Matt had blown seven saves in 22 chances and struggled to a 4.76 ERA, prompting Twins manager Ron Gardenhire to switch to Nathan again. Matt finished the season with a 4–7 record and only 15 saves. He hopes to rebound with the Twins in 2012.

THE FACE OF FAITH

At the start of the 2009 season, when Matt was still a Pirate, David Daly had something he wanted to show Matt and Jenn. David recently had been named the Fellowship of Christian Athletes' national baseball director, and the ministry had published an exciting new product.

So David took the couple to dinner at Jerome Bettis' Grille 36 restaurant, wedged in between PNC Park and Heinz Field on the Three Rivers waterfront. There, over tuna, steak, and salad, he showed them a mock-up version of the new FCA Baseball New Testament. Matt was on the cover.

David expected smiles and giddiness. Instead, Jenn started crying.

The culprit wasn't sorrow, though. She was simply overwhelmed by the shocking contrast: The face of the man who once rebelled against God with an upraised fist was now on a Bible.

A smile altered the path of the tears rolling down her cheek. "I never thought God could use you like this," she said.

God loves paradoxes that bring Him glory. Matt, like all Christians, was once "dead in . . . transgressions and sins" (Ephesians 2:1). But now, he is a new creation, boldly proclaiming his life-giving faith.

When David asked Matt to join FCA Baseball's national board of directors, he jumped at the chance. Before the 2010 season, Matt shared his testimony before four hundred people at an FCA breakfast during the American Baseball Coaches Association's annual convention in Dallas. He has also spoken to hundreds of kids at off-season FCA clinics.

Still, Matt is a relatively private man. He wants to make a difference, not a headline. So he serves in ways that aren't in the camera's lens. There are financial gifts, hospital visits, and other personal interactions we know nothing about.

Matt's most poignant testimonials are often simple gestures during games. Each time he takes the mound, he removes his hat, bows his head, and says a short prayer before his first pitch. It's a powerful, public witness of where his faith rests.

There's this, too: when the bullpen stirs to life in the middle innings, Matt often places cups of water by the mound for his teammates. This loudly echoes Jesus' words in Matthew 23:11: "The greatest among you will be your servant."

"It's exactly what Christ would've done," David said.

And so Matt continues down life's path, trying all along to affect others and grow himself. It's a mysterious, sometimes circuitous route, filled with death and life, grief and hope, failure and victory. Nothing is guaranteed . . . except the Lord's steadfast love.

"I know that God loves me and there's a purpose for me being here," Matt said. "There's a reason why I struggle. There's a reason why I have success. And it's not really for me or you to understand. But there's a higher meaning behind all of it. I don't believe my sole purpose in this world is to be a professional athlete or to do anything on the baseball field.

"There's a greater reason, a better reason, for me to be on this earth. Baseball is the resource God has put in front of me to spread the gospel and make other people aware."

As Matt's father once said, someone has to be.

10

MARK TEIXEIRA:
HITTING ON ALL CYLINDERS

Rarely does a single set off this much celebration.

But on August 17, 2004, Mark Teixeira's leadoff single in the top of the seventh inning electrified the crowd at Ameriquest Field in Arlington, Texas.

No, Mark's hit didn't win the game. The Texas Rangers were already ahead 16–1 against the Cleveland Indians.

And no, it wasn't his three thousandth base knock, because the twenty-four-year-old had only been in the majors for a couple of seasons.

But Mark's single did make history because he'd already collected a triple, home run, and double in his previous three at-bats. So his "meaningless" single in the seventh had plenty of meaning, putting Mark in a select group of athletes who have hit for "the cycle."

Since statistics have been kept, a player has hit a single, a double, a triple, and a home run in a nine-inning game less than three hundred times in Major League Baseball's 135-year history.

On May 25, 1882, Curry Foley of the Buffalo Bisons became the first player to hit for the cycle. Since that time, nearly four hundred thousand major league games have been played . . . and still fewer than three hundred players have ever hit for the cycle.

For Mark, it took him less than two full seasons to accomplish this rare feat. More impressively, he became only the seventeenth switch-hitter to do it.

Mark's evening against the Indians didn't start out in a historical manner. He struck out in his first at-bat. But the second time he came to the plate, he smacked a two-run double. Then he hit a three-run home run in the fourth inning and a triple in the fifth that scored two more runs.

By the time Mark came up to bat in the seventh, he had already collected seven RBIs and just needed a single to complete the cycle.

"[My teammates] were kidding me, telling me to trip over first base if I hit one into the gap," Mark joked.

But Mark didn't have to trip or fake an injury to stay on first; he hit a line-drive single up the middle. A pinch runner came in for Mark as 24,864 fans gave him a standing ovation.

That wouldn't be the last standing ovation this 6-foot, 3-inch, 220-pound power hitter would receive. Since 2003, Mark has been one of the best players in baseball.

In 2003, his first year with the Rangers, Mark hammered 26 home runs and was voted the American League Rookie of the Year. His home run total jumped to 38 the following year (to go along with 112 RBIs).

But 2005 turned out to be his breakout year. That season, Mark crushed 41 homers and drove in a staggering 144 runs—the most for a switch-hitter in baseball history. In addition, he scored 112 runs, batted .302, and recorded his one hundredth career home run (he ended the year with 105) to become one of just five players in major league history to hit a hundred homers during his first three seasons. Joe DiMaggio, Ralph Kiner, Eddie Mathews, and Albert Pujols are the others.

Through 2010, Mark had won three Silver Slugger awards (which go to the best offensive player at each position in the American and National leagues) and four Gold Gloves (which are awarded to the best defensive player at each position in each league). In fact, in 2005 and 2009, Mark won the Silver Slugger *and* Gold Glove awards—honoring him as the best offensive *and* defensive first baseman in the American League.

How does a player get this good this young? A lot of factors combine to create an All-Star baseball player. But one word leaps to mind when studying Mark: *discipline*.

Mark shows discipline in nearly all areas of his life. From practicing his faith to practicing baseball, he has a consistent mind-set.

"I've always tried to be disciplined," Mark said. "If you're not, then it's easy to stray from the straight road. I always did my homework and took extra swings or extra ground balls."

Players around Mark have joked that his routine can sometimes border on obsessive-compulsive, but he takes his preparation and the game of baseball very seriously. From his pregame peanut butter and jelly sandwich to how he stands for the "The Star-Spangled Banner," Mark's disciplined behavior shines through.

While some players blow bubbles or look at the scoreboard during the National Anthem, Mark has a distinct routine.

"He stands perfectly straight, head down, shirt tucked in—every single time," former teammate Torii Hunter said. "He doesn't say a word. He doesn't even have a hair out of place."

Mark's laser-like focus and awe-inspiring statistics caused people to take notice. And as his fame grew, so did his bank account. Before the start of the 2006 season, the Rangers gave him a two-year, $15.4 million contract. But Mark didn't finish out his contract in Texas. In 2007, he was traded to Atlanta. He also had a brief stint with the Los Angeles Angels of Anaheim during the 2008 season.

Before the 2009 campaign, Mark made headlines by becoming the highest-paid first baseman in baseball when he signed a $180 million, eight-year deal with the New York Yankees. His $23,125,000 salary in 2011 ranked him fourth among the highest-paid players in the sport. Only Yankee teammates Alex Rodriguez and C.C. Sabathia and Angels outfielder Vernon Wells made more.

While the awards and money are nice, they're not the reason Mark plays baseball. He knows God has given him a gift, and he wants to honor God with how he goes about his business on the diamond.

"I try to live and play baseball the way that I think the Lord would want me to," Mark said. "I try to do the right things on the field and off the field."

Some players may just say those words, but Mark lives them out with his actions and his wallet.

PUTTING HIS MONEY WHERE HIS FAITH IS

Faith has always been important to Mark Charles Teixeira, who was born in Annapolis, Maryland, on April 11, 1980. His Portuguese surname is pronounced te-SHARE-ah.

During his early elementary school years, Mark showed tremendous athletic ability. He played baseball, soccer, and basketball, and he often participated in tournaments in which he competed in five or six games every weekend. But no matter where the family was, Mark found himself in church on Saturday nights or Sunday mornings.

"At a very young age, I learned about Jesus and how important your faith is," Mark said. "My parents were definitely the most influential people in my life . . . and they taught me the right values."

Mark dedicated his life to God as a child and has continually sought to serve Him, so as he got older and was rewarded monetarily for his athletic talents, he gave back to God.

This started in 2001 after Mark signed his first major league contract. The Rangers drafted him fifth overall and signed him to a four-year, $9.5 million package with a $4.5 million signing bonus. Once the ink was dry, Mark went back to his old high school, Mount St. Joseph, and talked with principal Barry Fitzpatrick.

During Mark's junior year, one of his best friends, Nick Liberatore, was killed in a car accident when a truck driver fell asleep at the wheel and plowed into his parked car. The loss devastated the Liberatore family . . . and Mark. Now that he had the means, Mark wanted to create a scholarship to honor his friend.

The principal told Mark that it would cost $75,000 to start the scholarship. Without hesitation, Mark wrote the check and created the Nick Liberatore scholarship program. He still funds that scholarship, helping make the college dreams of kids from his hometown a reality. In fact, President Barack Obama talked about Mark's generous spirit when the Yankees visited the White House in 2010 to celebrate their World Series victory.

"For the president to single me out, I was very honored," Mark said. "I've always thought baseball is just a tool for me to try to do work for other people. I've been very blessed in my career, and the first thing I did when I had a chance was that scholarship."

But that certainly wasn't the last thing he did. Mark gives his money and his time to a number of important causes.

After graduating from Georgia Tech, Mark established a $500,000 baseball scholarship called the Mark C. Teixeira Athletic Scholarship. Mark received a scholarship to attend the Atlanta-based university and wanted to fund the collegiate aspirations of other players.

He also gave back in a big way to Mount St. Joseph in 2008. His former high school in Baltimore was in the middle of a $10 million "Building Men Who Matter" campaign to update and expand its facilities. Mark's million-dollar donation helped make that happen.

Over the years, Mark also has created college scholarships for deserving high school seniors in the Dallas area.

Based on Mark's giving, it's obvious that education and sports are important to him.

"Ever since I started [my foundation], it has been very involved with college scholarships, education, and children's needs," Mark said. "Whether it's the Police Athletic League, or the Boys & Girls Clubs, those sort of things are really close to my heart."

So when Mark moved to the Yankees in 2009, it was no surprise that he got involved in Harlem RBI.

Started in 1991 when a handful of volunteers turned an abandoned lot in East Harlem into two baseball diamonds, Harlem RBI now serves a thousand boys and girls ages five to twenty-one. With year-round academic, sports, and enrichment programs, this organization has seen huge success in giving hope to children who come from seemingly hopeless situations.

Since 2005, 98 percent of Harlem RBI seniors have graduated high school with 94 percent of them earning acceptance into college.

In May 2010, Mark donated $100,000 and agreed to join the board of directors. But in 2011, he stepped up his commitment by giving $1 million and becoming the co-chair of a $20 million Harlem RBI capital campaign. In all, the goal was to build an $85 million, thirteen-story building that will become the home to Harlem RBI headquarters, its DREAM charter school, and ninety affordable housing units.

Groundbreaking for the Harlem RBI building is scheduled for the summer of 2012 with the project completed in 2014. Since Mark signed an eight-year deal with the Yankees in 2008, he should be able to watch the buildings go up the entire way.

"I became involved with Harlem RBI and DREAM charter because I believe the work we are doing is truly changing lives," Mark said.

Although Mark has plenty of well-paid teammates, he doesn't pressure them to give. The president may have singled out Mark, but he said a number of his Yankee teammates are involved in their own charitable endeavors. He doesn't think it'd be fair to ask them to donate when they're already doing so much in areas that are close to their hearts.

Mark enjoys being hands-on. He likes meeting kids and making a difference in their lives. But sometimes those kids have a bigger impact on him than he does on them.

That was the case when Mark visited Brian Ernst at Children's Hospital in Atlanta in 2010.

Brian loved baseball. As a star pitcher at West Hall High School in Oakwood, Georgia, he dreamed about making it to the big leagues. But shortly after his seventeenth birthday, Brian was diagnosed with Ewing's sarcoma, a rare cancer found in bone or soft tissue. Brian battled valiantly but died at nineteen.

Before Brian's death, Mark visited him through the Make-A-Wish Foundation. Originally, Brian had planned to fly to New York and play catch with Mark at Yankee Stadium. But his failing health limited travel. Instead, Mark traveled to Atlanta in February. When Mark walked into the hospital, a Make-A-Wish representative met him and said that Brian might not be feeling well enough to see him in person. But by the time the Yankee All-Star made it to Brian's room, the teen was sitting up in bed and wearing Mark's No. 25 Yankees' jersey.

Although Brian hadn't been too responsive the previous few days, he and Mark talked for several hours—not only about baseball, basketball, and football, but also about Brian's desire to help other people, especially children, fighting similar diseases.

During Brian's time at the hospital, he had kept a positive attitude and helped cheer up younger children who had cancer.

"I've visited hospitals before and worked with the Make-A-Wish Foundation," Mark said. "You think you're giving a kid something, but after I left Brian, he gave me something. . . . Brian changed lives. He really did.

"Brian didn't lose his battle with cancer. He won the battle. It didn't break him down. He showed everybody that you can live through cancer, make a difference, and inspire people no matter what circumstance you have."

After Brian died, Mark invited his family to Yankee Stadium for the home opener on April 13, 2010. Brian's father, mother, and brother made the trip. The Ernsts sat with Mark's wife, Leigh, and his parents during the game. Mark also gave Brian's parents his game cap, which had been inscribed with "Brian, Faith, #5"—the number of Brian's high school baseball uniform. Mark wore that inscription the entire 2010 season.

"The thing that was so amazing about Brian was his faith throughout his ordeal," Mark said. "He was so upbeat, and he knew that God gave him this [trial] to teach other people about faith."

Meeting Brian strengthened Mark's faith, and he wants to have a similar effect through his actions on and off the field. At the same time, Mark doesn't want to give people the wrong idea that good actions can earn favor with God.

Mark gives his time and money to help others out of gratitude for how much God has blessed him—not to earn brownie points with his heavenly Father.

"Our deeds don't make us righteous," Mark said. "Our deeds don't make us worthy to be in God's presence or to be in His Kingdom. . . . God's righteousness is given to us, and His grace is given to us as a gift."

GIFTED ATHLETE MAKES GOOD

Mark knows his athletic abilities are also a gift. He grew up in the Baltimore suburb of New Canaan with a ball of some sort always nearby.

"My parents brought me up in a home where we worked very hard and did our best," Mark said. "But we also realized the gifts that we had were from God."

His parents didn't force him to play baseball. In fact, they wanted him to try lots of different sports. He played soccer and basketball competitively, but he always came back to America's pastime.

By the time Mark was nine, he had announced to his mom that he wanted to be a major league baseball player. That shouldn't have been too surprising. Baseball ran in his blood. His mom's brothers were good baseball players, and his dad had played for the United States Naval Academy in college. His uncle even made it into the Braves' minor league system.

Most of Mark's favorite athletes growing up were baseball players. While Mark normally bled orange and black, the team colors of his hometown Baltimore Orioles, he had a special affinity for New York first baseman Don Mattingly. The popular Yankee played from 1982 to 1995 and was known for his smooth swing, competitive drive, and defensive skills.

Mark put a poster of Mattingly in his bedroom and chose to wear No. 23 in honor of his favorite player. He even risked ridicule and injury by donning a Yankees' cap to Baltimore Orioles games when the Bronx Bombers were in town.

The preteen continued to play youth baseball, but he didn't do a whole lot to further his professional aspirations until he finished middle school. That's when the family decided to send Mark to Mount St. Joseph, an all-boys high school with a solid baseball program.

"People would think I'm crazy, but it was the greatest thing for me," Mark said about attending the private school. "I didn't have to worry about impressing girls or having distractions. . . . During those school hours, it was very important to be focused."

Mount St. Joseph did have two sister schools, so the athletic teams had cheerleaders, and the schools enjoyed dances together. But Mark was serious about his schoolwork and playing baseball.

Mark saw a little varsity action his freshman year, but when he took over third base duties as a sophomore in 1996, he never gave them up. While he sprinkled seven home runs in his first two seasons, Mark grew into a power hitter his last two. He was an All-Metro selection as a sophomore, but he gained a lot of recognition as a junior by hitting .518 with 10 home runs. During his senior year, he belted 12 homers while knocking in 36 RBIs. The slugger also batted a staggering .568.

By the time he graduated, Mark's 29 career home runs stood as a Maryland Interscholastic Athletic Association record, as did his 108 RBIs and 128 hits.

The *Baltimore Sun* named Mark its 1998 Baseball Player of the Year, which looked pretty good along with *USA Baseball* calling him Maryland's top junior the previous season.

Baseball America projected Mark as a first-round pick in the 1998 draft. But when the June draft day rolled around, the Boston Red Sox selected Mark in the ninth round.

Baseball insiders were perplexed at how someone with first-round talent, intelligence, and attitude would drop so low. Some felt it may have been because agent Scott Boras was advising Mark. Boras, one of the top agents in the game, was known as a tough, hard-nosed negotiator. Others speculated that teams felt Mark (who was a member of the National Honor Society and graduated twelfth in his class) planned to go to college, so it wasn't worth wasting a pick.

Despite picking Mark so low, Boston still offered the teen first-round money—a $1.5 million signing bonus to be exact. Boras felt the offer was on the low end.

Instead of signing, Mark turned down $1.5 million and enrolled at the Georgia Institute of Technology on a baseball scholarship.

Most teens wouldn't have patience and foresight to walk away from that kind of money. But Mark wasn't a typical teenager. In addition to losing one of his best friends in a car accident, Mark had witnessed his mother fight breast cancer during high school. Seeing firsthand that life can be short made Mark serious about working toward his dreams.

Going to Georgia Tech turned out to be a great decision. Not only was Mark at a highly ranked academic school with a good baseball program, but, more importantly, he also met his future wife, Leigh, at a party during his freshman year. The couple married in December 2002.

Those were "the best three years of my life," Mark has often said. Looking at his statistics and what those years led to, it's hard to argue with him.

As a freshman, Mark batted .387 with 13 home runs and 65 RBIs. Those numbers earned him the 1999 National Freshman of the Year and ACC Rookie of the Year honors. He followed that up with an even bigger year as a sophomore: his .427 batting average, 18 home runs, 80 RBIs, and 104 runs scored put him near the top of every batting category in his conference. His 67 walks were tops in the nation.

With Mark leading the way, the Yellow Jackets posted a 50–16 record and made it to the College World Series. The sophomore was nearly a unanimous selection as the National Player of the Year.

After playing a summer of baseball with the Maryland Battlecats in a twenty-and-under league, Mark looked forward to bolstering his professional stock with an even bigger junior year.

Seven games into the season, however, Mark broke his ankle and missed nearly the entire year.

In Mark's three years at Georgia Tech, he batted over .400 and helped the school win 129 games. (He was inducted into the Tech Hall of Fame on November 9, 2011.) He declared himself eligible for the 2001 draft and was picked fifth overall by the Texas Rangers. USA Today wrote that he was "at least as good a hitting prospect as past college stars Barry Bonds, Mark McGwire, J.D. Drew, and Pat Burrell."

Mark quickly lived up to the hype by collecting hits in twelve consecutive games at Class A Charlotte in the Florida State League. Before the summer of 2002 was over, Mark was playing for the Double-A Tulsa Drillers, where he drilled 24 extra-base hits in 48 games. He ended the year playing fall ball in Arizona, hitting seven home runs and knocking in 23 RBIs in just 27 games.

When Mark entered spring training in 2003, he did it with just one goal: make the big league ball club. His spectacular play made it easy for the Texas management. After hitting a team-record eight homers in spring training, his name made the list on Opening Day.

With Hank Blalock entrenched at third base, Texas looked for ways to get Mark on the field. He played outfield, first base, and several games at third. In 146 games, he batted just .259, but his 26 home runs and 84 RBIs were tops for rookies.

By 2005, Mark had established himself as one of the best first basemen in the game. Had Texas been a perennial playoff contender, casual fans would've known his exploits. As it was, Mark was quietly making a name for himself.

During the 2007 season, with the Rangers out of the playoff picture and Mark in the middle of contract negotiations, he was traded to Atlanta. The deal came just two weeks after he had turned down an eight-year, $140 million contract extension.

Right away, Mark looked at home in his former hometown. He homered in each of his first three games as a Brave. A few weeks later, Mark put together back-to-back multiple home run games. On August 19, he hit two jacks from the left side of the plate. The next night he went yard twice from the right side.

In 54 games with Atlanta, Mark batted .317 with 17 home runs and 56 RBIs. The Braves signed their new first baseman to a one-year contract worth $12.5 million.

But Mark didn't finish the 2008 season with the Braves: he was traded to the Los Angeles Angels of Anaheim in July. Batting third for the Angels, he helped lead the team to its first-ever hundred-win season. The first round of the playoffs didn't go as well, though, as the Angels fell to Boston.

With the season and his contract over, Mark became a free agent in November 2008. The Angels, Red Sox, Orioles, and Washington Nationals all bid for his services. But in the end, Mark found himself in the Big Apple.

BIGGEST STAGE ON EARTH

The move made sense for Mark. Not only was the money outstanding, but the contract also came with a full no-trade clause. Plus, it got Mark and his young family closer to their families on the East Coast.

Not that the decision didn't come without a cost. Mark had to give up his favorite number 23 because the Yankees had retired Mattingly's jersey. He chose to wear number 25. But perhaps more difficult for Mark was the fact that he was now playing in the fishbowl known as Yankee Stadium.

"No one's going to expect more out of me than me," Mark said. "I believe I have yet to tap my potential. I'm trying to get better. I haven't accomplished anything yet—I don't have a World Series ring on my finger."

After being announced as a Yankee on January 6, 2009, and going through spring training, the season started out in typical fashion for Mark—poorly.

Since entering the big leagues, he's been a notoriously slow starter.

During the month of April, Mark batted .200 with just three homers and 10 RBIs. That wasn't what the New York faithful were hoping to get from their new $180 million man. The cheers that greeted Mark at the beginning of the season quickly turned to boos.

Mark started putting in extra time with Yankees hitting coach Kevin Long, who pointed out a couple of mechanical tweaks but told Mark to stay positive.

"I let him know that I was behind him all the way," Long wrote about conversations with Mark in his book *Cage Rat*. "I knew that it was just a matter of time."

In six Aprils before joining the Yankees, he amassed a total of 19 home runs and 65 RBIs. During those same six seasons in the month of September, Mark had 44 homers and 152 RBIs.

Yankee fans aren't known for their patience, and they let Mark hear their displeasure. But even in the midst of his early season slump, Mark gave them something to cheer about.

On June 12, 2009, the Yankees hosted the New York Mets in an interleague game. Mark contributed early by blasting a two-run home run in the third inning, but in the bottom of the ninth his team trailed 8–7 with two outs. The Yankees still had hope as Derek Jeter was on second and Mark stood on first with Alex Rodriguez at the plate. However, A-Rod popped the ball up in shallow right field, and Mets' Gold Glove second baseman Luis Castillo drifted over to make the final out.

Not taking anything for granted, Mark started sprinting around the bases. And then the unthinkable happened: Castillo dropped the ball!

Never slacking his pace, Mark rounded third and slid into home plate to give the Yankees a 9–8 victory.

"When you're on the bases, why not run hard?" Mark said. "There's no reason not to play the game hard. . . . It was the third month I was with the Yankees, so [the fans] were still getting to know me. So to see that play hopefully gave them a little bit of an insight into the kind of player I am and the pride that I take in playing the game."

That pride and determination eventually resulted in solid numbers at the plate. Batting third all season, Mark helped lead the Yankees into the playoffs. He even led the American League with 39 home runs and 122 RBIs—not bad considering his incredibly slow start.

New York began the American League Division Series against Minnesota. After the Yankees easily won the first game 7–2, Mark lifted his team to a 4–3 victory in Game 2 with a walk-off home run in the eleventh inning. It was Mark's first postseason homer and couldn't have come at a better time.

The Yankees swept the Twins and earned the right to face Mark's former team, the Angels, in the AL Championship Series. New York jumped out to a quick 2–0 lead in the best-of-seven series and beat the Angels four games to two.

In the World Series, New York battled Philadelphia. The Phillies won Game 1 in New York and led early in Game 2 before Mark helped jump-start the offense. His solo homer in the fourth inning tied the game 1–1. New York added runs in the sixth and seventh to win 3–1.

New York notched victories in the next two games in Philly as Mark scored a run in each game. By the time the series returned to New York, the Yankees were leading three games to two.

The Yankees claimed their record twenty-seventh World Series title on November 5, 2009, with a 7–3 victory. Mark tallied a run and an RBI in the game.

Despite struggling in the playoffs (he batted just .136 in the World Series and .180 for the postseason), celebrating his first World Series victory was sweet for Mark.

"For us to be holding the trophy at the end of the season, it was a special year," Mark said. "We're very blessed to win the World Series in my first year here."

Mark knows he's blessed off the field as well. He and Leigh have three young children, Jack, Addison, and William, and live in Greenwich, Connecticut.

Mark enjoys getting away from baseball and spending time with his family. Hours with his kids are special, considering the amount of time he's gone during the regular season, but he says his children have also had a profound impact on his faith in Christ.

"When my first son was born in 2006, I just realized the love that God has for all of us," Mark said. "It was seeing my son born and knowing the unconditional love that I have for him."

Being a father has also increased Mark's ability to quote children's movies. One of his favorite things to do at home is pop a bag of popcorn, go into his theater room with his kids, and watch a film. His kids liked *Kung Fu Panda* so much that they wore out a couple of DVDs.

"I can probably quote the entire movie start to finish," Mark said.

Having a strong family and firm faith help Mark deal with the ups and downs of the long baseball season and with the brutal New York media.

He had his worst April ever in 2010, hitting just .136 for the month. Headlines were written that bashed Mark's abilities, including one that read: "Tex Mess." In the midst of the slump, Mark never doubted himself or God.

"Baseball is a game of failure," Mark said. "There are plenty of opportunities to be down, to feel sorry for yourself . . . but when you have God in your life and you follow Christ, you're never going to be let down. Every time you fail, He's there to pick you right back up."

And Mark's season did pick up. He rebounded to post respectable numbers by the end of the year: 33 home runs, 108 RBIs, and a .256 batting average. He even had a three-home-run game against Boston in May, making him only the second player in the Yanks' history besides Lou Gehrig to accomplish the feat against the Red Sox.

The 2011 season started differently for Mark. Because he worked out less with weights and spent more time in the batting cage, his bat felt quicker. He responded by hitting home runs in his first three games. By the end of June, he already had 63 RBIs and 25 homers, including a monumental one he hit on the last day of the month.

On June 30, Mark launched the three hundredth home run of his career in a 5–0 victory over the Milwaukee Brewers. Only 130 other major league players have ever hit this benchmark. But just like hitting droughts don't get him down, this milestone didn't impress him.

"That's not a major milestone," he said. "I'm not trying to downplay it; it's not 500 or 600 or anything like that." Mark finished the 2011 season by earning his keep with 39 home runs and 111 RBIs to go with his .248 batting average.

Mark has bigger goals for his baseball career. He knows the numbers will come as long as he keeps playing the game the right way and following the right path.

"My faith keeps me grounded," Mark said. "I know no matter my success or failure on the field that there's a higher thing for me with God and with Jesus. To have that kind of faith, it makes the failures here not as important because the most important thing is my faith and my relationship with God."

11

BRIAN ROBERTS:
BIG TRIALS, BIG FAITH FOR A SMALL PLAYER

Each year, millions of tourists from around the world flock to Florida like an enormous migration of birds, enticed by the state's warm weather, natural wonders, and wide array of attractions. The famed beaches. The tropical waters. The Magic Kingdom. Universal Studios. Miami's South Beach. Fort Lauderdale. St. Augustine. The Everglades. The Keys.

Within the continental United States, you can't get much closer to paradise.

But in the summer of 2011, one man was trying desperately to escape Florida. For him, the Sunshine State felt more like a balmy prison cell with palm trees. All of Florida's allurements notwithstanding, Brian Roberts wanted to get the heck out of Dodge.

Brian, the Baltimore Orioles' longtime second baseman, spent most of the season confined to his off-season home in Sarasota, thanks to a concussion he suffered during a headfirst slide into first base in Boston in the middle of May. For an ultra-competitive athlete and the face of a hapless franchise, few things are worse than being restricted by the invisible shackles of a medical clearance that never seems to come.

According to Brian, his extended time on the disabled list was the "toughest stint" of his career. "Certainly for me," he said, "it's the hardest thing that I can go through."

That's saying something. From the moment Brian was born, trials have been flying at him like fastballs from a JUGS machine gone berserk. There have been, to name a few:

- a huge health scare as a child
- a steroids scandal in 2006–2007
- multiple career-threatening injuries

And don't forget the seemingly endless epidemic of losing that has plagued the Orioles throughout Brian's career.

That's not to say there haven't been good times. Brian, a diminutive overachiever with ruffled good looks, is a two-time All-Star with a fat contract and a model for a wife. He is also a genuinely humble man who has become a poster boy for all sorts of charity work with kids.

But Brian's life has been defined by, as much as anything, a gauntlet of faith-testing ordeals. Baseball, in particular, has been like a spiritual surgeon's knife, a precise tool of sanctification that incrementally cuts away the remnants of his old self. He has grown in peace, patience, and contentment. He has learned volumes about himself and others. He has felt God's discipline and love.

Most of all, he has learned to trust the Lord.

"Proverbs 3:5–6 have really been my verses that I've lived by as much as I can," Brian said, before quoting them: "Trust in the Lord with all your heart and lean not on your own understanding. In all your ways, acknowledge him and he will make your paths straight."

This, Brian quickly admits, is easy when things are peachy, but not so much when they're painful.

First, the pain . . .

"BUGGY-WHIPPING" TO THE BIG LEAGUES

The screams echoed off the walls of North Carolina Memorial Hospital in Chapel Hill.

Mommy! I don't want to go!

Little five-year-old Brian had a death grip on his mom's neck. He was doing everything in his half-pint power to avoid being wheeled down the long, ominous hallway to the operating room.

It wasn't supposed to be like this. He should've been in La-La Land already, but the medical orderly hadn't timed the anesthesia correctly. The kid was awake . . . and terrified.

Eventually, they peeled Brian off his mom. Mike and Nancy Roberts watched helplessly as Brian's gurney rolled through the double doors and out of sight.

Brian, the younger of Mike and Nancy's two children, was born October 9, 1977, with an atrial septal defect, a congenital heart disorder where the wall separating the upper heart chambers does not close completely. In other words, he had a hole in his heart. The condition eventually necessitated open heart surgery. Today, he still bears a Y-shaped scar on his chest from the surgeon's incision.

Before long, little Brian—and we do mean *little*—was back on his feet and playing baseball. No surprise there. He came from a Southern, baseball-crazy family. His grandfather, Edd Roberts, loved the game, even though he had never played much, unless you count the makeshift games in North Carolina cow pastures. (Watch your step rounding first.)

Edd grew up in the 1930s as a Cardinals and Indians fan mainly because the radio stations he could pick up were KMOX out of St. Louis and WTAM out of Cleveland. He spent many a night transfixed by the static-saturated tales of Dizzy Dean and the Gas House Gang, and Bob Feller throwing bullets off Lake Erie. During the Great Depression, Edd worked long hours hauling logs in Asheville, but he often stopped off on his way home at McCormick Field, the Asheville Tourists' home since 1924, to catch some minor league action.

Later in life, when Edd lived in Kingsport, Tennessee, he presided over the Kingsport Boosters' Association and became the town's main liaison to whatever Appalachian League team called Kingsport home.

Edd transferred his passion to his son, Mike, who eventually became the head baseball coach at the University of North Carolina, holding that position from 1976 to 1998. Brian spent countless afternoons on campus, cavorting around the field with college stars like catcher B.J. Surhoff and shortstop Walt Weiss, both first-round picks in the 1985 major league draft.

Becoming a star himself, though, was going to take a lot of work. Brian was always a pipsqueak without much over-the-fence pop. So Pop decided to teach him how to drive the ball like nobody's business. By the time Brian could walk, Mike was teaching him elementary hitting drills from both sides of the plate. At age ten, Brian was hitting tennis balls from Mike, who threw them as hard as he could from thirty feet away—over and over and over.

It was all about creating quick wrists and bat speed. Mike called it "buggy-whipping" your hands through the strike zone. Back when Mike was a catcher in the Kansas City Royals' farm system, the prevailing wisdom held that good hitters needed to be strong only from the elbows down. Players were discouraged from lifting weights in favor of building Popeye forearm strength. So Mike learned to buggy-whip. It was a term taken from the arm motion Edd would use to snap a whip over a stubborn mule to make his buggy go.

"We tried to hit the ball flat—line drives," Mike said of his hitting sessions with Brian. "A ground ball wasn't right. A fly ball wasn't right."

Mike knew that a scrawny kid who could hit for average but not field worth a lick wouldn't go far. So father and son worked nonstop on defense, too. During games of catch, Mike would use neighborhood objects to incrementally increase Brian's throwing distance—mailbox to mailbox, mailbox to manhole cover, mailbox to that car way down the street, and so on. Mike made Brian throw with a ball painted half black so he could track his son's grip and spin on the ball. Every detail mattered.

Brian enjoyed a great high school career. But his size scared off most college coaches . . . except one. Want to guess who it was?

For two years, Brian made his dad look like a recruiting genius. In 1997, he won the national Freshman of the Year award by hitting a school-record .427 and setting other Tar Heel benchmarks with 102 hits, 24 doubles, and 47 stolen bases. The next season, he led the country in stolen bases with 63.

After Mike lost his job following the 1998 season, Brian transferred to South Carolina, where he earned second-team All-American status as a junior with a .353 average, 12 home runs, 36 RBIs, and a national-best 67 stolen bases.

For three years, Brian had treated college pitchers like his personal piñata and base paths like a dragster strip, but major league scouts were still wary of his size. He was passed over for the first forty-nine picks in the 1999 draft before the Orioles took a chance on him with a supplemental first-round selection.

It was a magnificent moment for Brian and his family. God had blessed all his hard work and dedication.

But pro baseball would test Brian's faith like never before.

PAIN AND PERSEVERANCE

As deep as Brian's baseball roots go, his family's spiritual roots go just as far. He remembers waking up at his grandfather's house one morning at 5:30 and shuffling downstairs, bleary-eyed, only to see the kitchen light on and Edd doing his quiet time at the table. He recalls seeing his mom studying her Bible every day as well.

"I saw the way they lived out their faith, not only around other people, but in their own time," he said. "I had incredible examples of what it meant to really put your faith first in your life."

Mike and Nancy took Brian and his older sister, Angie, to Hope Valley Baptist Church in Durham twice a week. At age twelve, Brian placed his faith in Christ during a church revival, but he slowly drifted into worldliness. By the time he was a UNC freshman, he was trying to fit in with his teammates a little too much.

Nancy, like all good moms, could see her son was struggling, even without a word from Brian. So she gave him a copy of *Victory: The Principles of Championship Living*, a book by NBA star A.C. Green, whose bold faith included a now-famous acknowledgment that he remained a virgin until he got married. That December, during a family vacation to Hawaii, Brian devoured *Victory* and the Bible, and committed to his faith for good.

"I was trying to show my teammates that I wasn't going to run and tell Dad everything," Brian said. "I wanted to show them I was a teammate, not just Coach's son. I did a lot of things I probably shouldn't have done, but now I know that I had to go through those things to really be drawn back to the relationship with God that I needed to have."

Brian's renewed spiritual dedication came at the right time. For a select few players, the minor leagues are merely a pit stop en route to The Show. For everyone else, they are a crucible of perseverance. Count Brian among the latter group.

Despite making his major league debut on June 14, 2001, Brian spent significant time at various levels of the Orioles' farm system from 1999 to 2003, battling Jerry Hairston, Baltimore's eleventh-round draft pick in 1997, for playing time every step of the way. The constant uncertainty forced Brian to ask tough questions about his faith.

But when Hairston went on the disabled list early in 2004 spring training, the door of opportunity swung open. Brian began the season as the team's starting second baseman and leadoff hitter.

Brian's physical stature was not lost on others, certainly not opposing fans. During a game in Seattle one year, Brian made it safely to first base, where the Mariners' Richie Sexson, a massive human being, awaited. At 6 foot, 8 inches, Sexson was a whole foot taller than Brian. Noticing the disparity, a Seattle fan yelled out, "Hey Richie, I didn't know it was Bring Your Kid to Work Day!"

Brian laughed, but the moment illustrated a question on many people's minds: Could a player the Orioles generously listed as 5 foot, 9 inches tall and 175 pounds really be an everyday impact player in the major leagues?

The answer was a resounding yes.

In 2004, Brian hit .273 with 107 runs scored and an American League–leading

50 doubles, which marked the most by a switch-hitter in AL history. That made the Orioles' choice easy. The following February, they packaged Hairston in a trade to the Cubs for slugger Sammy Sosa. At age twenty-six, Brian was the team's second baseman of the future. The little buggy-whipper with the patchwork heart had made it.

Still, few outside Baltimore took notice. After all, the Orioles finished the season 78–84 and a distant third in the AL East. The team was a blip on baseball's radar.

But if 2004 was a modest foreshadowing of the AL's newest star infielder, 2005 was a megaphone announcement. With previously unseen power, Brian took the league by storm that year, hitting .345 with 15 home runs, 49 RBIs, 18 stolen bases, and a 1.007 OPS (on-base-plus-slugging) percentage at the All-Star Break. His torrid start propelled the surprising Orioles into first place in the AL East early on, and he earned the starting nod at second base for the AL All-Star Team.

It was like someone popped a bottle of "Instant Stardom" champagne and sprayed it all over Brian. Suddenly, his locker became a media magnet, which, of course, prompted much ribbing from his teammates.

"In batting practice, the guy couldn't even hit a home run," Jay Gibbons, an Oriole from 2001 to 2007, joked in May 2005. "I told him in spring training one day, 'Please, just hit one out for me so I can see it.' He's like, 'I don't think I can do it, man.' He finally hit one out, and I gave him a standing ovation. And a month and a half later, the guy is leading the league in homers."

Then the bubbly ran out. On September 20—less than two weeks before the season ended—Brian suffered a gruesome arm injury. A collision at first base with New York Yankees base runner Bubba Crosby dislocated his left elbow, tore his ulnar collateral ligament, and ripped his flexor mass muscles off the bone. It hurt as bad as it sounds.

Poof! Just like that, Brian's amazing season was over—and worse, his career was in jeopardy. Baseball's best second baseman was left sitting in excruciating bewilderment on the infield dirt, cradling his left arm like a mother holds an infant. Haunting questions swarmed his mind: *Why did this happen? Why now? Is my career over?*

Some players never return from such a thunderclap of physical violence. Brian did. But the recovery process was brutal.

He underwent surgeries to replace his elbow ligament (procedures also known as "Tommy John surgery") and reattach his forearm muscles to the bone. Then he had to endure six months of rehab that were both physically and psychologically taxing.

His parents spent a month with him at his off-season home in Arizona to help with his most basic needs, such as cooking, cleaning, and getting dressed. He had to learn to throw again, too. Humble pie, anyone?

"I was basically like a child," Brian recalls. "I couldn't even put my clothes on."

Weak and utterly helpless, he was right where God wanted him. The truths of 2 Corinthians 12:9 hit Brian like never before. His frailty acted as a microscope that magnified God's power and love.

"It's easy to sit there and say, 'I love Jesus. This is great. God is good. He's a God that wants to bless you,' and all this when things are going great," Brian said. "But when everything comes crashing down on you, how do you handle it? Are you prepared and capable of saying, 'I still trust God. . . . I still think He's a perfect God and that He can't do anything wrong. This is right. Why not me?' "

From a numbers perspective, 2005 was still a marvelous season. Brian was named the "Most Valuable Oriole" after finishing among the AL leaders in batting average (.314), doubles (45), stolen bases (27), and on-base percentage (.387). He also set career highs to that point with 18 home runs and 73 RBIs.

But what could be expected of him in the future after such a traumatic ordeal? As it turns out, a lot.

Remarkably, Brian was ready to go by Opening Day 2006. Despite a slow start, thanks to lingering arm issues and an unrelated three-week stay on the disabled list, he managed to hit .286 with 34 doubles and 36 stolen bases. In 2007, he improved to .290 with 42 doubles, 103 runs scored, and an AL-best 50 stolen bases while earning his second All-Star nomination. That "buggy-whipping" stuff sure came in handy.

Brian had regained his status as one of the best second basemen in baseball. Off in the distance, though, storm clouds were gathering. The injury trials of 2005–2006 would feel like a quick spring downpour compared to the monsoon to come.

THE MITCHELL REPORT

The first lightning strike came on October 1, 2006, the final day of the regular season. That afternoon, Baltimore suffered a 9–0 defeat to Boston that marked a merciful end to a 92-loss season.

The Orioles were undoubtedly distracted. That morning's edition of the *Los Angeles Times* contained a story that implicated Brian and two teammates, Jay Gibbons and Miguel Tejada, as illegal performance-enhancing drug users, based on the reported testimony of former Orioles pitcher Jason Grimsley, who was under investigation for steroid use.

According to the story, Grimsley had named Brian, among others, as a steroid user in a federal affidavit. According to the article, the *Los Angeles Times* got the information from a source who viewed a copy of the document, which was filed in federal court in Arizona in May 2006, before Brian and the other players' names were redacted.

Brian flatly denied the report. A day later, he was exonerated by comments from Grimsley's attorney and the case's lead investigator in a separate story. Eventually, the *Los Angeles Times* ran a correction admitting that Grimsley had not named Brian or his teammates in the affidavit. The squall died down.

Then, on December 13, 2007, the big one hit.

Twenty-one months earlier, Major League Baseball commissioner Bud

Selig had asked former U.S. senator George Mitchell to investigate allegations of widespread steroid use in baseball. When MLB released the Mitchell Report, it sent Richter-scale-rattling shockwaves through baseball.

In all, the Mitchell Report alleged eighty-nine players as steroid users. While many names in the documents weren't surprising, one was: Brian Roberts.

Page 158 of the Mitchell Report included the following excerpt:

> *Brian Roberts is an infielder who has played for the Baltimore Orioles since 2001. He has been selected to two All-Star teams.*
>
> *Roberts and Larry Bigbie were both rookies in 2001. According to Bigbie, both he and Roberts lived in [David] Segui's house in the Baltimore area during the latter part of that season. When Bigbie and Segui used steroids in the house, Roberts did not participate.*
>
> *According to Bigbie, however, in 2004 Roberts admitted to him that he had injected himself once or twice with steroids in 2003. Until this admission, Bigbie had never suspected Roberts of using steroids.*
>
> *In order to provide Roberts with information about these allegations and to give him an opportunity to respond, I asked him to meet with me; he declined.*

After four days of silence, Roberts publicly admitted that he had tried steroids once—and only once—in 2003, a year in which he started the season at Triple-A Ottawa and was still trying to solidify his place on a major league roster.

"In a moment of weakness, I made a decision that I knew wasn't right from the beginning," he told the *Baltimore Sun*. "My size, my ability, whatever it was—none of that is any reasoning for making a decision like that."

The news shook baseball and rocked Baltimore. In the wake of Cal Ripken Jr.'s retirement in 2001, Brian had become the face of the franchise. He was a lovable, homegrown underdog with a quiet humility, a soft spot for kids, and boy-next-door looks. And now, like a twenty-first-century baseball version of *The Scarlet Letter*, he had been branded with an ignominious "S" on his chest.

Public reaction was harsh. On December 18, 2007, the *Baltimore Sun* ran a column titled "Hard to Believe Roberts." Opposing fans mocked him on the road. It was a painfully raw period of soul-searching and combating spiritual condemnation.

"It was really hard for me to forgive myself and not beat myself up over it and worry about what other people were thinking and take everything that fans yelled personally," Brian said.

In the days that followed, Brian felt God calling him to use his mistake as a teaching tool. So in 2008, he participated in a candid, seventeen-minute video with the Fellowship of Christian Athletes (FCA) and also spoke to a large group of student athletes in the Baltimore area for an anti-steroids campaign called "Playing Safe, Fair and Sober."

Slowly, the truth of 1 John 1:9 and other scriptures related to confession and forgiveness started to have their intended effect.

"We're all sinners," Brian said. "We can't look in the mirror and say we've always made the right decisions. I've been forgiven by a lot of people that I've hurt, and for that, I'll forever be grateful. Forgiving yourself and knowing that God forgives you, that's a huge part of it."

David Daly, FCA Baseball's national director, who has known Brian since 1997, believes every word of Brian's steroids confession.

"There's no reason not to believe him," Daly said. "He's not a user. He did it one time and immediately knew it was the wrong thing to do. He never did it again. Even though he made a mistake and readily acknowledged that publicly, he knew forgiveness comes from God. And his strong faith got him through that."

A HEART FOR ONE

Often, an individual's qualities are best seen through the eyes of another. And David Daly's eyes have been on Brian for a long time.

The two met when Brian was a UNC freshman and David was a local pastor. The next year, David became the Tar Heels' chaplain, and his ten-year-old son, John, became the team batboy.

John and Brian, both second basemen, immediately hit it off. Brian treated John like a little brother, instructing him (knowingly and not) in the pursuits of baseball and godliness. Brian was one of the best college players in the nation, yet he made plenty of time for his wide-eyed shadow. When John noticed that Brian wrote his favorite scripture passage, Proverbs 3:5–6, underneath the bill of his cap, the boy did the same thing.

Growing up, John never had to buy his own batting gloves. He always had a customized Brian Roberts pair in his bag. Brian also made sure John had a wooden bat to hit with. None of that aluminum junk.

During the 2004 season, Brian found out that a friend of John's was struggling with drug abuse, and he called John. There was a lot of static on Brian's end of the line, so John asked where he was. Brian was in the middle of an exhausting West Coast road trip.

"I'm in Oakland," Brian said, "but we need to talk."

After John's high school graduation in 2007, Brian asked David if he could host John for a weekend during a Baltimore home stand.

"Sure," David said. "I'll book his hotel and make the arrangements."

"No, just put him on a plane," Brian responded. "I'll take care of him. Oh, yeah, tell him he can bring a buddy, too."

When John arrived in Baltimore, a car and driver were waiting for him at the airport. That weekend, John and his friend stayed at Brian's place, attended the Orioles series, and went out to eat with Brian after games. For John, it was the weekend of a lifetime.

"That's how Brian is," David said.

David had grown very close to Brian, too. Both men believe strongly in the mission of FCA, and Brian has been involved with the Christian sports ministry since he was a first grader. In 2008, he accepted David's invitation to join FCA Baseball's board of directors. For years, David has supplied Brian with FCA New Testaments to give to kids he comes in contact with. David considers Brian "part of our family."

Inevitably, the Mitchell Report hit the Daly family hard. Brian called David after the news broke. It was an emotional conversation, especially when Brian asked to speak to John. The two friends both shed tears as Brian asked for John's forgiveness.

"He felt like he had let me and John down," David said. "He hadn't let anyone down. We will always love him."

John, who now coaches baseball at Hickory Christian Academy in Hickory, North Carolina, still texts regularly with Brian. His prized possession remains an autographed, game-worn Roberts jersey with the inscription: "To John, the little brother I never had." That treasured jersey hangs framed on the wall over John's bed.

"Here's the thing about Brian," David said. "He's a better man than a baseball player, and he's an All-Star baseball player."

A HEART FOR MANY

Diana Chiafair witnessed the effect Brian has on people—his compassion and tenderness, particularly with sick and disadvantaged kids. In fact, that's what she credits for her becoming Mrs. Diana Roberts. Cue the love ballad.

Brian and Diana met on a blind date. Well, that's not exactly true—they *tried* to meet on a blind date of sorts. It was spring training 2007, and Brian was expecting to see Diana, a briefcase model on the NBC game show *Deal or No Deal*, in the stands at Fort Lauderdale Stadium, the Orioles' former spring training home. But every bottom half of the inning, he scanned the seats behind home plate. No Diana. *Ouch*. It was only a blind date, but still. . . .

Diana was oblivious to Brian's angst. Baseball was a foreign language to her. She had never been to a baseball game, and for all she knew, Baltimore Orioles were rare, winged creatures that nest in Maryland's largest city. So she arrived at the game with some girlfriends in the sixth inning, completely unaware that teams often pull their starters much earlier in spring training games. Brian was done for the day. When he called her later that night, they cleared up the confusion and laughed it off.

Three nights later, they went out to dinner. He was nervous and shy. She found his reticence cute. But it wasn't until she visited the University of Maryland Hospital for Children in Baltimore with him that she knew he was "the one."

Recalling the fears and difficulties of his own experience as a child, Brian had been visiting the hospital for years. If there's one thing he loves doing besides "buggy-whipping" a baseball, it's bringing smiles to the faces of hurting children. During the season, he usually goes to the hospital every month or two. And since 2006, he had hosted "Brian's Baseball Bash," an annual hospital fund-raiser at the ESPN Zone in Baltimore that raised more than $500,000 in its first five years.

Once, when Brian found out a young friend of former Orioles chaplain Chris Adomanis had a heart condition, he sent the child a note. No fanfare. No accompanying PR campaign. He didn't even tell Adomanis. He just wanted to bless the kid.

"He's just a solid rock," Adomanis pointed out.

When Diana saw Brian's compassion firsthand, she marveled. Here was this famous athlete stooping down to play with sick kids, his face beaming as much as theirs. She had never seen someone reflect so well the heart of Christ toward children.

"I think that's the first thing I fell in love with about him because it's something we're both so passionate about," Diana said. "I was thrilled when I found out. I remember the first time we visited children at the hospital together, seeing him light up. The kids loved being around him. We were there for three hours, but it felt like five minutes. I fall in love with him all over again when we play with kids."

Brian and Diana got married in January 2009. They share a single, powerful heartbeat for broken people. In recent years, Brian has embraced Diana's passion for the Foster and Adoptive Family Connection, a ministry based in Greeneville, Tennessee. Since 2009, he has also mentored inner-city men at Baltimore's Helping Up Mission, which cares for the poor, homeless, and drug-addicted.

Whenever possible, Brian works at FCA clinics and speaks at FCA events. In 2009, he gave his testimony to about 150 baseball coaches at an FCA breakfast during the American Baseball Coaches Association annual meeting in San Diego.

In the Orioles' clubhouse, he's a trusted and well-respected spiritual voice—the guy with the Bible in his locker and a noticeable aversion to bawdy locker room banter. He has been the team's Baseball Chapel representative for many years. His faith is evident, but he's not pushy with it.

"My goal is always to learn more about why God has put me in this position and to follow the doors He opens speaking-wise, working with kids, or whatever it might be," Roberts said. "I realize that I'm in a position that not many people are in, and I have a chance to reach a lot more people than I would otherwise."

MORE TRIALS, MORE FAITH

In 2008 and 2009, Brian enjoyed good health and fine seasons. In 2009, he set the major league record for doubles by a switch-hitter with 56, joining Hall of Famers Tris Speaker, Paul Waner, and Stan Musial as the only players in MLB history with three or more seasons of at least 50 doubles. He also set career highs in runs scored (110) and RBIs (79).

But the injury bug crept back in 2010. Brian spent three months on the disabled list with a herniated disc in his back and a strained abdominal muscle. Then he missed the last six games of the season after giving himself a concussion by hitting his helmet with his bat in frustration after a ninth-inning strikeout. He battled headaches and nausea until Christmas.

Self-inflicted wounds truly hurt the most.

"Kids out there," Brian said in a moment of self-deprecating humor in an April 2011 video blog, "whatever you do, no matter how frustrated you are, no matter how down you get, *do not* hit yourself on the top of the head with a bat. Bad idea."

The disabled list, Brian's albatross, struck again in 2011. A headfirst slide in Boston in May forced him to miss the rest of the season with concussion symptoms. He even had to cancel his children's hospital fund-raiser in Baltimore.

Without their star leadoff hitter, the Orioles sputtered to a 69–93 record, their fourteenth straight losing season. In various Internet chat rooms and social media platforms, long-suffering Orioles fans voiced their restlessness with Brian, an oft-injured player who signed a four-year, $40 million contract extension in February 2009.

"Mr. [Peter] Angelos [the Orioles' owner] has put a lot of investment into me and my family, the Orioles have tried to count on me for a lot and I haven't been there, and that's hard for me," Brian said in early September 2011, when he drove from his Sarasota home to St. Petersburg to visit his teammates, who were in town to face Tampa Bay. "It's hard for me to walk in there and look guys in the eye, especially knowing what they've been through the last five months. I've been there and I've done it, and it's hard."

It was another trip to life's shadow lands, where the Almighty's presence sometimes feels distant, and questions of *Why, God?* and *How long, O Lord?* hide behind every jagged rock and echo in every gulch. So Brian turned once again to Proverbs 3:5–6 and let his favorite scripture illuminate the darkness.

He also took refuge in the Psalms. He loves their realness and their rawness. Many were written by men who opened breaking hearts to God and asked tough questions. Brian especially loves reading psalms by King David, a great yet flawed man who enjoyed God's favor, endured God's discipline, and suffered through numerous life-threatening trials. David didn't approach God with canned prayers. He came with agony, tears, joy, and praise—all genuine and unfiltered. That ministers to Brian.

"Look at David," Brian said. "He was upset and angry. We can be honest with God. That's part of our relationship. That's why it's called a relationship. God isn't a lucky charm. It's a real relationship. That's why He should be your best friend, one you can talk to through the ups and downs, the good and bad. Our feelings should be relayed to Him in that same way, and I believe that He hears that and understands that."

So what are we to make of Brian's trial-riddled career so far? Perspective helps. By any standard, he has enjoyed great success. Entering 2012, he's a career .281 hitter in eleven big league seasons and ranks among the Orioles' all-time leaders in hits, doubles, extra-base hits, walks, and runs. He also plays a strong second base with a .987 career fielding percentage there.

Still, you can't help wondering how much more he could've accomplished if fully healthy. No one can blame Brian for entertaining similar thoughts. Or questioning whether he'll ever play for a winning team.

Ultimately, though, the conjecture is all moot. Life doesn't offer 70-mph, down-the-middle fastballs for long. It always mixes in the tougher stuff. What matters most, Brian has learned, is how you handle life's high heat and off-speed junk. He has come to trust in the wisdom of James 1:2–4, the mysterious paradox that life's trials are to be embraced, not cursed.

So the persistent, undersized underdog stays at it—trusting, praying, serving, and buggy-whipping all the way. Few thought he would get *this* far. But it's already been a great career. And it's not over yet.

"I can rely completely on God, and it's very rewarding to know that," Brian said. "Even when we feel inadequate physically or mentally or spiritually, it helps to know that we're not counting on ourselves. It's not about us. It's been fun. It's been frustrating. It's been a little bit of both. And that's the awesome part about it. That's our journey—the ups and the downs."

12

JOSH WILLINGHAM:
UNDERSTANDS THE LORD
GIVES AND TAKES

By any reckoning, June 13, 2009, was the worst day of Oakland Athletics out-fielder Josh Willingham's life.

The previous night, Josh, who was playing for the Washington Nationals at the time, had suffered an 0-for-4, two-strikeout performance in a 4–3 loss at Tampa Bay, dropping his batting average to .252. The Nationals, at 17–43, were 18½ games back in the National League East and freefalling toward a 59–103 final record, the franchise's worst showing since the 1976 Montreal Expos lost 107 games.

Josh's head finally hit the hotel pillow after midnight. Blessed relief—but relief that was short-lived.

At 5:30 a.m., an abrupt knock startled Josh from slumber. Groggy and perplexed, he opened his hotel room door. Standing there was Rob McDonald, the National's travel director. He told Josh that he had received an urgent message from Josh's father, David Willingham.

McDonald swallowed hard. Then he delivered the terrible news: Josh's little brother, Jon, was dead.

What do you do when life blindsides you with a crushing roundhouse? How do you react? To whom do you turn? Where do you go?

Josh hurried home as soon as he could pack his suitcase. Home for Josh was Florence, Alabama, a modest town (population 39,319) in the state's "Shoals" area—a place that fancies itself as "Alabama's Renaissance City."

The good people of Florence like to puff out their cultural chests a bit with art shows, film festivals, renaissance fairs, and a popular annual music celebration honoring native son W.C. Handy, the "Father of the Blues." Renowned architect Frank Lloyd Wright chose Florence as the site of his only house in Alabama. The city also features the Fame Recording Studio, whose microphones have been graced by the likes of the Queen of Soul, Aretha Franklin, as well as rhythm and blues legends Etta James and Wilson Pickett.

Otherwise, life in the Shoals ambles by like a boat drifting down the Tennessee River. The Shoals, like Alabama in general, is college football country. Baseball? Not so much. Florence's main university, North Alabama, is an NCAA Division II outpost whose greatest baseball alumnus was Terry Jones, a career .242 hitter in 227 big league games from 1996 to 2001. The city certainly isn't on any major league scouts' radars.

But Josh wasn't just anyone. His prodigious power stuck out like a Handy trumpet solo from "St. Louis Blues." After the low-key slugger set plenty of records at tiny Mars Hill Bible School—a Christian institution founded by his great-grandfather in 1946—and the University of North Alabama, the Florida Marlins drafted him almost as an afterthought in the seventeenth round in 2000. Six years later, though, he became a full-time big league starter.

At 6 feet, 2 inches and 215 pounds, Josh is a chiseled collection of fast-twitch muscles who can hit the ball a country mile. In his first six full big league seasons (2006–2011), he averaged 22 homers and 71 RBIs in only 128 games a year. He's also a career .262 hitter.

But injuries, especially a troublesome disc in his back, have long been his kryptonite. In 2006, he missed two weeks with a sprained hand. In 2008, he missed 50 games with a lower back strain. A knee injury that required surgery wiped out the last 44 games of 2010 for him. And his back and a sore Achilles' tendon nagged him in 2011.

What, one wonders, could he do in a full, healthy season? It's not a question Josh dwells on. He deals in reality, not his imagination, so he turns to scripture for reminders that trials are for his spiritual good—and to trust God no matter what.

"I just take it day by day," he said in his syrupy-sweet Southern twang. "You're not guaranteed a day in life, or in baseball, so I'm just trying to do today what I can to help us win and to do my best."

Josh's even-keeled outlook is actually a product of a strong faith that took root in a loving home. His parents, David and Denise, took him and his brother, Jon, to Cross Point Church of Christ in Florence three times a week. By 2000, when he was twenty-one years old and experiencing his first season of professional ball a thousand miles from home in Utica, New York, with the Utica Blue Sox (Class A), Josh made his family's deep faith his own by trusting in Christ for the forgiveness of his sins.

"That's where my faith grew," he says. "I had to stand on my own."

Suddenly, on June 13, 2009, Josh felt very alone.

He and Jon, his only sibling, did everything together growing up. As kids, Josh and Jon (who was three and a half years younger) fished, biked, pelted each other in acorn fights, and created a mini chip-and-putt golf course in their yard. They loved to watch University of Alabama football together—and don't even utter the word *Auburn* nearby.

"They were very close," David Willingham said. "They kept up with Alabama football constantly. I guarantee that up to the week Jon died, they were talking football and recruiting and what was going to happen that season."

Jon's death felt surreal to Josh—for both the sudden shock and the mysterious details surrounding it. According to a June 14, 2009, article in Florence's *TimesDaily* newspaper, twenty-seven-year-old Jon was pronounced dead at a local hospital after leading police on a chase for several minutes before losing control of his 2003 Ford Explorer and slamming head-on into a tree around

1:45 a.m. A male passenger in Jon's car was placed in the intensive care unit but survived. According to the article, police were trying to pull over Jon for reckless driving and speeding.

Josh took a weeklong bereavement leave for the funeral. Death felt too familiar. Just forty-two days earlier, his paternal grandfather, a patriarch of the family faith, had passed away.

As the week's end drew near, Josh told his father, "It's going to be hard for me to go back. I don't have my heart in it." Eventually, with David's encouragement, he boarded the plane for D.C.

Sporting two wristbands and a necklace bearing Jon's name, Josh caught fire and raised his average to .309 by early August before cooling off in September for a respectable line of .260, 24 homers, and 61 RBIs in 133 games.

A left medial meniscus tear derailed another solid season in 2010 (.268 batting average, 16 home runs, and 56 RBIs in 114 games) before life rattled his comfort zone again: in December 2010, the Nationals traded Josh to the Athletics.

Florence, Alabama, and Oakland, California, are as different as the twenty-three hundred miles between them would suggest. It wasn't easy for Josh to get used to the West Coast lifestyle. Plus, with an off-season home in Florence, Josh's college-sweetheart wife, Ginger, and their two young sons couldn't fly to Oakland for extended visits as much as they had when Josh played in D.C. For all of its glamour, life in the major leagues also presents some challenging realities.

Josh's batting average dipped to .246 in 2011, but he continued to show that he's a dangerous hitter when healthy, as evidenced by his 29 home runs and 98 RBIs in 136 games. On July 15, he smashed the first home run into the Oakland Coliseum's second deck since Frank Thomas accomplished the feat in August 2006.

Josh capitalized on his power-hitting 2011 season and signed a three-year deal with the Minnesota Twins during the off-season. His career has been marked by trials and ordeals, so Josh has learned to lean more on the Rock who never moves.

"Being so far away from home and family, I have to lean on Him more," he said.

Josh thinks about his little brother every day. But life goes on, and there is much to be thankful for. He has a wonderful family, financial security, and a dream job.

Job, the Bible's archetypal sufferer, endured utter devastation and still exclaimed, "The LORD gave and the LORD has taken away; may the name of the LORD be praised" (Job 1:21). This, too, is Josh's attitude. Whether it's death, exasperating injuries, or a difficult cross-country move, he knows where to turn for hope and peace.

"I can't understand how people do it if they don't have faith, especially [regarding] eternal life," Josh said. "What kind of hope do people have? You have to really lean on God when [a trial] happens. He has basically showed me that He is the boss through difficult times."

13

MARIANO RIVERA:
THE CLOSER WHO GOT SAVED

Looking for a good argument? Just walk up to any die-hard baseball fan and start talking about the greatest players of all time.

Who's the best center fielder ever to play the game? Is it Willie Mays, Joe DiMaggio, Ty Cobb, Mickey Mantle, or Ken Griffey Jr.?

How about third basemen? Good cases can be made for Mike Schmidt, George Brett, Brooks Robinson, Alex Rodriguez, and Chipper Jones.

And don't even dare to bring up first basemen, where Lou Gehrig, Jimmie Foxx, and Albert Pujols top most lists.

The truth is, baseball fans love to argue the minutia of the sport and whether the bigger, stronger players of the modern era are better than the greats from the past. No other American sport has the history and voluminous statistics that baseball affords, so the debates over the "best ever" can be never-ending.

But the position of closer is one where there's virtually no argument. When the bullpen gate swings open in the ninth inning with a game on the line, one player has dominated more than any other pitcher in history: Mariano Rivera.

In seventeen seasons since coming up with the New York Yankees in 1995, Mariano has earned 603 saves—the most in baseball history. Only he and Trevor Hoffman (601 saves) have passed the 600 mark . . . and that doesn't count Mariano's 42 postseason saves, which are also a major league record. When he's on the mound, the Yankees nearly always secure a victory. His save percentage is a hair under 90 percent—the best ever for pitchers who have had 250 or more save opportunities.

In the playoffs, where things really matter, Mariano has been nearly unhittable. And playing for the Yankees, he's had plenty of postseason experience. He has helped New York win five World Series titles and was named the Most Valuable Player of the 1999 World Series. His earned-run average in the playoffs is an unheard-of 0.70.

Only twenty-one pitchers in the history of baseball have tallied *half* the number of saves that this slender hurler known as the "Hammer of God" has earned. Mariano has won the Rolaids Relief Man Award five times for the American League and has been voted an All-Star twelve times.

Despite the accolades and accomplishments, Mariano stays humble and firmly rooted in his Christian faith. He lets his actions, instead of his words, do the talking. Not exactly the demeanor of a typical big league closer.

Almost everything about Mariano is the opposite of what most people think of when they picture a relief pitcher. This normally high-strung bunch is known for their bushy beards, waxed mustaches, big rope necklaces, nervous tics, and unpredictable behavior on the mound.

"Look at Mo's delivery, look at how he repeats it," teammate Joba Chamberlain marveled. "He does the same exact thing every time. That's a very hard thing to do—I try, but I can't do it like Mo. There's never any added stress on his arm because all the parts move the same way every time."

If Mariano could be described in one word, it would be *predictable.* He warms up the same way before every appearance. He never looks rushed or worried. His demeanor is the same, whether it's a spring training game or the World Series. Even his signature pitch—the cut fastball—is predictable. Batters know it's coming, but they still can't hit it.

Jim Thome, who has hit more than 600 home runs in his career, called Mariano's cut fastball the greatest pitch in baseball history. Longtime Minnesota Twins manager Tom Kelly once said, "He needs to pitch in a higher league, if there is one. Ban him from baseball. He should be illegal."

When asked if being called the greatest closer ever embarrasses him, Mariano answered: "Yes, it does. It does make me uncomfortable because I don't like to talk about myself. I just want to be able to contribute as much as I can for the team. And the rest is just blessings from the Lord."

In reality, he doesn't have to say anything. Teammates, opponents, and sportscasters say it for him.

"You're seeing the greatest closer of all time," Yankee catcher Jorge Posada said. "I don't care about ERAs. There's nobody better. No one can even compare. His body doesn't change. He doesn't change. He's the same Mariano as he was as a setup man, as a closer, and as a friend."

Yankee shortstop Derek Jeter has equally high praise for the kind of person Mariano is. "He's like my brother," said Jeter, who came up in the minor leagues with Mariano. "Anytime you play with someone that long, there's a connection there. . . .He's been the exact same person he was since the first day I met him."

That person is deeply committed to God, his family, and his teammates.

Mariano is the first to say that he never could've collected so many saves if his team hadn't put him in the right situation. In order to earn a save, a pitcher must record at least three outs with his team in the lead by no more than three runs. Every save opportunity brings pressure, but Mariano handles it with ease.

He appears strangely peaceful on the mound—and it's a peace that only comes from knowing the Prince of Peace.

"I don't know if we'll ever see it again," Yankee manager Joe Girardi said after Mariano notched his 600th career save. "This is a guy who I believe is the best closer that's ever been in the game, and I've had the fortune of catching him, coaching him, and managing him, and it's a treat."

Hitting against him is anything but a treat. However, Mariano has earned the respect of opposing batters, including Boston Red Sox great David Ortiz. "If you talk to him at an All-Star Game, it's like talking to somebody who just got called up," Ortiz said. "To him, everybody else is good. I don't get it. To him, everybody else is the best. It's unbelievable. And he is the greatest. . . . Good people, you want to do well."

And Mariano has done well. *Very* well, especially considering that when the Yankees first saw him, he was a *shortstop*, not a pitcher.

DEVELOPING THE MIRACLE PITCH

Kansas City Royals scout Herb Raybourn first witnessed Mariano on a baseball field in 1988. He was playing for Panamá Oeste (Panama West) in the national championship game. At 6 feet, 2 inches and around 160 pounds, Mariano made an impact as a rangy shortstop with a good arm. His batting stroke, however, was less than impressive.

A year later, Panamá Oeste again qualified for the national tournament. But with his team's pitching floundering, Mariano volunteered to step onto the mound. He had thrown some growing up and, as a child, was always good at hurling rocks at a target.

Mariano wasn't overpowering as a pitcher, but he was accurate. So accurate, in fact, that he caught the eye of Chico Heron, a Yankees scout. Heron set up a tryout with Raybourn, who had since become the head of Latin American scouting for the Yankees.

Mariano traveled to Panama City for the audition. Raybourn immediately recognized him. The skinny shortstop took the ball and walked to the mound. He had thrown just nine pitches—all of which registered in the mid-80s on the speed gun—when Raybourn stopped him. Mariano thought he'd blown it. But Raybourn had seen enough.

"The radar wasn't really being lit up," Raybourn said. "But what I liked about Mariano was his looseness, a nice loose arm. And his fastball had a lot of movement. I could picture him pitching in the majors."

Raybourn figured that with some professional coaching and weight training, Mariano's fastball could gain some extra pop. He'd also have to learn a few other pitches.

The twenty-year-old signed with the Yankees on February 17, 1990, and received a $2,000 signing bonus. He had never thought about being a professional baseball player until he inked his name on the contract.

"Usually a player prepares for years," Mariano said. "Here I was signing, and I wasn't even [planning on becoming] a pitcher."

Even though Mariano didn't feel like a pitcher, he looked like one on the diamond. He was assigned to the Gulf Coast League Yankees, where he competed against other rookies. In 22 games, he pitched 52 innings and gave up one earned run while striking out 58 and walking just seven.

In 1991, he advanced to the Class A Greensboro Hornets (North Carolina). While his record (4–9) was subpar, he posted an impressive 2.75 ERA and 123-to-36 strikeouts-to-walks ratio. After the season, Mariano enjoyed a greater highlight when he flew home to Panama and married Clara Younce, whom he had known since elementary school.

Over the next several years, Mariano worked his way up to the Triple-A Columbus Clippers in Columbus, Ohio, but his 87-mile-per-hour fastball didn't impress the big league club.

Early in the 1995 season, though, injuries to several Yankees starters gave Mariano a chance to pitch in pinstripes for the first time. His major league debut turned out to be a dud when he gave up five runs and eight hits in just three innings to the California Angels. In his first four starts for the Yankees, he notched a 10.20 ERA and was quickly sent back to Columbus.

The Yankees still liked Mariano, but they wanted someone with more pop on his fastball. They considered trading him to the Detroit Tigers for David Wells. Then two weeks after Mariano shipped back to the minors, something amazing happened—he added ten miles an hour to his fastball.

On June 26, 1995, Mariano pitched a five-inning no-hitter against the Rochester Red Wings that ended early due to bad weather. But what impressed the Yankees organization most was that his fastball registered a smoking 96 miles per hour on the radar gun.

Nobody could explain where the extra speed came from, but Mariano had an answer: it was a gift from God.

The hurler had recently accepted Jesus Christ as his personal Savior. During his career in the minor leagues, Mariano had seen God show up for him time after time, often through the kindness of other people who would come forward to help at key moments. When his wife was in the hospital, a pitching coach offered to stay with the couple's first son so Mariano could be with her. Another time a lady in Panama helped out his wife while he had to play.

"Every time I was going through a hard time, somebody was there to help," Mariano said. "Even though I had nobody here, I was never alone. That made me accept Jesus as my Savior. I knew it wasn't a coincidence. It was the Lord putting someone there for me."

The extra oomph on his fastball earned Mariano a return trip to New York. This time he fared much better. On July 4, 1995, he struck out 11 in eight shutout innings against the Chicago White Sox.

In 1995, Major League Baseball's first season of expanded, four-teams-per-league playoffs, New York qualified for the playoffs as the wild card. Mariano made the postseason roster and earned a victory in Game 2 against Seattle. The Mariners won the series three games to two, but Mariano pitched well each time out—even striking out Mike Blowers in the eighth inning of Game 5 with the bases loaded.

By 1996, Joe Torre had taken over as manager of the Yankees, who were loaded with young talent, including Jorge Posada, Derek Jeter, Andy Pettitte, and Bernie Williams. With enough starting pitching, Torre knew he wanted Mariano coming out of the bullpen; he just didn't know what role Mariano would play.

The Yankees soon figured out that Mariano was the perfect setup man for closer John Wetteland. With Mariano and Wetteland coming out of the bullpen that year, the Yankees notched a 79–1 record in games in which they held a lead after seven innings.

After failing to win a World Series since 1978, the Yankees claimed the 1996 championship by defeating Atlanta four games to two. Wetteland earned Most Valuable Player honors in the Series, but everybody knew the season belonged to Mariano. He even finished third in Cy Young Award balloting, which goes to the best pitcher in each league. No setup man had ever finished that high.

A FASTBALL THAT'S A CUT ABOVE

If God had given Mariano a gift by adding extra zip to his fastball, He was about to perform a miracle that has kept Mariano at the top of the game for years.

The Yankees let the high-priced Wetteland go in the off-season and moved Mariano to closer. The decision seemed like a no-brainer. But after the 1997 season started, Mariano blew four of his first six save opportunities.

The slow start resulted in a meeting with Torre and Yankees pitching coach Mel Stottlemyre. Mariano felt terrible. He hated letting down the team.

"The harder I tried, the tougher it got," Mariano said. "It was like moving in quicksand. I kept sinking. Joe told me that, 'As long as you are here, you'll be the closer.' That's exactly what I needed to hear."

Shortly after the meeting, something remarkable happened. Mariano had made it into the majors with a four-seam fastball that sometimes had good movement. He got batters out with velocity and accuracy. But as he warmed up before a game with pitcher Ramiro Mendoza, Mariano tried holding the ball a bit differently as they played catch. Mariano noticed that his throws dipped and darted when he gripped the ball a certain way, moving so much that Mendoza had a tough time even catching them.

Mariano had always liked fiddling with how he held the baseball. His long fingers and flexible wrist were perfect for a pitcher. But now he had a problem . . . or did he?

At first, Stottlemyre tried working with Mariano to remove the cutting action and make the ball go straighter. But after discovering his new pitch, Mariano recorded the save that day. He converted his next three save opportunities as well.

Suddenly, Mariano possessed a pitch that looked like a fastball but acted like a slider when it got close to the plate. And it wasn't long before Mariano developed perfect precision with his signature cut fastball. He controlled its location by putting different pressure on the ball with his fingers. Greater pressure with his middle finger made it move one way. Using the index finger a little more caused it to move another.

From a hitter's perspective, Mariano's delivery looked effortless. But in an instant, the ball exploded past the plate at more than 95 miles per hour.

Scientists have studied thousands of Mariano's pitches. What makes him so devastating is that he throws the cut fastball and four-seam fastball with the exact same motion. Contrary to popular belief, big league batters don't possess supernatural reflexes and reaction speeds. What allows a batter to hit a ball are visual cues and tons of practice. If a pitcher drops down in his delivery or flicks his wrist, a batter can anticipate where the ball is going to be.

"You can't see the spin on it," six-time All-Star Lance Berkman said about Mariano's cutter. "A four-seam fastball rotates a certain way. A slider or a cutter is going to spin a certain way—you see a red dot on the ball as it's coming at you from the seams as it spins. And once you see the rotation on it, you react a certain way. The good cutters, like Rivera's, rotate like a four-seamer—you don't see the red dot, you don't know it's going to come in on you until it's too late."

Batters often think they're seeing a hittable pitch over the plate, but by the time they make contact, the ball has moved several inches and is either in on their hands or hit off the end of the bat. Mariano has unofficially led the major leagues in broken bats every year since he developed his cut fastball. Some sportscasters have joked that bat-maker Louisville Slugger should pay Mariano a bonus because of all the business he's brought its way.

But this pitch is no joke to Mariano—it's a blessing.

"That is my miracle pitch," Mariano said. "That's what I call it, because it's God's gifting. I didn't have that pitch before and nobody taught me that. It came as a miracle."

Since mastering the pitch, Mariano throws his cutter more than 90 percent of the time. He might mix in an occasional two-seam fastball. And about four times a year, he'll throw a changeup just to keep batters honest.

Once Posada became the Yankees' everyday catcher, it got to the point that he didn't flash signs to tell Mariano what pitch to throw. Posada would simply signal to throw the pitch over the inside or outside *corner* of the plate. Mariano rarely throws one down the middle. With pinpoint accuracy and a determination to win, Mariano goes after the black edges of the plate.

Unlike a lot of closers, Mariano doesn't resort to intimidation. He doesn't believe in throwing brushback pitches. One, because he isn't out there to show up hitters. And two, because that would waste a pitch. All Mariano wants to do is throw strikes.

"My mental approach is simple: get three outs as quick as possible," he said. "If I can throw three, four pitches, the better it is. I don't care how I get you out, as long as I get you out."

HIS OLD MAN AND THE SEA

Mariano developed his workmanlike attitude as a child, thanks largely to his father.

Mariano was born on November 29, 1969, the son of a fisherman in the little town of Puerto Caimito, located about thirty miles north of Panama's capital, Panama City. His house sat about a hundred feet from the Pacific Ocean and consisted of concrete blocks and a corrugated tin roof.

Mariano's sport of choice as a child was soccer, but he also played baseball . . .if using a stick to hit a ball made of electrical tape wrapped around fish netting counts as baseball.

During his early elementary years, Mariano and his friends would make a ball, cut a few straight tree branches for a bat, and form gloves and chest protectors out of cardboard. Games were played on a stretch of beach at low tide or in the streets.

When Mariano was twelve, his father bought him a real leather glove. The youngster was so excited that he slept with the glove and took it everywhere with him, even to school.

Mariano's father worked hard as a fisherman, earning around $50 a week, to provide for his four children. He was also a strict disciplinarian. Mariano remembers receiving a lot of spankings, but he knew his father punished him for his own good.

"My childhood was wonderful," Mariano said. "Basically, I didn't have anything. But what we had, I was happy."

As Mariano entered Pablo Sanchez High School, he dreamed of becoming a professional soccer player. He had quick feet and a smooth athleticism. What he didn't have was the ability to stay healthy. Numerous ankle injuries caused him to give up on his *fútbol* aspirations.

Instead of bending it like Beckham, Mariano was going to try to fish 'em like Roland Martin. Following his graduation from high school at sixteen, Mariano tried his hand at the family business. He wasn't afraid of hard work, but he soon realized that fishing wasn't for him. The boats would go out for six days a week. Everybody slept on board, and sometimes it got dangerous when the seas were up. Once, his boat full of fish capsized and sent the crew into the ocean. Fortunately, everyone made it to the safety of a nearby vessel.

"It's hard. Extremely hard," Mariano said of being a fisherman. "I wanted to study to be a mechanic. Obviously, I didn't do it because the Lord had different plans for me."

While Mariano didn't follow his father's footsteps into fishing, he did pick up a lot from Mariano Sr.—including his strong character and generous spirit. If his father can help someone, he will, Mariano says—even if that means giving a person his last ten dollars. (Panama uses the American dollar as its currency.)

Mariano's generosity shows through in numerous ways. After making it with the Yankees, he always made sure to give back to his home country. Mariano purchased baseball equipment for local children. He donated medical equipment and supplies to a hospital. He sent Christmas presents. He honored area mothers by holding a party on Mother's Day (which is celebrated on December 8 in Panama) and giving away furniture and appliances. He even built a church in his hometown.

Mariano is also helping rebuild a church in his new home city. During the summer of 2011, Mariano and his fellow Spanish-speaking congregants at *Refugio de Esperanza*—Refuge of Hope—announced they were buying and restoring the historic North Avenue Church in New Rochelle, New York. Built in 1907, the church had been under public ownership for decades and fallen into disrepair. Renovation costs were estimated at $3 million.

Mariano fell in love with the building from the moment he saw it and has big plans for the church.

"We have a lot of goals to work with the youth," Mariano said. "That is my passion. We are working hard to make it open as soon as possible."

Mariano added that he plans to devote himself to the church full-time once he retires from baseball. Yankees fans, of course, hope that's years down the road, but it isn't the first time they've heard that kind of talk from their closer.

In July 1999, Mariano stood on the mound in Yankee Stadium as the Bronx Bombers hosted the Atlanta Braves. Between pitches, he heard something that he'd never heard before—a joyous yet powerful sound. He described it as the voice of God telling him, *I am the One who has you here.*

When the season ended and the Yankees had won their second straight World Series, Mariano went back home to Panama and spoke to a church, saying that he planned to play baseball four more years before retiring to become a minister.

Obviously, Mariano didn't end up walking away from baseball in 2003. But his desire to serve God hasn't changed.

"This was something special, and God wants me to concentrate on bringing Him to other people," Mariano said of the encounter. "That meant the only reason I'm here is because He's my strength. He put me here. Without Him, I'm nothing. I think it means that He has other plans for me, to deliver His Word."

Mariano is an extremely private man who's protective of his wife and three sons: Mariano Jr., Jafet, and Jaziel. But when it comes to his faith, he will boldly step out. He often reads his Bible in the Yankees locker room and is a regular at team chapel services.

Mariano also stays involved with a number of charities and was honored for his charity work with the 2003 Thurman Munson Award, named for the great Yankee catcher.

BIG MO

When it comes to great Yankees pitchers, Mariano already tops most lists—above other legends such as Lefty Gomez, Whitey Ford, Ron Guidry, Red Ruffing, and Goose Gossage.

At the end of the 2011 season, Mo—as his teammates call him—held twenty-nine MLB pitching records and eight career Yankee records, including a couple he set during an incredible streak from 1998 to 2000.

During those years, the Yankees won three consecutive World Series—and Mariano was nearly unhittable. In 1999, Mariano actually recorded more saves (45) than hits he allowed (43) all season. That was also the year he won the World Series Most Valuable Player award. A week later, Panamanian president Mireya Moscoso gave him the Order of Manuel Amador Guerrero, one of the country's highest honors.

The following year, when Mariano notched the final out against the New York Mets in the World Series, it marked the first time in MLB history that the same pitcher had nailed down the last out in three straight Series.

Following their 2000 championship, the Yankees had to wait nine years before getting back on top. At times, Mariano carried some of the blame, like when he committed a throwing error on a bunt in the bottom of the ninth inning in Game 7 of the 2001 World Series against the Arizona Diamondbacks. Arizona capitalized by scoring two runs off broken-bat hits and winning the game 3–2, claiming the Series four games to three.

But even after the disappointment, Mariano saw God's hand at work. Had the Yankees won the game, a ticker tape parade was planned for the whole team. Without a championship, Yankees' teammate Enrique Wilson changed his plane flight and went home to the Dominican Republic early. He had originally planned to be on American Airlines Flight 587 on November 12, 2001. That plane crashed in Queens, New York, killing all 260 passengers on board.

"I'm glad we lost the World Series," Mariano said, "because it means that I still have a friend."

The Florida Marlins defeated the Yankees in the 2003 World Series, but New York earned its record twenty-seventh world championship on November 5, 2009. And who was on the mound when the Yankees recorded the decisive out against the Philadelphia Phillies? Mariano, of course. By his side were Jeter, Pettitte, and Posada—four players with five world championship rings apiece.

"That comes from God, having the ability to perform," Mariano said. "I always thank God that He has given me the chance to be part of a team like the New York Yankees and to be able to do my job every time I get there."

Mariano's consistency and dominance are truly amazing. Sportswriters have predicted his decline for years. After several blown saves early in one season, the *Albany Times Union* published the headline, "Rivera No Longer Mr. Automatic." That was in 2002. Since then, he's had some of his best years and has been every bit as automatic as he was in the late nineties.

In 2004, he earned a career-high 53 saves.

In 2011, at age forty-one, Mariano had one of his best seasons by amassing 44 saves, including two record-breaking performances.

On May 28, 2011, Mariano appeared in his one thousandth game as a Yankee. Fourteen pitchers before him had appeared in a thousand games, but he was the first one to do it with one team. His stats that night: four batters, three outs, and twelve pitches—ten of which were strikes.

On September 19, Mariano became baseball's all-time saves leader when he closed out a game against the MinnesotaTwins. With a 6–4 lead in the ninth, Mariano took the mound, retired three batters, and preserved the win. The final out came in typical Mariano fashion. He started Minnesota's Chris Parmelee with a belt-high strike on the outside edge of the plate. Mariano followed with an inside strike that Parmelee fouled off, breaking his bat in the process. With new lumber in his hands, Parmelee could only watch as

Mariano's signature cutter caught the outside corner for strike three.

Three pitches. Three strikes. One historic out.

Yankees fans and players jumped around with emotion as Mariano calmly took the game ball from catcher Russell Martin and smiled. After Mariano hugged his fellow Yankees, Posada nudged him back onto the mound to accept the adulation of the fans. He blew a kiss to the faithful at Yankee Stadium and took off his hat to thank the fans who had cheered for him for seventeen years. He looked almost embarrassed by the applause as he smiled and threw up his arms.

Immediately following the game, Mariano deflected attention away from himself and toward his teammates and God.

"The whole organization, my whole teammates have been a pillar for me," Mariano said. "I always have to talk about God, because that's the most important thing in my life. Yes, there have been bumps in the road, but God gave me the strength."

Mariano credits his longevity to God's blessing and to living a clean lifestyle. After most games, he hurries home or to his hotel, where he's in bed about an hour after throwing the last pitch.

The fact that Mariano takes care of himself and has avoided major arm problems, following his elbow surgery in 1992, makes people believe that the closer may have a number of years ahead of him.

When asked about his future, Mariano joked that he could pitch until he's fifty. But more seriously, he said he's under contract for the 2012 season, and he'll evaluate how he feels and how much he can contribute after the season is over.

No matter what the future holds for Mariano on the mound, one thing is certain in the minds of many fans: they'll never see a pitcher like Mo again.

"When you talk about the greatest relievers of all time, there's only one guy," Yankees teammate Mark Teixeira said. "That conversation begins and ends with Mo."

Posada agreed. "Amazing that he's been able to do it with one pitch over and over again," the catcher said. "There will never be anybody like Mariano Rivera."

Mariano, on the other hand, honestly doesn't care where he'll be remembered in baseball history. He does hope, however, to be remembered for the impact he made on people.

"I don't pay too much attention to that," Mariano said when asked if he cared about being called the greatest relief pitcher who ever lived. "I just want to be the greatest person you've ever met. If I am, then I'm comfortable with that."

ABOUT THE AUTHORS

Mike Yorkey, a former *Focus on the Family* magazine editor and author, co-author or editor of more than seventy-five books, has written about sports all his life for a variety of publications, including *Breakaway*, *Brio*, *Focus on the Family Clubhouse*, *Tennis*, *Skiing*, and *City Sports* magazines. Mike's a lifelong baseball fan, thanks to his parents, who are San Diego Padres season ticket holders. He has collaborated with former San Francisco Giants pitcher Dave Dravecky (*Called Up* and *Play Ball*) and is also the coauthor of *Every Man's Battle* with Steve Arterburn and Fred Stoeker and ten other books in the *Every Man's Battle* series. He is also a novelist who, with Tricia Goyer, coauthored the World War II thriller *Chasing Mona Lisa*, which was released in early 2012. Mike and his wife, Nicole, are the parents of two adult children, Andrea and Patrick. They make their home in Encinitas, California. Mike's website is www.mikeyorkey.com.

Jesse Florea has worked at Focus on the Family for more than eighteen years. He is currently the editorial director for youth magazines. He oversees *Focus on the Family Clubhouse* (for kids eight to twelve) and *Clubhouse Jr.* (for three- to seven-year-olds). He also cohosts the biweekly "Official Adventures in Odyssey Podcast," which often exceeds 100,000 listeners. Jesse is an avid sports fan who has written thousands of high school sports stories and more than a hundred magazine articles on sports personalities, and he was the coauthor of two devotional books for sports-minded children: *The One-Year Devos for Sports Fans* and *The One-Year Sports Devotions for Kids*. He's cowritten or edited more than a dozen other books as well. Jesse's greatest baseball memory is taking batting practice in Coors Field in the mid-1990s with the Colorado Rockies and alongside the "Blake Street Bombers": Andrés Galarraga, Dante Bichette, and Larry Walker. He lives in Colorado Springs, Colorado, with his wife, Stephanie, and two teenagers, Nate and Amber.

Joshua Cooley, a former full-time sports editor/writer at the *Baltimore Examiner* and *The Gazette* newspapers in Maryland, has worked in the sportswriting industry since 1996. His first book—*The One-Year Sports Devotions for Kids* (Tyndale), a collaboration with Jesse Florea and Jeremy Jones—was published in October 2011. Joshua currently works full-time at his church, Covenant Life, in Gaithersburg, Maryland, and freelances for a variety of publications. His freelance credits include *Sports Illustrated*, the *Atlanta Journal-Constitution*, the *Baltimore Sun*, the *Orlando Sentinel*, the *Pittsburgh Tribune-Review*, *Bethesda Magazine*, *Orioles Magazine*, and *Nationals Magazine*. He has also written for Christian publications such as *Sports Spectrum*, *Sharing the Victory*, *Breakaway*, *Brio*, *Focus on the Family Clubhouse*, and *Susie*. In 2006, he contributed to the International Bible Society's "Path to Victory" *Sports New Testament*. Joshua bleeds Baltimore Orioles' black and orange, for better or worse. He and his wife, Kelly, are the parents of four children. The Cooleys make their home in Germantown, Maryland.

SOURCE MATERIAL
PLAYING WITH PURPOSE: FOOTBALL

Introduction

"The number of traffic tickets issued to Tim Tebow . . ."
"That's the Ticket," *San Diego Union-Tribune*, January 4, 2010, page D2.

"I've interviewed all three players . . ."
Author's interview of *Sharing the Victory* editor Jill Ewert, April 5, 2010.

"People have used the term 'perfect storm' . . ."
Author's interview of Reagan Lambert, April 7, 2010.

"Green Bay Packers quarterback Aaron Rodgers says . . ."
"Hardest, Riskiest, Toughest, Greatest Job in Sports," by Peter King, *Sports Illustrated*, September 7, 2009, and available at http://sportsillustrated.cnn.com/vault/article/magazine/MAG1159769/2/index.htm

". . . framed poem on his wall . . ."
"SEC Preview: Florida's Odd Couple Give Gators Bite," by Kelly Whiteside, *USA Today*, August 23, 2007, and available at http://www.usatoday.com/sports/college/football/sec/2007-08-23-florida-oddcouple_N.htm

1. Sam Bradford: The Dynamite Draft Pick

"Where's Rudy When You Need Him?"
"Bradford's Dad Wants to Avoid Spotlight," by John Helsley, *The Oklahoman*, August 22, 2007, and available at http://www.newsok.com/article/3107688?searched= %22Kent%20Bradford%22&custom_click=search

"It wasn't even Halloween."
"Sooner (and Cowboy) Born," by John E. Hoover, *Tulsa World*, November 28, 2008, and available at http://www.tulsaworld.com/site/printerfriendlystory.aspx?articleid=20081128_92_B1_TOPKen88370

". . . show off his ball collection . . ."
"Parents Are Wind beneath Bradford's Wings," by Jenni Carlson, *The Oklahoman*, December 12, 2008, and available at http://www.scrippsnews.com/node/39089

". . . put me on a soccer field today, I would be clueless."
"Q&A with Oklahoma QB Sam Bradford," by Eric Edholm, *ProFootballWeekly.com*, April 5, 2010, and available at http://sports.yahoo.com/nfl/news?slug=pfw-20100406_qa_with_oklahoma_qb_sam_bradford

"We can't move to Canada. Our lives are in Oklahoma."
"Hockey and the Heisman: Sam Bradford," by Danielle Bernstein,
USA Hockey magazine, issue 3, 2009, and available at http://www
.usahockeymagazine.com/article/2009-03/hockey-and-heisman-sam-bradford

"I definitely think their attitudes had a great deal of impact . . ."
"Heisman Hopeful Oklahoma Quarterback Sam Bradford Has Been Boosted
by the Love and Support of His Parents," by Jenni Carlson, *The Oklahoman*,
December 12, 2008, and available at http://newsok.com/the-one-and-only
/article/3329566

"Sam's cello ended up in a closet . . ."
"A Different Tune for Bradford," by Thayer Evans, *New York Times*,
December 6, 2008, and available at http://thequad.blogs.nytimes.com/tag
/sam-bradford/page/2/

"Hockey is so fast and unpredictable . . ."
"Hockey and the Heisman: Sam Bradford," by Danielle Bernstein, *USA Hockey*
magazine, Issue 3, 2009, and available at http://www.usahockeymagazine.
com/article/2009-03/hockey-and-heisman-sam-bradford

"We were playing sports every weekend, and it's not like I didn't know who
God was . . ."
"More Q&As with Bradford and Robinson," by Jenni Carlson, *The
Oklahoman*, April 29, 2009, and available at http://blog.newsok.com
/jennicarlson/2009/04/29/more-qs-as-with-bradford-and-robinson/

"No Off-Season"
"Three-Sport Threat: Sam Bradford," by Andrew Gilman, *The Oklahoman*,
March 25, 2005.

"Hanging out with friends, listening to an engaging middle school pastor . . ."
"Sam Bradford's Strategy for Success," by Jonathan Cyprowski and Shawn
Brown of *The 700 Club*, and available at http://www.cbn.com/700club
/features/amazing/sam_bradford041509.aspx

"Meet Sam Bradford, High School Sophomore Quarterback"
"Sam Bradford, Putnam North," *The Oklahoman*, September 4, 2003, and
available at http://www.newsok.com/article/1070234?searched=Sam%20
Bradford%2C%20Putnam&custom_click=search

"Sam came in and showed us he was the guy."
Author's interview with Putnam North head football coach Bob Wilson,
April 9, 2010.

". . . watched the boy fashion a swing. The ball rose in flight . . ."
"Q&A with Oklahoma QB Sam Bradford," by Eric Edholm,

ProFootballWeekly.com, April 5, 2010, and available at http://sports.yahoo .com/nfl/news?slug=pfw-20100406_qa_with_oklahoma_qb_sam_bradford

"Then Long learned something about Sam that sealed the deal . . ."
"Golf Was OU Quarterback Sam Bradford's Special Link," *The Oklahoman,* March 2, 2009.

"If I come here, I'm coming to play . . ."
"Seeking Depth, Oklahoma Got Much More," by Thayer Evans, *New York Times,* December 6, 2008, and available at http://www.nytimes .com/2008/12/06/sports/ncaafootball/06oklahoma.html?_r=1

"According to reports, Bomar had an arrangement . . ."
"Oklahoma Bombshell," by Stewart Mandell, SI.com, August 2, 2006, and available at http://sportsillustrated.cnn.com/2006/writers/stewart _mandel/08/02/mandel.bomar/

"Kent Bradford was on cloud nine."
"OU Names Bradford Starting Quarterback," by John E. Hoover, *Tulsa World,* August 21, 2007, and available at http://www.tulsaworld.com/ sportsextra/OU/article.aspx?subjectid=92&articleid=070821_2 __Oklah55185&archive=yes

"Sam told CBN's Shawn Brown that his patience and perseverance . . ."
"Sam Bradford's Strategy for Success," by Jonathan Cyprowski and Shawn Brown of *The 700 Club,* and available at http://www.cbn.com/700club/ features/amazing/sam_bradford041509.aspx

"Bradford said it's not that he identifies with David, even though there are similarities."
"Bradford Solves Sooners' Problems with Ease," by Evan Maisel, ESPN.com, published January 6, 2009, and available at http://sports.espn.go.com/ncf/ bowls08/columns/story?columnist=maisel_ivan&id=3812989

"Coach Wilson was on board . . ."
"Sooners Eyeing the No-Huddle; All the Top Teams in the Big 12 Are Using It," by Jake Trotter, *The Oklahoman,* March 17, 2008, and available at http:// www.newsok.com/article/3217125?searched=Sam%20Bradford%2C%20 Bob%20Wilson&custom_click=search

". . . they vaulted themselves to the top of the major college football polls . . ."
"Sooners No. 1 in Major College Football Polls," by John E. Hoover, *Tulsa World,* September 28, 2010, and available at http://www.tulsaworld.com /sportsextra/OU/article.aspx?subjectid=92&articleid=20080928_298 _Okla002744&archive=yes

"The Texas quarterback saw the Red River pairing as special."
"Heisman Showdown," by John E. Hoover, *Tulsa World*, October 10, 2008, and available at http://www.tulsaworld.com/sportsextra/OU/article.aspx?subjectid=92&articleid=20081010_92_B1_TomGil584717&archive=yes

"Sometimes," she said, her voice cracking, "you just have to pinch yourself and realize what's happening."
"The Toast of New York," by John E. Hoover, *Tulsa World*, December 13, 2008, and available at http://www.tulsaworld.com/sportsextra/OU/article.aspx?subjectid=92&articleid=20081213_92_B1_Heisma497939&archive=yes

"Earlier, the three of them had sat in the green room together . . ."
"It's Not Fair to Rip Tebow for His Faith," by Woody Paige, *Denver Post*, May 4, 2010, and available at http://www.denverpost.com/paige/ci_15011076

"I first need to thank God . . ."
Transcription of Sam Bradford's Heisman Speech from this video: http://www.youtube.com/watch?v=VN-Nm-rRVCY&feature=PlayList&p=89EC30B3EC5D9DB9&playnext_from=PL&playnext=1&index=7

"Kent and Martha Bradford, whose memory banks must have flashed through the hundreds of peewee ballgames . . ."
"Sam's Club," by John E. Hoover, *Tulsa World*, December 14, 2008, and available at http://www.tulsaworld.com/sportsextra/OU/article.aspx?subjectid=92&articleid=20081214_92_B1_Olhmur737076&archive=yes

"Something else neat happened in New York: Sam clicked with Colt."
"QB Triumvirate Share Common Bond," by Ivan Maisel, ESPN.com, published August 12, 2009, and available at http://sports.espn.go.com/ncf/preview09/columns/story?columnist=maisel_ivan&id=4391994

"The day after Sam cradled the Heisman Trophy, Jeremy Fowler of the *Orlando Sentinel* laid down a Gator gauntlet when he wrote . . ."
"Loss Will Only Fuel Tebow's Fire," by Jeremy Fowler, *Orlando Sentinel*, December 15, 2008, and available at http://www.tulsaworld.com/sportsextra/OU/article.aspx?subjectid=92&articleid=20081215_92_B2_NEWYOR613627&archive=yes

"The trash talk began when Sooners cornerback Dominique Franks . . ."
"Oklahoma DB Dominique Franks Says Tim Tebow Would Be 4th-Best QB in Big 12," by Jeremy Fowler, *Orlando Sentinel*, January 5, 2009, and available at http://articles.orlandosentinel.com/2009-01-05/sports/bcstebow05_1_franks-oklahoma-defensive-oklahoma-sam-bradford

"Florida linebacker Brandon Spikes, however, couldn't resist the microphone . . ."
"Tebow Responds: Gator Spikes Calls Big 12 Defenses 'A Joke,' " by Guerin

Emig and John E. Hoover, *Tulsa World*, January 5, 2009, and available at http://www.tulsaworld.com/sportsextra/OU/article.aspx?subjectid=92&artic leid=20090105_92_0_MIAMIF579650&archive=yes

"You don't want to wake up a sleeping giant . . ."
"Florida's Tebow, Defense Power Past Oklahoma in BCS Title," by B. G. Brooks, *Rocky Mountain News*, January 8, 2009, and available at http://www .rockymountainnews.com/news/2009/jan/08/florida-tops-oklahoma-bcs -title-game/

"Kent also knew something about insurance policies . . ."
"Texas' Colt McCoy Joins Elite Quarterbacks Who Have Insurance," Matt Murschel, *Orlando Sentinel*, July 26, 2009, and available at http://blogs. orlandosentinel.com/sports_college/2009/07/texas-colt-mccoy-joins-elite-quarterbacks-who-have-insurance.html

"Kent declined to state how much insurance the family took out . . ."
"Good Thing Sam Bradford Has Insurance," The Sports Culture website, and available at http://thesportsculture.com/2009/09/07/good-thing-sam -bradford-has-insurance/

"One of the first questions asked was whether he had any regrets about deciding to return to the University of Oklahoma . . ."
"Bradford Says Farewell," by Guerin Emig, *Tulsa World*, October 27, 2009, and available at http://www.tulsaworld.com/sportsextra/OU/article.aspx?sub jectid=92&articleid=20091027_92_A1_SamBra540297&archive=yes

2. Colt McCoy: The Eyes of Texas Are upon Him

"Inside the Rose Bowl locker room . . ."
"Anguished McCoy Did All He Could to Change Ending," by Mike Lopresti, *USA Today*, January 8, 2010, and available at http://www.usatoday.com /sports/columnist/lopresti/2010-01-08-mccoy-anguish_N.htm

"It seemed like millions to Colt . . ."
"Agonizing Night for Texas QBs," by Dan Wetzel, Yahoo Sports, January 8, 2010, and available at http://rivals.yahoo.com/ncaa/football/news?slug=dw -texasqbs010810

"During a lull in that game's action . . ."
"Title-Seeking QBs Share Football Pasts, Big Dreams of BCS Glory," by Kelly Whiteside, *USA Today*, January 6, 2010, and available at http://www .usatoday.com/sports/college/football/2010-01-06-bcs-mccoy-mcelroy -cover_N.htm

"Keep your head up. Keep plugging away . . ."
"Garret Gilbert Bounces Back from BCS Title Game," by Chip Brown at

Orangebloods.com, March 4, 2010, and available at http://texas.rivals.com
/content.asp?CID=1059086

"They also like to torture him by pretending to punch him in the man region . . ."
"The Eyes of Texas Are upon Him," by Rick Reilly, ESPN.com, published
October 14, 2009, and available at http://sports.espn.go.com/espn/columns
/story?columnist=reilly_rick&id=4557869&sportCat=ncf

"The story goes that Colt's mom, Debra . . ."
"Brad and Debra McCoy: Leaving a Legacy," by Mike Giles, *Dallas Christian
Family* magazine, and available at http://dfwchristianfamily.com/cover
/McCoy-Leaving-Legacy.php

"I can't remember," he said. "I was a little baby . . ."
"Christian Faith Fuels Heisman Front-Runner Colt McCoy," by Peter Elliot,
EverydayChristian.com, October 9, 2009, and available at http://www
.everydaychristian.com/features/story/5053/

"And be a leader . . ."
"Title-Seeking QBs Share Football Pasts, Big Dreams of BCS Glory," by
Kelly Whiteside, *USA Today*, January 6, 2010, and available at http://www
.usatoday.com/sports/college/football/2010-01-06-bcs-mccoy-mcelroy
-cover_N.htm

"Only middle names, please . . ."
The information that Colt's brothers go by their middle names comes from
an interview Colt did with ESPN's Dan Patrick on October 15, 2008. The
link is: http://www.youtube.com/watch?v=pw5sYBa9VlM&feature=related

"They would prepare their children for the path, not the path for their
children . . ."
"Brad McCoy: Four Principles for Raising Godly Children," a blog written by
Amy of Everyday Bless, April 9, 2010, and available at http://walkman4
.blogspot.com/2010/04/brad-mccoy-4-principlesraising-godly.html

"Brad says he raised Colt and his brothers in a disciplined home . . ."
"Brad & Debra McCoy: Leaving a Legacy," by Mike Giles, *Dallas Christian
Family* magazine, and available at http://dfwchristianfamily.com/cover
/McCoy-Leaving-Legacy.php

"His father signaled in the play for a screen pass . . ."
"Father Brad Adds to Colt Lore," by Danny Reagan, GoColtGo.com, October
18, 2006, and available at http://blogs.scripps.com/abil/colt/2006/10/father
_brad_adds_to_colt_lore.html

"Athletes do not drink soda . . ."
"ESPN Covers Century Council: Olympic Athletes Take Time to Teach

Kids," by Alyssa Roenigk, *Century Council*, February 24, 2010, and available at http://www.centurycouncil.org/content/espn-covers-century-council-olympic-athletes-take-time-teach-kids

"We were at On the Border by Six Flags in Arlington . . ."
"The Real McCoy," by Jason King, Yahoo Sports, October 16, 2008, and available at http://rivals.yahoo.com/ncaa/football/news?slug=jn-mccoy101708

"A guy told me after the third game Colt played as a seventh grader . . ."
"The Heart of Texas," by Clay Meyer, *Sharing the Victory* magazine, December 2009, and available at http://www.sharingthevictory.com/vsItemDisplay.lsp?method=display&objectid=3DE967BD-C29A-EE7A-E1312EF7698DA498

"I caught some criticism for it . . ."
"The Real McCoy," by Jason King, *Yahoo! Sports*, October 16, 2008, and available at http://rivals.yahoo.com/ncaa/football/news?slug=jn-mccoy101708

"Sign it," Lavallee replied. "It'll probably be the first of many."
"The Real McCoy," by Jason King, Yahoo Sports, October 16, 2008 and available at http://rivals.yahoo.com/ncaa/football/news?slug=jn-mccoy101708

"We got beat on a cold night . . ."
"Texas' Star-Studded Colt Not Playing Like a Freshman," by Todd Henrichs, *Lincoln Journal Star*, October 19, 2006, and available at http://journalstar.com/sports/football/college/article_67340ae3-0675-52d7-a147-1d952b523e11.html

"I kind of did this [committing to the Longhorns] to get it off my shoulders . . ."
Danny Reagan, *Abilene Reporter-News*, May 18, 2004, and available at http://blogs.reporternews.com/colt/UTcommitment.html

"At the start of training camp . . ."
"Title-Seeking QBs Share Football Pasts, Big Dreams of BCS Glory," by Kelly Whiteside, *USA Today*, January 6, 2010, and available at http://www.usatoday.com/sports/college/football/2010-01-06-bcs-mccoy-mcelroy-cover_N.htm

". . . Greg Davis remembers Colt approaching him the day . . ."
"Colt McCoy of Texas Says He's the Best QB in NFL Draft," by Mary Kay Cabot, *Cleveland Plain Dealer*, April 17, 2010, and available at http://www.cleveland.com/browns/index.ssf/2010/04/cleveland_browns_prospect_colt.html

"I'm not listening to you, dude. You're a freshman . . ."
Q&A with QB Colt McCoy, posted on the 49ers.com website April 12, 2010, and available at http://www.49ers.com/news-and-events/article-2/QA-with -QB-Colt-McCoy/508b5c93-73d0-483a-9d09-782f36328e6f

"I thought Vince would come back . . ."
"Mack's Media Day, Part One: The Quarterbacks," by Peter Bean, Burnt Orange Nation website, July 25, 2006, and available at http://www .burntorangenation.com/2006/7/25/142512/092

"You never enjoy losing, but losing to the Aggies is even worse . . ."
"McGee Accounts for 4 TDs, Aggies beat No. 13 Texas before A&M Coach Franchione Resigns," Associated Press, November 24, 2007, and available at http://www.usatoday.com/sports/scores107/107327/NCAAF763617.htm

"This is Patina. Ken and I are on the dock . . ."
Author's interview of Patina Herrington by the author, April 16, 2010.

"It seems the translators had pooled their money . . ."
"Colt Hero," by Alyssa Roenig, *ESPN Magazine*, August 18, 2009, and available at http://sports.espn.go.com/ncf/news/story?id=4395897

Reagan Lambert, who has been working with . . ."
Author's interview with Reagan Lambert, April 28, 2010.

"Nobody knows who you are. You can just be yourself for a week . . ."
"Colt McCoy: Missionary Man," by Bill Frisbie, Inside Texas.com, March 10, 2009, and available at http://insidetexas.com/news/story.php?article=930

"It's not a slump because I feel like I grew so much . . ."
"Bradford, McCoy Debunk Predictions of Doom," by Dave Sittler, *Tulsa World*, October 8, 2008, and available at http://www.tulsaworld.com /sportsextra/article.aspx?subjectid=202&articleid=20081008_202_B1 _NORMAN313265&archive=yes

"McCoy escapes from seemingly impossible situations so often . . ."
"Texas' McCoy Barely Beats Out OU's Bradford on My Final Ballot," by Gene Menez, Sports Illustrated.com, December 8, 2008, and available at http://sportsillustrated.cnn.com/2008/writers/gene_menez/12/08/final .heismanwatch/#ixzz0llF4xifh

"Colt dedicated his 2008 season to the cousin . . ."
"McCoy Dedicating Season to Late Marine Cousin," Associated Press, November 25, 2008, and available at http://cbs11tv.com/sports/Colt.McCoy .Season.2.873700.html

"It would mean a lot [to win against Alabama]. . . ."
"2009 Sporting News College Athletes of the Year: Colt McCoy, Texas QB,"
by Ken Bradley, The Sporting News, December 17, 2009, and available at
http://www.sportingnews.com/college-football/article/2009-12-17/2009
-sporting-news-college-athlete-year-colt-mccoy-texas-qb

3. Tim Tebow: The Chosen One

"He's been called the NFL version's of a total solar eclipse . . ."
"Fame, Fortune and Being Tim Tebow," by Johnette Howard, ESPN.com,
April 22, 2010, and available at http://sports.espn.go.com/espn/commentary
/news/story?page=howard/100422

"His agent, Jimmy Sexton, predicts Tim will become the best marketable
athlete in history . . ."
"Fame, Fortune and Being Tim Tebow," by Johnette Howard, ESPN.com,
April 22, 2010, and available at http://sports.espn.go.com/espn/commentary
/news/story?page=howard/100422

"The Davie-Brown Index . . ."
"Not Even in NFL Yet, Tim Tebow Already a Marketing Trendsetter," Associated
Press, April 19, 2010, and available at http://www.usatoday.com/sports/football
/nfl/2010-04-19-tim-tebow-marketing_N.htm?utm_source=moggy&utm
_medium=twitter&utm_campaign=GatorWire&utm_source=GatorWire&utm
_medium=twitter&utm_campaign=MoggySocialMedia

"Growing up, I knew my goal was to get a job and make a million dollars . . ."
"Tebow's Family Vision Runs Much Deeper Than Just TDs," by Dave Curtis,
South Florida Sun-Sentinel, August 8, 2008, and available at http://www.sun-
sentinel.com/sports/other/sfl-flsptebowdad08sbaug08,0,5446800.story

"Bob and Pam became friends, and their first date came a year after they met . . ."
"Coaching Character," by Suzy A. Richardson, *Gainesville Sun*, October 7,
2007, and available at http://www.gainesville.com/article/20071007
/NEWS/710060317?p =all&tc=pgall

"It wasn't always easy, but it was a wonderful time for our family . . ."
"Coaching Character," by Suzy A. Richardson, *Gainesville Sun*, October 7,
2007, and available at http://www.gainesville. com/article/20071007
/NEWS/710060317?p =all&tc=pgall

"I was weeping over the millions of babies being [aborted] in America . . ."
"You Gotta Love Tim Tebow," by Austin Murphy, *Sports Illustrated* July 27,
2009, and available at http://sportsillustrated.cnn.com/vault/article
/magazine/MAG1158168/index.htm

"Dysentery is common in developing and tropical countries like the Philippines . . ."
"Amoebic Dysentery: How Common Is It?" by the British Medical Journal Group in association with the *Guardian* newspaper, March 9, 2010, and available at http://www.guardian.co.uk/lifeandstyle/besttreatments/amoebic -dysentery-how-common

"They didn't really give me a choice. That was the only option they gave me . . ."
"Mothering Tebow," by Joni B. Hannigan, *Florida Baptist Witness*, January 8, 2009, and available at http://gofbw.com/News.asp?ID=9758

"It was amazing that God spared him, but we knew God had His hand on his life . . ."
"Mothering Tebow," by Joni B. Hannigan, *Florida Baptist Witness*, January 8, 2009, and available at http://gofbw.com/News.asp?ID=9758

"If I could get my kids to the age of 25 and they know God and serve God . . ."
"Tebows to Headline Evangelism Conference Sessions," *Florida Baptist Witness*, January 29, 2008, and available at http://www.gofbw.com/news. asp?ID=8334

"But the Tebows *were* into competition . . ."
"Competitive Fire Fuels Tebow," by Guerry Smith, Rivals.com website, December 8, 2007, and available at http://collegefootball.rivals.com/content .asp?cid=748732

"Some of his teammates were picking at the ground without even paying attention . . ."
"Competitive Fire Fuels Tebow," by Guerry Smith, Rivals.com website, December 8, 2007, and available at http://collegefootball.rivals.com/content .asp?cid=748732

"One time, Tim wrote a report on why athletes' bodies need more protein . . ."
"Pam Tebow's Labor of Love," by Lindsay H. Jones, *Denver Post*, May 10, 2010, and available at http://www.gainesville.com/article/20100510/ARTICL ES/100519941?p=all&tc=pgall&tc=ar

"Guess that's my claim to fame . . ."
"Tebow Caused a Stir Even as a Youngster," by Dave Curtis, *Orlando Sentinel*, December 5, 2007, and available at http://articles.orlandosentinel.com/2007 -12-05/sports/tebowthekid05_1_quarterback-tim-tebow-hess-allen

"That's not what Bob Tebow wanted for his son, though . . ."
"Team Tebow," by Robbie Andreu, *Gainesville Sun*, January 31, 2006, and available at http://www.gainesville.com/article /20060131/GATORS01/20131 0351?p=all&tc=pgall&tc=ar

"We wanted to give Tim the opportunity to develop his God-given talent . . ."
"Parents, High School Officials at Odds over Motivation for Athletes' Transfers," by Ray Glier, *USA Today*, November 21, 2006, and available at http://www.usatoday.com/sports/preps/2006-11-21-transfers-cover_x.htm

"We were willing to make that sacrifice. We have made sacrifices for all our children . . ."
"QB Facing College Challenges Grounded in Christ," by Barbara Denman, *Florida Baptist Witness*, January 17, 2006, and available at http://www.gofbw .com/news.asp?ID=5351

"People can always lead with words but not always with actions . . ."
"A Gator for God," by Suzy Richardson, *Charisma*, October 2008, and available at http://www.charismamag.com/index.php/features/2008 /october/17874-a-gator-for-god

"We had six road games my sophomore year . . ."
"Tim Tebow Draws from High School Days at Nease," by Mitch Stephens at MaxPreps.com, February 16, 2010, and available at http://www.maxpreps .com/news/AmVWLhtREd-UswAcxJTdpg/tim-tebow-draws-from-high -school-days-at-nease.htm

"Chris Leak is our quarterback . . . "
"Orange Defeats Blue in a Less Than Spectacular Spring Finale," by Dennis Culver, *Gainesville Sun*, April 26, 2006, and available at http://www .gainesville.com/article/20060422/GATORS0108/60422003?p=all&tc=pgall

"There's room for another one next year, Timmy Tebow . . ."
"Leak, Wuerffel Share Lifetime Gator Bond," by Pat Dooley, *Gainesville Sun*, January 14, 2007, and available at http://www.gainesville.com /article/20070114/GATORS24/70114040?p=all&tc=pgall&tc=ar

"The story noted that Tim had sung 'She Thinks My Tractor's Sexy'. . . "
"A Florida Folk Hero Prepares to Face Reality," by Pete Thamel, *New York Times*, September 1, 2007, and available at http://www.nytimes .com/2007/09/01/sports/ncaafootball/01florida.html?_r=1

"After the Tennessee game, the *Gainesville Sun* collected the best quotes . . ."
"UF's Tebow a Legend of the Fall," *Gainesville Sun*, September 20, 2007, and available at http://www.gainesville.com/article/20070920/NEWS/709200331

"It makes you realize that everything that happens in this game doesn't really mean that much in the grand scheme of things . . ."
"Notebook: UF's Tebow Takes Losses Hard, Gains Perspective," by Brandon Zimmerman, *Gainesville Sun*, October 30, 2007, and available at http://www .gainesville.com/ar-ticle/20071030/NEWS/710300310?tc=ar

"Tim took some hits from the media . . ."
"John 3:16—Latest Bible Verse to Be Featured on Tim Tebow's Eye Black,"
by Tom Herrera, *NCAA Football Fanhouse*, January 9, 2009, and available at
http://ncaafoot-ball.fanhouse.com/2009/01/09/john-3-16-latest-bible-verse
-to-be-featured-on-tim-tebow/

"He's just an amazing young man, an amazing football player . . ."
"Tebow Wins Wuerffel Award," by Robbie Andreu, *Gainesville Sun*,
December 9, 2008, and available at http://www.gainesville.com
/article/20081209/NEWS/812090943

"You knew he was going to lead us to victory . . ."
"Tebow Engineers Comeback," by Kevin Brockway, *Gainesville Sun*,
December 7, 2008, and available at http://www.gainesville.com
/article/20081207/NEWS/812060925

"I was pretty excited . . ."
"Best Player Ever? I'll Take Tebow," by Pat Dooley, *Gainesville Sun*, January 9,
2009, and available at http://www.gainesville.com/article/20090109/COLUM
NISTS/901090279?p=all&tc=pgall&tc=ar

4. Plenty of Predraft Drama

"I look at myself as a pretty self-motivated person . . ."
"Tebow Will 'Just Be Me' at Senior Bowl," Associated Press, January 24, 2010,
and available at http://www.gainesville.com /article/20100124/ARTICLES/10
0129731?p=all&tc=pgall

" 'It's simple,' said one NFL scout . . ."
"Tim Tebow Senior Bowl: Disaster or First Step to NFL?" by Mark
Sappenfield, *Christian Science Monitor*, January 31, 2010, and available at
http://www.csmonitor.com/USA/Society/2010/0131/Tim-Tebow-Senior
-Bowl-Disaster-or-first-step-to-NFL

"Scouts Inc. gave Tim a D+ grade . . ."
"2010 Senior Bowl: Tim Tebow's Performance Adds to His Plummeting NFL
Draft Stock," by Daniel Wolf, Bleacher Report.com, January 30, 2010, and
available at http://bleacherreport.com/articles/336387-tim-tebow-senior
-bowl-performance-adds-to-plummeting-nfl-draft-stock

"No mention of abortion . . ."
"Tim Tebow's Brilliant Fake Leads to Pro-Life Score," by David Gibson,
PoliticsDaily.com, February 7, 2007, and available at http://www
.politicsdaily.com/2010/02/07/tim-tebows-brilliant-fake-leads-to-pro-life
-score/

"At a speech held at Lipscomb University in Nashville . . ."
"Tebow Laughs Off Jerry Jones Video, Talks about Losing Sponsors Because of His Super Bowl Ad," by Ben Volin, *Palm Beach Post*, April 18, 2010, and available at http://blogs.palmbeachpost.com/gatorbytes/2010/04/18/tebow-laughs-off-jerry-jones-video-incident/

"It's more of a tweak . . ."
"Tim Tebow's New Team Honing His Technique," by Sam Farmer, *Los Angeles Times*, February 27, 2010, and available at http://articles.latimes.com/2010/feb/27/sports/la-sp-nfl-combine27-2010feb27

"Kurt Hester, the corporate director of training at D1 . . ."
"What's It Like to Help Tim Tebow Prepare for the NFL? D1's Kurt Hester Is Here to Tell You," by Ben Volin, *Palm Beach Post*, February 22, 2010, and available at http://blogs.palmbeachpost.com/gatorbytes/2010/02/22/whats-it-like-to-help-tim-tebow-prepare-for-the-nfl-d1s-kurt-hester-is-here-to-tell-you/

"You're investing a lot of money in some of these guys . . ."
"Future Pros Tackle Grueling NFL Combine," by Kevin Acee, *San Diego Union-Tribune*, February 28, 2010, and available at http://www.signonsandiego.com/news/2010/feb/28/future-football-pros-tackle-grueling-days-combine/

"You get dizzy from it all . . ."
"Underwear Olympics," by Phil King, *Sports Illustrated*, p. 61, March 8, 2010.

"I'd like to say I was six-foot-four . . ."
"Colt McCoy Doesn't Shy Away from Brees Comparison," by Jason Feller, NFL.com, February 27, 2010, and available at http://blogs.nfl.com/2010/02/27/colt-mccoy-doesnt-shy-away-from-brees-comparison/

"Here are some sample questions from the Wonderlic test . . ."
"So How Do You Score?" ESPN page 2, and available at http://espn.go.com/page2/s/closer/020228test.html

"For all the television time, Internet bandwidth . . ."
"Florida's Pro Day Was a True Circus, with Tim Tebow Front and Center," by Andy Staples, SI.com, March 18, 2010, and available at http://sportsillustrated.cnn.com/2010/writers/andy_staples/03/17/tim.tebow.pro.day/index.html

"The 15 minutes passed by way too quickly . . ."
"Tebow Quickly Impressed McDaniels, Broncos as a Genuine Gem," by Lindsay H. Jones, *Denver Post*, April 25, 2010, and available at http://www.denverpost.com/broncos/ci_14953999

"I like this workout better . . ."
"McCoy Satisfied He Aces Test at Texas Pro Day," by Charean Williams, The

Sports XChange/CBSSports.com, and available at http://www.cbssports.com
/nfl/draft/story/13141671/mccoy-satisfied-he-aces-test-at-texas-pro-day

"Colt said he enjoyed his 'pitch and catch' . . ."
"McCoy Accurate in Workout," Associated Press, April 1, 2010, and available
at http://sports.espn.go.com/nfl/draft10/news/story?id=5044786

5. The 2010 NFL Draft

"When quarterbacks Peyton Manning and Ryan Leaf were in the running . . ."
"Leaf's Pro Career: Short and Unhappy," by Damon Hack, *New York Times*,
August 4, 2002, and available at http://www.nytimes.com/2002/08/04/sports
/pro-football-leaf-s-pro-career-short-and-unhappy.html

"Everything you hear about him, that's said, it's legit . . ."
"Rams Keeping a Close Eye on Bradford as Prospective No. 1," by Jim
Thomas, *St. Louis Post-Dispatch*, April 21, 2010, and available at http://www.
stltoday.com/stltoday/sports/stories.nsf/rams/story/604C46ED60B319BB862
576F10005F645?OpenDocument

". . . Devaney learned a valuable lesson when it came to drafting
quarterbacks . . ."
"Evaluating Quarterbacks Is a Tough Part of the Draft," by Jim Thomas, *St.
Louis Post-Dispatch*, April 12, 2010, and available at http://www.stltoday
.com/stltoday/sports/stories.nsf/rams/story/EB21CD1FB9FB34B686257703
000EA4B3?OpenDocument

"It's a once-in-a-lifetime thing . . ."
"Bradford Discusses Decision to Attend NFL Draft," by John E. Hoover,
Tulsa World, April 22, 2010, and available at http://www.tulsaworld.com
/sportsextra/OU/article.aspx?subjectid=92&articleid=20100422_92_0
_NEWYOR504083&archive=yes

"In a conference call with St. Louis reporters . . . "
"St. Louis Rams Get Their Man in QB Sam Bradford," by Jim Thomas, *St.
Louis Post-Dispatch*, April 23, 2010, and available at http://www.stltoday.
com/stltoday/sports/stories.nsf/rams/story/25E7CB0AEC82E9348625770E0
0146973?OpenDocument

"It would have been exciting to be here . . ."
"Tebow Declines Invitations to Attend Draft, Decides to Return Home," by
Jason La Canfora, NFL.com, April 21, 2010, and available at http://www
.nfl.com/draft/story?id=09000d5d817aa5ce&template=with-video-with
-comments&confirm=true

"Tim's former teammate at Florida, Cincinnati Bengals wide receiver Andre
Caldwell . . ."

"Bengals' Andre Caldwell: Right Spot to Pick Tim Tebow Is 'Late Second Round,'" *USA Today*'s The Huddle, March 31, 2010, and available at http://content.usatoday.com/communities/thehuddle/post/2010/03/bengals-andre-caldwell-right-spot-to-pick-tim-tebow-is-late-second-round/1

"Miami Dolphins quarterback Chad Henne . . ."
"Dolphins' Chad Henne on Tim Tebow: 'He's Not an NFL Quarterback,'" *USA Today*'s The Huddle, March 18, 2010, and available at http://content.usatoday.com/communities/thehuddle/post/2010/03/dolphins-chad-henne-hes-not-an-nfl-quarterback/1

". . . Tim did an interview on ESPN Radio with host Freddie Coleman . . ."
"Tim Tebow Does Not Take Mel Kiper's Criticism Kindly, Calls Him Out on Air," by Will Brinson, NCAA Football Fanhouse, December 19, 2008, and available at http://ncaafootball.fanhouse.com/2008/12/19/tim-tebow-does-not-take-mel-kipers-criticism-kindly-calls-him/

"On the morning of the NFL draft . . ."
"Tim Tebow: Is He a Miracle Worker, or Just an Average QB?" by Jon Saraceno, *USA Today*, April 22, 2010, and available at http://www.usatoday.com/sports/football/nfl/2010-04-21-tim-tebow_N.htm

"If you want Tim to be on your football team . . ."
"Great Tebow Draft Debate Will Finally Be Answered," by Robbie Andreu, *Gainesville Sun*, April 21, 2010, and available at http://www.gainesville.com/article/20100421/ARTICLES/100429878?p=all&tc=pgall&tc=ar

"Whether it's Tim Tebow . . . you look for a guy with good character . . ."
"Report: Tebow Plans Team Workouts," by ESPN.com, March 8, 2010, and available at http://sports.espn.go.com/nfl/draft10/news/story?id=4974087

"Kiper and his ESPN sidekick, Todd McShay, stuck to their guns . . ."
"Great Tebow Draft Debate Will Finally Be Answered," by Robbie Andreu, *Gainesville Sun*, April 21, 2010, and available at http://www.gainesville.com/article/20100421/ARTICLES/100429878?p=all&tc=pgall&tc=ar

"Klis then offered these reasons . . ."
"Will the Broncos Draft Tim Tebow?" by Mike Klis, *Denver Post,* April 21, 2010, and available at http://blogs.denverpost.com/broncos/2010/04/21/the-case-for-tebow/

"And that's when Tim's cell phone rang with a 303 area code . . ."
"Tim Tebow Drafted by Denver Broncos in First Round of NFL Draft," by Jeremy Fowler, *South Florida Sun-Sentinel,* April 23, 2010, and available at http://articles.sun-sentinel.com/2010-04-23/sports/sfl-tim-tebow-broncos-10_1_tim-tebow-25th-selection-later-round

"Coach McDaniels was on the line, but he didn't seem at all in a hurry . . ."
"Mile-High on Tebow," by Robbie Andreu, *Gainesville Sun*, April 23, 2010,
and available at http://www.gainesville.com/article/20100423/ARTICLES/4231
012?p=all&tc=pgall&tc=ar

"I just think I showed them [the Broncos] I was willing to do whatever it
took . . ."
"Tim Tebow Drafted by the Denver Broncos," Alligator Army website, April
22, 2010, and available at http://www.alligatorarmy.com/2010/4/22/1437123/
tim-tebow-drafted-by-the-denver

"Tim Tebow is a lightning rod . . ."
"Colorado Evangelicals Singing Praises of McDaniels' QB Pick Tebow," by
Electa Draper, *Denver Post*, April 24, 2010, and available at http://www
.denverpost.com/news/ci_14948943

"A couple of NFL scouts, speaking anonymously, told CBS Sports . . ."
"Clausen's Fall to Second Round and Panthers Gets Personal," by Clark
Judge, CBSSports.com, May 6, 2010, and available at http://www.cbssports
.com/nfl/story/13355576/clausens-fall-to-second-round-and-panthers-gets
-personal

"Devaney said afterward that Colt was extremely impressive . . ."
"Rams Impressed with Colt McCoy During Private Workout," by Laken
Litman, SportsDayDFW by *Dallas Morning News*, April 9, 2010, and
available at http://collegesportsblog.dallasnews.com/archives/2010/04/rams
-impressed-with-colt-mccoy-during-pr.html

"Don't worry, Son, you're in a great place . . ."
"Browns' Mike Holmgren Takes an Ordinary Joe in Colt McCoy," by Rick
Gosselin, SportsDayDFW by *Dallas Morning News*, April 24, 2010, and
available at http://www.dallasnews.com/sharedcontent/dws/spt/columnists
/rgosselin/stories/042410dnspogosselincolumn.410e13f.html

"Nobody expected Colt to have the career that he had at Texas . . ."
"Browns' Mike Holmgren Takes an Ordinary Joe in Colt McCoy," by Rick
Gosselin, SportsDayDFW by *Dallas Morning News*, April 24, 2010, and
available at http://www.dallasnews.com/sharedcontent/dws/spt/columnists
/rgosselin/stories/042410dnspogosselincolumn.410e13f.html

"Tim bowed his head and delivered a wonderful prayer . . ."
"Tim Tebow Closes National Prayer Breakfast in Prayer, but Obama Leaves,"
by Steven Ertelt, LifeNews.com, February 4, 2010, and available at http://
www.lifenews.com/nat5964.html

6. Their First Two NFL Seasons

"A. J. would be the guy. Maybe I should put that on tape . . ."
"A. J. Feeley Remains Ahead of Sam Bradford on Rams' Depth Chart," by Mike Florio on the NBC Sports Pro Football Talk blog, August 6, 2010, available at http://profootballtalk.nbcsports.com/2010/08/06/aj-feeley -remains-ahead-of-sam-bradford-on-rams-depth-chart/

"Sam was asked if he would be reading the story of David and Goliath . . ."
"Sam Bradford Reads Bible Before Game," by Anna McDonald, ESPN .com, January 2, 2011, available at http://sports.espn.go.com/espn/page2 /story?id=5976560

"I think one of the reasons [we lost] is we never got in a rhythm . . ."
"It's a Stinging Loss for Bradford," by Bill Coats, *St. Louis Post-Dispatch*, January 3, 2011, available at http://www.stltoday.com/sports/football /professional/article_52ee05aa-1702-11e0-b02e-0017a4a78c22.html

"I take a lot [of pride] in that," Sam told the *St. Louis Post-Dispatch* . . ."
"Rams' Sam Bradford Has Displayed an Unexpected Quality: Durability," by Sam Farmer, *Los Angeles Times*, January 1, 2011, available at http://www .latimes.com/sports/la-sp-nfl-sunday-spotlight-20110102,0,4721013.story

"You can tell that he is a natural-born leader . . . "
"Browns Find Leader with Texas Twang," by Mark Kaboly, *Pittsburgh Tribune-Review*, October 18, 2010, available at http://www.pittsburghlive .com/x/pittsburghtrib/sports/steelers/s_704839.html

"Tim needs to work on the fundamentals of being a pocket passer . . ."
"Elway Says Young QB Tebow Needs Work as a Pocket Passer," by Lindsay H. Jones, *Denver Post*, January 6, 2011, available at http://www.denverpost .com/broncos/ci_17021315

PLAYING WITH PURPOSE: BASKETBALL

Introduction: It's Not an Easy Gig, Playing in the NBA

"The NBA Player Who Never Scored" by Rick Reilly, *Sports Illustrated*, December 9, 1999, and available at http://sportsillustrated.cnn.com/inside _game/magazine/life_of_reilly/news/1999/12/07/life_of_reilly/

"When *Sports Illustrated* followed up with A.C. in the summer of 2008 . . ." by Adam Duerson, *Sports Illustrated*, July 14, 2008, and available at http:// sportsillustrated.cnn.com/vault/article/magazine/MAG1141820/index .htm?eref=sisf&eref=sisf

"Watching Bobby Jones on the basketball court is like watching an honest man in a liars' poker game . . ." and "He's a player who's totally selfless, who runs like a deer . . . ," both from a Bobby Jones entry on Wikipedia, available at http://en.wikipedia.org/wiki/Bobby_Jones_(basketball,_born_1951)

"Bobby didn't see what all the fuss was about . . ." from "Bobby Jones: The Gentleman of the NBA," a feature on the NBA.com website and found at http://www.nba.com/sixers/features/bobby_jones_090506.html

1. Dr. James Naismith: Inventing with Purpose

"One time while at rugby practice . . . ," anecdote from *Big Game, Small World,* by Alexander Wolff, Warner Books, New York, 2002, page 12.

"His belief was reinforced when a man from Yale University . . ." from *James Naismith: The Man Who Invented Basketball,* by Bob Rains, Hellen Carpenter Books, page 25.

"Naismith, I want you to see what you can do with those students . . ." from "Springfield College: The Birthplace of Basketball," found on the Springfield College website at http://www.springfieldcollege.edu/home.nsf/The -Birthplace-of-Basketball

2. Chris Kaman: Getting Off the Meds

"He can use both hands, and he can run the floor . . ." from "Central Michigan vs. Duke," *USA Today,* March 22, 2003, and available at http://www.usatoday .com/sports/scores103/103081/20030322NCAABDUKE------0nr.htm

3. Jeremy Lin: Welcome to the Show

"Jeremy has a better skill set than anyone I've seen at his age . . ." from "Harvard's Hoops Star Is Asian. Why's That a Problem?" by Sean Gregory, *Time* magazine, December 31, 2009, and available at http://www.time.com /time/nation/article/0,8599,1951044,00.html

"He knew exactly what needed to be done at every point in the basketball game . . ." from "An All-Around Talent, Obscured by His Pedigree," by Chuck Culpepper, *New York Times,* September 14, 2010, and available at http://www .nytimes.com/2010/09/15/sports/basketball/15nba.html

"Many college-age Christians lose interest in their faith . . ." from "NBA Rising Star Jeremy Lin Not Too Busy to Pray," by Gordon Govier, *Charisma News,* February 15, 2012, and available at http://charismanews.com/culture/32833 -nba-rising-star-jeremy-lin-not-too-busy-to-pray

"Jeremy Lin is probably one of the best players in the country you don't know about . . ." from "What They're Saying about Harvard Basketball and Jeremy," Harvard sports website, December 11, 2009, and available at http://www .gocrimson.com/sports/mbkb/2009-10/releases/091210_MBB_Quotes

"This fascinating interview between Lacob and *San Jose Mercury News* columnist Tim Kawakami . . ." from "Lacob Interview, Part 3: On Jeremy Lin, Ellison, Larry Riley, Bold Moves, and Poker," conducted by Tim Kawakami on the Talking Points website, August 17, 2010, and available at http://blogs .mercurynews.com/kawakami/2010/08/17/lacob-interview-part-3-on -jeremy-lin-ellison-larry-riley-bold-moves-and-poker/

"His schedule was Navy SEAL Team 6 material . . ." from "Jeremy Lin's HS Coach Is Surprised, Too," by Tim Keown at ESPN.com, February 14, 2012, and available at http://goo.gl/0wbQU

"At the time, I was thinking if this doesn't work out . . ." from "Exclusive: Jeremy Lin Says 'Lin-Sanity' Was Triggered by Leap of Faith," by Marcus Thompson II, *Silicon Valley Mercury News*, February 13, 2012, and available at http://www.mercurynews.com/jeremy-lin/ci_19954877

"The Knicks offense didn't get a huge boost Tuesday . . ." from "Knicks Claim Harvard Grad Off Waivers," by Sean Brennan, *New York Daily News*, December 27, 2011, and available at http://goo.gl/lGhQm

"I had no opportunity to prove myself . . ." from "Exclusive: Jeremy Lin Says 'Lin-Sanity' Was Triggered by Leap of Faith," by Marcus Thompson II, *Silicon Valley Mercury News*, February 13, 2012, and available at http://www .mercurynews.com/jeremy-lin/ci_19954877

"I think they messed up their coverage . . . " from "Lin, Knicks Scale Wall's Wizards in Washington," by Frank Isola, *New York Daily News*, February 8, 2012, and available at http://goo.gl/FGH8o

"The fluke no longer looks so flukey . . ." from "Lin Leads Again as Knicks Win 3rd in a Row," by Howard Beck, *New York Times*, February 8, 2012, and available at http://goo.gl/9eD9I

"So we wanted to go out there and do something that was lighthearted and not too serious . . ." from "Jeremy Lin's Religious Pregame Ritual," thestar.com website, February 13, 2012, and available at http://goo.gl/CeKvW

4. Luke Ridnour: Heir to Pistol Pete

"Really, when I started reading the Word with my chaplain, everything changed . . ." from "Super Sonic: Seattle's Luke Ridnour Talks Small Towns and Big Faith," by Jill Ewert, *Sharing the Victory* magazine, a publication of Fellowship of Christian Athletes, and available at http://www. sharingthevictory.com/vsItemDisplay.lsp?method=display&objectid=F10AF 9D8-5E91-416A-959F5BAC3AA6B942

"Coach Kent summed up his point guard's contribution this way . . ." from "Cool Hand Luke" by Jeanne Halsey, *Sports Spectrum* magazine, and available at http://faithsite.com/content.asp?SID=808&CID=59253

"My mom wouldn't be too happy about it . . ." from "The Inside Track," the *Los Angeles Times*, December 17, 2002, and available at http://articles latimes.com/2002/dec/17/sports/sp-quotebook17

"You must have made a big impression on him, then . . ." from "Super Couple: Kate Ridnour Q&A," by Jill Ewert, *Sharing the Victory* magazine, a publication of Fellowship of Christian Athletes, and available at http://www .sharingthevictory.com/vsItemDisplay.lsp&objectID=E22C67AB-BE6F -4326-86C9D58F7DC1BC2B&method=display

5. They're Playing with Purpose, Too

"It turns out that Dr. Orsino is a blogger . . ." from a blog called "End of Me" by Guy Stanton, April 21, 2008, and available at http://stantonmarcfreyendofme .blogspot.com/2008/04/stephen-curry-i-can-do-all-things.html

"I have like a deal for my pastor . . ." from "Brazil's Nene Vows to Retire by 2016 Olympics to Focus on Religion," by Chris Tomassen, *AOL News*, October 4, 2009, and available at http://www.aolnews.com/2009/10/04 /brazils-nene-vows-to-retire-by-2016-olympics-to-focus-on-religi/

"It was scary, but I believe in God . . ." from "Nene 'a Survivor' after Cancerous Testicle Removed," by Benjamin Hockman, *Denver Post*, March 8, 2008, and available at http://webcache.googleusercontent.com /search?q=cache:asPckLRh0aAJ:www.denverpost.com/ci_8498637%3Fsourc e%3Dbb+nene+a+survivor+after+cancerous+testicle+removed&cd=2&hl=e n&ct=clnk&gl=us&source=www.google.com

"It's a good play for our defense . . ." from "Feisty Nick Collison Takes Charge," by Mike Baldwin, *The Oklahoman* newspaper, March 9, 2010, and available at http://newsok.com/fiesty-nick-collison-takes-charge /article/3444923

"In short, Kevin Durant is endorsement gold right now . . ." from "Kevin Durant is D'Man: An Endorsement Diamond in the Midwestern Rough," by Patrick Rishe, *Forbes* magazine, May 20, 2011, and available at http:// blogs.forbes.com/sportsmoney/2011/05/20/kevin-durant-is-dman-an -endorsement-diamond-in-the-midwestern-rough/

"It's tough, man. I can't lie about that . . ." from "NBA All-Star Kevin Durant on Faith, Family, and Fame," by Chad Bonham of *Inspiring Athletes*, and available at http://blog.beliefnet.com/inspiringathletes/2011/05/nba-all-star -kevin-durant-on-faith-family-and-fame.html

"I'm keeping strong at it, just trying to make my walk with faith a little better . . ." from "Thunder's Kevin Durant Commits to Daily Bible Reading," by Darnell Mayberry, *The Oklahoman* newspaper, April 21, 2011, and available at http://newsok.com/thunders-kevin-durant-commits-to-daily-bible -reading/article/3560862

"I've got Jesus in my heart . . ." from "Bill Sorrell: Faith Sustains Young Griz Players," by Bill Sorrell, published on the Faith in Memphis website on April 8, 2011, and available at http://faithinmemphis.com/2011/04/08/bill-sorrell -faith-sustains-young-griz-players/

"It helps me in every aspect of my life . . ." from "NBA Rookie in the Habit of Thanking God" by Lee Warren, *Christian Post*, May 11, 2011, and available at http://www.christianpost.com/news/nba-rookie-in-the-habit-of-thanking- god-50190/

"I'm lucky to get a second chance . . ." from "Heart Condition Ends Notre Dame Player's Career," *Los Angeles Times*, September 29, 1990, and available at http://articles.latimes.com/1990-09-29/sports/sp-1229_1_notre-dame

"To this day, the doctors can't understand what happened . . ." from "A Perfect Character for the Blazers," by Brian Meehan, *The Oregonian* newspaper, August 21, 2005, and available at http://www.4hcm.org/forums /archive/index.php/t-10311.html

"We came up with a tool that will help people take certain verses and chew on those verses for a week . . ." from "New Orleans Hornets Coach Monty Williams Lifted by Faith," by Jimmy Smith, *New Orleans Times-Picayune* newspaper, December 25, 2010, and available at http://blog.nola.com/hornets_impact/print .html?entry=/2010/12/new_orleans_hornets_coach_mont_22.html

Overtime: Pistol Pete Maravich, the Prodigal Who Played with Purpose

"His canvas was the basketball floor, and his brush was his basketball . . ." from "Sixty Cool Pistol Pete Facts," compiled by John Hareas, Andrew Pearson, and Chad Sanders for the NBA.com website and available at http:// www.nba.com/features/sixty_pistol_pete_facts_070622.html

"Whenever I went to the movies I'd take my ball with me . . ." from "I Want to Put on a Show" by Pete Maravich with Curry Kirkpatrick, *Sports Illustrated*, December 1, 1969, and available at http://sportsillustrated.cnn .com/vault/article/magazine/MAG1083101/index.htm

"A former teammate, "Sweet Lou" Hudson, summed it up this way . . ." from "No One Can Cap the Pistol" by Curry Kirkpatrick, *Sports Illustrated*, December 4, 1978, and available at http://sportsillustrated.cnn.com/vault /article/magazine/MAG1094399/index.htm

"Then he tore up one knee in classic Maravich style . ." from "NBA Encyclopedia: Pistol Pete Maravich," found on the nba.com website and available at http://www.nba.com/history/players/maravich_bio.html

"For two years, I remained in seclusion . . ." from *Heir to a Dream,* by Pete Maravich and Darrel Campbell, Thomas Nelson Publishers, 1987, page 187.

"I don't want to play ten years [in the NBA] and then die of a heart attack when I'm forty. . ." from "Maravich's Creative Artistry Dazzled," by Bob Carter, a SportsCenter Biography on the ESPN.com website and available at http://espn.go.com/classic/biography/s/Maravich_Pete.html

"Even my greatest records would someday be broken . . ." from *Heir to a Dream*, by Pete Maravich and Darrel Campbell, Thomas Nelson Publishers, 1987, page 189.

"I've cursed you and I've spit on you . . ." from *Heir to a Dream,* by Pete Maravich and Darrel Campbell, Thomas Nelson Publishers, 1987, page 190.

PLAYING WITH PURPOSE: BASEBALL

1. Clayton Kershaw: Standing on the Precipice of Greatness

All quotations used are from personal interviews between coauthor Joshua Cooley and Clayton Kershaw, except the following:

"Probably the best in the world . . ." from "Clayton Kershaw's Great Expectations," by Jeff Passan, *Yahoo! Sports*, May 14, 2008, and available at http://sports.yahoo.com/mlb/news?slug=jp-kershaw051408

"Might as well go by Zeus . . ." and "These guys don't come along often . . ." from "Kershaw Takes the Stage," by Jeff Passan, *Yahoo! Sports*, May 26, 2008, and available at http://sports.yahoo.com/mlb/news?slug=jp-kershaw052608

"Ceiling? There is no ceiling . . ." from "Kershaw Looking Ahead to Life without Limits," by Ken Gurnick, MLB.com, February 23, 2010, and available at http:// losangeles.dodgers.mlb.com/news/article.jsp?ymd=20100223&content _id=8120062&vkey=news_la&fext=.jsp&c_id=la

"There's no reason to really set limits . . ." from "Dodgers' Clayton Kershaw Continues to Shine," by Ben Bolch, *Los Angeles Times*, August 13, 2011, and available at http://www.latimes.com/sports/la-sp-0814-dodgers

-astros-20110814,0,6852499.story

2. Ben Zobrist: The PK Who's a Zorilla on the Field

All quotations used are from personal interviews between coauthor Mike Yorkey and Ben Zobrist and his father, Tom Zobrist, except for the following:

"Ben first attracted notice for playing his wife's . . ." from Julianna's page on the Zobrists' website at www.thezobrists.com and available at http://goo.gl/hrl5g

"Dad, this is more important to others than it is to me . . ." from "Former AIA Player Makes It to the Big League," by Elaine Piniat, published June 25, 2009 on the Athletes in Action website and available at http://goo.gl/S5uqY

"She was just this awesome, godly woman . . ." from "Ray of Light: Tampa Bay All-Star Ben Zobrist," by Jill Ewert, published in *Sharing the Victory* magazine and available online at http://goo.gl/DRquR

3. Albert Pujols: A Home Run Hitter with a Heart for Others

"That was me twenty-five years ago . . ." from the *60 Minutes* segment "The Incredible Mr. Pujols," which aired on April 10, 2011, on CBS, and available at http://www.cbsnews.com/video/watch/?id=7362328n

"Believe it or not, baseball is not the chief ambition of my life . . ." from "A Message of Faith from Albert Pujols," by the Pujols Family Foundation, and available at http://www.pujolsfamilyfoundation.org/faith/

"Growing up in the Dominican, that's pretty much all I did is play baseball . . ." from "Albert and Dee Pujols: Giving Honor to God," *Focus on the Family,* Daily Radio Digest, August 15–16, 2006.

"It's the farthest and hardest I've seen a baseball hit . . ." from "Albert Pujols: Revisiting the Early Years" by Arne Christensen, *The Hardball Times,* June 15, 2010, and available at http://www.hardballtimes.com/main/article/albert-pujols -revisiting-the-early-years/

". . . Have power even if he used a toothpick . . ." from "Albert Pujols: Revisiting the Early Years," by Arne Christensen, *The Hardball Times,* June 15, 2010, and available at http://www.hardballtimes.com/main/article/albert-pujols-revisiting -the-early-years/

"He's the best hitter I've coached or seen . . ." from "Albert Pujols: Revisiting the Early Years," by Arne Christensen, *The Hardball Times,* June 15, 2010, and available at http://www.hardballtimes.com/main/article/albert-pujols-revisiting -the-early-years/

"I'll never, never get over it . . ." from the *60 Minutes* segment "The Incredible Mr. Pujols," which aired on April 10, 2011, on CBS, and available at http://www .cbsnews.com/video/watch/?id=7362328n

"I went to church every once in a while growing up . . ." from "Albert Pujols Testimony," Baseball Chapel video, July 20, 2011, and available at http://www .youtube.com/watch?v=n9yz9inU5XY&feature=youtube_gdata_player

"I wouldn't say it was easy and that the Lord starting turning things around [right away] . . ." from "Albert Pujols Testimony," Baseball Chapel video, July 20, 2011, and available at http://www.youtube.com/watch?v=n9yz9inU5XY&feature =youtube_gdata_player

"I had been praying for God to be able to use Albert to share Jesus and wanted it to be bigger . . ." from "Albert and Dee Pujols: Giving Honor to God," *Focus on the Family,* Daily Radio Digest, August 15–16, 2006.

"It must've been the highlight of the year for them . . ." from the *60 Minutes* segment "The Incredible Mr. Pujols," which aired on April 10, 2011, on CBS, and available at http://www.cbsnews.com/video/watch/?id=7362328n

"One thing I have learned is that it's not about me; it's about serving the Lord Jesus Christ . . ." from "Albert Pujols Testimony," Baseball Chapel video, July 20, 2011, and available at http://www.youtube.com/watch?v=n9yz9inU5XY&feature =youtube_gdata_player

"He's like the best baseball player in baseball now . . ." from "My Wish: Albert Pujols," *ESPN Sports Center: My Wish*, July 19, 2010, and available at http://espn .go.com/video/clip?id=5392781

"Albert is such a great player . . ." from "My Wish Q&A: Debbie Trammel," by Scott Miller, ESPN.com, July 21, 2010 and available at http://sports.espn.go.com /espn/features/mywish/news/story?id=5367335

"I'm glad it was him . . ." from "For Pujols, a Game for the Age," by Tyler Kepner, *New York Times,* October 23, 2011, and available at http://www.nytimes. com/2011/10/24/sports/baseball/for-albert-pujols-of-st-louis-3-home-runs-for -a-record-night.html

"I think the last month of the season . . ." from "Cards Win World Series, Beat Texas 6–2 in Game 7," Associated Press, October 28, 2011, and available at http:// sportsillustrated.cnn.com/baseball/mlb/gameflash/2011/10/28/40004_recap .html

"Enjoy it. Respect it. Appreciate it . . ." from "Pujols Is a Faith-Based Mystery," by Jeff Passan, *Yahoo! Sports*, July 14, 2009, and available at http://sports.yahoo. com/mlb/news?slug=jp-pujols071409

"Albert has no glaring weaknesses, and he doesn't chase many bad pitches . . ." from "Albert Pujols Quotes," *Baseball Almanac*, and available at http://www.baseball-almanac.com/quotes/albert_pujols_quotes.shtml

"I'd rather walk in a run than give up four . . ." from the *60 Minutes* segment "The Incredible Mr. Pujols," which aired on April 10, 2011, on CBS, and available at http://www.cbsnews.com/video/watch/?id=7362328n

"He's the face of baseball . . ." from the *60 Minutes* segment "The Incredible Mr. Pujols," which aired on April 10, 2011, on CBS, and available at http://www.cbsnews.com/video/watch/?id=7362328n

"I would never do any of that . . ." from "Cardinals Slugger Albert Pujols Is Batting Cleanup for Baseball," by Bob Nightengale, *USA Today*, July 13, 2009, and available at http://www.usatoday.com/sports/baseball/nl/cardinals/2009-07-12-pujols-cover_N.htm

"I don't believe in all that science stuff . . ." from "Pujols Is a Faith-Based Mystery," by Jeff Passan, *Yahoo! Sports*, July 14, 2009, and available at http://sports.yahoo.com/mlb/news?slug=jp-pujols071409

4. Carlos Beltran: Praying All the Way to the Ballpark

All quotations used are from personal interviews between coauthor Joshua Cooley and Carlos Beltran.

5. Adrian Gonzalez: Gonzo for God

All quotations used are from personal interviews between co-author Joshua Cooley and Adrian Gonzalez, except for the following:

"I still have my reports on him . . ." from "On Baseball: Gonzalez Recalls Time in Portland," by Kevin Thomas, *Portland Press Herald*, April 20, 2011, and available at http://www.pressherald.com/sports/say-goodbye-to-winter_2011-04-01.html

"Everybody is just going crazy over him. . ." from "The Secret Is Out on Gonzalez," by Bob Nightengale, *USA Today*, July 12, 2011, and available at http://www.usatoday.com/SPORTS/usaedition/2011-07-12-Cover-Adrian-Gonzalez_CV_U.htm

6. Josh Hamilton: Baseball's Bat Man Comes Back from the Brink

"But that wasn't the amazing thing . . ." from "180 Degrees of Separation," by Jeff Pearlman, *Sports Illustrated*, April 12, 2004, and available at http://sportsillustrated.cnn.com/vault/article/magazine/MAG1031772/index.htm

"I've gotten a lot of trophies over the years, but the Ashley Pittman Memorial Award is special to me . . ." from *Beyond Belief: Finding the Strength to Come Back* , by Josh Hamilton with Tim Keown (New York: Hachette Book Group, 2008), page 33.

"We've watched him for a long time . . ." from "Rays Feel Hamilton Has Makings of a Star," CNNSI.com, June 2, 1999, and available at http://sportsillustrated.cnn .com/baseball/mlb/1999/draft/news/1999/06/02/hamilton_lamar/

"I'm thinking three years in the minors, then fifteen years in the big leagues . . ." from *Beyond Belief: Finding the Strength to Come Back,* by Josh Hamilton with Tim Keown (New York: Hachette Book Group, 2008), page 37.

"Their fears became real in our first game . . ." from *Beyond Belief: Finding the Strength to Come Back,* by Josh Hamilton with Tim Keown (New York: Hachette Book Group, 2008), pages 7–8.

"I didn't expect you'd be out here tonight . . ." from *Beyond Belief: Finding the Strength to Come Back,* by Josh Hamilton with Tim Keown (New York: Hachette Book Group, 2008), page 38.

"I got saved when I was eighteen years old . . ." from the *Larry King Live* show on CNN, October 28, 2008, and available at http://www.youtube.com /watch?v=rJ2xN_xHT0g

"He plunged the needle into my spine till it felt like it was grinding on bone . . ." from *Beyond Belief: Finding the Strength to Come Back,* by Josh Hamilton with Tim Keown (New York: Hachette Book Group, 2008), page 76.

"I had a lot of 'firsts' that night . . ." from the *Larry King Live* show on CNN, October 28, 2008, and available at http://www.youtube.com/watch?v=rJ2xN _xHT0g

"The display still hadn't been fixed and was covered by a banner that promoted the team's website . . ." from "If You Build It, They Will Come, or Will They?" by Matt Martz, Bakersfield.com, October 17, 2008, and available at http://people .bakersfield.com/home/ViewPost/78184

"Everybody knew who Josh was in high school . . ." from "Josh and Kate Hamilton, Parts 1–3 Live Interview, February 14, 2010," West Lonsdale Baptist Church, February 14, 2010, and available at http://www.youtube.com /watch?v=dM_M8JTjkvM&feature=related

"I was a shell of a human, a soulless being . . ." from *Beyond Belief: Finding the Strength to Come Back,* by Josh Hamilton with Tim Keown (New York: Hachette Book Group, 2008), page 150.

"I was a wreck—dirty, twitchy, barely coherent . . ." from *Beyond Belief: Finding the Strength to Come Back,* by Josh Hamilton with Tim Keown (New York: Hachette Book Group, 2008), page 154.

"I went back in the room where I'd just been using drugs, grabbed a Bible, and the first verse I read was James 4:7 . . ." from "Josh and Kate Hamilton, Parts 1–3 Live Interview, February 14, 2010," West Lonsdale Baptist Church, February 14, 2010, and available at http://www.youtube.com/watch?v=dM _M8JTjkvM&feature=related

"Baseball is third in my life right now, behind my relationship with God and my family . . ." from "I'm Proof That Hope Is Never Lost," an excerpt from *Beyond Belief,* by Josh Hamilton with Tim Keown, *ESPN: The Magazine,* July 5, 2007, and available at http://sports.espn.go.com/mlb/news/story?id=2926447

"God has given me such a platform to share what He's done in my life . . ." from "Hamilton's Drug Comeback 'Beyond Belief,'" Associated Press, October 19, 2008, and available at http://www.youtube.com/watch?v=942OxgJT0ec&fe ature=relmfu

"I was out there for three weeks and stopped praying, stopped doing my devotions, stopped reading the Word . . ." from "Josh and Kate Hamilton, Parts 1–3 Live Interview, February 14, 2010," West Lonsdale Baptist Church, February 14, 2010, and available at http://www.youtube.com/watch?v=dM _M8JTjkvM&feature=related

"I'm embarrassed about it for my wife, Katie, for my kids, and for the organization . . ." from "Hamilton Admits to Relapse with Alcohol," by Joe Resnick of the Associated Press, August 8, 2009, and available at http://www .breitbart.com/article.php?id=D99UTUGG1&show_article=1

"When he walked in the door, and I [saw] how broken and repentant and remorseful he was . . ." from "Josh and Kate Hamilton, Parts 1–3 Live Interview, February 14, 2010," West Lonsdale Baptist Church, February 14, 2010, and available at http://www.youtube.com/watch?v=dM_M8JTjkvM&feature=related

"Rooted in his Christian beliefs and his rigorous daily devotions . . ." from "Josh Hamilton Finds Strength after Misstep in Recovery from Addiction," by S.C. Gywnne, *Dallas Morning News,* October 4, 2010, and available at http://www .dallasnews.com/incoming/20101003-Josh-Hamilton-finds-strength-after -misstep-1474.ece

"Just another night in the life of the best player in baseball went something like this . . ." from "Hamilton Leaving No Doubt He Is the Best Player in Baseball" by Tom Verducci, SI.com, August 17, 2010, and available at http://sportsillustrated. cnn.com/vault/article/web/COM1173399/index.htm

"Everybody yelled 'Ginger ale!' and I just jumped in the middle of the pile and they doused me with it . . ." from "Josh Hamilton Included in Celebration" by Richard Durrett, ESPNDallas.com, October 12, 2010, and available at http://sports.espn.go.com/dallas/mlb/news/story?id=5679952

"Could I have reached people being that clean-cut kid coming out of high school?" from "Hamilton's Drug Comeback 'Beyond Belief,'" Associated Press, October 19, 2008, and available at http://www.youtube.com/watch?v=942OxgJT 0ec&feature=relmfu

"One thing I can't live without is obviously Jesus . . ." from "Josh and Kate Hamilton, Parts 1–3 Live Interview, February 14, 2010," West Lonsdale Baptist Church, February 14, 2010, and available at http://www.youtube.com /watch?v=dM_M8JTjkvM&feature=related

7. Stephen Drew: Good Things Come in Threes

All quotations used are from personal interviews between coauthor Joshua Cooley and Stephen Drew.

8. Jeremy Affeldt: *Solus Christus*—By Christ Alone

All quotations used are from personal interviews between coauthor Joshua Cooley and Jeremy Affeldt, except the following:

"Jeremy Affeldt. We go way back . . ." from "Giants' Biggest Hero in Game 6 Fits Team's 'Improbable' Bill," by Joe Posnanski, *Sports Illustrated*, October 24, 2010, and available at http://sportsillustrated.cnn.com/2010/writers/joe _posnanski/10/24/nlcs.game6/index.html

9. Matt Capps: Opening a Once-Closed Fist to God

All quotations used are from personal interviews between coauthor Joshua Cooley and Matt Capps.

10. Mark Teixeira: Hitting on All Cylinders

"[My teammates] were kidding me, telling me to trip over first base if I hit one into the gap . . ." from "Teixeira Hits for Cycle in Rangers' Win," August 18, 2004, and available at http://www.redorbit.com/news/general/79812/teixeira_hits_for _cycle_in_rangers_win/index.html

"I've always tried to be disciplined . . ." from "Mark Teixeira Works on His Form," by Lee Warren, *Breakaway* magazine, September 2007, page 19.

"He stands perfectly straight, head down, shirt tucked in . . ." from "Straight-up Talent," by Lee Jenkins, *Sports Illustrated*, November 11, 2009, and

available at http://sportsillustrated.cnn.com/vault/article/magazine
/MAG1162901/2/index.htm

"I try to live and play baseball the way that I think the Lord would want me
to . . ." from "Mark Teixeira Works on His Form," by Lee Warren, *Breakaway*
magazine, September 2007, page 20.

"At a very young age, I learned about Jesus and how important your faith is . . ."
from "Mark Teixeira Works on His Form," by Lee Warren, *Breakaway* magazine,
September 2007, page 19.

"For the President to single me out, I was very honored . . ." from "President
Barack Obama Singles Out New York Yankees First Baseman Mark Teixeira for
Charitable Works," by Mark Feinsand, *New York Daily News,* April 27, 2010, and
available at http://articles.nydailynews.com/2010-04-27/sports/27062767_1
_college-scholarship-mark-teixeira-white-house

"Ever since I started [my foundation], it has been very involved with college
scholarships, education, children's needs . . ." from "Yankees' Teixeira Goes to
Bat for Kids," by Jim Wilkie, ESPN.com: The Life, May 4, 2010, and available at
http://sports.espn.go.com/espn/thelife/news/story?id=5161392

"I became involved with Harlem RBI and DREAM charter because I believe the
work we are doing is truly changing lives . . ." from NYC Department of Housing
Preservation & Development press release, by Eric Bederman, June 13, 2011,
and available at http://www.nyc.gov/html/hpd/html/pr2011/pr-06-13-11.shtml

"I've visited hospitals before and worked with the Make-A-Wish foundation . . ."
from "Inspired by Young Cancer Patient, Yankees' Mark Teixeira Shares Life
Lesson" by Jason Rovou, Larry King Live Blogs, April 13, 2010, and available at
http://larrykinglive.blogs.cnn.com/2010/04/13/inspired-by-young-cancer
-patient-yankees%E2%80%99-mark-teixeira-shares-life-lesson/

"The thing that was so amazing about Brian was his faith throughout his
ordeal . . ." from "Teixeira's Mission: Raise Awareness for Cancer to Honor
Ernst's Memory," by Ashley Bates, *Gainesville Times,* April 28, 2010, and available
at http://www.gainesvilletimes.com/archives/32589/

"Our deeds don't make us righteous . . ." from "Bright Light in the Big City," by
Chad Bonham, *Sharing the Victory*, October 2009, and available at http://www
.sharingthevictory.com/vsItemDisplay.lsp?method=display&objectid=EDA17
9A5-C29A-EE7A-E8E85C89FA8CE71A

"My parents brought me up in a home where we worked very hard and did our
best . . ." from "Program 246," *Personally Speaking with Jim Lisante* podcast, Jim
Lisante, Catholic Communication Campaign, January 16, 2011, and available at
http://old.usccb.org/audio/psradio.shtml

444 PLAYING with PURPOSE: BASEBALL

"People would think I'm crazy, but it was the greatest thing for me . . ." from "Program 246," *Personally Speaking with Jim Lisante* podcast, Jim Lisante, Catholic Communication Campaign, January 16, 2011, and available at http://old.usccb.org/audio/psradio.shtml

"No one's going to expect more out of me than me . . ." from "Mark Teixeira's Wife Leigh Nudged Hubby toward Yankees," by Anthony McCarron, *New York Daily News*, January 6, 2009, and available at http://articles.nydailynews.com/2009-01-06/sports/17913844_1_mark-teixeira-yankees-offer

"I let him know that I was behind him all the way . . ." from *Cage Rat: Lessons from a Life in Baseball by the Yankees' Hitting Coach,* by Kevin Long with Glen Waggoner (New York: Ecco, 2011).

"When you're on the bases, why not run hard?" from "Mark of Excellence," by Bob Bellone, *Sports Spectrum*, Summer 2010, page 38, and available at http://mydigimag.rrd.com/display_article.php?id=426780

"For us to be holding the trophy at the end of the season, it was a special year . . ." from "Mark Teixeira Interview Post 2009 World Series," Steinersports, November 10, 2009, and available at http://www.youtube.com/watch?v=Uewfl9vfUJw

"When my first son was born in 2006 . . ." from "Bright Light in the Big City," by Chad Bonham, *Sharing the Victory*, October 2009, and available at http://www.sharingthevictory.com/vsItemDisplay.lsp?method=display&objectid=EDA179A5-C29A-EE7A-E8E85C89FA8CE71A

"I can probably quote the entire movie start to finish . . ." from "Yankees' Teixeira Goes to Bat for Kids," by Jim Wilkie, ESPN.com: The Life, May 4, 2010, and available at http://sports.espn.go.com/espn/thelife/news/story?id=5161392

"Baseball is a game of failure . . ." from "Bright Light in the Big City," by Chad Bonham, *Sharing the Victory*, October 2009, and available at http://www.sharingthevictory.com/vsItemDisplay.lsp?method=display&objectid=EDA179A5-C29A-EE7A-E8E85C89FA8CE71A

"That's not a major milestone . . ." from "Derek Jeter to Play in Trenton This Weekend Before Returning to Yankees," by Zach Berman and Conor Orr, *The Star-Ledger*, June 30, 2011, and available at http://www.nj.com/yankees/index.ssf/2011/06/derek_jeter_will_play_in_trent.html

"My faith keeps me grounded . . ." from "Mark Teixeira Texas Rangers—Today's Christian Videos," Trinity Broadcasting Network, and available at http://www.godtube.com/watch/?v=JCC291NU

11. Brian Roberts: Big Trials, Big Faith for a Small Player

All quotations used are from personal interviews between coauthor Joshua Cooley and Brian Roberts, except the following:

"Toughest stint . . ." and "Certainly for me . . ." from "Roberts Plans to Be Part of Orioles' Future," by Jeff Zrebiec, *Baltimore Sun*, August 16, 2011, and available at http://www.baltimoresun.com/sports/orioles/bs-sp-orioles -roberts-0817-20110816,0,5149721.story

"Brian Roberts is an infielder . . ." from "The Mitchell Report," which was released December 13, 2007, and is available at http://mlb.mlb.com/mlb/news /mitchell/index.jsp

"In a moment of weakness . . ." from "Roberts Admits He Used Steroids," by Jeff Zrebiec, *Baltimore Sun*, December 18, 2007, and available at http://www.baltimoresun.com/sports/bal-te.sp.roberts18dec18,0,769248.story

"Kids out there . . ." from Brian's video blog entry entitled "Improved Team Chemistry Could Result in Improved Record," April 22, 2011, and available at http://www.masnsports.com/brian_roberts/2011/04/improved-team-chemistry -could-result-in-improved-record.html

"Mr. Angelos has put a lot of investment . . ." from "Emotional Roberts Admits That 2011 Return Not Looking Good," by Jeff Zrebiec, *Baltimore Sun*, September 2, 2011, and available at http://weblogs.baltimoresun.com/sports/orioles /blog/2011/09/emotional_roberts_admits_that.html

12. Josh Willingham: Understands the Lord Gives and Takes

All quotations used are from personal interviews between coauthor Joshua Cooley and Josh Willingham.

13. Mariano Rivera: The Closer Who Got Saved

"He needs to pitch in a higher league, if there is one . . ." from "Mariano Rivera's a True Yankee, Almost Mythical in His Dominance," by Joe Posnanski, SI.com, July 2, 2009, and available at http://sportsillustrated.cnn.com/2009/writers /joe_posnanski/07/01/rivera/index.html

"Yes, it does. It does make me uncomfortable, because I don't like to talk about myself . . ." from "The Michael Kay Show," ESPN New York (1050 AM) podcast, September 16, 2011, and available at http://espn.go.com/new-york/radio /archive?id=2693958

"You're seeing the greatest closer of all time . . ." from "Mariano Saves," by Tom Verducci, *Sports Illustrated*, October 5, 2009, and available at http://

sportsillustrated.cnn.com/vault/article/magazine/MAG1160757/index.htm

"He's like my brother . . ." from "Modern Yankee Heroes: From Humble Beginnings, Mariano Rivera Becomes Greatest Closer in MLB History," by Christian Red, *New York Daily News*, March 13, 2010, and available at http://articles.nydailynews.com/2010-03-13/sports/27058930_1_puerto-caimito-cardboard-cousin

"I don't know if we'll ever see it again . . ." from "Mariano Rivera Gets 600th Save," by Andrew Marchand, ESPNNewYork.com, September 14, 2011, and available at http://m.espn.go.com/mlb/story?w=1b0rl&storyId=6968238&i=TOP&wjb=

"If you talk to him at an All-Star Game, it's like talking to somebody who just got called up . . ." from "Mariano Saves," by Tom Verducci, *Sports Illustrated*, October 5, 2009, and available at http://sportsillustrated.cnn.com/vault/article/magazine/MAG1160757/index.htm

"The radar wasn't really being lit up . . ." from "Modern Yankee Heroes: From Humble Beginnings, Mariano Rivera Becomes Greatest Closer in MLB History," by Christian Red, *New York Daily News*, March 13, 2010, and available at http://articles.nydailynews.com/2010-03-13/sports/27058930_1_puerto-caimito-cardboard-cousin

"Usually a player prepares for years . . ." from *Mariano Rivera*, by Judith Levin (New York: Checkmark Books, 2008), page 18.

"Every time I was going through a hard time, somebody was there to help . . ." from "The Secret of Mariano Rivera's Success," by Peter Schiller, baseballreflections.com, November 7, 2009, and available at http://baseballreflections.com/2009/11/07/the-secret-of-mariano-riveras-success/

"The harder I tried, the tougher it got . . ." from "Yanks' Rivera Continues to Learn," by Mel Antonen, *USA Today*, October 9, 2006, and available at http://www.usatoday.com/sports/soac/2006-10-09-rivera_x.htm

"You can't see the spin on it . . ." from "This Is the Game Changer," by Albert Chen, *Sports Illustrated*, June 13, 2011, and available at http://sportsillustrated.cnn.com/vault/article/magazine/MAG1187105/index.htm

"That is my miracle pitch . . ." from "Mariano Rivera's Cutter 'The Miracle Pitch,'" interview with Pastor Dewey Friedel, courtesy the Trinity Broadcasting Network, and available at http://www.youtube.com/watch?v=L0tTLssCKZU

"My mental approach is simple: Get three outs as quick as possible . . ." from "Mariano Saves," by Tom Verducci, *Sports Illustrated*, October 5, 2009 and available at http://sportsillustrated.cnn.com/vault/article/magazine/MAG1160757/index.htm

"My childhood was wonderful . . ." from "Modern Yankee Heroes: From Humble Beginnings, Mariano Rivera Becomes Greatest Closer in MLB History," by Christian Red, *New York Daily News*, March 13, 2010, and available at http://articles.nydailynews.com/2010-03-13/sports/27058930_1 _puerto-caimito-cardboard-cousin

"It's hard. Extremely hard . . ." from "Modern Yankee Heroes: From Humble Beginnings, Mariano Rivera Becomes Greatest Closer in MLB History," by Christian Red, *New York Daily News*, March 13, 2010, and available at http:// articles.nydailynews.com/2010-03-13/sports/27058930_1_puerto-caimito -cardboard-cousin

"We have a lot of goals to work with the youth . . ." from "Yankees Pitcher to Open Church," by Danielle De Souza, *New Rochelle Patch*, June 28, 2011, and available at http://newrochelle.patch.com/articles/yankees-pitcher-to-open-church

"This was something special, and God wants me to concentrate on bringing Him to other people . . ." from "Baseball; Love of God Outweighs Love of the Game," by Jack Curry, *New York Times*, December 10, 1999, and available at http://www.nytimes.com/1999/12/10/sports/baseball-love-of-god-outweighs -love-of-the-game.html

"I'm glad we lost the World Series . . ." from "The Confidence Man," by Buster Olney, *New York Magazine*, May 21, 2005, and available at http://nymag.com /nymetro/news/sports/features/9375/index2.html

"That comes from God, having the ability to perform . . ." from "World Baseball Classic Pool D: San Juan," an interview with Mariano Rivera by ASAP Sports, March 7, 2009, and available at http://www.asapsports.com/show_interview .php?id=54723

"Look at Mo's delivery, look at how he repeats it . . ." from "Mariano Rivera Pitches in 1,000th Game for Yanks and Has a Lot of Mo," by Bob Klapisch, *The Record*, May 28, 2011, and available at http://www.post-gazette.com /pg/11148/1150003-63-0.stm?cmpid=sports.xml

"The whole organization, my whole teammates have been a pillar for me . . ." from "Mariano Rivera Gets 602 to Become All-Time Saves Leader," by Bryan Llenas, *Fox New Latino*, September 19, 2011, and available at http://latino. foxnews.com/latino/sports/2011/09/19/mariano-rivera-gets-number-602-to -become-all-time-saves-leader/

"When you talk about the greatest relievers of all time, there's only one guy . . ." from "Mariano Rivera: Saving with Grace," by Kevin Baxter, *Los Angeles Times*, September 17, 2011, and available at http://articles.latimes.com/2011/sep/17 /sports/la-sp-0918-down-the-line-20110918

"Amazing that he's been able to do it with one pitch over and over again . . ." from "Modern Yankee Heroes: From Humble Beginnings, Mariano Rivera Becomes Greatest Closer in MLB History," by Christian Red, *New York Daily News*, March 13, 2010, and available at http://articles.nydailynews.com/2010-03 -13/sports/27058930_1_puerto-caimito-cardboard-cousin

"I don't pay too much attention to that . . ." from "The Michael Kay Show," ESPN New York (1050 AM) podcast, September 16, 2011, and available at http://espn .go.com/new-york/radio/archive?id=2693958